AF872838

COMPLEXITY ECONOMICS FOR ENVIRONMENTAL GOVERNANCE

In *Complexity Economics for Environmental Governance*, Jean-François Mercure reframes environmental policy and provides a rigorous methodology necessary to tackle the complexity of environmental policy and the transition to sustainability. The book offers a detailed account of the deficiencies of environmental economics and then develops a theory of innovation and macroeconomics based on complexity theory. It also develops a new foundation for evidence-based policy-making using a Risk-Opportunity Analysis applied to the sustainability transition. This multidisciplinary work was developed in partnership with prominent natural scientists and economists as well as active policy-makers with the aim to revolutionise thinking in the face of the full complexity of the sustainability transition, and to show how it can best be governed to minimise its distributional impacts. The book should be read by academics and policymakers seeking new ways to think about environmental policy-making.

Dr Jean-François Mercure is Senior Climate Economist in the Chief Economist Office of the Vice Presidency for Equitable Growth, Finance and Institutions at the World Bank and Associate Professor in Climate Change Policy at the University of Exeter. His research focuses on developing models and methods for public policy appraisal in low-carbon innovation based on complexity science, and for assessing the macroeconomic impacts of diverse types of low-carbon, energy and climate policies. Jean-François Mercure has worked at several universities including the University of Cambridge, where he was Deputy Director of the Cambridge Centre for Climate Change Mitigation Research, and now remains fellow of the Cambridge Centre for Energy, Environment and Natural Resource Governance (C-EERNG). He regularly engages with policy-makers from across UK government, in developing countries, the European Commission and other governments internationally.

CAMBRIDGE STUDIES ON ENVIRONMENT, ENERGY AND NATURAL RESOURCES GOVERNANCE

Cambridge Studies on Environment, Energy and Natural Resources Governance publishes foundational monographs of general interest to scholars and practitioners within the broadly defined fields of sustainable development policy, including studies on law, economics, politics, history, and policy. These fields currently attract unprecedented interest due both to the urgency of developing policies to address climate change, the energy transition, food security and water availability and, more generally, to the progressive realization of the impact of humans as a geological driver of the state of the Earth, now called the "Anthropocene."

The general editor of the series is Professor Jorge E. Viñuales, the Harold Samuel Chair of Law and Environmental Policy at the University of Cambridge and the Founder and First Director of the Cambridge Centre for Environment, Energy and Natural Resource Governance (C-EENRG).

Complexity Economics for Environmental Governance

JEAN-FRANÇOIS MERCURE
University of Exeter

CAMBRIDGE
UNIVERSITY PRESS

CAMBRIDGE
UNIVERSITY PRESS

Shaftesbury Road, Cambridge CB2 8EA, United Kingdom

One Liberty Plaza, 20th Floor, New York, NY 10006, USA

477 Williamstown Road, Port Melbourne, VIC 3207, Australia

314–321, 3rd Floor, Plot 3, Splendor Forum, Jasola District Centre, New Delhi – 110025, India

103 Penang Road, #05–06/07, Visioncrest Commercial, Singapore 238467

Cambridge University Press is part of Cambridge University Press & Assessment, a department of the University of Cambridge.

We share the University's mission to contribute to society through the pursuit of education, learning and research at the highest international levels of excellence.

www.cambridge.org
Information on this title: www.cambridge.org/9781108428828

DOI: 10.1017/9781108553650

© Jean-François Mercure 2023

This publication is in copyright. Subject to statutory exception and to the provisions of relevant collective licensing agreements, no reproduction of any part may take place without the written permission of Cambridge University Press & Assessment.

First published 2023

A catalogue record for this publication is available from the British Library.

Library of Congress Cataloging-in-Publication data
NAMES: Mercure, Jean-Francois, author.
TITLE: Complexity economics for environmental governance / Jean-Francois Mercure.
DESCRIPTION: [New York?] : Cambridge University Press, 2023. | Series: Cambridge studies on environment, energy and natura | Includes bibliographical references and index.
IDENTIFIERS: LCCN 2022037406 (print) | LCCN 2022037407 (ebook) | ISBN 9781108428828 (hardback) | ISBN 9781108451116 (paperback) | ISBN 9781108553650 (epub)
SUBJECTS: LCSH: Environmental economics. | Environmental policy. | BISAC: LAW / Environmental
CLASSIFICATION: LCC HC79.E5 M45136 2021 (print) | LCC HC79.E5 (ebook) | DDC 333.72–DC23/eng/20220826
LC record available at https://lccn.loc.gov/2022037406
LC ebook record available at https://lccn.loc.gov/2022037407

ISBN 978-1-108-42882-8 Hardback

Cambridge University Press & Assessment has no responsibility for the persistence or accuracy of URLs for external or third-party internet websites referred to in this publication and does not guarantee that any content on such websites is, or will remain, accurate or appropriate.

Contents

Figures

Tables

Preface

Climate change is progressing, as humans fill the atmosphere up with greenhouse gases. This pulls our world into unchartered territory in which it becomes increasingly difficult to predict what will happen next. At the same time, the world of technology and human behaviour also evolves, where old ways of making a living are replaced by new ones through 'creative destruction'. This also pulls our society and economy into unstable territory, although we have seen technological revolutions before and what impact they have had. They recur every half century, and every time they cause havoc. This time around, we face both environmental and economic turbulence at the same time, as the socio-technical change that we are precipitating in order to avoid climate change is beginning to cause upheaval all over again, but might not even entirely solve climate change. Can the low-carbon transition be well planned from a public policy point of view? This is the broad challenge that this book attempts to address.

According to many environmentalists, the solution is simple: Just eliminate greenhouse gas emissions, right now. It sounds easy, but why is it in fact so difficult? To paraphrase Nicholas Stern, why are we waiting? Well, the transition is not easy, but, worst of all, it is not well understood. Many proponents of radical emission reductions tend, in my view, to understand the climate fairly well, but do not fully understand the dynamic economic process that rapid emission reductions imply. In fact, I am not sure the economics profession fully understands it either.

A sufficiently abrupt low-carbon transition that achieves present-day objectives of net-zero in 2050 implies putting society on a track of very rapid economic and social change. However, as it operates, the economy runs continuously on 'promises' that it fulfils in the future. I am not saying this is bad, I am saying that we must understand that this is how it really works. Purchasing power is created, and activities are carried out with that purchasing power, activities that usually prove themselves to have been worth it. Everyone's day-to-day activities are justified by unstated promises of flows of economic value that make it possible to move forward. Therefore, when the economy cannot clearly foresee its own promises being fulfilled, it loses direction, panics and grinds to a halt, until it finds its bearings again. By then, lots of promises will have been abandoned, and, as a result, some activities will never return.

A rapid transition has three main implications. First, investment in the capital of the future is a continuous process, and the creation and use of the purchasing power invested fuel the machinery that enables the creation of that very capital. When the future becomes so uncertain that return on investment is too difficult to ascertain, whole sections of the economy unavoidably pause activity. Second, when return on investment is unclear, the very valuation of capital, assets, skills, goods and services and even money can change very quickly. This is because their value is contingent on the belief in promises of future flows of economic value. Third, the promises of those flows of value are created through innovation with which, entrepreneurs believe, more value will be created at less effort than used to be possible. If change in the way the economy operates is so rapid that innovation does not have time to generate the returns it promises, then the pause in economic activity could be much worse than we intuitively think.

This is therefore what this book really sets out to understand. It takes for granted the imperative of achieving climate goals, and the reasons to do so are well explained in many other books dealing with earth system dynamics. What this book seeks to understand is the real economic process that must happen to achieve the low-carbon transition, and how best to mitigate its negative impacts, with a very tangible attention to the policy process required. What is clear is that, as with any other wicked problem, the processes of understanding and solving the problem go hand in hand, and to some degree are one and the same. We learn, and we act.

However, in this broad context of environmental policy, there is one thing that makes me nervous; it is dogmatism. Dogmatism sees the world, in high-contrast black and white, as one big battle for ideology, and this makes me, for some reason, uncomfortable. Sometimes, dogmatism happens under the name of science, and it puzzles me. To me, science does *not* have all the answers, since if it did, science would have completed itself and ended, uncertainty would have been eliminated, and everything knowable would be known. But obviously science never ends and can never fully explain anything, and furthermore, it never stops building ever taller and precarious evidence cathedrals, upon which accepted knowledge sits. Parts of those cathedrals sometimes collapse, with small or large avalanches. Knowledge is incomplete almost by its own definition, and its precariousness is the very definition of science. How could one be so certain of one's knowledge to feel justified in imposing one's normative interpretation of the facts, if the latter are only ever established in an approximate manner, onto others? One can with no difficulty be certain of one's own moral stance, but not of one's knowledge.

Science cannot really completely determine one's moral position, or establish one's higher moral ground. Science only just helps men and women wade through the mists of deep uncertainty, that is, just like business observations help businesses take decisions that determine their companies' futures. The world is mostly not composed of saints and evil men; it is composed of people trying their best at what they do, mostly lacking direction or coordination, because no social planner exists, and no-one really knows what's best for everyone.

I wrote this book in response to a wide gap in knowledge regarding, very practically, how to be honest regarding real uncertainties when informing the direction of public policy, on the basis of scientific analysis, to reduce greenhouse gas emissions and avoid climate change. This book is mainly inspired by very resourceful civil servants, at the UK government and the European Commission, and other policy agents elsewhere around the world, who are doing everything they can to solve climate change and/or better their nations. What they continuously need most is convincing evidence bases and narratives upon which to build their work. Climate and earth system science evidence is abundant, clear and convincing; that is not a problem anymore. What is lacking most, in my view, is reliable science informing the way out of the high-carbon paradigm, the deep implications of doing so, and how to mitigate those.

Policy analysts can easily find various versions of The Green Gospel: the free market Green Gospel, the socialist Green Gospel, the 'repent for your carbon sins' Green Gospel. But the dilemma for governance that comes with embracing any gospel is that it requires to either convert everyone into followers of a particular denomination of the Green Church, or marginalise a large number of people. It seems to be hard at the moment to find such a broad Green Church that everyone can fit in.

Indeed, the world has recently become polarised to the extreme, and environmentalism is, I am afraid to say, mixed up in it. In the United States and in the United Kingdom alike, following green ideologies has, for good or bad, become associated with other political divisions, in relation to immigration, social exclusion, inequality, race, gender, governance and international cooperation. When the economy moves from one socio-technical regime to another, the people already operating in the new regime praise its merits as they only see the opportunities, while others become trapped by socio-economic and post-industrial decline as economic life as they know it ends. Some people look towards the future, others towards the past. Some people's livelihoods fit in with the new futuristic paradigms developing; others' are becoming trapped as the old ways of doing things are phased out. Those who accidentally find themselves the 'nouveau riche' might on top of that claim a higher moral ground, but those being left behind will not quietly accept their fateful economic decline especially if they are to be told that their livelihoods are now 'morally wrong'. Climate change is real. But the climate 'crisis' will not likely be solved, or solved 'well', by imposing by force onto good and honest working-class workers in oil, gas and coal, the automobiles, steel and heavy industries, the concept that they have somehow done something wrong.

Ultimately, resilient political action relies upon creating a 'sufficient' degree of consensus. And therein lies the dilemma: should climate action focus or not on spreading the Green Gospel and converting the remaining non-followers? Or is there another way to create consensus? If anything, history teaches us that spreading gospels worldwide is neither possible nor peaceful. A lot of people around the world have a lot to lose in the low-carbon transition, and may feel it is their moral duty to block the green agenda. The 'truth' that may be uncomfortable to the Greens is, if some people disrupt the green agenda, it might not actually be for lack of scientific literacy or education; science often ends up the tool of politics one way or another.

As I see it, and that's just my personal opinion, one should attempt to create narratives that most can accept, and offer compromises to those at the losing end. To be honest, these narratives should be created using transparent science, recognising that it is full of uncertainty. This is difficult, but is this not precisely what political leadership is all about? Political leadership could, in principle, rely on evidence bases that people do not have to question, but this relies on trust in research institutions and on scientific integrity. Here, I use the word 'science' very broadly to include scientists such as myself who delve into both the non-normative social sciences and economics as well as the natural sciences. Economic science indeed is a thing, or should be.

Thus here is my proposal: how about creating an economic science that is reliant to a minimum degree on moral axioms, and maximally on observation of complex societal dynamics, and I would like to call it *Complexity Economics*. This term was coined by Brian Arthur, who plotted a revolution in collaboration with renowned complexity scientists Phil W. Anderson and David Pines back in the eighties, the latter both physicists whom I also admire for their own enormous contributions to physics and the sciences of complexity. I would urge the reader to consider this: policy-making before and during a major societal transformation in reality mostly deals with deep uncertainty, rather than opposing worldviews and conflicting morals. The challenge is not about spreading a gospel, it is about figuring out what to do that leads to achieving some stated goals. In my view, we can use this Theory of Complexity Economics to try to inform policy-making in the deep midsts of a tempestuous storm. Policy-makers can decide what to do with the evidence.

This book focuses on identifying and understanding the process of societal transformation implied by the low-carbon transition that many policy-makers are attempting to put in motion. The first part focuses on identifying conceptual and self-consistency problems in current environmental economics and the concepts driving policy narratives in the present. These are the problems that drive all of the interpretation issues and lack of distinction between scientific analysis and philosophical theorising that plague the field.

In the second part, a theory of complexity economics is proposed. This is new science that goes from understanding the source of uncertainty in prediction for dynamical systems, before exploring the process of innovation and technology transformation, finance and macroeconomics. Socio-technical change itself implies deep structural changes in the economy as some industrial value chains and the dependent occupations come to economic death while new ones are born. This causes torsion in society, where some people win and others lose. An endogenous theory of growth based on process and product innovation is formulated. While debates have raged over how many percents of gross domestic product (GDP) should be expected to be lost during the transition, it would seem, from a complexity science perspective, that it is not GDP but rather economic, financial and political stability that weakens. This implies a radically different narrative to understand the social change to be expected during the low-carbon transition.

Lastly, a normative theory for the operation of the science–policy interface, where complexity science could inform environmental (or other) policy-making in situations of transformational change, is proposed. This is as close as this book comes to a gospel, and it is a broad and hopefully inclusive science–policy gospel. Following that, the complexity analysis is applied to three chosen case studies. First, the complexity of the highly interconnected economy-environment system is explored, where a blurred line exists between formulating policy and understanding the problem. Second, an analysis of the dynamics of diffusion of low-carbon innovations is explored, with policy implications, in a micro-level perspective. Third, the macroeconomic impacts of the low-carbon transition are explored in detail, exploring issues of structural change in the economy (winners and losers regionally and sectorally), and problems of financial instability caused by rapid technological change and stranded assets. These three case studies, I hope, illustrate the essential of what needs to be known for policy-making that seeks a successful while not too 'unhappy' or unstable low-carbon transition.

As a guide to this book, I have attempted to please both the general policy reader and the more mathematically minded economist and complexity scientist. I have kept the mathematics mostly out of sight, in appendices at the end of chapters for those wondering what they are. The policy reader not interested in theory could in principle skip Part II entirely. However, Part II is where most of the new scientific juice is, therefore the economist or scientist could in principle focus on Part II.

Although the process started many years ago, publishing this book also comes in the context of leading the project 'Economics of Energy Innovation and System Transition' (EEIST, `www.eeist.co.uk`) jointly funded by the UK Government's Department for Business, Energy and Industrial Strategy (BEIS) and the Children's Investment Fund Foundation (CIFF). This is a project that I co-designed along with many colleagues including Simon Sharpe from the UK's Cabinet Office, Hector Pollitt from Cambridge Econometrics, Jorge Viñuales, Pablo Salas and Laura Anadon in Cambridge, Michael Grubb of UCL, and Doyne Farmer from Oxford.

This book formulates what I believe could be a complexity theory of economics applicable to the goals of this project, and notably, Chapter 12 on 'Risk-Opportunity Analysis' was written in that context.

—

The reader may be curious to know how I came to write a book about complexity science *and* innovation economics. I started my research career in the experimental sciences studying the physics of complex systems, and thus I received a highly rigorous quantitative natural sciences training in the sciences of complexity. However, I was an experimentalist, and therefore came to appreciate the meaning of uncertainty. I completed a PhD on the complexity of the phase diagram of the liquid of electrons in the magnetic layered material $Sr_3Ru_2O_7$, where something called 'Quantum Criticality' is thought to arise (Mercure et al., 2009, 2010). Prior to that, I studied the dynamics of the complex networks of amorphous silicon (Mercure et al., 2005). After my PhD I went on and measured the very strange properties of superconductivity in one dimension (Mercure et al., 2012). The complexity of interactions of particles of matter in such systems that sit between ferromagnetism, simple metal, insulator, superconductivity, glasses and other phases is staggering.

The zoology of physical properties one can get by assembling just one, two or three element types in complicated structures is huge. But also, perhaps unexpectedly, working in experimental physics labs gave me a deep understanding of technology, innovation and entrepreneurship. I was not born to be a physicist, I was born to be a social scientist, as it is people and societies I am interested in. Over time, through studying energy systems, economics and climate change I have drifted towards macroeconomics, innovation and the science–policy interface. My re-training as a social scientist took the best part of ten years, and I took it most seriously. It is an interesting observation that many complexity scientists have jumped into economics as a key area needing the application of complexity concepts, not least Nobel Prize-winning Phil Anderson who also strived to explain the complex properties of magnetic materials. Thus it all starts with Anderson (1972), really, although a lot was done by Kauffman (2000). However, not many have gone further into the real social sciences, and I hope to think that I have.

Acknowledgements

I owe much the writing of this book becoming a reality to the moral support of my beloved, Dr Lorinda Turner, especially during our two isolation spells (yes, not just one). First, I had cancer and had to self-isolate for about a year. Here I thank colleagues at Radboud University, my then academic home in the Netherlands, for giving me great flexibility. Second, shortly after returning to my spiritual (if not natal) home, the United Kingdom, we ran into the COVID-19 crisis, in which I was not ill for once, but everyone else was. Lori was working day and night in the University of Cambridge, processing blood samples and interpreting data to try to understand what happens to the immune system following an infection from that new disease.

In the literature, I owe all of my economic inspiration to Schumpeter, while morally, I owe everything to Antoine de Saint-Exupéry. But in practice, I owe all of my inspiration to my academic family, which includes, first and foremost, Hector Pollitt, with whom I have had a 10-year long conversation trying to understand why there exists no really coherent macroeconomic theory of growth and what it should be if we were to create one ourselves (and I think we may be on the verge of succeeding); Jorge Viñuales, through whom I learned what I know of political science, environmental law and realpolitik; Neil Edwards, from whom I learned a lot about statistics of Earth System models, how to write as well as how to herd cats and govern a large group of scientists; and the creative mind of Phil Holden for all kinds of unexpected insights across the disciplines. They are the key architects of our precarious collective knowledge cathedral in our small circle between the University of Cambridge, Cambridge Econometrics, the Open University and the University of Exeter. More recently, I have learned and absorbed a lot from Andrew Jarvis at the University of Lancaster taking a metabolic systemic view of evolutionary systems, and Gregor Semieniuk at University of Massachusetts looking at complex financial networks and economic history.

Most of what I know of policy-making, however, comes to me through various civil servants in government whom I have met over the years, notably Simon Sharpe, who was, at the time, at the Cabinet Office of the UK government, and colleagues at the European Commission, including Joan Canton, and now Florian Knobloch at the German government. The energy of policy officers never ceases to amaze me; I cannot claim equal amounts of tenacity to what I do nor their tolerance towards the vagaries of the real world.

While I wrote this book myself, the work would not have been possible without the enormous contributions of many co-authors in previously published articles and reports on which some of the research in this book is based. These authors are as follows.

- **Chapter 2**: Hector Pollitt, Andrea M. Bassi, Jorge E. Viñuales, Neil R. Edwards.
- **Chapter 3**: Florian Knobloch, Hector Pollitt, Leonidas Paroussos, Serban Scrieciu, Richard Lewney.
- **Chapter 6**: Florian Knobloch.
- **Chapter 9**: Hector Pollitt, Femke J. M. M. Nijsse.
- **Chapter 10**: Hector Pollitt, Phil B. Holden.
- **Chapter 11**: Hector Pollitt.
- **Chapter 12**: Simon Sharpe, Jorge E. Viñuales, Matthew Ives, Michael Grubb, Hector Pollitt, Florian Knobloch, Femke J. M. M. Nijsse.
- **Chapter 13**: Maria Augusta Paim, Pierre Bocquillon, Soeren Lindner, Pablo Salas, Paula Martinelli, Issa Berchin, José Baltazar S. O. Guerra, Cristiane Derani, Celso L. de Albuquerque Junior, João Marcello, Florian Knobloch, Hector Pollitt, Neil R. Edwards, Phil B. Holden, Aideen Foley, Sibyll Schaphoff, Rafael Faraco, Jorge E. Viñuales.
- **Chapter 14**: Aileen Lam, Florian Knobloch, Yeliz Simsek.
- **Chapter 15**: Gregor Semieniuk, Phil B. Holden, Pablo Salas.

Partners in crime are many, but most importantly Pablo Salas and Aileen Lam, since we have spent around ten years working together trying to build models that make sense of things, and Florian Knobloch, whose deep mind never ceases to inspire me, and together with whom I've learned to understand the science–policy interface. The more recent additions to the academic family are Pim Vercoulen, Femke Nijsse and Yeliz Simsek, the whole EEIST group. Mentors include Michael Grubb, Heleen de Coninck, Tim Lenton, Richard Lewney and the one who started it all, Terry Barker. I also salute all of the integrated assessment modelling crowd for paving the way, the old Cambridge Centre for Climate Change Mitigation Research (4CMR) and Cambridge Centre for Energy, Environment and Natural Resource Governance (C-EERNG) and all the hard-working consultants at Cambridge Econometrics, in particular Unnada Chewpreecha for keeping things going and for making good practical use of our collective work with real world stakeholders. Dear colleagues abroad include Soocheol Lee in Japan, and José Baltazar Salgueirinho Osório de Andrade Guerra and his Greens team in Brazil.

Lastly, as mentioned, I must not forget that I was a physicist before becoming an economist, and I would not have become a complexity economist had I not been a complexity scientist to start with. Recognition goes to physics professors at the Université de Montréal, François Schiettekatte and Richard Léonelli, who early on shaped my scientific thinking, and my University of St Andrews condensed matter physics PhD supervisor Andy Mackenzie and colleagues, Bristol University colleague Nigel Hussey and Cambridge University colleagues Gil Lonzarich, Neil Wilson and Sibel Özcan. This goes back a long journey from complex systems in superconductivity and magnetism all the way to Schumpeterian and post-Keynesian economics. I thank my supportive friends Henri, Vaughan, Andrew, Will, Becky and the girls Amelia and Lucy. Amelia and Lucy, you will carry the flame one day.

PART I

The State of Knowledge and Its Use in Environmental Economics

MAP FOR PART I

Part I of this book reviews the current state-of-the-art economic theory and modelling methods and practice that are relevant to the assessment of environmental and low-carbon policy. It focuses on the main issues hindering progress in devising effective environmental or low-carbon policy, which stem from model and theoretical constructs in the mainstream theory. Part I justifies the need for a new Complexity theory of Economics that is developed in Part II. Part I is structured along four chapters that cover the following:

1. an introduction to complexity in environmental problems, looking at how understanding and solving environmental issues are most of the time two faces of the same coin;
2. an overview of four key issues in standard environmental economics, looking at the diffusion of innovations, the macroeconomics of environmental innovation, uncertainty, human behaviour and policy effectiveness;
3. a detailed exploration of the implications of current assumptions in economic models over finance and innovation systems onto the results of economic assessments and information delivered to policy-makers;

4. a detailed analysis of the philosophy of science used in economics and economics models, the lack of discipline that exists in that respect which creates confusion over the meaning of analyses made, between what are *normative* questions and what is *descriptive* analysis, in relation to insights provided to policy-makers. A list of building blocks is then given for the development of a complexity theory of economics, to help the development of Part II.

Part I is hopefully written in sufficiently simple and general terms to be read by the general reader and policy-makers. The goal is to make clear how current theory and models and their application are not fit for purpose for informing policy-making for environmental governance, especially in the case of managing the low-carbon transition. This will lead to the new theory given in Part II, and the solutions offered in Part III. In principle, the reader who is not so interested in the theoretical details of complexity economics could skip Part II and land directly in Part III to explore the space of solutions.

1

Introducing Complex Environmental Economics

In this first chapter, the emergent complexity of problems in environmental and climate policy is raised and summarised. These issues are described as 'wicked': the process of solving them coincides with the scientific process of understanding their nature and the internal mechanisms driving them. While in many scientific areas of enquiry, statistics can be accumulated using repeated experiments, this is not possible here, and moreover, each time an attempt is made to solve an environmental problem with a chosen policy strategy, the problem typically transforms into something new. The case is made why optimisation approaches are fundamentally flawed in analysing environmental problems, as they assume the access and availability of knowledge and data by analysts that is not realistic. This introductory chapter motivates the various issues raised and discussed throughout this book.

1.1. THE PROBLEM OF ENVIRONMENTAL GOVERNANCE

1.1.1 *'Wicked' Environmental Problems*

Climate change is set to transform the world in unpredictable ways. If greenhouse gas (GHG) emissions remain unabated, it could warm the planet on average up to 4°C, bringing the world towards a situation of mass extinction of species, runaway sea-level rise and a high frequency of extreme weather events. However, some degree of climate change is already committed, and the world is already changing.[1] Climate change is a highly complex environmental problem combining human and natural factors, which is not yet fully understood.[2] Climate change is an example of humans

[1] The reader is referred to the IPCC's reports (IPCC, 2013, 2014, 2018) and the thousands of references therein.

[2] Climate change is fairly well understood, and the evidence is overwhelming. However, some complex processes are not fully understood, which could in general make matters worse.

reaching a so-called planetary boundary,[3] where the carbon cycle is irreversibly disturbed. Other planetary boundaries exist, including biodiversity, land-use change, freshwater use, the nitrogen cycle (disturbance by the use of fertilisers). Knowledge on the carbon cycle boundary is extensive; however, knowledge on the other boundaries is mostly scarce. For example, deforestation is progressing at an alarming pace in tropical countries, promoted by intensive commoditisation of agriculture, closely associated to economic globalisation and global trade networks.[4] Biodiversity is declining due to excessive land-use change (Chapin III et al., 2000). Freshwater use is disturbed by both climate change and by human use for agriculture. As with climate change, each of these problems is highly complex and involves a combination of human and natural factors, and threatens the survival of humanity on Earth. Solutions do exist, technological and regulatory, and to address these issues requires effective science-based environmental governance. But which kind of governance?

Environmental governance faces what has been famously called a 'wicked problem',[5] in which 'the process of solving the problem is identical with the process of understanding its nature'. This would not necessarily imply analytical near-intractability, if it weren't combined to a very high degree of complexity. In common planning problems, such as the management of bus timetables, traffic, road networks, the traditional approach, since computers have become widely available, has been to build a database, and deploy brutal optimisation mathematical algorithms to identify best possible solutions. Sometimes, problems could have several solutions, and finding the best out of them all could take considerable time and computing resources.[6] Since the sixties, this has fuelled the development of the field of operational research. A large number of planners think in terms of optimisation, prominently among which are energy modellers. This mathematical tradition has been well established and maintained.

Operational research, however, necessitates some very basic inputs in order to be possible at all. It sits on the assumption that the analyst has sufficient knowledge of the system he attempts to plan, such that all possible outcomes of planning can be enumerated and ranked, and the best solution identified. This, unfortunately, sits at odds with science, because key premises in the work of a scientist include, first, that he is searching for knowledge that he doesn't already have; second, that he makes incremental progress; and third, that there can be aspects he has yet to discover

For instance, the interactions between atmospheric change, forest dieback, changes in evapotranspiration, water runoff and river flows is not, at the time of publication, modelled with a high degree of detail, mostly due to the sheer complexity of the task. An eventual Amazon collapse could radically change the global climate (Lenton et al., 2008).

3 Rockström et al. (2009); Steffen et al. (2015).

4 For example, in Brazil, see Lambin and Meyfroidt (2011); Lapola et al. (2014); Malhi et al. (2008).

5 This term was coined in the influential paper on planning by Rittel and Webber (1973).

6 E.g., the 'travelling salesman problem', finding the shortest route that connects a large number of stopover points, common in all sorts of engineering problems. See Wikipedia `https://en.wikipedia.org/wiki/Travelling_salesman_problem`.

or has missed. Therefore, almost by definition, the scientist at work will never fully understand any system that he studies to be able to reliably optimise it. Some doubt will always remain whether he is actually optimising something other than the real problem, and worse, the optimisation solution may keep flipping almost randomly subject to new knowledge becoming available.

In other words, one can optimise the bus timetable to minimise the sum of the durations of all possible routes, but one cannot optimise a problem under scientific investigation, and particularly not one of environmental science. For example, searching for optimal policy to avoid climate change, or optimal policy to stop deforestation, leads to an ambiguous problem or to using false premises. Doing so would greatly over-claim the existing degree of scientific knowledge (natural and social), or, alternatively, make assumptions that are not supported by any evidence. Since stating an optimisation problem require to 'know everything' about it, or in other words, to have a perfectly known representation of system responses to controls (i.e. policy), a large number of assumptions not supported by evidence must be made for every bit of missing knowledge. For some, it then becomes a problem of finding out why reality does not behave similarly to the optimisation solution, but this inevitably sends one back to scientific research. But more to the point, such models are being extensively used to inform, and sometimes potentially to mislead, decision-makers, under the false impression that optimal solutions can reliably be identified.[7] Claiming that something is optimal is a truly big claim, as it involves assurances that nothing exists that could be superior. Naturally, users of science love this, but can it be defended?

One area where this is increasingly becoming problematic is with the identification of 'optimal' climate policy. Environmental policy in the United States and the United Kingdom requires, as a matter of process, a Cost-Benefit Analysis (CBA) to be carried out. Nobel prize winning Nordhaus (2017) follows this normative tradition, as did Stern (2007) to set the UK's climate agenda, to estimate the optimal carbon price by setting the marginal cost of abatement equal to the marginal cost of emitting carbon, the social cost of carbon.[8] In this normative frame, one argues that social justice should require that the polluter pays for emitting waste to the environment a price that equals the value of the damage that he causes. This therefore requires to know both the costs of emissions reductions and the value of the avoided damages. In Nordhaus' scenarios of thus normative nature, this has had the result of effectively recommending waiting until the *discounted* damages of climate change become sufficiently high for mitigation action to be worth being undertaken.[9]

[7] Depending of course on how the results are used; but modellers can never prevent non-subtle interpretations by policy-makers that scenarios are truly optimal.

[8] Note that CBA is not in fact generally used in the UK to develop the broader strategic vision but rather, it is used to test individual projects, using notably cost-benefit ratios. The strategic vision is understood to be political.

[9] A discussion on which discount rate has subsequently raged for some time (see Stern and Taylor, 2007; Nordhaus, 2007a,b, and many more), as this result entirely depends on whether one uses

However, Weitzman (2009) identified the key problem: probability distributions of extreme future climate events and damages generated by climate change (storms, floods, famines, etc.) have heavy probability tails, to the extent that the sum of damage values times their probability may not converge or may generate very large uncertain values. Therefore, the monetised benefits of avoiding climate change may be infinite or close to infinite, given that the sum of damages is infinite or close to, making the CBA exercise ambiguous. Whether the benefits of avoiding climate change are infinite or simply large with large uncertainty, the method is fundamentally flawed for assuming that one *can* estimate them accurately.

In both countries, this problem re-surfaces in many applications of CBA in which the benefits face fundamental or radical uncertainty, while costs are relatively well defined. This unavoidably leads to the outcome that decisions are systematically biased towards the *status quo*. The reason behind this is that one uses values assuming certainty or known converging probabilities, for the sake of getting an answer, in places where one should instead assume fundamental uncertainty, *and* that there is an asymmetry between existing knowledge of the *status quo* and that of possible new ways forward. In UK and US climate policy, this leads to adopting emissions reductions targets as objectives, while at the same time most policy proposals are blocked as they cannot get past the cost-benefit test done in government departments for not generating sufficient benefits to overcome costs, and for no action being taken. The insufficient valuation of benefits, especially in relation to valuing innovation and natural capital, are pointed to. But estimating with certainty the returns on specific investments in low-carbon innovation is truly asking to know the unknowable.

Rittel and Webber (1973) propose a method to approach planning problems that is more consistent with the gradual process of scientific discovery. They develop the concept of the 'wicked' policy problem, in which

(1) Understanding and solving the problem is in fact the same process, which implies that finding a solution is an incremental scientific process;
(2) There are no 'true' or 'false' answers to a wicked problem, only outcomes subsequently subjectively judged 'good' or 'bad' by different interested parties;
(3) No prior experiments are possible, and decision-makers typically have only one opportunity for taking action;
(4) Due to limited scientific knowledge, solutions to wicked problems are not exhaustively enumerable, let alone rankable;
(5) Actions taken change the problem, and
(6) The choice of explanation determines the nature of the problem's resolution.

a social discount rate (3% or less) or something closer to consumer or corporate discount and interest rates. Ultimately, these discussions are normative and besides the science.

These basic issues of knowledge and decision-making are typical particularly for environmental governance problems, notably climate change: they involve a combination of human and natural processes, and they involve knowledge in almost every field of science and research.[10] A common problem in environmental science is to find individuals able to acquire broad knowledge in a sufficiently large number of distinct areas of research, able to cross the traditional disciplinary boundaries. Otherwise, solutions become excessively biased by particular individuals' disciplinary training, which constrains the breadth of solutions considered. For instance, engineers will tend to focus on technological solutions and seek to maximise efficiency, but will not typically translate this into legally workable policy proposals. Their solutions may face difficulties when individuals or agents involved in operating associated new machinery do not behave as they were assumed they 'ought to' in the engineering models. But this only betrays a lack of understanding of human behaviour. It is one thing to identify how, ideally, a system ought to be configured. It is another to find which combination of incentives, rules, laws and policy levers, in the hands of authorities, will lead agents involved to realise that system.

1.1.2 A *Truly Multidisciplinary Field*

Progress in environmental science requires knowledge in a large multitude of disciplines. However, a few are really important, representing two main domains, namely natural processes, and human processes. Within the natural processes are included systems such as the climate, geology, biology and zoology, while human processes include demography, politics, economics, trade, agriculture, industrial production and pollution. These processes are in constant change, however, and therefore two additional phenomena of evolutionary nature must be added: natural selection and evolution in the natural world, and, correspondingly, technological change and innovation in the human world. Here, focus goes towards the latter, as innovation forms the major component of the solutions favoured by environmental governance. Indeed, this makes the problem even more 'wicked', since the study of innovation as a human process must become central to environmental scientific analysis, and the prospect of innovation so radically changes the spectrum of solutions that it makes enumerating and optimising solutions ever less plausible.

Of note therefore are the disciplines of technology and innovation research, economic science, physical and human geography, and biology. Here, economic science refers to the study of individual and group behaviour of humans with their purchasing power. In this book, economics is not merely a theory of moral philosophy, such as searching for how best to behave, or how best to allocate

[10] For example, climate change mitigation research involves a combination of at least the fields of climatology, physical geography, chemistry, mathematics, computer science, engineering, economics, sociology, psychology, political science and law.

resources, since, as the reader will realise, normative considerations only appear rather late, in the last part of this book (Part III). Economic science refers to a scientific analysis of human economic behaviour, and thus is not as value-laden as it should necessarily be when restricted to pure moral philosophy. It is not necessarily only an analysis or search for best course of policy action based on subjective objectives and values. This can be called 'applied economics'. As in physical geography, which seeks an understanding of Planet Earth, its atmosphere, oceans and continents, and human geography, which seeks to understand human behaviour in relation to its environment, economic science seeks to understand how the economic process actually works, as opposed to how it ought to. Naturally, economic models that attempt to describe economic reality are never truly value-free, but that does not invalidate the aspiration to develop models that are as objectively empirically grounded as possible.

As seen in Chapter 3, there is currently *no consensus* over the mechanisms underpinning the economic process, and it is important to recognise that. And the choice of theory does not, or should not, depend on one's political leaning. In fact, both current mainstream microeconomic and macroeconomic theory currently possess deep shortcomings, flaws, which have been criticised in depth, but have not been unanimously addressed, and thus as opposed to, say, physics, no universally accepted basic theory of economics exists. It has become clear recently that most current macroeconomic models are incorrectly formulated since they could not foresee the recent 2008 financial crisis, highlighting that these models do not explain reality as humans experience it.[11]

The innovation of this book brings into the picture a relatively new discipline of its own called complexity science.[12] It is a 'meta-science' that refers to the study, in any type of system (social or natural) of phenomena emergent from interactions between sub-systems, and searches for 'universality classes' of problems for which common analysis methods could be used. For instance, while subatomic physics studies the properties of electrons, protons and neutrons, chemistry is not simply 'applied subatomic physics', because substantial amounts of chemical behaviour do not directly depend on the basic properties of electrons, protons and neutrons in vacuum; instead, many chemical phenomena stem from interactions between these particles when found in large numbers. Understanding the staggering diversity of phenomena in biology is not done on the sole basis of chemistry knowledge.

The same applies with people and institutions: collective human behaviour cannot be easily understood on the sole basis of the psychology of isolated individuals;

[11] See Keen (2017).

[12] Many scholars have contributed to the diverse field of complexity science. However, substantial knowledge originates from physics, and one author particularly stands out, Philip Warren Anderson, with his seminal contribution (Anderson, 1972). For an application to economics, see Anderson et al. (1989); Arthur et al. (1997b); Arthur (2014).

it requires analysis of how humans interact with one another, and with groups of peers. For instance, it is thought in social anthropology that consumption habits of people are socially determined, and therefore that knowing individual preferences is insufficient to predict consumption habits of a group.[13] '*Emergence*' is the phenomenon by which new properties arise out of the interactions between components, the existence of which is not straightforward to predict from known properties of individual system components.

Emergent phenomena exist in economics, which stem from interactions between economic agents,[14] including bubbles (in which agents attempt to outplay each other in financial markets, see, e.g., Arthur et al., 1997b; Palmer et al., 1994) and fashions (in which agents influence each other's consumption habits, see, e.g., Arthur and Lane, 1993; Brock and Durlauf, 2001; Mercure, 2018). These are crowd effects not predictable from the psychology of isolated individuals, but emerge in groups.

In any system in which large numbers of interactions are at play, the enumeration of 'easy to guess' emergent phenomena quickly becomes impossible. When drawing a model of such a system, it becomes ever more difficult to guess what unexpected emergent phenomena could arise that defies initial expectations. Environmental systems are such: many observed complex phenomena are unexplained, even if all components of the system are perfectly well known. For example, as seen in Chapter 13, deforestation in the tropics is caused not just by a myriad of direct factors, but also by indirect factors through a highly complex chain of events that circumvent existing legislation, thus interacting even with policy-making. It originates from a combination of climate change and trade through globalised networks, provoking complex chains of indirect land-use changes and stresses that ultimately destroy the rainforest. And this system evolves faster than the pace of progress at which scientists get to grips with understanding it.

1.1.3 *Science and the Policy Cycle*

Part of the ambiguity in conventional, normative, environmental economics is the lack of clarity regarding which process of the policy cycle it seeks to address, whether for agenda-setting or for impact assessment. Environmental governance requires

[13] In particular, comsumption habits of individuals follow the dividing lines of social groups such as due to income, social class, cultural belonging, country of origin, industry type, etc. The work of Douglas and Isherwood (1979) sets the stage for understanding consumption on the basis of social interactions, something that is supported by a myriad of sociological research. Wilk and Cliggett (2007) offer a good starting point to explore economic anthropology.

[14] Other than through prices in the economy. As seen in Chapter 2, standard general equilibrium economic models assume that agents interact solely through prices and supply-demand relationships; however, this fails to represent many other observed phenomena.

scientific knowledge inputs to be integrated at particular stages of the policy cycle. Classical descriptions of the policy cycle involve the stages of (e.g., see Crabbé and Leroy, 2008):

(1) agenda setting;
(2) policy formulation;
(3) *ex ante* impact assessment and decision-making;
(4) policy implementation;
(5) *ex post* monitoring and evaluation.

Scientific information can help intervene in the policy cycle either for *agenda setting*, in which the policy agenda is decided (whether or not to address a problem), for *impact assessment*, in which the impacts of the policy agenda onto natural and social systems are assessed, in order to decide whether or not to adopt proposed new legislation, or for *evaluation*, to determine whether an intervention has had the desired result, in order to revise that policy program.

Agenda-setting is clearly a more fundamentally prescriptive process than impact assessment, as it attempts to establish a vision and direction for future policy-making: what future do 'we' collectively want? In that respect, it is appropriate to imagine and establish various idealisations of the world which could be aspired to. For example, one can search for the configuration of a global energy system with zero greenhouse gas emissions that fulfils all applications required in some chosen definition for human need and well-being. Such a normative analysis can, in principle, be carried out using cost-optimisation energy models, because the possible system idealisations thus designed can be entirely hypothetical. For a hypothetical, idealised world, missing data can be themselves hypothesised. Crucially, to carry out an optimisation requires to choose a number of subjective criteria and valuation methods, which are understood to reflect objectives determined by political consensus: for example, the value ascribed to a unit of greenhouse gas emissions, the value of ecosystem services, the value of energy security, the value of environmental protection. Standard methods exist to determine such values, including using surveys and other ways to gather people's subjective opinions.[15] These methods are outside of the scientific process, since they do not deal directly with *observable quantities* and their explanations. They deal with normative preferences that are not formally quantifiable.[16]

Meanwhile, impact assessment is more of a descriptive science process, in which an analyst attempts to predict what the likely outcome could be of a chosen policy pathway, in order to build an evidence base that can be used to defend a policy

[15] See the methods in Hanley and Barbier (2009); Bateman et al. (2002).

[16] Note that one cannot demonstrate the reliability of a measurement of subjective preference for a person or a group, since one can at best use for such quantification measurements of what people say, or observations of what people do, neither of which measure their true intent or their beliefs. Thus the interpretation of such measurements is philosophical and outside of the realm of positive science.

proposal designed to achieve the set agenda (e.g., through a vote in parliament). Models used for this purpose logically should ideally represent the objective world as observed, through its underlying governing mechanisms as they are known. Thus, models used cannot, according to the philosophy of science, be of the same idealised, normative type as used for agenda-setting. In particular, optimisation tools are not suitable for the impact assessment purpose, since they cannot establish a clear causal connection between policy and outcome.[17]

Serious errors in policy-making can easily be made on the basis of using the wrong models for the questions asked. However, it is not the sole responsibility of policy-makers to choose the correct models for the questions; analysts share a large part of the responsibility. Since descriptive models are scarce, optimisation models are widely used for predicting the outcomes of policy, which, as shown in Chapter 3, is a dangerous game. It currently leads to substantial amounts of disagreement and lack of consensus in both academic and policy circles. It is not, strictly speaking, the remit of the policy-maker to identify the validity of models. When the outcomes of a model supports a particular policy vision, it is likely that it will be used by policy-makers, whether the process is scientifically valid or not. Using the wrong models for the questions can lead to supporting decisions that are ultimately detrimental to the environmental problem one attempts to solve, if they mis-represent the real dynamics of system evolution.

1.1.4 *Risks and Opportunities Instead of Costs and Benefits*

As could be inferred through discussions with high ranking UK and EU civil servants in energy and climate change-related positions of governance, it would seem that assessing risks and opportunities is often more useful to policy-makers than assessing costs and benefits.[18] The reason is intuitively simple: fundamental uncertainty can

[17] The debate in this respect, i.e. whether optimisation models can be used for impact assessment, is one that can be expressed as whether one believes that system-wide optimisation is a good description, or approximation, of the real observed collective economic processes. This book spends a great deal of space showing why it almost certainly does not. In short, optimisation of a whole system is *not* equivalent to the collective behaviour of a group of individually optimising agents, even if one was inclined to believe that agents optimise, or knew exactly what they optimise: a coordination problem exists between the two, see Arthur et al. (1997b); Palmer et al. (1994).

[18] In fact it depends what activity is undertaken by government officials, and there remains debate about this, but the 2020 amendment to the UK's Green Book guidelines for policy appraisal (HM Treasury, 2020a, Annex 7) attests to the need for information beyond CBA. The EEIST project (Economics of Energy Innovation, funded by UK government and formerly coordinated by the author) has organised a number of discussions with officials across UK government departments. When assessing whole programs, risks and opportunities are understood as helpful if it is clear that costs and benefits cannot be identified with certainty, and if the methodology provides additional insights (see Chapter 12). For prioritising among large numbers of possible small projects, it remains to be determined if anything more complicated than CBA is practical for these stakeholders' day-to-day use.

be used to advantage and understood for its potential for generating opportunities, especially through innovation, while it can also encompass various types of disasters. If one is not able to establish reliable probability distributions over the outcomes of a decision to estimate expected costs and benefits, one will seek ways to improve the likelihood of opportunities and options (escape routes) arising, and decrease the likelihood of disasters and dead-ends taking place. The latter implies carrying a risk assessment, for which standard methodologies exist (see Chapter 12). For the former, uncertainty is a generator of potential positive outcomes, especially through innovation.

This is typically how a company manager would think: positioning his company such that it can capture market opportunities if they arise, and thus deliberately placing it in a situation of fundamental uncertainty. Full certainty is bad news for business, since it eliminates all options to improve, and therefore impedes growth as it dis-incentivises innovation and productivity change. Instead, ambitious entrepreneurs obtain finance from venture capitalists precisely because they think they have a chance of achieving something big, even if this is unquantifiably uncertain. And furthermore, venture capitalists precisely seek these types of risky ventures, since this is how they make money. Few high return ventures exist that do not involve high risks, and truly visionary technological change necessarily involves taking big risks.

When public authorities seek ambitious technological projects or a radical change of technological direction (such as going to the moon, or the low-carbon energy transition), they necessarily accept that high risk technological ventures will have to be undertaken. Since the government is, at the same time, the '*lender of last resort*', the '*spender of last resort*' and the '*innovator of last resort*' (see Chapters 8, 10 and 11), the institution with the deepest pockets and the highest ability to absorb risk, it expects to at least partly finance and absorb the risk involved in such ambitious projects. These projects can improve a society's ability to capture social and economic opportunities by creating new capabilities (Mazzucato, 2013). In such a perspective, it would make sense for policy-makers to assess proposed policies based on their potential to generate risks and opportunities. This is shown in detail as a decision-making framework proposal in Chapter 12.

1.1.5 *Few Realistic Descriptive Models Exist*

The complex linkages between the economy, the geography (or environment), social systems and environmental degradation are not described satisfactorily by any self-consistent descriptive model, and indeed the challenges are substantial. Yet, as seen in Chapter 2, lack of realism in many economic and technology models used in science–policy circles is the most important and pressing flaw. Many mainstream, or orthodox, representations of social systems are deficient in large parts due to the widespread use of optimisation algorithms beyond their application remit, which are not really grounded in evidence regarding individual and collective agent behaviour, even if they are often rich with data. Furthermore, there is also a problematic tendency of researchers to mix up both descriptive and normative models to carry out what becomes interpreted as predictions. This is reviewed in Chapter 4.

Social scientists often argue that the difference between natural science models and social science models is that human behaviour cannot be predicted, while in the natural sciences, the behaviour of objects, fundamental particles and organisms can be. In fact, this is not true. In the physical sciences, Schrödinger's and Heisenberg's equations, that govern the evolution of matter in the universe, are fundamentally about the uncertainty over the behaviour of fundamental particles. Yet more importantly, fundamental uncertainty emerges through all the possible imaginable and unimaginable ways system components can interact, and reality constructs itself by creating more possible paths forward than it eliminates possibilities. This is explored in Chapters 5 and 6. It seems clear that the philosophy of science underpinning model of human processes requires more rigour and clarification than currently happens. It is in practice not always clear even to social science modellers what the philosophy of science of their own models is, as it even sometimes changes according to the problem when the methodology does not (Chapter 4).

In this book, a blueprint is created for a coherent predictive model of human-environment systems, for use in impact assessment, and a framework for policy appraisal based on assessing risks and opportunities is formulated. This book does not delve deeply into the inherently political area of agenda-setting, since the philosophy of why humans should address environmental concerns is extensively covered elsewhere. It may be argued that in many countries, the past two or three decades have been spent setting the climate change agenda. This has generated several generations of highly qualified agenda setters in academic circles. This has been supported by further developments in the field of operational research. However, in the case of climate change, following the Paris Agreement, the agenda is essentially now solidly set in most countries, and where it is not, no substantial additional agenda-setting research will really make a difference, as it is now purely driven by politics. Policy circles are in fact moving towards detailed impact assessment for assessing the form of interventions, and require substantial information and analysis capacity which is not currently available.

It would be easy to keep using the agenda-setting arsenal to try and identify the optimal policy to use under real and assumed certainties; however, this may be a fundamental mistake happening over and over that is costing substantial time in trying out policy that ultimately does not achieve the goals set in the agenda. Instead, researchers must now devote their time and energy into creating detailed predictive models for impact assessment, which must involve true scientific research on humans and their behaviour, and the deeper impacts of socio-technical change.

1.2. CLIMATE CHANGE AND PLANETARY BOUNDARIES

1.2.1 *Planetary Boundaries*

Many in the general public are developing a strong conviction that humans are squandering Planet Earth at an alarmingly fast pace. In which way exactly is this happening? Many think that the planet just cannot sustain the current rate of economic growth, and therefore clamour for a so-called 'de-growth' economy. What exactly would that entail? The oceans are currently filling up with plastic, mistaken for food by wildlife. Deforestation is progressing at a fast rate in the tropics, to make space for agriculture. Agricultural land is gradually degrading with intensive agriculture. And finally, but not least of all, the climate is changing with the accumulation of greenhouse gases in the atmosphere, which originate primarily from human processes.

How should these issues be addressed in environmental governance, and crucially, using which legal and policy instruments? Some hope for a deep social revolution against neoliberal capitalism, which in their view would solve all of these problems. However, it is not clear that anyone really fully understands dynamics of environmental issues in order to know with certainty how to solve them. It is hard to resist the temptation to propose new dogmas on how to be 'green' as solutions to these emergent problems. Surely, some may think, if people had had the 'right morals', these issues would not have emerged? The unfortunate likely truth is that, not one of the issues above are likely to be solved using simple interventions or behavioural dogmas. Human society is globalised and interconnected, such that problems occurring somewhere induce other problems elsewhere.[19]

A framework called 'planetary boundaries' has been developed by a consortium of environmental scientists, that seeks to quantify the impacts of human processes on the environment, summarising the main global environmental issues.[20] These include the carbon cycle (climate change), the nitrogen and phosphorus cycles (related to fertilisers in agriculture), freshwater use, land-use change (including deforestation), ocean acidification, ozone depletion and biodiversity loss (Figure 1.1). Planetary boundaries quantified global limits in these domains, but perhaps more importantly, the work quantified also the current state of knowledge over these processes. However, they do not suggest policy approaches to deal with these issues, and rightly so, since policy is context and geography-dependent, not globally set.

Climate change originates from a large disturbance in the planet's carbon cycle. The carbon cycle involves all living matter and some non-living matter around the planet, through which the carbon element flows and is carried and stored, including plants, trees and living creatures on land, marine ecosystems, volcanoes, soil carbon

[19] E.g., see Lambin and Meyfroidt (2011).

[20] Originally defined in Rockström et al. (2009), further developed by Steffen et al. (2015).

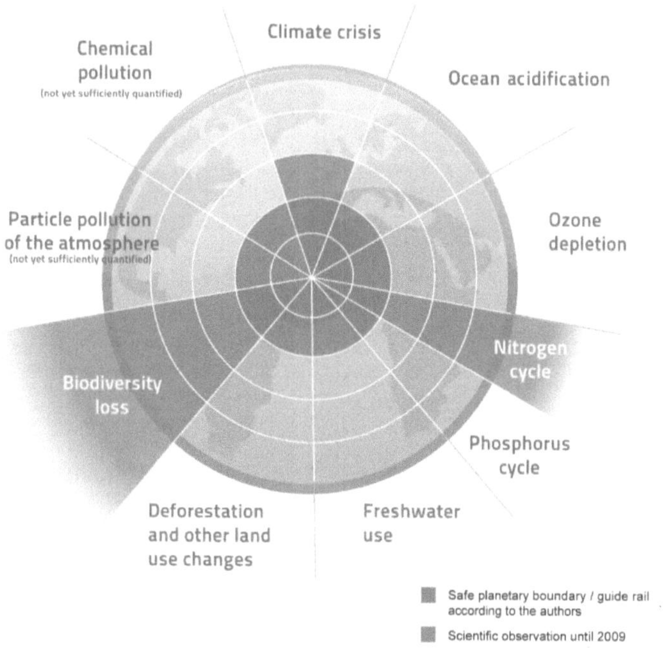

FIGURE 1.1 Planetary boundaries (originally from Rockström et al., 2009). Reproduced from Wikipedia.

and the decomposition of dead matter, fossil fuels and of course human processes. Carbon flows between all of these natural processes and stocks, going from plants to the atmosphere and back to plants, but also from the atmosphere to the ocean and back. Marine ecosystems take up this carbon, in the form of carbonic acid, and form calcium carbonate shells, which eventually fall to the ocean floor. With tectonic plate movements, some of these calcium carbonate sediments become buried underground, and some of the carbon comes back out through volcanoes, while some of the carbon becomes stored in the crust in the form of fossil fuels.

Carbon compounds contain energy that can be converted to heat by combustion. For centuries, humans have been partly preoccupied with finding powerful sources of energy, in order to operate economic processes that gradually increased their living standards (see Smil, 2019). Fossil fuels are deposits of carbon compounds underground, that feature a relatively high energy density, in comparison to other combustible materials found on the land, for example wood.

Fossil fuels are leftovers from living matter, onshore or marine, that became buried underground. Energy exists underground: heat is present inside the core of the earth. It originates from decaying unstable heavy elements, themselves originating from how the planet was formed out of interstellar matter condensed. This decay process continuously heats the inner parts of the planet, heat that gradually escapes to the

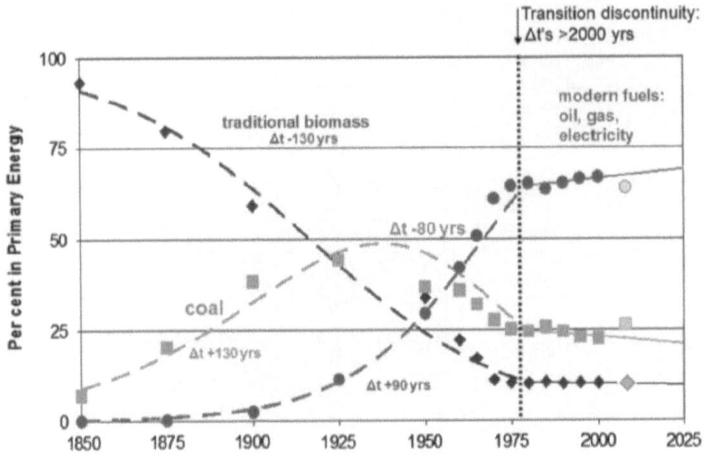

FIGURE 1.2 History of use of primary fuels. Reproduced from Grubler (2012).

cosmos, but that is also used by various natural processes. In the case of organic matter buried underground, this heat gradually upgrades its energy content by slowly changing its chemical structure. Thus oil, gas and coal form over millennia, and contain a high energy density that can be converted to heat when combusted.

Various technological revolutions have characterised human history, involving changes in energy sources.[21] As seen in Figure 1.2, the world changed from using primarily biomass from the land towards more energy dense coal, which itself became gradually replaced by more energy dense oil, which is now gradually being replaced by more energy dense gas. These changes coincided with, or were driven by, changes in the industrial structure then in place. Wood was used in household fireplaces, but coal came to be understood as more efficient for new steam engines being developed for providing mechanical work in developing textiles industries. This gave rise to a higher availability of coal and other materials made with it (e.g., iron and steel), and thus coal became used in most energy-using activities, including notably mobility. However, the subsequent rise of the internal combustion engine made clear that liquid fuels could enable a higher diversity of mobility activities (e.g., cars and planes), due to its more convenient form and higher energy density. A new chemical industry developed around all the compounds made available by the developing oil industry, enabling an ever higher number of new activities and industrial processes. However, oil prices rising with scarcity and important geopolitical tensions led to a decline of its use where it is least important, notably for electricity generation, as it became increasingly replaced by higher energy

[21] See Freeman and Louçã (2001) for a detailed account of Kondratiev waves and related technological revolutions, or industrial revolutions, that took place over history.

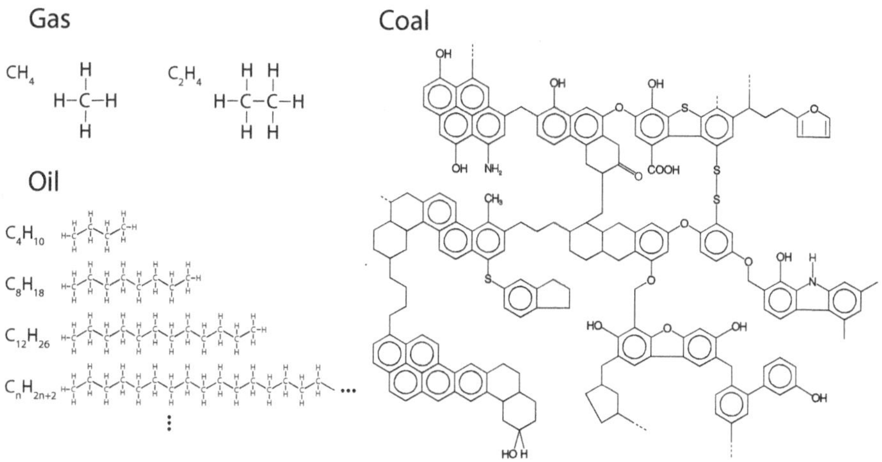

FIGURE 1.3 Illustration of chemical structures of fossil fuels. The heavier the fuel, the longer and complex molecules are, and the lower the number of hydrogen to carbon bonds in comparison to carbon to carbon bonds, the lower the energy content.

density gas. Nowadays, the energy system uses a roughly similar amount of coal, oil and gas.[22] Figure 1.3 shows the chemical origin of the energy density hierarchy of the three fuels.

The combustion of these fuels emits carbon dioxide (CO_2) in the atmosphere, alongside other gases in lower quantities (NO_x, SO_x and particulate matter). This is *new* carbon added to the existing carbon cycle, which was prior to that trapped underground. This new (or perhaps old) carbon disturbs the carbon cycle in such a way that the oceans become more acidic, due to the excessive flux of carbonic acid, and the atmosphere traps more light from the sun due to absorption bands in the spectrum of CO_2 which is found in higher concentrations. This increased amount of energy changes the climate, as oceans and the atmosphere warm up. The absorptive capacity of the land surface increases as snow melts and falls less frequently, and as glaciers, ice caps and the ice covers of the poles melt permanently. The volume of sea water expands with additions of freshwater from glaciers and due to simple thermal expansion, leading to sea-level rise. The frequency and strength of storms and extreme weather events (floods, gales, droughts, fires) increases measurably. As the average temperature increases, animals, plants and ecosystems either need to migrate or cannot survive.[23]

22 Each of between 140 and 180 EJ (10^{18} Joules) of fuel use globally (see the data in IEA, 2020).

23 See Houghton (2015) and of course the IPCC (2013) report for a review.

1.2.2 *The Energy–Water–Food Nexus*

As global demand for energy, water and food expands, with rising population and, more crucially, income, it is likely that humans reach the limits of what Planet Earth can supply.[24] But what are these limits, and are there specific measurement indicators that could tell humans when they are exceeding these? Unfortunately, the answer is no, but instead, the complexity of issues obscures substantially any assessment of such limits. This issue has been named the 'Energy–Water–Food' nexus, to illustrate the strong interdependency of a whole range of environmental issues forming a 'perfect storm'.

Deforestation is one of the key issues of environmental governance, as it touches almost all other environmental issues: climate change (through emissions), biodiversity loss (through loss of habitat) and freshwater availability (through the ability of trees to transfer moisture between the atmosphere and the land). For example, destruction of the Amazon forest could lead to a substantial re-structuring of the whole Earth's climate system because of its role in managing moisture (Malhi et al., 2008). In fact, a vicious cycle exists between human deforestation, forest fires, and forest dieback (Brando et al., 2014). Therefore what is the motivation for humans to deforest the Amazon?

China has undergone substantial economic transformation over the past few decades, which has substantially changed the purchasing power of Chinese people. They enjoy consuming pork products, and as their income grows, they consume pork with increasing frequency. The very large pork industry in China and elsewhere uses soybeans as feed, as it contains substantial amounts of protein. Chinese agriculture produces soybeans, but in insufficient quantities for the size of the Chinese pork industry, in part due to a decline related to gradual desertification (Brown-Lima et al., 2010a). With globalisation, this has historically offered a very important opportunity for exports to South-American countries such as Brazil and Argentina, which have substantial amounts of suitable land. The growth of a large soybean industry required substantial growth in land area dedicated to agriculture, which has ultimately come at the expense of the Amazon and the Cerrado forests.

Deforesting the Amazon is essentially illegal. Soybean producers usually appear not to be directly involved in deforestation. In fact, soybean producers primarily expand by buying land legally. However, the suppliers of this land are mostly cattle farmers who are thus displaced by the soybean industry, in what is called 'indirect land-use change'.[25] Cattle ranchers are most likely the ones carrying out the deforestation, mostly by setting fire to the forest. However, since this is illegal, the way in which recently deforested land eventually comes into legal ownership

[24] The Energy–Water–Food Nexus as a concept became popular following papers such as those by Beddington (2012) and Hoff (2011), and remains a topic of investigation.

[25] Arima et al. (2011); Barona et al. (2010).

and sold legally to soybean producers remains unclear. It nevertheless takes place at an alarming rate, through a complex chain of direct and indirect causal effects motivated by the opportunities of globalisation. This subject is explored in detail in Chapter 13. However, it is clear that chains of events cannot be understood or predicted using optimisation models; the complexity of all possible chains of events is simply overwhelming, and it is furthermore not clear who is maximising what. These chains evolve over time, where policy solutions are designed and implemented to tackle the problem, delivering moderate success as the problem changes again. It is a wicked problem, and must be treated as such.

1.2.3 *Growth, Intensity, Boundaries, Natural Resources*

Economic growth is an expression that summarises simply a large variety of economic processes. Growth of gross domestic product (GDP) corresponds to the growth of the sum of value-added in all sectors of the economy. In popular thought, growth is often associated with the growth of natural resource extraction, to which of course it is closely related, but not exclusively and not simply. Between value-added and natural resource extraction, an evolving process of efficiency exists, at both ends. The quantity of natural resources needed in each economic process typically gradually declines, per unit of economic process done, at rates that change according to context. This is due to innovation, in which entrepreneurs seek ways to cut costs and increase profits.

For example, the quantity of fuel demanded by vehicles per kilometre driven declines over time, as vehicle engines are gradually improved. The total amount of fuel demanded for road transport increases, since the demand for transport services increases faster than the rate of fuel efficiency improvements, and thus GHG emissions increase. Thus growth and efficiency have opposing effects, to the extent that the economy, when seen as a metabolic system, 'runs to standstill', where efficiency apparently changes in a way that only just overcomes, on average, the increasing complexity and loss of efficiency of the natural resource delivery network due to its own growth.[26]

Economic growth is not just related to population and consumption growth. It is in fact primarily related to innovation and productivity growth. Entrepreneurs continuously seek ways to reduce the inputs into their production processes in order to make a profit. Innovation also increases product diversity in the economy, which attracts spending. Profit made on innovation is spent in the economy, leading to increasing demand for products and services. However, as inputs required for production decline with cumulative innovative activity, the overall costs decline

[26] See the work of Andrew Jarvis (Jarvis et al., 2015; Jarvis, 2018) for a metabolic description of the energy–economy system.

and eventually prices decline as well, leaving households with leftover income after buying 'the usual basket of goods', which can be spent on additional products and services, also leading to the growth of overall consumption. Meanwhile, the increasing efficiency upstream reduces demand for labour which ultimately becomes reallocated to the production of novelty goods.[27]

The resource intensity of the economic process changes continuously over time. The economy can be seen as a macro-organism, which extracts resources, processes them with a certain intensity, and produces waste with another type of intensity. These intensities are closely related to the process of growth. For example, it is observed that, without a decline in the intensity of use of fossil fuels, the growth process would not be possible, due to the increasing inefficiency that results from growth as the fuel delivery to end-users in the economy complexifies, and due to constraints over how much energy can be physically extracted from the environment (Jarvis et al., 2015). The induced innovation apparently creates a balance between primary energy extraction and the efficiency of delivery to, and use by, the end-user, and the two continuously push and pull one another.

Therefore, economic growth does not necessarily lead to the depletion of all natural resources on Earth, since when scarcity sets in, innovation typically reduces the energy intensity of the economic process to do more with less: the economy is adaptive. In that sense, advocating GDP 'de-growth' in the economy may be premature without better understanding innovation and the economic process. De-growth might in fact only be a smokescreen, a red herring, inferred from moral philosophy more than from observed economic mechanisms.

1.3. MODELS OF ENVIRONMENTAL AND HUMAN PROCESSES

1.3.1 *Innovation and Technological Change*

In climate change mitigation research, as well as in other areas of environmental policy, technological developments make up a large portion of the solutions debated. In fact, innovation is generally expected to solve most environmental problems, and the governance discussions revolve around finding how to foster innovation. For example, governments ban the sale of certain products, and promote other more environmentally friendly products in replacement. Ironically, the process of innovation itself is mostly unknown or misunderstood by scientists and economists, even if they are themselves to some degree part of it. What are the social processes involved? Studying innovation as a social phenomenon is a field in its own right.[28]

[27] This goes back to Schumpeter (1934) and his *Theory of Economic Development*, discussed in Chapters 8 and 11.

[28] See for example the works of Freeman and Perez (1988); Hekkert et al. (2007); Bergek et al. (2008); Nelson and Winter (1982); Grübler and Wilson (2013).

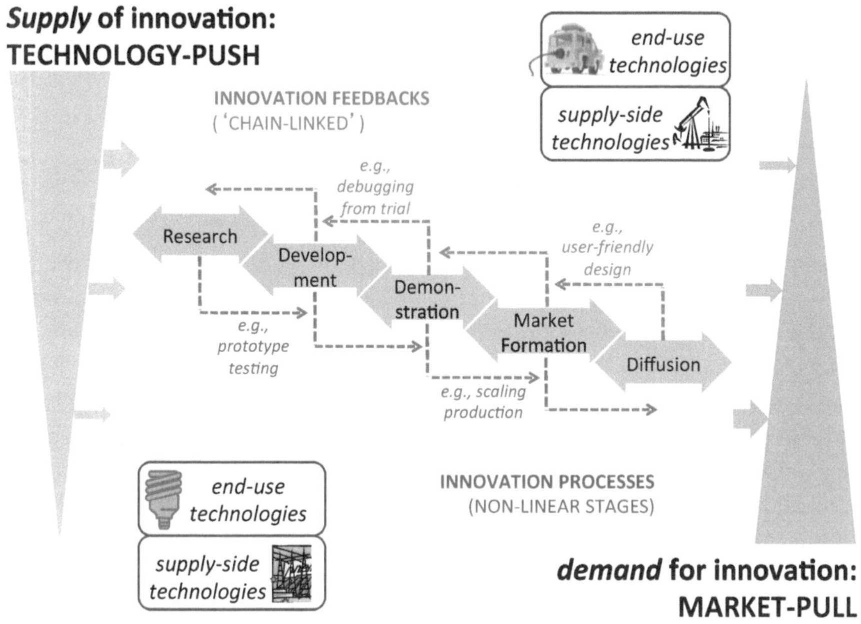

FIGURE 1.4 The innovation chain (Grübler and Wilson, 2013).

Innovation lies with the development of knowledge, which is then applied to developing new products to be sold in markets, or improving existing ones. Innovation follows a complicated chain of events, in which many different types of agents interact. Each agent can be seen to fulfil one or more functions in the innovation system (Hekkert et al., 2007). The innovation chain itself is normally described as following a certain order (Figure 1.4), with feedback between various steps.

Each step is also financed in a fairly different way from different sources. Early stages of innovation are typically publicly financed and carried out at universities and public research institutions. Ideas are generated that could, in principle, lead to the development of products. The highly risky process of taking academic ideas and transforming them into working devices is not very often done by private companies; it is often left to publicly funded institutions, financed by governments (see e.g., Mazzucato, 2013). However, the packaging of such devices and ideas into working sellable products is more frequently done by the private sector, often through start-up companies, financed by, for example, venture capital and angel investors. Demonstration projects are frequently done through public-private partnerships. Meanwhile, the push and marketing of products into mass markets is typically done by private sector firms, with their own internal funding or on the back of privately owned financial assets. This is described in Chapter 8.

What accelerates the creation and diffusion of low-carbon products to reduce emissions is typically a combination of technology push (technology creation and deployment) and market pull (what makes them economically attractive) policies (Grubb et al., 2014). This is discussed in Chapters 7 for theory, and 14 for application to real policy.

1.3.2 *Creative Destruction with Low-Carbon Innovation*

The process of innovation is not entirely inoffensive. Firms live in a world of cut-throat competition. They face an innovation race, in which they must out-innovate their competitors in order to attract sales. This is clearly observed in the innovation race for smart phones and applications of artificial intelligence. Innovation and new products often replace older systems, which thus become obsolete. For older systems that have been dominant, this sometimes leads to the decline of very large industries and companies, along with their suppliers, and the latter's suppliers, and everyone they employ. Technological change can lead to mass unemployment, particularly in locations in which large industries have been concentrated but have gone into decline. For example, many coal mining and steel-making towns in North America have become ghost towns, and some cities around the Great Lakes dominated by the car industry have gone through spectacular declines. Scars from this process can be seen long after it has taken place, for example, where the steel industry has once been dominant in the North of England. Industry has continuously changed over history, going from one industrial revolution to the next.[29]

Schumpeter (1942) coined a famous expression for this process of innovation destroying existing industries: 'creative destruction'. In the Schumpeterian world, creative destruction is not a term with any normative connotation. Schumpeter did not intend to imply that creative destruction is a desirable, or undesirable, process. Rather, it is an observed phenomenon, that arises from the search of entrepreneurs for profits, wealth and power. Creative destruction underpins much of the process of productivity change and economic growth. However, it also leads to periodic crises of structural adjustment, in which some people are left behind while others benefit periodically leading to social dislocations (Freeman and Louçã, 2001). The macroeconomic implications of this are discussed in Chapters 11, for a theoretical model, and 15 for application to understanding the dynamics of global decarbonisation, industrial change and the decline of fossil fuel markets.

Creative destruction is also a financial process. Following Schumpeter (1934), entrepreneurs typically have ideas about how to reduce the use of inputs in particular production processes (whether labour, energy, capital or even knowledge inputs), but do not typically own the necessary funds to implement their ideas. They either apply to financial institutions by showcasing their ideas, or find willing private investors, and their projects become financial assets to parties who become financially involved

[29] The best references on this topic are Freeman and Louçã (2001) and Perez (2001), in the tradition of Schumpeter (1939), reviewed in Chapters 8 and 11. See also Semieniuk et al. (2021).

in the process. If the innovation process is successful, the entrepreneur as well as his financiers gain a profit. However, the entrepreneur may also fail, and possibly default on his loan repayments and declare bankruptcy. In either case, entrepreneurial action is not possible without interaction with the financial sector.

Over history, many financial bubbles have arisen as a result of some group, or constellation of technological innovations, which have led to financial crises and economic recessions or depressions.[30] Thus, innovation can be responsible for both crises of structural adjustment and financial crises, as creative destruction takes place. It therefore means that even studying finance, and the financial sector, is relevant to environmental science. For example, one may ask the question whether Europe, still in a state of recovery from the last financial crisis, is in a position to finance a large-scale transformation towards a sustainable society. This is because innovation and technological change is capital intensive, and a society riddled with debt may or may not be in a position to undertake a large amount of additional debt. The answer to this question is unknown. This is discussed in Chapters 10 for a model of financial instability, and 15 for application to the financial impacts of a rapid low-carbon transition.

1.4. STRUCTURE OF THIS BOOK

In this book, it is hoped that all the issues raised in this introduction are addressed in a holistic manner, in order to prepare the reader for and propose a new approach for environmental governance. The approach emphasises the study of complex systems in order to fully understand the dynamics at play, both in natural and human processes, which are typically intertwined. The objective is to put forward a method that fully distinguishes between moral philosophy (normative models) and positive science (descriptive models), and makes scientific use of available data, and quantification of uncertainty, to effectively inform environmental governance.

Part I of this book explores the current state of knowledge and practice in environmental governance. Chapter 2 focuses on describing the degree of agency (decision-making power) in environmental governance problems, looking at the representation of agents in models of human processes, and discussing the distinction between normative and positive theories. Chapter 3 describes equilibrium and non-equilibrium economic models, their origin, their underpinnings and their implementations, including innovation and finance. Chapter 4 focuses on the policy cycle and the philosophy of science, to explain why a complexity approach is necessary and unavoidable, with a list of required scientific developments necessary to make this possible.

30 Perez (2001) records this in detail, building on Freeman and Perez (1988); see also Semieniuk et al. (2021).

Part II proposes the various components of a comprehensive positive theory for environmental complexity economics. Chapter 5 sets out key elements of complexity science to be used. Chapter 6 explores the structure of knowledge and uncertainty, focusing on how to understand outcomes of scientific research within the uncertainty they are embedded in, and the structure of probability and predictability of complex systems and human behaviour. It also explores representations and theories of human behaviour, in order to build a knowledge base upon which to build models of human processes. Chapter 7 proposes a model with micro-foundations for a theory of technological diffusion. Chapter 8 proposes a model with micro-foundations for a theory of innovation. In order to explore financial stability issues in relation to low-carbon innovation, Chapter 9 describes the nature of money and the financial system, and its peculiar characteristic of recurrent instability. Chapter 10 explores the finance of innovation by offering a quantitative model, with micro-foundations, of debt, ownership and financial instability. Chapter 11 proposes a macroeconomic model (this time with both micro-foundations and *macro*-foundations) that is true to the evidence found in economic history and the evolutionary economics literature.

Part III of this book formally sets out theoretical foundations for normative complexity economics, followed by three case studies. In Chapter 12, a framework for decision-making in complex environmental problems is given, driven by a method to work with pervasive uncertainty, to replace equilibrium and cost-benefit models that are unsuitable to study problems of policy intending *transformational change*. Chapter 13 provides a case study on the Energy–Water–Food Nexus in Brazil. Chapter 14 explores the effectiveness of policy for incentivising the diffusion of low-carbon innovation. And finally, Chapter 15 provides an analysis of the macroeconomic impacts of a low-carbon transition on structural change, employment and financial wealth ownership and stability.

2

Complexity, Heterogeneity and Uncertainty as Basis for Policy Analysis

This chapter raises key questions on the current state of practice in policy appraisal and analysis, in academia and government. It proposes a fundamental methodological shift in the modelling of policy interventions for sustainability transitions in order to account for complexity, uncertainty and agent heterogeneity. It identifies the main shortcomings of present methods of the equilibrium and optimisation-based approaches most frequently used to inform sustainability policy: (i) their normative, optimisation-based nature, (ii) their unrealistic reliance on the full-rationality of agents, (iii) their inability to capture self-reinforcing feedback processes, (iv) their inability to represent multiple solutions and path-dependency and (v) their inability to properly account for agent heterogeneity. A proposal is made for dynamical systems analysis in policy appraisal that could lead to a paradigm shift in the ability of governments to understand and solve complex environmental issues. This chapter is adapted and updated from earlier work published in Mercure et al. (2016a).

2.1. AGENT DIVERSITY, UNCERTAINTY AND COMPLEXITY

Chapter 1 summarised the key issues involved in addressing with policy problems qualified as 'wicked', or in other words, issues of transformational scope. The use of optimisation was criticised, but without yet a clear scientific underpinning; however, the chapter offered a roadmap for the rest of the book. This chapter substantiates this criticism by narrowing down more specifically on the issues that affect policy analysis in current methods, namely agent diversity, uncertainty and complex dynamics.

2.1.1 *The Chilling Effect of Uncertainty*

National and international public policy-making must confront the unprecedented challenge of effectively managing the complex interaction of economic development, energy systems and environmental change. The effects of stringent climate policies are subject to uncertainty and disagreement, which hinders policy action, and the lack of policy clarity has, in turn, a chilling effect on the private sector's incentives to shift investment towards sustainable options and opportunities. In the context of damaging policy indecision, investors are often inclined to wait before committing to new long-term capital investment decisions. Meanwhile, carbon budgets are increasingly consumed (IPCC, 2018), and the likelihood of avoiding dangerous climate change is rapidly decreasing. Consensus on desired outcomes achieved through international agreements urgently needs to be translated into consensus on actions, to identify effective climate policy and facilitate its rapid global adoption.

At the roots of policy indecisiveness lie conflicts in the current understanding of the complex interactions between technology, society, the macroeconomy and the environment. Policy-makers often consider that important trade-offs exist between, on the one hand, improving the sustainability of the economy and, on the other hand, adequately supporting economic growth. The ensuing reluctance to act contrasts with the signals from an increasing body of reports produced by think-tanks and international organisations arguing that wealth could be generated by new green technology. Decision-makers thus face dissonant signals, causing them to hold back their action. Indeed, successful public (and related private) initiatives of the scale required to stabilise emissions and adapt to climate change have no precedent, and they are unlikely to develop unless the important uncertainty as to their full implications is properly tackled. To make the analysis more intelligible, four major areas are identified where uncertainty contributes to climate policy indecisiveness:

1. the dynamics of technology adoption and diffusion;
2. macroeconomic impacts of low-carbon policies;
3. interaction between human and environmental systems;
4. policy implementation and effectiveness.

As stated in Chapter 1, solutions to environmental degradation largely rest on the diffusion of mostly energy-related innovations, technologies and practices throughout industries and between households. In most cases, low-carbon alternatives already exist. However, whether their adoption can be incentivised in time to avoid dangerous environmental change, and whether this is economically or technically possible, remain open questions, although the outlook is changing rapidly.[1] Similarly, the extent to which the diffusion of new low-carbon products could support

[1] Note that, in many countries, the cost of solar electricity is breaking parity with the lowest alternative, usually coal electricity, which suggests that things are changing. Electric vehicles

economic development is not well understood. Moreover, it is also unclear whether climate policies may influence access to food, water and energy, and – if so – how. Hence, guidance on how to better understand the complex interactions between technology, the macroeconomy and the environment is much needed.

This chapter introduces a methodological approach that could significantly improve the ability of decision-makers to anticipate the effects of environmental policy options by integrating behavioural and non-equilibrium complexity science and environmental feedbacks into environmental policy analysis, with a framework consistent across relevant disciplines. It is in some sense a blueprint for the rest of the book, anticipating many of the deeper aspects presented in later chapters.

2.1.2 *Shortcomings of Equilibrium Analysis in Standard Social Science Models*

Equilibrium and optimisation-based approaches,[2] despite their contribution to date, have five main shortcomings for the analysis of the uncertainty identified in the preceding section.

The first shortcoming concerns the concept underpinning these approaches, as stated in Chapter 1, namely that of an effective social planner coordinating society to minimise total cost or maximise the aggregate utility of a hypothetical representative agent. The implicit corollary is that there exists a unique stable economic equilibrium to which a social system tends to return after exogenous disturbances (e.g., see Mas-Colell et al., 1995). This method leads to approaches that are generally to be interpreted as *normative* in their philosophy of science (i.e., they seek to identify *desirable* strategies; see Chapter 4) rather than *positive/descriptive/predictive* (where one would instead seek to describe observed system behaviour with a high degree of rigour).[3] While a normative approach, or mixing up normative and descriptive, may appear attractive for policy purposes, it is fundamentally undermined by the fact that no such central coordination or equilibrium exists, while the assumption

remain more costly than alternatives, but perhaps not for long. Other technology costs are declining rapidly as well.

[2] E.g., cost-benefit analysis (CBA), general equilibrium, cost-optimisation or even simple regressions. Most of the work to date has been done with equilibrium approaches. Simple models have been highly influential and include Nordhaus (2010) and Stern (2007), while more complex studies include the larger integrated assessment models (IAMs) reviewed in IPCC (2018) and, for instance, in Kriegler et al. (2015a).

[3] This is a recurrent concept in this book. Utility/cost optimisation is interpreted in either of two possible ways: (1) the philosophy of science is *normative* and the model identifies what ought to be desired by the decision-maker, or (2) the philosophy of science is descriptive but the modeller believes there exists a force that coordinates the actions of agents such that a utility maximum is realised as an emergent phenomenon – something yet unsupported by any evidence (Kirman, 1992; Trutnevyte, 2016; Jaxa-Rozen and Trutnevyte, 2021).

of optimality neglects critical aspects of economic reality such as unemployment of labour and other resources, and market disequilbria (something analysed in detail in later chapters).

A second, closely related shortcoming is that equilibrium theories do not sufficiently allow for *the possibility that agents may not be unboundedly rational.* Indeed, equilibrium theories typically involve finding the maximum across time of an aggregate utility function (or, in cost-optimisation models, the minima of total system costs). Such a maximum (or minimum) results from the sum of the utility (or cost) functions of the underlying agents, who are assumed to carry out an exhaustive ranking of their preferences over all possible products in all existing markets, and all possible life strategies, and to optimise their goods basket and life choices given an economic context (see Mas-Colell et al., 1995). Underpinning this understanding is the assumption that the aggregate behaviour of a system of utility-maximisers can always be expressed as that of a single average utility-maximising representative agent with the same behavioural rules.[4] However, if one accepts that it is not reasonable to expect that economic agents carry out exhaustive rankings of all goods in all markets (which is technically described as *boundedly rational*) and that instead, agents may influence and learn from one another, the utility of the representative agent becomes too complex or impossible to optimise due to increasing feedbacks and emergent complex dynamics. In fact, in those conditions, what happens is not anymore the solution to an optimisation calculation.[5] It then becomes unclear whether optimisation methods can be used at all, and using it comes at the price of losing touch with reality.

Third and relatedly, equilibrium theories do not capture the possibility that agents *may influence one another, leading to positive feedbacks and crowd effects.* And indeed, it is clear in the empirical evidence that agents learn about what they can consume through their peers (Chapter 7). In this regard, the conventional equilibrium perspective may be termed *reductionist*, in the meaning ascribed to this term in complexity theory (Anderson, 1972), where the macro system behaviour is inferred from assumed micro agent behavioural rules, but without considering to a full extent the interactions (including mutual influence) between agents. Following complexity theory, one may consider interactions as *additional elements* that lead to the emergence of additional *collective phenomena* (Chapter 5). In economics, the inclusion of multi-agent interactions (specifically, the possibility that agents influence the

4 See Kirman (1992) for a critique. The representative agent concept makes the assumption that macro-level collective behaviour can be approximated by the behaviour and motives of one single (human) agent. The representative agent is one possible (trivial) solution that solves the aggregation problem, the case in which agents do not interact with one another, but not the only solution (Chapter 7). Observed reality shows that macro-level behaviour can be structurally quite different from micro-level behaviour, notably with the emergence of collective instabilities, as seen in Chapters 9 and 10.

5 This is reviewed and supported by a mathematical model in Chapter 7.

behaviour of other agents) actually determines the difference whether processes due to crowd effects are allowed to emerge, including technology transitions and economic cycles. Allowing for multi-agent interactions is very important in practice because such interactions are at the roots of essentially all self-reinforcing economic processes (crowd effects), and these are excluded in equilibrium economics.

In the theory of complex systems, many properties emerge solely from the interactions between agents, not from the behaviour of the agents themselves (regardless of whether these are in homogeneous or heterogeneous contexts). This includes important economic phenomena such as the profile of diffusion of innovations, learning-by-doing, expectations in finance and economic fluctuations, trends and fashions, technology lock-ins and many more. These phenomena exist, but do not stem from microeconomic behaviour of isolated individual agents. Therefore, they cannot be studied with a methodological understanding that ignores interactions between agents. With multi-agent interactions, the representative agent, if we still consider the concept useful, could be understood to gain *additional emergent behavioural traits* that the underlying agents do not possess. Thus while there is a good rationale for desiring a macro theory built upon micro-foundations, the latter must include not just agent behavioural rules (e.g., individual preferences, spending patterns and income elasticities) but also how groups of agents as a whole behave, which can be different (as is clear, for example, during bubbles and crashes, where the group does not behave rationally).

Again relatedly as a corollary point, since optimisation only works if the utility of the representative agent strictly decreases (or the system cost increases) away from the equilibrium, the method has a problem when facing self-reinforcing phenomena. This includes, for example, a decline in prices resulting from cumulative investment (learning), leading to investments that increase the likelihood of more similar investments (e.g., sales in solar panels make their cost decrease which attracts more sales). In an optimisation framework, such positive feedbacks lead to numerical instability of the model solver, due to the emergence of multiple solutions. Yet, processes with increasing returns are a very important feature of the real world, particularly as regards climate policy. For example, early investments in solar energy may lead or have already led the technology, through learning, to competitiveness and possible market dominance, while a lack of early investments would have confined the technology to niche applications.

A fourth shortcoming, also related, is the difficulty of optimisation models to deal with *multiple solutions and path-dependence*. Indeed, when increasing returns are introduced, several solutions to the optimisation problem emerge, and it becomes unclear which optimum is the correct one. In the investment example above, two different possible future solutions evolve from different early investment decisions. Real-world technological and economic change is thus *path-dependent*. Technology adoption typically follows S-shaped patterns, which stem partly from social influence and interactions, where adoption of innovations increases the likelihood of further adoption of the same innovations (Rogers, 2010). This is explored again in full detail in Chapter 14. Full path-dependency is a key property missing in many current economic models and integrated assessment models (IAMs).

Finally, equilibrium theories do not sufficiently account for *agent heterogeneity*. The representative agent is understood as the aggregate collective behaviour emerging from the actions of the underlying multitude of agents, which in reality have different preferences. No clear role is ascribed to differences in the distribution of income or other socio-economic and industry parameters. Following expected utility theory (EUT), only one type of behavioural response exists, namely a decision based on the expected utility associated with different choices multiplied by their respective probabilities (assumed to be known). In the real world, at least two types of deviations from EUT typically arise: *behavioural diversity* (variations around a central value),[6] and *behavioural biases* (systematic deviation from EUT).[7] Agent heterogeneity can also be interpreted, in a utility maximisation perspective, as some degree of ambiguity in terms of agent perceptions of optimality. Agent heterogeneity is important in the representation of consumer or investor choices, which is critical in the process of the diffusion of innovations, technologies and practices (Knobloch and Mercure, 2016). As can be inferred from standard innovation diffusion theory (Rogers, 2010), behavioural response, its diversity, the diversity of social groups and unequal distribution of information are precisely what determines actual rates of adoption of innovations. This is standard knowledge in the field of marketing research,[8] where firms seek profits out of matching products to diverse consumer profiles. In addition, utility maximisation under budget constraint is known empirically to be an incorrect representation of attitudes towards risk, gains, losses and uncertainty.[9]

These shortcomings imply that the use of equilibrium models comes at a price. Such analytical omissions are reflected in the types of policies that are advocated on that basis. Specifically, they lead to the expectation that a simple internalisation of environmental costs, in the form of a pricing instrument (e.g., a carbon price or tax) will optimally and effectively incentivise technology adoption and diffusion. And, standard CBA fails to explain why, in the real world, such instruments do not play out and deliver as expected (Grubb et al., 2014). In point of fact, the expected optimal success of such mechanisms is but a reiteration of the initial assumptions of the model, rather than a result of the actual analysis: efficient markets, rationality, etc. In other words, these policies would work if real people behaved simply as they

6 E.g., as represented in discrete choice theory (Domencich and McFadden, 1975; Anderson et al., 1992).

7 E.g., as represented in prospect theory, Kahneman and Tversky (1979); see also Sorrell et al. (2011) for a review and taxonomy.

8 E.g., on product differentiation (Smith, 1956).

9 As shown in prospect theory (Tversky and Kahneman, 1974; Kahneman and Tversky, 1979).

do in the imaginary world of equilibrium theory. With real agents, these policies are almost certainly not optimal, if optimality could actually be defined.

2.1.3 A *Paradigm Shift*

Integrating both complexity and behavioural sciences as applied to economics could bring path-dependency and agent heterogeneity to the core of the analysis. Complexity science is the cross-disciplinary field that specifically studies properties that emerge from interactions between system components, initially studied in physical, biological and computer sciences.[10] By introducing better descriptions of how agents behave and interact, theories and models turn from *normative to positive/descriptive* and their methodology evolves from optimisation to simulation, where the analyst relies on 'what if' approaches. Here, such a paradigm shift in thinking is proposed for re-framing models. However, this is not simple, and will in fact take the whole of this book to justify and substantiate. It requires in fact the elaboration of a whole theory of complexity economics. In Chapters 3 and 4, the shortcomings of the current paradigm are analysed more deeply to fully justify why a change is needed, while Part II of the book lays out a complete theoretical framework. In the rest of this chapter, an overview is given.

It is understood that in simulations of complex systems, uncertainty plays an important role partly because the theories do not necessarily predict a propensity to return to equilibrium. This is an aspect well understood and managed in the climate sciences, and no inherent reason prevents modellers from using the same concepts in economics. Indeed, humans behave in unpredictable ways, partly dictated by diverse contexts. The fact that humans have agency or 'free will', is a frequent objection raised by social scientists, to the modelling of behaviour. This argument does not contradict the complexity approach, however, for the following reason. Humans do not behave randomly (unlike physical particles); however, while the actions of individuals cannot be predicted, they almost always lie within known bounds, from which statistics can in fact be developed when considering large groups of people.[11] The result is a theory of collective behaviour. As seen in later chapters, however, it may not always have statistics described by normal distributions. But in complex systems (e.g., the climate, the economy), both natural and social systems face the same complexity challenges, and their description can be modelled in broadly the same way.

In practical terms, the complexity-based methodological approach proposed in this book follows an analytical structure in which many scenarios are simulated based on possible policy choices, and acceptable results are filtered based on a

[10] See Chapter 5.

[11] As for physical particles – e.g., the multinomial logit in social sciences is conceptually identical to the Boltzmann factor in statistical physics.

multidimensional range of outcomes that reach given objectives. For example, such an approach can involve filtering scenarios, in multidimensional human and environmental sets of criteria, to determine ranges of policy options that enable society to avoid exceeding planetary boundaries while ensuring continued human development globally.[12] Ambiguity or conflicting perceptions of optimal policy-making between diverse policy-makers or model users is avoided by leaving subjective outcome value judgments outside of the scientific framework. Indeed, unlike conventional multi-criteria analysis, where optimisation is carried out using subjective weighting of all factors considered given by the modeller, in the context proposed here, one obtains feasible points in a multidimensional outcome space, and the policy-maker can target a possible subspace in accordance with her/his political platform, itself designed to address concerns of his/her voters.

In the rest of this chapter, some concrete examples are given of how complexity and behavioural sciences can be used for the assessment of sustainability policies, with emphasis on model uncertainty analysis, in order to build a powerful approach for next-generation public policy analysis. Four key areas of environmental policy analysis are identified where uncertainty is high and where the proposed methodological approach would be particularly useful: dynamics of technology adoption and diffusion; macroeconomic impacts of low-carbon policies; interaction between human and environmental systems; and policy implementation and effectiveness. Four specific applications are provided of the proposed methodological shift in connection with: the diffusion of transport technology; impact of low-carbon investment on income and employment; processes with cascading uncertainty; and cross-sectoral impacts of biofuels policy.

2.2. FOUR KEY POLICY AREAS OF HIGH UNCERTAINTY

2.2.1 *Technology Adoption and Diffusion*

As established above, the diversity of consumers and investors influences the choice of environmental technology. Consumers' choice of certain technologies, such as vehicles, takes place within contexts of distributed income that span several orders of magnitude (see below). The diversity of incomes, social groups and attitudes is known to determine the rates and profiles of diffusion of innovations (early and late adopters, etc., see Rogers, 2010). For present purposes, this means that agent heterogeneity matters in real life, and it must therefore be integrated into models. This is true not only regarding how policies may affect each income group, but also, how each income group responds to policy signals. Modelling the impacts of policy incentives to the consumer using averages over too few consumer group parameters can indeed

[12] More on this in Chapter 12; see also Rockström et al. (2009); Steffen et al. (2015); OXFAM (2012).

be misleading, since differences in income and other socio-economic parameters across consumers lead to highly diverse consumption habits.

Meanwhile, interactions between agents are also crucial to consider when analysing technology adoption, since technology generally features *increasing returns to adoption*: the adoption of technology by agents is increasingly more probable the more agents adopt and use the technology. Transitions build upon themselves with dynamics following a pattern comparable to that of infectious diseases (see Mansfield, 1961). Thus, increasing returns may generate resistance to change in socio-technical regimes (lock-ins), but they may also give momentum to technological transitions.[13] This aspect is an important feature of historical narratives found in evolutionary economics (e.g., Freeman and Perez, 1988) and transitions theory (e.g., Geels, 2002).

For obvious reasons, anticipating how diverse agents may respond to different policies is of great interest to policy-makers. However, studying the impact of incentives to consumers with differing incomes and social groups is also a tradition of marketing research,[14] anthropology[15] and behavioural economics.[16] However, the contribution of those areas of research to the understanding of climate policy has so far been mostly overlooked in climate change mitigation modelling or environmental assessment research. Its use thus remains a promising but emerging field.[17] Grubb et al. (2014) emphasise the need for future research on behavioural aspects of emissions reductions. Insufficient efforts have been devoted to understanding the aggregate behavioural response to sustainability policy instruments, and this is related to a possibly overstated expectation that an efficient equilibrium should emerge on its own in technology markets.

Empirical marketing research literature shows that technology substitution in many different contexts follows simple S-shaped diffusion profiles.[18] More generally, a tradition exists to describe the competition between several technologies for market space using coupled Lotka–Volterra systems, which can be derived from simple statistics of industrial and consumer dynamics.[19] This is also called the 'replicator dynamics' system of evolutionary theory, in which natural selection is carried out by the consumer, who filters successful innovations based on their fitness to the

[13] See Anderson et al. (1989), pp. 9–10, and Arthur (1989, 1999, 2014).

[14] E.g., see Bass (1969); Fisher and Pry (1971); McShane et al. (2012).

[15] Douglas and Isherwood (1979); Sahlins (1972).

[16] Discrete choice modelling, e.g., Ben-Akiva and Lerman (1985); Domencich and McFadden (1975), and behavioural economics, e.g., Kahneman and Tversky (1979); Tversky and Kahneman (1974).

[17] See, e.g., Köhler et al. (2009); Axsen et al. (2009); Giraudet et al. (2012); Rivers and Jaccard (2006).

[18] A lot of empirical research exists on this, including Fisher and Pry (1971); Grübler et al. (1999); Mansfield (1961); Marchetti and Nakicenovic (1978).

[19] Bhargava (1989); Karmeshu et al. (1985); Safarzynska and van den Bergh (2010); Mercure (2015, 2018), see Chapter 7.

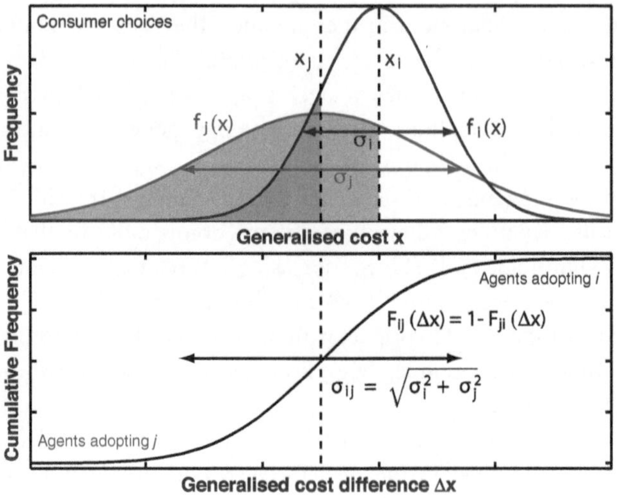

FIGURE 2.1 Schematic representation of a binary logit (Mercure, 2015).

market, while entrepreneurs strive to improve their products in order to increase their fitness by better matching consumer taste. This natural selection, however, involves decision-making by consumers under bounded rationality, who are naturally highly diverse, and the diversity of consumers drives product differentiation and increasing product diversity.

Equilibrium/optimisation models neglect agent heterogeneity and interactions, as they look at average agents in isolation facing choices (with perfect information), rather than at socio-technical systems where agents influence what other agents do. Agent heterogeneity could, however, be represented to some extent in models by introducing statistical distributions over agent perspectives (see Figures 2.1 and 2.3: preferences are often simply distributed), instead of using mean values only. In such a framework, the modeller disposes of *both* mean values as well as ranges. Then, when evaluating aggregate agent propensities towards technology substitution, one simply faces comparisons between distributions of preferences: counting how many people prefer option A to option B, and the converse, according to who they are.[20]

This is an area where our methodological shift may advance the understanding of sustainability policy by moving the research focus from the generation of 'desirable' energy sector storylines (policy formulation) to the forecasting of 'likely' policy outcomes (policy assessment) based on existing technology, knowledge of the market, and technology diffusion dynamics. It would clarify whether modellers consider themselves as dealing with how they think that agents behave based on the empirics, versus how they think they ought to behave.

[20] As for instance in a binary logit.

2.2.2 Green Growth: Macroeconomics and the Finance of Innovations

Complexity and agent heterogeneity are also important to understand the interactions between technology diffusion, lenders' expectations and macroeconomic fluctuations, which are part of the process of economic growth, and are affected by climate change mitigation policies. Theories based on utility-maximising non-interacting agents assume full employment of economic resources, essentially because that's what happens in optimised systems. Under full employment, policies that lead to a re-allocation of resources away from an assumed optimal starting-point in the use of resources are unavoidably detrimental to economic performance, which is some kind of tautology. However, obviously, full employment is never observed in reality, and most readily observed is unemployment of labour. In real life, expectations as to the performance and return of innovations drive most investment, and ultimately, economic growth. Importantly, expectations as a process arise from multi-agent interactions.[21]

Policies for the diffusion of low-carbon innovations present significant opportunities for both the private sector and job creation. But the feedback between the diffusion of new sustainability technologies and economic development and growth is poorly understood. There is an apparent contradiction between observations of highly lucrative activity arising in successful low-carbon ventures (e.g., Tesla electric and Toyota hybrid cars, wind turbines, solar photovoltaic), and the perception that the use of lowest-cost fossil energy with conventional technology is indispensable for development and growth. This type of dichotomy pervades climate and environmental policy-making.

In basic conventional equilibrium economics, full employment, which results from maximising the utility of the representative agent, entails that all resources (labour, fixed capital, financial capital) are currently allocated in the economy in the most productive way they can be. This is of course not what is observed, where instead, it is found that different countries lie at varying distances from theoretically defined efficiency or productivity frontiers (Grubb et al., 2014). Effectively, the use of economic resources depends upon the economic development trajectory followed by an economy (investment, fixed and human capital and labour).

Importantly, in equilibrium-based theories, savings are understood as a share of fixed national income (GDP), equal to investment, resulting from a choice by agents between spending on consumption in the present or in the future. Thus if a fixed share of income were allocated to investment, naturally, all firms would compete for this fixed allowance, and this would lead to so-called crowding-out, equilibrating supply and demand for finance. Since in equilibrium total investment and the allocation of labour are fixed in this way, equilibrium-based theories cannot reproduce financial

21 E.g., see the artificial stock market by Arthur et al. (1997b), and works by econophysicists (e.g., Sornette, 2017).

fluctuations or crises, or involuntary unemployment, as periodically observed. This is explained in more detail in Chapter 3.

In a broader non-equilibrium complexity economics perspective, income is not fixed to a pre-defined trajectory, and investment does not need to be a constant share of national income. Instead, causality is reversed: income in part depends upon investment, and investment decisions depend upon expectations by financial institutions. This link, however, opens the door to fluctuations: interacting investors in technology ventures can influence each other into frenzies or panics. Indeed, the finance of technology and innovation leads to productivity change, but also, to speculation and bubbles,[22] which, in turn, create economic cycles.[23] Investment fluctuations heavily influence the rate of economic development. This dynamic was arguably at the roots of the great recession,[24] after which quantitative easing was used to offset the reluctance of financial institutions to provide credit. This dynamic cannot be understood without taking into account the interactions between technology diffusion, lender expectations and macroeconomic fluctuations. In reality, equilibrium macro-models should have been dismissed immediately following the financial crisis for failing to provide a suitable intellectual framework to understand what was going on.

More realistic economic modelling that allows for variable amounts of finance and investment is possible if one abandons the restrictive assumptions of equilibrium approaches. In a theoretical approach that allows for crowd effects to emerge, the amount of investment in the economy is determined by investment decisions by lenders acting upon expectations of return. This is not new, it is at the roots of both Schumpeterian (Schumpeter, 1934, 1939) and Keynesian (Keynes, 1936) forms of demand-led economics. A post-Schumpeterian or post-Keynesian perspective also allows for fluctuating amounts of *money* in the economy, and indeed, this is what is observed, called *endogenous money*.[25]

As understood in the tradition of Schumpeterian economic history, the emergence of new technologies is characterised by important increasing returns to investment and adoption, and it involves strongly path-dependent cross-sectoral spill-overs that often lead to economy-wide activity accelerators (Freeman and Louçã, 2001). For example, in the industrial revolution, new textile machinery required better iron and steel. Investment in iron and steel led to the emergence of an industry as well as cost reductions that reshaped the so-called '*design space*' for other products to be made out of those materials more cheaply. This, in turn, enabled many related and clustered innovations to emerge and economically reach the marketplace. In the Schumpeterian economic tradition, the clustering of investment stemming

22 See Keynes (1936); Minsky (1982).
23 The evolutionary economics literature is broad on this. See, e.g., Perez (2001); Freeman and Louçã (2001). Schumpeter (1934, 1939) argued the same.
24 See Keen (2011, 2017) and Guttmann (2015).
25 See McLeay et al. (2014); this is explained in detail in Chapters 3 and 9.

from the clustering of innovation leads to both economic prosperity and depression periods in alternation.[26] Risks of financial crises arise when finance is raised using financial assets as collateral, a phenomenon that has taken place periodically over history.[27]

Formal modelling of path-dependent, non-equilibrium macroeconomics is possible on the basis of two assumptions. Firstly, under the principle of *cumulative causation of knowledge accumulation*, productivity change is described by sets of aggregate sectoral learning curves where productivity growth is derived from cumulative investment and is roughly consistent with the trends observed in economic history.[28]

With regard to climate change mitigation, it is well established that an amount of investment in the energy sector larger than in a business-as-usual scenario will be necessary (e.g., McCollum et al., 2018). This scale of investment in new technology sectors is likely to result in substantial economic reallocations due to, first, substantial money creation by financial institutions, and second, innovation and cross-sectoral spill-overs (e.g., new materials, new design and engineering methods, etc.), both of which would not have happened otherwise. Importantly, in models without the constraint of full-employment of resources, capital and labour, the impact can be either beneficial or detrimental, depending on many factors, such as the trade balance, energy imports, international competition and relative prices. When the implications are beneficial, the transition can be termed as *green growth*, where new investment and employment are generated from technology policy, although possibly with important relative price changes. An example is given below in which climate change mitigation policy leads to increased employment and GDP as a result of enhanced investment in the electricity sector. That said, technology policy does not necessarily lead to beneficial impacts because such policies can take many forms. In an equilibrium-based theory, however, the possibility of beneficial outcomes is entirely ruled out, and by assumption rather than as a result of calculations. Indeed, equilibrium models *always* predict detrimental impacts for climate mitigation efforts, such that the debate is framed in terms of *burden*, and economic opportunities of climate policies are not extensively examined.[29]

Thus, and importantly, it is clear that the incorporation of multi-agent interactions (by accounting for feedback loops, delays and nonlinearity) leads to key consequences for theory and its application: in a theory where investment is determined by expectations, information flow between variables runs from variable or fluctuating savings/investment to income, back to investment, and allows for beneficial impacts

26 Freeman and Louçã (2001); Perez (2001); Schumpeter (1939).

27 Perez (2001), see also Keen (1995, 2011).

28 E.g., as in Kaldor (1957), see Chapters 8 and 11.

29 This is a recurrent problem in debates of the IPCC, which, one may possibly argue, are driven by the expected or desired policy, rather than driving the policy strategy. On growth in models, see Grubb et al. (2014), Ch. 9; see, also Ekins et al. (2011); Lee et al. (2015).

of technology policy while in equilibrium-based theories, information flows from fixed income to investment, and beneficial impacts are ruled out.

2.2.3 *Uncertainty Analysis in Human-Environment Interactions and Climate Change*

Models based on complexity theory can better describe the complex interactions between the socio-economic and the natural (environment) systems. Such interactions are at the heart of climate policy. Feedbacks between the economy and the natural environment take place through direct human intervention (e.g., land-use change) or indirectly through the impact of economic activity.[30] The natural environment influences, in turn, human action leading to a highly complex system of feedbacks. The allocation of land for agriculture, including crops for biofuels, interacts directly with the climatic system through phenomena such as deforestation, land-use change, emissions and desertification, but also indirectly through the economy. The extensive use of water further constrains the availability of natural resources for human use, in what is increasingly referred to as the energy–water–food nexus (Chapter 1). At the same time, natural resource use stems directly from economic processes, involving the demand for agricultural, energy and forestry commodities that are traded in international markets.

At this stage, the best guess of modellers to integrate human and natural environment processes is to connect an ever larger number of complex models from both camps together (Figure 2.2). The danger in doing this is that one eventually generates data that is difficult to interpret due to the level of complexity. Nevertheless, it is

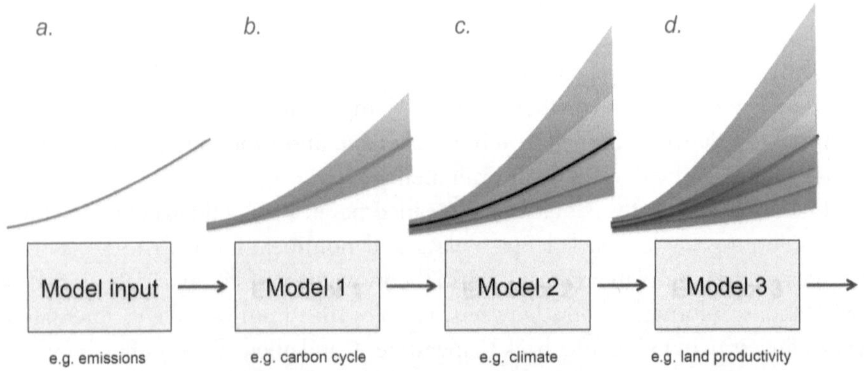

FIGURE 2.2 Schematic representation of cascading uncertainty across complex models.

30 E.g., the generation of air pollution or the emission of greenhouse gases causing climate change.

not better to try to simplify the dynamics to obtain more tractable answers, if these are going to risk being entirely wrong. Connecting complex models thus requires to explore the range of projections that remain within what is considered feasible.

The cascading of uncertainty that arises when connecting models to one another increases with simulation timespan, which stems from the general property of complex non-linear models that produce scenarios that diverge from each other exponentially for arbitrarily small changes in starting parameters (i.e. the sometimes termed 'butterfly effect' in chaos theory), typical of climate models (discussed in Chapter 6). This type of uncertainty is also a property of an economic model with positive feedbacks, as well as of diffusion-based technology models. Current practice is in fact inconsistent as it treats economic projections as deterministic (e.g., a unique GDP trajectory in equilibrium), while treating climate projections as probabilistic (e.g., 95% probability range for a global warming trajectory). It is entirely possible to assign 'uncertainty bounds' to projections of a socio-economic model through the use of statistical analysis. Thus, the uncertainty faced in climate policy-making can be effectively tackled through statistical representations. Depending on the sensitivity of each sub-system to perturbations (i.e. the rate of divergence of scenarios, and conversely, the possible presence of 'attracting states') the cloud of uncertainty may increase moderately or dramatically as it propagates through the chain. This in turn provides a clear quantification of one's ability to reliably model the ensemble of systems.

The prevailing view, however, seems to be that natural systems are suitably modelled by complex data-driven simulations, while the economy is suitably modelled by simple axioms-based normative optimisations. This makes no scientific sense at all, since if anything, social systems are equally if not more complex than natural systems. There is no reason for complex human systems to be treated any differently than complex environmental ones.

2.2.4 *Policy Effectiveness, Behaviour and Implementation*

Tools from marketing research, anthropology and behavioural economics can be very useful to improve our understanding of consumer and investor behaviour. They provide a powerful addition to economy-environment modelling, namely the ability to predict quantitatively the most likely aggregate response to policy instruments. Valuable insights can be gained in this way. In climate change policy, which requires action sooner rather than later, there is significant value in the ability to predict the effectiveness of emissions reduction measures.

However, assessing such feasibility requires knowledge of their legal and political implications and constraints (e.g., political feasibility, legal consistency), which may be just as important. Apparently minor differences in the applicable legal framework[31] may, in fact, make certain developments less effective, or more vulnerable to challenge, or even block them entirely.

Much policy analysis has been carried out in connection with specific policies proposed to address externalities such as pollution or environmental degradation, including taxes and other financial incentives imposed on households, firms or consumers. The justification for taxes is often based on considerations of ethics and social justice; it less frequently results from the analysis of their likely effectiveness.[32] Indeed, policies are often chosen and adopted without much prior knowledge of their likely effectiveness, which ultimately lies with investor and consumer decisions.

Policy analysis for climate change mitigation is complex, and realistic proposals should ideally take into account the political and institutional context (legal – both domestic and international). For example, some environmental differentiation techniques (e.g., certain subsidies or feed-in tariffs), may be inconsistent with international economic law and can attract significant legal difficulties (Viñuales, 2012). Furthermore, the introduction of carbon pricing mechanisms[33] can be politically very different from that of energy/fuel standards or emissions taxation, and it would therefore have a different likelihood of success. Thus, studying the effectiveness and feasibility of policy measures requires integrating expertise on the mechanisms of policy-making and law with expertise on the modelling of decision-making by investors and consumers. However, such a broad integration of expertise is extremely rare in contemporary state-of-the-art climate change mitigation research.

This book proposes, as part of the working structure of model-based sustainability policy assessments, a two-way feedback with knowledge of domestic/comparative politics and environmental, investment and trade law. This would effectively guide the 'what if' approach to scenario-creation for testing potential policies, as opposed to proposing policies that are already 'optimal'. Effectively, in a model that is not based on optimisation, policies are assessed on the basis of their ability to effectively achieve certain objectives through the simultaneous use of several policy instruments that interact with one another. Such an approach avoids the more common siloed assessments, and it accounts for policy impacts across sectors.[34] A more detailed proposal for a policy assessment framework is given in Chapter 12.

31 E.g., the modalities for the acquisition of land, the modalities for the initial distribution of emission reductions or for their banking, the local content requirements added to a feed-in-tariff scheme.

32 This is well reflected by the IPCC (2014, 2018), and primarily originates from the 'polluter pays' normative principle. This is discussed in detail in Chapter 4.

33 E.g., a cap-and-trade system where the allowances are freely allocated – at least initially – on the basis of prior emissions.

34 This approach is in fact recommended by the European Commission in its Impact Assessment guidelines (EC, 2009, 2015).

2.3. PRACTICAL RELEVANCE OF THE PARADIGM SHIFT: APPLICATIONS TO FOUR CLIMATE POLICY ISSUES

In this section, the practical meaning of the discussion above is applied in context using four case studies. These case studies are expanded upon in the rest of this book in various chapters. Ultimately, these four cases together demonstrate that it is possible to go beyond the standard framing of environmental policy, but providing a detailed underpinning justifying what is shown here will require all of Part II of this book.

2.3.1 *The Impact of Consumer Heterogeneity on the Diffusion of New Transport Technology*

The importance of agent heterogeneity for technology adoption can be empirically established using private passenger vehicle purchases, as shown in Figure 2.3. In the UK, the distribution of car purchase prices follows closely the income distribution (panel a). Cars of different prices have different manufacturer-rated emissions, which are thus similarly distributed (panel b). Vehicles with alternative engine technologies have yet a different distribution, and this stems from their gradual process of diffusion, which takes place unevenly with respect to the distribution of conventional vehicles (panel c). Finally, rated emissions are correlated with vehicle prices through a log-linear relationship.

Car purchase choices largely depend upon each consumer's respective social group, through social interactions, as is known in empirical work.[35] This generally explains the relationship between consumption behaviour and income distribution shown above. Consumers do not attempt to minimise their transportation costs; instead they apparently purchase what is most common in their visible surroundings, and the diversity of social groups is what forms the lognormal distribution shown above. Alternatively, we can suppose that consumers maximise some definition of utility within a subset of the market (bounded rationality) defined by their social interactions (discussed in Chapter 7).

It thus appears necessary to analyse each band of income, and each type of consumer, separately. If one explores possible substitutions between models that could result from emissions reduction policies in the car market, one can calculate elasticities of substitution from these distributions by determining statistically which vehicle models are most likely to be chosen within the same new price band (after tax). Therefore, the rate of adoption of consumer technology, including low carbon systems, stems precisely from this diversity, which varies across the world. This enables us to determine the effectiveness of certain low-carbon policies

35 For example, see McShane et al. (2012), as well as Pettifor et al. (2017a,b).

(taxes, subsidies) at incentivising technology substitution, using market data. In fact, this is exactly what marketing research does to forecast sales before placing new products in the market.

Such information can be fed into technology diffusion models that aim to reproduce typical S-shaped profiles[36] to provide expected rates of adoption (Figure 2.5, see also Chapter 14). Such a representation reproduces technology lock-ins. This picture is incomplete, however, as it does not represent attitudes and culture. Yet, just as with firms attempting to place new products in the market, the more

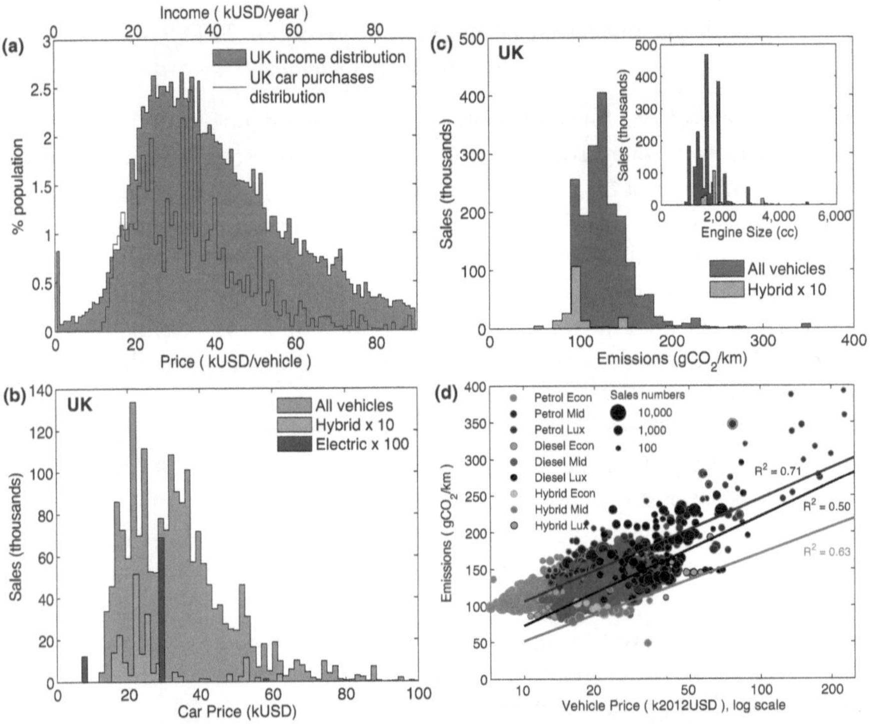

FIGURE 2.3 Data from 2012 relating the impacts of consumer diversity and market structure on the effectiveness of emissions taxation in the private personal mobility sector (reproduced from Mercure and Lam, 2015). (a) Comparison of the UK income distribution to the price distribution of recent vehicle purchases. (b) Comparison of UK market coverage between conventional and unconventional vehicle engine technology. (c) Associated distribution of vehicle carbon intensities. (d) Structure of the UK vehicle market for prices and emissions from which likely effectiveness of taxes can be deduced. These properties were found to vary across economies (Mercure and Lam, 2015).

36 E.g., see the 'Future Technology Transformations' (FTT) model Mercure (2012); Mercure et al. (2014, 2018b).

detailed information thus gained helps to better characterise the rates of technology adoption that could result from proposed policies throughout the diffusion cycle. By contrast, optimisation-based models would typically characterise variations in consumer behaviour, at best, by parameterising different discount rates for technologies attributed to particular market segments (McCollum et al., 2016).

2.3.2 *Green Growth: Employment and Income Impacts of Low-Carbon Investments*

The importance of accounting for the interactions between lenders' expectations, technology diffusion and macroeconomic variables can be illustrated by reference to the link between low-carbon investments, income and employment. Figure 2.4 is based on the non-equilibrium macroeconomic model E3ME-FTT, which is not subject to the full employment constraint. It shows a possible causal chain in the process of technology finance based on expectations impacting the economy in the electricity sector.

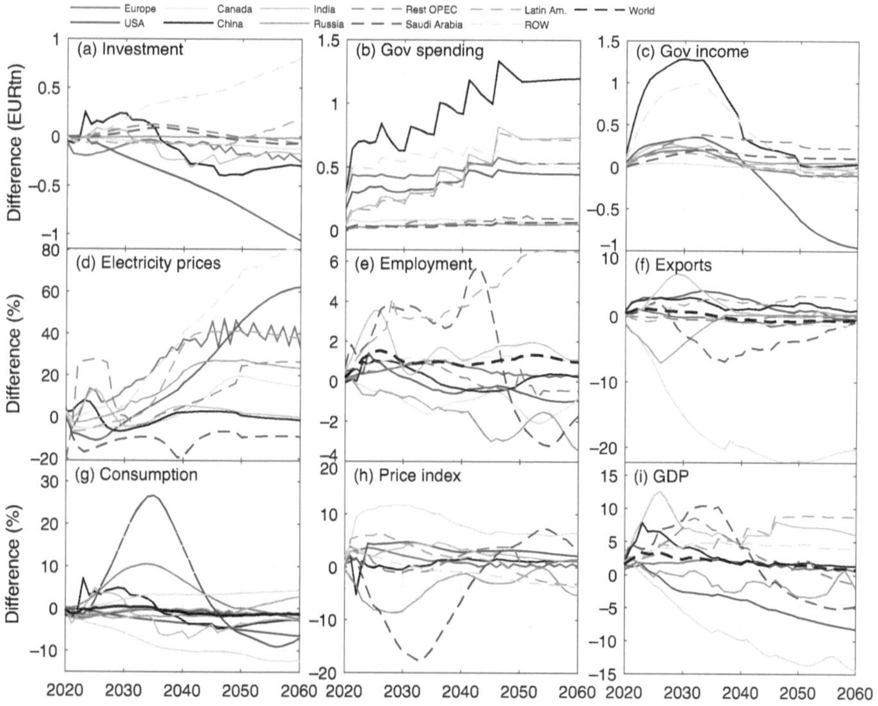

FIGURE 2.4 Example of possible economic impacts of investment in low-carbon technology, when studied using a non-equilibrium post-Keynesian model, E3ME-FTT (see Mercure et al., 2018a). Vertical axes refer to changes from the baseline, in billion current USD for the top three panels, and in percentage points for the six lower panels.

In this model, no limit is imposed on finance for technology developments, in contrast to an equilibrium model where interest rates adjust to clear the money market.[37] In other words, financial resources are given to entrepreneurs by banks for low-carbon investments through credit creation. The model's critical assumption is only the solvency of entrepreneurial activity, that is, economic viability of low-carbon projects ensured by policy. Therefore it is not claimed that the economic system has no limit at all on money creation: it is assumed that all technology ventures that are financed in any scenario are profitable, and that government and private debt is not indefinitely increased. This supposes that situations that could lead to financial instability through unsustainable debt growth are not created. This example is selected to show that economic outcomes of mitigation policy in models are primarily dependent on model architecture, and that impacts can be (but are not necessarily) beneficial if one allows for non-equilibrium effects.

In this example, the global energy system is largely decarbonised by 2050 and has a probability of not exceeding 2°C of 75%. Higher costs of low-carbon electricity generation technologies (e.g., wind turbines, solar panels, carbon capture and storage) are passed on by utilities into their bills to customers, that is, into higher prices of electricity, proportionally to the evolving technology composition. Entrepreneurial activity requires loans to finance new low-carbon capital, which requires more investment than existing fossil fuel generators. *Banks create money to finance these ventures as they create loans*. Loans are paid back over capital lifetime by firms using a higher price of electricity, and *the additional money is gradually destroyed* as the loans are paid back. In the model, as shown in Figure 2.4, the higher level of money flows from investment (panel a) creates jobs (panel e), increases exports (panel f) and consumption (panel g), with possible effects on inflation (panel h).

Meanwhile, higher prices of electricity increase operational costs of most sectors, and thus decrease employment, household income and consumption (same panels), therefore an offsetting force. These two effects were observed to roughly cancel each other out in many regions in the model and scenario. A positive 'green growth effect', in this particular case, is generated in part due to redistribution policy and in part due to increased employment. Revenue raised by fuel taxes (panel c) aimed at incentivising technological change (carbon pricing), minus spending on technology subsidies (panel b), is indeed recycled to lower income tax. This moves the system's balance towards a higher income level than in a baseline scenario in some countries (higher GDP, panel i). Where GDP goes down relates to losses of fossil fuel exports, a form of creative destruction, as will be seen in Chapter 15. The positive GDP effect subsides in later years (e.g., Europe, China) when low-carbon construction

[37] Here, interest rates remain constant, as they are assumed to depend on other things than the demand for money, as credit risk is assumed not to change due to the government ensuring the viability of projects with credible policy.

slows down and investment and redistribution declines, while the price of electricity remains high. The GDP effect may even reverse when the technology transformation is completed and society faces servicing debt only. Debt servicing takes place through consumers paying a higher price for electricity.

Note, therefore, that while economic growth is enhanced in this scenario, private debt is also increased beyond the end of the simulation. In non-equilibrium theory, borrowed investment flows indirectly contribute to increased aggregate demand in the short run, when loans are issued, and to decreased demand in the long run, when loans are gradually paid back. Increasing the level of borrowing generates debt-based growth, which if done indefinitely, generates significant prosperity but eventually leads to collapse through a financial crisis. It is unlikely that climate change mitigation would lead to indefinite borrowing. But it will likely require significant amounts of finance.

According to Keen (2017), extended debt-based growth and excessive debt levels have been the underlying cause of the recent banking crisis.[38] This points to a complex entanglement between strategies for economic recovery after the economic crisis, and strategies for climate change mitigation policy. The financial crisis involved banks refusing to lend despite quantitative easing, while mitigation, a potential economic stimulant, requires increased amounts of finance in the energy sector.

In other words, while with equilibrium economic theory, the economic question to address in climate change mitigation concerns what level of GDP growth loss can be deemed acceptable, with non-equilibrium economic theory, the question concerns instead what level of debt and systemic financial risk can be sustained by economies and their financial systems. Thus, the normative implications of using complexity economic theory are substantially different, suggesting that the evidence base of many political discussions may have been misguided.

Further investigation is clearly required to understand the levels of debt and risk, private and public, that economies can realistically undertake to reduce global emissions, as well as to clarify the collective expectations on their economic returns. This motivates the development of theory and analysis in Chapters 5 all the way to 15, where Chapters 9 and 10 specifically analyse the propensity for instability in the financial sector as it creates debt. In a complexity/non-equilibrium perspective, the impact of collective expectations appears to be the key issue to explain, rather than simple welfare effects of different allocations of fixed amounts of capital typically analysed with current optimisation models. In the context of scenarios of rapid decarbonisation, the analysis of debt and access to finance becomes particularly crucial.

[38] And possibly many other economic cycles historically (Perez, 2001; Minsky, 1982).

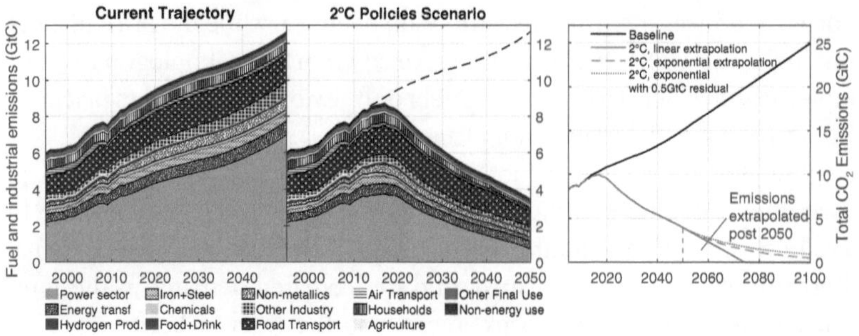

FIGURE 2.5 Global emission scenarios using E3ME-FTT, to feed to the GENIE climate model.

2.3.3 *Model Integration across Processes with Cascading Uncertainty*

Large models of the natural world have many imperfectly known parameters as well as – through multiple combinations of those parameters – a considerable number of possible output values arising from variations in those parameters (even 10 settings of only 10 parameters would generate 10^{10} possibilities). Statistical modelling techniques are required to interpret such a large space of uncertain outcomes. When several models are linked in a causal chain, the uncertainty of models upstream inevitably generates higher uncertainty downstream as ever wider ranges of parameters are given to models. Figures 2.5 and 2.6 give an example of this with soft-linked models, starting with individual emissions scenarios from E3ME-FTT,[39] their emissions trajectories coupled to the GENIE earth system model.

These emissions scenarios are fed to the carbon cycle and climate model GENIE, which generates GHG concentration outputs with probability ranges (Figure 2.6). The model is operated using E3ME-FTT emissions on the basis of multiple runs, each of which uses a random selection of parameter variations (including the climate sensitivity), in order to explore the full range of uncertainty that can be generated by the model. By counting the number of outcomes in various warming ranges, one can determine the probability of reaching a certain climate target (e.g., 2°C , 1.5°C).

2.3.4 *Is Higher Model Complexity a Bonus or a Drawback for Policy-Makers?*

Lower complexity or reduced-form models are often argued to be advantageous to use due to their higher apparent transparency, and thus more appropriate for policy-making. An example is the use of Nordhaus' DICE model, which was originally designed for illustrative purposes using sketchy data, but has been used for policy-making purposes in some countries, including the USA and the UK.

39 Note that these scenarios are the same as in Figure 2.4.

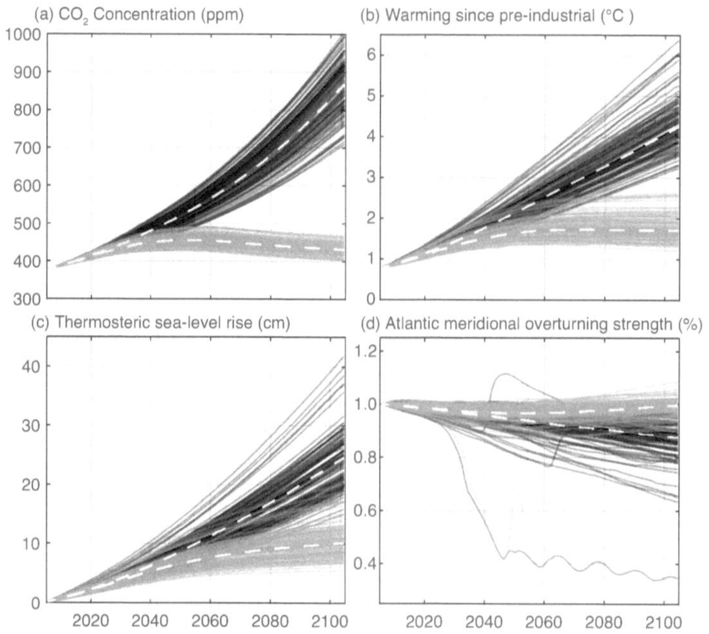

FIGURE 2.6 Uncertainty treatment in the GENIE earth system model. The model is run under many runs with random parameter variations, and the distribution of outcomes is used to determine the per cent chance of meeting a certain climate target.

Lower complexity *does not mean better science*, and simplifications can, in some cases lead to potentially plainly incorrect conclusions.[40] Moreover, and more fundamentally, the use of deterministic economic projections without uncertainty[41] is not a scientifically correct methodology. It is clearly inconsistent with the way complexity-based climate modelling is conducted. No one would find realistic someone claiming the ability to predict the exact climate or mean global temperature in 2100, therefore why would it be acceptable to do so with economic projections?

This book thus argues that while higher complexity models may be more difficult to use in policy circles, such difficulty is clearly offset by their greater realism and rigour. Simple illustrative models may be able to generate simple storylines that fit some policy-maker's agenda, but it is disingenuous for the scientist to do so. The key consideration is not whether simpler or more complex models should be used,

[40] Notably, for the reasons given in this chapter, despite being very simple, tractable and understandable by just about anyone, the very famous Nordhaus (2010) DICE model is not a good representation of a real economy. Its simplicity does not prevent it from being simply wrong and misleading.

[41] E.g., in policy-making based on optimal carbon prices derived from intersecting deterministic curves for the social cost of carbon and the marginal abatement cost, which are inevitably heavy-tailed with ill-defined means, see Chapter 12.

but whether the science–policy interface is capable of relaying the results of more powerful and realistic models to policy circles.

2.4. CONCLUSION: A WORLD OF NEW POSSIBILITIES FOR SUSTAINABILITY POLICY-MAKING

Equilibrium and optimisation-based models are appropriate to use for normative exploration and identification of desirable future configurations of the technology–economy–environment system. Given the fact that they are comparatively highly detailed and tested, they are currently treated as the standard approach. This is possible because normative analysis relies entirely on assumptions and does not require empirical knowledge of actual human behaviour. However, such models support only certain steps of the policy cycle, as they provide ambiguous information regarding how to achieve – through policy interventions – the ideal configurations they portray or how likely they may be. This gap is a direct consequence of a *lack of causal relationships with human behaviour*. Producing scenarios that accurately forecast the future course of events as a result of policy choices, with any likelihood (however low), requires fine-grained representations of human behaviour, its diversity and multi-agent interactions. These representations are as necessarily imperfect as they are necessary to come close to real life.

It is often argued that forecasting is not possible, and that serious sustainability science can only express itself in the form of exploratory scenarios (e.g., van Vuuren et al., 2011). This book submits in contrast that forecasting is both necessary and inevitable, and can be improved within the bounds of finite predictability with increased attention to known nonlinearities and interaction effects. The climate sciences provide a major example of an area where outcomes are expressed in terms of likelihood levels based on model statistics. Conditional forecasts are not always accurate, but they are nevertheless useful due to their careful quantification of probabilities, parameters and their uncertainty. There is no inherent reason why this is not possible in the social sciences.

The main challenge lies in the quantification of likelihood, which is not possible with current mainstream socio-economic models. It is not claimed, however, that one should be able to predict the onset of wars, election results, natural disasters, strategic political choices or other unique events. Thus, an important caveat must be made, in that our methodological approach excludes the occurrence of some events.[42]

Yet, the modelling paradigm shift proposed here opens a large spectrum of possibilities for sustainability policy-making. It allows for the quantification – within

[42] Just as in weather forecasts, which do not take into account possibilities of volcanic eruptions, even in active areas.

uncertainty bounds – of the expected effectiveness of specific policies aimed at inducing particular agent groups to take particular decisions.[43] The ability to conduct such forecasts entails significant advantages, including the reduction of the uncertainty involved in creating policy portfolios, and the possibility to explore their impacts across sectors through the coupling of several sectoral models.

The rest of this book addresses in detail each problem raised in this chapter. This goes from the philosophy of science used in modelling and policy appraisal, which is most of the time not clear (Chapter 4). It goes through the aggregation problem in economics: how to determine the macro-behaviour of groups of heterogeneous agents using complexity science (Chapter 5). It covers uncertainty and how to use it (Chapter 6). The structure of the diffusion of innovations, and the innovation system are covered (Chapters 7 and 8). The issue of money as a gauge of trust is explained (Chapter 9), as are financial and macroeconomic dynamics (Chapters 10 and 11). In Chapter 12, a detailed proposal framework for policy appraisal based on non-equilibrium models identifying risks and opportunities is given, which explains how using complexity science could work in practice. Applied examples are given in Chapters 13–15, where complexity economics analysis is used to explore the Brazilian energy–water–food nexus, effective policy for the diffusion of low-carbon innovations and the macroeconomic, financial and structural change impacts of a rapid low-carbon transition. However, next are discussed in more detail the implications of model assumptions over finance and innovation for model outcomes and policy recommendations made, unpacking Pandora's box which was opened in this chapter.

43 E.g., consumer purchases, investment choices, land-use decisions.

3

Modelling Innovation and the Macroeconomics of Low-Carbon Transitions

Equilibrium and Non-equilibrium Paradigms

Energy and climate policies may have significant economy-wide impacts, which are regularly assessed based on quantitative energy–economy–environment models. These tend to vary in their conclusions on the scale and direction of the likely macroeconomic impacts of a low-carbon transition. This chapter traces the characteristic discrepancies in models' outcomes to their origins in different macro-economic theories, most importantly their treatment of technological innovation and finance. The relevant branches of macro-innovation theory are analysed grouped into two classes: 'Equilibrium' and 'Non-equilibrium', which yield opposite conclusions for the economic impacts of low-carbon policies. It is shown that model outcomes are mainly determined by their representations of monetary and finance dimensions, and their interactions with investment, innovation and technological change. This chapter is adapted from work first released as a European Commission report in Mercure et al. (2016b), and later in a journal in Mercure et al. (2019a).

3.1. INTRODUCTION

Climate and energy targets could be met via different pathways and combinations of supply-side and demand-side technological and socio-economic options. Significant debate exists on strategies for achieving an efficient and cost-effective sustainable energy transition.[1] Macro-models are used extensively in this context to inform policy-making, notably through the IPCC process, and in national, European and international policy-making.

It was discussed in the previous chapter that, following the context of economic instability in many countries across the globe, due first to the 2008 crash and more

[1] Stern (2007); Edenhofer et al. (2010); Nordhaus (2010); IPCC (2014); Kriegler et al. (2014); Nordhaus (2015); Rogelj et al. (2015, 2018).

recently to the COVID crisis, it has become of primary importance to determine whether climate policies will hinder or boost economic growth, lead to unsustainable debt levels, generate economic opportunity or impose an economic burden.[2] It was suggested that depending on how economists viewed and conceptualised the process of finance, different normative interpretations were derived in relation to low-carbon policy and their macroeconomic implications. The issue goes further than that, as it is in fact the whole process of innovation, and how it is understood, that lies at the heart of this schism. Innovation as a driver of economic activity is a recurrent theme in current discourses on economic development, as well as public and private aggregate debt, and it remains rather misunderstood, not least because there is no widely accepted theory of innovation[3] (the topic of Chapters 8 and 11). This particularly relates to low-carbon and energy innovation, which could, as seen earlier, either fuel future prosperity or become an economic burden, its scale being sufficiently large to influence the macroeconomy.

This chapter zooms in on this critical question. Energy–economy–environment (E3) models are typically designed to inform policy-makers precisely on technology or economic scenarios for achieving low-carbon transformations. However, as discussed in Chapter 2, current models do not address in the required detail some of the key features of low-carbon innovation, including the necessary investment and finance of technology transitions, leaving unanswered questions for actual policy application.[4] This problem has some history in economics, and consensus has never been reached over how to treat innovation and technological change, and financing, in basic economic theory. Since underlying model assumptions on such theory determine model outcomes and policy recommendations, results are in fact often exactly opposite for different models.[5] This is an issue that has been debated for many years and remains unresolved.[6] While there is an ongoing debate on how to improve the realism of technological change and agent behaviour by using model experiments, none of these experiments challenge representations of investment, money and finance.

This problem reflects partly the underestimation of the role of finance and money on the real economy,[7] including stranded assets[8] or assets at risk from climate change

[2] Stern (2007, 2015); Mercure et al. (2016a). See Rogelj et al. (2013); Clarke et al. (2014); Kriegler et al. (2015a,b); McCollum et al. (2018); van Vuuren et al. (2020) for engineering estimates of mitigation costs/investment.

[3] See NCE (2018); OECD (2015); EC (2017). See also McLeay et al. (2014); Mazzucato (2018).

[4] Grubb et al. (2014); Mercure et al. (2016b); Pollitt and Mercure (2017).

[5] See, e.g., Carbon Trust (2005); Edenhofer et al. (2010); Cambridge Econometrics (2013, 2015).

[6] Michael Grubb has reviewed the evidence and modelling practices on induced innovation since the nineties (Grubb et al., 1993, 2002, 2006, 2021b), a body of work that shows how little progress has been made.

[7] Pollitt and Mercure (2017); Guttmann (2016); Monasterolo and Raberto (2018).

[8] McGlade and Ekins (2015); Mercure et al. (2018c).

and climate policy,[9] and partly the difficulty in modelling energy-related innovation, technological change and the effectiveness of policy instruments. Few of the current E3 models[10] have representations of the financial sector, its relevance for a large scale decarbonisation transition and its impact on the macroeconomy. This is a major shortcoming because such a transition will require large-scale investment in non-traditional sectors and put at risk existing investment and assets.[11] As discussed earlier, it also requires a better understanding of the complex behaviour of agents and their response to policy incentives than what currently exists in the community. While the need for a more explicit representation of the financial sector in macroeconomic models has been widely discussed after the 2007 global financial crisis (e.g., for models as they are used by central banks), such a discussion in the context of climate policy has yet to take place.

In this chapter, current modelling methodologies for assessing energy and climate policies are reviewed. A critical comparative analysis of various approaches to modelling policy-induced energy innovation and technological change is given, in order to critically justify why improvements need to be made to models, and which improvements, something that is then addressed in Part II of the book. For this purpose, features and factors in theory and models are identified that result in particular modelling outcomes. This requires looking at their underlying theoretical basis and methodological assumptions: how does the community currently understand innovation? Several reviews on the representation of energy-related innovation in E3 models have been written.[12] However, none of these reviews cover the theoretical underpinnings of the various existing implementations, especially with regards to finance. Furthermore, many analyses have been made of how innovation may be induced by prices or policy,[13] going back to Nordhaus (1973) and Hicks (1932), but again, these do not cover the role of money and finance in technological change.

In Section 3.2, how innovation and finance are addressed in recent economic theory and models is reviewed. Section 3.3 shows how different underlying theories imply different perspectives on the macro-economic effects of policies, how this can be considered in policy-making, and under which conditions models could converge. Section 3.4 concludes and proposes a research agenda covering key gaps in the future energy–economy–environment modelling of low-carbon transitions.

9 BoE (2015); Carney (2015); Battiston et al. (2017); Campiglio et al. (2018).
10 E.g., see GEA (2012); IPCC (2014); Kriegler et al. (2014).
11 BoE (2015); Carney (2015); Battiston et al. (2017); Mercure et al. (2018c).
12 Grubb et al. (2002); Löschel (2002); Köhler et al. (2006); Popp (2006); Clarke et al. (2008); Gillingham et al. (2008); Baccianti and Löschel (2014); Hall and Buckley (2016).
13 Goulder and Schneider (1999); Popp (2002); Acemoglu et al. (2012); Nordhaus (2014); Goulder et al. (2016).

3.2. INNOVATION IN ECONOMIC THEORY AND MODELS

3.2.1 *Technology and Innovation in Economic Theory*

It was already argued in Chapter 2 that economic theory can be roughly grouped into two different schools, each with different perspectives on innovation and the macroeconomy: equilibrium economics and non-equilibrium economics. This book uses the non-equilibrium approach, for clear theoretical reasons given in Chatpers 5 and 6. Nevertheless, it is helpful to first explore the impact that the current, more widely used equilibrium methodology has on actual policy decisions, and to identify the current knowledge frontier. It is notable that the schools are currently converging, and that improving critical elements of the equilibrium school could in principle help overcome some of the problems raised. However, this book suggests that pushing forward the non-equilibrium school is much more likely to be productive for fundamental theoretical reasons given in Chapter 6.

The equilibrium economics school explains finance, innovation and productivity change based on post-Walrasian neoclassical economics.[14] The central assumption is that prices coordinate the actions of all agents that adjust so as to equilibrate the markets for production factors (labour, capital/finance, knowledge, etc.). The decisions of representative agents (usually one per economic activity) ensure that given technology and resource constraints and market imperfections (labour unemployment), all remaining factors are always fully employed in the most efficient way, determining the state of the economy. This underpins most models used to assess energy–economy issues in the climate change community.[15]

In the non-equilibrium economics school, the economy is seen as being in perpetual dynamical change. At its heart is Schumpeter's foundational work[16] on the role of the entrepreneur and of the enabling financial institutions (Schumpeter, 1934, 1939, 2014), and Keynes' analysis of investment and macroeconomic dynamics (Keynes, 1936), which has been extended by the 'post-Keynesians' into a comprehensive theory of macroeconomics (e.g., Lavoie, 2014). Models that focus on money and finance follow this theoretical underpinning.[17]

14 Arrow (1962b); Romer (1986); Aghion et al. (1998); Acemoglu (2002).

15 E.g., see Capros et al. (2014); Clarke et al. (2014); Kriegler et al. (2014, 2015a); Nordhaus (2017).

16 Schumpeter's telling representation of innovation has resurfaced in various forms throughout modern economics, for example in Endogenous Growth Theory (Aghion et al., 1998), Evolutionary Economics (Freeman and Louçã, 2001), Sustainability Transitions Theory (Geels, 2002), Energy Technology Innovation Systems (Hekkert et al., 2007; Grübler and Wilson, 2013), directed clean innovation (Acemoglu, 2002; Acemoglu et al., 2012), and 'planetary economics' (Grubb et al., 2014).

17 E.g., Dafermos et al. (2017); Bovari et al. (2018); Lamperti et al. (2018); Mercure et al. (2018c); Monasterolo and Raberto (2018).

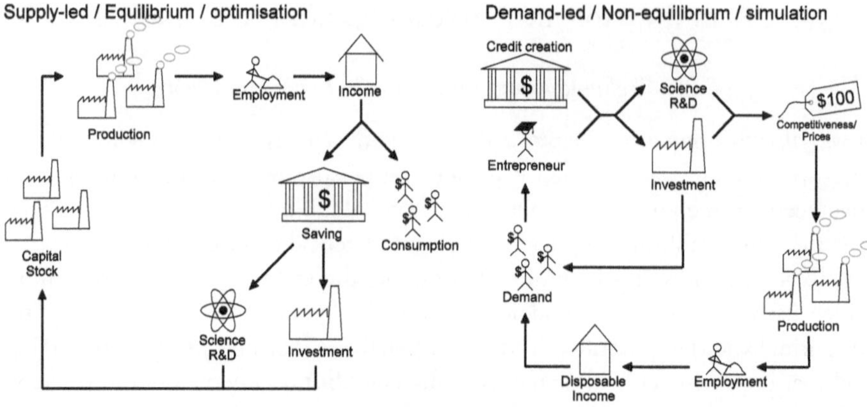

FIGURE 3.1 Contrasting representations of economic growth in the post-Keynesian/post-Schumpeterian (non-equilibrium) schools to the neoclassical (equilibrium) school.

The basic view of the *equilibrium school* is one of optimal allocation of scarce economic resources given technology at each point in time, and of optimal capital accumulation over time (Figure 3.1 left):

1. Firms produce by fully using all available production factors (full employment of capital)[18] to meet the demand for their products, given the technology options and households' preferences for consumption.
2. Firms decide on investment that maximises their net present value, and seek financing from the capital market, which the interest rate clears.
3. Firms' revenues from selling products are paid out to households, according to their provision of labour and capital ownership to the production process. Based on an intertemporal utility maximisation, households choose how to allocate this income between consumption (of various goods) and saving.[19]
4. Savings are used to finance firms' investments. Investment accumulation defines the capital stock available for production, which includes: physical production facilities (e.g., new factories, replacement of retired machinery, etc.), and investments into knowledge stock (e.g., technical progress, R&D).

[18] This reflects a standard assumption in textbook models. Contemporary equilibrium theory can allow for partial employment, market imperfections, oligopolisitic competition (Dixon and Jorgenson, 2013).

[19] Noting the distinction between *saving* (the action of not spending a fraction of income) and *savings* (a certain amount of accumulated wealth). Here the verb saving is used, which implies a yearly flow of income not spent on consumption.

5. The increased amount of capital, labour (population) and their improved factor productivity (resulting from R&D expenditure) expand the production frontier, which allows higher volumes of production.

Meanwhile, the *non-equilibrium school* contends that economic development takes place through entrepreneurial activity and the creation of purchasing power by banks (Figure 3.1 right):

1. Entrepreneurs sense where potential demand is not satisfied and see potential applications for their ideas. They apply to financial institutions to finance either innovative improvements to the existing capital stock, or the development of new products. Banks offer loans and create deposits, based on entrepreneurs' credit-worthiness and the expected profitability of the investment project.
2. Bank-funded investment in new capital or knowledge involves R&D expenditure in various connected technologies and sectors, which increases their productivity or creates new products entirely.
3. Productivity improvements reduce production costs, while new products attract spending. This can result in a mixture of (1) profits for the entrepreneurs and (2) price reductions in consumer markets. Both can result in higher income for households (depending how profits are spent), higher demand for the new products, and/or (3) reduced imports, and/or (4) increased exports.
4. Higher income leads to higher effective demand (for all products) and higher saving.
5. Higher demand and profits incentivise firms to re-invest in R&D and to expand their capital stock.

These two representations are radically different in their key principles and lead to contrasting approaches when implemented quantitatively, with opposite directions in the flow of information.

In the equilibrium school, a representative agent maximises utility by allocating fixed resources between possible uses, so that the methodology is generally tied to constrained optimisation.[20] In this perspective, the economy is driven by its ability to produce (it is *supply-led*).

In the non-equilibrium school, the state of the economy at every time step primarily depends on its states in previous time steps and expectations of the future and financial resources are unconstrained, so that the methodology is generally tied to dynamical systems simulations (simulation henceforth). In that perspective, the economy is driven by demand (it is *demand-led*). These are independent traditions

[20] Optimisation henceforth; every point in time is optimal and in a steady state within its context.

of mathematics research, often pursued independently from one another, and this often hinders communication between the two camps.

While the simulation/optimisation terminology may be neither exhaustive nor always exact,[21] in practice it classifies effectively the methodology used in most contemporary models, and captures a marked methodological division that reinforces theoretical differences and perceptions for policy-making.

The theoretical difference between the schools has at its heart a difference in the treatment of risk and uncertainty in investment and finance, something defined more precisely in Chapter 6, which is dedicated to this.[22] Keynes describes risk as quantifiable probabilities of outcomes of an action (e.g., investment), while uncertainty is unquantifiable. In post-Keynesian theory, it is assumed that investment takes place under fundamental uncertainty, which makes it impossible for agents to reliably estimate the likelihood of return on investment. Keynesian theory assumes that due to lack of detailed information, it is not possible for agents to devise a strategy that fully uses reliably all resources, as opposed to neoclassical theory, in which even under uncertainty, agents would find ways through markets to coordinate the use of all resources. For example, in the non-equilibrium school, under uncertainty over variations of demand, the investor plans for spare production capacity, so that he/she can respond to sudden demand changes (see Chapter 6). This implies that investment depends on investor and bank confidence in markets, and drives income and employment (or unemployment) of resources.

Meanwhile, in pure equilibrium theory in its most basic form, income determines investment through the propensity to save. Since demand can be relied upon and be foreseen (probabilistically), capital is optimally planned and used. Thus, capital accumulation determines production, and the theory functions the other way around. Therefore, the different direction of economic causality in equilibrium and non-equilibrium theory is a consequence of their respective treatments of risk and uncertainty.

A difference in philosophical interpretation also arises: in basic equilibrium theory, agents behave in a way that leads to maximal utility for all. This therefore identifies a normative or aspirational scenario, and deviations, ascribed to real-world effects and policy decisions, are discussed as distortions or frictions. Meanwhile, in non-equilibrium theory, no scenario is deemed more aspirational than any other; each scenario describes the economy in a different trajectory, and scenarios diverge from one another over time.

[21] For instance, Goodwin (1982) model could be classified as Marxian although it uses some optimal conditions to yield a closed-form.

[22] See Fontana (2008). Note that DSGE models do attempt to integrate uncertainty to macroeconomic modelling (Christiano et al., 2018). However, the uncertainty addressed is that which concerns the modeller's knowledge, not the modelled agent's knowledge and expectations, since the rational expectations assumption prevents systematic errors in agent predictions, making the predictions of agents the same on average as the model's themselves.

3.2.2 Technology and Innovation in Contemporary Low-Carbon Transition Models

Taxonomy of Theories and Models Used for Informing Climate Policy

Representations of money, innovation, technology, methodology and the source of economic change are enumerated in ten schools and research areas in economics, grouped into equilibrium and non-equilibrium (Table 3.1). This list is not exhaustive, but represents the main contemporary currents of economic thought.

Current macroeconomic and macro-sectoral economic models are classified along the categories of general equilibrium, partial equilibrium, macro-econometric, systems dynamics and agent-based (Table 3.2). Within each of these, sub-categories exist. A taxonomy of approaches is given according to the types of assumptions adopted for the structure of technological change, its representation at the micro and macro levels, and their representation of the entrepreneur at both levels.

The main methodologies are classified in terms of their representation of energy-related innovation, and representation of agents, at the micro and macro levels. Here 'micro' and 'macro' are used to refer to the level of aggregation: 'micro' means for example distinguishing individual technologies (e.g., solar PV), while macro means modelling aggregates at the sectoral or economy-wide level (e.g., the electricity or automotive sectors as whole). Innovation indicates representations of cost-reducing or productivity-enhancing activity, while agents refer to representations of decision-making and behaviour (e.g., investment decisions).

Representations of endogenous innovation and induced/endogenous technological change (ITC/ETC) were explored extensively a decade ago, and applied to energy and climate policy (Edenhofer et al., 2006). The result was that, according to the models, the capital costs and hence investment requirements to roll out technological change become less over time if learning-by-doing and technological progress is allowed to take place endogenously in those models.

The change towards ITC/ETC has been crucial: in earlier neoclassical models with inter-temporal optimisation, the representative agent was optimising utility over a trend of productivity predetermined with certainty. This had the perverse effect that the representative agent could anticipate future gains in efficiency and so postpone investing in low-carbon energy if this was not cost-optimal. The presence of so-called back-stop technologies[23] also had the same effect, promising future solutions that would appear with certainty once made economical. This in general meant that pre-ETC model results were to a great extent determined by exogenous assumptions (Grubb et al., 2002). With ITC/ETC, results emerged regarding the clustering of different possible types of optimal path-dependent states of the energy system, whether high or low-carbon (Gritsevskyi and Nakićenovic, 2000).

[23] A backstop technology is a hypothetical future technology that, assuming the consumer is willing to pay a high enough price, could provide infinite amounts of clean energy (e.g., solar photovoltaic or nuclear fusion).

TABLE 3.1 *Schools of economic thought*

		School Name	Micro-foundations		Money	Estimation method	Innovation & technology	Economic change
			Rational	Agent				
Equilibrium	Neoclassical	Solow[1]	RE	RA	Commodity	Optimisation	Exogenous	Capital accumulation
Equilibrium	Neoclassical	Endo growth[2]	RE	RA	Commodity	Optimisation	Knowledge in production functions	Capital & knowledge accumulation
Equilibrium	Neoclassical	GE[3]	RE	RA	Commodity	Optimisation	Knowledge in production functions	Capital & knowledge accumulation
Non-equilibrium	P-S	EE[4]	Behavioural Heterogeneous		Asset (Credit creation)	Dynamical systems (EE), Historical approach[9]	Knowledge networks, Diffusion, learning	Entrepreneur, Innovation, creative destruction
Non-equilibrium	P-S	TT[5]					Historical	
Non-equilibrium	P-S	TIS[6]					Case studies	
Non-equilibrium	P-K[7]	Horiz. Struct.	Behavioural Heterogeneous		Asset (Credit creation)	Time series econometrics	Sectoral tech. progress functions	Investment & innovation
Non-equilibrium	Behavioural[8]		Numerous agents		–	Empirical	–	–
Non-equilibrium	Marxian		Classes		–	Econometrics	–	–

Notes: P-S: Post-Schumpeterian. P-K: Post-Keynesian. GE: General Equilibrium. EE: Evolutionary Economics. TT: Transitions Theory. TIS: Technology Innovation Systems. Horiz: Horizontalists. Struct: Structuralists. RE: Rational Expectations. RA: Representative Agent.

[1]Nordhaus (Nordhaus, 2010), [2]REMIND (PIK, 2016), [3]IMACLIM (CIRED, 2018), AIM (NIES, 2012), GEM-E3 (E3M, 2018), [4]Safarzynska and van den Bergh (2010), [5]Geels (2002), [6]Hekkert et al. (2007), [7]E3ME-FTT (Cambridge Econometrics, 2014), GINFORS (Lutz et al., 2009), [8]Kahneman and Tversky (1979), Domencich and McFadden (1975), [9]Freeman and Louçã (2001), Geels (2002).

TABLE 3.2 *Macro-models and summary of their assumptions.*

		Assumption type	Micro innovation	Macro innovation	Micro agent	Macro agent
Optimisation		Optimal growth[1]	Does not have detailed dissagregated sectors	Knowledge accumulation in economy production function	Normative social planner optimising utility inter-temporally	
Optimisation	GE	CGE[2]	Can be linked to detailed technology models	Endogenous productivity in sectoral production functions	Representative agent with rational expectations (deterministic) optimising utility, prices adjust to clear all markets	
Optimisation	GE	DSGE	Can be linked to detailed technology models	Exogenous technological change	Heterogeneous stochastic representative agent	
Optimisation		Partial equilibrium cost-optimisation[3]	Learning curves, exogenous diffusion rates, vintage capital	Productivity not defined, can be linked to a CGE model	Can be heterogeneous, market segments	The normative social planner
Simulation		Macro-econometric[4]	Can be linked to technology models	Technology progress indicators (fn. of cumulative investment)	Can be linked to detailed t echnology models	Investment behaviour derived economet-rically
Simulation	SD	Discrete choice[5]	Vintage capital (fleets), learning curves	Productivity not defined, but can be linked to any macro-model	Multinomial logit regressions, heterogeneous agents	Can be linked to macro-model
Simulation	SD	Diffusion[6]	Selection-diffusion evolutionary model, learning curves	Can be linked to a path-dependent economic model	Decision-making under bounded rationality, social influence	Can be linked to macro-model
Simulation	AB	Sectoral[7]	Vintage capital (fleets), learning curves	Can be linked to a path-dependent economic model	Decision-making under bounded rationality, social influence	Can be linked to macro-model

Notes: GE: General Equilibrium; CGE: Computable General Equilibrium; DSGE: Dynamic Stochastic General Equilibrium; SD: Systems Dynamics; AB: Agent-Based.

Model examples: [1] RICE/DICE (Nordhaus, 2020), FUND (Anthoff and Tol, 2014), QUEST (DG ECFIN, 2015); [2] GEM-E3 (E3M, 2018), IMACLIM (CIRED, 2018); [3] MESSAGE (IIASA, 2013), TIMES (IEA-ETSAP, 2016), PRIMES (E3MLab, 2018); [4] E3ME (Cambridge Econometrics, 2014), GINFORS (Lutz et al., 2009); [5] IMAGE-TIMER (Bouwman et al., 2006); [6] FTT (Mercure et al., 2014); [7] MATISSE (Köhler et al., 2009).

Exogenous productivity has been equally problematic in post-Keynesian or post-Schumpeterian simulation models. For example, if the efficiency of new energy-using technology did not endogenously respond to a change in prices, models would predict continuous slowdowns of energy-based service demand (e.g., transport, energy intensive goods, and perhaps economic growth) in scenarios of increasing energy prices, something not observed in reality.[24] In reality, price rises incentivise investment in higher efficiency and faster technological turnover, while price falls do not imply technology regression (though they may encourage behaviour that uses more energy, see Grubb et al., 2014).[25]

However, at the time of these modelling innovations, there was no consensus on the meaning of economic costs, an ongoing issue. Indeed, in some studies, costs are identified with total energy system costs, in other cases with additional investment costs, and yet in other cases, with changes in GDP or changes in (conceptualised) utility or welfare.[26]

Many contemporary models now feature representations of some degree of ETC/ITC in principle, although it is not always clear to which degree these mechanisms are relied upon in studies, as they are not always reported, an issue that can lead to ambiguity for interpretation.[27] These representations can be radically different, tracing back again to basic economic theory, namely the neoclassical, post-Keynesian and post-Schumpeterian schools of thought.

Innovation and Technological Change in Macroeconomic Models

Consistent with the underlying philosophical assumptions about flows of causality in economic systems, the two theoretical paradigms embody the following, opposite, directions of causation with respect to the treatment of innovation and technological change:

24 See Grubb et al. (2014), p. 209 and Grubb et al. (2018).

25 Jorgenson and Wilcoxen (1993) found, using a CGE model, that the oil price shocks of the seventies suppressed total factor productivity growth temporarily. This result, however, is fully dependent on the assumption of crowding-out discussed below, as the dynamics involve changes in savings, originating from changes in consumption, that are forced by model construction to generate equal changes in investment. Without crowding-out, lower (higher) consumption would not be directly linked to higher (lower) investment.

26 Which is still the case, see, e.g., IPCC (2014), ch. 6, Grubb et al. (2014), ch. 11 and van Vuuren et al. (2020).

27 ETC/ITC generates difficulties when introduced in optimisation algorithms, and therefore, it is known that such features, although available, are sometimes (or potentially often) switched off in order for modellers to improve model stability and/or reduce computational time, as inferred from private communications with modellers. Thus, while nearly all model descriptions and papers claim or have claimed representations of learning curves, it is currently not possible to know when they are used and when not.

(a) In the equilibrium/supply-led paradigm, the representative household chooses between consuming its income now or in the future (i.e. to save). The financial resources made available by saving in the present are exhausted in investment, increasing (with certainty) the production capacity and productivity for supplying consumption in the future, through the accumulation of physical capital and knowledge. Capital resources in each year are finite, and are allocated to their most efficient use (that provides the highest rate of return). Because in deterministic equilibrium models investment outcomes are known with certainty, only the efficient portfolios are selected (technology risk-returns relationships are exogenously specified).

(b) In the non-equilibrium/demand-led paradigm, the entrepreneur decides under fundamental uncertainty whether to borrow funds for investing in production capital, R&D and technology. When banks agree to offer loans, money is created in the form of deposits (the finance for investment), and saving and investment both increase equally. Since investment is not constrained by households' savings, this increases debt and income simultaneously (unless the economy is operating at full employment). Individual investments may or may not lead to their intended productivity improvements and profit; at the aggregate level, however, they all contribute to an increasing body of knowledge. Economic growth can be driven by increasing debt (although not indefinitely). The clustering of innovation leads to economic cycles.

In computational implementations, the current model zoology is not so clear-cut, and many models are hybrid.[28] In particular, when equilibrium models feature elements that cannot be changed even when it would be optimal to change them (e.g., physical capital with long lifetimes, sticky prices), solutions are 'sub-optimal' and models deviate from 'aspirational' efficient markets towards descriptions that more closely reflect real-world 'imperfections'. Furthermore, the representative agent can be given limited foresight.[29] Finally, if a financial sector is introduced, savings can be borrowed from abroad and repaid in the future.

A similar division of paradigms also exists in the bottom-up technology modelling literature: an optimisation versus simulation methodological divide, with a large number of partial equilibrium cost-optimisation models of technology being in use and forming the most common model type. Furthermore, the adoption and diffusion

28 E.g., IMACLIM (CIRED, 2018) and GEM-E3 (E3M, 2018; E3MLAB, 2018a), see Mercure et al. (2019a) for details.

29 Often called the 'myopic mode', relaxing the constraints of rational expectations.

of innovations are processes that are not modelled very well in the community: energy models are found to produce typically pessimistic outcomes in comparison to observed diffusion trends. This points to a clear need to improve this representation, which is currently addressed in ongoing research initiatives.[30]

3.3. THE ROLE OF MONEY AND FINANCE IN CURRENT MACRO-MODELS

A transition to a decarbonised energy system requires significant amounts of investment in energy R&D, supply chains, infrastructure and physical capital, which could substantially exceed what might have been invested in this sector in an otherwise business-as-usual scenario. Even in contexts favourable for entrepreneurs to invest in low-carbon technology, they require access to funds in order for the transition to take place. Such investments could, in principle, displace other (arguably more productive) investments, a detrimental 'crowding-out' effect. A debate also exists as to whether government or other finance of innovation in the early stages of the innovation chain 'crowds-out' or 'crowds-in' other private finance in later stages.[31]

In the context of this work, a general meaning of 'crowding-out' is used: when an agent (government, firms, individuals) borrow(s) significant amounts of funds in order to invest into productive capital, this demand could (under certain conditions) divert funds that otherwise would have been used elsewhere in the economy, by bidding upwards the price of finance (the interest rate), therefore pricing out competing projects. Crowding-out can also apply to physical capital or labour, in which case prices or wages clear the respective markets.

The potential extent of 'crowding-out' depends on the amounts of funds available in the economy, and the degree to which crowding-out is assumed to take place in the model is determinant for model results.

This subject is once more fundamental to economic theory, with same two paradigms of equilibrium and non-equilibrium theory, this time with a focus on money. For policy contexts favourable for entrepreneurs to invest significant amounts of funds into low-carbon ventures (e.g., due to carbon pricing), outcome narratives will differ:

(a) In the equilibrium/supply-led paradigm, investment is determined by saving, which is a fixed proportion of income. Entrepreneurs compete for this restricted finite amount made available through financial markets/institutions. Demand for money by different sectors at the same time is cleared by the rate of interest, so that some entrepreneurs are outbid by the willingness of others to pay, and are thus crowded-out.

[30] Wilson et al. (2013); for initiatives see McCollum et al. (2016); Knobloch and Mercure (2016).

[31] Mazzucato (2013); Popp and Newell (2012); Hottenrott and Rexhäuser (2015); Mazzucato and Semieniuk (2017, 2018).

Money is a commodity in a finite quantity chosen by the central bank; if the central bank prints more money, the value of money decreases proportionally (the 'neutrality of money'). Thus equilibrium models need not have any representation of money or inflation, but only of relative prices. In the climate policy context, low-carbon investments promoted by policy crowd out other investments key to the economy. This leads to underinvestment in other key sectors for growth, leading to less productive use of capital, higher cost of capital and hence overall high costs to the economy.

(b) In the non-equilibrium/demand-led paradigm, investment is unrestricted and determined only by the willingness of entrepreneurs to invest and the willingness of banks to lend (unless funds are re-invested profits), determined by the perception by banks of the credit-worthiness of entrepreneurs. Banks are not solely intermediaries, but have a balance sheet and strategy. Banks borrow from each other, to diversify risk, and to/from the central bank, to gain reserves necessary to underwrite their lending activities (they minimise/optimise the risk and return of their balance sheet, constrained by financial regulation). Money, whether in paper form, or in commercial bank accounts, is a form of asset-liability pair, between two entities, the bank (debtor) and the owner (creditor). Thus all forms of money are financial instruments that can be created or destroyed by financial institutions.[32] Money creation is thus not constrained by savings, but only limited by the supply of credible lucrative ventures (in the prevailing context). In times of economic optimism with high returns on investment, banks expand lending, leading to growth and prosperity; in times of high perceived risk of default, financial institutions restrict lending, leading to economic recession. Thus GDP can increase in periods of optimism, high borrowing and investment, while it can slump in periods of pessimism, credit rationing and low confidence.

In line with those perspectives, equilibrium models take the premise that banks only play the role of intermediary between creditors and lenders, and that their role as money creators is neglected. Current non-equilibrium models, when they lack explicit representations of the financial sector, assume the allocation of finance 'on demand' by banks exogenously (i.e., how much money is created) according to how much investment is required. Notwithstanding the overwhelming role that money and finance play in driving low-carbon transitions, the modelling literature that provides a satisfactory representation of such monetary elements is extremely scarce.

[32] Lavoie (2014); McLeay et al. (2014); Schumpeter (2014); Wray (2016).

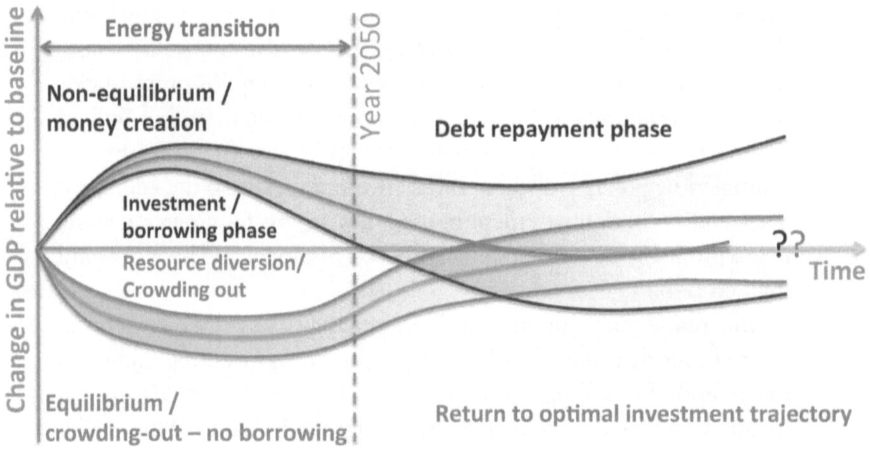

FIGURE 3.2 Illustration of GDP changes, relative to a baseline, of a policy-driven sustainability transition for the two groups of modelling schools of thought, equilibrium and non-equilibrium, in the current state-of-the-art. In this hypothetical example, a sustainability transition is financed (self-financed or via borrowing) from time zero until the vertical dashed line, after which low-carbon finance stops (figure co-designed by the authors). It is to be noted that for equilibrium models, recovery post-transition is strongly related to innovation processes such as productivity change, which mitigate the negative effects. However, even without representations of learning-by-doing and innovation, equilibrium models may still display a recovery post-transition due to processes such as reductions in fossil-fuel imports. Meanwhile, without representations of debt burdens, non-equilibrium models would not likely display a convergence post-transition.

3.4. IMPLICATIONS OF MODEL CHOICE FOR CLIMATE-RELATED POLICY-MAKING AND MACROECONOMIC IMPACTS

3.4.1 *Model Outcomes and Policy Implications by Model Type*

The key message of this chapter is shown in Figure 3.2, based on work using state-of-the-art models from both sides of the theoretical spectrum.[33] In the case of equilibrium models (grey curves below zero), with crowding-out of investment, an investment-intensive energy transition displaces resources that would have been used more productively elsewhere in the economy, leading to a sub-optimal equilibrium at lower GDP in the short run.[34] As the transition completes itself and high carbon equipment becomes replaced by low-carbon technology, this displacement ceases and investment returns to normal (undistorted) purposes. In the long run, with learning-by-doing, productivity increases, while lower operational expenses (e.g., fuel

33 This diagram was agreed by consensus between the E3ME and GEM-E3 model teams. In other words, the authors agreed on exactly how they disagree by designing this diagram.

34 Unless, for instance, if the baseline initially included distortions that were then removed in a mitigation scenario.

costs) may be incurred, and GDP recovers, or may even be improved above the baseline due to improved productivity and trade balance.

It is noted that a reverse 'crowding-out' effect can also arise in equilibrium in cases where policy forces the shutdown of an economic sector (e.g., oil and gas during decarbonisation). In the equilibrium case, this frees-up capital, which, with optimal allocation, increases the capital available for investment in other sectors, thereby compensating for the output loss. Thus, the effect goes both ways.

In the case of non-equilibrium models without crowding-out (black curves above zero), an investment-intensive energy transition program is predicted to create additional employment and to boost GDP in the short to medium run, due to higher investment (which is not offset by the impact of higher interest rates since financing is assumed to be abundant). It is followed by a possible reduction in macro-economic gains or even decline in the long run as debts are paid back, depending on debt servicing conditions. This is due to money being created by banks for investment in the early phase, which funds construction and results in activity across the economy, but also increases the debt burden, which remains in the longer term. For similar reasons as in equilibrium models, long-lasting productivity increases typically remain in the long run, following cumulative investments in better technology and equipment. These can offset the burden of debt repayment.

The 'reverse crowding-out' effect observed in equilibrium models also does not occur in non-equilibrium models. In the latter, losses of market share in particular sectors means that related capital and investment opportunities are truly lost and not replaced, leading to job and income losses despite the aggregate possible positive impact of investment-led growth in other sectors. This means that rapid structural change instead leads to stranded capital, for example stranded fossil fuel assets, which do not arise in equilibrium models.

This explains why models of different classes exhibit essentially opposite outcomes for the macroeconomics of an energy sustainability transition (i.e. GDP and employment). Uncertainty also behaves differently: in equilibrium, due to the use of optimisation, uncertainty of solutions is linearly related to the uncertainty in parameters, as it primarily represents the gradient of the optimisation function in the vicinity of the optimal point. In contrast, non-equilibrium models are strongly path-dependent. This means that uncertainty on parameters accumulates over simulation time, as path-dependence generates alternate scenarios that diverge from each other, differing minimally in the short run but becoming significantly different in the long run. As such, model outcomes in the far future are more uncertain than those in the near future.[35] This property is standard for complex systems, and arises, for example, strongly in climate models.

[35] Lower apparent uncertainty bounds in equilibrium models should not be understood as better treatment of real-world uncertainty, but rather, as the uncertainty that can be represented in optimisation algorithms, which are not strongly path-dependent, see Chapter 6.

3.4.2 *Is a Convergence of Models Possible?*

To move beyond conceptual arguments about different economic paradigms and the models that result, the author's team of economists worked together with economists of the opposite camp in enhancing two models based on these different fundamental perspectives – equilibrium (GEM-E3)[36] and non-equilibrium (E3ME)[37] – and focused on how to represent the crucial processes of innovation and finance applied to climate change mitigation. The collaboration was facilitated by the fact that both models already had an advanced treatment of induced innovation, and have been given similar parameterisation inputs.

These two models make explicit the mark-up faced by borrowers over a 'benchmark' interest rate, where the mark-up is intended to capture the risks that are specific to the project / industry sector / country. One such risk is the capacity of borrowers to service additional debt, and the models construct estimates of the existing debt carried by each industry (or other institutional sector) based on the history of previous investment and assumptions for how that investment was financed. The models differ in their determination of the benchmark interest rate, reflecting their respective origins in the equilibrium (GEM-E3-FIT) and non-equilibrium (E3ME-FTT) traditions.

In both models, the developments allow financial constraints to be explored explicitly in scenarios. For example, a scenario of rapid decarbonisation in power generation would be associated with a higher rate of investment and a higher level of debt carried by the firms undertaking the investment. This will have the effect of making the power generation sector a riskier prospect for lenders, reflected in a higher cost of capital and a higher price ultimately passed through to consumers. This can be mitigated by policy, for example through some form of public underwriting of the higher risk (transferring the risk, and the cost to taxpayers).

In summary, in equilibrium models, the factor limiting the total amount of borrowing is the interest rate, which clears the market. In non-equilibrium theory, credit-worthiness is what ultimately determines the confidence of banks to invest.

Based on comparison of preliminary results from the models E3ME-FTT and GEM-E3-FIT, incorporating the developments described above, the two models appear to converge in their outcomes. As discussions and debates intensify regarding investment levels required in the context of the low-carbon transition, it is possible that improving the representations of money and finance in both model types could bring much needed coherence and clarity in the macroeconomic messages conveyed to energy and climate policy-makers. However, as seen later in this book, this in fact opens a Pandora's box of complexity.

36 GEM-E3-FIT: General Equilibrium Model for Energy Economy & Environment with Financial and Technical progress modules.

37 E3ME-FTT: Energy-Economy-Environment Macro-Econometric model with Future Technology Transformations. See Mercure et al. (2016b) for details on both models.

3.4.3 *Clarifying the Purpose of Models: Normative or Positive?*

The use or not of an optimising representative agent or social planner construct, as a model representation of human populations, raises questions, as already mentioned in Chapter 2, regarding the nature, purpose and methodology of models deployed in climate policy-making, which appear to be confused: are they *normative* (identifying best configurations or strategies in order to make recommendations, i.e. what agents ought to do) or *positive* (describing observed reality, i.e. what agents are observed to do)? By definition, an economic allocation identified by systems optimisation is the best possible allocation (under certain chosen criteria and constraints, and according to existing knowledge). The finding that an optimal resource allocation is not achieved due to frictions and market failures, ultimately reflects a normative philosophy of science. Meanwhile, allocations that are identified and described because they are considered likely to arise, whether good or bad, reflect a descriptive scientific approach. The science philosophy question debated here concerns what the research question is, whether agents are understood to behave in such a way that optimal outcomes are realised in scenarios, and whether those scenarios are in themselves recommendations or descriptions of reality. Unfortunately, there exists a deep lack of clarity in the position of modellers on that question in the field. Chapter 4 explores this in more detail, but more needs to be said here.

Scenarios calculated using normative optimisation models are by definition 'possible/plausible', but they are not necessarily 'likely'. Specifically, it is not possible to determine the likelihood of optimal scenarios occurring in reality, simply because, even if agents were inclined to contribute to an optimal economic allocation, they would have no way of finding out, individually, which strategies would make the correct contribution (Kirman, 1992). The degree of control and coordination necessary exceeds the capacity of law-makers. Naturally, what is analysed in optimisation scenarios are the differences from the optimum, not the optimum itself, while in descriptive models, it is differences from current trajectory that are analysed. Thus, when dealing with optimal scenarios, the difference between the 'baseline' (no intervention) trajectory and an optimal situation (albeit with market failures) is sometimes blurred. If not treated carefully, the interpretation of optimisation results could pre-determine the result, in that any market distortion of the baseline scenario would automatically lead, by construction, to a detrimental performance outcome, even though it corrects market failures (for instance, its impact on GDP).

Furthermore, a danger exists in interpreting results of optimisation models – inherently normative – in a descriptive philosophy. For example, cost-optimisation and pure representative agent equilibrium models offer the attractive but potentially misleading suggestion that pricing policies are the best way to correct market failures such as climate change, since agents, when assumed to behave optimally, always find the best possible use of resources according to prices. Indeed, many such models equate 'marginal/social cost of carbon' (what the models produce from a constraint or externality) with 'carbon price' (the assumed policy instrument). However, policy practice has shown that pricing is usually not the only policy lever to be known to work: while pricing policies do offer incentives to correct market failures, their likelihood of achieving actual normative objectives is not as clear as basic equilibrium theory would suggest.[38] As suggested earlier, finding out whether carbon pricing is likely to reach its stated objective requires studying how agents take decisions, including how they take account of such incentives. The distinction between normative and descriptive approaches to science is not frequently identified, but it is crucial if one is to understand the meaning of model results. Ultimately, the danger lies in the interpretation of model results in terms of causality between intervention and outcome.

The normative/descriptive paradigms are reflected in model behaviour. In optimisation-based models, allocations at each point in time modelled are in equilibrium steady states, and thus only change when exogenous variables change, as for example, population, regulations, trade agreements, the price of carbon, technology costs or taxation. The converse is that configurations do not change unless an external parameter changes (e.g., the price of an internalised externality). This has the result that, for climate change mitigation, additional emissions abatement only takes place when the (shadow) price of carbon increases.[39] Low-carbon technology diffusion stops if the (real) price of carbon or other incentives becomes constant.[40] In the scenario database of the IPCC (2014), this has led to some models reporting very high real carbon prices, of order \$10,000/tCO_2 or more, that are required to abate the last remaining sources of emissions in the marginal abatement cost curve. However, in a largely decarbonised world, as carbon markets decline in relevance, and older socio-technical and industrial systems based on fossil fuels are abandoned and replaced by newer innovative low-carbon systems, it is not necessarily clear how, in reality, the carbon price would behave.

In a non-equilibrium perspective, model states typically evolve without end even if the policy context does not change, in part pre-conditioned by their history, momentum and inertia. Thus, technological change does not solely take place when relative prices change, but instead, happens continuously, since the methodology

38 Notably, most optimisation models assume and require the application of a carbon price to all sources of carbon emissions, including those in which other policy instruments are currently used and for which no plans currently exist in most countries to use emissions trading or carbon taxes (e.g., personal mobility, household heating, agriculture). The assumed effectiveness of a carbon price to reduce emissions in consumer-based sectors is at best conjectural, and not informed by extensive behavioural research.

39 With the exception of policy instruments involving setting standards which optimisation models reflect by reducing the menu of technological choices, eliminating those polluting technologies that do not meet the standards imposed. In this case emission reductions can still occur as a response to setting standards without changes in the carbon price.

40 In models without non-convexities, technology composition is a unique function of the carbon price.

does not involve searching for a steady state. In this paradigm, taxes create incentives to re-orient an ever-changing system towards a new course.[41] Indeed, the system may be permanently altered and the policies which drove the transition to a new path may then become either embedded, or redundant (or possibly both). Unchanging but significant policies are not in this case equivalent to zero incentive.

This difference in model behaviour matches a divide within the policy sphere as well. The world of climate policy is divided along two lines of thought. On the one hand, in the equilibrium paradigm, policy-makers see carbon pricing as a tool for re-allocating scarce funds to fix a market failure, climate change, focusing on the marginal abatement cost and social cost of carbon. As a result, it is generally argued that linking or merging carbon markets increases market efficiency.

In the non-equilibrium perspective, energy and climate policy-makers see the carbon price as a signal instrument to incentivise faster economy-wide innovation and low-carbon technological change. The experienced and expected future price of carbon must be sufficiently high to communicate the current and future value of low-carbon investment to firms (including R&D), but it is not the only policy available. Regulation can play an important role, allowing a lower carbon tax, using for instance technology or sectoral policies, including both 'push', and 'pull' policies such as the combination of R&D, feed-in tariffs and regulatory changes which have driven the revolution in renewable energy technologies. It is then argued that different national innovation systems, facing different contexts, are likely to require different magnitudes of incentives (e.g., what creates incentive for R&D, innovation and investment in China is not the same as in Germany), and thus carbon markets should not necessarily be linked internationally to accelerate decarbonisation.

3.5. DISCUSSION AND POLICY IMPLICATIONS

Innovation is one of the determining factors in the long run costs of climate change mitigation, a finding that may also be relevant for other major structural economic transformation processes. Climate policies that stimulate innovation have a plausible prospect of yielding economic benefits, but are also as likely to generate economic challenges. In fact, climate policies may well be found to generate both at the same time, depending on sectors and regions, the net effect depending on contextual policy design and mode of implementation.

41 Diffusion is not a simple function of the carbon price or other incentives: increasing the carbon price does not always incentivise the same number of agents deciding to purchase a particular durable good; it depends on history. But also, due to inertia in diffusion, an unchanging (real) carbon price/tax signal can sustain low-carbon technology diffusion.

Climate and energy policy assessment often involves the use of large complex multi-sectoral computational economic, energy technology and environmental models, to carry out quantitative analysis. However, innovation, and the financing requirements of capital-intensive systems transformations, remains generally not well represented in models deployed for informing climate and low-carbon energy innovation policy planning. Furthermore, long-run models that do not explicitly include endogenous innovation have a higher chance of yielding potentially erroneous results which could become quickly outdated (notably technology cost data that often drive model results).

Depending on the model choice, model results imply that the structural characteristic of the climate change mitigation problem may or may not be one of burden-sharing to deliver a global public good. Instead, they could rather point towards the challenge of crafting smart domestic policies combined with international mechanisms for accelerating low-carbon technology and policy diffusion, and for reducing the cost of capital by cementing policy commitments in international agreements. Ultimately, with further development, models may over time depart from the standard framing of climate policy as a prisoner's dilemma, replacing it by another type of game with rules based on the consequences of financing low-carbon innovation and structural change (see Chapter 15).

The observed differences between the models in their treatment of innovation, money and finance reflect the lack of consensus among economists and social scientists. While both approaches are seen as theoretically rigorous and self-consistent, it is important for policy-makers to have some insight into this state of conflicting knowledge. It needs to be recognised by both the policy and modelling communities that this schism exists, that representations are incomplete, and therefore that further research is critically needed in order to further our ability to effectively inform climate policy-making. Otherwise, model types can be chosen solely according to whether their results support or not particular political platforms. In this context, it is reasonable to make the recommendation that, in the interests of transparency for policy-makers and researchers, all modelling studies should state clearly their underpinning theoretical school and their treatment of finance and innovation, whether they use learning-curves, or represent finance explicitly, something not usually currently done.

Finally, and most importantly, it emerges here that developing representations of the monetary and financial sectors is crucial in models used for studying the economic impacts of energy system transformations and emissions reductions. Model differences completely hinge on whether crowding-out of financial resources takes place or not, which thus needs empirical verification. In addition to this, improving representations of behavioural features in agent decision-making (e.g., technology adoption, bank lending) can improve the accuracy of models to assess the effectiveness of proposed policies. It is thus imperative that in existing science–policy interfaces, in which policy-makers routinely commission modelling studies, strong incentives are given to modellers to improve their representations of money and finance. This is critical in order to clarify model outcomes with respect to policy proposals, and attempt to reduce model uncertainty, robustness of results, and spur a conciliatory methodological dialogue.

4

Philosophies of Science and the Policy Cycle

Chapter 4 concludes Part I by summarising the scientific consistency problems with current economic analysis of policy, offering a way forward to rebuild a consistent framework under the umbrella of complexity economics. A standard simple representation of the policy cycle is used, in order to place the role of scientists and economists into the policy-making process, and thus identify what kind of evidence is used in which stage of the policy-making process. Normative and positive traditions of policy analysis are described, with their respective roles in the policy cycle, and current inconsistencies identified. Contradictions in the philosophy of science currently used in economics are discussed. The Lucas critique is reviewed, arguably one of the main problems in economic modelling. A shortlist is drawn for desired empirical evidence as building blocks to develop a complexity theory of economics.

4.1. INTRODUCTION

There are two broad types of landscape painters. Those who paint a landscape as accurately as they can as it appears to their eyes, and those who paint a landscape the way they think it ought to be shown, seen and remembered, according to how they like to see it and what they find beautiful. Clearly, beauty is in the eye of the beholder, while ugly objective reality is what lies in front of the artist. Whether right or wrong, it is usually the idealised landscape that is remembered after the artist's time is gone, since this is how humans like to shape the world they see. However, accurate visual depictions of the world as it is or has been do matter and for different purposes in documenting and remembering. The same happens with economists and social scientists, for whom a blurred line exists between idealised and empirical representations of human reality. Both types of messages are useful to policy-making; however, they play different roles.

Representations of reality are used for informing policy-making for solving societal problems. Scientists, economists and modellers in the climate change, environmental science and sustainability fields entertain more and less idealised representations of how they understand actual economic behaviour by economic agents, contrasting to various degrees against how they think they 'ought' to behave morally. Analysts have an intuitive understanding of how policy-making works in governments and international institutions, and thus, of how their understanding of human reality can inform this. However, how analysts picture both economic reality and policy-making may not always be the most accurate representation of actual reality, of what is called by political scientists the 'policy cycle' and the 'science–policy interface'.

Members of the public and students in natural science degrees often imagine the science–policy interface to be a process in which university professors barge into policy-makers' offices and impose on them *'recommendations'* regarding what the policy *'should be'* based on their analysis of *'objective reality'*. Alternatively, policy-makers are imagined knocking on the university professor's door, in an ivory tower, and asking, 'I heard of this new climate change thing, what do you recommend we should do?', following which the scientist designs an optimisation calculation to 'objectively' answer the question. It may also be imagined that whether policy-makers duly implement such recommendations depends on whether they have suitable values and political views, or otherwise follow the advice of their corrupt friends and cronies in the fossil fuel industry. In this representation, *agency* is transferred from the policy-maker to the winners of a battle between competing ideologies, sets of values and lobbying groups. This is sometimes true, but thankfully, not always.

The structure of policy-making and of the science–policy interface is in reality not just much more complex than this; it possesses a recurrent form that does not resemble this at all. Notably, there is often (though not always) an important process and procedural difference between policy and politics, and between setting the agenda and gathering evidence to assess the impacts of proposed policies, between setting a vision of what could be aspired to, and determining concrete steps to get there. These phases are frequently confused by scientists and students.

The notions of objective reality, regarding how economic agents are observed to behave, versus moral philosophy, regarding how economic agents 'ought to' behave according to some normative principles, is recurrently confused in science and economic theory, which does not improve clarity in evidence-based policy-making. Policy-making based on an idealised reality can lead to policy failure, something that often goes unchallenged for what it may in fact be: scientifically misguided and possibly ideologically driven, where the ideology itself is embodied in the idealised reality.

This whole book is in fact about quantitative methods for evidence-based policy-making. It is therefore necessary to understand what it is. In this chapter, the structure of evidence-based policy-making and of the science–policy interface, the role of models, and the philosophy of science are jointly discussed. Problems are identified in the existing science–policy interface with regards to the economics used. The problems lie with the models and theory used, not the actual science–policy process. Important discrepancies are identified between the current philosophy of science adopted in models used to analyse climate, industrial and economic policy questions, and the questions that modellers attempt to address with models. These inconsistencies partly stem from age-old divisions and debates in economic theory, which bring with them their own inconsistencies in their underlying philosophy of science and originate from old traditions of moral philosophy and ideology. It is found that these inconsistencies fundamentally impede progress in developing an effective science–policy interface when it involves economics. Scientific ways forward are suggested for developing a complexity science-based decision-making framework, later developed in Chapter 12.

4.2. THE POLICY CYCLE

4.2.1 *Steps of the Policy Cycle*

Figure 4.1 shows the basic accepted model of the structure of policy-making.[1] In this model, policy-making begins with various actors influencing the broader political debate, pushing certain issues and interests into the political agenda. For help with their task of relatively weighing the demands from stakeholders, policy-makers sometimes commission scientists, economists or analysts to provide a summary of the existing evidence over a certain question. For example, the Intergovernmental Panel on Climate Change (IPCC) has, over the last 2–3 decades, played an important role in rounding up the necessary knowledge base upon which to set the agenda for climate policy (IPCC, 2007, 2014, 2018). This has informed the development of the Paris Agreement (UNFCCC, 2015), in which most countries of the world have collectively agreed to adopt some form of policy to reduce greenhouse gas emissions. In a similar example, the UK government commissioned what became known as the Stern Report (Stern, 2007) which assembled an evidence base on the economic impacts of climate change, and this has contributed to the adoption of the UK's Climate Change Act. With the climate agenda at least partly set for many countries, in other words, having decided whether to address climate change or not, it has become possible to increasingly focus on how to reach newly adopted climate agendas as set out in the Paris Agreement.

As the agenda becomes set, through a framing of policy problems, policy-makers can draft a set of formulations of possible policy strategies that could potentially

[1] See the textbook by Crabbé and Leroy (2008), which provides a detailed overview of present understanding of the policy cycle. A similar perspective can be found in the UK's policy appraisal guidelines (HM Treasury, 2020a).

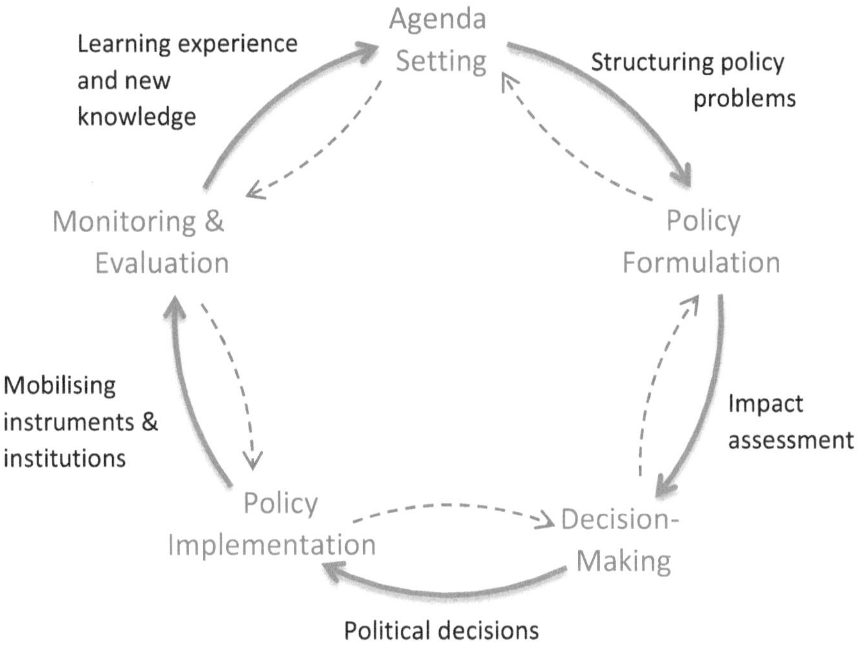

FIGURE 4.1 Simple schematic representation of the policy cycle. After Crabbé and Leroy (2008).

achieve the target.[2] However, for any policy solution to gain legitimacy, several institutional steps are generally required. In most countries, some degree of evidence base is needed in order for policy proposals to be taken seriously by the legislative assembly. In some countries and supra-national regions, including the EU, an impact assessment is required by law before any new legislation can be adopted (EC, 2009, 2015). In other countries such as the US and the UK, a cost-benefit analysis is required. When such an exercise is requested, several policy formulations may be tested and their multidimensional impacts assessed, generally using qualitative or quantitative models.[3] The paper trail of all debates, communications and analyses carried out are made publicly available in order to gain legitimacy across stakeholders and the voting population. Using this level of transparency helps to protect the policy-making process from popular and legal challenge. These steps are common at the highest level of government in the UK, the USA and the EU notably. This may be less common in other countries, constituencies or lower levels of governance, and in fact differs everywhere. However, when well established science–policy interfaces exist, they tend to work in this way.

[2] Called 'longlist appraisal' in UK policy-making, see HM Treasury (2020a).
[3] Called 'shortlist options appraisal' in UK policy-making.

Following a successful impact assessment stage, political decisions are taken, laws are amended and policies becomes implemented. Policy packages do not always become implemented in the way that they were initially formulated, due to various debates, interests and power relations putting pressure on policy-makers, and the latter, generally seeking compromises and consensus, alter the policy proposals in ways that makes them acceptable to different stakeholders. It is thus not uncommon at that time for proposals to be sent back to the policy formulation stage, if policy-makers, or members of the legislative assembly, amend or refuse to adopt them.

At the point at which policies are implemented, creating and mobilising policy instruments and related institutions (e.g., regulatory bodies), policies are normally (or ideally) required to be monitored, which allows their performance to be evaluated after the fact. When this is done well, a learning effect can arise following what is identified when evaluating policies. New external knowledge may also become available and new contexts arise, and the political agenda can be amended, depending what new priorities arise.

The above may seem, especially to readers who understand policy-making processes, as mainly driven by politics, like an idealisation of the process of evidence-based policy-making, where reality is instead much more messy. This cannot be denied. However, this framing and simplification is sufficiently accurate and effective for structuring thought when considering informing the policy-making process, and was validated by colleagues working within UK government and at the European Commission. However messy, each part of the policy process can be categorised into one of the steps given above, with feedbacks and iterations with previous steps. And clearly, the process can at anytime go back to any of its earlier phases in order to progress again, or be terminated altogether.

4.2.2 *Three Different Views of the Policy Cycle*

Policy-making is generally analysed through one of three types of lenses, depending on analysts' background training and professional perspectives: the '*technocrat*' scientific view, the *political* view and the *legal* view. Scientists, economists and engineers tend to see policy-making as a rational problem-solving process, while social and political scientists tend to see a balancing of interests and power relations or a constructing of reality, and lawyers see institutional and legislative issues, precedents and constraints (Crabbé and Leroy, 2008). These three viewpoints are as valid as each other and complementary, but raise different issues and lead to different interpretations of the nature of problems and strategies for solving them. Ideally, one should look at policy problems through all three lenses simultaneously, but due to specialism in most analysts' unique disciplinary training, this is a great challenge.

'Technocrats' (scientists, economists and engineers) tend to see policy issues as rational processes for identifying problems and seeking and adopting solutions based on scientific evidence gathered. Thus, scientists, economists and engineers often expect decisions to be taken based solely on the basis of scientific evidence, and may tend to overlook, misunderstand or underestimate why power relations and legal issues matter. The technocrat view may work well in informing the agenda setting and policy formulation phases, but often breaks down at the decision-making and implementation stages, in which power relations and legal issues shape processes. Technocrats frequently ascribe implementation failure to what to them is a black box they may call 'political feasibility'. Scientists specialise in identifying why problems are problems, and how one should ideally solve them, but the solutions they propose may lie outside of the institutional and political framing in which action can realistically take place, or they may simply be inconsistent with existing legal structures and treaties (Crabbé and Leroy, 2008). The scientific perspective includes all aspects of natural and social science, economics, business, and will often use computer models to derive evidence to support the soundness of policy proposals against chosen evaluation criteria.

Scholars trained in political science will be able to understand why a particular policy has failed to become implemented, or why it changed form before being implemented. Sometimes policies are reduced in ambition to an extent that renders them ineffective at the implementation stage, but acceptable to stakeholders. While scientists and engineers may think it makes little sense to reject well-studied proposals, or to adopt ineffective policies, the political scientist will be able to identify which power relations led to what outcomes, often using interview methods as an empirical basis. The implementation of effective policies takes place through rare political windows of opportunity. Political science scholars will well understand power relations, the legitimacy of policy proposals in the view of stakeholders and the public, and understand the composition of the political space.

Legal scholars will understand policy-making in a legislative context, through what has a legal precedent, what is legally feasible (consistent with existing law) and what is not. When proposed policies are not legally consistent, they may be challenged in court (e.g., firms or individuals suing the government) and ultimately revoked. For instance, if a precedent exists for a policy approach having been successfully challenged in court, it later becomes impossible to implement anything with a similar formulation. Legal challenges can delay or block effective policy-making substantially. Furthermore, legal scholars can also see and predict what could be feasible, by studying existing law in detail. Thus, while political scientists tend to work primarily by interviewing people, not necessarily aware of the legal details, lawyers do not necessarily understand the full set of political power relations at play, but they know what is legally feasible. One must note that there can be an important difference between the intended use and the actual use of legal instruments. Lawyers will understand their intended use, while political scientists will identify what they are being used for in practice. Legal scholars will have a deep understanding of the resilience to legal challenge of policy formulations, the institutional context in which they must be treated, and the legislative process through which they can be put in place or removed.

A notable example of discrepancy between the three views is with the history leading to the successful adoption of the Paris Agreement (Viñuales, 2015), which stands in stark contrast with the failure of the Copenhagen negotiations, in which an attempt was made to agree on a framework of global climate policy. In Copenhagen, technocrats were requesting a global uniform pricing mechanism to be imposed on carbon emissions. The realities of sovereignty and agency meant that globally coordinated climate policy could not materialise, while uncoordinated but widely adopted climate policy was possible (see e.g., Falkner, 2016). As discussed in this chapter, the proposal of uniform pricing originates from particular principles of moral philosophy, rather than from some sort of science. Some technocrats continue to ascribe the failure of Copenhagen to what they see as mis-informed 'political feasibility' (see, e.g., Bertram et al., 2015) and that time has been wasted since. This is not the view held by lawyers and political scientists, however, whose message is more subtle: progress has been made where it could be made, and there are more ways than one to incentivise change.

4.3. THE PHILOSOPHY OF SCIENCE IN ECONOMICS

4.3.1 *The Core Issue: Lack of Discipline*

The basic premise in evidence-based policy-making is that policy-makers cannot, a priori, be certain of the potential of any policy actions of achieving their stated objectives, even given their accumulated experience. In order to publicly defend their decisions, they commission external experts to produce evidence that supports their policy proposals. The advantages of evidence-based policy-making, in contrast to taking decisions solely on the basis of addressing as many interest groups as possible, is that it offers a publicly stated rationale, based on a (it is assumed) defensible methodology, on the basis of which decisions can be defended against challenge by those interest groups whom those decisions do not favour. Indeed, if challenged publicly or in courts, policy and law-makers could simply say that they decided on the basis of the implications of the evidence regarding the effectiveness of their strategy at achieving social and economic objectives, produced by recognised external experts, who used defensible analysis methods, and thus the decision was not made preferentially towards any particular interest group. It is important to note that in doing so, policy-makers partly delegate responsibility for their decisions, to those experts upon which they relied.

Various approaches and methods are used to inform policy-making, belonging to various traditions of the philosophy of science, in the social and natural sciences, engineering and moral philosophy. Specifically, it is frequent to adopt a 'normative' (or 'prescriptive') approach, typical of welfare economics, to develop a narrative addressing the normative question of whether a policy objective should be adopted or not, based on a chosen axiom or set of axioms. For example, in climate policy, one can adopt the normative axiom principles of 'the polluter pays', somewhat based on social justice, and 'internalising externalities', rooted in the Pareto principle of welfare economics, and carry out a cost-benefit analysis for identifying an optimal emissions reduction target. One can then derive an 'optimal carbon tax' that satisfies these normative principles: it is deemed socially just that polluters should pay only the amount that equates to the damage that they cause, unless they choose to eliminate their contribution to the externality. In that, the carbon tax is normatively derived from the axioms of the theory.

Another example could be to seek to identify the unique imaginary optimal state of an existing system (e.g., the energy system), of all possible states, under certain constraints (e.g., budget, climate change), that reaches a stated set of objectives (e.g., minimal cost, maximal security). This identifies a vision, an aspiration, that decision-makers could adopt and seek to realise. It identifies whether and in what form an objective is achievable in principle, and whether it is desirable. In this case, the philosophy is based upon an axiom stated by the objective function, where for instance, minimising whole system cost could be interpreted as socially superior to other configurations. This is rooted in utilitarian theory and axioms (see Wilk and Cliggett, 2007).

As part of a 'positive' (or 'descriptive') philosophical approach, one can assess the potential impacts of particular policy proposals or set of actions, against certain stated objectives, based on observation of how social systems work, irrespective of any normative axioms. This is a 'conditional forecasting' exercise that analyses what is deemed the likely outcomes of those actions in relation to progress towards those objectives, as well as unintended or undesirable outcomes. Here, analysis can search through action space for different proposed strategies to achieve a certain stated objective, in each case analysing in detail their impacts on systems and stakeholders, and whether an objective is achieved or not, and at what 'cost' in relation to undesirable side effects.

The key difference between the normative and the positive methodologies, in general, is that in the former, the driver for the choice of action is rooted in the action itself meeting pre-defined axioms of normative, moral philosophy, while in the second, the driver is rooted in the outcome meeting the objective. Thus in normative analysis, one searches for what meets normative principles seen as expressing the expectations and values representative of a social group, while in positive analysis, one searches for what can be reasonably expected to work in practice. Both of these approaches can be assigned independent useful functions in the policy cycle, and have different input requirements. Notably, identifying optimal system configurations does not typically need accurate representations of how system components, notably humans, behave, since it is ultimately bound to suggest how they 'ought to' behave. Meanwhile, positive assessment of the impacts of policy action normally requires scientific knowledge grounded in observation, and large amounts of data. Identifying an objective is different than choosing a strategy to achieve that objective, and both are important components of the policy cycle.

The state of philosophy of science in policy analysis is unfortunately currently not as clear as the above, since one observes with experience that the two philosophies are confused with one another and applied inconsistently across the policy cycle. It is clear from philosophical reasoning that optimisation is suitable for setting a policy agenda, while positive approaches are suitable for the impact assessment stage. But this is not usually what happens in practice. It is often the case that impact assessment is done on the basis of whether a choice of action meets a normative axiom, rather than a likelihood of achieving an objective, or meeting an axiom is interpreted as achieving an objective, where consistency with observation is confused with meeting axioms.

4.3.2 *Using Normative as Descriptive*

Using optimisation, utility maximisation or cost-benefit tools to *predict* the outcomes of policy choices is a strange concept from the viewpoint of the philosophy of science. It implies a belief by the analyst that agents in a system under study behave in such ways that meet moral philosophy axioms chosen by the analyst himself.[4] Take for example, a utilitarian economist who assumes that everyone behaves in ways that maximise their personal utility. It is difficult to prove what moral philosophy axioms people in society follow (Wilk and Cliggett, 2007); however, it can reasonably be deemed unlikely to be true that everyone should be utilitarians in practice, since it is readily observable that many traditions of philosophy (and spirituality) are followed by different people within and across geographies. It is also notably the case that utilitarian economics does not claim to have identified any definitive empirical basis for its own justification (Wilk and Cliggett, 2007). Indeed, for someone to follow a philosophical doctrine, no empirical basis is needed by that person. However, to infer

[4] Rather than the axioms of those agents themselves. To be consistent, one should assume that the actions of agents meet those agents' own axioms of moral philosophy which may not be the same as the analyst's. For example one assumes that agents may give to the poor if they believe in altruism, etc., but there may exist a large diversity of axioms within a population of agents. In other words, economists often assume that agents in their models are economists similar to themselves.

that others than oneself follow a doctrine, evidence is in principle needed, and what someone believes is often not observable.

Optimisation approaches in part originate from either engineering and normative economic traditions. Since engineers are trained to solve problems by inventing technical solutions, their disciplinary training leads them to think that a technical solution exists to every problem. For example, how to best organise a power network, a public transport network schedule or the use of resources in a hospital. To someone with a hammer, every problem looks like a nail. Meanwhile, normative economic methods find their roots directly in utilitarian moral philosophy: when economic agents seek to maximise their utility, they carry out optimisation exercises over their various possible courses of action under the constraints (budgets, etc.) that they face.

As stated in Chapter 1, to carry out an optimisation successfully requires one to have complete and certain knowledge of the system under study in order to exhaustively list the options for the solver. For some problems of technical nature, this is often feasible, and optimisation can be very effective to build planning tools. Optimisation can still be carried out with some levels of uncertainty, in which case the treatment of knowledge and likelihood can be interpreted in relation to a certain confidence over the exact parametric location of the optimal solution, or an uncertainty over the exact nature of the action to take.[5]

Clearly, certainty and complete knowledge sit at odds with the positive philosophy of science, and with science in general. Scientists exist precisely because some things are not known, and their job is to figure these things out. One can in principle know everything about a professionally designed rail system, but generally not about a whole society and economy. Thus for the positive tradition, the use of systems optimisation is scientifically inconsistent. If one wishes to base policy action choice on observation and induction, rather than moral philosophy, one cannot then choose to use an optimisation tool, because that tool is designed with the goal of meeting an axiom of moral philosophy, and notably, requires to know everything with certainty about everything involved. No evidence exists to suggest that the economy cost-optimises in the way implied by these models, and in fact, evidence exists to the contrary.[6] Obviously, since complete knowledge is frequently an impossible requirement, especially when people are involved, this puts pressure on analysts to use proxies for missing knowledge, and this typically implies interpreting axioms of moral philosophy as objective observations of agent behaviour (notably, assuming that people really are centrally coordinated utility maximisers).

Optimisation tools are widespread possibly simply due to convenience. Why not answer all questions with the same tools already available? In truth, they are also much easier to build since they require in general substantially less empirical

5 For example, uncertainty on the exact value of a carbon tax that meets normative axioms.

6 Trutnevyte (2016); Trutnevyte et al. (2019); Jaxa-Rozen and Trutnevyte (2021).

knowledge. Thus this may be where the legitimacy of the optimisation and cost-benefit methods in policy analysis frequently breaks down: when they are applied to everything, including as both descriptive and normative tools, and too many parameters and relationships are assumed, and with insufficient appreciation of uncertainty. Or worse, unknowable quantities may be assumed.[7] When used in normative mode, the analysis tools do not require complete empirical bases (on human behaviour, notably), and analysts do not seek that either. However, this then implies that no empirical basis is sought to demonstrate the validity of the tools when they are subsequently used in descriptive mode, which thus invalidates their claim of being science-based. Clearly, that empirical basis would not be found if it was really sought, as this would require demonstrating, notably, that all people follow the analyst's particular choice of moral philosophy, something clearly contradicted by everyday observation. Lastly, optimisation tools used for descriptive purposes suffer from interpretation issues, in that they may be interpreted solely in normative terms by evidence users.[8]

It is in many ways unfortunate to note that despite the considerations above, optimisation is so widespread in policy analysis that it has become an institutionalised standard, to the extent that some users of evidence in governments express a sentiment of being trapped by the limited range of evidence these models offer access to.[9] Lax habits of analysts have asserted themselves through a methodological lock-in: it is often assumed that all policy problems should be solved by optimisation, and that *optimal policy can always be identified*. However, the philosophy of science is unclear and seems to be situated somewhere in the middle: somewhat normative, somewhat descriptive. Missing information, however, most of the time concerns human behaviour, and this information, replaced by idealised assumptions over human beliefs and responses to situations meeting particular axioms of moral philosophy, leads to mistaken expectations over the response of real people to real policy. The interpretation frequently goes some way towards claiming that if agents behaved 'the way they really *ought to*', according to someone's specific axioms of moral philosophy, then the real outcome would match the expected outcome. And thus, to some degree, the message can be transformed into one of moral philosophy once again in the tautology that 'if everyone behaved the way they ought to, the social good would be realised'.

7 Notably, assigning probability distributions to quantities over which the set of known possible outcomes is not complete, or possess heavy-tails such that expected values are largely uncertain or diverge. This is discussed in detail in Chapter 12.

8 Projections interpreted as recommendations. Notably, there is a recurrent interpretation issue with socio-economic scenarios of the IPCC (2018).

9 This was the rationale behind the UK government (BEIS) funding the project 'Economics of Energy Innovation and System Transition' (EEIST), to support the development of alternate model formulations. Chapter 12 has been developed in the context of EEIST.

4.3.3 *Economics: Science or Moral Philosophy?*

Standard mainstream ('orthodox') economics is a particular case in point. In what is often termed 'first best' solutions[10] of a standard economic model, agent behaviour and beliefs are essentially assumed, without reference to existing knowledge on behavioural science or anthropology, to follow the utilitarian moral philosophy. These postulates underpinning economic theory have unavoidably been discussed at length in economic anthropology, and it is no surprise to find that no clear support or refutation has emerged from this (Wilk and Cliggett, 2007). Notably, the difficulty lies in empirically proving what moral philosophy people follow in their daily lives, and empirically measuring beliefs is arguably not something within the realm of science, as this cannot be falsified. However, substantial evidence exists to show the huge variety of philosophical models that exist and have existed in human society (Wilk and Cliggett, 2007; Graeber, 2014). The real practical question arguably may be how close average human behaviour is to utility maximisation, which is more amenable to be determined empirically (see Chapter 6).

Thus, standard economic theory has a peculiar relationship with the normative philosophical tradition as it attempts to describe reality under a normative or moral frame, to the extent that one may legitimately ask whether it is in fact meant to be interpreted just simply as moral philosophy. And indeed, many of the great thinkers in economics (e.g., Smith, Locke, Pigou, Coase, Hume; see Graeber, 2014) have been traditionally interpreted as moral philosophers as opposed to scientists attempting to describe reality. And thus, to the uninformed reader, this may well beg the question as to whether the whole of economics is merely a theory of Anglo-American moral philosophy or whether there exists something called '*economic science*'.

Does all of economics as a discipline only seek to determine what people 'ought' to do in particular situations, just as any of the spiritual denominations do, based on the axioms of moral philosophy? An important part of the answer to this question depends on the degree of agency that economists have believed can be ascribed to individuals and groups of humans. If social groups possess very strong agency, homogeneous beliefs and high internal coordination, then how they collectively behave becomes mostly a question of moral philosophy. If they do not, and that their behaviour is determined by heterogeneous individual circumstances, history and 'behavioural biases', then one is dealing with a social science problem. As discussed below, this disagreement over agency in part determines and delineates the various branches of applied economics, between the Marxists, the Walrasians, the Keynesians and the Schumpeterians.

10 Solutions of models with idealised agent behaviour assumptions are often termed 'first best', while solutions that include so-called 'behavioural failures', in which agents fail to act according to moral philosophy axioms are termed 'second best' (Lipsey and Lancaster, 1956). Model solutions with assumptions that may be informed empirically, are thus also termed 'second best'. In that sense, some degree of positive science is introduced under that terminology.

However, economic science does indeed exist, since there are and have been economic thinkers who were more interested in developing accurate descriptions of economic reality than in preaching over what people ought to do. Arguably, thinkers such as Keynes, Schumpeter, Kaldor, Minsky, the behavioural economists such as Kahneman, McFadden, Tversky, the economists of the evolutionary tradition[11] and those in economic anthropology[12] fall in that category. One can see but little trace of moral philosophy in their texts. Instead, particularly in the case of anthopologists, one finds analyses of debates on the role that moral philosophy has had in economics (e.g., see Wilk and Cliggett, 2007). It is also notable that for those who developed quantitative models, the methodologies are often not related at all to optimisation algorithms, but instead, are in the realm of dynamical systems, a completely different field of mathematics. Furthermore, those theories are amenable to the inclusion of heterogeneity and uncertainty (see Chapter 6).

4.3.4 *The Lucas Critique*

It is thus asked here, which is, exactly, the philosophy of science that economists *believe* they use? Is there one, more than one, or perhaps none? This is a complex question, in particular when one is concerned with textbook neoclassical theory, as predominantly taught to students. A good example is found in Robert Lucas' Nobel Inauguration Lecture (Lucas Jr, 1996), where he argues the empirical reality of monetary neutrality, whether an increase in the money supply causes a proportional decrease in the value of money. His argument starts from the premise of utilitarian economic models in which agents intertemporally optimise their own personal individual utility under 'rational expectations'.[13] Following some reasoning and mathematics, Lucas eventually concludes that money neutrality should hold in the real world. This should be interpreted as a prediction based on theory. However, money neutrality is not in fact always observed in the real world, especially not during depressions or periods of hyperinflation (discussed in Chapter 10). Lucas' result is of course contingent upon behavioural assumptions derived from moral theory, but interpreted as observations. Indeed, many more contradictions are found in neoclassical theory in the same way, notably that the theory does not allow for endogenous financial crises which results from assuming that people only borrow when they *know for certain* that they will pay back their debts.

[11] E.g., Freeman and Louçã (2001); Nelson and Winter (1982); Perez (2001).

[12] E.g., Graeber (2014); Douglas and Isherwood (1979); Sahlins (1972).

[13] Rational expectations were originally defined by (Muth, 1961), but subsequently substantially re-interpreted. It suggests that agents have sufficiently good knowledge of the future not to make errors when they intertemporally optimise their utility, which simplifies theory and optimisation algorithms a great deal (it makes them mathematically tractable). It also postulates that uncertainty is risk with quantifiable probability, and that expected utility theory holds.

The Lucas critique (Lucas et al., 1976) states that policy-relevant predictions cannot be made on the basis of models calibrated solely against historical data, if history does not contain a precedent for the policy studied. It contends that economic models should, in order to have policy relevance, be grounded in *assumed* microeconomic behaviour of agents, preferentially to being inferred from historical time series of aggregate trends, because, it argues, information over the response of agents to future stimuli may not be present in data characterising the past, while past policy may influence those trends. The overwhelming response of economists has been to assume axioms of moral philosophy for agent behaviour where empirical data is missing, or often even *instead* of empirical data.

Under that impetus, a widespread preference developed towards the use of models based specifically on axioms of utilitarian moral philosophy instead of observable aggregate variables. This so-called micro-foundations 'revolution' has been celebrated as a great victory for positive macroeconomics (see, e.g., Capros et al., 1990). It also made life easier, since substantially less empirical evidence was all of a sudden needed to build and calibrate micro-founded models in comparison to macroeconometric or other behaviourally based models.

A great fallacy of complexity science exists in the micro-foundations revolution, however. It is shown in Chapter 5 that in fact, even if the rules that govern individual agent behaviour under various economic contexts were to be known in detail, for example, if one could empirically support that individuals are utility maximisers, one would nevertheless not be able to fully predict the aggregate macro-behaviour of groups of agents due to emergent phenomena that appear through the interactions between agents. The '*emergence*' phenomenon is a key principle of complexity science, where one generally still has to make some use of aggregate observed trends since defining micro-foundations is not in fact sufficient to derive all the possible macro-states. In other words, knowing that agents are utility maximisers individually is not sufficient to be able to claim that the economy as a whole optimises utility. But as stated above, the microeconomic rules (people's behaviour and beliefs) are not known with any certainty to start with, and thus the micro-foundations revolution in practice consists in imposing axioms of utilitarian moral philosophy onto people's motives, individually and collectively. It also results in normative tautologies (e.g., 'if people invested rationally, financial crises would be avoided').

4.4. POLITICAL PHILOSOPHY IN LAW AND ECONOMICS

4.4.1 *Normative Analysis: A Question of Social Justice*

It may be argued that two types of reasoning exists in environmental science and economics. In the first, analysts frame problems similarly to medical doctors, where society, the economy and the environment, can be found in either healthy or unhealthy states. This framing puts the purpose of most policy action in the realm of diagnosing and fixing problems, as a medical doctor would with antibiotics and remedies. For example, an engineer will diagnose failures of a water delivery system and devise a new machine that prevents these failures from occurring. This is denoted here as the '*medical*' approach, which provide solutions to areas where agency is lacking. In contrast, the second type of reasoning is one in which society is neither healthy nor affected by disease, but instead has aspirations in relation to its current state and capabilities. This is denoted as the '*entrepreneurial*' approach.

The 'medical' approach will be typically found in circles of environmental policy-making and macroeconomics, where the health of the economy and the environment is debated in relation to a return to normality (ending the recession, solving climate change). Meanwhile, the 'entrepreneurial' approach will be observed with policy-makers involved in innovation policy, business and trade, where opportunities for growth, job creation and the creation of new markets is the topic of debate. This thus suggests that the way in which society and the economy is understood, and how problems are framed, depends strongly on one's disciplinary training as well as one's role. Notably, is climate change a disease that needs to be cured in order for the environment to return to normal, or is it a particular turn that the industrial system has taken, compared to other paths it could have followed? And crucially, is solving climate change a sacrifice that one must make, or is it an opportunity for creating new things?

Featured centrally in the 'medical' tradition, modern welfare and environmental economic theory is founded upon the theory of externalities of Pigou and the Coase theorem (Coase, 1960), in which the concept of market failure and economic efficiency, the latter achieved by setting property rights and pricing externalities, takes the centre stage. The Coase theorem is indeed about normative solutions, where assigning property rights to public goods affected by externalities, allowing their trade and giving them a price, is expected to return to economic efficiency in the allocation of that good, in other words solve the problem and return to normality (provided of course that agents are utilitarians). If that doesn't work, there must have been more than one externality at play. Making a parallel with human health, disease and remedies, economic efficiency is the normative healthy state, externalities and market distortions are the symptoms diagnosed, and property rights and pricing the general remedies.

It is often asserted that the Coase theorem demonstrates that, for example, having a global carbon price covering all sectors is the most efficient way to address climate change with policy, since it will produce the right incentive for all industries and consumers to reduce emissions by the right amount that maintains economic efficiency.[14] The corollary is also used to argue that any other policy approach is inferior. More generally, pricing externalities improves the inter-temporal utility of

14 See for instance Bertram et al. (2015) and references therein.

the representative agent, although it generally reduces consumption in the short term. In such a world, environmental questions become framed in terms of social justice, and indeed, this is the tradition. Depending what the discount rate of the representative agent is chosen to be,[15] by pricing externalities, one is making a choice in terms of the utility of present-day citizens versus that of future citizens, opening a question of intergenerational equity. This question of social justice is again of the realm of moral philosophy, and emphasises that there is no clear dividing line between standard economics and moral philosophy. Thus, it can be concluded that the 'medical' approach is one that, among other things, seeks social justice.

4.4.2 *Positive Analysis: A Question of Achievement*

One aspect that is not substantially discussed in the theory of externalities is that some agents may have a pronounced entrepreneurial spirit, aspiring to get involved in endogenously changing the state of industry and the economy using new ideas, not necessarily as utilitarians. In a neoclassical model, agents have perfect knowledge, and specifically, rational expectations. There is no uncertainty but only quantifiable risk, which implies that the representative agent knows probabilistically what future innovations and discoveries will be made, and can normatively trade the future off against the present day. Since he foresees that the costs of innovations are going to be lower in the future due to the future work of scientists and other innovators, there is going to be no point in paying more to develop them today, since they will arise inevitably. But that very decision implies that innovations are never developed at all, leading to a paradox.[16] A similar problem arises with venture capital: there being no uncertainty but only quantifiable probabilities, investment and venture capital finance is a predictable zero-sum game, in which the representative agent loses as much as he gains on average, and thus cannot make any money.

In reality, future innovation is by definition not known by anyone, while many productivity advantages exist in being the first to develop or adopt innovations, although they involve uncertainty. What maximises business profitability appears to be a clever combination of commitment to innovation, breadth and careful selectiveness (Klingebiel and Rammer, 2014; Meifort, 2016). This helps understand why in reality entrepreneurs and venture capitalists do thrive economically. Not knowing the future incentivises economic agents to take action under different frames, notably increasing the chances of opportunity through deliberately generating more uncertainty (e.g., through disruptive innovation), or minimising perceived risk with a precautionary approach.

[15] In this case, a normative social discount rate, the present-day valuation of future expenditures recommended by economists, see the Nordhaus-Stern debate mentioned in Section 1.1.

[16] This is notably at the root of Directed Technical Change theory by Acemoglu (2002); Acemoglu et al. (2012).

In the 'entrepreneurial' approach, the framing for environmental and economic policy is one in which stock-taking is made of the present situation, and an objective is identified as to where to go from here. Public policy-makers in business and industry departments usually seek to improve business environments that allow for a better capture of innovation, market and trade opportunities, whether this involves trade policy, subsidies for innovation, tax breaks or foreign diplomacy. More broadly, the 'entrepreneurial' approach seeks to improve capabilities in order to achieve more ambitious goals, firm growth and market power, as well as solve existing problems. In such a worldview, public policy signals such as taxes and the carbon price do have an important role; however, they have less to do with fixing market failures by pricing externalities and more with serving as market shaping signals to incentivise changes of direction in the decisions of entrepreneurs and potentially to induce them to innovate.

4.4.3 *Political Philosophy at the Root of the Debate*

Legal scholars have for the longest time also been divided along two broad traditions of philosophy, the normative and positive schools of law, which ultimately stem from corresponding branches of moral philosophy seeking a theory of justice (see, e.g., Kymlicka, 2002). Both traditions are important as they fulfil different roles. On the one hand, normative lawyers take inspiration from philosophy and social justice to formulate legal frameworks based on normative principles. Examples of such normative principles include human rights and property rights. Meanwhile, positive law tends to be more grounded in observation, relying less on philosophy, social justice and principles, but formulate law based on experience of what leads to desired outcomes. Examples of such positive frames includes systems of power sharing (executive, legislative and judicial).

Moral philosophy in law is understood as the theory of justice, which establishes how institutions should be built to distribute advantages and disadvantages equitably. The problem is to define 'equitably' (Kymlicka, 2002). The driver of legislation and legal definition is most of the time moral philosophy, and the opposing schools, the 'consenquentialist' and 'deontological' branches of moral philosophy, offer a critical tension that has shaped the development of law and legal systems since at least as far as the Greeks. The basic source of tension is that the deontological school (Kant and religious schools) contends that what should be deemed 'good' is the intent of an agent, not the consequence of his/her actions, while in the consequentialist school (Bentham, Mill, Sidgwick), it is the reverse, an action may be judged based on whether the outcome was good or bad.

It is clear that in the deontological school, the outcome is by definition disregarded, and the onus is on proving intent. Meanwhile, in the consequentialist school, the onus is on whether an agent was able or not to predict the outcome of his actions.

In the latter, being able to forecast events and understand causation in a complex path-dependent world is a central issue, on which complexity science has something interesting to say (Chapters 5 and 6).

4.4.4 *Normativity and Positivitism in Law: Principles versus Collective Utility*

In the deontological view of moral philosophy,[17] a certain norm setting a conduct must be followed because of the intrinsic value of the norm.[18] It is really the intent of agents that is scrutinised, not the outcome of their actions. In that, Kant argues that a person's intentions cannot be judged by the outcome, because the outcome could be influenced by other factors: both good and bad outcomes could arise by accident. This is to some degree a reaction to uncertainty in causation, inherent in the course of historical development.

Religious philosophy (or divine command) is also deontological but from a different point of view: principles and norms are derived from the word of God, which in practice means from sacred texts. The source of law is thus already in parts written, and moral philosophy can be derived from these principles by reason. While in Kant, the rational man makes moral law universal, in divine command it is God that makes moral law universal. The critical advantage in the deontological view is that it does not have to deal with uncertainty in relation to causation; however, it does have to deal with uncertainty in relation to intent. In the world of God, events are deterministic and history is already written. But proving intent is not straightforward.

The consequentialist view must, for obvious reasons, consider uncertainty in causation, whether outcomes can be ascribed with confidence to certain actions by agents. The attribution problem is a key issue in legal analysis, notably for climate change. Who caused climate change, and what fraction of climate change has been or would be caused by, for example, someone investing in a coal power plant? The attribution problem causes difficulties for compliance to legally binding emissions reduction targets, such as the UK's climate change act, because the moment in time at which it can be unambiguously proved that non-compliance occurred is when it is too late. Law would otherwise have to deal with the uncertainty that is inherent with predicting the future outcome of a decision taken in the present.[19]

The irony is that the root of the consequentialist view lies with Bentham and utilitarianism, where, the value of a norm is given by the overall utility it achieves if the norm is observed. It originates with the view that law must be decided by attempting to maximise collective utility, by which it is implied to also maximise individual utility. From this can be derived the consequentialist view: that

[17] E.g., Kant's Foundations of the Metaphysics of Morals or Critique of practical reason.

[18] E.g., the prohibition of torture or racial discrimination or genocide.

[19] See `http://climatecasechart.com/non-us-case/urgenda-foundation-v-kingdom-of-the-netherlands/`.

actions can be judged by their outcome, in relation to whether they improved the public good or made it worse. However, utility itself is a concept challenging to define clearly, something that most classical economists spent considerable time working on (see Chapter 7).

In practice, most laws are formed by a combination of both sources of moral philosophy: they derive from some principles, and have some consideration to outcomes. There are aspects of 'norming' (i.e. setting what is right and wrong), and aspects of 'regulating' (maintaining a system within certain bounds of stability and safety).

4.4.5 *Normativity in Economics*

Utilitarianism possibly finds some of its roots in Bernard de Mandeville's fable of the Bees,[20] in which an illustration was made regarding how 'private vices' benefited the public good through their contribution to markets and incomes that benefited everyone, including those who criticised the said 'vices'. A similar concept later arose in Adam Smith's Invisible Hand, in which agents pursuing their own self interest collectively made the economy and ultimately the wealth of nations. What was considered simply the actions of any rational person, was also turned into something that is desirable for society. The descriptive happened to be identical to the normative. Thus normativity and positivity have been mixed since as far as the discipline goes (at least in the Anglo-American tradition), where utilitarian rationality is deemed a good description of agent behaviour *and* it is desirable. It is difficult in contemporary neoclassical economic theory to disentangle the good/bad from explanations/predictions.

The Fable of the Bees and the Invisible Hand in fact defined what is arguably the key problem at the core of economics, that is called the 'aggregation problem'. The aggregation problem is to determine the connection between the actions of agents at the microeconomic level, and the observed trends at the macro level. Between the two lies all the possible emergent collective movements, trends, and phenomena that we commonly see. Emergent collective movements are really meta-agents in the economy, for example, social groups, institutions and fashions. Agency existing at the meta-level becomes of the realm of Marxist theory, where group behaviour is analysed, something ignored in utilitarianism, which focuses on the individual.

An interesting implication arises in relation to the role that complexity science can take in economics as a result of this. Complexity science and the theory of dynamical systems can inform rigorously on causation in systems formed of interacting agents, such as the economy. In the aggregation problem, it is the

[20] `https://en.wikipedia.org/wiki/The_Fable_of_the_Bees`.

emergence of collective phenomena that causes challenges to the consequentialist view that one could reliably predict the outcomes of action, whether they benefit the public good, and establish unambiguously causation. In complex systems (see Chapter 5), one can never be completely certain of causation, since some macro phenomena arise as a result of *collective* but not necessarily *intended* action. A prime example is the concept of systemic risk, the risk of systemic collapse generated by collective action of numerous agents, actions not risky at the individual level but risky at the community level. This arises notably during bubbles and financial crises. A contribution to systemic risk is a particular kind of collective externality imposed, possibly unconsciously, by agents and their decisions, onto every other agent part of the same community.[21] Causation of systemic risk is challenging to attribute and price, and a measure or metric for systemic risk is needed for its quantification (this is discussed in later chapters). In such cases, pursuing one's self-interest does not lead to improving the public good, but rather system collapse, and attribution of wrongdoing is not possible.

4.4.6 *Agency: Who Are the Decision-Makers?*

A natural question that arises in the philosophy of science of economic models is who has agency and to what degree, or in other words, who has the power to influence the evolution of the economic system. Understanding agency is important, as otherwise, under incorrect assumptions one could accidentally or consciously invoke and 'use' imaginary policy levers to claim to solve real problems, and public accountability is at play. For example, a policy for the central bank to print money to accelerate lending may be imaginary, since most of the money supply is created by private banks and only underwritten by the central bank (Keen, 2011, 2017). Another is reducing public deficit in order to improve economic activity.[22] In the real world, every person has a little bit of agency, some more than others, and no central planner exists. In the realm of models, while central planner-based algorithms are by definition normative, in other types of models, particular agents and meta-agents are endowed with agency by the modeller, in particular through the creation of exogenous policy inputs.

In optimal systems planning, agency arguably belongs to the social planner. For a company, this could be some sort of decision board of investors. Some national energy systems are centrally planned and a tradition of optimisation to help planning originates from such institutions. For the economy, a social-planner-based model would resemble more a centrally planned economy than a capitalist economy,

[21] Examples of this include certain types of financial transactions, but also behaviour such as travelling during a disease pandemic, which may or may not lead to disease transmission at the individual level, but increases transmission at the population level.

[22] Reinhart and Rogoff (2010), analysis that has been questioned by Herndon et al. (2014).

even though it is capitalist economies that are most frequently represented in such models. A failure to represent uncertainty, innovation, the entrepreneur and financial institutions, who have their own endogenous agency and do not obey any central planner, is a failure to represent capitalism. Even centrally planned economies do not really behave as fully optimised systems, since implementation failure and gaming by agents always emerges somewhere.

Thus, agency in utilitarian economic models appears to be in addressing externalities using pricing mechanisms. But this is not likely to agree with wide diversity of agents that make up governments, their departments and devolved institutions. As discussed in Chapter 12, agency arguably comes in three forms, strategy (setting the direction of travel), accounting (prioritising the use of resources) and regulating (maintaining systems with acceptable bounds of operation and managing risk). Optimal systems planning arguably makes the latter two redundant if resources are by definition 'optimally' allocated and risks by definition eliminated. However, this may be seen as unsatisfactory by some model users.

4.4.7 *The Role of Science versus Doctrine*

Current mainstream macroeconomics undoubtedly yields policy recommendations that agree with the currently widespread global neoliberal ideology. If one believes that agents are endowed with rational expectations and complete knowledge of all goods in all markets, that agents have a transitive ordering in their preferences and optimise intertemporally their choices, then a policy of free market, in which government regulation is minimised, yields maximal economic efficiency. Pursuing one's self-interest is good. These concepts happen to be the central pillars of neoliberalism.

Neoliberalism is an ideology, not a theory of economics, while neoclassical economics is a theory, not an ideology, although it is derived from moral philosophy axioms. In neoclassical economics, it would appear as if the theory architecture had been chosen to fit an ideology. In reality, the theory, the ideology and real life events have co-evolved over the past centuries since Adam Smith and De Mandeville's fable of the bees, with pronounced application since the Thatcher-Regan period. Neoliberalism is a relatively young ideology in the context of human history (Graeber, 2014). Recent excesses ascribed by many to neoliberalism may have generated high degrees of inequality (Piketty, 2013), and that may potentially explain recent or ongoing social and political instability observed in the USA, France, the UK, the Middle East and many other regions. Neoliberalism has also been accused of leading to the 2008 financial crisis. Thus it is being debated whether the pursuit of one's own self-interest benefits the public good.

Neoliberalism has been very successful politically, but neoclassical economics could not foresee, due to its formulation of agent behaviour, and lack of the concept of systemic risk, the 2008 financial crisis and subsequent great recession. The crisis probably led to a new wave of skepticism towards neoliberalism in the public (Graeber, 2014), and of neoclassical economics in academic circles (Battiston et al., 2016a). Neoclassical economists often ascribe financial crises to errors by the central bank in managing the money supply.[23] But this is increasingly discredited.[24] Is it the theory or the ideology that is wrong? Indeed, the origin of the crisis is now increasingly argued to lie more with prior gradual relaxing of financial regulation, than with erroneously printing too much or too little money.[25] Importantly, it points to the financial sector missing in economic models, since in neoclassical theory, rational agents do not, on average, default on their loans.

The explanatory power of neoclassical theory is plagued by its grounding in moral philosophy axioms instead of observation. Whether agents maximising collective utility causes economic dynamics is something that is impossible to prove, not least because there is no objective measurement of utility for individuals, and even less of collective utility. Utilitarism is a strand of moral philosophy that itself strives to find a satisfactory definition for utility (Kymlicka, 2002). As such, economic theory based on maximising utility is unfalsifiable. Many social scientists argue that all theories are value-laden, even if only through how problems are framed, while policy-makers seek narratives not explanations (Heilbroner, 1973). Other social scientists argue that humans cannot be modelled since they cannot be predicted (Heilbroner, 1973). These views devoid science of any explanatory power, and in fact suggest that evidence is always chosen for its driving narrative, which defeats the existence at all of a science–policy interface.

To conclude, economics can in principle be a descriptive science with explanatory power, however, to do so, it must be formulated independently from doctrine. And to do that, it must include three levels of analysis grounded in observation: the micro, the meso and the macro scales. The micro-scale can be informed by social, psychological and anthropological observations. The macro-scale can be grounded in statistical measurement of economic quantities. But crucially, the connection between the two can be made using complexity science.

4.5. EMPIRICAL BUILDING BLOCKS FOR A COMPLEXITY THEORY OF ECONOMICS

The process of aggregating micro-foundations into a macro theory is not simple, and can lead to radically different outcomes according to which assumptions are deemed important. It has been argued by post-Keynesians that macroeconomics cannot be derived from micro-foundations, but instead, should be inferred from

23 See Lucas Jr (1996); Galí (2015); Friedman and Schwartz (1965).

24 By many economists including the Bank of England (see, e.g., Wray, 2016; McLeay et al., 2014; Keen, 2017; Graeber, 2014; Haldane and May, 2011).

25 Keen (2017); Graeber (2014).

macro-foundations (King, 2015). It is clear that theory and model outcomes should reproduce observations at the macro-level. But also, theory and models should be consistent with what is observed at the micro-level, including all the observed diversity of agents and agent behaviour. The Lucas critique remains at least partially valid in that inferring what may happen in projections solely on the basis of what happened in the past excessively restricts the range of possible projections, particularly in cases of the application of policies without precedent. It would, therefore, be most powerful if progress on solving the aggregation problem could be made, going from micro to macro, with an appropriate methodology. It allows us to better model the impacts of policy, but this does *not* mean equating macro with micro as is currently done in general equilibrium theory. This could be inspired from, for example, research on the statistical properties of systems out of equilibrium and agent-based models.[26]

In Chapters 7–11, possible macro-models are constructed out of micro-foundations inferred from observation, for the diffusion of innovations, process innovation, financial dynamics and the macroeconomy. While these models are far from complete, they do suggest workable and empirically grounded entry points into the aggregation problem for key problems in economics. In the remainder of this chapter, a number of elements of micro and macro foundations are suggested that could be part of an ideal complexity theory of economics.

4.5.1 *Heterogeneity, Culture, Social Belonging, Entrepreneurship*

As opposed to atoms or molecules in a statistical physical problem, humans are not identical, and have different ways of taking decisions and different motives. Different persons live in different contexts, often radically different cultural settings, in which elements of life are not given the same importance or weight, and decisions are not taken considering the same factors. It is quite clear that outside of economics, (e.g., anthropology, management, history or psychology), few academics consider the representative agent to have much explanatory power (Haldane and Turrell, 2018).

First, a body of literature exists on observed cultural traits of different nations across the World, which can be classified into a number of primary cultural dimensions (Hofstede, 2001). Some cultures feature pronounced preference for decisions based on tradition, others are more pragmatic; in some the influence of peers is important, in others it is the influence of what is considered a consensus across the national population; in some cultures, the opinion of elders is most highly valued, while in others it is the views of cultural leaders.

Second, heterogeneity exists beyond values, some individuals may take decisions using elaborate calculations, while others may use heuristics and rules of thumb

[26] Farmer and Foley (2009); Haldane and Turrell (2018); Kauffman (2000); Arthur (2014); Anderson et al. (1988).

(see, e.g., Knobloch and Mercure, 2016). Agents have different levels of time preference (notably due to income disparities), different evaluation methods for decisions (notably due to different domains of training and levels of education), and different domains of knowledge (notably due to different domains of work and cultural belonging; for example, public servants, factory workers, artists, entrepreneurs, members of the upper class).

Third, multi-agent interactions matter. Insights can be taken from economic anthropology: the individualistic view of decision-making in neoclassical economics is contrasted against the group or social class basis of collective decision-making in other traditions such as Marxists. A theory for the anthropological nature of entrepreneurship as a driver of social change is needed.[27] While these three pillars are not sufficient to build solid micro-foundations for a macro theory; they are undoubtedly necessary.

4.5.2 *Brief Overview of Economic Anthropology*

Economic anthropology is the sub-field of anthropology that attempts to maintain a dialogue with economists regarding conceptualisations of human nature in economic theory. Wilk and Cliggett (2007) emphasise various conceptualisations of human nature as have been proposed and used in various traditions of philosophy, anthropology and economics. They argue that these can be categorised within three alternate models of human decision-making: the self-interested model, the social model and the moral model.

The self-interested model is a representation of the human as a free individual decision-maker, behaving using a strategy that maximises his utility. This is a model that does little to explore the interactions between persons and with institutions. The human in this case is seen as having a clear set of ranked preferences, such that he is able to clearly decide every action he takes in terms of his individual preferences. It is often criticised for being enthnocentric, but this model can understand motivations for entrepreneurship.

The social model sees humans as inherently social beings, and action motivated by a desire to promote the interests of communities and social groups, underpinning much of what is termed the *political economy*, finding its roots in Marx. Humans belong to social groups, communities and classes, which shape choices through norms, and group interests trump individual self-interest. Power relations are the drivers of economic change. In this view, encompassing Marxist theory, humans are seen with little autonomy or entrepreneurship.

The moral model is based on analyses of agent worldviews, beliefs and perceptions of what they think is the right thing to do. Culture, beliefs and religion shape

[27] See the innovation (e.g., Klingebiel and Rammer, 2014; Meifort, 2016; Hekkert et al., 2007; Grübler and Wilson, 2013) and business literatures (e.g., Porter, 1991; Porter et al., 1996).

human action. Worldviews are socially determined by culture and norms, and a wide variety of worldviews can co-exist. Preferences of individuals may exist, but may not necessarily be rankable, as agents may not all see the same meaning in things. For instance, the value of some action may depend on who it takes place with or whom it is intended for. Anthropologists in this area analyse the meaning of gifts, exchange and other multi-agent interactions.

All three models have strengths and weaknesses, are limited individually but are able *together* to explain most types of human action and motivations (Wilk and Cliggett 2007), and neither of the three can definitely be empirically proven wrong. However, given a problem of public policy, each of these models used on their own may suggest radically different approaches.

4.5.3 *The Anthropology of Consumption*

Basic neoclassical theory conceptualises agents as being infinitely lived, having knowledge of all goods and services that exist, and as having a strict unambiguous ranking of preferences for all of these things on which they could spend their money. This implies that agents consume goods and services for their absolute 'value' according to these preferences rankings independently from their peers.

In the anthropological evidence, objects appear to be desired by agents because they have 'meaning', as opposed to absolute utility. For example, different brands of clothes sell at different prices because of their meaning in social circles. Douglas and Isherwood (1979) argue that consumption always happens in a social context, as it has little value when carried out in isolation. For example, the type of wine one purchases when inviting guests for dinner depends strongly on the context, who the guests are and what is expected within social relations. Cars and clothes are outlets for expressing a form of identity to peers. It is clear from sociological research that cars are bought with strong consideration of what other agents in neighbouring areas also purchase, through visual influence (McShane et al., 2012). Chapter 7 reviews the evidence and offers a self-consistent model of diffusion of consumption habits.

4.5.4 *The Anthropology of Debt and Money*

Neoclassical theory understands money as a commodity of exchange and store of value, which solves the problem of non-coincidence of wants that arises with barter. Graeber (2014) shows with ample anthropological evidence spanning the last 5,000 years that barter was never widespread as a mode of exchange, but instead, that complex credit systems predate the development of currency. In fact, evidence suggests that money is a metric for assets and debts, as described by evolutionary and post-Keynesian theory.[28]

[28] E.g., Minsky (1982); Keen (2011); Wray (2016); Lavoie (2014).

Meanwhile, substantial evidence from econophysics show the financial system as self-organising in 'scale-free' networks constructed by a process of preferential attachment. Statistical physics applied to financial data shows that prices of financial assets behave in particular ways not described by equilibrium models, but rather, by models exhibiting a punctuated equilibrium interrupted by periods of instability. In Chapters 9 and 10, a suitable dynamic model of creation of unstable complex networks is given that reproduces the key properties of financial time series.

4.5.5 *Psychology and Behavioural Science*

The neoclassical self-interested utilitarian model uses a particular choice of rationality, in which agents have perfect knowledge of everything that can be known in the economy, with 'rational expectations' over the future. Most of the criticism it has received revolves around its definition of rationality within the bounds of self-interested individual decision-making.

A first critical dimension is perfect knowledge, in replacement of which has been proposed the use of 'bounded rationality' (Simon, 1955), where agents have knowledge of subsets of all the knowledge that exists in the economy, and use simple heuristics for decision-making. Second, rational expectations have been replaced by various conceptualisations of myopia, where agents optimise but do not see beyond a certain horizon.[29] Most notably, biases with respect to a utilitarian rationality baseline have been measured, where losses are not valued equally to gains when evaluated under the same monetary metric. This includes 'prospect theory' (Kahneman and Tversky, 1979; Tversky and Kahneman, 1974). This is explored in Chapter 6.

4.5.6 *The Anthropology of the Entrepreneur*

There are few anthropological models of the entrepreneur as an agent with motivations with social contexts. Economic anthropologists have focused on the theory of value, the gift as well as debt, but do not offer a reliable basis to explain entrepreneurship. Analyses of entrepreneurship remain philosophical or normative, focusing on what makes an entrepreneur successful. In some cases the entrepreneur is seen as the hero, in others as the culprit of financial instability or monopoly creation.[30]

29 Notably in recursive dynamic general equilibrium models.

30 For example, Baumol (1996) looks at good and bad allocations of available entrepreneurs, seen as a scarce resource, to various activities deemed good or bad for society. Steyaert and Hjorth (2008) explore how to promote better social entrepreneurship and social change.

Part of the problem may be that anthropologists have not been able to agree on a definition for the entrepreneur. Bull and Willard (1993) propose a theory of the entrepreneur in which motives and enabling factors are a combination of:

1. task-related motives associated to a desire not to work for someone else, but instead self-define the tasks;
2. a likelihood of success due to acquired specialist expertise and networks;
3. expectations of personal gain, financial and social;
4. the existence of a facilitating environment.

It does not, however, explain for instance how entrepreneurial opportunities are identified, and under what circumstances a new combination of input resources leads to new outcomes.

Many theories exist for the nature of innovation and innovation systems. Klingebiel and Rammer (2014) and Meifort (2016) show that what appears to make firms more successful in their innovation strategies is a combination of

1. commitment to innovation,
2. breadth of in-house experimentation,
3. a good selection mechanism for which innovation project to invest resources in, and which to terminate.

Definitions have been developed for an innovation system as a network of agents and institutions, and their functions, involved in the development, diffusion and use of innovations, including the entrepreneur himself, the financial institution or investing agent, diffusers of information, institutions protecting intellectual property, policy-makers, scientists and academic institutions.[31] A model of innovation is given in Chapter 8.

4.6. CONCLUSION AND WAYS FORWARD

The goal of this chapter was to attempt to pin down two ambiguous concepts in economics. The first was what philosophy of science is used in the dominant paradigm of economics, utilitarian model-based neoclassical theory. The second was whether economics can be a positive scientific theory. These two simple questions have opened a complex pandora's box of problems and inconsistencies in mainstream economics that date back to the classical authors such as Adam Smith and Jeremy Bentham. These problems have influenced to this day the shape and form of how economics has been done.

It was found that the dominant paradigm of economics is predominantly normative in practice, but with an ambiguous philosophy of science in which it claims to be sometimes normative, sometimes positive. This may be related directly or

[31] Hekkert et al. (2007); Bergek et al. (2008).

indirectly with the main currents of thought and frames in moral philosophy, policy-making and law, which are by nature normative, notably whether pursuing one's self interest benefits the public good. However, utilitarian *economic science* as a positive discipline based on theory and observation does not have a clearly stated foundation. That agents collectively maximise utility is not verified nor verifiable, and one cannot coherently make predictions using an unfalsifiable theory.

An opportunity exists to create a widely accepted falsifiable *complexity theory of economics*[32] by providing it with clear foundations, much like any other natural or social science grounded in observation, to make predictions that can be verified empirically. It would first be helpful for the discipline of economics to more fully integrate empirical evidence from the other social sciences (Haldane and Turrell, 2018).

The field would likely have to let go of the self-interested homo economicus, which is arguably just an ethnocentric representation of Anglo-American moral philosophy rather than an empirical observation. There appears to be nothing credible nor verifiable in the representative agent with rational expectations from the viewpoint of anthropology and sociology. However, since the economy is composed of interacting agents, and since this implies that emergent phenomena exists, it is not just the representation of individual agents that require empirical foundations, but also, the multi-agent interactions. A complexity theory of economics requires the use of an empirical basis from anthropology, sociology and other fields, to correctly calibrate the nature of economic agents and of their mutual interactions, in order to build, using complexity science tools, macro-models from the micro scale, through the meso level, that explain observed macroeconomic trends.

This therefore concludes Part I and motivates Part II of this book. In Part I, a hopefully comprehensive overview of the limitations of current mainstream models of analysis for environmental and other policy was laid out, and some empirical building blocks were proposed for developing a better theory and better models. Part II of this book takes this forward and develops key components of a complexity theory of economics.

[32] 'Complexity Economics' (Arthur, 1999) could be an umbrella term for all positive traditions of economics, including post-Keynesian, post-Schumpeterian, Ecological Economics and Econophysics.

PART II

A Positive Theory for Complexity Economics

MAP FOR PART II

Part II is like a book within a book. It develops key elements of complexity economics relevant for environmental and low-carbon policy. The choice of topics follows the issues raised in Part I, Chapter 2: the diffusion of innovations, the dynamics of innovation, the financial sector and macroeconomic dynamics, the last two in relation to technological change described in the first two. The reasons for this choice are that the information required by policy-makers to carry out suitable appraisals of low-carbon and environmental policy concerns the effectiveness of different policy options at triggering the required changes, and understand their main socio-economic tradeoffs. In a complexity view, pricing mechanisms as suggested by the theory of market failures are not sufficient, or at least, not the most effective policies to achieve stated environmental goals, and this requires developing a theory of the diffusion of innovations and innovation itself. Furthermore, since in a complexity view, the tradeoffs involve not exactly a general loss of national income, but rather, structural change, unemployment and financial instability, theory for those three has to be developed too.

First, some relevant elements of general complexity theory are presented (Chapter 5) followed by a detailed analysis of uncertainty in economics providing a basis and justification for non-equilibrium theory (Chapter 6). After that, the focus turns to key theory components that matter for environmental and low-carbon policy:

(1) the diffusion of innovations and the evolution of markets (Chapter 7),
(2) the dynamics of innovation systems, process innovation and the design space (Chapter 8),
(3) the monetary system and the dynamics of the financial network (Chapters 9 and 10),
(4) macroeconomic dynamics and socio-economic change as a result of innovation and technological change (Chapter 11), building upon all prior chapters of Part II.

The theories developed in Part II will be applied in case studies in Part III. Part II could in principle be skipped by the reader who might be less interested in pure theory, but interested in the new insights generated by complexity models. Such a reader can safely land in Part III, Chapter 12 and carry on from there. However, Part II is the main academic contribution of this book to the literature, in that, it formulates the key building blocks for a fairly comprehensive theory of complexity economics for environmental governance.

5

Concepts of Complexity for Economics

In this chapter, a number of key concepts from complexity science are introduced in order to provide the tools, methods and philosophy of science necessary for later chapters. Focus is given to concepts needed in a complexity and network theory of money, finance, innovation and macroeconomics. In particular, the notions of emergence, interactions, non-linearity and path-dependence are explored, and their relationship with equilibrium, non-ergodicity, stability and chaos, and the theory of evolution. A simple classification of complex systems is given. The particular case of self-organised criticality is explored as it becomes later used as a basis to explain complex dynamics and fluctuations in innovation networks and the financial system.

5.1. INTRODUCTION TO COMPLEXITY SCIENCE

Complexity science is an area of research, as well as an organising system for science, that transcends disciplines. Its main contribution is that it enables scientists to make predictions without being tied to the particular system it is applied to, whether in physics, biology or the social sciences. Its power lies in defining universality classes of scientific problems and mapping common solutions to these classes across fields of science. It is, in that sense, a meta-science. If one can identify the universality class of a problem, then one can infer the solution, or the behaviour to expect, from what is known of another system of the same universality class, if one is known to exist. This can transcend disciplines, for example economics, biology and physics, if common universality classes can be identified.[1]

[1] Good references for complexity science and complexity economics include Thurner et al. (2018) and Anderson et al. (1989). The seminal piece defining the discipline is arguably Anderson (1972).

Complexity science simply studies the properties of systems comprised of many interacting elements evolving over time. It is a relatively young discipline, and offers many tools of analysis that have never been available or known in most fields of research until relatively recently. It finds its roots mostly in physics and evolutionary biology, in which thinking along similar lines has existed for a long time, but has more recently permeated many other fields of application such as economics. The field is also gradually becoming something different and more precise: a theory of complex networks, and this has a huge scope for application in social science.

In this chapter, an introduction to complexity science is given, covering the concepts most relevant for the purpose of this book. Complexity science tools are used in order to develop a positive complex theory of environmental economics, to replace existing static theories of environmental economics, which are mostly grounded into normative principles using the theory of externalities, and into static equilibrium analysis. Since, as argued in Chapters 2 and 3, many problems of interest in environmental governance involve evolving systems, rather than static ones, a dynamical theory of environmental economics will one day have to replace the traditional static theory for descriptive purposes, although it also has normative implications (Chapter 12).

The economic theory discussed in this book is evolutionary in nature. Complexity science ultimately is the theory that is closest to explaining the theory of evolution, and to making verifiable predictions. It can explain many stylised facts observed in evolutionary history in biology. These concepts and stylised facts are also observed in economics, and substantial evidence exists showing that the approach of complex networks is the correct one from a scientific standpoint. Therefore, this chapter gradually builds complexity theory in a simple way for the non-expert using relatively simple concepts up to the point at which a networks-based theory can be defined for evolutionary systems. This is used throughout Part II of the book thereafter. Few equations are used, simply because most evolutionary problems are not solvable in the traditional analytical sense; they require a quantitative algorithmic approach, for example, using agent-based models. But the results are not always intuitive, especially for the reader trained in traditional equilibrium economics.

Some policy implications emerge from considering the economy as a complex system. Path-dependence implies a shaping role for governance. That economic agents interact also implies that emergent collective movements can be destructive for the economic system, which implies the existence of systemic risk. These are discussed in the conclusion and in the rest of this book. In this chapter, an introduction to complexity science is first given, followed by analysis of relevant properties of systems of interacting agents. Scale-free networks are discussed, followed by the peculiar phenomenon of self-organised criticality governing many aspects of evolutionary systems. A conclusion then summarises what matters for this book.

5.1.1 *The Hierarchy of the Sciences*

In physics, a very simple problem has been studied without a complete solution being found for many decades if not centuries: the three-body problem.[2] In the classical two-body problem, a solution for the movement of two interacting entities (for example, two planets interacting through gravity) can generally be identified that predicts their movement indefinitely and with infinite precision, so long as the two-body condition is valid. In the three-body problem, no such solution can be found, and instead, one can only calculate with computers the trajectory of three interacting entities, and the outcome is ever more inaccurate the further ahead in time one makes a forecast. While most of classical science is based on theories such as for the two-body problem, supporting a false sense of scientific triumph, most real problems of science are more akin to the three-body problem, betraying a real sense of inadequacy. Science must attempt to solve problems that involve complexity.

In 1972, a theoretical physicist, Philip W. Anderson, who was to become famous,[3] wrote an influential article named 'More is different' (Anderson, 1972), which helped kick-start a new field of research, 'complexity science'. The key point he made was to distinguish two approaches in science, one of which he calls 'reductionist', in which one seeks fundamental laws governing the behaviour of fundamental system elements, and another that embraces the complexity involved in a particular science. In the reductionist approach to science, some scientists who researched fundamental laws governing the behaviour of individual fundamental particles, or system parts, have gone so far as to claim that they had discovered a 'Theory of Everything',[4] and that the rest was applied science. The fallacy in this way of thinking is that, to quote Anderson (1972), 'The ability to reduce everything to simple fundamental laws does not imply the ability to start from those laws and reconstruct the universe.' To paraphrase Laughlin and Pines (2000), 'We have succeeded in reducing all of ordinary physical behavior to a simple, correct Theory of Everything only to discover that it has revealed exactly nothing about many things of great importance.' But what prevents scientists from doing so?

[2] A popular novel by Liu (2014) uses the three-body problem as a centre-piece for an interesting plot in a science-fiction setting in the context of characters working in the physical sciences. This may be one entertaining way to learn about the scientific context surrounding the three-body problem, and why it is interesting. It gives the reader a greater sense of the nature of information and science, if not complexity science itself.

[3] P. W. Anderson won the Nobel Prize in Physics in 1977 for his discoveries in magnetism and disordered systems. He was always interested in all sorts of research fields in which complexity appears. He contributed to setting up the now influential Santa Fe Institute, a world-leading centre for the study of complexity (see Anderson et al., 1989).

[4] A subsequent paper aptly titled 'The theory of everything' discusses the same problem (Laughlin and Pines, 2000). D. Pines was also a founding member of the Santa Fe Institute.

Interactions between system parts is what prevents scientists from doing so. For example, in condensed matter physics, Schrödinger's equation describes perfectly well the behaviour of individual electrons, simple atoms and simple molecules in isolation. However, when looking at a real system such as a piece of material or a bit of liquid, while Schrödinger's equation remains valid, too many states of matter are possible as one assembles atoms together, and the equation is not very helpful at predicting the real observed macro properties. This includes, notably, magnetism and superconductivity, two very common phenomena that are still not fully explained despite decades of research and hundreds of thousands of papers.

These are phenomena that were first observed, and later explained by finding the particular solution to Schrödinger's equation that explains them. But it is not a great triumph for theoretical condensed matter physics if predictions happen after the observations, rarely making predictions of what new things could be observed. Indeed, in areas of science mostly driven by complexity,[5] the discovery and characterisation of whole zoologies of unexplained phenomena is far ahead of the development of any quantitative theory to explain them.

In physics, these states of matter arise out of mutual *interactions* between system parts (electrons and atoms), and to a lesser degree on the specific properties of these underlying elements. The fact that more properties or phenomena can arise than would be predicted from knowing the fundamental properties of system elements is what is called 'emergence'. In many areas of science, these are the properties that dominate and produce all of what puzzles scientists and non-scientists. For example, in social systems, interactions between individuals can lead to social influence or crowd effects, such as bubbles in the financial sector, economic recessions and social change in general, which could not be imagined with theories in which individuals do not interact with each other, however well one understands the psychology of isolated individuals. A theory for isolated individuals is simply not a good enough building block for a theory of social behaviour, let alone economics.

In Anderson's view, fields are connected through a hierarchy, from the most fundamental to the most complex, in which 'the elementary entities of science X obey the laws of science Y' (Table 5.1). That is to say, one level obeys the laws of the previous, but adds new laws of its own, through complexity and emergence, which generates the wide diversity of phenomena observed at each level. Meanwhile, each level's laws do not depend substantially, if at all, on the laws of science fields two or more levels below, while they do not influence the laws observed two or more levels above. For example, the behaviour of molecules in biological systems do not depend substantially on the behaviour of the nuclei of atoms.

[5] Notably, condensed matter physics (magnetism, superconductivity), biology (genetics, proteins, cell biology), social science (financial markets, social behaviour).

TABLE 5.1 *Anderson's hierarchical ordering of the sciences.*[a]

X	Y
Solid state or many-body physics	Elementary particle physics
Chemistry	Many-body physics
Molecular biology	Chemistry
Cell biology	Molecular biology
•	•
•	•
•	•
Psychology	Physiology
Social sciences	Psychology
Economics	Social sciences

[a]Reproduced from Anderson (1972).

Similarly, the behaviour of social systems do not depend substantially on the internal workings of the human body or individual cells.

A key property of complex systems is that they feature intrinsic uncertainty, mainly due to one's limited capacity at calculating the infinitely difficult problems involved in complex systems: one cannot resolve on a computer the collective behaviour of 10^{23} molecules in a small quantity of chemical substance, just as one cannot resolve the collective behaviour of 68 million interacting economic agents in the United Kingdom, or the animals in an ecosystem. One has to rely on shortcuts and approximations, which are inherently uncertain. Furthermore, the actual behaviour of particles or people are themselves uncertain.[6]

What results from this is that for *any* complex system modelled on a computer, uncertainty increases exponentially with the time span modelled.[7] However, the rate of increase of uncertainty is context-dependent. A reflection of this is, for example, the fact that the weather cannot be forecast further ahead than around two to three weeks, and these forecasts are ever more uncertain the closer they are to this limit. However, global warming can be predicted 300 years ahead within reasonable uncertainty ranges, since it depends on different longer-term climate dynamics, but nevertheless faces the same structure of uncertainty. Thus, scale is an important parameter in complex systems.

6 A note on computing: creating an agent-based model for all economic agents of the UK is not likely to run very quickly, and may even take years to generate scenarios covering the same amount of years, potentially even calculating more slowly than reality itself materialises. The complexity means processing amounts of information of a large scale difficult to appreciate.

7 As characterised, for instance, by the Lyapunov exponent, see https://en.wikipedia.org/wiki/Lyapunov_exponent.

5.1.2 *Interacting Entities and Emergent Properties*

A general lesson for all sciences can be found in the history of modern physics. In the year 1926, Schrödinger wrote down his equation, as a postulate, to explain the movement of fundamental quantum particles through time and space; it became one of the most important equations in physics. Schrödinger's equation generates predictions that are realised within remarkable degrees of accuracy, in simple systems in which measurement accuracy is also high.[8] This has implied a very important success for quantum mechanics, a theory that enabled finding solutions to many fundamental contradictions in the classical theory.[9] This may have seemed at the time (together with Einstein's relativity) as if a 'theory of everything' had actually been finally found, and that the rest were just details to be worked out. Some very pompous claims were even made to that effect. However, following these successes, and an increasing motivation for understanding complex materials as opposed to individual particles and atoms, Schrödinger's equation turned out to be a difficult tool to use to make scientific predictions that would be verified for anything really practical.

The equation did not greatly facilitate developing a theory for superconductivity, a peculiar state of matter in which metals, below a certain critical transition temperature near to zero Kelvin (−273°C), conduct electricity infinitely well with near-zero resistance, known to exist since 1911. A solution was found in 1957 by Bardeen, Cooper and Schrieffer (BCS), who used Schrödinger's equation, but applied it to new unknown composite particles, instead of known individual particles. By invoking '*quasi-particles*' (groups of particles acting as one), they were able to 'discover' the emergence of superconductivity in the equation. They modelled the *collective behaviour* of *groups of particles*, and found solutions, whereas if they applied the equation to known individual particles (electrons, atoms), they could not explain observations. The discovery was that one needed to find the right basis upon which to apply the equation.

A few decades later, in 1989, a new type of superconductivity not explained by BCS theory was discovered, so-called 'high-temperature' superconductivity (referring to superconductors with critical transition temperatures well above −200°C), and remains unexplained to this day, despite the efforts of tens of thousands of physicists and hundreds of thousands of scientific papers on the topic and substantial funding during the last thirty years. The collective basis upon which to apply the equation has never been found. What is clear is that the solution should probably involve more

8 See for instance the verified prediction of the electron's anomalous magnetic moment using quantum electrodynamics, with the astounding success of being correct within 10 significant figures. All of these experiments relate to individual particles in vacuum. This level of accuracy has never been possible in any systems with any higher degree of complexity, let alone materials or magnetic systems.

9 Notably, the problems of black body radiation and the photoelectric effect, both solved by Einstein.

complex types of collective behaviour, and could perhaps give rise to an entirely different theory. It is unclear, however, whether the approach used, starting from simple constructs to develop more complex ones, is ever going to work, especially given that interest and research funding for this is dwindling.

High temperature superconductors are materials with very complicated structures, where higher transition temperatures tend to come with higher material complexity. The conventional tools of theoretical physics appear to have failed to explain the phenomenon, despite its potential revolutionary technical applications.[10] Similarly, complex magnetic materials were never fully explained by a brute force use of basic quantum theory. Instead, the search for a solution laid some of the groundwork for developing a theory of complex systems.

The discovery of 'Cooper pairs' by BCS, composite particles that solve Schrödinger's equation, is an example of 'emergent' collective behaviour of particles that work together to create something new. In this case, the pair involves coherent movement betwen two electrons and vibrations in the material. They lead to a radically different state of matter than would be expected from the normal application of Schrödinger's equation, which indicates that the application of the 'theory of everything' in fact promises to explain very little of the observed everyday real-world complexity. Ideally, a 'theory of everything' would explain the emergence of much more complex self-organised systems such as proteins and chemical cycles in cell biology, evolution in zoology, the climate, the economy or innovation systems. Such a theory does not exist, but it would seem that its roots might already exist as part of complexity theory, rather than quantum theory. This would mean that instead of focusing on knowing the properties of individual building blocks in a system, the focus could instead be re-directed towards the interactions between these blocks, to decipher all the different ways that they can work together. The problem mainly lies with the fact that it is essentially not possible to be exhaustive in enumerating all the ways in which system components can work together cooperatively.

Complexity science strives to define universality classes of problems, rather than to explain specific observations. It is remarkably frequent that independent scientific problems in different fields of research (notably, in condensed matter and evolutionary biology) turn out to have the same dynamical behaviour (e.g., the frequency of systemic collapse). It is sometimes the case that the universality class is discovered to be the same between two independent problems, which then suggests that the solution found for one of the problems applies to the second, within its context. For example, it has been shown that some theoretical representations of evolutionary

[10] Notably, physicists cannot determine whether or not there can be a room temperature, ambient pressure superconductor. This would enable various unusual applications based on magnetic levitation and infinite electrical conductance, large magnetic fields, and perhaps, more accessible methods for quantum computing. See Castelvecchi (2020); Snider et al. (2020).

dynamics are the same as some theoretical representations of magnetic systems,[11] Or that financial crises are similar to earthquakes (see Chapter 9).

5.2. PROPERTIES OF INTERACTING SYSTEMS

5.2.1 *Increasing and Decreasing Returns*

Brian Arthur (2014) argues that what makes systems complex is the existence of strong feedbacks between processes. By strong feedbacks, it is the interactions between the actions of agents in a system that is meant. If the actions of agent A influence the actions of agent B, then a feedback exists.

He gives the example of technological diffusion: imagining two equivalent but different innovations, that provide the same service, that agents can adopt, none of which have been adopted by anyone, and of which the costs are the same. The situation is symmetric. If a positive feedback on the adoption of technology exists, it means that one agent adopting innovation A implies an increased likelihood of a second agent adopting innovation A (and the same for B). If a negative feedback exists, then an agent adopting innovation A leads to a decreased likelihood of a second agent adopting innovation A. With positive feedbacks (or, as Arthur calls it, *increasing returns*,) as soon as one agent adopts one of the innovations, and if that action influences other agents to do the same, then the symmetry is broken and a path-dependence emerges in the overall process of innovation. It makes the process strongly depend on events happening early on.

Increasing returns are important in many aspects of the real world, not least in economics. In mainstream equilibrium economics, *constant* or *decreasing returns* are often assumed for the sake of theoretical convenience and model tractability. If an economic resource is used to a certain level, using it more generally implies an increased marginal cost in the standard model of economics. It is convenient theoretically because of the use of optimisation algorithms that maximise utility (or minimise cost): if instead the use of a resource became less costly with increasing use, the optimisation would run away to infinity. Decreasing returns maintain optimisation calculations between bounds. For economists, this makes intuitive sense: the use of any resource is maintained in a certain balance by increasing costs, and economic agents allocate their use of resources between different types according to the cost of their use and the amount of utility they obtain from it.

Utility functions also feature decreasing returns: the consumption of a certain good generates decreasing amounts of marginal utility at higher consumption levels, and this property serves the same theoretical purpose. However, some cases of

[11] Specifically, Stuart Kauffman's NK model maps onto frustrated versions of the Ising model of magnetism, see Thurner et al. (2018). Note that this is a comparison of theoretical models, not of real problems as observed.

increasing returns clearly exist that makes this theoretical standpoint difficult: what to do with technological learning curves? With learning-by-doing, the marginal cost of deployment of technologies goes *down* with the level of deployment, notably with solar energy. As discussed in Chapter 2, this creates difficulties in optimisation algorithms as it generates different possible, equally optimal, model outcomes. This is because *path-dependence emerges*. For the standard models, this is problematic, as several storylines emerge at the same time, and models cannot choose between them which one has lower cost or higher utility. With a relatively low amount of positive feedbacks, the number of solutions increases to a degree that is unmanageable, or perhaps, a degree that makes the optimisation algorithm lose meaning. It then becomes a question whether avoiding increasing returns for theoretical convenience and model tractability is a correct scientific procedure, if increasing returns really are important in the real world.

In a set of seminal papers, Arthur et al. (1987) and Arthur (1989) created a simple mathematical system that illustrates very well the implications of increasing returns, and of the emergence of path-dependence. It is based on the so-called 'Polya urn'. One imagines an urn in which coloured balls are added, for a start black and white. With different rules, the content of the urn changes. Imagine that the urn starts with two balls, one of each colour, and that the rule is that a ball is randomly picked from the urn, put back in, and that a ball of the same colour to what was picked is also added to the urn. The outcome is quite interesting: the proportion of white to black balls initially changes rapidly but later tends to converge towards a particular fixed value, any shade of grey between all black and all white with equal probability. It is literally impossible to predict what the end proportion will be. This is because, each time a ball is added, the proportion changes slightly, which alters the probability of picking a colour, but the changes influence the composition less and less as more and more balls are added, and the system is locked-in to a state that it re-inforces. What determines the outcome value? Is is the very sequence of events at the earliest stage, and given that they are random, there is no way to predict what the outcome will be (Figure 5.1 a).

The model can also be run with different types of returns, by creating a non-linear interaction: instead of adding just one white ball when picking a white ball, one could add two, or a probabilistic fraction greater or lower than one. Obviously, two types can be explored, whether returns increase, or whether they decrease (Figure 5.1 a and b respectively). The probability of the outcome is not equal anymore, but a clustering of the outcomes emerges, that diverges for increasing returns, and that converges for decreasing returns.

This demonstrates two features of social systems. First, interactions between events create chains that force the outcome to converge towards ever more specific storylines, and are strongly influenced by all events that took place along the way. In the case of a choice model to describe agent behaviour, even in the case where one choice is demonstrably inferior to another, historical events may drive

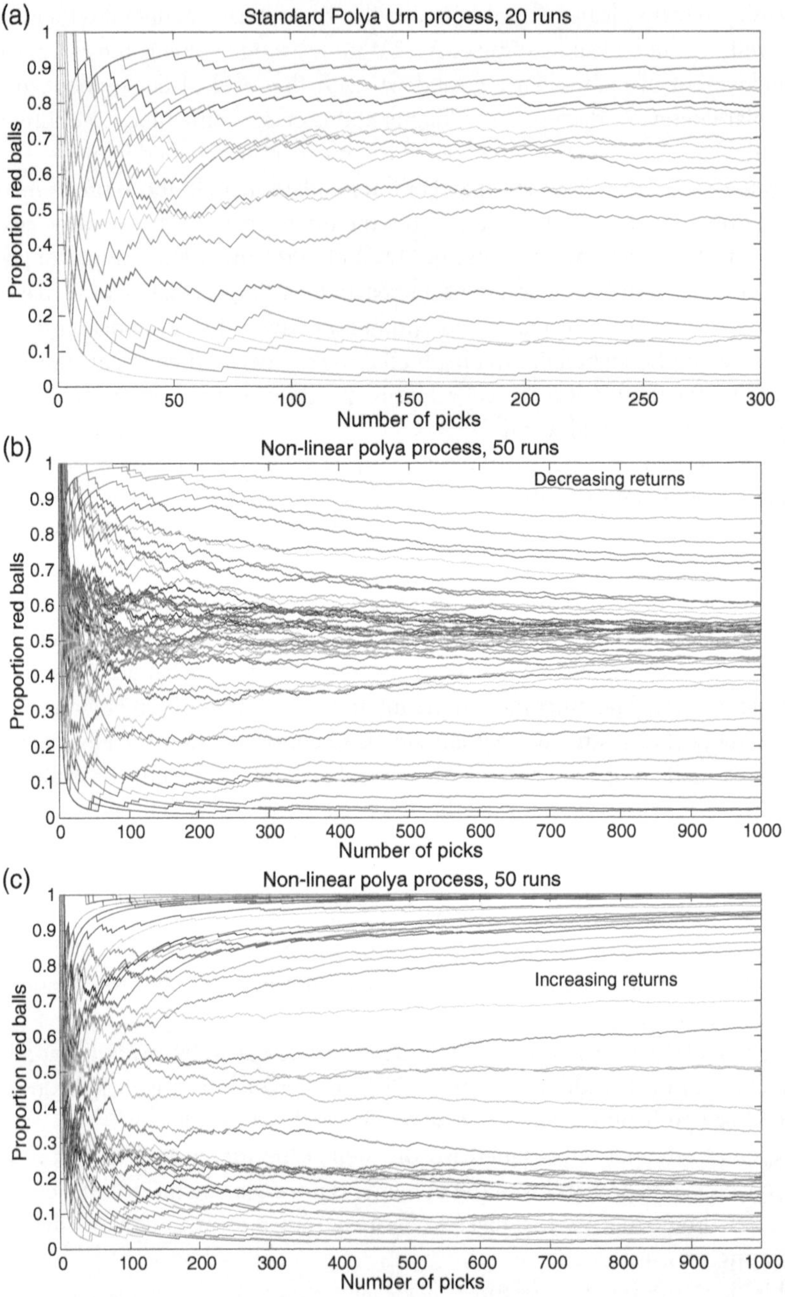

FIGURE 5.1 Pólya urn process, following Arthur et al. (1987), using the linear Polya process (a) and non-linear process with decreasing returns (b) and increasing returns (c).

the macro system towards unexpected outcomes that become 'locked-in'.[12] Second, the outcome depends strongly on the type of interaction between events, whether feedbacks are positive or negative. In the case of negative feedbacks, outcomes, although still path-dependent, tend to converge towards each other. For increasing returns, storylines diverge from each other.

5.2.2 *Equilibrium, Out-of-Equilibrium and Chaotic Systems*

A key set of classes of systems of interacting elements is between situations of equilibrium, non-equilibrium and chaos. To make it simple, in equilibrium, systems interact in such a way that the statistical distributions of their properties are independent of any initial conditions: the system forgets its past and where it came from. When a disturbance arises, a temporary non-equilibrium situation emerges in which the disturbance dissipates, and the system returns to equilibrium, and forgets this ever happened. Consider for example a liquid in thermal equilibrium, with no gradients of temperature. If one measures the velocity of individual molecules, one finds a well-defined statistical distribution that is predictable from theory with very good accuracy. Every molecule travels at a different velocity, and transfers kinetic energy with other particles as it collides with them, but the overall average velocity remains constant across the population (the temperature remains constant). If the system had initially been heated, such that convection took place (temperature gradients existed, and collective movement of the liquid happened), when the heating stops, after waiting for a sufficiently long period, the system gradually returns to equilibrium and gradually 'forgets' it ever was heated as the liquid mixes, heat is conducted across the liquid and temperature gradients gradually disappear.

In an economic system, this would correspond to a situation in which prices, demand/supply or productivity have no relationship with history, which may be realised in particular cases, for example, in some types of auctions and markets. In biological systems, a biological body (e.g., the human body) recovers after a disease or an accident such that the body shows little trace of it ever having happened or any consequence from it. In terms of the earlier section, equilibrium can only arise with decreasing returns, in which the system gradually forgets earlier events and returns to a fixed pre-determined state independent of its past.

Non-equilibrium situations describe all other possible situations, in which systems do not find an equilibrium independent from the past, but instead are strongly conditioned by their history. Such systems 'remember' their history, sometimes forever, and display all sorts of 'scars' that can tell the story of their existence. Early events in their life often have a determinant impact on the rest of their existence, as in the Polya urn example. A person's choice of career may be highly influenced

[12] The story of the QWERTY keyboard is the classical example (David, 1985).

by learning events at school and or perhaps even by one single conversation with a teacher. The emergence of an industry in a region could be due to the work of one particular entrepreneur who kick-started something that lasted, as has notably been the case in most industrial revolutions, from which landmarks often remain (e.g., Brunel in nineteenth century Great Britain). In biological evolution, branching processes, or the creation of new species, can revolutionise and destabilise whole ecosystems. Non-equilibrium systems may be stable or unstable, but their principal characteristic is that they remember the past.

Chaotic systems, for their part, are systems with very strong interactions that are dominated by noise and cannot be well described by any theory. Such systems display noise of such an intensity that they forget the past, but never reach any stable equilibrium. These systems are of lesser interest here, other than to mention that they exist and sometimes emerge. However, many systems exist on the edge of chaos.

A key concept in relation to whether systems are in equilibrium or not is that of 'ergodicity', where equilibrium and chaotic systems can be said to be 'ergodic' while non-equilibrium systems can be said to be '*non-ergodic*'. Peters (2019) describes the degree to which ergodicity matters for economics.

Ergodic systems do not remember the past, while non-ergodic systems do. The important distinction for economics is as follows. Imagine a situation in which one is offered to buy a ticket to participate to a game in which one either wins money equal to 50% of one's own wealth, with 50% probability (e.g., the flip of a coin), or loses 40% of one's own wealth with 50% probability. Standard expected value theory would suggest that this is an attractive game since one should on average win 5% of one's own wealth by playing this repeatedly, thus increasing one's wealth by 5% per game played, on average. However, the reality turns out to be quite different: Figure 5.2 shows that one *always* loses all of one's wealth if one plays this game a sufficient number of times, on average at a rate of -5% per turn, but with a large standard deviation. This paradox should puzzle deeply any economist who has only ever considered equilibrium systems.

The explanation of the paradox is explained simply by considering the non-ergodicity of the problem. At each turn, one risks winning more than losing; however, once one has lost a couple of times or more, it becomes unlikely to ever recover. Imagine the following series: $(1-0.4)\times(1+0.5)\times(1+0.5)\times(1-0.4)=0.81$; even though one has won the game twice out of four, one still loses 19% of one's original wealth. This seems intuitively correct, and few would be willing to play this; therefore the question is why standard economics should claim that one can expect to win 5% per turn? In fact, standard economics effectively assumes that the player rewinds time every time he plays and plays many times, and therefore, in standard economics' mathematical artillery, the player does not follow a real storyline. Winning 5% on average would be true for the average outcome for a large group of people playing just one turn. But it stops being true starting with the second turn when people replay the game. Thus people should really play it only once in order to have, on average,

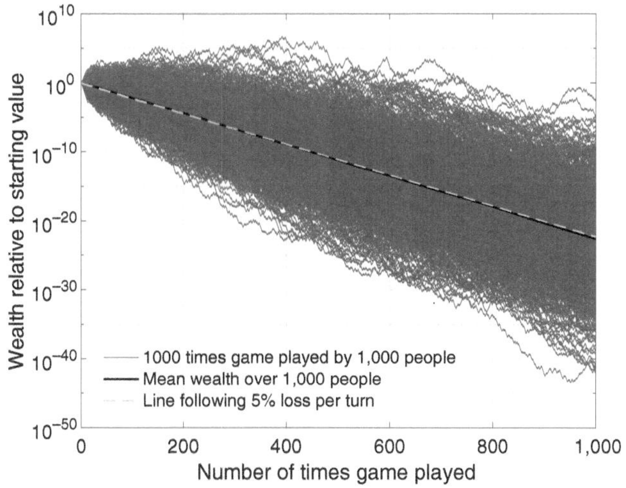

FIGURE 5.2 Game described in the text played 1,000 times by 1,000 different persons, their wealth shown as grey lines showing 1,000 different storylines. The average wealth at each time step is shown with a black line, which appears to follow exactly a decline rate of 5% per turn. The white dashed line shows an actual decline rate of 5% per turn.

a real chance of winning money. It is also notable in Figure 5.2 that some storylines lose wealth very quickly, while others win for a certain duration, but all storylines ultimately lose in the end with virtual certainty. There is thus some logic in wanting to get out of the game early when one is winning.

This system is non-ergodic, in that every storyline fully remembers its past, and no-one in the game loses his/her wealth at exactly 5% per turn. However, Peters (2019) offers a huge additional insight: people understand this intuitively, as social experiments appear to show. People don't appear to believe in expected value theory, according to the empirical evidence. In some sense, people understand what game they are playing when at the casino. People intuitively understand non-ergodicity – that is, with the exception of equilibrium economists. One can therefore suspect that economists might persist and lose all their wealth if they decide to play this game, but ordinary people would likely decide to quit the game early on, if they play at all. There is no stable equilibrium corresponding to expected values in this game, not even when averaging over the stories of 1,000 people.

The economy is very clearly made of a collection of path-dependent stochastic systems that remember their full history. Looking at GDP trends before and after the 2008 financial crisis, a scar very clearly appears. While the rate of growth has to some degree recovered, although not everywhere in the World, the absolute GDP value is forever scarred, it will never become what it should otherwise have been had the crisis not happened. If the economy is non-ergodic, and remembers all of its history, then all of expected value theory should not apply to any quantity. *The reality is that since one cannot enumerate all possible futures in non-ergodic systems, one cannot form stable probability distributions to calculate expected values.* This becomes a key concept for policy analysis in Chapter 12.

5.2.3 *Non-ergodicity and Path-Dependence in the Economy*

Where non-ergodicity and path-dependence matter most for one's understanding of the economy is in how one pictures the future, whether in the form of diverging storylines or in the form of disturbances and return to a normal trajectory. The reader might remember the 1985 film 'Back to the future' featuring Michael J. Fox, in which the protagonist travels through time. He goes to the past, accidentally changes history, and then finds himself having to fix the past or cease to exist. In the sequel, he returns to a bleak future, and thus wants to go back to the past to fix the future again. The director clearly saw history as path-dependent. And so is the economy, no storyline is preferred to any other, and it is impossible to enumerate all possible futures the present and past could lead to.

Kauffman (2000) focuses on this with the goal of defining the statistical properties of a theory of evolution. His way to understand non-ergodicity in the economy is to consider the storyline the economy is on as a chain of amino acids that make proteins. Proteins are molecules performing specific tasks in biological cells, and each different protein in existence is defined by a unique coded chain of amino acids, and there are twenty possibilities for each chain link. When proteins are made like that, once completed they fold up into a unique shape according to their unique code, and perform a unique function. Starting from one random amino acid, each time step passing in the economy is akin to adding one of the twenty possible amino acids, to the front of the chain. Each time this happens, the new amino acid added improves the definition of what the function of the protein is or could become, in part by adding new functionality, and in part by ruling out a number of possible proteins that the current system is not becoming. The evolution of the economy through time is the same: each time step increases functionality in the economy as agents create and destroy things, through all the innovation and events marking the economy forever, while at the same time ruling out a number of futures that have become impossible or unlikely.

Consider the COVID-19 pandemic. It has considerably changed what the future can be, by severely curtailing activities and the finances of economic agents, even after the economy returns to 'normal' (although according to this chapter, there is no 'normal'). But also, it has changed the behaviour of agents and most importantly, policy-makers. Many businesses and activities that were profitable have ceased to exist and will not come back. But agents will also have discovered new possibilities, for instance offered by remote work and remote meetings, reducing future travel and commuting, which might never have become so popular had this not happened.

This could potentially reduce expenses on office space, improving firm productivity, inciting people to move to the countryside, but also have knock on effects on fossil fuel markets with downward pressure on oil prices. Meanwhile, governments may improve the capacity of the health system and the economy at absorbing large similar future shocks. Pre-COVID times are over forever.

This view of the economy contrasts starkly with an equilibrium view, in which there are 'normal' and 'abnormal' states, and a tendency to return to normal after disturbances. This is unproven, and notably, economic time series readily show non-ergodicity and memory.[13] In neoclassical theory, disturbances are remembered because they are made exogenous, which implies that they are effectively written as a storyline in God's Grand Book of Events. In reality, non-ergodicity in time series suggests that possible future states of the economy are determined by *cumulative causation* in its past, and present day choices, but cannot be enumerated, at least not beyond the next round of choices. It is a possibility, however, that the global economy has some sort of attractor state with growth at 3% p.a. (Jarvis, 2018), towards which the economy is attracted following disturbances. Thus even though it is unstable, going through all sorts of crashes, and despite that it remembers all of its past, global GDP growth hovers around 3%. But this does not imply that absolute GDP is tied to a particular storyline as implied by basic neoclassical theory (e.g., Nordhaus, 2017).

5.2.4 *Phase Transitions*

Systems with no interactions can be predicted until the end of time with infinite accuracy using the classical theory, or at least, with as much accuracy as is available from empirical measurement.[14] This applies for instance to the movement of simple cosmic objects when only two interact (planets, stars), pairs of fundamental particles (e.g., the hydrogen atom) or individuals with well-defined assumptions of utilitarian rationality. The property extends to systems of *non-interacting* components, such as the ideal gas in physics (a gas made of non-interacting atoms, e.g., helium) or an economy made of non-interacting agents. Unfortunately, none of the systems that are observed empirically match predictions of theories of non-interacting systems. As such, they are instructive in telling us how the world *does not work*. For instance, as shown in Chapter 7, as soon as learning interactions of any degree are introduced in a theory of the diffusion of innovations, the concept of the representative agent loses clear interpretation, as social groups form.

[13] In the statistical distribution of their noise and its autocorrelation in time (Silverberg et al., 1999).

[14] The 'classical theory' here refers to classical physics before the development of statistical physics and complexity science, and classical economics in equilibrium before the inclusion of Schumpeterian, Keynesian and Minskian economics. Marx arguably developed a non-equilibrium dynamical theory, although later became rejected. Neoclassical theory follows the classical structure.

Furthermore, almost all phenomena of interest stem from interactions between system components. Of particular interest are moments of substantial change, such as financial crises, species extinctions and phase transitions in matter such as from solid to liquid, metal to magnetic, ordered to disordered. In fact, many such sudden events could arguably be called phase transitions. Phase transitions are unique moments and situations in which a system with many interacting components finds itself at a transition between two distinct macro states, in some sort of superposition between both, at which many measurable quantities record drastic changes and fluctuations. For instance, a change in expectations of investors in a financial market generates a sudden change surrounded by volatility in asset prices, or water boiling sees a drastic change and fluctuations in density. As one approaches this transition from one state or the other, fluctuations appear that seem to 'anticipate' the coming transition, such as bubbles in water or price volatility (Lenton, 2020). The transition point usually displays unique properties where fluctuations become as large as the system itself.[15] The transition takes place less and less locally, and the notion of 'local' gradually loses clear meaning. In fact, it is the notion of scale that disappears at the transition point, as fluctuations appear at all scales (all price scales, all length scales, all timescales: it is not clear what is small and large). This is called a 'scale-free' state (Figure 5.3).

The transition point is characterised by specific statistical signatures. At the transition, fluctuations (e.g., bubbles and price variations) appear at all scales, large and small, following specific distribution statistics: their frequency as a function of their magnitude follows a power law. This means that on a log-log graph, the number of events (bubbles, price drops) follows a linear function of the associated magnitude, the larger being less frequent.

Take for example the Ising model of ferromagnetism, in which magnetic spins (magnetically oriented elements on a regular spatial lattice) influence neighbouring spins in pointing in the same direction. When they are at low temperature, they have insufficient energy to overcome the force from neighbouring spins that induces them to all point in the same direction. The direction is random but collectively determined. Increasing the temperature towards a critical point, some spins fluctuate in all directions, overcoming neighbouring forces, and some patches of spins of limited size pointing collectively in different directions appear in various places. Past the critical point, all spins point randomly in any direction. But at the critical point between the ordered and disordered states, patches of spins pointing in different directions emerge in all possible sizes, and their size is governed by power-law statistics, and so are many observable macro properties of the magnetic system.

Similarly, in financial networks, traders influence each other by imitation. As buyers push up asset prices, the upward trends attract more buyers. Similarly, sellers

[15] See for instance the treatment of financial crashes by Sornette (2017).

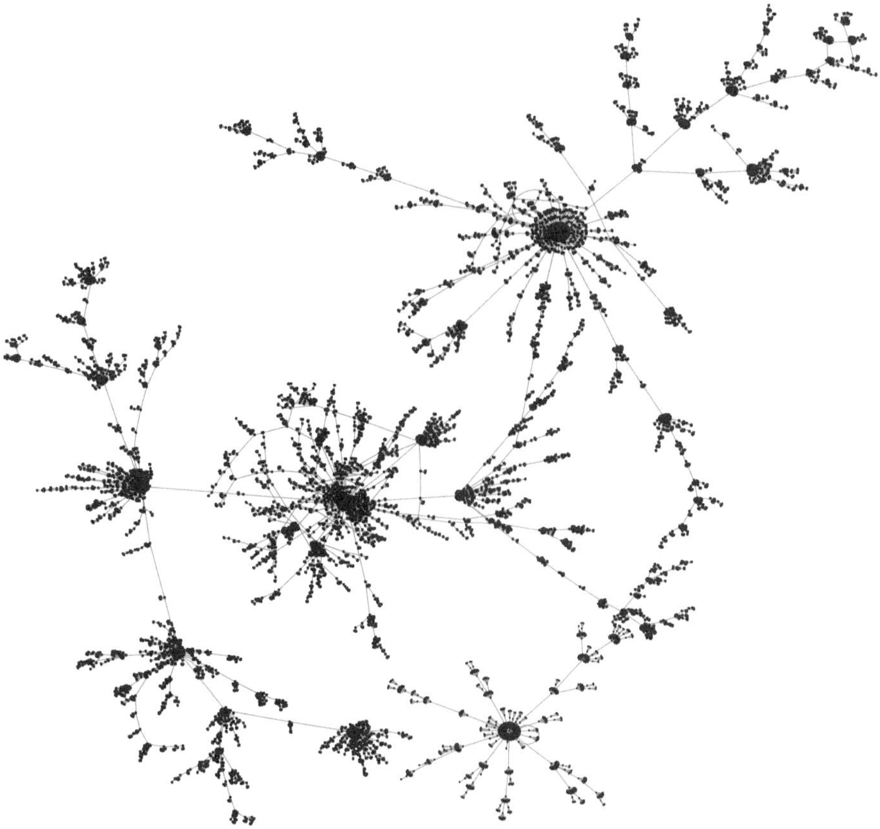

FIGURE 5.3 Illustration of a 'scale-free' network with an exponent of −1.4, similar to equity networks in finance.

push down asset prices, attracting more sales. Phase transition points exist at which large collective sales take place, sometimes even leading to financial crashes. It is the interactions between financial agents that lead to these fluctuations, which are also governed by power-law statistics (Sornette, 2017).

The theory of power-law statistics in phase transitions is well understood since many decades, based on work in statistical physics, notably by Kadanoff (2000). This field of enquiry has made important contributions to present understanding of matter as it evolves in the physical world. However, most of statistical physics describes equilibrium, steady state or static systems, going from one equilibrium state of matter to another, and mostly avoids the complexities of non-equilibrium or non-ergodic science. It does not describe or explain self-organisation, the key concept at the heart of evolutionary theory. But, before going there, the topology of networks must be explored.

5.3. SCALE-FREE NETWORKS

Networks are, loosely speaking, systems of interacting entities, represented as nodes and links. Networks can be static or dynamic, and can have many types of topologies. For instance, in some networks, the number of links per node may be the same for every node, for example, a lattice in which every point has the same number of neighbours (e.g., houses in neighbourhood). Other networks may have random numbers of links per node (e.g., trees in a forest). 'Scale-free' networks instead have particular topologies, in which some nodes have enormously larger numbers of links to other nodes than most nodes (e.g., networks of friends or professional colleagues).

Many, if not most, observed network systems are scale-free or approximately so, including friends, cities connected by roads, ecosystems, Facebook, Instagram and Twitter, telecommunications, internet and so on. Of interest for this book are patent, financial, citation and social networks.[16] The peculiarity of scale-free networks is that their way of being scale-free is the same as the behaviour of phase transitions: their statistics follow power laws. In citation or patent networks, for instance, patents or papers with larger numbers of citations to other patents or papers are less frequent than patents or papers with fewer citations, and this follows a power law with a particular exponent. The exponent is the slope of the function in log-log space, generally a negative number between −1 and around −6.

Scale-free networks have the key property that they are formed and grow into hubs of varying sizes, following the scale-free statistics (Barabási and Bonabeau, 2003). They are ubiquitous for a good reason: they arise naturally through the so-called process of '*preferential attachment*', where new nodes and links attach themselves to the network with preference to nodes that are already well-connected. If the likelihood of attaching themselves to particular nodes is proportional to the connectivity of hubs, then the network naturally becomes scale-free, it just forms that way. Think of roads between cities of different sizes, and the saying 'all roads lead to Rome'. However, if the likelihood of links attaching themselves to nodes increases faster than linearly with connectivity, the networks tend to form something else, at the limit a star network with only one node connecting every other.

Scale-free networks have particular properties in terms of connectivity: they are more robust than most other network topologies to random node failures. With random nodes failing, the network most of the time remains operational, and this matters for information networks, notably the internet. However, and conversely, they are vulnerable to targeted attacks on chosen well-connected nodes, which can fragment the network into small pieces.

Network topology matters for applied science. In disease propagation during epidemics (as observed with COVID-19), the scale-free nature of social networks has consequences for how to contain the situation. In random networks, there normally

16 See Katz (2016); Barabási and Bonabeau (2003); Thurner et al. (2018).

exists a transmission rate threshold below which small epidemics die out, due to lack of connectivity. For scale-free networks, this threshold can be demonstrated to be zero. This means that such networks are so well connected that diseases with any transmission rate however low propagate easily, and that reducing connectivity is a good way to stop propagation. Immunisation programs that are applied to random individuals usually have a low rate of success, as the likelihood of immunising well-connected individuals by chance is relatively low. Instead, it is clear that targeting small numbers of well-connected hubs is more effective, but it is not always straightforward to identify who they are. It would be, for instance, more effective to immunise acquaintances of random people than these people themselves, as this naturally has a much higher likelihood of reaching well-connected hubs, although this is not ethical in practice.

5.4. SELF-ORGANISED CRITICALITY TO EXPLAIN EVOLUTION

5.4.1 *Per Bak and His Insightful Contribution*

In contrast to the continuous process Darwin expressed in his theory of evolution, the fossil record shows that evolutionary systems evolve through periodic bursts of intensified change between long spells of tranquility, something that has been called the 'punctuated equilibrium'.[17] For a long time, no theory could explain the peculiar timeline of the fossil record, as Darwin's theory suggests that evolution happens gradually following a constant rate of mutation, giving rise only to gradual changes in biological systems. But substantial evidence exists over the occurrence of extinction events of all magnitude at all times, interspersed between long periods where nearly nothing changed (Gould and Eldredge, 1977). This is an observation that can also be made of financial systems, in which price falls of all magnitudes can be observed between periods of relative stability, something that can hardly be described as an equilibrium (Gopikrishnan et al., 1999).

In 1987, an important universality class was identified, what is called *self-organised criticality* (SOC), by Per Bak and co-authors.[18] Per Bak is arguably the creative mind who found the first algorithmic solution that could begin to explain the theory of evolution with its punctuated equilibrium behaviour. He started as a condensed matter physicist, but later became an important influence in complexity science across fields. He established that many systems, in many domains, that possess high degrees of *internal contingency* (where elements working normally depend on many other elements working normally), display the so-called 'punctuated equilibrium'

[17] To appreciate how uneven the rate of evolution of the earth system has been, see Lenton and Watson (2011).

[18] Bak et al. (1987, 1988); Bak and Sneppen (1993); Bak (1996). See Bak's detailed account of this phenomenon in all sorts of domains (Bak, 1996).

property, and proposed convincing mechanisms to explain them. This includes financial systems, production chains, ecosystems, brain activity and even traffic on roads and railroads. These systems are placid and peaceful in between bursts of activity and collapse. This happens due to knock-on effects that systemic collapse have on other parts of the system. Take notably the UK rail network: train delays cause delays, which accumulate throughout the day, leading sometimes to spectacular systemic failures across the whole network.

Such systems cannot be thought of as being in equilibrium, unless one deludes oneself in searching for 'ad-hoc' exogenous causes for disturbances every time a burst of activity occurs. These bursts are not periodic in time, but occur with *heavy-tailed* power-law (scale-free) probability distributions, which cannot be explained satisfactorily just by invoking a long list of external shocks that happen to follow exactly that probability. These bursts arise endogenously, due to internal mechanisms.

SOC arises in systems in which the components display strong internal mutual contingency, where some randomness (or stochasticity) exists and where slow driving forces arise that are not too strong to become chaotic. For example, in network traffic, every train or car arriving on time depends on every other car or train arriving on time. Increasing traffic density leads to fluctuations in flow, where trains accumulate small delays, and cars slow down and accelerate again. At high traffic density, small fluctuations become amplified to large fluctuations, sometimes to complete stops, traffic jams or major network failures. The same issue arises in delivery networks and production chains for composite goods.

SOC lies in a region of parameter space that is between equilibrium systems and chaotic systems, exactly at a phase transition. SOC systems are 'self-organised' because they feature forces that continuously push (or bring back) the system towards the edge of the phase transition. SOC systems arise in completely unconnected domains.[19] SOC systems feature avalanches of events triggered by small disturbances, or simply endogenously, of all possible magnitudes described by a power-law probability distribution (the log of the frequency of events against the log of their 'severity'), with a particular exponent, generally between -1 and -4, similar to phase transitions at the critical point.

What this means is that bursts of activity in SOC systems can be of any magnitude imaginable, the larger events less probable, the smaller events more probable. For example, if the slope of the linear trend, in a base ten log-log graph, is equal to one, then an avalanche ten times larger than another reference avalanche happens ten

[19] Collapses in piles of sand (Bak et al., 1987), earthquakes (Sornette and Sornette, 1989; Bak et al., 2002), evolutionary change in biology (Bak and Sneppen, 1993, see Thurner et al., 2018), financial disturbances and crises (Gopikrishnan et al., 1999), neuron activity in the brain (Stassinopoulos and Bak, 1995; Thurner et al., 2003) and heart function (Bak, 1996, see Thurner et al., 2018), and even innovation systems (Arthur and Polak, 2006).

times less frequently than that reference (this is the case, for instance, with earthquakes). However, events are also clustered in time, and this clustering determines their severity (and probability). These events are thus also said to be 'scale-free': they occur at all timescales and all length scales, from big to small, from frequent to rare, without known limits. The upper limit for measuring the likelihood of large events is that they do not occur sufficiently frequently, with respect to the time at hand (or historical data at hand), to generate reliable statistics. Conversely, the lower limit for measurement of frequent small events is that they may escape detection if sufficiently small. Importantly, due to the stochastic source of fluctuations (small random events trigger large events), if one was to 'replay the tape' of the story of any self-organised critical system, the emergent story would be different every time, although it would respect the same statistics (Bak, 1996).

A true law of nature appears to operate underneath this phenomenon (Bak et al., 1987). By their contingent nature, SOC systems drive themselves naturally towards a critical state prone to fluctuations. For example, earthquakes are created by the accumulation of pressure as tectonic plates move against each other. When a section of rock ruptures or moves, given the pressure accumulated in a multitude of points in the rock, this can trigger other ruptures or movements in the crust in multiple places. In fact, every movement can trigger a comparatively large chain reaction, or not very much, depending on the configuration of the network. Large clustering of events can lead to large earthquakes. As the geological system accumulates pressure, it continuously self-organises into a critical state. This state is characterised by shock events, chain reactions of movements, at all scales, from small to large, and at all timescales, from rare to frequent. Earthquakes are described by the Gutenberg-Richter law, a probability power law that is respected over many orders of magnitude (and forms the basis for the Richter scale), the same as what is found computationally.

As shown in Chapter 9, another example is price fluctuations in the financial system. The perceived value of financial assets is created through complex operations involving other assets: a firm borrows funds and purchases stocks or bonds from other institutions; firms borrow or issue shares or bonds in order to finance projects of which the value depends on the performance of other markets or assets. As the complexity of financial instruments and their contingency on others, and total debt accumulates (entities move closer to the insolvency limit), the financial system reaches self-organised criticality where unexplained price fluctuations of all magnitude arise.

In brief, several signatures indicate self-organised criticality (Watkins et al., 2016):

1. contingency between elements;
2. intermittent avalanches of all sizes at all timescales clustered in time;
3. avalanche thresholds;

4. a driving force that is orders of magnitude smaller in magnitude and slower in its variations than the avalanches themselves,
5. power-law distribution of avalanche frequencies against their magnitude, characterised by a critical exponent between −1 and −4.

5.4.2 *The Punctuated Equilibrium*

The punctuated equilibrium is a state that resembles an equilibrium when between bursts. However, it is very far from it, where in fact, it is during calm periods that pressure builds that will eventually be relieved through an avalanche. In Bak's sandpile model, grains of sand are sprinkled slowly, which gradually builds a sandpile, of which the slope gradient increases up to the critical point. At the critical point, any single grain of sand added, or any other disturbance, can trigger an avalanche, its magnitude determined by the very details of how the grains of sand precariously stand upon one another. In that sense, it is pointless to search for ways to predict the exact nature of the next avalanche, unless one is in a position to measure the position of each grain and model the pile on a computer. And even then, large numbers of small uncertainties would cumulate and lead the model to give wrong predictions for the exact nature and timing of the event, although the predicted statistics may be correct.

This does not make the study of SOC systems pointless, as it is a different type of quantity that matters. While one cannot predict the magnitude or timing of the next big earthquake with any degree of accuracy, one could, in principle, predict the likelihood of its magnitude, as a probability distribution, with very high accuracy, just by knowing the power-law exponent. Since avalanches cluster in time, as they trigger each other, the longer the time span since the last large event, the longer one can expect to wait until the next event. With earthquakes, the notion that one is 'due' to happen is in fact rather incorrect understanding of statistics, even if one knows the mean time span between earthquakes in the recent past. The punctuated equilibrium between events is really just that, a lull between storms the duration of which is determined by power statistics, during which pressures build for the next avalanches, but high pressures do not automatically imply that a large event is imminent.

5.4.3 *The Theory of Evolution*

The most important implication of the development of the general understanding of SOC is that it offers a potentially powerful quantitative theory to explain evolutionary dynamics, in biology as much as in economics. Evolution in biology (and economics) takes place through several steps (Thurner et al., 2018):

1. species (types of economic agents/activity) co-exist in a stable ecosystem and interact (e.g., through food chains, parasitic or mutualist interactions);
2. a species mutates, gaining new characteristics;
3. the new species either dies out or proliferates;
4. if it proliferates, it becomes part of the ecosystem by changing it;
5. other species are affected, and either adapt, collapse or proliferate more, potentially causing knock-on disturbances to other species, until a new stable state is found again.

The Bak and Sneppen (1993) model is the first model of SOC that attempted to explain punctuated equilibrium evolutionary dynamics. It is a very simplistic model, designed in this way to explain the most salient features of the data rather than to make realistic predictions. In his standard style, Bak thought that the details could be filled-in by others.[20] In this model, Bak and Sneppen hypothesised species as nodes on a circular network, each with two neighbours.[21] Each node is assigned a fitness that is relative to the average fitness, and each node depends for its own survival on the survival of its two neighbours. When the fitness of a species drops substantially below the average, it is thought to be on the brink of extinction. At each time step, a mutation is assumed to take place with the least fit specie, as well as its two neighbours. This is because the specie is assumed unfit, and its extinction cuts off resources to its two neighbours in the ecological network. All three are replaced by new species with random fitnesses.

The system starts with random fitnesses between zero and one, and when a species mutates, it gets assigned a new random number between zero and one (as well as its neighbours). The result is that after a number of iterations, the average fitness rises rapidly, as the system runs out of low values and accumulates high values. It gradually converges towards a seemingly steady state in which all fitnesses are above two thirds. However, every so often, a large avalanche takes place, since as neighbours, which were relatively fit, are assigned new random numbers, they may obtain low values that bring their own neighbours with them, and so on, and this can in

[20] It is notable that Bak sadly passed away in 2002 arguably at the peak of his career, relatively shortly after writing his influential book 'How Nature Works' (Bak, 1996). He would otherwise have likely participated in refining his theory of evolution, and tested it against empirical data in more detail. Although incomplete, Bak's theory of evolution is an important building block for current work in the field, see Thurner et al. (2018).

[21] In reality, ecological networks are often, unsurprisingly, scale-free (Montoya and Solé, 2002), although too complex to characterise without substantial uncertainty. This implies the resilience properties noted above: resilience to random node failure, but vulnerability to hub failure.

principle propagate indefinitely, or die out quickly. The system displays the signature behaviour of punctuated equilibrium.

This is shown in Figure 5.4. Three signatures of SOC emerge: the punctuated equilibrium for each species, and scale-free distributions for waiting times between bursts and the duration of bursts (in imagined genetic terms), or in other words linear in a log-log graph. These signatures leave little doubt for the existence of SOC in this model, which also provides a clear representation of punctuated equilibrium.

This system is simple, and its connection to evolution not necessarily obvious or complete. What it represents well is the co-evolutionary race between species, where species compete with one another through mutation to avoid extinction: 'it takes all the running you can do, to keep in the same place'.[22] It does not, however, represent very clearly how species depend on one another, where the topology of the network in fact matters.

5.4.4 *The Adjacent Possible*

Stuart Kauffman is one of the most prominent evolutionary theorists and has proposed some substantial progress as for the structure of an overarching theory, going even beyond biological systems. In 'Investigations', he describes how he senses there should exist a fourth law of thermodynamics that could underpin, better than the second law, self-organisation in complex systems leading to evolution through reproduction, selection and mutation (Kauffman, 2000). The second law of thermodynamics explains how disorder naturally increases in nature through irreversible processes, but does not explain how, conversely, order tends to be created through self-organisation.

Kauffman defines the autonomous agent as a system able to carry out at least one thermodynamic cycle, where, just like a thermodynamic engine, the agent uses energy or temperature gradients to generate work to create 'new constraints on the release of energy'. It is constraints on the release of energy that prevent complete conversion of energy into entropy (through irreversible processes, as the second law of thermodynamics suggests), which improve its ability to generate useful work. The channelling of energy flows is what allows agents to collectively create structures that enable ever better control over energy flows.

In the economy, the parallel extends readily, where agents sense demand for final or intermediate products from consumers and firms, and develop companies

22 This is a famous quote from Lewis Carroll's *Through the looking glass*, i.e. Alice in Wonderland. The effect is called the 'Red Queen' hypothesis, in which species are involved in a never-ending arms race against one another. This is well proven to take place, notably in the immune system, which co-evolves with bacteria and viruses.

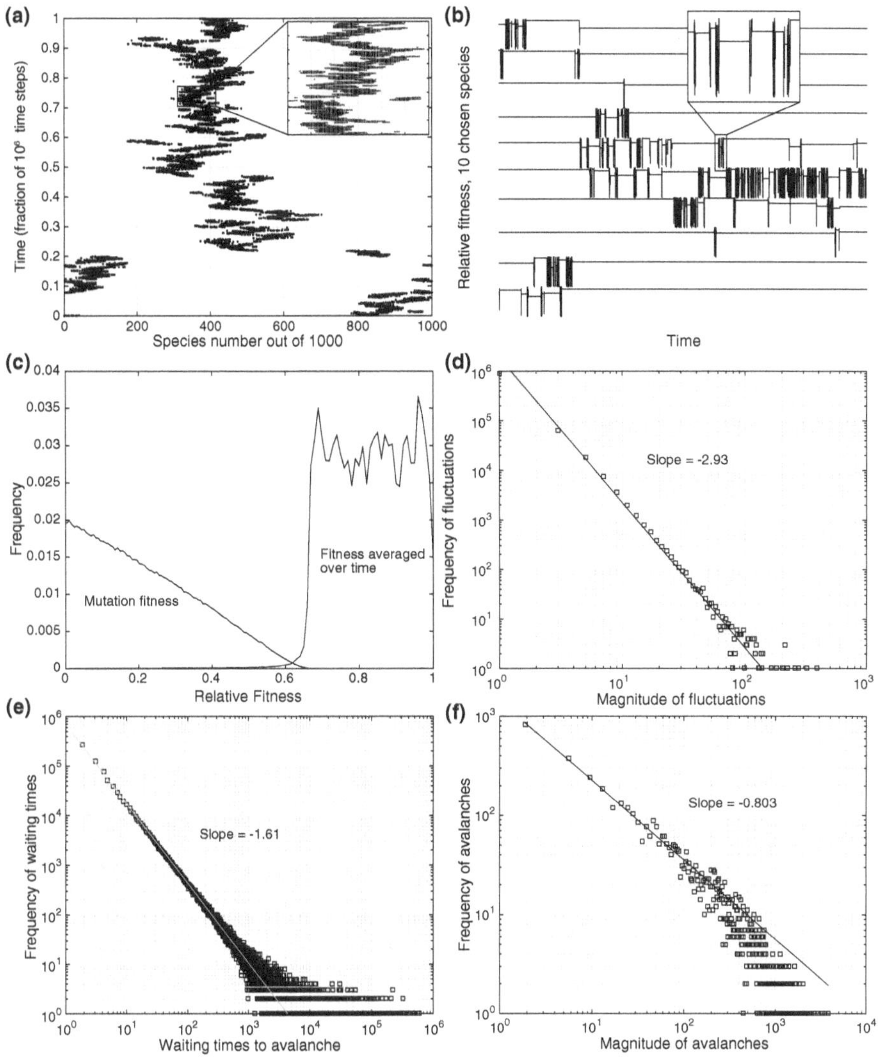

FIGURE 5.4 Outputs from the Bak and Sneppen (1993) model (calculated by the author based on the paper, using 1,000 species, see text). (a) Mutation activity over time for all species. Inset: the image is a fractal (self-similar when one zooms in) (b) Fitness over time for 10 consecutive species. The punctuated equilibrium is visible. Inset: the nature of the bursts is self-similar (fractal), appearing at all possible timescales (c) *Left curve*: distribution of fitnesses of mutating species. *Right curve*: distribution of average fitnesses. (d) Distribution of species distances between consecutive mutations. (e) Distribution of waiting times between bursts of activity. (f) Distribution of the duration in time of bursts of activity.

and build physical capital in order to respond to that demand, make a profit and re-invest part of those profits into further ways to respond to demand. The economy similarly builds onto itself, self-organising and creating order, and this is the nature of economic growth.

Agents build those constraints by adopting ever newer 'ways of making a living' (Kauffman, 2000) that collectively make those constraints materialise, in niches that they discover through a continuous search process. Effectively, this happens through selection and random trial on the basis of existing structures. People or species search for ways to make a living, and when they find one that works, they stick with it, and the fact that they do enables others to find new ways to make a living that build upon that. Existing structures therefore offer a range of niches and new systems that could be discovered and built if agents get to it. The range of immediate possibilities that existing structures offer agents in terms of feasible innovation is what he termed the 'Adjacent Possible'.

Again, this translates exactly in economics, where, for example, innovation builds upon existing knowledge, and the Schumpeterian development of 'new combinations' of inputs to production is made possible by the continuously increasing availability of new products that could be joined up into new combinations. Essentially, as new technological components, materials, know-how and management structures become available, they can become incorporated into production processes, but obviously cannot be introduced until they are invented and made available in markets.

The 'Adjacent Possible' offers a way to organise theory in relation to emergence. Emergence can only stem from what exists in the ensemble of possibilities in the Adjacent Possible. In technological space (the full range of 'ways of making a living'), innovations must be adjacent to what already exists, and thus are not entirely random. However, there are deeper implications than this. First, the number of possible innovations that are members of the Adjacent Possible increases at a pace faster than exponential with the growing number of active innovations becoming widespread, themselves expanding the Adjacent Possible. Second, the system cannot explore all of the Adjacent Possible, as it expands faster than it can ever be explored. Third, the direction of development of the Adjacent Possible is not random but obviously, by definition, path-dependent. Fourth, all of the above makes the evolution of the system non-ergodic. In fact, it is a good and simple explanation of why economic (and biological) evolutionary systems are non-ergodic and out of equilibrium: economies are unable to explore all of their possibilities, because the number of possibilities expands too fast. The pace of growth of the Adjacent Possible in relation to the pace of evolution of the economy prevents the economy from exploring all of its possible states and therefore, by definition, it never has time to find an equilibrium.

5.5. CONCLUSION: COMPLEXITY MATTERS FOR ENVIRONMENTAL GOVERNANCE

5.5.1 *New Concepts for Governance Derived from Complexity*

This chapter brought the reader rather far from the central topic of environmental governance. However, as indicated in earlier chapters, the paradigm of economics that is used in this book is an evolutionary one, a complex adaptive economy. This implies a self-organised evolutionary system. As it turns out, one of the most recurrent features of complex dynamical systems are phase transitions and SOC, observed in a large number of different contexts but with universal behaviour. Most importantly, the economy, just as evolutionary systems, earthquakes and magnetic systems, display a recurrent punctuated equilibrium. In the economy, this takes the form of creative destruction (Chapter 8) and episodic financial crises (Chapter 9). This very distinctive feature arises only in SOC mathematical models, as far as it is currently known. This suggests that the economy, financial and innovation systems could be scale-free networks that exhibits SOC.

One broader insight that can be gained from this chapter is that in systems in which agents strongly interact with one another, fluctuations become amplified and transmitted across the system, to possible spectacular and dramatic effect. This has implications for the stability of systems that policy-makers design using our systems of governance. A system that is highly tuned such that it should theoretically work on time like clockwork is more likely to collapse spectacularly than a system which is designed in a less rigid manner with room for movement that can absorb shocks. Everyone understands this intuitively, for example by using buffers such as capital requirements in finance, spare capacity and time buffers in rail networks, redundancy in communication and road networks, and so on. Humans often understand complex problems intuitively, and in regards to this, governments design regulatory institutions in charge of overseeing the stability of societal components. There is an intuitive trade-off between the 'tuning' of the performance of systems, and their risk of systemic failure (or resilience), and there is also a mathematical description of that.[23]

Two key concepts to take from this chapter are *path-dependence* and *systemic risk*. Path-dependence expresses the idea that every point in time has an equal potential to completely impact and transform the future, such that the future is partly determined by its own past. The economy is not deterministic, and there is no equilibrium path it can return to after a disturbance.

[23] Doyle and Carlson (2000); Carlson and Doyle (2002).

Meanwhile, systemic risk is akin to a statistical externality. It is risk of systemic collapse that accumulates through the uncoordinated action of agents who collectively fragilise the wider network. While they only act on a small component of the system, the interaction between the risk associated with individual nodes collectively adds up to something larger than the sum of its parts. Notably, risky behaviour of small investment funds pose little risk to themselves or the economy on their own, but their proliferation constitutes a systemic danger that can bring down the largest and safest banks.

Lastly, the implications of heavy-tailed statistics have to be mentioned. As seen above, many quantities in complex systems feature noise, or fluctuations, described by heavy-tailed statistics. This includes train and delivery system delays, traffic density, the magnitude of asset price fluctuations, power cuts, supply chain failures and many more. Crucially, the outcomes of policy action may often be plagued by heavy-tailed statistics. The most important implication is that one or more moments of such variables typically become infinite, generally their variance, and in extreme cases their average. If the variance of a variable becomes infinity, then by definition the value of its mean is unreliable. This means that expected values, as used notably in cost-benefit analysis, are not meaningful and likely misleading. For example, the distribution of climate change damages is a well known heavy-tailed variable, and the benefits of avoiding climate change are either infinite or very large and extremely uncertain (Weitzman, 2009).

For economic and environmental governance, four key issues matter:

1. Events at every time point constrain what possible trajectories the future can follow, including through governance. The 'path is made by walking it', where technology diffusion and learning continuously generate a new normal in the economy.
2. It is not possible to unambiguously attribute systemic risk to the behaviour of individual entities. There can be so many elements unknowingly at fault that it may be impractical to act upon an attribution of wrong-doing if known.
3. Measurements of systemic risk must become part of the information used for decision-making, alongside system performance.
4. Heavy-tailed statistics over outcomes of policy choices must be understood and become integrated to thinking, and it implies that expected values cannot be used (for example, in cost-benefit analysis).
5. A tradeoff exists between performance and resilience: optimising systems leads to building systems prone to recurrent failure.

These issues are revisited in Chapter 12 to develop a 'risk-opportunity analysis' framework for decision-making. The next chapter takes these concepts to the next level by exploring all of the contributions to what makes economic projections uncertain. This goes from uncertainty over predictions of individual agent behaviour and decisions, uncertainty that those agents perceive when taking decisions, and uncertainty over how the economy behaves as a whole. This can then be used to better understand the behaviour and predictability of the economy and the structure of what can be known and the reliability of that knowledge. This will be used later on when discussing the science–policy interface in Chapter 12.

6

Fundamental Uncertainty

This chapter introduces the concepts and implications of uncertainty in complex economic models. Uncertainty is driven by different levels of analysis: from the concept of the agent and how he makes decisions (behavioural economics), from the aggregation of interacting agents that leads to emergent outcomes and heavy-tailed statistics (complexity science), and from the non-ergodicity and strong path-dependence of evolutionary models. These sources are analysed and explained, which generates a foundational definition for *fundamental uncertainty*, and delivers a narrative for how to use information generated by complex models attempting to mimic an infinitely more complex reality.

6.1. INTRODUCTION

The world is inherently uncertain – particularly so when dealing with expectations of the future, with human decision-making, with complex systems, or a combination of the three. It is not known for certain what will happen in a century, in a decade, or even in a day from now. Often, one does not fully understand the underlying mechanisms, dynamics and feedback that govern what one observes. In many cases, one is not even aware of what is uncertain, as it is still beyond imagination, which is constrained by the perspective of one's current knowledge base. It is a long debated question in the philosophy of science if certainty of knowledge is even possible, and if so, to what extent and under what circumstances.

Policy success depends to a large degree on policy-makers' ability to anticipate the outcomes of the feasible options they face, in order to formulate strategies that are not only feasible but also effective. The theory of externalities is not sufficient to anticipate policy success. Estimating the uncertainty over the outcomes of policy choices goes in parallel with determining their outcomes: it is what gives confidence in analyses. Standard economics does not typically analyse uncertainty, through some sort of tradition. Indeed, if systems did return to known equilibrium, there would be no uncertainty. But smart policy-makers are not likely to accept that, and thus, why not be honest and simply quantify the confidence ascribed to model predictions? Weather forecasts do this routinely. This is part of the paradigm shift proposed in Chapter 2.

However, this is not simple. The achievement of complete deterministic certainty is obviously not possible, not least because in quantum physics and in social systems, some quantities cannot be measured without disturbing them, and are therefore unknowable. Additional research and analysis may improve levels of understanding of a given system, but can never lead to complete knowledge. Sometimes, research may even discover new, previously unknown or overlooked aspects of a system, thereby increasing the known uncertainty instead of reducing it.

In this chapter, the various sources of uncertainty are discussed, both in the real world and in complexity economics models. An accurate definition for Keynes' and Knight's 'Fundamental Uncertainty' will be derived that will drive much of the rest of the book, as well as underpin how this book recommends to interpret information originating from economic models for use in policy-making. A particular focus lies with analysing the uncertain impacts of policy instruments and the underlying facets of behavioural uncertainty, at the individual and collective levels, which is of central importance for policy-making and any attempts at anticipating policy impacts. The term 'behavioural uncertainty' refers to the uncertain behaviour of individuals and collectives who need to make decisions under uncertainty.

When modelling behaviour, uncertainty is present at two levels: at the system level (agents making decisions, individually or collectively), and at the model level (conceptualising an abstract representation of such decisions). At the system level, agents face uncertainty in their decision-making, which impacts the way in which they decide between alternative choices (e.g., technologies, courses of actions). At the model level, the analyst must formalise a structural representation of such decision-making, for example, in order to anticipate the impacts of potential policy choices. Modelling representations remain of course uncertain themselves, in their structural form and/or their parameterisation. Importantly, behavioural uncertainty determines the potential impact of any kind of policy instrument, even of those that are primarily concerned with natural or technological systems. Lastly, the complexity phenomenon of emergence (Chapter 5) implies the emergence of additional uncertainty originating from the interactions between system parts. Non-ergodicity implies growing cones of uncertainty looking forward, and the potential for heavy tails. This has implications on the ability of policy-makers to steer the direction of travel as opposed to achieving exact end goals.

6.2. WHAT IS UNCERTAINTY?

Despite its importance for all realms of life and science, there is no universally shared definition of uncertainty. Different terminologies are used for the same type of uncertainty in different scientific fields or even by different scientists within a field. At the same time, seemingly common terms might refer to different types of uncertainty. Here, the terminology suggested by Walker et al. (2003) is adopted, who define uncertainty as 'any deviation from the unachievable ideal of completely deterministic knowledge of the relevant system' (p. 5). This definition applies to a wide spectrum of uncertainties, ranging from 'know' to 'not know' and 'not know that we do not know'. It covers uncertainty due to a lack of information, as well as uncertainty due to variability that is inherent to a system, and may persist even when plenty of information is available.

6.2.1 *Uncertainty in the Philosophy of Science*

The nature of uncertainty is deeply rooted within philosophy, and has been discussed intensively throughout the centuries: what can one know about the world in its current and future states, and what are the role and limits of science? The origin, nature, methods, and limits of human knowledge are at the heart of a whole branch of philosophy, referred to as epistemology.

The main epistemological position in natural science and modelling is positivism in the tradition of Descartes. It is based on the premise that it is possible to systematically inquire reality, for example by means of measurement, mathematical and quantitative methods. From this perspective, science is seen as 'the search for and prediction of empirical regularities to make universal, true statements that can be falsified [against observation] in the Popperian sense' (van Asselt and Rotmans, 2002). Accordingly, uncertainty is seen as the absence of knowledge, which can be reduced by means of further scientific enquiry. However, as argued by philosophers such as Hume and Hegel, the knowledge obtained can never be perfect and complete. There always remains a gap between reality and observation, and that gap cannot be fully bridged by reason. In the words of Werner Heisenberg (1958): 'What we observe is not nature itself, but nature exposed to our method of questioning.'

This line of arguments leads to two epistemological perspectives opposite to positivism, namely post-modernism (describing knowledge and value systems as socially-conditioned through history) and social-constructivism (describing knowledge as constructed through interactions with others). Both stress the inherent subjectivism of scientific enquiry. From both perspectives, science is seen as 'a creative process in which social and individual values interfere with observation, analysis and interpretation' (van Asselt and Rotmans, 2002). Taken to its extremes, scientific knowledge is seen as nothing but social 'conventions'. Therefore, although science can lead to knowledge, this knowledge is never certain. This perspective is more dominant in the social sciences than in the natural sciences. Multiple theories aiming at explaining the same phenomena can co-exist, without any one theory having a higher claim to the truth. Uncertainty is not just the absence of knowledge, but can exist in the presence of extensive information. If new enquiry reveals that something is more complex than previously thought, additional information may even increase the overall level of uncertainty. In the words of Shackle (2010): 'There would be no uncertainty if a question could be answered by seeking additional knowledge. The fundamental imperfection of knowledge is the essence of uncertainty.'

While positivist and non-positivist epistemological positions stand at opposite ends with regard to the nature and limits of scientific reasoning, the positivist approach to uncertainty in the tradition of Hume and Hegel is not in fact fundamentally different from, say, a more moderate constructivist position, in that both acknowledge that scientific knowledge cannot be seen independently from the chosen means of enquiry, and they stress that some forms of uncertainty inevitably remain.

6.2.2 *Risk versus Uncertainty*

In Knight (1921) and Keynes (1921), uncertainty is distinguished from pure risk in that uncertainty cannot be quantified using probabilities, while risk can. This is a definition that economists often use, but it sits at odds with definitions used elsewhere. Elsewhere (notably in policy and regulatory practice), risk is defined as the degree to which a valued asset could be destroyed, damaged or affected by specific or unspecified events, while uncertainty refers to a lack of knowledge, without reference to damage. This specific terminology is adopted in this book in order not to confuse different types of readers.

In the practice of risk assessment,[1] risks are defined as the product of hazards, exposure and vulnerability. Respectively, these refer to the degree to which dangers exist in a system (e.g., the frequency of storms and their strength), the degree to which an asset is exposed to those dangers (e.g., whether a ship generally runs into storms, or whether it has the ability to avoid them), and the damage that could be caused (e.g., the degree to which a ship can be damaged by a storm, i.e. the value of that ship that the storm puts at risk).

Quantifiable risk (what Keynes and Knight call risk) can be defined as a situation in which one does not know the future outcome of a system and its impact on valued assets, but knows with confidence the probability distribution of all possible future outcomes and their impacts. This can arise for instance if one has perfect knowledge of a system, but known natural variability exists in that system, so that a known probability can be assigned to every possible realisation, the latter being bounded.

[1] E.g., see the guidelines of UK government in HM Treasury (2020b), and in relation to climate change, see Warren et al. (2017).

Since this is rarely realised, quantifiable risk is mostly confined to a few well-defined situations with rules deliberately created, for example, at a casino.

In contrast, unquantifiable risk (what Keynes and Knight call uncertainty) concerns situations in which one neither knows the future outcome of a system, nor the underlying probability distribution. One does not have perfect knowledge of the system, and hence one cannot assign objective probabilities to all possible outcomes, even if in some cases one can quantify natural variability. In fact, one is not usually aware of all possible outcomes. A prominent example of uncertain outcomes are the future damages from climate change: it remains uncertain in which exact ways the climate system will dynamically react to changing greenhouse gas emissions, and how the resulting changes in the climate will dynamically interact with other natural systems. Thus some situations in which the existence of unquantifiable uncertainty matters is where the likelihood of damaging events is comparatively low, although not vanishingly low, while impacts or vulnerability is very high:[2] taking expected values implies multiplying and adding up small and large numbers, which is inherently unreliable (Weitzman, 2009). In such cases, the variance is very large and not stable even with the inclusion of larger amounts of data.[3]

'Fundamental (or deep) uncertainty' is where not all relevant outcomes are known nor knowable. As neither objective nor subjective probabilities can be assigned to unknown events and outcomes, fundamental uncertainty also precludes the meaningful application of Bayesian statistical approaches, based on conditional probabilities given subjective degrees of belief. Fundamental uncertainty is a shorthand way to express the fundamental property of the economy that the future is not already written somewhere waiting to be accurately discovered, but instead, that uncertain events are contingent upon other uncertain events leading to a complex compounding of uncertainties. This is unpacked below.

6.2.3 *Uncertainty in Policy-Making*

Since there is no escape from uncertainty, decisions need to be taken in a context of incomplete knowledge. While it is sometimes possible to wait or look for additional information that reduces some uncertainty, it is never possible to wait for complete

[2] So-called heavy tails in probability, see Coronese et al. (2019) for the case of extreme climate events.

[3] Note that when heavy tails exist, while the mean is unreliable, as it involves summing up all outcomes times their likelihood, estimations of medians, quintiles or percentiles remain more reliable. Notably, to estimate a median, one only assumes that half of measurements fall below the median, and thus one does not require detailed knowledge of the frequency of rare events above the median. The median does not 'creep' as much as the mean with the inclusion of larger amounts of data (Coronese et al., 2019).

information that eliminates all uncertainty. It was mentioned in Chapter 1 that Rittel and Webber (1973) classify such decision situations as 'wicked problems'. Due to inherent incomplete information and limited understanding of all relevant properties of the system, the process of solving the policy question becomes identical with the process of understanding its underlying drivers. As a result, all decisions are sub-optimal by definition, sub-optimal to what could have been decided had all knowable knowledge been known! Knowledge and understanding continues to improve incrementally as decisions are taken, after which policies may need to be adjusted, which leads to a search for further knowledge and understanding, and so forth, in a never-ending cycle. It becomes clearer why the term 'optimal policy' has no clear meaning.

In the scientific literature, situations in which high-stake decisions on 'wicked problems' must be informed in the context of fundamental uncertainty (such as long-term climate policy) are also classified as 'post-normal science'.[4] Post-normal science contrasted against 'normal science' as defined by Kuhn, where iterative experimentation allows one to resolve testable hypotheses: in post-normal science, experimentation as such is not possible. The system is characterised by both quantifiable and unquantifiable uncertainties, and the process of reducing these uncertainties cannot be separated from attempting to solve the policy-question. Notably, the true impact of any policy decision can only be known after its implementation. While such a policy implementation may be seen as a large-scale experiment, it is never reproducible, as the context is constantly evolving, meaning that the attribution of cause and effect relationships is rarely fully established even after decisions have been taken.

6.2.4 *Uncertainty within Models*

Since uncertainty is inherent to all aspects of the observed world, it also applies to all types of models, artificial representations of that world, that can be defined as 'any kind of abstraction of the system of interest' (Walker et al., 2003). Since '*positive*' (or non-normative) models are simplified representations of cause-effect relationships in real-world systems (either of existing or of hypothetical future systems), the modeller also needs to consider all of the underlying uncertainties. Although models themselves are often deterministic (always yielding the same outcome for the same set of input parameters), the represented system is presumed not (see below). While the model can be an important tool for enhancing the understanding of a system, uncertainties will remain. They are thus an essential component of any modelling activity, and should be analysed and communicated accordingly.

4 The term is not meant to downplay the role of science in any way, and must not be mixed up by present-day discourses on 'post-truth' and 'alternative facts'.

Within models, three different dimensions of uncertainty can be distinguished (Walker et al., 2003):

1. *Location of uncertainty*: where in the model does uncertainty manifest itself?
2. *Level of uncertainty*: how can the uncertainty be classified on a spectrum from completely deterministic knowledge to total ignorance?
3. *Nature of uncertainty*: what is the fundamental epistemological reason behind the uncertainty?

Notably, uncertainty over the outcome of a model that identifies a course of action (a normative model) is not the same as the uncertainty over projections from a model that conditionally forecasts the future (a positive model), and the interpretation is different. In the first, one estimates the uncertainty over whether the policy really is the best course of action, while in the second, one estimates the reliability of the forecast.

The first dimension is the location of uncertainty. Possible locations of uncertainty may be summarised under the following generic classifications:

1. *context uncertainty*, ambiguity in the definition of boundaries of the system modelled;
2. *structural uncertainty*, from the chosen structure and implementation of the model;
3. *parametric uncertainty*, from input data and parameter calibration;
4. *outcome uncertainty*, over model outputs of interest.

The context of a model determines which aspects of the real-world system are represented within a model, and which parts are treated as exogenous to it. Within this process, context uncertainty originates from 'the conditions and circumstances (and even the stakeholder values and interests) that underlie the choice of the boundaries of the system, and the framing of the issues and formulation of the problems to be addressed within the confines of those boundaries.' (Walker et al., 2003). Different people (modellers, policy-makers, stakeholders) can have different perceptions of the real-world system that should be modelled, possibly being related to different world views, framings and prior knowledge. This may translate into different choices of the modelling context and the framing of the research question: what should be included in the model, what are its boundaries, and what are the variables of interest? Such decisions can be explicit or implicit, resulting from tacit values.

Once the system boundaries are defined, a model representation must be formalised and implemented, leading to two different types of structural uncertainty: model structure uncertainty (about the conceptual model formulation), and model technical uncertainty (arising from the technical implementation of a given model formulation).

Structural uncertainty refers to the uncertainty that can result from incomplete understanding of the represented real-world system: the behaviour within a system, its relevant elements, and how they relate to each other. If the true structure and dynamics are not fully known, there is uncertainty about the most appropriate model representation of the system of interest.

Parametric uncertainty refers to the uncertainty arising from the input data, which either describe the characteristics of the system to be modelled, or the external drivers of the system. For models of natural systems, this may be the description of a terrain, map, geophysical properties, or stocks of matter in different locations. For socio-economic models, it may describe the stock of technologies in different economic sectors, the existing infrastructure, or flows of economic value. External driving forces determine the changes within a system, and are not modelled endogenously, which can be uncertain, and include, for example, population and external decisions.

Parametric uncertainty also originates from uncertainty regarding the choice and calibration of model parameters, which are then typically fixed within a model run or scenario. Parameters are determined by calibration, for example, by comparing model outcomes with historical data. Typically, parameters are chosen so that they minimise the difference between observed outcomes and model outcomes, for example, over a period of known history. Importantly, parametric uncertainty cannot always clearly be separated from structural uncertainty. Depending on the model formulation, the same system may either be represented as a model with a very simple structure and only few parameters, or as a very complex model with many parameters.

6.3. DECISION-MAKING AS A SOURCE OF FUNDAMENTAL UNCERTAINTY

6.3.1 *Uncertainty as Part of Decision-Making*

In the context of modelling socio-economic systems, agents can be people who act within a system of interest – either as individuals (e.g., as consumers), or within organisations (e.g., firms or political institutions) – or agents can be institutions and organisations formed of multiple agents. Since the future is uncertain by definition, agents are constantly required to make decisions under uncertainty, while decisions are taken within the context that agents individually and collectively see.

It is a common finding that empirically observed decisions are inconsistent with basic economic concepts of rationality, profit or utility maximisation as defined in standard Expected Utility Theory (EUT).[5] For example, decisions by individuals and

5 Kahneman and Tversky (1979); Tversky and Kahneman (1991); Kahneman (2003), see also Thaler (2016). Note that EUT (Morgenstern and Von Neumann, 1953) is used as the baseline against which 'biases' are defined.

firms are found empirically to be much more sensitive to upfront costs (monetary or otherwise) than to future benefits, which may be related to subjective degrees of time preferences (preferring present over future consumption), loss aversion (relatively higher impact of subjectively perceived losses on decisions), or risk aversion.[6] Such forms of decision-making are not necessarily 'irrational'.[7] Instead, they can possibly be interpreted as a rational strategy for making decisions under uncertainty. For example, when future benefits are uncertain, it makes sense to focus on tangible upfront costs.

Uncertainty is a key element not just for explaining the decisions of individuals, but also of firms. In the Keynesian theory of economics, future demand for products is considered to be fundamentally uncertain, and firms need to plan accordingly.[8] Under such conditions, it is not possible to truly maximise profits over time.[9] Instead, firms base their investment decisions on their subjective expectations, which may or may not turn out to be realised. For example, short of having reliable forecasts, firms may expand production capacity beyond expected demand in order to ensure capacity to cope with potential scenarios of unexpectedly high demand.

In a context of uncertainty, decisions by firms and individuals are not taken in isolation. Instead, decisions by one agent may impact decisions of others. For example, new technologies are typically first adopted by a relatively small fraction of the population, which is characterised by lower risk aversion and higher curiosity (Rogers, 2010). These early adopters provide valuable information to the rest of the population: is the new technology reliable, and does it provide the promised benefits? Waiting and observing the experiences of others can thus be a strategy for reducing uncertainty. This kind of behaviour is common not just for individuals and firms, but has also been observed in primates and possibly other animals.[10]

The modeller must decide how to represent human decision-making under uncertainty in a stylised and mathematically tractable way. As such representations are always imperfect, they lead to uncertainty within the model – be it uncertainty about the appropriate functional form, or uncertainty regarding the input data for a given functional form. There is thus behavioural uncertainty in any descriptive (positive) model that attempts to represent how social systems and decision-making operate and evolve in the real world.

For being useful to policy-makers, a model for the simulation of policy effects must be based on a representation of human behaviour which is as close to reality as

6 Anderson and Newell (2004); Jaffe and Stavins (1994); Gillingham and Palmer (2014).

7 In any other way than for deviating from EUT.

8 See Bellais (2004).

9 In the sense of being certain that no other strategy could generate more profits.

10 For individuals, Bikhchandani et al. (1998); Bala and Goyal (1998); Young (2009); Abrahamse and Steg (2013); for firms, Kapur (1995); Jochem and Gruber (2007); for primates, van de Waal et al. (2013).

possible, in order to plausibly estimate responses of households and firms to changing variables: based on which criteria and evaluation principles do they decide, what do they know, how do they influence each other?

6.3.2 *The Fundamental Uncertainty: How Does Our Brain Work?*

The uncertainty regarding human decision-making starts at a very fundamental level: it remains an unsolved riddle what constitutes consciousness, and how the biological brain and its neurological processes relate to thoughts, behaviour and decisions.

In the dualist school of thought, which can be traced back to Plato ('Theory of Forms') and Descartes ('cogito ergo sum'), a clear divide is postulated between the mind and brain. In this line of thinking, the mind and brain are like software and hardware: the (unphysical) mind as software depends on the brain as its underlying hardware, but both are separate and clearly distinguishable from each other. If this were true, it would hypothetically be possible to reverse-engineer the mind's source code, and to replicate the working of the mind by means of computer algorithms. This is not only a popular theme in science fiction, but also in real science. For example, a large research project in Europe, the 'Human Brain Project', aims at replicating the human brain as computer software – so far without clear success in terms of replicating the brain (Amunts et al., 2016).

From both a philosophical and a natural science perspective, it remains unclear if this will ever be possible. While there is growing knowledge about the neurological functioning of the brain, there is no consistent theory on how the neurological level connects to the mind: While scientists can observe and map neural brain activity, they cannot observe how the biological process of neurons activating each other lead to the emergence of thoughts, dreams, wishes and memories, to name only a few of the processes which likely constitute our personalities. This is further complicated by the observation that the functions of the brain are not as 'hard-wired' as they might appear to be. Various studies with brain-damaged patients show how the brain can adapt, sometimes in surprising ways, and 'relocate' many functions to different parts of the brain.

To further complicate things, it is not only the brain that matters. In fact, it can be argued that it is the whole body that determines our perception of reality, and thus our conception of ourselves, our desires and wishes, and in the end our decisions. Wouldn't we behave differently if we were bats, and can we ever know what the world looks like from their perspective (Nagel, 1974)?

6.3.3 *Decision-Making from the Behavioural Science Perspective*

Due to the inherent difficulty of explaining human behaviour from a bottom-up perspective, today's psychology and behavioural science mainly try to tackle the question from the opposite direction than neuroscience. Instead of analysing mind and brain from first principles, behavioural scientists essentially treat them as a black box, and focus their investigations on the relationship between inputs and outputs to that box. This method of systematic enquiry for understanding the behaviour of humans (and animals) originates in '*behaviourism*', which started in the 1900s, as classical depth psychology (e.g., Freud) proved insufficient for making testable predictions about behaviour.

In contrast to the introspective methods of depth psychology, behaviourism focuses on predictions that could be tested experimentally, by measuring observable behaviours and events. An early famous example is the work by Pavlov, who demonstrated the predictable reaction of dogs to certain external stimuli, and how a dog's behaviour can be conditioned on such stimuli (Pavlov and Gantt, 1928). Obviously, this is a rather deterministic perspective on behaviour, unfit for revealing anything about the inner workings of the brain. The mind–body problem is effectively ignored: it is irrelevant if there is a mind and to what extent the mind is separable from the biological brain. In fact, the methodology of behaviourism could as well be applied to robots – it is irrelevant if a conscious mind or a simple automaton is being observed and studied.

By treating the brain as a black box and thus circumventing the perhaps unsolvable mind–body problem, behaviourism has proven to be a powerful tool for gaining insights into human behaviour from a positivist point of view: how do people behave and make decisions, given different contexts? If asked directly, this is a question that even people themselves could not answer honestly in many cases: they make decisions all the time, often without being certain why a particular decision has been made. In hindsight, people will come up with explanations for their decisions and defend them, but these explanations might have nothing to do with the factors that led to their decisions in the first place. This is hardly surprising: neurological research shows that the brain is ready to execute a voluntary action half a second before someone becomes conscious of his intention to execute this action (Libet et al., 1983).

6.3.4 *Decision-Making from the Economics Perspective*

As seen in Chapter 4, classical economics is interested in identifying the optimal allocation of scarce resources from a normative point of view: how can efficiency be achieved, costs minimised, utility maximised? In microeconomics, these questions are addressed from the (hypothetical) perspective of a perfectly rational decision-maker, the rational agent of economic theory (also known as 'homo oeconomicus'). Importantly, this hypothetical agent is not supposed to describe how individuals do behave and make decisions in the real world. Instead, the rational agent is a construct for describing how people ought to make decisions, if they were indeed acting in line with the axioms of rational utility maximisation. For classical economics and its rational agent, both the mind–body problem and the uncertainties of behavioural science are thus without further relevance.

In behavioural economics, the normative framework of microeconomic theory is taken as a benchmark, against which observed decision-making of people are measured and evaluated. Since no real person is a perfectly rational automaton that maximises utility across time with mathematical precision, such a comparison between observed decisions and hypothetically optimal decisions inevitably reveals discrepancies.

Empirical studies and experiments provide overwhelming evidence that observed decision-making at the micro-level is inconsistent with the axioms of perfect rationality, irrespective of all economic and technological factors (Kahneman, 2003). Therefore, Simon (1955) suggested to replace the assumptions of unbounded maximisation with satisficing behaviour: agents are assumed to behave rationally, but within cognitive limits. Manifestations are heuristics in the form of rules of thumb or the replacement of an originally complex decision problem with a simpler, roughly accurate one. In the decades that followed, several dozen behavioural biases have been identified (Thaler, 2016) – such as the 'availability heuristic' (people estimate the frequency of some event by the ease with which they can recall instances of that event), the 'salience bias' (where people give more weight to facts that are prominently visible, relative to known facts that are not as visible) and the 'endowment effect' (where humans value things that they already possess relatively more).

A famous example for the 'endowment effect' is the classical experiment by Knetsch (1989). Half the participants were given a mug, the other half a candy bar. After a few minutes, those who initially received the mug are asked whether they would like to exchange it for the candy, and those who initially received the candy, whether they would like to exchange it for the mug. Given the assumptions of classical economics, for a rational decision-maker, preferences and the resulting decisions should be independent of the reference point: it should not matter whether a participant was initially given a mug or a candy bar. Contrary to this assumption, however, only around 10% of participants decided to give up the mug to obtain the candy, but also, in plain contradiction of the classical theory, only around 10% of participants would give up the candy to obtain the mug! 90% preferred to keep what they were initially (and randomly) given. Without an initial assignment of these goods, around half of the participants in fact preferred the mug and half the candy.

Such biases are not only random fluctuations (which are irrelevant on average), but constitute systemic deviations from the normative benchmark of the rational agent – which implies that EUT cannot be used as a positive description of human behaviour. The systemic nature of behavioural decision-making was famously demonstrated by Tversky and Kahneman (1974), who systematically mapped apparent 'biases' in human decisions, and conclude that optimality considerations are less relevant than the question, 'What course of action seems most natural in this situation?' (Kahneman, 2003). Based on psychological foundations and empirical observations, Kahneman and Tversky (1979) proposed Prospect theory as a descriptive alternative to Expected Utility Theory (EUT) and its rational agent. The theory is not interested in optimal decision-making, but in actual behaviour as observed in reality. It thereby helps to explain not only the 'endowment effect', but also other biases – such as 'asymmetric loss aversion' where losses are typically weighed roughly twice as much as gains; and the 'status quo bias' where humans are reluctant to changes and tend to stick to default choices.

The predictive power of Prospect Theory rests on three central properties, which were derived from decision-making experiments with people:

1. *Reference dependence* reflects experimental evidence that people do not derive utility from absolute levels of wealth or pleasure (as in EUT), but from changes relative to a reference point (usually the status quo). Positive changes are evaluated as gains, and negative changes as losses.
2. *Loss aversion* describes the empirical observation that peoples' choices are more sensitive to losses than to gains, relative to their subjective reference points. Even when both are of the same absolute magnitude (e.g., in monetary terms), they are perceived and valued differently in the process of subjective decision-making: Experiments show that the relative impact of losses on choices is roughly twice as strong. As a result, people perceive deviations from their current situation as less attractive than what EUT would imply, and therefore show stronger than expected preferences for the status quo and their current entitlements – referred to as 'status quo bias' and 'endowment effect'
3. *Diminishing sensitivity* implies that people tend to be *risk averse* over the probability of gains, but *risk seeking* in the domain of losses: People typically prefer a certain gain of £100 to a 50% chance of winning £200, but also prefer a 50% chance of losing £200 to a certain loss of £100.

From a policy perspective, the insights from behavioural economics imply that the real-world impacts of policies could be very different from what would be expected based on rational decision-making. For example, ignoring the implications of loss aversion can overestimate the market uptake of new technologies by households, and thereby result in expectations of the effectiveness of climate policies that are far too optimistic. In model simulations of heating technology uptake by households with and without the consideration of loss aversion, loss aversion results in higher projected CO_2 emissions by households, and the need for much stronger policy instruments for achieving decarbonisation targets (Knobloch et al., 2019). Even for similar degrees of decarbonisation, accounting for loss aversion implies substantial changes in the underlying technology composition: technology choices become subject to a 'conservative shift' towards low-carbon technologies which are relatively less efficient, but already more established in local markets.

On the other hand, policy-makers can also try to use the knowledge of systematic biases in decision-making to their advantage, for steering people into the desired direction – an approach which is often referred to as 'nudging' or 'libertarian paternalism' (Thaler and Sunstein, 2009). For example, due to behavioural biases, the choice between two options A and B is typically affected by designating either A or B as a default option. The default option is much more likely to be chosen, even in the case of high-stake decisions. For example, Johnson and Goldstein (2003) find that the enrollment in organ donor programs in seven European countries was 97.4% when this was the default option, and only 18% otherwise. Such insights lead to the creation of various 'nudging units' by governments around the world. While nudging can help to increase welfare, such attempts also face the criticism of manipulation (Sunstein, 2015).

6.3.5 *Behavioural Uncertainty from a Macro Perspective*

In addition to behavioural biases, one also needs to consider behavioural diversity. For example, Gaechter et al. (2007) estimate that 88% of participants are loss-averse, with an interquartile range for the loss aversion coefficient of 1.3–3.0. Due to the diversity of perception and heterogeneous decision-making parameters, decisions by agents often differ even when faced with the same problem and data. Given that agents apply heterogeneous decision protocols, it is generally not possible to forecast individual choices. However, possible values of parameters used for decisions across individuals in a group are bounded, and based on plausible assumptions on parameter distributions, it is therefore possible to construct an overview of how the choices are distributed among a sufficiently large number of decision-makers (Knobloch and Mercure, 2016).

Still, the insights of behavioural science remain limited to the systematic mapping of inputs to outputs, given the context of observation or experimentation. While the results might thus have a large degree of internal validity (i.e. the results are consistent and replicable within a given context), their external validity is less well established. This means that while much is known about how people behave and make decisions in experiments, how to make inferences about human behaviour in real-world settings is less clear. Furthermore, behavioural science usually focuses on analysing the decisions of individuals, but has less to say about how people behave in social contexts.

Generally, one has to be careful with the generalisation of behavioural science (such as Prospect Theory) to societal contexts that differ from those under which experiments were made. For example, although loss aversion has been observed in a variety of contexts for individual decision-making, it remains unclear to which extent it also applies to groups of people, which is of interest for policy-making. It is arguably an oversimplifying generalisation that a group should behave like an individual. In reality, it is not clear that all people evaluate choice options using similar reasoning, and to which degree people influence each other (Chapter 7). For example, while people may exhibit loss aversion when facing choices individually, this effect could be weaker or stronger in social contexts, where social interactions produce new collective behaviours.

In addition to an accurate representation of choices by individuals at the micro level, it therefore needs to be considered that choices are not made in isolation, but within a broader context of social dynamics.[11] As discussed earlier, from a more general anthropological perspective, decision-making can be seen under three different theoretical lenses (Wilk and Cliggett, 2007): (1) the self-interested (utilitarian) model, used in microeconomics, in which choices are directed by individual utility; (2) the social model in which decisions are made by social groups, and (3) the moral model in which agents make decisions according to beliefs, values, culture and tradition. Behavioural economics studies biases in relation to the utilitarian model, and has less to say about the other two.

The various possible interactions between humans and their decision-making in societies can thus lead to different outcomes of the decision-making processes: The sum of millions of individual choices made in isolation can be very different from the decision-making of millions of interacting people, who can influence, observe and imitate each other. Agent interactions at the micro-level can lead to unexpected dynamics and outcomes at the macro-level (such as path-dependent, non-linear profiles of technology adoption, Rai and Henry, 2016).

For example, the behavioral bias of loss aversion can help explain why people reject seemingly beneficial choices on an individual level. However, the perceived 'loss' is not set in stone, but depends on a subjective reference point – what is considered 'normal' or as the default choice. In a societal setting, such a reference point is likely to be influenced by others and their decisions, for example, based on observation or societal norms. As long as the societal reference point is well-defined, loss aversion can help explain why societies prefer conservative choices, for example, when choosing between the existing policy and an alternative policy proposal (Alesina and Passarelli, 2019). Once a certain threshold is crossed, the reference point of many individuals could well change. At this point, conservatism can turn into a form of 'fear of missing out':[12] when most of one's neighbours suddenly drive an electric car, this can be the new reference point, against which all choice options are evaluated.

[11] Such as social influences between individuals, see Abrahamse and Steg (2013); Rogers (2010); Steg et al. (2015); Pettifor et al. (2017b); McShane et al. (2012).

[12] Also known as 'keeping up with the Joneses'.

6.3.6 *Uncertainty Aggregation*

It is often assumed, offhand, that the behaviour and uncertainty observed at the micro-scale (individual agents) can be translated or compounded to the macro-scale (groups of agents) simply, such that it is structurally the same. For example, assuming that the 'representative agent' behaves in the same way as individual agents, and that the uncertainty over 'his' behaviour is structurally the same as for individual agents. This notion, true only by assumption, has led the economics community to perhaps become blinded by a focus on behavioural biases observed at the micro-scale to debate problems with theory for the macro-scale. For example, many biases in relation to 'rational behaviour' at the micro-scale have been identified (Thaler, 2016), and many would think they should invalidate macro-scale models based on simple rational behaviour utility maximisation.

Friedman (1953) suggested that lack of realism, or perhaps uncertainty, in model assumptions, can be justified if the predictions of models are validated. He held that to be true notably for firms maximising returns, since otherwise 'it seems unlikely that they would remain in business for long' (Friedman, 1953, p. 22). In his view, agents do not necessarily have the improbable capacity to solve the complex calculations required to maximise utility, but they are found to behave 'as if' they did.

Complexity science indeed suggests that not all rules of behaviour observed at the micro-level are relevant to infer behaviour of the macro-scale. But just as interactions generate the emergence of new behaviour rules at the macro-scale, it similarly generates new types of uncertainty over that macro-behaviour. This is not to say that 'assumptions do not matter', as many have interpreted Friedman's text to mean. Nor that behavioural biases should necessarily fully determine the macro-scale either. In physics, the non-interacting ideal gas case, in which micro rules match macro outcomes, is studied precisely for the sake of showing that it does not exist in reality. Solving the aggregation problem is what links observed micro- and macro-behaviour, through which new sources of uncertainty arise. To paraphrase Anderson (1972), 'more is different', thus uncertainty at the macro scale is more than just N times the micro-scale, the sum of its parts. Thus there is no scientifically valid reason to expect the 'representative agent' to necessarily behave in the same way as individual agents in isolation.

6.4. COMPLEXITY AS A SOURCE OF FUNDAMENTAL UNCERTAINTY

6.4.1 *Uncertainty in Complex Systems*

Much modern economics treats uncertainty as quantifiable, in order to be able to make use of averages and expected values over time and space, and assume equilibrium or steady states. However, the validity of this approach is increasingly challenged as phenomena such as systemic risk and heavy-tailed uncertainty are identified, notably in finance. Is it always possible to calculate objectively expected values, for example of investment portfolios, reliably? The answer is generally it is not,[13] and worse, it may even be best to avoid doing so, in case of undiagnosed heavy tails due to insufficient amounts of data or due to not measuring for long enough to observe extreme events. In those cases, imposing short-tailed uncertainty distributions can be very misleading in the expected values that they generate. And in fact, careful uncertainty treatment becomes important precisely in those cases: understanding the dynamics of the 2008 financial crisis, or the wild propagation of the COVID-19 disease. Can one establish metrics for systemic risk? This may well just be the key question.

Take an investor involved in highly speculative investment schemes, that person 'imposes' a systemic risk externality to everyone else who is an investor. If he is the only one doing so, this may have little to no consequence. But if an accumulation of agents systemically involved in speculative investment arises, the *whole* financial network increases its risk of systemic collapse, although one cannot estimate its likelihood with sufficient accuracy to price it (Chapters 9 and 10). In complex systems, frequency distributions of events often have heavy tails and as a consequence, the standard concept of 'externality' needs to be broadened to encompass systemic risk. Being a collective phenomenon, it cannot be attributed to anyone in particular, and thus it cannot be priced and traded away in a Coasian way. A trade-off also exists between the performance of systems and their stability, which has important consequences for planning and decision-making (Chapter 12).

Complex systems as defined in Chapter 5 have particular properties with regard to uncertainty. Since they are characterised by the emergence of phenomena that stem from the interactions of internal elements, they are characterised by emergent uncertainty as well. It is not possible to exhaustively enumerate all the possible ways in which internal micro-elements can cooperatively produce different types of macro-phenomena, and therefore, unquantifiable uncertainty exists over whether one should expect to see unexpected things. This may offer a better and clearer definition for fundamental uncertainty and why it exists and pervades most observed real systems.

Take the two-body problem of physics (see Chapter 5, e.g., an isolated pair of orbiting cosmic objects). Their collective behaviour, due to gravity, can be predicted with very high accuracy, for all practical purposes forever, with little to

[13] However, it is always possible in principle to calculate expected values subjectively, in other words, to the best of one's knowledge, which is not so much objective as it is contingent to the information available and its subjective interpretation. Investment risk in this case is dependent on that information's interpretation.

no uncertainty. The uncertainty compounds 'linearly', in that the total is the root of the sum of the squares of the measurement uncertainties, the latter known to be unrelated to one another.[14]

For the three-body problem, since the accuracy of prediction declines with forecasting time span, necessarily the uncertainty, initially stemming from uncertainty over exact starting conditions, grows over time to something larger than parametric (root sum square) uncertainty. It grows due to the non-linearity of the problem.

In the more general and common situations dealing with complex systems, one is often not even certain which are truly independent variables, and thus whether the full range of uncertainty can be estimated using just a root sum square rule. But furthermore, uncertainty distributions are not knowable, since if 'long-range correlations' exist, unobservable weak relationships between variables can become driving factors during extreme events, where everything begins moving together. In such cases, probability distributions typically have heavy tails, with heavy weighting towards one or both ends that declines more slowly than the normal distribution. Take the sandpile model of evolution of Chapter 5: most elements are normally not connected to others, except during large collapses, where everything collapses together. That system possesses a heavy uncertainty tail.

6.4.2 *Uncertainty in Collective Action: Emergence*

In complex systems and complex networks, two general features of uncertainty arise that may not be seen in non-complex systems:

1. uncertainty is unquantifiable because emergent phenomena cannot be exhaustively enumerated;
2. uncertainty tends to be heavy-tailed because too many known and unknown relationships exist between elements of the system.

The second point relates to the first in that one can generally not assume knowledge of all connections that exist in a system and thus cannot exclude that the uncertainty is not heavy-tailed. Since tail uncertainty is challenging to measure, as extreme events are rare and data is limited, what probability distribution one chooses is critical

[14] Measurement uncertainty is usually normally distributed. If every point in a normal distribution is itself uncertain and normally distributed, the resulting probability distribution is a 'convolution' of the two probability distributions. The resulting standard deviation is the root of the sum of the squares of the two underlying distributions, i.e. if $Z = f(X,Y)$, then $\Delta Z = \sqrt{\left(\frac{\partial Z}{\partial X}\right)^2 \Delta X^2 + \left(\frac{\partial Z}{\partial Y}\right)^2 \Delta Y^2}$. This is called 'uncertainty propagation', and can be calculated across models so long as theoretical relationships are known, and that uncertainties are uncorrelated (no relationship exists between X and Y).

to one's understanding and expectation of uncertainty. For example, assuming a normal distribution for the damages of climate change allows one to calculate expected damages as a simple function of cumulative emissions, while assuming a heavy-tailed distribution, depending on its heaviness, can generate either infinite or near-infinite damages with as large uncertainty. The choice of a probability distribution equates to making some inference about missing data. It is to be noted that for policy-related purposes, it is only the use of expected values that is to be abandoned; however, important policy-relevant information also exists in the tail. The reasons this arises are as follows.

The micro-level behavioural analysis discussed in the previous section, over the system micro-foundations, is in many ways similar to the fundamental Heisenberg uncertainty that exists in quantum physics over the position and momentum of individual particles or atoms. In the same way that the behavioural rules governing individual components of one system level do not completely determine whole system behavioural rules governing a higher level of collectivity, since many behavioural features emerge from collective action across interacting parts, system uncertainty finds new sources that stem from limits to knowledge on all the different ways system elements can interact. That uncertainty can 'overwhelm' the micro-level parametric or structural uncertainty, since uncertainty on whole system behaviour is more than the sum of uncertainty over the individual components.

Take a domino chain standing idle in a noisy environment:[15] while one domino has a well-defined likelihood of falling over on its own due to the ambient noise (e.g., wind, vibrations), estimating its likelihood of falling over due to its neighbours falling over is complex as it depends on the likelihood of its neighbours' neighbours falling over, which depends on their respective neighbours, and so on. These teleconnections generate a compounding effect that spans as far as the whole chain of dominoes, the so-called long-range correlations. Here, the likelihood of a domino falling due to its neighbours is much higher than the likelihood of it falling over due to the ambient noise, and the likelihood of the whole chain falling over collectively (the systemic risk of an extreme event) is many orders of magnitude higher than the likelihood of all individual dominoes falling over on their own independently due to the ambient noise.[16] Thus, the fact that elements are chain-linked means that this system has a high likelihood of extreme events (the collapses are likely to be big), and thus the likelihood of systemic collapse is heavy-tailed but the exact probability function is not straightforward to determine.

Examples of policy-relevant problems include the failure of transport, water or power networks, financial crashes, disruption in industrial supply chains, and other types of cascading failure problems.[17] Since variations trigger variations, just like

15 The noise being parametric uncertainty over external forces acting on individual dominoes.

16 The uncertainty obtained from the root sum square rule.

17 See Gallos et al. (2005); Kishore et al. (2011); Vespignani (2012); Bak (1996).

earthquakes trigger earthquakes, and financial losses trigger financial losses, it is in fact often the study of noise in complex systems that reveal information about their propensity to produce extreme events, and to possess tipping points.[18] Looking at the 2007 financial crisis, the widespread use of a normally distributed compounding of parametric uncertainty led to vastly underestimating systemic risk (Adams and Thornton, 2013).

6.4.3 *The Adjacent Possible*

The emergent fundamental uncertainty in complex systems is often but not always larger than the compounded uncertainty over the behaviour of all agents or constituent parts combined. For example if it was known that agents in a collectivity were certain to act in complete harmony and coordination, then the collectivity would behave just like one individual. However, if creativity exists in the ways agents decide to interact with one another, then substantial emergent uncertainty of yet another kind arises.

It is useful to return the concept of the 'Adjacent Possible' (Kauffman, 2000) introduced in Chapter 5, which suggests that self-organisation in economic systems creates structures, which are used as a basis to create more structures, such that the range of possibilities of what can be created increases faster than the economy can explore them. This is the true reason why the economy is never in an equilibrium, as it does not have time to explore all of its internal possibilities before they have changed. But also, it implies that the economy is path-dependent and non-ergodic, as it builds upon its own successes as agents continuously search for and adopt new 'ways of making a living' (Kauffman, 2000).

As with the three-body problem, path-dependence has particular implications for uncertainty. It implies that uncertainty necessarily must increase with the distance to any time horizon that may be considered by agents when forming expectations over the future, as well as for the observer/modeller himself. The uncertainty over what could take place in the economy is contingent on all the possible path-dependent directions that the economy could take from its present state through innovation.

Imagine for a moment that one agent (who could usefully be called the 'social planner' or 'representative agent') is in possession of all knowable knowledge, the present economy's configuration and immediate possibilities, the economy's Adjacent Possible. Even with that degree of comprehensive knowledge, that agent could not foresee all the possible futures and what they imply, in effect, just due to the sheer number of such possible futures contingent on present-day possibilities and all of the future possibilities contingent on the full range of innovations developed at each future moment. That sheer number rises faster than exponentially, simply due to its combinatorial nature. It may well take a very large and fast computer longer

18 See, e.g., Lenton (2020); Lenton et al. (2008).

than the age of the universe to foresee all of those futures; in fact it may well take a computer longer to generate and parse that information than it takes the future to materialise.

For example (following Kauffman, 2000), take the OECD's PATSTAT database for patents (see Chapter 8). It forms a large 'scale-free' network of several million entities recorded since the 1970s. Innovative activity implies entrepreneur agents using one or more of these patents and combining them with one another and/or new resources in order to file more patents. The number of new patents that can be formed by the combination of these $N \sim 10^7$ patents is the Adjacent Possible. The size of the Adjacent Possible is in principle approximately $N^N = 10^{70,000,000}$, representing all possible recombinations of patents to make new technologies. However, this is too large since no innovator is likely to combine a large number of patents. Imagine that up to $n \ll N$ patents can be combined, where n may be of the order of 10–20. Then the size of the Adjacent Possible is of the order of 10^{60} to 10^{114}, which is still a large number.[19]

Actual innovation during the next time period, say a year, will comprise a very small subset of this range of possibilities. But this small addition, call it $\Delta N \ll N$, will expand the source that generates the new Adjacent Possible, which becomes $(N+\Delta N)^n$, which is approximately $(N^n e^{\frac{\Delta N}{N} n})$,[20] necessarily greater than N^n, even if not that much greater, and even for relatively small ΔN. If the economy cannot explore all of the vast Adjacent Possible's N^N, or more realistically N^n, possible innovations at time t, it has a declining ability of ever exploring its even vaster future Adjacent Possible at every subsequent time $t+1$, $t+2$ and so on.

Thus, the notion that an agent would be capable of enumerating and optimising the range of possible futures is readily shown to be impossible. But more importantly, the above fact provides a good explanation over why it is not possible to form probabilities over future events in order to take expected values to form expectations. The combinatorics are impossible for an agent, or for that matter a modeller, to fathom. Rational expectations are thus not humanly or even computationally possible. That is the true nature of fundamental uncertainty. It emerges out of multi-agent interactions, from the tendency of agents to search for and adopt 'new ways of making a living' that build upon those of others, or in other words to innovate in a way contingent on all previous innovations and existing capabilities of the economy, generating too many possible futures for anyone to be able to enumerate and compare them.

19 In principle this number is $\sum_{k=1}^{n} \frac{N!}{(N-k)!k!}$ with k increasing in the sum up to $n \ll N$. However, keeping only the largest component of the sum, this whole expression can be approximated using Stirling's formula and determine that it is at least equal to N^n/n^n.

20 Since $(N+\Delta N)^n \simeq e^{n(\log N + \log(1+\frac{\Delta N}{N}))} \simeq N^n e^{\frac{\Delta N}{N} n}$.

Another way to look at that uncertainty problem is to consider what would happen if one were to 'replay the tape' of history. Assuming that history is not pre-written in God's Grand Book of Events, or in other words, that the tape records but does not prescribe history, then at each unit of time, events and creations by autonomous agents impose to the system new possibilities that become part of the Adjacent Possible, and influence the range of possible choices the collectivity of agents can make. The collectivity never has time to evaluate what is the absolute best way forward, due to the sheer number of possibilities, and thus continuously makes sub-optimal but sufficiently good choices for the economy to keep growing, although some periods of mass extinction (or perhaps financial crises) and disasters do arise with power law-distributed frequencies. If one replayed it several times, the tape of history would necessarily be vastly different every time, and there would in fact be as many tapes of history as one has time to play them, all of which gradually diverge from each other exponentially in configuration space over the tape length. The rate of divergence is simply related to the rate of innovation. The rate of innovation is not so fast that innovations have time to prove themselves and become widespread before becoming threatened with creative destruction by other innovations. However, the rate is greater than zero.

6.4.4 *A Complex Systems Definition for Fundamental Uncertainty in Economics*

Keynes and Knight both wrote their respective books in the 1920s on probability, more or less simultaneously, describing risk and uncertainty for use in economics and the sciences of prediction. Economics is a science that analyses events as they take place in time, contingent to events that have taken place at earlier times, and thus benefits from such definitions. Recent work in post-Keynesian economics has generated a more precise definition for fundamental uncertainty (Fontana, 2008). However, Keynes and Knight certainly could have benefited from the concepts from complexity science that are now available, to formulate a more precise formal definition for fundamental uncertainty.

Perhaps it is the approach of Kauffman (2000) given above that is the most convincing. At each moment, the economy creates more economic and business opportunities than it has time to explore, and therefore the economy is, by definition, always away from and searching for an equilibrium. But since autonomous agents have some agency over their situations, they can in principle take consideration of the degree to which the future is uncertain to them according to their experience, and adopt an adaptive response. By expecting extreme events to arise, in which domino chains of arbitrary (power law-distributed) length collapse, agents build in some coping capacity. In other words, they expect to some degree the collectivity to fail, search for coping mechanisms and create elements of redundancy.

In economics, this would translate into a tendency for economic agents not to operate at full capacity and maximum profit, in order to maintain a buffer capacity to respond to sudden changes in system direction. *They invest in more capacity than they need to prepare for the unknown*. This leads to the existence of what is called the output gap, the difference between the economy's output and its maximum capacity to produce. However, to prove this point is not simple, and is not the intention in this chapter. Suggesting a full explanation and empirical justification for this will take the rest of this entire book and more.

6.4.5 *The Systemic Risk Externality*

Agents that are not coordinated by a superior force have no way of correctly forecasting the collective behaviour of other agents in order to optimise their own within that context.[21] Their behaviour can be more or less risky to their own situation, something on which they have to some degree of agency according to their risk preference. However, the risk that they impose to the collectivity can be more than the risk they impose to themselves as individuals.

Take for example risk-taking in financial networks in which agents invest in stakes in the profits of other agents who are also engaging in very similar risk-taking strategies (see Chapter 10). The risk they take is in fact compounded by the risk taken by others, which is compounded by the risk taken by yet others. If each agent has a reserve capacity to absorb losses, such that they do not transmit them to their peers, then sudden random losses might disperse rapidly in the financial network. However, some agents may not have a substantial capacity to absorb any losses; in comparison to what they observe around them, then, they are likely to pass on any losses that come their way to their peers if they default on their commitments. If many agents are in that position, it is likely that losses can travel and amplify far across the network, as in a large domino collapse. The closer the agents are to the insolvency limit, and the more numerous, in comparison to ambient noise, the higher the risk is to the whole collectivity of agents. This is the origin of systemic risk.

In standard normative welfare economics,[22] externalities add up linearly, in that agent behaviour that imposes an inconvenience (or benefit) to peers is generally considered attributable and to have a well-defined value, which can be compensated for by a well-defined Coasian transfer of money. In complexity economics, the value that compensates for systemic risk is not well defined since costs or benefits are

[21] See, for example, Brian Arthur's El Farol Bar Problem (Arthur, 2014), in which an agent tries to predict whether the El Farol bar will be too crowded on gig nights in order to decide whether to go or not, given that other agents are also trying to forecast the same and also making their decision to go contingent on their own predictions. There is no rational expectations solution to that problem. More generally, the problem of adaptive behaviour conditional on adaptive expectations is rich with complex dynamics (Arthur et al., 1997b).

[22] See Perman et al. (2003); Hanley et al. (2019); Hanley and Barbier (2009); Bateman et al. (2002).

heavy-tailed. In practice, it is difficult to appropriately price systemic risk and this is partly the reason why financial crises happen. Attribution of cause is also not possible, and thus who should pay the undefined price is also undefined.

Nevertheless, the externality exists. Its nature is that, as discussed in Chapter 5, the closer the system is to the edge of chaos where the SOC regime lies, the heavier the tail of the fluctuations and magnitude of extreme events becomes, where it becomes a power law at the boundary. The system becomes brittle and prone to collapse. Increasing the capacity of agents to absorb shocks is what reduces the externality. It is known to some degree that the more optimised systems are, the more they are prone to collapse.[23] This is obvious in financial networks (Chapter 10), but it is also the case in ecological networks.[24]

6.5. CONCLUSION AND OUTWARDS LOOK

Economics in general pays little attention to uncertainty. In some sense, it might just stem from a flawed intuition that one can always turn uncertainty into risk and sum up probabilities times quantity and only work with expected values, without paying much attention to what is going on with variances or higher moments. It is clear that in financial economics, more attention is generally given to volatility. But it is also known in that field that most time series are not stationary and have all sorts of peculiar properties such as clustered volatility, memory and non-ergodic noise (see Chapter 9). This is clearly an area under active development, particularly since the 2008 financial crisis; however, findings made by the rising field of econophysics are not generally taken seriously by economists in the mainstream.

Much of what comes next in this book revolves around issues of path-dependence and growing uncertainty with projection time spans. In many ways, if one could really enumerate and rank predictions of the future as easily as representative agents with rational expectations can, investment would be substantially less risky, and the world could indeed be as simple as it is in mainstream theory, and in equilibrium. In rational expectations, agents could be said to collectively agree to work cooperatively to make their collective behaviour simple to describe. But venture capitalism could hardly exist in a world in which everyone could equally well foresee the future, which in some sense requires future inventions to already be invented. And indeed, it is precisely through path-dependence that strategic behaviour pays off.

To paraphrase Thaler (2016), in the game of chess, what would happen if all players could foresee all possible chains of moves by both players and enumerate every possible way the game could end in order to optimise strategy? It would not make any player better off, but would make playing the game take a lot longer. It remains

23 See Doyle and Carlson (2000); Carlson and Doyle (2002), from which a literature has emerged on the brittleness vs performance tradeoff.

24 Bak (1996); Kauffman (2000).

an interesting question the sheer amount of computing power that it takes to beat humans at chess, or at 'go', and thus, humans truly are good at foreseeing the future in complex settings. But there is a clear limit: these games show remarkable emergent complexity despite that they are composed of such simple rules, and the real world of people is not so simple. The human mind cannot beat the complexity of the real world, let alone the complexity of the real world of interacting humans.

This ends the section of the book in which tools of pure complexity science are developed. The next chapter begins to apply the tools of non-equilibrium economics to key problems in environmental governance, starting with the diffusion of innovations and new low-carbon products.

7

Micro-foundations for Consumer Theory

In standard theories of innovation diffusion, agents have full knowledge of markets and products from birth. However, it is known from empirical research that the diffusion process takes time and is self-reinforcing. Here, it is shown that if one takes a standard model of innovation diffusion with utility-maximising agents, but modified to assume that heterogeneous agents start in life with no knowledge but learn through peers about the existence of products, one observes the emergence of clusters of agents with relatively homogenous sets of knowledge within the clusters, but knowledge that is heterogeneous across the clusters. Fads and fashions arise, transitivity in aggregate preferences is lost, and non-equilibrium path-dependent diffusion dynamics emerge. Aggregate utility cannot be optimised anymore. Instead, an evolutionary theory of the diffusion of innovations arises naturally. Elements of this chapter were adapted from Mercure (2018).

7.1. INTRODUCTION

The nature of most policy programs for reducing greenhouse gas emissions consists in a combination of low-carbon product creation, the diffusion of low-carbon durable and non-durable goods and some changes in behaviour. However, the larger part of the effort goes towards incentivising the adoption of existing low-carbon innovations by consumers and companies, goods such as solar panels and electric vehicles, using policies such as subsidies and carbon taxes. It is therefore of utmost importance that policy-makers understand how the diffusion of innovation process works. Yet, surprisingly, this process, well known empirically, is essentially absent from models, which tend to assume that innovations are adopted as soon as they are technically economical. This chapter develops a general theory and model that explains and reproduces empirically observed patterns of diffusion.

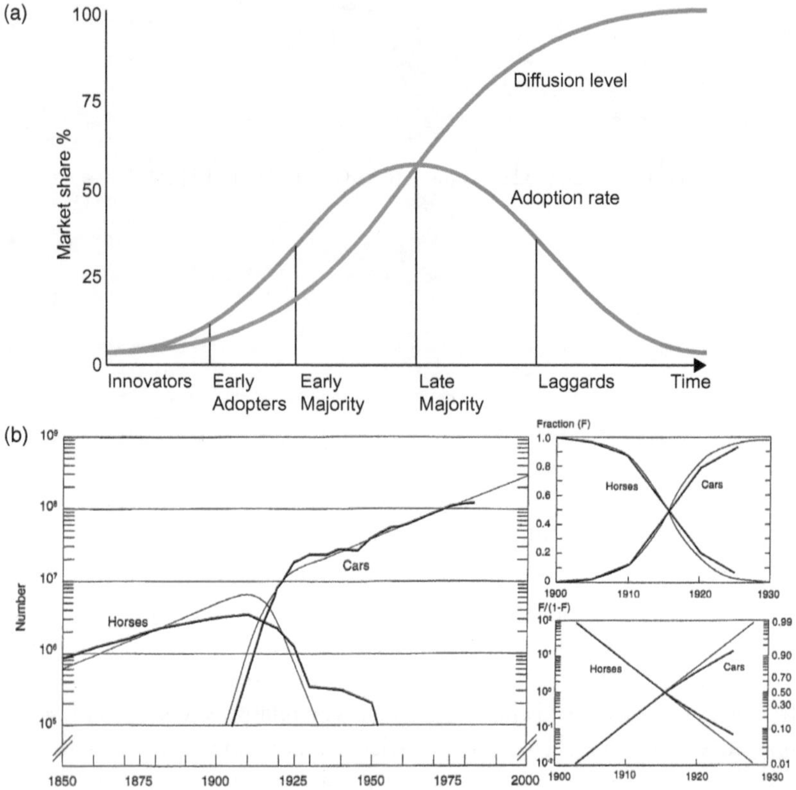

FIGURE 7.1 (a) The diffusion of innovations with different types of adopters. (b) Example of the replacement of horse-drawn carriages by internal combustion engine cars, reproduced from Nakicenovic (1986). Here, the total number of vehicles increases exponentially but the proportion of each type follows the S-shaped curve above.

The diffusion of innovations is not an instantaneous process, nor is it an equilibrium process. In 1943, researchers studied the uptake of farming innovations by US farmers, and observed a particular structure in which neighbour effects contributed to their wider acceptance, leading to a bell-shaped curve in rates of adoption (Ryan and Gross, 1943). In 1963, Rogers published his seminal work on the diffusion of innovations, in which he observed a recurrent feature: the uptake of innovations followed a slow exponential take-off, followed by a fast and steady linear adoption profile, which eventually slowed down in a saturation process (Rogers, 2010). This stems from interactions between adopters, starting with early adopters who influence the choices of various categories of later adopters. This process is now famously known as S-shaped diffusion profiles (Figure 7.1).

It is clear that diffusion processes are sufficiently slow that they can be well observed under a standard frequency of economic measurement (e.g., quarterly, yearly). This represents a process of change in which adoptions of innovations or new products influence and promote further adoptions of the same, and intrinsically implies a process out of equilibrium. For example, people having seen a movie influence others whether or not to go and see the same film, and thus the number of sales is never at a steady state, never in equilibrium. Even when external (exogenous) variables do not change (e.g., income and prices), sales of products grow and decline over time. Many examples of studies of S-shaped diffusion processes exist in the diffusion literature[1]. Just as in ecology, in which the growth of populations of some species can take place at the expense of others, it has been argued that diffusion profiles follow types of ecological mathematical systems called Lotka-Volterra[2]. In general, the diffusion process is one that involves communication across complex networks, some kind of epidemic process. Mathematically, diffusion problems are non-linear and therefore, standard equilibrium consumer theory, notably using equilibrium substitution functions, may not be appropriate to study the substitution of products when their diffusion is not stable.

This is a process involving inter-agent interactions. Trends and fashions are important factors driving the diffusion of innovations, in which, typically, the diffusion of a product reinforces its own ability to diffuse. Such crowd effects arise only in models that include multi-agent interactions. As stated in Chapter 5, complexity theory contends that the addition of multi-agent interactions in a model leads to the emergence of new structures, which depend predominantly on the nature of the interactions, and to a lesser degree, on the rules of behaviour of agents in isolation. Even if one used a utilitarian model, with interactions, what maximises the utility of individual agents does not necessarily maximise aggregate utility (Kirman, 1992). Crowd effects have been studied in contexts such as financial markets, technological lock-ins, information cascades and herd behaviour in firm decisions, the diffusion of innovations, and social influence in discrete choices.[3] In that context, since the representative agent is a theory without explicit multi-agent interactions,[4] and that it assumes that a steady state equilibrium takes place, it does not model the diffusion of innovations very well.

1 See, e.g., Grübler et al. (1999); Nakicenovic (1986); Sharif and Kabir (1976); Fisher and Pry (1971); Mansfield (1961); Farrell (1993); Kwasnicki and Kwasnicka (1996); Marchetti and Nakicenovic (1978).

2 Named after Lotka (1925) and Volterra (1939), normally applied to ecological systems. Volterra researched a solution to the problem of changes in fish populations in the Adriatic sea after the First World War, where the latter had prevented fishermen from fishing for some time, thus changing the balance of population growth and decline. The same Lotka-Volterra equation system has been used to model the evolution of technology, see, e.g., Morris and Pratt (2003); Karmeshu et al. (1985); Farrell (1993); Lakka et al. (2013); Mercure (2015).

3 Respectively, see Arthur et al. (1997b); Arthur (1989); Bikhchandani et al. (1992); Banerjee (1992); Young (2009); Kreindler and Young (2014); Brock and Durlauf (2001); Durlauf and Ioannides (2010).

4 Agents interact with one another through the economy only, i.e. through prices clearing markets, but agents do not influence the behaviour of other agents.

A deeper study of the problem reveals that information transfer between agents and its credibility is in large parts at the root of the issue.[5] In standard consumer theory, agents are infinitely lived and have full knowledge since all time of all goods in all markets and possess innate ordered transitive preferences over all of these things. Furthermore, the menu of consumption options does not change. However, if one allows that agents are not infinitely lived, and not born with complete 'objective' knowledge (albeit with preferences) of all goods in all markets, and that new goods are being introduced from time to time, then agents *must* learn in order to consume.[6]

Information acquisition models are known to behave similarly to disease propagation models,[7] as they possess the typical structure of an evolving complex network. The adoption of innovations extensively follows the same dynamics.[8] If knowledge of all goods is not equally shared by all agents, then knowledge of goods in markets, and their value, ceases to be 'objective', as different bits of knowledge become shared only by subsets of the population (social groups), and no product can be unambiguously established across the population as superior, on average, to any other.

To summarise the problem, in standard models, the list of products to consume does not change and all agents know in detail all products offered in all markets and their absolute preferences over each of them. The representative consumer is a model meant to represent all of that. The question is how to credibly introduce information acquisition in standard models of consumer behaviour, and what that means for quantitative economic modelling, consumer tax policy, market placement and innovation policy. More generally, the question can be framed as, starting with a simple utilitarian world (which is in fact disowned later), what are the rules governing the behaviour of the representative consumer in a theory where multi-agent interactions are included?

The representative agent may still be a utility maximiser. However, he unavoidably will have *additional behavioural traits* that individual agents do not have: the crowd effects. These emergent crowd effects between interacting utility-maximisers, as is known in complexity theory, cannot be exhaustively enumerated. The macro-behaviour may then differ considerably from the micro-behaviour. Considering this, then, one may enquire what the relationship is between a theory of learning agents, if there exists one, with standard classical consumer theory. And it is useful to do this as by doing so, one can understand the connection that exists between standard normative utilitarian models (Chapter 4) and path-dependent descriptive models of consumers.

5 Young (2009) positions diffusion as stemming from contagion, social influence, social learning, or a mixture of these. Here the meaning is not specifically about credibility as information asymmetry (Akerlof, 1970), although this could easily be included in the model.

6 Ultimately, one must acknowledge that agents are not infinitely lived, and are born without any knowledge at all. Every consumption habit that people learn will have been demonstrated by someone somewhere, in most likelihood someone near, e.g., a family member or friends.

7 See Arthur and Lane (1993); Lane (1997); Young (2009).

8 E.g., as known in empirical work, see Mansfield (1961); Fisher and Pry (1971).

The inclusion of agent preference heterogeneity in standard consumer theory lies in the realm of Discrete Choice Theory (DCT).[9] In DCT, one measures in data the heterogeneity of revealed preferences in a population of consumers (e.g., modes of travel in a city) regressed against a number of variables (e.g., income, distance travelled, age, gender, occupation) to determine aggregate preferences, and how choices would change if the underlying variables changed.

DCT models are equivalent to standard substitution models under budget constraints, and pave a way to define the representative consumer from statistical micro-foundations. This average man displays elasticities representative of the aggregate response to economic contexts of an underlying population of heterogeneous agents, behaving stochastically and/or having different preference ranking orders.[10] Even when taking into account imperfect information, optimal choices of information-seeking agents, facing costs of information acquisition, although influenced by prior beliefs, match the standard multinomial logit (Matêjka and McKay, 2015). DCT thus establishes quite clear micro-foundations for deriving the aggregate behaviour of a population of *non-interacting* heterogeneous agents in equilibrium, in which the representative agent has the same behavioural rules as individual utility maximisers in isolation. The issue is clear: DTC is a static picture – the list of choices cannot change because any change in the list of products available can lead to irreversible radical 'flips' in market allocations that violate the equilibrium assumption. Thus all agents are infinitely lived and know all products since the dawn of time until the end of time; there is nothing new to learn or discover, and market shares of products change marginally with marginal price changes (or other variables).

In a real economy, consumers have incomplete knowledge of markets, because entrepreneurs exist who create new products, and consumers can thus learn about and try new products. Schumpeterian entrepreneurs continuously strive to introduce new differentiated products in attempts to secure profits by capturing the interest of consumers. Agents are subject to the influence of other agents in their choices, attracted to novelty products. When following their peers, agents make choices that violate the ranking of preferences that would have been theirs without interactions with their peers while learning about products, existing or new. Their preference rankings change endogenously because of their peers. Thus the number of agents who know any product at any time continuously changes, as trends come and go, making knowledge in the economy 'subjective' (i.e. context- and agent-dependent).

If the standard model of consumers was approximately correct, it could be acceptable; the problem is that for consumer markets, it is wildly incorrect,[11] and

9 The seminal work is by McFadden (1973) and Domencich and McFadden (1975). A great review textbook was written by Anderson et al. (1992).

10 Stochastic theories of economic behaviour take the same stance and mathematical form (Aoki and Yoshikawa, 2007).

11 In problems such as transport mode choice, it is reasonable to assume that agents are equally aware of all the options they have, and their characteristics, and may be less likely to follow

leads to important structural problems, despite that it enables economists to keep using the optimisation approach. It is challenging, however, to offer a replacement model, because it is bound to become path-dependent, and path-dependence is a challenge to work with. Here, the goal is to construct the simplest possible theoretical microeconomic foundations for a non-equilibrium consumer macro-theory involving the diffusion of innovations, and the introduction of differentiated products by entrepreneurs.

This is the aggregation problem for consumers. Standard DCT is modified to include social influence. However, instead of looking for equilibria, focus is kept on the dynamics. Indeed, the connection between discrete choices and the dynamics of diffusion is not clearly established in existing literature.[12] The reason to focus on dynamics is that fads and fashions, originating from social influence, inherently change over time, and this is critical for consumer markets.

For example, imagine the case of the market for moving pictures. People may, on average, see one film or less per week. People often choose which films to watch through peer recommendations. They do not already know all the films on show, obviously. If agents require, say, between one and three recommendations to decide to watch a film, and usually see one film a week, the timescale of diffusion for a film to take off will be several weeks, longer than the quarterly timescale of economic measurement. This ordinary system is not in equilibrium under the measurement timescale. In fact, for an equilibrium to exist in a market when prices and income are constant, choices must settle to a steady state under a timescale much shorter than the measurement frequency, which is often not the case for consumer goods and services (especially durables).[13] As for moving pictures, most consumer goods markets are in continuous flux and change, and thus, it is explicitly chosen not to look for fixed points in the theory, and time as a variable becomes important.

For the sake of clarity of the model, standard discrete choice consumer theory is first reviewed, and subsequently modified. A theory of interacting consumers is built from micro-foundations by incorporating social influence (i.e. learning) in a standard discrete choice model, and the non-equilibrium dynamical implications explained. Were there no new products appearing in the market, consumption habits would indeed converge towards a small number of homogenous goods in equilibrium. This never happens in reality, and thus innovation is explicitly included, and the model leads to product diversity with a composition that changes over time. It is shown that

their peers, and for that, DCT is shown to work well (DCT in fact was developed for problems of transport mode choice). However, to assume that the same is true in consumer markets is problematic, because agents do not know all their options, they are influenced by peers in their choices, and, new products appear all the time.

12 See Kreindler and Young (2013, 2014); Matějka and McKay (2015); Young (2009).

13 The analysis of social influence in equilibrium of Brock and Durlauf (2001), used, for example, in choices between schools or other long-term social choices, does not apply to the problem here. Brock and Durlauf (2001) analyse *choices* (e.g., voting) but not *adoption* (e.g., purchasing), the latter involving a rate of change of market shares and thus time.

by decreasing the strength of multi-agent interactions to zero, standard consumer theory is restored, where a phase transition takes place. The roles of innovation, diffusion and the entrepreneur, of an evolutionary nature are discussed. Finally, it is concluded that in a model of heterogeneous learning agents, the meaning of facts and knowledge is subjective to context, and thus the concept of utility of the representative agent, normally used in welfare theory, is ambiguous in a model where agents learn. It is noted that while consumer tax policy acts as an incentive orienting the diffusion trajectory, problems of optimal tax policy have no solution.

In this chapter, some mathematics unavoidably have to be used, because the mathematical root of current theory is modified. For the sake of this book and style, maths are kept to a minimum, at the unfortunate cost of losing exactness, but improving readability. Detailed maths are given in Mercure (2018) and summarised in the appendices.

7.2. REVIEW OF EQUILIBRIUM CONSUMER THEORY

7.2.1 *Choice Modelling in Equilibrium*

Standard DCT in equilibrium is reviewed first, upon which is later built a non-equilibrium DCT. DCT provides a consistent methodology to determine aggregate (or most frequent) choice of a group of non-interacting heterogeneous agents that face a menu of options, for example, a list of model-brands of cars, or different house-heating devices, microwaves or other appliances with different characteristics but providing the same service. Consumer theory is not always expressed in the form of DCT, but as helpfully demonstrated by Anderson et al. (1992), all equilibrium consumer theories are equivalent.[14] Agents are considered who make choices between products to purchase, in diversified markets, in order to maximise their personal utility. Agents do not substitute variable quantities of all products, not due to budget constraints, but because they cannot or do not need to.[15] Product diversity means that goods exist in sets that achieve the same purpose, but that possess varying characteristics and prices.

Heterogeneous utility maximisers have preferences that are described in DCT using probability distributions.[16] Thus the choice process is described as the

[14] Mathematically, they can be transformed into one another.

[15] E.g., in choosing between cars, restaurant meals, they do not choose between two of A versus one of B, they compare one for one.

[16] For which the Gumbel distribution of width σ (or double exponential) is appropriate: $F_i(U) = e^{-e^{-\left(\frac{U-U_i}{\sigma}\right)}}$, $f_i = e^{-e^{-\left(\frac{U-U_i}{\sigma}\right)}} e^{-\left(\frac{U-U_i}{\sigma}\right)} dU$, where f is the probability distribution, F the cumulative distribution, U is an arbitrary utility value, U_i is the mean utility associated to product i and σ is the diversity of the population. This statistical distribution is widely used to describe extreme values, such as daily maximum wind speeds.

comparison between the frequency distributions of utility maxima (how often, in a population, one product is preferred to another one). The measurement of how frequently an option is the favourite across the population is interpreted as a likelihood of it being realised. Anderson's 'Linear Random Utility' logit regression model is used here, in which utility is regressed against a number of socio-economic variables V^x that vary across agents, for the set of choice options denoted $i = 1, 2, 3, \ldots$

$$U_i^* = \beta_i^1 V_i^1 + \beta_i^2 V_i^2 + \beta_i^3 V_i^3 + \cdots + \epsilon_i, \tag{7.1}$$

where the βs represent various socio-economic parameters (elasticities), the Vs are the matching socio-economic variables (e.g., income, prices, preferences, etc.), and ϵ_i is the remaining unexplained error. The star denotes the stochastic nature of U_i^* (it is distributed). In the binary choice case, one computes the frequency at which option i generates, on average over a diverse population, more utility than option j. This yields the well-known logistic function of the binary logit model (see Appendix A):[17]

$$P_{ij} = \frac{1}{1 + \exp\left(-\frac{U_i - U_j}{\sigma}\right)}, \tag{7.2}$$

where depending on whether the mean utility is higher for option i or j, the preference P_{ij} tips towards one or the other options following a smooth step function of width σ, which represents general heterogeneity (see Figure 2.1).

Choices, however, are generally not binary, and the problem is to find the preference in a wider set of options. To treat more than two options simultaneously, one evaluates the probability that an arbitrary utility value U is higher for one choice than for all possible alternate choices in a set of n possibilities (see Appendix A),

$$P\left(U > \max\left[U_1^*, U_2^*, \ldots U_n^*\right]\right) = P\left(U > U_1^*\right) P\left(U > U_2^*\right) \cdots P\left(U > U_n^*\right), \tag{7.3}$$

and then one determines the probability that the utility of option i is greater or equal to U, given that U is greater than the utility of all other choices:

$$P\left(U_i^* > U \middle| U = \max\left[U_1^*, \ldots U_{i-1}^*, U_{i+1}^*, \ldots U_n^*\right]\right) \tag{7.4}$$

One finds that the probability P_i of agents choosing option i over all others is the simple weighted ratio of exponentials:

$$P_i = \frac{e^{\frac{U_i}{\sigma}}}{\sum_j e^{\frac{U_j}{\sigma}}}, \quad \sum_i P_i = 1, \tag{7.5}$$

which is called the the standard multinomial logit (MNL).

This, as it happens, is identical to the thermodynamics of simple gases of non-interacting atoms or molecules, and some insights from there can therefore be

[17] Here, when $U_i \gg U_j, P_{ij} = 1$, while when $U_j \gg U_i, P_{ij} = 0$, with fractional values between. The utility difference required for either option to have $1/(1+e)$ the probability of the other is $|U_i - U_j| = \sigma$, the width of the distributions.

borrowed. It is of the exact same universality class. Ultimately, all theories of non-interacting agents have to be similar within their universality class. Thus here, agents are like atoms in a vessel running around consuming and bumping into each other but not exchanging any information. All of what they know, they have always known.

In DCT, all changes in prices or other variables that induce increases in the utility of the representative consumer correspond to Pareto improvements, and thus are interpreted as beneficial to the community. In equilibrium, one finds that the utility of the representative consumer is maximised with respect to marginal changes in variables, which respects the principles of welfare economics. When variables change (e.g., prices, income, age, occupations), choice allocations re-arrange themselves in such as way that the utility of the representative agent remains maximised. For example, if one option becomes more expensive, agents consume it less frequently and consume more of the other options, but the utility remains maximised.

The utility of the representative consumer has also been given interpretations in terms of information theory (information minimisation, see, e.g., Anas, 1983), and has been used directly as an indicator of aggregate welfare for choices in public policy.[18] Note that this system is a reversible one in which the passage of time is not considered, nor innovation or the introduction of new products. The introduction of new products would change the menu of choices, would be irreversible, and would therefore involve non-equilibrium dynamics, ultimately leading to a different equilibrium. This is because with the addition of a new product, a complete discontinuous re-organisation would result.

From the above detailed microeconomic first principles, the model of constant elasticity of substitution can be derived (see Appendix B). Maximising utility in a model of *Constant Elasticity of Substitution* (CES) under budget constraint generates exactly the MNL equation. This indicates that the MNL is not only consistent with a standard utility maximisation model; it actually forms its micro-foundations. The choice of products in the MNL thus matches general equilibrium theory.[19] The problem discussed here in fact pervades all of general equilibrium theory. Thus it implies that in any general equilibrium model, there is no learning by agents, and making new products available is to some degree inconsistent, as agents cannot discover them. Effectively, the assumption is that agents knew these new products existed all along but they were never able to access them before. And indeed, the damning fact is that none of this theory can reproduce the standard S-shaped diffusion pattern observed empirically in all goods and services (Figure 7.1), unless prices move in such an odd way that by accident this profile is generated.

18 See, e.g., McFadden (2001); de Palma and Kilani (2009); Small and Rosen (1981).

19 CES models underpin much of Computable General Equilibrium (CGE) modelling (see, e.g., Dixon and Jorgenson, 2013), widely used for quantitative economic analysis.

7.2.2 Limits of Equilibrium Consumer Theory

Equilibrium consumer models are quite restrictive: they *require* that agents (1) *do not interact* with one another, (2) *know from birth* all products in all markets, (3) are able to express a complete ranking of their preferences for every product, and (4) have an *unchanging stock of knowledge.*[20] Such a system is, in fact, equivalent to systems of individual agents interacting with the economy only through demand/supply signals, but not with each other. Unchanging stocks of knowledge imply no novelty products, which implies no innovating entrepreneurs, and no diffusion of innovations, and thus no entrepreneurial profits nor productivity change and therefore even no economic growth!

Indeed, if one allows that agents find value in consuming products that *other agents* also consume (non-price interactions), then the corresponding discrete choice theory model that incorporates fashions and trends inevitably takes a radically different form. Formally, if agent *k finds value in consuming product i because other agents* ℓ *also consume it*, with intensity α, then a term that links the utility between agents must be added to the utility equation (valuing other people's views):

$$U_i(k) = \beta_i^1 V_i^1(k) + \beta_i^2 V_i^2(k) + \beta_i^3 V_i^3(k) + \cdots + \alpha f\left(\sum_{\ell} \beta_i^4 V_i^4(k,\ell)\right) + \epsilon_i(k). \quad (7.6)$$

When such interactions are introduced, the absolute ranking of options breaks down in ways unpredictable with standard consumer theory, since preferences of agents depend on preferences of agents recursively. For example, popular items become more popular, because their popularity makes them more visible than other items. However, if this valuation of others' preferences is weak and reduced to a smaller and smaller α value, then the original equation and standard theory is restored again.[21] These are the limits of a non-equilibrium consumer theory with multi-agent interactions, which falls back to the standard theory. However, the above model cannot be treated using optimisation algorithms, because optimisation finds no solution to recursive problems; it searches forever.

Taking a step back, it is clear that preferences are *subjective*, and vary over space and time, rather than have a unique equilibrium. Agent rankings of preferences that exclude social influence could be seen as unrealistic, since what then drives agent preferences, if not his/her surroundings, cultural and family context, social class, social role, etc.? (e.g., see Benhabib et al., 2010) Trends and fashions *do* occur, and the popularity of novelty products *can* generate significant prosperity to particular entrepreneurs, while old products become disused. They also drive product diversity

[20] The unchanging stock of knowledge is implied because agents have no way of discovering new products.

[21] Note that an optimisation is guaranteed to have a unique solution only when $\alpha = 0$.

through consumption that is homogenous within social groups and heterogeneous across them.[22]

7.3. A GENERAL THEORY FOR INTERACTING CONSUMERS IN ECONOMICS

7.3.1 *The Problem of Heterogeneous Knowledge: When Everyone Knows Different Things*

A model is now introduced in which agents, before purchasing goods, must learn about their existence: people are born without knowledge of any product. Product use is social group dependent. Product diversity is large, and there is no need to assume that agents know of all available products at all times. Manufacturers adjust product diversity over time to match consumer tastes, in such a way that consumers do not need to search the whole market for goods; they are offered goods mostly tailored to their differentiated tastes. Firms consider that consumers do not need to be made aware of all the possible products that, individually, they are not likely to desire (firms do not spend unnecessarily on unproductive marketing).

Product diversity in vehicle markets was characterised by Mercure and Lam (2015), who found that it is comparatively large, and the frequency distribution of vehicle purchase is related to the income distribution, and differs by region of the world, even though in principle all vehicle models are technically available everywhere. This suggests that preferences are subjective, contextual and vary geographically.

It is known in sociology that purchase choices are often made through visual influence. In vehicle markets, it has been shown empirically that choices are made through visual influence within social groups, geographical areas, even price brackets (e.g., McShane et al., 2012). Households of a particular level of income and social identity do not therefore seek to know the full breadth of goods that target other income and social identity groups, as they already know in which market they will be searching. Explanations are suggested by socio-anthropological theory and observations, for example, in the 'anthropology of consumption' (Douglas and Isherwood, 1979), which describes consumption as an act of context-dependent social interaction.[23]

Agents are unlikely to purchase goods that they have never heard of, seen, used or seen used (e.g., as observed by Rogers, 2010). Instead, they are more likely to purchase goods that peers own or buy (credible information sources), such that they know what they are buying. In the present model, influence happens through *interactions* between agents. For example, the more people own a particular type of vehicle, the

[22] E.g., see Young (2001). See also Burke and Young (2011) for a good introduction to this topic.

[23] I.e. consumption does not happen solely for maximising the utility of lone individuals, but rather, as an act of communication of social identity between several individuals.

more often it is observed by peers, and the higher the likelihood of new sales of the same. In such a model, across the choice probabilities of agents, options cannot be equally weighted. Instead, they must be weighted by their *popularity*. The diffusion of innovations occurs through the diffusion of knowledge that stems from interactions across agents. This allows a theory where knowledge of the existence of new products starts from zero.

When everyone knows different things (*heterogeneous knowledge*), the stock of knowledge varies between agents, with only partial overlaps between any possible pair. When communication interactions exist between agents, the stock of knowledge of each agent changes over time. If products also change over time, the stock of knowledge of agents over products does not increase indefinitely; they can forget about older products gradually discontinued (e.g., landline phones) and learn about new ones (e.g., smart phones). Agents increase their (subjective) utility by purchasing amongst the products that they *know*, but each agent can maximise his own utility on a different set of choices (with a different maximum welfare).[24]

Social groups are defined here loosely as groups of agents having a relatively homogenous stock of knowledge and preferences, agents linked to one another by the *popularity* of particular consumption habits. This gives rise to product differentiation between, for instance, social, cultural and economic classes.[25] It leads to a so-called local conformity/global diversity effect (Burke and Young, 2011). Such a theory provides a robust basis to define *bounded rationality* in discrete choices beyond 'satisficing' (Simon, 1955), as shown below.

7.3.2 *Theory for Strongly Interacting Consumers in Economics*

For the sake of following standard consumer theory in its own utilitarian universe, a representative consumer is defined in a bounded-rational system of information-sharing utility maximisers, but where utility includes valuing other people's

[24] Here, the assumption is kept that agents maximise their individual utility, in order to keep some comparability and consistency with the standard model. Of course, as discussed widely in the literature and in Chapter 4, it is not clear that humans are self-obsessed utility maximisers. In the context of DCT, and in the case here, evolutionary DCT, whatever utility is, it ultimately disappears from the equations, and in some sense, does not really matter, as long as agents are allowed to compare certain products upon a certain basis for ranking their preferences. In other words, absolute levels of utility are never used in this theory, which only uses comparisons, and the similarly ill-defined term 'cost' could be used instead.

[25] E.g., some social groups, may be choosing amongst products of a completely different nature to other social groups, for example, across social classes or cultural groups. As emphasised by Douglas and Isherwood (1979), these groups of consumption norms are often separated by price barriers.

views, actions and purchasing behaviour. This drives the model away from the self-interested model and towards the social and moral models as defined by economic anthropology (Chapter 4).

The popularity/visibility of choices can be represented by correctly weighing option choice probabilities in the equations given above. The more an option is chosen, the more it is valued, and the reverse is also true. In a random sampling of information-sharing agents, the relative frequency of picking agents who use product i is the share of the market occupied by product i, denoted S_i.

What one obtains is a recursive problem of the form (see Appendix C):

$$P_i = \frac{S_i e^{\frac{U_i}{\sigma}}}{\sum_k S_k e^{\frac{U_k}{\sigma}}} + [\cdots], \tag{7.7}$$

which is not anymore exactly the MNL. The problem is that the second term $[\cdots]$ arises that makes things complex to solve. Effectively, as the utilities change, the number of consumers acquiring and getting to know these products change, and their ability to communicate about them changes, and thus the stock of knowledge changes. This is a recursive problem, and recursive problems must be analysed to see if they converge to anything.

7.3.3 A *Unique and Shared Equilibrium Set of Knowledge Does Not Exist*

The equilibrium solution does not exist! Formally, it can be shown that if one assumes an equilibrium, one obtains an absurdity. The equilibrium is a steady state; this means that all agents who could increase their utility have done so, otherwise they would change their choices, and it would not be a steady state. This means that the shares of the market should have converged to the choices, as is the case in the MNL.

It can be shown (see Mercure, 2018) that for a general form of the preferences as depending on other variables, the only solution is for one of the preferences to be equal to one, while all the others are zero, where all agents have converged to the same preference, and all prefer just one thing. This would be the case if one waited for a sufficiently long time, for example, waiting for everyone to have finally become convinced to behave like everyone else, but the time to wait for all preferences to settle on one single product would be very long, since social influence and diffusion take a long time to operate. Here, it is not the point of the model to wait for years until everything settles. For shorter timescales, this breaks the basic assumption and observation of existing product diversity. Thus it is concluded that the market shares of products cannot be equal to the probabilities of agents choosing them, but always lag behind (unless one waits for a very long time) and thus that one cannot have an equilibrium in this system and product diversity at the same time.

7.3.4 *Knowledge Propagates Like a Disease*

The adoption of innovations is never instantaneous, and this is due to the fact that consuming a product takes time: consumers have dinner once a day, purchase a new car every few years, change their mobile phone when the contract finishes, and tend to use up the eighty tea bags in a box before they purchase a new box or change brand, given a change in context (price, characteristics, etc.). Thus, whereas preferences P_i are instantaneous (if one surveys consumers, they are always able to give their opinion immediately), the shares of product use S_i lag behind preferences with a time delay, due to the time it takes to act on those preferences.

This has far-reaching consequences. Imagining that a large price change takes place all of a sudden (e.g., the introduction of a tax): it does not make the shares of product sales change at the same instantaneous rate. This is because agents need to, for example, finish the box of tea bags, wear out or pay off their car, finish their mobile phone contract or decide to eat out, each of which imply a different average statistical time lag. A price or utility change inducing changes in the preferences gives an *incentive* for agents to change their actual choices, which pulls product sales in a particular direction at a rate that is the inverse of the time lag. The actual value of the market share strongly depends on what its value was at a time just before the change in price or utility took place. Thus, product shares may lag behind preferences with an average time lag, but market shares could also have any value depending on their history. Meanwhile, preferences also evolve as the shares change, and 'aggregate tastes' evolve with agents discovering products and telling each other. Thus, the probability of agents choosing a product depends on its market share, and its market share depends on the probability of agents choosing that product at previous times.

For example, imagine that the Mini Cooper is popular, and gradually drains sales of other vehicle models. However, a subsidy is granted all of a sudden on electric vehicle sales including the much less visible Nissan Leaf. The Leaf may begin to absorb market shares from the Mini for a high enough subsidy, but its sales may not necessarily jump to a new level above the Mini instantaneously. It will take time for people to first reach the need to change vehicle, second to reform their preferences according to what the new market looks like, and thus to take advantage of the subsidy. Therefore, one can expect that Leaf sales will change direction and grow faster, perhaps at the expense of the Mini, whose sales may grow more slowly at the expense of other brands. This may take several years to happen, because the lifetime of cars is around eleven years, while if this happened in the smart phone market with time lags of two to three years, it could evolve much more quickly.

These are hallmarks of a dynamical system, in which the market shares are *hysteretic*, and *path-dependent*, that is, the shares are multi-valued functions, the preferences depending on configurational history. In other words, different market shares can arise for the same utility, depending on what happened before. Such a problem cannot be analysed with a standard linear regression, because of this multiple valuation and hysteresis issue. In such a system, multiple equilibria (or limit cycles) may exist, but they are not necessarily straightforward to identify (Hofbauer and Sigmund, 1998); however, equilibria take too long to reach (years for durable goods), and therefore their existence is not searched for; focus is kept on the properties of the dynamics.

Thus while the preferences provide a signal of agent choices, it only applies to those agents who are witness to product use, and this is a fraction of agents equal to the shares. The simplest possible adoption model is constructed below, which involves a rate of replacement equal to the inverse of the time lags. In a dynamical model of adoption, there is an in-flow of market shares for each product category when people buy products, and an out-flow of shares when people finish consuming the products and choose something new.

After some mathematics (Appendix D), one in fact obtains the general form of the replicator equation of evolutionary theory (Hofbauer and Sigmund, 1998). The replicator equation expresses the evolving populations of interacting species in ecosystems. Here, they are 'ecosystems' of consumer goods, and this shows that in fact, consumer markets are evolutionary.

One form of this system is the Lotka-Volterra finite differences equation of population dynamics in competing species,[26]

$$\frac{dS_i}{dt} = \sum_j S_i S_j \left(A_{ij} F_{ij} - A_{ji} F_{ji} \right), \tag{7.8}$$

where the matrices A_{ij} and F_{ij} are rates of substitution and preferences when given a choice between product options i and j. This equation has been used, for example, for modelling technological change in low-carbon transitions,[27] but it is also used in ecosystem biology and other fields of enquiry.

To make this clearer for the reader, this equation is the S-shaped diffusion equation for the case of many options interacting at the same time. If the number of options is reduced to two, then this reduces to a logistic curve, and produces exactly the pattern observed in Figure 7.1. The length in time of the S-shaped curve depends on the product of the matrices A_{ij} and F_{ij} (rate of replacement times the rate of preference). This equation is also very easy to use in models.

Figure 7.2 shows a comparison of model behaviour between this non-equilibrium (NEQ) replicator dynamics model and the MNL model. While the NEQ model shows continuous evolution even when utilities are constant, the MNL displays changes only when the utilities change. This means that, for example, a new tax

[26] See Mercure (2018) for a derivation based on the arguments here; see also Mercure (2015) for another derivation based on the population dynamics of technology systems.

[27] See Mercure (2012); Mercure et al. (2014, 2018c).

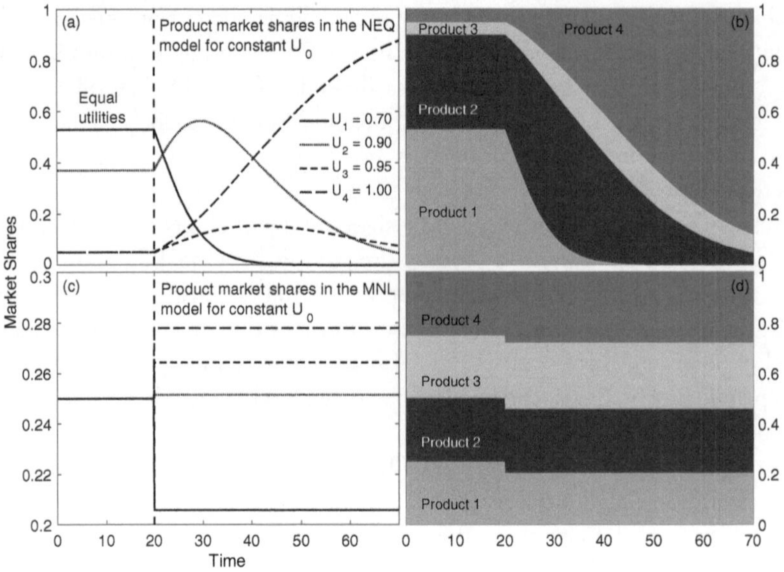

FIGURE 7.2 Outcomes of the non-equilibrium (NEQ) (Eq. 7.8) and the multinomial logit (MNL) models, for a set of 4 competing products, with constant utilities U_0 and different shares at the starting point. At $t > 20$ (in arbitrary time units), utilities become different. In (a) and (b), the NEQ model displays a gradual process of diffusion of products. In (c) and (d), the MNL gives constant market shares before and after $t = 20$, settling instantaneously at new values.

or subsidy will kick-off the diffusion of new products in the NEQ model, while in the MNL a tax must continuously change in order for the diffusion of products to proceed continuously, since an equilibrium is reached for each value of the tax. This implies a fundamental difference between models, and an important policy implication: in equilibrium models, to completely disincentivise the consumption of a particular product using a tax directed at that product only, the good must be taxed with an infinitely high rate! This is not the case with an evolutionary model, where an ordinary constant tax rate could drive down preferences over time for one product to such an extent that it just disappears from markets.

7.3.5 *On Stochasticity, Irreversibility, Path-Dependence and Lock-ins*

A system in equilibrium would be so independently of the configuration of product use and knowledge. In the present case it is not, and furthermore, it can be shown that it is generally irreversible, meaning that the state of the market will depend on configurational history. The simplest way to demonstrate irreversibility is to take the system and make it travel around a circle in product space and back to its starting point, and see if things have changed (Appendix E).[28] One finds that as the system travels around a closed path (by, for example, creating a tax, and removing it afterwards), the utility of the representative consumer does in fact go back to its original position, suggesting that the system is reversible and not path-dependent.

However, this changes when the choice menu is changed during the process, in particular when adding new products. As opposed to the MNL, this can be done without substantially disturbing the system by including new innovations with very small market shares, consistent with how innovations normally diffuse. New products appearing with very low shares have little immediate impact on the market even if they are very attractive, as it takes time for consumers to discover them and tell their friends. If a path is considered in which an innovation is added to the list along the way, the system becomes path-dependent, and not reversible, since once products are discovered, they remain in the memory of agents. But furthermore, this system also becomes path-dependent for any level of small disturbances in shares or utilities, and the system cumulates these small disturbances, as with Arthur's Polya Urn (Chapter 5). Thus, unless the system is considered perfectly deterministic, with no fluctuations, it remains just about reversible; but small fluctuations break this reversibility very quickly, as shown next.

Changes taking place in time are now considered, where a path of utility that goes back on itself is created, such that the start and end points have the same utility value set for all products (e.g., with tax policy that is introduced, and later withdrawn, making some products more attractive for a time, and then not anymore). This should not generate a change of the utility of the representative consumer at the start and final point, as the shares evolve but afterwards undo themselves back to where they started.

Including small random events, one can imagine that the shares and the utilities vary with the noise. These small contributions to the diffusion of market shares do not cancel out, but instead, accumulate over time. Even for vanishingly small amplitude disturbances from random events, because the system is non-linear, its evolution becomes path dependent due to that accumulation, which can readily be observed computationally.[29] For slightly different series of fluctuations, the system takes slightly different directions, but these minute changes of directions accumulate to produce completely different paths. The name is given of 'weak path-dependence', which leads to a typical 'butterfly effect', where different simulations have outcomes that diverge from one another exponentially with simulation time span, due to

[28] Note that learning-by-doing experience curves are not yet included, which are sources of irreversibility. Once these are included, the system is unavoidably path-dependent, but for clarity, consumer systems already have some type of path-dependence without those implied by the accumulation of technical expertise at making products in learning curves. Learning is explored in Chapter 8.

[29] E.g., it is observable on a computer due to rounding error on 16 bit floating point variables.

different accumulated random fluctuations, just as was discussed in Chapter 5. This emerges strongly due to the non-linearity of the recursions in the diffusion model where variables depend recursively on themselves: a very slightly higher popularity induces a slightly higher level of sales, which in turn means an ever slightly higher popularity, and so on, which accumulates. Very small initial differences can mean large differences in the long term.

Now, in the case of new products, it is imagined that along the path, a new product is created by entrepreneurs and introduced in the market, at time t_1, with very small but non-zero shares, denoted as choice option ℓ. Assuming that it is an attractive product, shares will leak out from other competing products towards this new product as people buy it. The process before this happens is reversible, but afterwards, it is not possible to 'un-invent' product ℓ, since as time passes, it may have acquired growing shares (i.e. not vanishingly small any more), when reversing the context (e.g., removing a policy), the change in the utility of the representative consumer does not go back to its starting value. This denoted 'strong path-dependence': introducing new products in the market opens new possibilities that did not exist before, and new degrees of freedom in which the system can evolve.

A key property of this system is that it implies increasing returns to adoption of innovations (i.e. adoptions leading to increased likelihood of adoptions). Increasing returns have been discussed extensively,[30] including in Chapter 5. There, it is shown how the existence of increasing returns to adoption in a system of two products with identical benefits leads to a situation where the dominance of a technology is determined by comparatively insignificant historical events in early stages. In the presence of decreasing returns, small fluctuations would instead cancel out and disappear in the aggregate, maintaining path-independence. In the presence of increasing returns, fluctuations cumulate, resulting in path-dependence.

The introduction of an innovation in the market involves work (including in the thermodynamical sense): it represents an injection of potential utility that the system can henceforth reach. This allows the average utility, and the utility of the representative agent (which represents welfare in standard models) to reach a new range of values. This is irreversible, meaning that this new amount of utility cannot be taken out afterwards.

Strong path-dependence is radically different from weak path-dependence: the system takes a new trajectory, enabling, in effect, the exploration of areas of utility inaccessible in the past. Intuitively, one expects that only innovations providing users with higher utility are likely to successfully diffuse in the market. With a flow of innovations, the system can feature indefinitely increasing utility of the representative agent, as new products with higher utility are gradually adopted, and products with lowest utility are gradually phased out and forgotten. This, in effect,

30 See Arthur (1989); Arthur et al. (1987); Anderson et al. (1989).

corresponds to Schumpeter's process of economic development, as discussed below. Innovations can also fail, and policy can also play a role in changing the state of the system.

7.3.6 *Theory for Weakly Interacting Consumers in Economics*

It is now possible to develop micro-foundations for a non-equilibrium consumer theory, and this is the critical step. It is challenging to do without mathematics at all, and thus the non-mathematical reader is urged to bear with the author, it will be translated to every day language in the following section, and this can be skipped. Starting from the random utility function of *individual agents* who are interacting with their peers, the macro (collective) behaviour is derived. Having interactions means that *consumers value information gained from other consumers*, and thus the interaction term of Eq. 7.6 can be fleshed out:

$$U_i = \beta_i^1 V_i^1 + \beta_i^2 V_i^2 + \beta_i^3 V_i^3 + \cdots + \alpha \log \left[\frac{1}{N} \sum_k^N \delta_{ki} \right] + \cdots + \epsilon_i, \tag{7.9}$$

$$\delta_{ki} = \begin{cases} 1 & \text{if agent } k \text{ owns or uses product } i \\ 0 & \text{otherwise} \end{cases},$$

where N is the number of agents. Here, $\log \delta_i(k)$ gives $-\infty$ amounts of utility for an unknown option i, and zero otherwise, reflecting that agents cannot choose what they do not know. α is a scaling parameter that is discussed below, in arbitrary units of utility. Importantly, the parameter α determines how comparatively strongly agents value other agent's behaviour amongst other things.

Appendix F derives the utility of the representative agent that this leads to, and the replicator equation that emerges from arbitrarily weak interactions (of strength α) between agents. This is

$$\frac{dS_i}{dt} = \frac{1}{\tau_i} \left[\frac{\tau}{\tilde{\tau}} \frac{[S_i]^{\frac{\alpha}{\sigma}} \exp\left(\frac{U_i^0}{\sigma}\right)}{\sum_k [S_k]^{\frac{\alpha}{\sigma}} \exp\left(\frac{U_k^0}{\sigma}\right)} - S_i \right], \tag{7.10}$$

which, for durable products, can also be expressed as

$$\frac{dS_i}{dt} = \sum_j S_i^{\frac{\alpha}{\sigma}} S_j^{\frac{\alpha}{\sigma}} \left(A_{ij} F_{ij} - A_{ji} F_{ji} \right). \tag{7.11}$$

It is already known that if the time for consumption τ_i is reduced towards zero, one obtains an equilibrium model. One now also finds that if, in addition to tuning τ_i to zero, one also tunes the multi-agent interactions α towards zero, one recovers the equilibrium MNL, where

$$S_i = \frac{\exp\left(\frac{U_i^\circ}{\sigma}\right)}{\sum_k \exp\left(\frac{U_k^\circ}{\sigma}\right)}. \tag{7.12}$$

This shows what the connection is between equilibrium and non-equilibrium consumer theories. Adding learning interactions between agents and time lags in consumption in this model takes the model from the MNL of standard consumer theory, to the replicator equation of evolutionary theory. When $\alpha/\sigma \to 0$, if the price context changes much more slowly than the product purchase turnover rate $1/\tau_i$, standard consumer theory is recovered, the MNL, in other words utility optimisation under constraint.

7.3.7 *Translation into Standard English*

In the above calculation, the utility of agents was amended from the linear model of the standard theory to include the process where agents value what other agents consume in their decisions. A formulation was added of this in which agents have nothing to value if they do not know the products in question, in other words they do not choose a product that nobody uses, but add substantial value when the products are used. With just that, the evolutionary equation already discussed (Lotka-Volterra) is discovered! This requires the inclusion of the time lags involved in consuming products, and a certain relative influence of the social influence effect in relation to other considerations in product choice such as prices and perceived product qualities. As stated above, this evolutionary equation reproduces the S-shaped diffusion curve of Figure 7.1. In fact, it is clear in the theory of Rogers (2010) that the diffusion pattern happens through interactions between agents, therefore this is consistent.

It is also found that if the time lags are assumed to be so small that they do not matter, then the preferences and the market shares become equal again, as in the standard MNL theory. Furthermore, if the social influence parameter is so small that it does not matter in relation to other considerations, then the standard MNL choice model is also recovered. This is important, as it shows under what conditions one obtains an evolutionary consumer model: where there are time lags, and where there is social influence (or any kind of influence), again consistent with Rogers (2010).

This result also means that this problem is one of correlations between agents and their behaviour, a complex 'many-body problem', where interactions in this case imply a 'frustrated' dynamical system without equilibrium. As soon as learning interactions are included between agents, however small, the model becomes non-linear and goes out of equilibrium, and complexity, hysteresis and path-dependence arise. This is a phase transition, which exists between the MNL and the evolutionary model.

7.4. THE SUPPLY OF NEW PRODUCTS: BUSINESS, INNOVATION AND DIFFUSION

7.4.1 *Innovation and the Supply of New Products*

In this model, for any degree of social influence, however small, if the context remained static for a sufficiently long time, shares would catch up with preferences where either all utilities associated with all products are equal (unstable equilibrium) or one product dominates the market (stable equilibrium). In the latter case, the model would also reach nil product diversity, inconsistent with observed reality. Product diversity does not mean maintaining the same products, as new/old products continuously enter/exit the market. This in/out flow provides ever higher utility to users, and not a steady state.[31]

In post-Schumpeterian theory,[32] entrepreneurs create new products motivated by the prospect of securing monopoly rents. In the present model, this means a stream of products offering ever higher amounts of utility (through increased functionality, lower cost) which allows the utility of the representative agent to increase as long as the flow of innovations does not cease, in an ever evolving market.[33]

As has been shown here, this process is irreversible and perpetually out of equilibrium. The evolutionary replicator dynamics (Lotka-Volterra) equation above expresses the *selection* process filtering innovations generated by entrepreneurs. The popular ones take off, the unpopular ones fail. This is illustrated in the top panels of Figure 7.3 (panels a and b). The succession of innovations generates ever increasing utility for the consumer (panel c). The source of irreversibility, which disrupts the equilibrium, is investment in R&D leading to the introduction of new products (as well as fluctuations in adoption or utility). In this model, this implies continuously expanding the set of existing products.

Three important aspects of this are to be noted. (1) The introduction of new products at vanishingly small shares does not discontinuously disturb the system even though it generates irreversibility. (2) A flow arises away from old products towards new ones that replace them. (3) The utility of the representative consumer indefinitely increases, and thus cannot be maximised in an optimisation algorithm, as it is not bounded.

The behaviour of the MNL (and standard general equilibrium or CES models) is radically different to this when faced with innovation. The allocation of consumer choices changes instantaneously if either utilities change, or if the list of

[31] For example, the rate of innovation can change over time, and indeed changes all the time, for example, if entrepreneurs in a particular area run out of ideas, or if a breakthrough happens. See for instance Arthur and Polak (2006).

[32] E.g., Safarzynska and van den Bergh (2010); Perez (2001); Freeman and Louçã (2001).

[33] For example, consider the mobile phone market, which continuously evolves, every generation offering higher numbers of possible applications, gradually transforming the way communication is done by users.

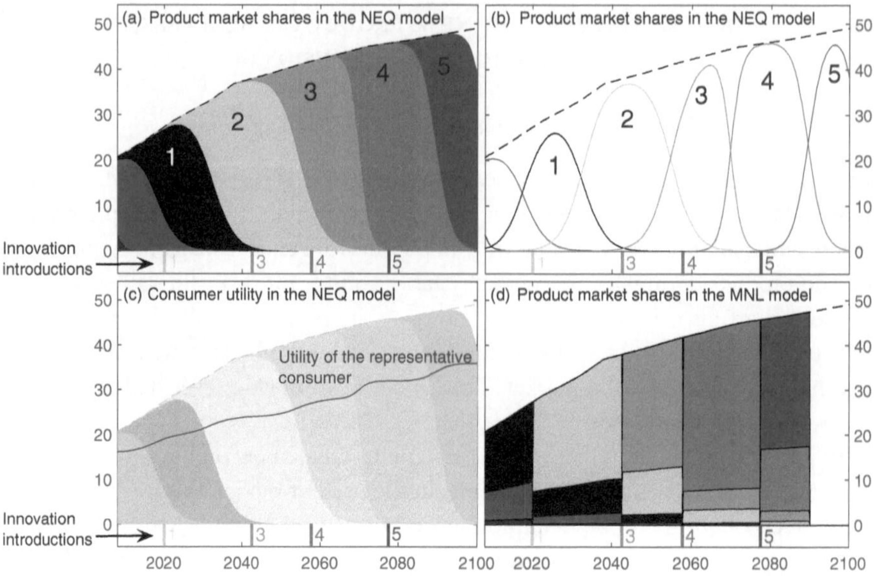

FIGURE 7.3 Illustration of the non-equilibrium (NEQ) and multinomial logit (MNL) models, in a case where 5 innovative variants of a product are introduced at particular points in time (numbers 1–5 at bottom of the charts). (a) and (b) Diffusion of these successive generations of innovations. The dotted line is the total number of units. (c) The utility of the representative agent increases indefinitely. (d) Outcomes of the MNL in a similar context: it discontinuously changes each time an innovation is introduced.

products changes. Where new products are introduced, the allocation of market shares changes discontinuously every time a new product is introduced (panel d), because agents know this immediately and change their behaviour accordingly. This information or product access reaching consumers instantaneously is contradicted by large amounts of empirical literature.[34] However, in practice, equilibrium models are not typically used with changing lists of products. But then this is inconsistent with assuming the existence of economic growth!

7.5. CONCLUSIONS

In standard consumer theory, given that choice options can be ranked, are transitive and known by all agents, the representative consumer is able to exhaustively rank his preferences based on those of the underlying population that he represents. It was shown that in a model of learning agents with heterogeneous knowledge, the representative agent is not able to establish a ranking of his preferences, because he represents agents each of which establish their preferences on a different subset of

34 See, e.g., Fisher and Pry (1971); Bass (1969); Rogers (2010); Mansfield (1961).

options, and none of which know all products in the market. Every agent maximises their utility on a different subset of products that he knows. However, preferences of agents 'attract' the preferences of other agents through interactions (social influence), and therefore preferences cluster in groups (social groups). In a model with learning agents and heterogeneous knowledge, there does not exist any 'objective' set of preferences shared by everyone, and no product or social choice is 'objectively' superior to any other, since consensus on any cannot be obtained across all agents simultaneously.

The deeper meaning of this finding is that in a theory of learning agents with by heterogeneous knowledge, preferences and choices are subjective to context and whom it refers to: social identity groups, income classes, cultural origins, professional classes, etc. The meaning of utility is itself subjective to every agent and their context, and not comparable, aggregable or averageable across agents. This model of learning by heterogenous agents has a number of implications.

First, the representative agent loses meaning as soon as infinitesimally small interactions (social influence) occur between agents. With non-zero interactions and a rapidly changing context, the multinomial logit becomes the non-equilibrium replicator dynamics system of evolutionary theory. That is, a dynamical evolutionary model of selection and diffusion. It also follows that standard consumer models (MNL, elasticity of substitution models) are only adequate for systems of isolated agents without interactions and in a relatively static context.[35]

Second, optimisation is not a reliable analysis tool for models of learning agents. Such systems are dynamical, in perpetual motion without equilibrium, but with hysteresis. Timescales for equilibrium are typically longer than measurement timescales, and longer than the average waiting times at which innovations are introduced, innovations that push systems further out of equilibrium.

Third, the utility of the representative agent thus *cannot reliably be used as a measure of social welfare*, since:

1. *It does not represent everyone equally* – at any time, some agents gain more utility from contextual changes (e.g., taxes) than others.
2. *Its meaning is ambiguous* – its relationship with the utility of any particular individual agent is not straightforward to determine.
3. *It cannot be maximised (its maximum cannot be found)* – with increasing returns, fads and fashions appear, and utility is unbounded and path-dependent. Path-dependence makes the state of the economy subjective to its context and configurational history.

Fourth, the purpose of the act of consumption is clearer in a model of learning heterogeneous agents, which enables linking to standard socio-anthropological theory, in which consumption is context-dependent (Douglas and Isherwood, 1979).

[35] E.g., in which the market settles much faster than changes in context or the rate of innovations.

This is, for example, expressed as different consumption habits held by different income, social, cultural or professional groups. Particular cultural groups consume particular types of food products much more rooted in their tradition, in order to follow their kin, rather than based on their relative price (in comparison to what other groups consume) and the absolute utility (e.g., nutrition) they derive from it. In other words, the utility associated with tradition (behaving like peers) is at least as important as the utility associated with the product itself.

Fifth, in standard theory, it is typically difficult to explain the simultaneous observations of (1) relative product diversity across social groups and (2) relative product homogeneity within social groups (Young, 2001). It is tenuous with the representative agent to explain why prices can differ markedly across markets serving different subgroups, for products serving near identical purposes.[36] It is much more plausible that different social groups choose within submarkets for goods that perform similar functions, and do not delve very strongly in each other's submarkets (as in McShane et al., 2012). The present model is consistent with these observations.

Sixth, while in standard models, optimal tax policy determines the quantities of goods consumed in equilibrium, in a non-equilibrium model, tax policy influences the trajectory of diffusion, but not directly the quantity of goods sold. This becomes important in Chapter 12.

As a last reflection, this is a theory of consumer behaviour in a context of policy. This is particularly useful in contexts in which policy-makers want to know how large a subsidy to impose onto, for example, the price of low-carbon durable goods, to reduce environmental footprints. Alternatively, they may want to know how long it would take to eliminate a certain type of good, for example, petrol vehicles. The evolutionary model shown here is ideally designed for that. What the model does not do is find out what makes new products appear at all in the market, or what makes them more attractive and less costly as their scale and market share increases. This is what comes next in Chapter 8.

7.6. MATHEMATICAL APPENDICES

Appendix A: Deriving the Standard Discrete Choice Model

Heterogeneous utility maximisers have preferences that are described using probability distributions, the Gumbel distribution (or double exponential, Domencich and McFadden, 1975), of width σ:

$$P(U > U_i) = F_i(U) = e^{-e^{-\left(\frac{U-U_i}{\sigma}\right)}}, \quad f_i = e^{-e^{-\left(\frac{U-U_i}{\sigma}\right)}} e^{-\left(\frac{U-U_i}{\sigma}\right)} dU, \tag{7.13}$$

[36] E.g., cars, where prices vary by orders of magnitude (Mercure and Lam, 2015).

where f is the probability distribution, F the cumulative distribution, U is an arbitrary utility value, U_i is the mean utility associated to product i and σ is the diversity of the population. One defines a Linear Random Utility Model (LRUM, Anderson et al., 1992) in terms of a number of socio-economic variables that make agents heterogeneous, for choice options i

$$U_i^* = \beta_i^1 V_i^1 + \beta_i^2 V_i^2 + \beta_i^3 V_i^3 + \cdots + \epsilon_i, \tag{7.14}$$

where the βs represent various socio-economic parameters (elasticities), the Vs are the matching socio-economic variables (e.g., income, prices, preferences, etc.), and ϵ_i is an error term. In the binary case $N = 2$, computing the frequency at which option $i = 1$ generates, on average over a diverse population, more utility than option $j = 2$ yields a convolution of the cumulative distribution (F_j) of one option with the frequency distribution (f_i) of the other, where for an arbitrary U:

$$\begin{aligned} P_{ij}\left(U_j^* > U \middle| U = U_i^*\right) &= \int_{-\infty}^{\infty} f_i(U - U_i) F_j(U - U_j) dU \\ &= \frac{1}{1 + \exp\left(-\frac{U_i - U_j}{\sigma}\right)}, \end{aligned} \tag{7.15}$$

yielding the well-known logistic function of the binary logit model (BL).

To treat more than two options simultaneously, one uses:

$$\begin{aligned} P\Big(U_i^* > U \Big| U = \max\left[U_1^*, \ldots U_{i-1}^*, U_{i+1}^*, \ldots U_n^*\right]\Big) \\ = \int_{-\infty}^{\infty} f_i(U - U_j) \overline{F}(U - \overline{U}) dU, \end{aligned} \tag{7.16}$$

where $\overline{F}(U-\overline{U})$ is the cumulative utility distribution of the 'representative consumer' with unknown mean $\overline{U}$. This is similar to the binary logit case. The representative consumer has a distribution of preferences that is the product of all distributions, from which the utility of the representative consumer $\overline{U}$ can be isolated:

$$\begin{aligned} \overline{F}(U - \overline{U}) &= \exp\left(-\sum_j e^{-\left(\frac{U-U_j}{\sigma}\right)}\right) = e^{-e^{-\left(\frac{U-\overline{U}}{\sigma}\right)}}, \\ \overline{U} &= \sigma \log\left(\sum_j e^{\frac{U_j}{\sigma}}\right). \end{aligned} \tag{7.17}$$

In statistical physics, this would be called the 'partition function'. Replacing U_j for $\overline{U}$ in Eq. 7.2, one obtains the standard multinomial logit (MNL),

$$P_i = \frac{e^{\frac{U_i}{\sigma}}}{\sum_j e^{\frac{U_j}{\sigma}}}, \quad \sum_i P_i = 1. \tag{7.18}$$

One can also obtain the MNL by taking partial derivatives of the utility of the representative consumer:

$$P_i = \left.\frac{\partial \overline{U}}{\partial U_i}\right|_{U_j} = \frac{e^{\frac{U_i}{\sigma}}}{\sum_j e^{\frac{U_j}{\sigma}}}. \tag{7.19}$$

The average utility across agents is different:

$$\langle U \rangle = \frac{\sum_i U_i e^{\frac{U_i}{\sigma}}}{\sum_j e^{\frac{U_j}{\sigma}}} = \frac{\partial}{\partial \frac{1}{\sigma}} \left(\frac{\overline{U}}{\sigma} \right). \tag{7.20}$$

One defines an 'entropy' type function $\mathbb{S}$ as the difference between $\overline{U}$ and $\langle U \rangle$, called the *consumer surplus*:

$$\sigma \mathbb{S} = \sigma \frac{\partial \overline{U}}{\partial \sigma} = \sigma \log \left(\sum_i e^{\frac{U_i}{\sigma}} \right) - \frac{\sum_i U_i e^{\frac{U_i}{\sigma}}}{\sum_j e^{\frac{U_j}{\sigma}}} = \overline{U} - \langle U \rangle . \tag{7.21}$$

It is effectively an entropy (Anderson et al., 1988) since it can be written as

$$\mathbb{S} = - \sum_i P_i \log P_i, \tag{7.22}$$

maximised in equilibrium. Note that the function $\overline{U} = \mathbb{S} + \langle U \rangle$ is conceptually the same as Helmholtz' free energy for a system of non-interacting physical particles, which is minimised in thermodynamic equilibrium.

Appendix B: Deriving the MNL from the CES Model

One starts from the CES utility function U and budget constraint Y

$$U = \left(\sum_j [X_j]^\rho \right)^{\frac{1}{\rho}}, \quad Y = \sum_i X_i p_i, \tag{7.23}$$

where X_i are quantities of goods and p_i are prices. One wants to maximise U under constraint Y. Define the Lagrangian $L = U - \lambda Y$ and take gradients over all parameters X_i:

$$\nabla_{X_i} L = 0 \Rightarrow \nabla_{X_i} U = \lambda \nabla_{X_i} Y, \tag{7.24}$$

from which is derived

$$\left(\sum_j [X_j]^\rho \right)^{\frac{1-\rho}{\rho}} X_i^{\rho-1} = \lambda p_i, \tag{7.25}$$

to obtain

$$\frac{X_i}{\left(\sum_j X_j^\rho\right)^{\frac{1}{\rho}}} = (\lambda p_i)^{\frac{1}{\rho-1}}. \tag{7.26}$$

This relationship is inverted by substituting X_j in the denominator for the value of X_i itself:

$$X_j = (\lambda p_j)^{\frac{1}{\rho-1}} \left(\sum_k X_k^\rho\right)^{\frac{1}{\rho}} = (\lambda p_j)^{\frac{1}{\rho-1}} U, \tag{7.27}$$

and obtain

$$(\lambda p_i)^{\frac{1}{\rho-1}} = \frac{X_i}{\left(\sum_j (\lambda p_j)^{\frac{\rho}{\rho-1}} U^\rho\right)^{\frac{1}{\rho}}}. \tag{7.28}$$

X_i can be isolated,

$$X_i = (\lambda p_i)^{\frac{1}{\rho-1}} \left(\sum_j (\lambda p_j)^{\frac{\rho}{\rho-1}}\right)^{\frac{1}{\rho}} U. \tag{7.29}$$

If one defines choices P_i as shares of expenditure, in which the term $\left(\sum_j (\lambda p_j)^{\frac{\rho}{\rho-1}}\right)^{\frac{1}{\rho}} U$ cancels out, then:

$$P_i = \frac{p_i X_i}{\sum_j p_j X_j} = \frac{(\lambda p_i)^{\frac{\rho}{\rho-1}}}{\sum_j (\lambda p_j)^{\frac{\rho}{\rho-1}}} = \frac{e^{\frac{U_i}{\sigma}}}{\sum_i e^{\frac{U_j}{\sigma}}}, \tag{7.30}$$

that is, equal to the MNL. Taking the utility U_i as a logarithmic function of prices $-\log \lambda p_i$ implies that

$$\frac{U_i}{\sigma} = \frac{\rho}{1-\rho} \log \lambda p_i, \quad \text{with} \quad 0 < \rho < 1. \tag{7.31}$$

This determines the price and cross-price elasticities. This shows a complete equivalence between the MNL and the CES. Further information can be obtained in Anderson et al. (1992), Section 3.7.

Appendix C: The MNL with Strongly Interacting Consumers

The expression 7.3 is evaluated by multiplying on each side the probabilities calculated individually for all N agents, with $N_1, N_2, \ldots, N_n$ the numbers of agents using products $1, 2, \ldots, n$ ($\sum N_i = N$),

$$\begin{aligned} &P(U > \max[U_1, U_2, \ldots, U_n])^N \\ &= P(U > U_1)^{N_1} P(U > U_2)^{N_2} \cdots P(U > U_n)^{N_n}, \end{aligned} \tag{7.32}$$

which, using $S_i = N_i/N$, can be written as

$$P(U > \max[U_1, U_2, U_3, \ldots, U_n]) = \prod_i P(U > U_i)^{S_i}, \qquad (7.33)$$

where the S_i are market shares, and $\sum_i S_i = 1$. One then finds the utility of the representative consumer, as a partition function for interacting agents:

$$\overline{U} = \sigma \log\left(\sum_i S_i e^{\frac{U_i}{\sigma}}\right). \qquad (7.34)$$

One then takes partial derivatives to obtain choice probabilities as in Eq. 7.19. Temporarily, it is proposed that product shares S_i are single-valued functions of utilities U_i, as in the MNL:

$$P_i = \frac{\partial \overline{U}}{\partial U_i} = \frac{S_i e^{\frac{U_i}{\sigma}}}{\sum_k S_k e^{\frac{U_k}{\sigma}}} + \sigma \frac{\sum_j \frac{\partial S_j}{\partial U_i} e^{\frac{U_j}{\sigma}}}{\sum_k S_k e^{\frac{U_k}{\sigma}}}. \qquad (7.35)$$

This expression is made complex by the second term involving the change in market shares S_i with respect to changes in the utilities of product categories U_i. This is a recursive problem, of which the convergence must be determined.

It is shown by contradiction that this implies that there is no equilibrium. A fairly general assumption is made about the form of P_i by expressing it in terms of the Fourier transforms of the numerator and denominator:

$$P_i = \frac{\sum_n A_{ni} e^{\alpha_n \frac{U_i}{\sigma_n}}}{\sum_{mk} A_{mk} e^{\alpha_m \frac{U_k}{\sigma_m}}}, \qquad (7.36)$$

where the A_{ni} are real Fourier coefficients and $\alpha_n = iu_n + v_n$ are complex frequencies. The derivative of this term is needed:

$$\frac{\partial P_j}{\partial U_i} = \frac{\sum_{nj} \frac{\alpha_n}{\sigma} A_{nj} e^{\alpha_n \frac{U_j}{\sigma_n}} \delta_{ij}}{\sum_{mk} A_{mk} e^{\alpha_m \frac{U_k}{\sigma_m}}} + \frac{\left(\sum_{nj} A_{nj} e^{\alpha_n \frac{U_j}{\sigma_n}}\right)\left(\sum_{mj} \frac{\alpha_m}{\sigma} A_{mj} e^{\alpha_m \frac{U_j}{\sigma_m}} \delta_{ij}\right)}{\left(\sum_{\ell k} A_{\ell k} e^{\alpha_\ell \frac{U_k}{\sigma_\ell}}\right)^2}, \qquad (7.37)$$

where δ_{ij} is Kronecker's delta, equal to zero unless $i = j$, in which case it equals 1.[37]

37 $\delta_{ij} = 1$ if $i = j$, but zero otherwise.

Inserting Eqs. 7.36 and 7.37 into Eq. 7.35 when imposing that $S_i = P_i$, we obtain, after cancelling terms in the numerators and denominators:

$$\frac{\sum_n A_{ni} e^{\alpha_n \frac{U_i}{\sigma_n}}}{\sum_{mk} A_{mk} e^{\alpha_m \frac{U_k}{\sigma_m}}} = \frac{\sum_n A_{ni} e^{(\alpha_n+1)\frac{U_i}{\sigma_n}}}{\sum_{mk} A_{mk} e^{(\alpha_m+1)\frac{U_k}{\sigma_m}}} + \frac{\sum_n \alpha_n A_{ni} e^{(\alpha_n+1)\frac{U_i}{\sigma_n}}}{\sum_{mk} A_{mk} e^{(\alpha_m+1)\frac{U_k}{\sigma_m}}} - \frac{\sum_n \alpha_n A_{ni} e^{\alpha_n \frac{U_i}{\sigma_n}}}{\sum_{mk} A_{mk} e^{\alpha_m \frac{U_k}{\sigma_m}}}. \tag{7.38}$$

This reduces to

$$\frac{\sum_n A_{ni} e^{\alpha_n \frac{U_i}{\sigma_n}}}{\sum_{mk} A_{mk} e^{\alpha_m \frac{U_k}{\sigma_m}}}(\alpha_n + 1) = \frac{\sum_n A_{ni} e^{(\alpha_n+1)\frac{U_i}{\sigma_n}}}{\sum_{mk} A_{mk} e^{(\alpha_m+1)\frac{U_k}{\sigma_m}}}(\alpha_n + 1), \tag{7.39}$$

where the $(\alpha_n + 1)$ cancel on each side. One is then led to equating $\alpha_n = \alpha_n + 1$ for any complex set of values for α_n, which is a contradiction. Thus this general form for P_i does not solve Eq. 7.35, unless one of the P_i equals one and the others equal zero, which is the trivial solution.

Appendix D: Deriving the Replicator Dynamics

The preferences are

$$P_i = \frac{S_i e^{\frac{U_i}{\sigma}}}{\sum_k S_k e^{\frac{U_k}{\sigma}}}. \tag{7.40}$$

The adoptions are

$$\frac{dS_i^{\uparrow}}{dt} = \frac{P_i}{\tau_i}\frac{\overline{\tau}}{\tilde{\tau}}; \quad \text{with } \frac{1}{\overline{\tau}} = \sum_i \frac{S_i}{\tau_i}; \quad \frac{1}{\tilde{\tau}} = \sum_i \frac{P_i}{\tau_i}, \tag{7.41}$$

with $\overline{\tau}, \tilde{\tau}$ the lifetime and the adoption rate, respectively. The out-flow is simply $\frac{dS_i^{\downarrow}}{dt} = \frac{S_i}{\tau_i}$, which means that the dynamical shares equation is

$$\frac{dS_i}{dt} = \frac{1}{\tau_i}\left[\frac{\overline{\tau}}{\tilde{\tau}}\frac{S_i e^{\frac{U_i}{\sigma}}}{\sum_k S_k e^{\frac{U_k}{\sigma}}} - S_i\right] \simeq \frac{1}{\tau}\left[P_i - S_i\right]. \tag{7.42}$$

This is correct since $\sum_i \frac{dS_i}{dt} = 0$. Furthermore, if the timescale of consumption is very short (or much shorter than the rate of observation), then a limit can be taken for when $\tau_i \to 0$, using also the transformation $y_i = \frac{1}{\tau_i} \to \infty$, multiplying 7.42 by τ_i on both sides:

$$\lim_{\tau_i \to 0} \frac{dS_i}{dt}\tau_i = 0 = \lim_{\tau_i \to 0} \frac{\overline{\tau}}{\tilde{\tau}} P_i - S_i = \lim_{y_i \to \infty} \frac{\sum P_i y_i}{\sum S_i y_i} = \frac{P_i^2}{S_i} - S_i. \tag{7.43}$$

This implies that $P_i = S_i$. Therefore, when the rate of adoption and consumption is much faster than the rate of observation, one falls back to a standard equilibrium state (as in Brock and Durlauf, 2001) in which market shares equal preferences, which, if one took out the multi-agent interactions, would also lead back to the MNL, where

$$S_i = \frac{\exp\left(\frac{U_i^\circ}{\sigma}\right)}{\sum_k \exp\left(\frac{U_k^\circ}{\sigma}\right)}. \tag{7.44}$$

This is the case for instance with transport decisions, which involves very short timescales, and not necessarily any social influence.

In the case of durable goods or production capital, there may be both a decision of adoption and a decision for scrapping (e.g., machines, vehicles), therefore with a lifetime τ_i and acquisition or production rate t_i, which gives:

$$\frac{dS_i}{dt} = S_i\left(\mathcal{F}_i - \overline{\mathcal{F}}\right), \quad \mathcal{F}_i = \frac{\frac{1}{\tau_i} S_i e^{\frac{U_i}{\sigma}}}{\sum_k \frac{1}{\tau_k} S_k e^{\frac{U_k}{\sigma}}} - \frac{\frac{1}{t_i} S_i e^{\frac{U_i}{\sigma}}}{\sum_k \frac{1}{t_k} S_k e^{\frac{U_k}{\sigma}}}, \tag{7.45}$$

where $\mathcal{F}$ is a comparative product 'fitness', or competitiveness, in the market, in the evolutionary sense. It can be transformed into a pair-wise exchange of market shares (imitation dynamics), a form of the Lotka-Volterra equation of population dynamics in competing species (see Appendix G for a derivation; see also Mercure, 2015),

$$\frac{dS_i}{dt} = \sum_j S_i S_j \left(A_{ij} F_{ij} - A_{ji} F_{ji}\right). \tag{7.46}$$

Appendix E: Irreversibility and Path-Dependence

Cross derivatives of the consumer surplus are evaluated, that is, the entropy:

$$\frac{\partial \mathbb{S}}{\partial U_i \partial S_i} = \left(\frac{P_i}{\sigma^2 S_i} - \frac{2P_i^2}{\sigma^2 S_i}\right)\left(\langle U \rangle - U_i\right) = \frac{\partial \mathbb{S}}{\partial S_i \partial U_i}. \tag{7.47}$$

When cross partial derivatives are not equal, the value of the function depends on its configurational history (e.g., whether we change U_i or S_i first). This system is thus conservative, and reversible, since the evolution of the entropy is not path-dependent. The utility of the representative consumer is also conservative (and therefore so is the average utility), which means that over any possible closed trajectory, the value of the utility of the representative agent $\overline{U}$ does not change:

$$\frac{\partial \overline{U}}{\partial U_i \partial S_i} = \frac{\partial P_i}{\partial S_i} = \frac{P_i}{S_i} - \frac{P_i^2}{S_i} = \frac{\partial \overline{U}}{\partial S_i \partial U_i} \Rightarrow \quad \oint_{\vec{T}} d\overline{U} = 0, \tag{7.48}$$

where $\vec{T}$ is any trajectory in S_i or U_i.

However, these things change when the technology list of innovations is changed. As opposed to the MNL, this can be done quasi-continuously by including new innovations with near-to-zero market shares, consistent with how innovations diffuse. If one considers a path $\vec{T}'$ in which one adds an innovation to the list along the way, this becomes path-dependent, and not reversible. But furthermore, this system also becomes path-dependent for any level of fluctuations in S_i or U_i. Thus, unless the system is considered perfectly deterministic, it remains conservative and in equilibrium; but vanishingly small fluctuations break this equilibrium rather quickly, which is shown next.

Changes taking place in time are considered, and a path of utility that goes back on itself is created, such that the start and end points have the same utility value set U_i (e.g., with tax policy that is introduced, and later withdrawn). This should not give a change of $\overline{U}$ at the final (start) point, as the shares progress but afterwards go back to their starting values. Choosing any trajectory $\vec{T}$ in time to carry out a line integral,

$$0 = \oint_{\vec{T}} \left[\sum_i \left.\frac{\partial \overline{U}}{\partial S_i}\right|_{U_i} \frac{dS_i}{dt} + \left.\frac{\partial \overline{U}}{\partial U_i}\right|_{S_i} \frac{dU_i}{dt} \right] dt \qquad (7.49)$$

$$= \sigma \sum_i \oint_{\vec{T}} \left[\frac{e^{\frac{U_i}{\sigma}} \frac{dS_i}{dt} + S_i e^{\frac{U_i}{\sigma}} \frac{dU_i}{dt}}{\sum_k S_k e^{\frac{U_k}{\sigma}}} \right] dt, \qquad (7.50)$$

which, using the fact that $\partial \overline{U}/\partial S_i = P_i/S_i$, while $\partial \overline{U}/\partial U_i = P_i$, can be written as

$$= \sigma \oint_{\vec{T}} \left(\left\langle \frac{1}{S_i} \frac{dS_i}{dt} \right\rangle + \frac{1}{\sigma} \left\langle \frac{dU_i}{dt} \right\rangle \right) dt = 0, \qquad (7.51)$$

that is, the preferences-weighted average relative changes of shares and change in utility in time.

Including small random events, the adoption S_i and the utilities vary with stochastic noise terms ϵ_i^S and ϵ_i^U.[38] This leaves two terms that do not cancel,

$$= \sigma \oint_{\vec{T}} \left(\left\langle \frac{1}{\epsilon_i^S} \frac{d\epsilon_i^S}{dt} \right\rangle + \frac{1}{\sigma} \left\langle \frac{d\epsilon_i^U}{dt} \right\rangle \right) dt \neq 0. \qquad (7.52)$$

This accumulates over time, leading to weak path-dependence.

In the case of new products, one imagines that along the path, a new product is created by entrepreneurs and introduced in the market, at time t_1, with vanishingly small but non-zero shares:

$$= \sigma \oint_{\vec{T}} \left(\sum_{i \neq \ell} \frac{1}{S_i} \frac{dS_i}{dt} + \frac{1}{S_\ell} \frac{dS_\ell}{dt} \right) dt \neq 0. \qquad (7.53)$$

This is also not zero and causes strong path-dependence.

38 To maintain $\sum_i S_i = 1$, ϵ_i^S must sum to zero.

Appendix F: Deriving the Weakly Interacting Replicator Equation

Agent k will learn about option i only if he can meet agent ℓ who has experience of option i,[39]

$$U_i = \beta_i^1 V_i^1 + \beta_i^2 V_i^2 + \beta_i^3 V_i^3 + \cdots + \alpha \log\left[\frac{2}{NN_p}\sum_k^N \sum_\ell^M \xi_{k\ell}\delta_{\ell i}\right] + \cdots + \epsilon_i, \quad (7.54)$$

$$\xi_{k\ell} = \begin{cases} 1 & \text{if agent } k \text{ knows/trusts agent } \ell \\ 0 & \text{otherwise} \end{cases},$$

M is the number of nearest peers that agents have, and the sum over M is carried out over each agent's set of accessible peers, and N_p is the average number of accessible peers per agent.[40]

Denoting U_i^0 as the random utility of non-interacting consumers for product i, inserting Eq. 7.54 into the utility of the representative agent Eq. 7.34, one obtains

$$\overline{U} = \sigma \log\left(\sum_i \exp\left[\frac{U_i^0}{\sigma} + \frac{\alpha}{\sigma}\log\left(\frac{2}{NN_p}\sum_k^N \sum_\ell^M \xi_{k\ell}\delta_{\ell i}\right)\right]\right). \quad (7.55)$$

Every pair of agents k and ℓ where agent ℓ has no knowledge of product i, one has a contribution of $-\infty$ to the utility, which gives a contribution of zero to the utility of the representative agent. Calculating further:

$$\overline{U} = \sigma \log\left(\sum_i \left[\sum_k^N \sum_\ell^M \frac{2\xi_{k\ell}\delta_{\ell i}}{NN_p}\right]^{\frac{\alpha}{\sigma}} \exp\left(\frac{U_i^0}{\sigma}\right)\right). \quad (7.56)$$

The approximation is taken that agents have on average N_p trusted peers, and the sum over agents k yields the number N_i of agents that use product i. Noting that N_i/N equals the share of product use S_i, one obtains

$$\overline{U} = \sigma \log\left(\sum_i [S_i]^{\frac{\alpha}{\sigma}} \exp\left(\frac{U_i^0}{\sigma}\right)\right). \quad (7.57)$$

When the ratio α/σ is equal to 1, we recover the utility of the representative consumer for strongly interacting agents, Eq. 7.34. When the ratio is equal to zero, one recovers that of non-interacting agents, the MNL.

Eq. 7.57 can be differentiated in order to obtain preferences P_i:

$$P_i = \frac{\partial \overline{U}}{\partial U_i} = \frac{[S_i]^{\frac{\alpha}{\sigma}} \exp\left(\frac{U_i^0}{\sigma}\right)}{\sum_k [S_k]^{\frac{\alpha}{\sigma}} \exp\left(\frac{U_k^0}{\sigma}\right)}. \quad (7.58)$$

39 See Durlauf and Ioannides (2010), in which the same form of utility function is used.

40 The average of M over agents equals N_p. The factor 2 avoids double counting pairs of agents. It is assumed that in a pair, interactions are bi-directional.

Appendix G: Connecting Different Forms of the Replicator Dynamics

Here the connection is made between a binary exchange model,[41] and the replicator dynamics obtained from adding social interactions in the MNL, Eq. 7.45. In order to obtain a binary exchange model, a system of boxes and marbles in fixed numbers is considered. The system consists in distributing and redistributing marbles from box to box according to rates determined by the constants t_i and τ_i, one time constant limiting the maximum rate of growth, and the other limiting the fastest rate at which a box can be emptied. This leads to dynamics extensively described in Mercure (2015), a Lotka-Volterra equation system expressed in the form of shares of the total.

A replicator dynamics of the classical form is considered,

$$\frac{dS_i}{dt} = \frac{S_i}{\overline{\tau}}\left(\mathcal{F}_i - \overline{\mathcal{F}}\right), \quad \mathcal{F}_i = P_i - P_i' \tag{7.59}$$

in which the fitness for survival in the market of product i is expressed using $\mathcal{F}$, and $\overline{\mathcal{F}}$ is the average fitness, and the fitness is related to the probability of adoption P_i and the probability of scrapping P_i'. The probability of adoption is greater the greater the utility (without interactions) U_i°, changes that arise at the average rate of turnover $\overline{\tau}$,

$$\frac{dS_i^\uparrow}{dt} = P_i = \frac{\frac{\bar{t}}{t_i} S_i \exp\left(\frac{U_i^\circ}{\sigma}\right)}{\sum_k \frac{\bar{t}}{t_k} S_k \exp\left(\frac{U_k^\circ}{\sigma}\right)}. \tag{7.60}$$

The economic decision to scrap products arises with a probability greater the lower the utility is,

$$\frac{dS_i^\downarrow}{dt} = -P_i' = -\frac{\frac{\overline{\tau}}{\tau_i} S_i \exp\left(\frac{-U_i^\circ}{\sigma}\right)}{\sum_k \frac{\overline{\tau}}{\tau_k} S_k \exp\left(\frac{-U_k^\circ}{\sigma}\right)}. \tag{7.61}$$

Then the total fitness for survival of the product in the market is

$$\begin{aligned}
\mathcal{F}_i &= \frac{\frac{\bar{t}}{t_i} S_i \exp\left(\frac{U_i^\circ}{\sigma}\right)}{\sum_k \frac{\bar{t}}{t_k} S_k \exp\left(\frac{U_k^\circ}{\sigma}\right)} - \frac{\frac{\overline{\tau}}{\tau_i} S_i \exp\left(\frac{-U_i^\circ}{\sigma}\right)}{\sum_k \frac{\overline{\tau}}{\tau_k} S_k \exp\left(\frac{-U_k^\circ}{\sigma}\right)} \\
&= \frac{\sum_j S_i S_j \left(\frac{\bar{t}}{t_i}\frac{\overline{\tau}}{\tau_j} e^{(U_i - U_j)/\sigma} - \frac{\bar{t}}{t_j}\frac{\overline{\tau}}{\tau_i} e^{(U_j - U_i)/\sigma}\right)}{\left(\sum_k S_k \frac{\bar{t}}{t_k} e^{U_k/\sigma}\right)\left(\sum_\ell S_\ell \frac{\overline{\tau}}{\tau_\ell} e^{-U_\ell/\sigma}\right)},
\end{aligned} \tag{7.62}$$

while the average fitness equals zero in this form. The denominator can be distributed as

$$\left(\sum_k S_k \frac{\bar{t}}{t_k} e^{U_k/\sigma}\right)\left(\sum_\ell S_\ell \frac{\overline{\tau}}{\tau_\ell} e^{-U_\ell/\sigma}\right) = \sum_{k,\ell} \frac{\bar{t}}{t_k}\frac{\overline{\tau}}{\tau_\ell} S_k S_\ell e^{(U_k - U_\ell)/\sigma} \tag{7.63}$$

[41] Imitation dynamics, see Hofbauer and Sigmund (1998).

and shown to be approximately constant, and reduced by symmetry, for every pair-wise k, ℓ case where the difference in utility is not large: assuming that τ_ℓ is not quantitatively very different from the average $\overline{\tau}$, and similarly for t_k, then it becomes approximately

$$\simeq \sum_{k,\ell} S_k S_\ell e^{(U_k - U_\ell)/\sigma} = \frac{1}{2}\sum_{k,\ell} S_k S_\ell e^{(U_k - U_\ell)/\sigma} + \frac{1}{2}\sum_{\ell,k} S_\ell S_k e^{(U_\ell - U_k)/\sigma} \quad (7.64)$$

$$= \sum_{k,\ell} S_k S_\ell \cosh(U_k - U_\ell)/\sigma. \quad (7.65)$$

If the value of $U_k - U_\ell$ is not much larger than that of σ, then $\cosh(U_k - U_\ell)/\sigma \simeq 1 + (U_k - U_\ell)^2/\sigma^2$, meaning that the denominator reduces to something very close to a value of 1. This will be the case when the sum of the Gumbel distributions of the alternatives has a single mode, in which case the weighted average of the distributions is not highly different from the distribution of the representative consumer.

However, whenever one option has a utility very different from the others ($U_k \gg U_\ell$), this will not be the case, as the exponential will have either a very large or near zero value (depending on the sign). In this case, the sum over k is carried out over only those cases i, replacing the alternate ℓ utility by the average utility $\overline{U}$ (i.e. $U_\ell \simeq \overline{U}$):

$$\simeq S_i \sum_\ell S_\ell \left(\frac{\bar{t}}{t_i}\frac{\overline{\tau}}{\tau_\ell} e^{(U_i - \overline{U})/\sigma} + \frac{\bar{t}}{t_\ell}\frac{\overline{\tau}}{\tau_i} e^{(\overline{U} - U_i)/\sigma} \right)$$

$$\simeq S_i \left(e^{(U_i - \overline{U})/\sigma} + e^{(\overline{U} - U_i)/\sigma} \right). \quad (7.66)$$

In this case, the denominator of Eq. 7.62 can be integrated to the numerator. If options i and j differ in utility significantly, and option i is identified as the option differing from the average, while j remains similar to the average, then the denominator, merged to the numerator, gives logistic functions of $U_i - U_j/\sigma$ (by identifying U_j to $\overline{U}$). If i and j do not differ much, the denominator remains close to 1 and the numerator close to 0, and thus this approximation remains correct.

Under these assumptions, the replicator dynamics becomes approximately

$$\frac{dS_i}{dt} = \frac{1}{\overline{\tau}} \sum_j S_i S_j \left(A_{ij} F_{ij} - A_{ji} F_{ji} \right), \quad (7.67)$$

where $$F_{ij} = \frac{e^{(U_i - U_j)/\sigma}}{e^{(U_i - U_j)/\sigma} + e^{(U_j - U_i)/\sigma}}, \quad F_{ij} + F_{ji} = 1, \quad A_{ij} = \frac{\bar{t}}{t_i}\frac{\overline{\tau}}{\tau_j}.$$

This is a pair-wise model of choice and substitution, analogous to a Lotka-Volterra model which can be derived under pair-wise interaction assumptions,[42] also called 'imitation dynamics' in Hofbauer and Sigmund (1998).

[42] As in the population dynamics of interacting species, see Mercure (2015).

8

Micro-foundations for an Economic Theory of Innovation

Modelling innovation is not generally part of economic modelling, and there exists no widely accepted method to quantitatively model innovation, beyond the standard simple learning curves at the micro or macro scales for process innovation, and nothing for product innovation. There exists, however, a wide range of established and empirically validated qualitative models of innovation systems that describe different stages of knowledge and product generation going from basic science to marketable products, and different functions of agents. Here, an overview is given of qualitative innovation theory, seeking to develop the basis for a quantitative model. A quantitative theoretical complex networks model of process innovation is then proposed that can be applied to patent network data that allows one to derive learning curves as well as productivity growth in the aggregate economy. This model could potentially explain differences in rates of learning observed between sectors and countries, according to how the topology of the network of ideas is organised to better understand economic growth.

8.1. INTRODUCTION: INNOVATION AS A COMPLEX SYSTEM

Innovation underpins the larger fraction of economic growth.[1] Despite how important innovation is for micro- and macroeconomics, it remains a field that is a bit of an outsider to economics. Economists do not tend to include endogenous processes of innovation in their models and theories, leaving it to outside forces

[1] Solow (1957) famously showed that if one accounts for the growth in the labour force and the accumulation of capital, one accounts for only three eighths of growth, and the rest is due to how these factors improve their productivity over time with innovation. However, this analysis is flawed to a large degree as the results of the regression originate more from the accounting methods for capital, which are themselves ambiguous, than from innovation (Shaikh, 1974). According to Kaldor (1957), there is no unambiguous way to quantify capital.

(see Chapter 3). As such, therefore, theories of innovation are not well integrated to the rest of economics, and public policy for innovation is not something that is formed using any formal theoretical basis in most nations.

This state of things is possibly explained by the fundamental fact that the impacts of investment in innovative activity are not knowable by definition and therefore challenging to predict even in aggregate. By definition, entrepreneurs strive at outplaying each other to capture markets and make profits, and as in any game of cards, if everyone could easily predict the outcome of the game, it would hardly be worth playing it. The same holds for venture capitalists, which make their entire living on choosing well which business initiatives to support financially and technically that will generate substantial return. It remains the case that out of ten startups funded by venture capital, typically about nine fail, but those that do not fail usually make enough return that they compensate for the failures and even leave a profit.

The state of knowledge in innovation scholarship is gradually changing as various traditions in the field have recently been making great progress. At the same time, due to the 2008 financial crisis, the recession caused by the COVID-19 crisis and the need for improving sustainability, governments and policy-makers, especially in the EU and the UK, are seeking solutions for industrial strategy that could help re-start the economic engine and create new jobs in new sectors in a sustainable way. The situation may be akin to a post-war context, in which policy-makers seek to know how to re-start the economy in a new direction.

Innovation is an evolutionary system very similar to ecosystems: technology is something that builds upon itself, just like science: 'standing on the shoulders of giants'.[2] Entrepreneurs generally seek to find new ways to combine what already exists to create something new and useful, and that involves existing technology and resources combined in new ways. Thus it follows that the economy is a system that 'complexifies' over time, as its technologies are made out of ever larger numbers of underlying components, ideas and knowledge that have been developed previously. In ecosystems, evolution works by adding new variations to an existing pool of genetic information, in a system of interacting phenotypes (e.g., animals, plants) themselves based on their genotypes. Technologies, companies and socio-technical systems are similar.

Kauffman (2000) describes evolution and innovation as a collection of autonomous agents who continuously search for 'new ways to make a living', until they find one, and then stick with it. Finding a new way to make a living means a way to constrain the flow of resources. To do this, they interact with their environment and build structures that enable them to create those constraints (e.g., building a canal diverting water from a river to power a mill). They continuously build upon the

[2] Kauffman (2000), the primary reference for this chapter, bases evolutionary theory on this concept.

constraints built earlier by other agents, and thus collectively develop and complexify their world as they continuously alter the range of things that can be built next on top of it. However, sometimes they also destroy the work of others or make it obsolete.

Innovation is classified into two broad types, product innovation, where new products with new functionality are created, and process innovation, where existing industrial functions are improved to perform the same with less resources. Sometimes, the result of product innovation is process innovation, but in that case this is considered process innovation. The reason to distinguish them is that their economic impact is different but complementary. In short, process innovation saves resources, and those resources can then be spent. However, unless process innovation develops products to spend profits on, those profits could end up accumulated into idle stockpiles of wealth, and therefore it is the combination of process and product innovation that lead to economic growth.

In this chapter, the state of knowledge in the economics of innovation is first reviewed in order to identify key components relevant for a non-prescriptive theory of macroeconomics, developed in later chapters. A theory of process innovation is then developed from a complex networks perspective, that is fully evolutionary. This allows to explain many unexplained features of economic evolution and offers quantitative micro-foundations for Schumpeter's theory of economic development. For that, extensive use is made of Kauffman's concept of the Adjacent Possible (Kauffman, 2000), and an attempt is made at characterising the source of the rate of learning and productivity change in macroeconomics. Macroeconomic implications are taken up again in Chapter 11.

8.2. SCHUMPETER AND THE ECONOMICS OF INNOVATION

8.2.1 *Schumpeter's Entrepreneur*

Schumpeter's Theory of Economic Development (Schumpeter, 1934) underpins most theories of entrepreneurship in economics, business and management. As opposed to descriptions of the economy in terms of the macroeconomic *circular flow* of value, as originally proposed by Walras,[3] Schumpeter's clear definition for the entrepreneur opened up a new way of thinking about the economy, innovation and business cycles.

Walras' macroeconomy, and that of neoclassical thinkers, is one of a constant circular flow of economic value and competitive markets, in steady state equilibrium characterised by full employment of resources (capital: human, produced, natural, financial). In the pure form of this perspective, private enterprise makes no profit, since in perfectly competitive markets, prices, determined by demand and supply, clear markets exactly and profit can only be the result of monopolistic power.

[3] Originally published in French in 1874, translated into English in 1954, see Walras (1956).

In models, technological progress is exogenously prescribed at each time step, and the economy is a static picture or a 'moving equilibrium'. Credit and debt exist, but they are only used to allocate savings (excess resources not consumed) between those who have it and those who want to use them, but no profit can be made out of lending money for investment, since profits do not exist in equilibrium. Investment originates from savings, which originate from forgoing consumption. Money is a commodity, and any change in its supply is offset by a change in its value, making money *neutral*, where inflation plays no role.[4]

Schumpeter uses this picture as a starting point, in order to explore the impact on the economy of adding an entrepreneur to the normal *circular flow*. The entrepreneur, in Schumpeter's very basic definition, is someone, with some kind of technical training, who has ideas on how to improve the performance of the production process of some good or service, by using lower quantities of inputs to produce the same amount of production, or improve the quality of a certain good or service for the same amount of inputs, or alternatively, create brand new products. Such *new combinations of inputs to production* allow the entrepreneur to make a profit at prevailing market prices, since either his production costs become lower than those of his competitors, or his product, of higher quality, sells at a higher price. He thus also opens the opportunity for creating a temporary monopoly for that good or service, during which markets are not competitive so long as only he can use or produce his innovation.

However, to concertise his ideas, the entrepreneur needs finance, and for simplicity, Schumpeter assumes that the entrepreneur has no savings available to pay for the capital costs required for experimenting or altering his production process.[5] This therefore requires the intervention of a financial institution, which, together with the entrepreneur and his business plan, enable the innovation to be developed and deployed, on the anticipation of profit.

The entrepreneur is not always successful, since, as it is with venture capital, typically nine out of ten ventures fail (see e.g., Klingebiel and Rammer, 2014). The entrepreneur cannot know with any certainty or probabilities whether his various ideas will work in practice, or whether he could be beaten in the race by competitors, until he tries and the future materialises. If he is unsuccessful, he loses someone else's money (the financier's) and, most likely, his own credit-worthiness in the face of the financial institution.

If the entrepreneur makes a return out of applying his innovations, he repays whatever funds he borrowed plus interest, keeps a profit, and enjoys a temporary monopolistic control of the market. However, other firms, those that do not go out of business for becoming uncompetitive, also innovate or imitate other firms'

[4] See Chapter 3; money, debt and finance are analysed more detail in Chapters 9 and 10.

[5] For simplicity of exposition Schumpeter separates the function of the financier from that of the entrepreneur, even if they may often be the same person/institution.

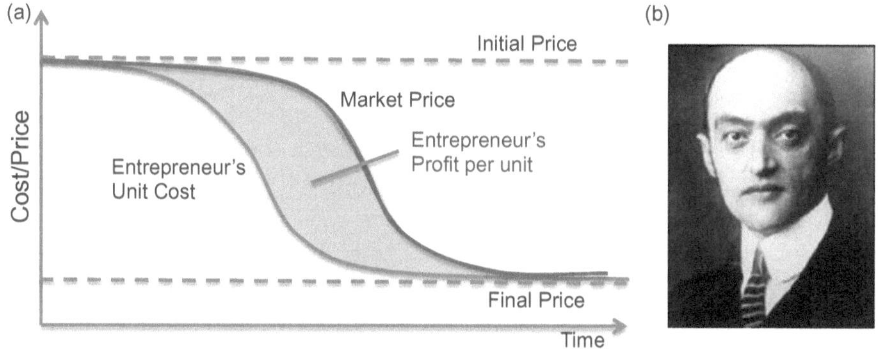

FIGURE 8.1 (a) The entrepreneur's cost, profit and price changes over time. (b) Photo of Joseph A. Schumpeter.

innovations, until their costs at least match those of the entrepreneur. This leads to the prices of the good or service eventually declining under market competition (Figure 8.1). At this stage, the entrepreneur's profit gradually declines and vanishes, unless he innovates further to decrease his costs even more. This process therefore implies a continuous innovation race between firms and entrepreneurs.

With cumulative innovative activity, as prices of goods and services relative to income gradually decline with cumulative innovative processes and market competition, the general population is eventually left with unspent income after enjoying normal consumption, which can be spent on a higher level of consumption. This is the basis of Schumpeter's economic development through innovation.

This theory was already developed in Chapter 3. Here, focus is given to Schumpeter's description of innovation and entrepreneurship in more detail. Developing an actual definition of the process of *creative destruction* is the goal of the chapter, something used recurrently thereafter in this book. But before going there, modern thinking on innovation is reviewed, looking at the innovation chain as a more detailed and accurate description of the innovation process than offered by Schumpeter.

8.2.2 *The Story of Sakichi Toyoda*

As a salient example, the case is taken of a man called Sakichi Toyoda, the founder of Toyota Industries Corporation in Japan.[6] Toyoda was a Japanese inventor and industrialist, which could be considered as the archetypical Schumpeterian entrepreneur.

[6] Sakichi Toyoda's story is explained on the Toyota Industries Corporation's website (`www.toyota-industries.com/company/history/toyoda_sakichi/`), as well as by Mass and Robertson (1996). But his story is much better told when visiting the Toyota Commemorative Museum of Industry and Technology situated in Nagoya, Japan (`www.tcmit.org/english/`), where the innovations that Toyoda, father and son,

As a young man, searching for ways to improve the economic performance of yet to be industrialised Japanese society, he became interested in improving resource use in industry. He focused on the textile industry, where he first developed a wooden hand loom, which enabled workers to use only one hand instead of two, which increased the quality of the product. It increased efficiency by 40–50%. He patented this in 1891.

Toyoda then went on to introduce further generations of innovations that increased ever more the productivity of the textile industry. This includes a continuously operating loom, improved spinning machines, the use of steam power, an automatic shuttle-changing mechanism, and famously, the circular loom. Each of these pieces of equipment led to a cumulative productivity improvement of over ten, possibly fifty, over forty-five years of R&D. A factor fifty in productivity ultimately means a factor fifty in potential price reduction. However, the successive introduction of innovations in his factories was partly motivated by competition. He eventually developed a fully automatic loom, which delivered the best performance worldwide in terms of productivity and textile quality. He licensed a patent for this machine to English and American corporations. The proceeds were later used by his son to expand business into the car manufacturing industry, leading to what is today Toyota vehicles.

This archetypical story is a good representation of Schumpeter's entrepreneur. A part of what matters in accounts of Toyoda's story, however, is his relationship with capital and credit creation (Mass and Robertson, 1996). Schumpeter's entrepreneur does not generally wait until the firm generates sufficient capital to invest in R&D. Toyoda's relationship with financiers and creditors was notably complex, as he fought with shareholders and executives for returns to be re-invested in R&D. Through credit creation at financial institutions, the Schumpeterian entrepreneur can make innovation take place much faster, and indeed, it is clear that credit is necessary for firms to maintain their rate of innovation as incentivised by competition and the prospect of going out of business if beaten in the innovation race.

As opposed to the circular flow, in which there is no return for credit creation, in Schumpeter, it is clear that the entrepreneur, shareholders and the financial institution share the profits from innovative activity. Therefore, returns exist on the creation of credit. This is true to the extent that innovative activity is successful and does indeed generate a return; a default on loans given out for expansion or R&D activities could any time lead to firm bankruptcy, unless further loans are given out to pay off earlier loans, in which case firms enter a speculative stage.

Schumpeter also interrogated himself over the nature of the business cycle.[7] Many explanations had already been proposed; however, his answer was in itself innovative

developed in their lifetime, are on display, some of them in operation, in both textiles and the automobile industry.

7 See *Business cycles* (Schumpeter, 1939).

and convincing: the business cycle is due to a natural tendency towards the clustering of innovative activity. Indeed, innovations often open up possibilities for further innovations, in particular constellations of related innovations (e.g., the textile industry or steam power). This clustering implies that at particular times of history, substantial credit would have been created to fuel successful innovation. These loans would have been given out by financial institutions out of expectations generated by previous successful return on investment. At times, it may have been perceived by financial institutions that potential innovative activity in a particular domain could be unlimited. However, with excessive credit creation, more risky or less productive ideas may have started to be financed out of such euphoric expectations. Typically, at a particular moment in the business cycle, an excessive number of business failures begin to emerge, at which point financial institutions begin to restrict access to further credit to limit risky speculative activity, based on newly formed expectations of loss on investment. This is when a recession or depression begins, with substantial unemployment and social strife. The economy recovers when a new wave of innovative activity starts again (Semieniuk et al., 2021).

Schumpeter's work on the business cycle has unfortunately lain almost dormant and misinterpreted for decades, under the dominance of the neoclassical synthesis in macroeconomics. The post-Schumpeterian approach has been incrementally developed by those who founded the school of evolutionary economics. Indeed, his plea for using a historical perspective in economic analysis has been enthusiastically taken up by some researchers.[8] There are also notable parallels with the works of Keynes and Minsky, which, however, have no clear treatment of innovation and technology, but instead, detailed accounts of the workings of the financial sector.[9] This suggests that Schumpeter may have indeed developed the only combined theory on money and innovation until the theories of endogenous growth emerged in the eighties with Romer and later Aghion.[10] As it emerged after his death in 1950, Schumpeter had indeed written a book specifically on money as credit in relation to innovation,[11] in addition to his original seminal contributions (Schumpeter, 1934, 1942).

What is important in Schumpeter's theory of money is that the creation of credit, tied to investment in innovative activity and productivity change, for a return of profit, is not constant over time, but instead is involved in the business cycle. This implies that the amount of money in the economy is not constant, and certainly not determined by the amount of money printed by the central bank. This would appear

8 Notably by Freeman and Perez (1988); Freeman and Louçã (2001); Perez (2001); Geels (2002); Dosi et al. (1988); Dosi (1982); Mazzucato (2013).

9 See Keynes (1936, 1930); Minsky (1982, 1986).

10 Romer (1986); Aghion et al. (1998)

11 'Treatise on Money' (Schumpeter, 2014), which he had been working on in the 20's but was never published until posthumously in German in 1970 and in English in 2014 (see the story in Schumpeter, 1991). This may have been related to Keynes' publication of his own 'A Treatise on Money' (Keynes, 1930).

to contradict standard equilibrium ideas that the role of banks is simply to lend the savings of others, that is, to transfer funds from one name to another, where since the propensity to save is considered relatively constant, the amount of saving each year is a constant proportion of total output (GDP), and therefore does not generate fluctuations. But fluctuations in the money supply are intrinsic in Schumpeter's theory of the business cycle. This is clear in his 'Treatise on money', where he develops a detailed credit theory of money as assets and liabilities.

In fact, Schumpeter foresaw what is now called the post-Keynesian theory of endogenous money,[12] in which money is created by commercial banks in order to finance investment, where the central bank provides on demand the necessary reserves to keep commercial banks solvent. In this case, investment still equates saving, but credit creation generates most of the savings, maintaining the validity of the identity. The process of credit creation in fact simultaneously creates both a liability to the borrower (the money deposit created by the bank) and an asset for the bank (the asset owned by the bank on which it expects a return), and there is no formal limit to the amount of credit that can be created. Focus is given on modern monetary theory in Chapters 9 and 10. What matters for innovation is the relationship between finance and innovative activity, since a substantial proportion of money creation ultimately finances some form of innovation and productivity change.

8.2.3 *Creative Destruction*

To summarise Schumpeter's thought on economic development, it originates from innovation by the invention of *new combinations of inputs to production*. These new combinations generate savings on inputs to production, which imply production at lower cost, or higher production at the same cost. With competition, the cumulative effect of new combinations lead to declining real prices, and these lead to leftover money in the hands of consumers, who can then increase their level of consumption, and their choice of products, as their real incomes rise over time. Innovation also leads to increased international competitiveness and exports, and increased exports implies markets expanding beyond national boundaries, offering substantial prospects for industrial and economic growth.

However, the development of innovations also often implies capturing markets at the expense of incumbent industries. In some cases, some industries characterised by a lack of ability to compete in the innovation race, could be led to decline. This may be inevitable in the innovation race, and these industry shutdowns could leave substantial numbers of workers without work, while the new industries create new types of jobs. An important example of such a process is given in Chapter 15, in which the possible decline of the fossil fuel sector, which has likely already started,

[12] Wray (2016); Lavoie (2014); Bell (2001); Minsky (1982).

is explored, through an energy transition towards a low-carbon economy, where stranded fossil fuel assets arise as a result of low-carbon innovative activity.

As Schumpeter put it himself,

> That the theorist's teaching, according to which capital 'migrates' from declining to rising industries, is unrealistic is obvious: the capital 'invested' in railroads does not migrate into trucking and air transportation but will perish in and with the railroads. (Schumpeter, 1947)

He called this phenomenon of industry decline due to innovation *creative destruction* (Schumpeter, 1942), an expression that has become one most associated with the author, and has been used even colloquially to refer to technological change in general. It is also often used in a normative sense, as if the duty of institutions or the state should be to creatively destroy existing economic activities in order to make progress. There is no evidence in Schumpeter's writings that such a subjective meaning had been intended. In other words, *creative destruction* was not intended to be a generator of normative principles.

Creative destruction is a key theme of this book. It involves the casualties of the innovation process, as technology, management and production methods gradually transform themselves and replace older ones. The process is conceptually the same as in evolutionary biology, when a mutated form of species gains an ability to successfully invade the resource space of another species, or even that of the earlier version of the same species. The result is a system going off-balance where potentially many other previously stable species sometimes see their world going upside down, creating opportunities for some and survival issues for others. The instability can resolve itself quickly, or go from one instability to the next, or occasionally even lead to catastrophic mass extinction (see Chapter 5). There is nothing 'good' in all this; however, what is clear is that genetic diversity increases as a result of mutation and selection, which itself increases resilience and systemic stability, but only until the next revolution. The calm lulls between instabilities, where ecosystems settle in steady states and each species finds its place and role, are only ever lulls waiting for the next storm of creative destruction. However, importantly, economic growth happens through processes of creative destruction.

The same thus arises with technology and firms, and it is helpful to see the parallels between natural and man-made ecosystems (Kauffman, 2000). The attraction of entrepreneurs towards large gains from innovation, creating 'new ways to make a living' occasionally pushes the system off-balance and creates cascades of creative destruction that are not normally peaceful.[13] However, there can sometimes be a centralised force incentivising the direction of innovation, and that is the state,[14] which happens through the innovation chain. This is developed next.

[13] Freeman and Louçã (2001); Freeman and Perez (1988).

[14] Mazzucato (2013); Mazzucato and Penna (2016).

8.2.4 *Fundamental Uncertainty*

Keynes never really made much of a point of describing technology and innovation. Even in his most highly regarded works (e.g., Keynes, 1936, 1930), technology appears only as a magical external force. In Keynes' description of 'animal spirits' guiding investment and of the archetypical 'bubble on a whirlpool of speculation' (Keynes, 1936), the purpose of investment and finance is not clearly associated with technology, improved methods of production and of productivity change, it is only assumed that some sort of return exists.

A key concept from Keynes is *fundamental uncertainty*[15] which, as he puts it, is what faces the entrepreneur. This was developed in detail in Chapter 6. The uncertainty that entrepreneurs face is an unquantifiable risk that is fundamental to the investment process: entrepreneurs cannot rely on probability distributions to determine the likelihood of return on investment, neither in R&D nor in production capacity expansion. However good their forecasting abilities are, as opposed to a game of chess, they cannot enumerate all possible futures, moves and countermoves of opponents. However, with what Keynes called *animal spirits*, entrepreneurs nevertheless invest, under certain enthusiastic beliefs over the state of the market, the economy, competition and their own capabilities in the face of these. Given fundamental uncertainty over the state of the economy, investors cannot predict in advance how much to invest, produce, or expand production capacity, and how much effort to devote to R&D. In Keynes, therefore, the uncertainty incentivises them to invest beyond the expected needs, in order to make sure that no market share is lost, in case the business context changes in unexpected ways. Therefore, spare capacity always exists to maintain systemic resilience, since forcing the economy to operate exactly at expected capacity would likely be unstable.

The concept of fundamental uncertainty implies an important feature of the Keynesian economy: demand volatility is anticipated, and spare capacity exists due to a lack of coordination and predictive power of entrepreneurs, which contrasts with neoclassical equilibrium theory. Equilibrium theory is supply-led, where according to Say's law, the equilibrium is reached by a process in which all production is consumed, and therefore by definition, production capacity is fully used. Fully using capacity would be least resource intensive; however it would also imply an unstable economy under any arbitrarily small degree of demand volatility, where occasionally demand could not be met.[16]

15 Chapter 6, Keynes (1921), see also Fontana (2008).

16 A good example of this is how markets behaved under substantial changes in demand patterns during the COVD-19 crisis, which exceeded capacity buffers in supply chains and inventories for many types of goods, and these then sold at highly inflated prices. At full capacity, the economy would have no capability to absorb any change in markets at all, and price instability would result. See Carlson and Doyle (2002); Doyle and Carlson (2000) for a discussion of the tradeoff between performance of systems and their stability, a general feature of complex interacting systems.

The inability of entrepreneurs to accurately predict future volatile demand also partly explains the development of bubbles and crashes: due to a lack of coordination between entrepreneurs, they sometimes collectively create too much or too little capacity in comparison to what is later needed. Since capital, once invested into physical equipment, cannot necessarily or easily be recycled back into liquid form, substantial capital can become stranded due to investor error when incorrectly anticipating demand and its evolution.

Lastly, it should be noted that the accurate measurement of capital and capacity in the economy is known to be problematic and riddled with contradictions. Should an unused, 20-years-old tractor, or low-productivity land on hillsides, or undeveloped but registered patent, be formally counted as part of the productive capacity of the economy? They could in principle come into the productive economy under certain circumstances, but also, they may never do so, and nevertheless, agents frequently keep these things in reserve.

8.3. INNOVATION THEORY

8.3.1 *The Innovation Chain*

That innovation happens in the obscure garages of bearded scientists is romantic, but far from reality. That innovation arises in R&D labs of large companies such as Apple and Microsoft is not entirely true either, although it has had its day. The full lifecycle of innovation happens at different levels in different institutions, going through a long complicated road, with duration spanning decades. It usually starts at universities and finishes in large companies going through small start-ups and spin-offs. It is also predominantly state-financed, and in more recent years, research has become concentrated into universities as companies have gradually downscaled or even shut their R&D departments.[17]

Take, for example, solar photovoltaic technology. The p-n junction at its heart was invented in the late forties along with spectacular scientific and technological developments with semiconductors happening back then,[18] notably at Bell Labs, then the R&D branch of the AT&T company (recently taken over by Nokia). Amongst many other applications, solar cells were first used in the fifties for power generation on satellites, on which no other source of power exists than solar radiation. It took decades of R&D and development in many applications until they could be considered for mainstream electricity generation, competing with primitive but inexpensive coal combustion. The technology life cycle has covered sixty to seventy years up to now.

[17] See Grubb et al. (2014) and Mazzucato (2013) for primary references.

[18] Notably, the LED cell, the solar cell, the transistor and most subsequent electronic device building blocks.

In modern theory of innovation, the innovative process takes place through a multitude of institutions working together, making Schumpeter's description of the entrepreneur and the innovation process too simplistic for modern purposes. Indeed, while the story of Sakichi Toyoda is a good historical representation of Schumpeter's entrepreneur and his view of the innovation process, this is hardly sufficient to describe what actually happens. Modern innovation theory describes innovation as taking place through a number of *stages*, enabled by a number of *functions* in the innovation process. Figure 1.4, already given in Chapter 1 (p. 21) provides a compact representation of the *stages* of the innovation process.

General knowledge is first generated, most of the time, through academic research at institutions funded most of the time by the public sector.[19] Out of this knowledge generation, some ideas are generated over technological, managerial or financial applications that could generate a profit. These ideas are thus developed into actual prototypes that can be tried and tested. In general, at this stage, the cost of producing prototypes is very high and not suitable for markets. Meanwhile, a demand for the new products under development does not necessarily exist already. A phase of demonstration often takes place, in which actual application can be introduced, potentially attracting investors and funders, towards a potential end product that could be sold in markets. At this stage, the private sector takes over, by investing in scaling up production and generating a sellable product at prices accessible to the wider public or industry. The last stage of the innovation chain is the process of mass production and diffusion.

It is to be emphasised that each step of the innovation chain involves feedback to previous steps. In particular, every failure requires going back one step, and learning processes lead to product improvements and production cost reductions. This feedback process is very important for the successful transfer of ideas across the innovation chain, towards a product sold on the market.

A key feature of the innovation chain is that each step is financed by a different range of the spectrum of types of investors (Figure 8.2). As is typically observed, basic research features prospects of return that are deemed too uncertain for most commercial enterprises to undertake. For that reason, basic research is predominantly funded by grants from the public sector, through research funding institutions.[20] Since this already takes place, private companies can access publicly accessible knowledge generated by public funds, and thus often do not feel the need to finance it themselves. This tendency of the private sector to appropriate knowledge produced by public institutions is discussed further below.

19 Universities, research institutes – note that sometimes basic research is funded by charities, and, more rarely, by the private sector, usually in partnership with the government.

20 For instance, in the UK, the various branches of UK Research and Innovation (UKRI), sub-functions of the Department for Business, Energy and Industrial Strategy, distributing public funds for basic research and R&D at universities and in start-up companies.

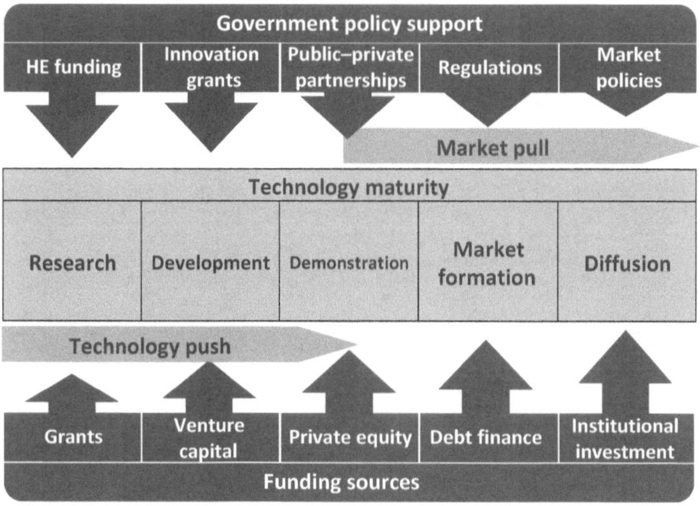

FIGURE 8.2 The innovation chain in a financial perspective. After Mercure et al. (2016b).

The second stage of the innovation chain is mainly financed by a combination of public funds and venture capital funds. Venture capitalists typically invest in start-up companies in order to offer them the time needed to develop ideas into products. They also typically offer experience and guidance in company management and development, skills that technical staff and scientists sometimes lack. They obtain return on their highly risky investments through hedging and investing in many different start-ups at the same time, the few successful ones paying for the failed ones and generating an overall profit. The majority of start-ups ultimately fail. However, substantial funding is also obtained directly from public institutions that support innovation.

As one travels rightwards across the innovation chain towards the market, one observes that increasing amounts of private funds gradually replace public funds. This is due to the perception in the private sector of lower uncertainty and more tangible returns the closer innovations are to the mass market. A trend has emerged over recent years in which large firms have become more likely to buy out smaller start-up companies than to carry out R&D themselves (Mazzucato, 2013). But large firms have the knowledge and skills necessary to identify suitable markets, scale up production and mass produce market-ready products. It is frequently the case that entrepreneurs create spin-offs from publicly generated knowledge, develop innovations and then either sell the intellectual property or the whole start-up company to large firms, since small start-up companies are generally not suited for scaling up their own products. Substantial profits can be made this way, although this is not the only possible model.

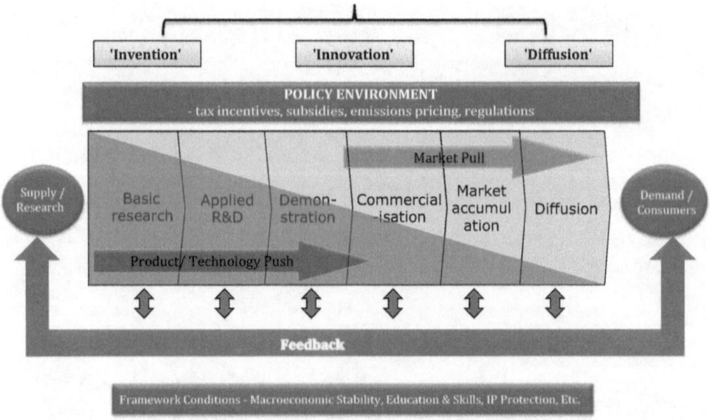

FIGURE 8.3 The innovation chain and public policy. After Grubb et al. (2014).

Due to the fact that the state finances the substantial amount of R&D that is deemed too risky by the private sector, and thus would not be financed otherwise, one could label the state as the '*innovator of last resort*'. This terminology is in reference to Keynes' description of the state as the '*spender of last resort*', where the state can fund public goods that the private sector would not be willing or able to fund, as well as Minksy's analysis of the '*lender of last resort*', in reference to the ability of the central bank to lend money for projects no other banks would be willing or able to finance. In general, the ability of the state to play a role 'of last resort' stems from the fact that the government tends to be the largest institution of the economy in terms of balance sheet, and can act as the ultimate venture capitalist, able to socialise risk and to finance needed innovation that no one else will finance. The state does this for the long-term public good in supplying fuel for future economic growth, despite the large uncertainties. By financing a sufficiently large and broad range of science and R&D, it pools and hedges innovation risk where no one else can.

Lastly, the policy regime has a strong influence on innovative activity. Public policies are classified into two broad types: technology push and market pull (Freeman, 1994, Figure 8.3). Technology push policies generally look at providing resources for innovation, and possibly, to give some direction to innovative activity where they are publicly funded. For example, the state may fund existing successful research, or can attempt to open up new research and innovation areas in which many findings are expected. But also, the state can propose partnerships with private companies to develop new technologies needed to achieve a certain policy objective, for example, reducing greenhouse gas emissions by co-financing low-carbon technology demonstration projects.[21]

[21] For example, in the UK, the government, through the Carbon Trust, has been supporting the development of offshore wind power in partnership with private companies. The goal in

At the other end of the innovation chain is the market. There, the state can also provide leadership and incentivise the direction of innovation, using market policy levers. A prominent policy tool for low-carbon innovation is carbon taxation and the carbon market, for instance, the EU's Emissions Trading Scheme. By changing the balance of costs to companies with high levels of CO_2 emissions, an incentive is created for investing in low-carbon technologies that are emerging in markets. This provides more space for low-carbon technologies to diffuse, a diffusion process that can self-reinforce as the technology spreads. Governments can also use taxes and subsidies (e.g., in vehicle markets) to level the playing field of innovations.[22] Thus, overall, the state can help direct the innovation process in two different ways, on both sides of the innovation chain.

8.3.2 *Socio-technical Regime Transitions and Technology Innovation Systems*

Two alternate, perhaps complementary descriptions of the innovation system have been developed during the last two decades, the Multi-level Perspective (MLP) on socio-technical change and technology innovation systems (TIS). These have been rising relatively independently, but share substantial amounts of common concepts.

The MLP has come to prominence with a seminal paper by Frank Geels (2002), in which he took Schumpeter's historical method to analyse the factors that contribute, or imposes barriers, to the diffusion of innovations, shown in Figure 8.4. In this perspective, innovations are initially developed and adopted in niche markets, where they find limited application (e.g., solar cells in satellites). Experimentation in innovation development plays an important part in the process (see the random arrows at the bottom). Depending on a socio-technical regime in place (arrows and elements in the middle), these niches may or may not grow to more mainstream use. However, changes in the socio-technical regime, and in the overall economic environment (wavy lines at the top, referring to population, macroeconomics, trade, etc.). When an innovation rises from a niche state towards mainstream use, a dominant design (Utterback and Abernathy, 1975) emerges out of a new technological trajectory (Dosi, 1982), increasingly accepted by mainstream actors and by the socio-technical regime. Innovations can eventually reach dominance; however, this strongly depends on enabling factors in the socio-technical regime, notably, policy, infrastructure, preferences, cultural influence and price/cost factors.

participating in the setting-up of such projects was to pave the way for more such projects by demonstration, reducing the perceived risk by private companies for such types of projects.

22 For example, electric vehicles have a high capital cost (vehicle price) but lower operation and fuel costs. This makes it difficult to attract consumers that may have high discount rates, or in other words, consumers who cannot afford high upfront costs, even if the lifetime cost is low. Capital cost subsidies can bridge that gap.

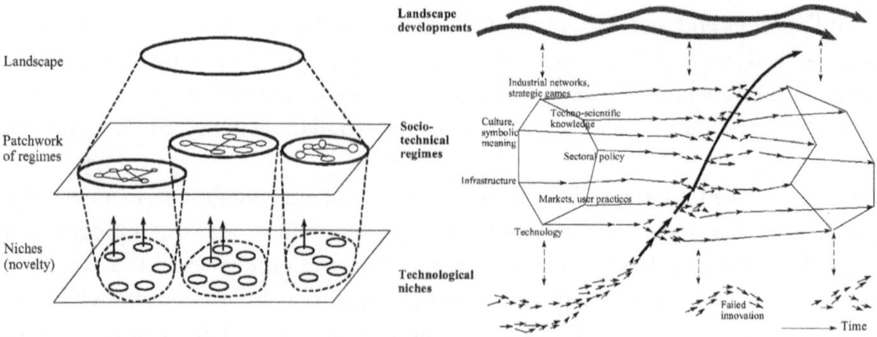

FIGURE 8.4 The multi-level perspective on technology transitions.

Substantial further work has been done on the MLP.[23] The MLP is a qualitative framework increasingly used to analyse how technological transitions have happened and how they may take place in the future, with some focus on sustainability transitions. Some of this literature focuses on a normative perspective of the MLP, in other words, how to nucleate and manage transitions, in the field of 'transitions management' (Rotmans et al., 2001). This approach, however, has been criticised as unduly normative and for not having a basis that is clearly validated historically (Genus and Coles, 2008).

The TIS analysis identifies the various institutions involved in the innovation process, and assigns to them particular *functions*:[24] (1) entrepreneurial activities, (2) knowledge development, (3) knowledge diffusion, (4) guidance of the search, (5) market formation, (6) resource mobilisation and (7) legitimisation.

(1) Entrepreneurs engage with other functions of the TIS and are enabled by them. (2) Entrepreneurial experimentation leads to accumulating experience in general, including ways to lower costs (e.g., learning curves). (3) Entrepreneurs share knowledge with other functions, including with policy-makers, which enables later facilitation. (4) Entrepreneurs and other functions make choices over what ideas/prototypes are worth focusing on and pushing through the TIS, a form of evolutionary selection. (5) Policy-makers and financiers create space for innovations to grow, either by niche management or directly by market pull policies. (6) Governments and venture capitalists mobilise finance, while research institutions may provide human resources. (7) Interest and advocacy groups raise awareness of innovations and help create a need for them. These functions work together

23 See, for instance, Geels (2005, 2006); Turnheim et al. (2015); Geels et al. (2016), with criticism, see Genus and Coles (2008), and response see Geels (2011). The origins of this line of research may be traced back to Freeman and Perez (1988); Freeman and Louçã (2001); Dosi et al. (1988); Dosi (1982).

24 The seminal papers in this literature are Hekkert et al. (2007) and Bergek et al. (2008). However, this line of research can be traced back to the work of Nelson and Winter (1982).

and enable innovation to progress. Missing one or more of these functions may substantially impede progress.

8.3.3 *Innovation Empirically*

Entrepreneurs and companies do invest in R&D to a certain degree endogenously, to attract business. Two extremes can be imagined that would show a cautionary tale to the entrepreneur who can use this as a rule of thumb for his/her choice of level of R&D investment. At one end of the scale, no investment in any innovation in a company means no development of new products at all. This can only happen temporarily, as it is hardly likely that existing products sell indefinitely. Companies must invest a minimum in developing new products that track changes in consumer tastes, evolving markets, selling prices and so on. Not doing so leads to almost certain business failure.

At the other end of the scale, one can imagine that large returns can be generated out of creating a revolutionary product, the success of which beats all competition. Investing big in R&D, more than the competition, with big ideas, can bring success; however, many small issues and problems can make it fail, not least the response from the competition that may change the market. Thus, investing a large fraction of resources available or that can be raised (e.g., cash, debt, equity) risks making the company fail through possible sequences of what with hindsight turns out to be strategic mistakes.

Klingebiel and Rammer (2014) show, using large surveys in Europe, that companies create their success by using clever combinations of breadth of experimentation, commitment to innovation, and good selection mechanisms. Breadth means that companies attempt to cover a good variety of innovation and product development projects in parallel, with different levels of risk. Commitment implies that companies commit to developing those products and do not cut off projects too early before they can see whether they are promising or not. Selection implies that companies have good and realistic ways to select which projects to support all the way to the marketing stage.

Meanwhile, in the time domain, there is a tendency to move, within a particular domain of technology, from seeking the maximisation of performance, towards the maximisation of sales and later towards the minimisation of costs (Utterback and Abernathy, 1975). This is related to the degree to which companies are committed to certain production processes, and how difficult or costly they are to change subsequently. Thus in the earlier stages during which products are designed according to the market, development is 'product innovation'-dominated. However, in the later stages of mass diffusion, innovation is 'process innovation'-dominated, where the product design is not substantially changed but the process to make it is improved. The lifecycle of products and the interplay of product/process innovation and their macroeconomic implications are taken up again in Chapter 11.

8.3.4 *Porter's Hypothesis*

In 1995, Michael E. Porter wrote an influential proposition regarding how environmental regulation can induce innovation, which itself could improve industrial competitiveness (Porter and van der Linde, 1995). This paper has been both controversial, since it contradicts many concepts of conventional environmental economics, and influential, as it offered new strategies for policy-makers. An extract of his text expresses this best:

> Competitive advantage, then, rests not on static efficiency nor on optimizing within fixed constraints, but on the capacity for innovation and improvement that shift the constraints. (Porter and van der Linde, 1995)

This therefore involves the innovation system at large interacting with the regulatory/policy regime. In this picture, firms are compelled by tightening regulation to search for ways to comply, and through this searching process, identify ways to improve their own cost-competitiveness, since innovative search often leads to such outcomes. Meanwhile, without any regulatory change, firms might see little incentive to invest in R&D.

Some evidence exists supporting Porter's hypothesis. In the learning curves literature, van Buskirk et al. (2014) empirically show that rates of learning, as functions of cumulative sales, have been changing in the USA for some types of household appliances (refrigerators, air conditioners, washing machines) each time a regulatory change took place. Another prime example is Japan's top runner program and, in particular, its influence in the automobile industry (Miyoshi and Kii, 2011). Periodic regulatory change increasing the ambition of efficiency standards based on the best technologies available incentivised an innovation race in Japan that saw rapid and widespread efficiency change, notably in energy efficiency and safety standards. This involved adaptive cooperation and communication between the private sector and the government.

8.3.5 *The State and the Innovation Chain*

Mazzucato (2013, 2018) argues that a romantic myth has been maintained in the Western World regarding the heroic role of sole entrepreneurs in shaping modern technology in the face of resistance, particularly prominent in Silicon Valley. The myth maintains that Silicon Valley 'garage inventors' and venture capitalists are to be attributed all the credit for rapid economic growth in California. It also maintains that their freedom from any sort of regulations was key to their success. Mazzucato suggests that this is a myth for the reason that most of the technologies that companies such as Apple, IBM, Intel and Microsoft used in their commercialisation processes were in fact developed not by them, but through publicly funded R&D, at universities and research centres.

The key role of these 'garage inventors' has been somewhat different to that maintained by the myth they themselves created: rather than inventing revolutionary gadgets in their garages, in fact they developed existing ideas, created by others in research labs, into the successful marketable products we see today. This is not to say that they have no merit in having done so, since commercialising innovations is one of the key processes and challenges of the innovation chain. However, disproportionate credit may have been given, in the public space, to entrepreneurs and venture capitalists, as a narrative designed to justify avoiding taxes and regulation, while insufficient credit may have been given to publicly funded research institutions. The public sector has received indirect returns for its investment in innovation through economic growth, improved employment and wages, and therefore tax income in public coffers. But the entrepreneurs of Silicon Valley created unassailable monopolies and accumulated unprecedented wealth, so much that it increased inequality in California to an extreme degree.

8.3.6 A *Wish List for Models of Innovation*

Innovation is not represented satisfactorily in traditional economic models, by which is meant models based on national accounts and on a social accounting matrix. In essence, forecasting innovation is about predicting the unknowable (see Chapter 6), and therefore, predicting how it shapes the economy is also unknowable to some degree. However, models that do not represent innovation at all are bound to make entirely incorrect macroeconomic predictions, which later on leads to recommending ill advised or ineffective public policy courses of action, and ideologies (see Chapter 4). If innovation did not exist, perhaps understanding the economy under an equilibrium Walrasian circular flow could be correct, where the economy has time to explore all of its possible states and settle on the best. But as discussed with the concept of the Adjacent Possible (Chapters 5 and 6), this is ruled out, as should all models based on equilibrium assumptions. There are not many models left after that. There remains post-Keynesian models, Schumpeterian models and complexity economics models (see Chapter 3).

However, it is reasonable to consider that the evolutionary pattern of innovation repeats itself, under some organising principle. Innovation is not random, nor is biological evolution. It builds upon itself. In principle, there is no reason why such a process could not be explored using simulations of agents exploring the Adjacent Possible. What models of innovation must generate are macro properties that emerge from that searching process, in which, ultimately, *creative destruction* leads, in aggregate, to some gradual productivity change in the economy, which itself incentivises increased effective aggregate demand for products and services. An attempt at creating the backbone of such a model is given in the next section. At the macroeconomic level, this is completed in Chapter 11.

8.4. MICRO-FOUNDATIONS FOR A THEORY OF INNOVATION

8.4.1 *Complex Innovation Networks*

In this section, micro-foundations are proposed for a theory of the entrepreneur and the process of innovation. The current representation of innovation in neoclassical equilibrium microeconomic theory is clearly deficient, primarily because it assumes that returns on investment in innovation are known probabilistically by entrepreneurs, who can then determine the optimal quantity of investment and optimal portfolio diversification to maximise profits. It is clear that if agents knew the future, science and R&D would not exist. In addition, the minimal representation of banking in neoclassical theory as only intermediates between savers and borrowers is also inadequate. This is clear since in times of optimism in the economy, there is more investment than in times of economic pessimism, such that the amount of investment is not entirely related to, or driven by, saving behaviour of households, as discussed in Chapters 9 and 10. It is related to the ability of the entrepreneur-finance collective to make finance materialise when and only when perceived risks are sufficiently low and substantial returns are expected.

The process of innovation is a complex network as it involves the recombination of existing ideas by entrepreneurs. When an innovation or invention is made, it is composed almost exclusively of a new combination of existing technology components. Thus, innovation builds upon itself continuously, and thus '*complexifies*', where the development new innovations is *contingent* on the existence of its components, developed through earlier innovative work by others. This is reflected by citations, in the filing of new patents, of earlier patents upon which they build. This forms a network of patents that develops over time. Given that innovations are contingent on earlier innovations, the temporal nature of innovation is highly non-ergodic and path-dependent. Sometimes, the same functionality or purpose is achieved by several innovations composed of different components, and if one of these becomes perceived as clearly 'superior', the components of the 'inferior' one can become obsolete and disused, leading to avalanches of technological abandonment, or in the words of Schumpeter, *gales of creative destruction*. Indeed, as Schumpeter famously claimed, the development of technology typically clusters in time, which requires investigation.

8.4.2 *Learning-by-Doing*

Despite the apparent chaotic behaviour of innovation systems when creative destruction occurs, it leads to remarkably regular organising principles and patterns: the *S-shaped diffusion* of innovations, as seen in Chapter 7, and the *learning curve*. The latter concept was famously invented by the Wright brothers, inventors of aeroplanes, who noted that the time required to build aeroplane frames appeared to decline following the cumulative number of frames built earlier in their factory, to an exponent of exactly $-\frac{1}{3}$ (Wright's law, Wright, 1936). This translated directly to a reduction of the cost of production of airplanes according to how many had been built before. This concept has been re-used countless times in economic modelling,[25] partly because it is very simple and easy to use for technological forecasting.[26] It describes production costs C as related to the cumulative number of units produced W over history through a power law (log-log) relationship:

$$\frac{C}{C_O} = \left(\frac{W}{W_O}\right)^{-b}, \tag{8.1}$$

where b is an exponent related to the learning rate through $\ln(1 - LR)/\ln 2$, the latter representing the percentage cost reduction for a doubling of cumulative production.[27]

Another observed regularity is Moore's law, which observes exponentially decreasing technological costs over *time*. This originated from computer technology in which the performance was observed to double every eighteen months (Farmer and Lafond, 2016). Given that technologies in early stages of diffusion normally diffuse exponentially, Moore's Law and Wright's Law are really alternate statements of the same basic regularity. Here it is assumed that Wright's law is the fundamental law, and Moore's Law is a consequence through the regularity of the S-shaped diffusion curve.[28]

Each cost reduction in Wright's Law stems from the actions of engineers and entrepreneurs over all sorts of aspects of the technology and its business model. One could expect this to be completely random, and this makes this regularity, which *emerges* from the complexity of the innovation system, quite remarkable. It is also remarkable that few if any attempts have really been made to quantitatively explain the learning rate out of concepts from innovation systems. One of the best attempts so far is that by McNerney et al. (2011), where learning rates are associated with technological complexity, something related to what is developed below.

[25] Arrow (1962a); Farmer and Lafond (2016); Weiss et al. (2010); McDonald and Schrattenholzer (2001).

[26] See, for instance, Grubb et al. (2014) Ch. 9, and Köhler et al. (2006). The cost of new solar panels is regularly compared with the learning curve for solar panels and the relationship appears respected over several orders of magnitude (see Yu et al., 2016).

[27] C_O, W_O are baseline costs and cumulative production at any chosen earlier position in the learning curve.

[28] One cannot prove that this is so; however, the relationship of economic quantities to time usually arises through investment, and if this is so, it is the diffusion that drives the learning curve, not time. If investment stopped (e.g., during a recession), cost reductions would almost certainly stop, generating a break in Moore's Law but not Wright's Law.

In contrast, many attempts have been made to *forecast* future costs of technology based on existing data and observed learning rates.[29] Learning rates are distributed within a range that spans 5 to 30 percent (Weiss et al., 2010), where smaller compact technologies improve faster (solar panels, computers), while larger bulkier systems improve more slowly. A key aspect may be that smaller units typically see vastly larger numbers of unit sales and vastly more repetitive production processes multiplying the impacts of small process innovations (Wilson et al., 2020). This seems intuitively correct, but remains unexplained, and it is a legitimate question whether patterns that could explain learning rates could be found in patenting data.

8.4.3 *Innovation as a Self-Organised Phenomenon*

Arthur and Polak (2006) identified self-organised criticality in a simple artificial innovation system simulated on a computer. The domain of logic operator development in computers was used as a schematic representation of an innovation system. All logic operators are constructed out of simpler logic operators down to a few most basic elements, and up to unlimited levels of sophistication (e.g., up to a micro-processor, made of large numbers of miniaturised transistors). Here, Arthur hypothesised agents randomly assembling operators until they find useful applications, keeping those and dismissing applications that become obsolete. This model is useful in many ways as it limits the sheer size of the growing Adjacent Possible.

Arthur's innovation system does not 'know' how to construct these applications, but quickly discovers how useful they can be. Setting a number of technological goals (desirable applications), the simulation randomly combines system parts (logical operators) until useful applications are 'discovered' (higher level logical operators), upon which can be built ever more elaborate systems. By running the computer software large numbers of times, Arthur could accumulate sufficient statistics to identify robust, recurrent scale-free distribution properties of self-organised criticality (Figure 8.5), even though the sequence of innovations discovered, and the time taken to discover them, differ at every run. In some runs, some innovations are never discovered, while new ones emerge. But the key outcome is: the statistics of self-organised criticality are recurrently observed.

Various phenomena are observed in this innovation system: (1) ever better applications are 'discovered', (2) the 'discovery' of useful innovations cluster in time and (3) existing combinations of elements providing existing useful applications can become obsolete by the discovery of simpler combinations supplying the same application, which with less system parts in numbers, are 'cheaper'. As when cutting a dead branch off a tree, the replacement of obsolete applications typically comes

[29] For example, see Farmer and Lafond (2016); Lafond et al. (2018) and references therein. Farmer, Lafond et al. develop a method to phenomenologically forecast Moore's law, but this does not explain the underlying mechanisms.

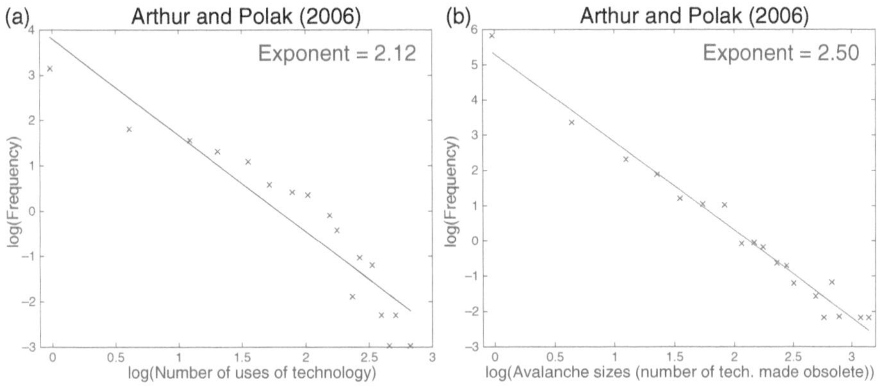

FIGURE 8.5 Self-similarity and avalanches in an artificial innovation system. Panel a shows uses of technologies by other technologies (innovation network node degrees), while Panel b shows avalanches of technology obsolescence. The data was taken from the paper by Arthur and Polak (2006) and fitted by the present author.

in whole groups, which Arthur calls 'avalanches'. He finds that the magnitude-frequency relationship of avalanches is like that of earthquakes, it is a power-law scale-free distribution. The clustering also suggests an observation of the punctuated equilibrium, with lulls during which search occurs, between bursts of new applications causing mass obsolescence.

The properties of this imaginary system suggests that real innovation systems may be self-organised critical, if indeed they follow similar dynamics. And it intuitively makes sense. But is this the case in the real world? To answer this, one needs to identify the phenomenon empirically, and this is more challenging, not least since critical systems have no bounds while datasets are normally of finite size.

8.4.4 *Innovation as Scale-Free Networks*

The scale-free nature of real innovation systems has been studied by various researchers.[30] In the patenting system, innovation forms networks, since patents must cite all patents they build upon. Backwards citation counting indicates other innovations that are used in the design of an innovation; forwards citation counting indicates which innovations are making use of an innovation. Here, data on patents in the EU and the USA are used to explore the topology of the innovation network.[31] By counting the number of innovations with N backwards citations, one observes that those with larger N occur less frequently than those with

[30] See for instance O'Neale and Hendy (2012), Brantle and Fallah (2007), Li et al. (2007), Valverde et al. (2007) and Hung and Wang (2008).

[31] The data used is the 2020 'OECD citations database', derived from PATSTAT (Webb et al., 2005).

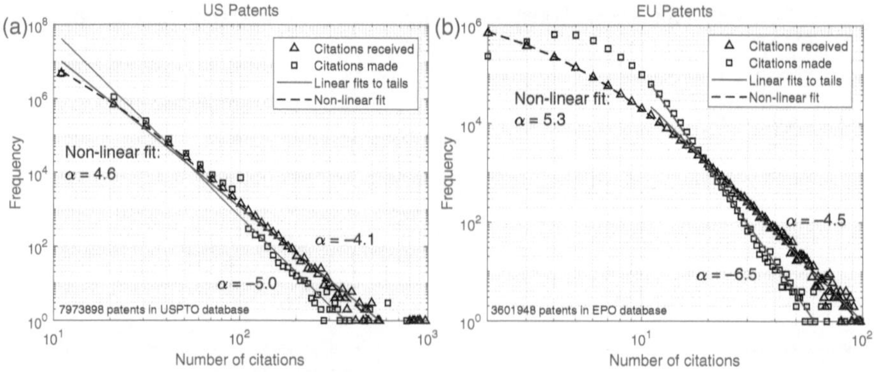

FIGURE 8.6 Frequency distributions of citations in US and EU patent citations datasets, with fits to the data. Linear fits in log-log space are made to the tails (solid lines) with exponents shown, and non-linear fits of the form $\log(F) = -\alpha \log(N + N_o) + C$ display more accurate representations of the data. The latter takes account of patent ageing (Valverde et al., 2007).

lower *N*, following a power law with specific exponents. Furthermore, by counting the number of innovations with *M* citations forwards, those with larger *M* are also more frequent than those with lower *M* with another power law.

This is demonstrated in Figure 8.6, where the numbers of forward and backwards citations in real data are shown, and exponents of between 4.5 and 5.5 are observed for citations received, and of between 5 and above 6 for citations made. The non-linearity observed in the data at low citation counts has been argued to be due to the process of patent ageing, where older patents receive less citations than new patents, which implies that citations initially increase faster for new innovations, before going towards some sort of a more steady citation flow converging to a scale-free state. Linear fits to tails and non-linear fits are both made which generate slightly different exponents.

That patent networks, or journal article citing networks, form complex networks with power law distributions of citation frequencies is well documented (Katz, 2016). It can be thought of as the branches of a tree. When creative destruction takes place, whole branches of that tree, large or small, get cut off by becoming obsolete due to the growth of new more effective branches. Thus the process illustrated in Arthur's artificial model of innovation may be seen as this continuous tree-pruning process. This could be called the 'Gardener's model', where a gardener cuts branches off a scale-free hedge randomly, and the frequency-size distribution of branches falling is calculated.

This then suggests that there may be a relationship between the well-known scale-free exponents of patent network topologies, and the scale-free exponents of hypothesised creative destruction avalanches. O'Neale and Hendy (2012) find that the frequency distribution of persons successfully filing patents is also scale-free. In fact, it is well known that the size of companies follows a Pareto (power law) distribution. If company value was to be quantified according to ownership of patents, O'Neale and Hendy (2012) suggest that similar distributions would be observed. However, their key finding is that differences in the scale-free exponents of patent ownership between countries are inversely related to R&D intensity and export product ubiquity in those countries. Thus some enabling factors must exist, such as R&D funding, that allows more innovators to file patents in countries where the measured exponent is lower.

In patent citation networks, the exponent is probably instead related to characteristics of technologies in particular domains of development. Rapid learning-by-doing rates are known to characterise the IT and micro- or nano-electronics domain, while slower learning rates characterise the heavy and chemical industries.[32] This may be related to the physical form and size of products, and the frequency at which steps are repeated in production lines, and the number of units overall sold. Large and heavy products, such as steel and thermal electrical plants, are not produced in large numbers, limiting the opportunities for process innovation, while small, packaged innovations, such as solar cells or computer processors, are produced repeatedly in astronomical numbers. This would likely be reflected in a higher density of patents of secondary importance on process innovation surrounding main domains in IT sectors compared with the heavy industries. This would translate to lower exponents in the former, and higher exponents in the latter.

8.4.5 *Rates of Innovative Activity and Learning Curves*

Rates of innovation may therefore be structurally related to the shape of the innovation network, for both '*who*' develops and patents ideas, and '*how*' ideas relate to one another. Highly concentrated ownership of patents is a sign of low R&D intensity, and highly concentrated patent connectivity (few large hubs, lots of leaves) indicates domains with slow progress and low learning rates. The converse appears also true. It is beyond the scope of this book to demonstrate the latter using the patent network, but the general relationship that is suggested here could exist, without yet empirical support, as follows.

In the Gardener's model, the innovation network makes progress, through creative destruction, by replacing existing ideas, and their dependent ideas, by new ideas that involve the use of less resources for their development and, *ceteris paribus*, higher returns on investment. Innovations are situated on a scale-free network '*hedge*' of connected ideas, and the '*creative destruction gardener*' cuts branches off that network, which are naturally attached by just one link, in terms of dependent ideas. The size of the branches that fall down is related to the magnitude of the cost

32 See Grubb et al. (2014), Farmer and Lafond (2016).

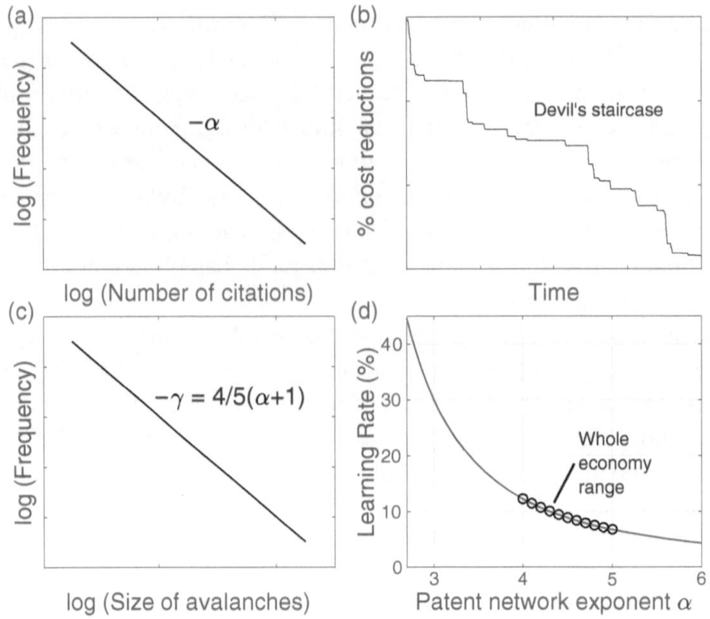

FIGURE 8.7 Illustration of the theory linking creative destruction in innovation networks and rates of learning-by-doing. (a) Innovation networks are scale free, characterised by exponent $-\alpha$. (b) As creative destruction brings small or large sections of the network of ideas to obsolescence, costs decline following a Devil's staircase. (c) The Devil's staircase cost reduction statistics are characterised by a scale-free distribution of innovation event frequency with exponent γ linearly related to α in the range of interest greater than about 2.5. (d) The learning rate is a function of the topology of the network of ideas α, which when approximated by the use of the patent network, yields a range of 4–5 when exploring all patents in the EU and the USA, which corresponds to learning rates of between 7 and 12%.

reductions that result from the R&D project of process innovation that led to their pruning. The hypothesis is that some will be large, and some will be small, with corresponding scale-free statistics. Cost reductions will follow a 'devil's staircase' downwards, where steps (branches) all have different sizes. This will lead, in the long run, towards declining costs (the total weight of dead wood accumulating); however, costs can only decline as a proportion of existing costs (the weight of the original hedge), as the innovation process gets rid of costly components and replaces them by less costly ones. Thus, relative cost reductions follow a devil's staircase, but absolute costs follow a power law decline, characterised by an exponent that is related to the network of ideas being creatively destroyed (Figure 8.7). The mathematics of this are given in Appendix A.

This model is in principle very similar to the one by McNerney et al. (2011). In that model, it is technological complexity that is suggested to determine the learning rate, which is a very similar proposal to the above, where it is the local topology of the network of ideas that is explored. In McNerney, through so-called 'design structure matrices', chains of dependencies of components to the elimination of other components serve the role that the topology takes here, but here this is proposed to be scale-free distributed, since the patent network is known to be. But furthermore, the shape of the frequency distribution of avalanche sizes is underpinned by the self-organised criticality process, providing a good explanation for its power law structure. It is certainly possible that both models are correct and complementary, and both require to be validated empirically.

It does turn out that one can show with a simple computer simulation that if one takes a scale-free network of ideas, and kills random nodes, and their dependent nodes, as the gardener prunes the branches of his hedge, the frequency distribution of the size of the branches falling is indeed a scale-free distribution. The exponent of the power law, denoted γ here, is linearly related to the scale-free exponent α describing the forward nodes of the network (i.e. in the direction looking towards the end of branches). The relationship appears be very close to $\gamma = \frac{4}{5}(1+\alpha)$.[33] The mathematics of Appendix A show that the prefactor in the log-log linear relationship between cost reductions and cumulated investment in the learning curve is $[(\gamma - 1)(\gamma - 2)]^{-1}$.

The 'learning rate' for the whole economy can then be estimated using the scale-free topology exponent for the whole patent network. With a topology exponent $\alpha \simeq 4.5 \pm 0.5$, the learning exponent that characterises the whole economy is $b = -0.12 \pm 0.04$. This would correspond to a cost reduction of $9 \pm 2\%$ for a doubling of capacity. The literature, however, shows that exponents cover the range between 3 and 30% with a mean around 15%, when looking at various household and industrial technologies (Weiss et al., 2010). The economy as a whole would therefore be slower than the rate of learning in electronics (up to 30–40%) but faster than that of the slower heavy industry (as low as 3%).[34] It has to be kept in mind that many sectors do not innovate in any substantial way. This is very crude, and more research is needed to establish this more solidly, in particular, by showing whether the equation above does indeed predict sectoral learning rates, out of local patent topologies, which is the hypothesis made here.

This model could explain whether the type of technology, its packageability, and how it combines components determines the rate of progress in relation to sales. If this is correct, then sectoral productivity growth following investment and expansion

33 This was obtained by creating random scale-free networks on a computer through the process of preferential attachment, and by randomly killing nodes and their dependents to create statistics of creative destruction. The result is scale-free with an exponent linearly related to the scale-free exponent of the original network. The experiment was carried out for network exponents between 2 and 6.

34 This analysis may, however, be biased by the known sector-specific propensity to patent ideas; more research would be needed to make this more accurate.

could be explained from micro-foundations in the network of ideas. Then the process of innovation, in particular process innovation, from R&D to creative destruction to profits sectoral output growth, all of that would become much clearer. If this can be demonstrated empirically, then a quantitative theory of innovation may actually emerge.

8.5. CONCLUSION

Innovation is the background process driving economic growth and development. It operates through Schumpeter's 'gales of creative destruction', in which old ideas, which cluster in constellations, are made obsolete by new ideas continuously generated by the inventiveness of agents, and their desire to solve problems and improve methods. Ideas build upon existing ideas by evolving through the Adjacent Possible. Such a process builds scale-free networks through preferential attachment. Such networks are described by scale-free exponents.

Innovation builds fragile cathedrals that undergo partial collapse through small and large technological revolutions, a process of self organised criticality. Innovation brings the innovation network close to the edge of chaos (Kauffman, 2000). Collapses follow a punctuated equilibrium. Each of those collapses lead to technological improvements and cost reductions in production processes that can diffuse across the economy, leading to either or both profits and lower prices, both of which increase spending and demand for new products or larger quantities of the same products as the 'usual basket of products' becomes less costly in real terms.

The exponents characterising the topology of the network of ideas ultimately control the shape of the creative destruction process as it describes what becomes obsolete and the magnitude of associated cost reductions. This is essentially because what periodically collapses is sections, large or small, of the existing network, which become obsolete following the development of other areas of the network.

However, variations exist between different technological domains, due to realities on the ground such as technology size, and the repetitive nature of the production process. It is the number of units coming out of factories that appear to drive learning rather than the volume of material or the economic value. Thus, small self-contained technological units have higher learning rates than large bulky and complex items. Learning rates are ultimately not explained quantitatively by any proposed theory. The theory proposed here suggests that analysing subsets of the network of ideas, for which one can take the network of patents as an inaccurate but available proxy, to predict learning rates for different sectoral subsets of the economy. This is beyond the scope of the present book, and therefore it cannot be shown here whether or not this approach makes reliable predictions. However, analysing distributions of patent ownership has predictive power on R&D intensity, and therefore it is reasonable to expect that the method discussed here may also have similar predictive power.

Now that innovation has been explored from a microeconomic point of view, it is important to explore the process, especially the interplay between product and process innovation, at the macroeconomic level with its relationship with economic growth. However, this involves finance, and thus finance must be discussed next. What is not simple is that there is no widely accepted theory for money and the financial sector. This therefore takes two chapters to develop, the first on money (Chapter 9) and one on the financial instability hypothesis (Chapter 10). The theory of money is important because it determines whether the quantity of finance is constrained by saving (in the sense of restricted consumption) or whether it is free to fluctuate and generate financial bubbles and crashes. Given the correct definition for money as asset-liabilities, then a self-organised critical model of the buildup of financial ownership can be constructed. This demonstrates how the accumulation of debt, for example, through the low-carbon transition, can lead to financial instability. This is developed next.

8.6. MATHEMATICAL APPENDIX

Appendix A: Connecting Networks of Ideas and Learning-by-Doing

The unit cost of a technology is defined as $C(t)$, and is defined as roughly equal to the ratio of the sum of the inputs to production over the production capital's lifetime I (capital investment in production capacity for that technology and fixed costs over the capital's lifetime), and the number of produced units during that lifetime P

$$C(t) \simeq \frac{I(t)}{P(t)}. \tag{8.2}$$

With more production of units at the same capital cost, or lower capital costs for the same production, unit costs go down. All of the cost components, investment or fixed, can in principle go down through innovation. It was discussed above that a learning curve usually exists, where costs go down as a power law function of cumulative production,

$$\frac{C(t)}{C(t_o)} = \left(\frac{\sum_o^t P(t)}{\sum_o^{t_o} P(t)} \right)^{-b}, \tag{8.3}$$

where t is the present time and the t_o is an earlier time, the starting point. As further units come out of the factory over time after t_o, costs decline below the value of C at t_o.

It is assumed that costs decline (and only decline) due to creative destruction. A number of engineers are imagined to combine ideas in innovative combinations searching for ways to cut costs by simplifying various parts of the technology. Thus the number of ideas they search through constantly rises, and the work is naturally ever more difficult. In the model of (Arthur and Polak, 2006), the number of successful ideas developed slows down roughly following the logarithm of time for a constant searching effort, which implies that the difficulty of finding a useful combination of ideas possibly rises exponentially. The most likely reason for this is that the space of ideas in which engineers search grows exponentially, as they develop it and constantly add to it. Alternatively, it may be that engineers search until they find ways to reduce costs, but go no further, as the Adjacent Possible is too large to search through, as discussed in Chapter 6.

Cost reductions ΔC are expressed using the factor ξ, as a fraction of current production costs $\Delta C = -\xi C(t)$, which follows a downwards devil's staircase during each unit time period Δt, where at each successful innovation event, a fraction of the inputs to production is eliminated and ξ becomes an ever smaller fraction of one. A key question is how frequently R&D attempts at reducing costs are done. It is postulated here that it happens every time a unit comes out of the factory, which is when the opportunity for identifying failures and inefficiencies in the production process arises. However, with R&D, the number of patents to search through for new combinations rises.

This devil's staircase scales linearly with R&D intensity β, which expresses a rate of innovation activity, depending how frequently attempts are made at reducing the inputs to production per unit of time t. Innovation attempts seek to eliminate inputs to production, and are repeated over and over at the rate of β. The number of inputs eliminated during each attempt are assumed to correspond to the number of patents becoming obsolete in an avalanche of creative destruction. The frequency distribution f of events eliminating n patents, generating changes in ξ in a unit time Δt, is scale-free and therefore a power law $An^{-\gamma}$, of exponent $\gamma > 2$. In a continuous limit approximation, the expected value for cost reductions is thus

$$\xi(t) \simeq -\left(\int_1^\infty f(n)n\,dn\right)\beta\Delta t = \left(\int_1^\infty An^{1-\gamma}dn\right)\beta\Delta t = \frac{A\beta\Delta t}{\gamma - 2}, \qquad (8.4)$$

where A is a normalisation constant $\simeq \int_1^\infty n^{-\gamma}dn = \frac{1}{\gamma-1}$. Thus the changes in costs are

$$\frac{\Delta C}{C} = -\frac{\beta\Delta t}{(\gamma-1)(\gamma-2)}, \quad \Rightarrow \log\frac{C}{C_0} = -\frac{\beta(t-t_0)}{(\gamma-1)(\gamma-2)}. \qquad (8.5)$$

This is an expression of Moore's law (Farmer and Lafond, 2016). For example, in computers, for several decades, costs per unit of computing power were halving every eighteen months.

To turn this into Wright's law, one needs to know how fast cumulative sales are growing. It is assumed that at each time step, investment in R&D takes place proportional to sales during that time step, as a fraction of the income is spent on R&D (total R&D scales with output). In the early phases of technological diffusion, where most of the learning cost reductions that matter happen, sales typically rise exponentially, at a rate that is related to β', $I_{R\&D} \propto P(t) \propto e^{\beta' t}$. However, knowledge does not depreciate, and it is cumulated knowledge that makes productivity move forwards, at R&D intensity β. This implies that

$$\log\left(\frac{\sum_{0}^{t} P(t)}{\sum_{0}^{t_0} P(t)}\right) = \beta'(t - t_0). \tag{8.6}$$

Here, the assumption is made, which cannot be proven here unless it is done empirically, that $\beta = \beta'$, in that the frequency of innovative activity is the rate of growth of sales, due to an implicit assumption that the effort applied to generate a constant rate of cost reduction over time rises exponentially. Meanwhile, the exponent of the scale-free avalanches γ is related to the exponent of the scale-free network α from which patents are eliminated, through $\gamma = \frac{4}{5}(1+\alpha)$, which as stated earlier, is something that is straightforward to show by computational experiments with the Gardener's model.

Therefore, the expression for learning-by-doing is obtained,

$$\log\frac{C}{C_0} = -\left[\left(\frac{4}{5}(1+\alpha) - 1\right)\left(\frac{4}{5}(1+\alpha) - 2\right)\right]^{-1}\log\left(\frac{\sum_{0}^{t} P(t)}{\sum_{0}^{t_0} P(t)}\right), \tag{8.7}$$

where the middle term in brackets is the learning exponent, related to the learning rate (% cost reduction for doubling of capacity):

$$LR = 1 - 2^{\left[\left(\frac{4}{5}(1+\alpha)-1\right)\left(\frac{4}{5}(1+\alpha)-2\right)\right]^{-1}}. \tag{8.8}$$

The hypothesis is made, however, that in the case where $\beta \neq \beta'$, Wright's law remains unaffected but Moore's law changes slope over time. Wright's law is independent of time and only relates to the topology of the network of ideas. To be respected, it does not require that sales increase exponentially, only Moore's law does. The above equation can be tested against innovation network data, and while this is simple mathematically, it requires an extensive patent data management effort outside of the scope of this book. A regression of learning exponents against local scale-free network exponents for various domains (software, electronics, biotech, chemicals etc.) could be made, which could determine whether $\beta = \beta'$, if the finding is that the relationship between the exponents is linear. This model is in principle very similar to that of McNerney et al. (2011), where the novelty concerns primarily the Gardener's model of self-organised criticality which states a relationship with the network of ideas and the possible link with the patent network to predict learning rates.

9

Empirical Foundations for the Nature of Money

The low-carbon transition is capital-intensive and requires the creation of substantial amounts of finance, and a premature depreciation of existing capital. It remains unclear what the impact of the transition will be for the financial sector. Current models lack clear causal representations between systemic risk, financial network dynamics, credit creation and instability. At the heart of this issue is a century-old debate on the nature of money, finance and debt. Here, empirical foundations are developed for a complexity and complex networks theory of macroeconomics by bringing together evidence from both economic anthropology and econophysics. Evidence from economic anthropology helps us to understand the origin, development and nature of money as liability-asset relationships between, and created by economic agents. At the same time, empirics from econophysics and complex networks analysis allow us to better understand the concept of systemic risk and financial dynamics during instabilities. These insights are brought together in a way that lays possible foundations for the development of a better understanding of the endogenous growth of financial networks, investment and economic growth.

9.1. THE SCHISM OVER MONEY

9.1.1 *Is the Quantity of Money Conserved?*

The previous two chapters explored the dynamics of technology diffusion and innovation. As was made clear in Chapter 8, innovation and finance generally co-evolve and feed off each other. The low-carbon transition is capital-intensive, in comparison to the incumbent high-carbon system. It replaces the fuel, the wages and the operational expenditures involved when producing fuel, by capital expenditures on technology. This implies that large amounts of finance must be created to build the low-carbon capital, while at the same time, large amounts of high-carbon produced capital (equipment and machinery) may depreciate prematurely. The impact of these two processes on the financial system and its stability is not well known, not least because the finance of innovation and technological change is not typically studied with suitable tools. Equilibrium models will not, by their definition, have the ability to study the financial instability.

The last financial instability before COVID, the 2007–2008 financial crisis and ensuing great recession, has changed perceptions of economics, and highlighted a deep unease, in academia and in the public, over the ability of economists to understand and predict basic characteristics and behaviour of the global economy (Haldane and Turrell, 2018). Her Majesty Queen Elizabeth II famously asked Prof. Tim Besley at the London School of Economics 'How come nobody could foresee it?' (Besley and Hennessy, 2009). Substantial discussions have taken place since, including the role of complexity science in economics for understanding complex financial network dynamics.[1] Despite this, no clear consensus has emerged yet on a theory of macroeconomics, across schools, that can understand endogenously the emergent onset of large financial instabilities.

How growth and economic change are understood takes its roots in how we understand the process of finance, credit creation and the nature of money.[2] Therefore, before exploring the financial impacts of the low-carbon transition, this chapter must develop an understanding of money. One would think that, if there is anything that economics should explain as part of its fundamental concepts, it should be money. But curiously, it does not. Two main currents emerge, the equilibrium and the non-equilibrium broad groupings of schools of thought, which offer exactly opposite stances on the direction of causation of events in the process of finance, innovation and economic growth (Chapter 3). In the equilibrium schools, loanable funds are created by economic agents saving and banks channelling savings from lenders to borrowers, with a clearing money market and a conserved exogenous quantity of capital (Nordhaus and Samuelson, 2009). In the non-equilibrium schools, banks simply just create credit and purchasing power as they lend, and savings arise as a result.[3]

It is clear with hindsight that the dominant economic modelling paradigm could not predict the financial crisis, since such a crisis is truly a far from equilibrium event and thus potentially lying outside of the remit of the theory (Helleiner, 2011). Economists in the equilibrium schools ascribe the origin of macroeconomic fluctuations to external productivity and monetary policy shocks,[4] which are typically independent from debt, leverage and likelihood of cascades of default. This is

1 Haldane and May (2011); Battiston et al. (2016a); Haldane and Turrell (2018).

2 Abel et al. (2014); Galí (2015).

3 McLeay et al. (2014); Werner (2014, 2016); Wray (2016).

4 DSGE models, see, e.g., An and Schorfheide (2007).

hardly helpful to policy-makers, as an endogenous theory in which instability arises from within would be preferable. Some economists were able to anticipate the crisis based on stock-flow models of private debt,[5] but only in relatively imprecise terms. Meanwhile, econophysicists and some researchers in quantitative finance use signatures observed in the data to predict price fluctuations (e.g., Sornette, 2017), with varying degrees of success.

Ultimately, the very conception that economists have over the nature of money lies at the very heart of the problem. This dates all the way back to the classical and neo-classical/monetarist economists (Smith, Marshall, Walras, Samuelson and Friedman) in opposition to Keynes and Schumpeter, Minsky and later followers. Economic theory has been divided on the nature and role of money for one hundred years or more. Werner (2014) describes the three main theories of money and banking: financial intermediation, fractional reserve and credit creation.

In the most basic form of the equilibrium school, money is a commodity-mediated means of exchange that serves as a store of value, the quantity of which is under government control;[6] it thus follows the financial intermediation theory of banking. In the non-equilibrium school, money is a contract created by agents stating a liability for someone, and an asset for someone else.[7] This is consistent with the credit creation theory of banking. The fractional reserve theory of banking sits in between these positions, where banks lend savings and reserves, but collectively re-lend these over and over until reserve requirements are reached (Abel et al., 2014).

The dichotomy seems strange, as since money is created by central banks, surely, to find out, one should only just need to ask central bankers what the nature of money is. But the answer remains controversial, since institutions such as the Bank of England have provided conflicting messages (Werner, 2014). Despite interventions by some central bank economists (McLeay et al., 2014), the wider economics community still cannot agree on any of the options.

Great progress was made in the nineties in developing micro-foundations for a theory of money by using theoretical models of random matching with agents randomly meeting other agents and trading, the so-called models of 'search equilibrium'. It was shown that one commodity or fiat commodity naturally arises as a medium of exchange, unless perfect information exists on past agent actions.[8] The micro-foundations of this 'New Monetarist' strand of literature are the mainstay of much of modern mainstream macroeconomic modelling. With some exceptions (Cavalcanti and Wallace, 1999a), these models assume, however, that agents do not know one another and that payment with credit instruments is ruled out. They support either

5 Bezemer (2009); Keen (2013).
6 Friedman and Schwartz (1965); Abel et al. (2014).
7 Innes (1913); see Bell (2001).
8 Kiyotaki and Wright (1989); Kiyotaki and Moore (1997); Kocherlakota (1998).

the financial intermediation or fractional banking theory, relying on theoretical models only, and thus empirical evidence remains scarce (Bigoni et al., 2020).

The existence of leverage and complex financial networks makes this particular understanding of the nature of money, defined strictly as a commodity of exchange existing in limited exogenous supply, potentially difficult to maintain. As is clear to most central bank modellers, the financial system is a complex network that spreads risk across multiple stakeholders. In contrast to post-monetarist search equilibrium models, credit creation theory postulates that the quantity of money cannot be completely controlled by public authorities since credit creation also happens at commercial banks.[9] Works in that tradition offer endogenous descriptions of the financial instability.[10] However, yet again, no comprehensive empirical or historical evidence is given, relying on theoretical models instead.

What remains notable is that whatever models are used, little to no empirical evidence is available to demonstrate whether they are valid explanations of why humans use money.[11] Options that have not been substantially explored include, first, works of economic anthropology, which may offer an alternative source of empirical insights that may be key to understanding the nature of money for people in various cultural settings. Second, works in econophysics could offer complementary empirical insights based on price time series regarding the dynamics of financial sector growth and instability.

In this chapter, it is shown how combining existing anthropological and complex networks evidence allows us to develop a possible, self-consistent and realistic complexity theory of money, banking and macroeconomics, and for Minsky's financial instability hypothesis. For that, consistent use is made of a basic thought experiment using a 'primitive'[12] economy and financial system. The latter is used in order to develop basic micro-foundations and avoid blindly walking into common traps that may exist in various existing theoretical frameworks. Anthropological evidence is first reviewed over the nature of value, debt and asset ownership, in order to establish in a more definitive way what the nature of money is. Empirical evidence from econophysics is then used to to identify stylised features of financial time series and dynamics. A conceptual model is developed to discuss various types of financial instability that can be explained by this model and combined evidence. Lastly, these findings are interpreted for a complexity theory of macroeconomics. Chapters 10 and 11 apply these findings to develop a model that can then be applied to understanding the financial impacts of the low-carbon transition.

9 Godley and Lavoie (2006); Lavoie (2014); Wray (2016).
10 Minsky (1982); Godley and Lavoie (2006); Keen (2011); Lavoie (2014); King (2015).
11 Werner (2014, 2016); Bigoni et al. (2020).
12 'Primitive' is used in quotes to express that the author does not believe in there being records of monetary systems having been 'primitive' as such, and especially not barter economies, that worked as thus described.

9.2. THE NATURE OF MONEY IN ANTHROPOLOGY

9.2.1 *Framing the Problem*

The standard, generally accepted theory of money postulates that the money supply is made of a commodity, or value-less fiat currency, that is used as a medium of exchange, that is minted or printed by a central bank, in quantities fully controlled by that institution.[13] To explain intuitively why money emerges in the economy, barter in a 'primitive' society is used as a thought experiment, raising the difficulties involved in the problem of double coincidence of wants (Jevons, 1876): if person A has item X and wants item Y, while person B has item Y but wants item Z, not item X, both need to find a third person who wants item X and has item Z, the solution of which the probability is low. To solve this, a durable commodity or value-less fiat currency naturally emerges as a convenient store of value used to exchange everything else, and everyone acquiring some of it becomes able to trade with everyone else (Kiyotaki and Wright, 1989).

The post-monetarist literature explores how commodity money can arise in settings in which agents search for other agents to trade with, and the possible optimal allocations of resources that are made possible. Kiyotaki and Wright (1989) show that fiat money endogenously emerges in search equilibrium models and allows welfare-enhancing allocations. Kocherlakota (1998) shows that the money commodity does not need to have intrinsic value since it serves a role equivalent to what could be a public record of past action, termed 'memory'. In other words, in that model money effectively keeps track of the cumulative 'goods' and 'bads' in the history of agents which then become rewarded through the allocation consumption goods; however, this can equally be achieved by accurate recording, as well as the issue of notes (Cavalcanti and Wallace, 1999b). Information asymmetries however can change this picture (Awaya and Fukai, 2017). The possibility of theft was argued to give incentive to keep money in banks (He et al., 2005). Interestingly, in the foundational work of Kiyotaki and Wright (1989), 'there is no credit since a given pair will meet again with probability zero', and this assumption, adopted by much of the following literature, is critical. Cavalcanti and Wallace (1999a) offer one rare discussion of the use of financial assets for payment, in their analysis of inside and outside money. Lastly, agent-based models have also been used to show how the use of a money commodity might arise (Moran et al., 2013; Lacopetta, 2019).

In the quantity theory of money that the above theoretical works mostly support, the quantity of money is determined by the mint (or central bank), and the 'stamp' of the mint on coins is an official certification of the value content (e.g., weight of gold). Under the gold standard, the money supply was understood to be determined by the quantity of gold held in the Treasury. The relatively recent emergence of

[13] Friedman and Schwartz (1965); Nordhaus and Samuelson (2009); Abel et al. (2014).

'fiat money', not redeemable in gold, since 1971 is generally understood to function under the same principles where the government chooses how much money to print. In the theory of the neutrality of money, the absolute total quantity of money available is arguably unimportant, since if the quantity changes, in equilibrium, the value changes inversely proportionally. Any possible non-neutrality is ascribed to information asymmetries (Berentsen et al., 2005).[14] Indeed, given the role of money representing some sort of 'memory' of past actions, debasing the coins should not change the purchasing power of the whole money supply. The role of commercial banks is thus, beyond safekeeping, to pass money around between those who need it and those who have it, charging interest for the service. However, the New Monetarist literature does not clearly address complex systems of borrowing and lending, in parts due to a possibly undue persistent belief that the money supply is fixed and exogenous.

9.2.2 *Thought Experiment*

A hypothetical 'primitive' society is now imagined as a thought experiment, in which villagers trade goods using coins of gold, of which the quantity of coins and gold content is controlled by the local authorities. No banking credit exists, all money borrowed is obtained from savings in the economy, and savings are kept inside bed mattresses.

One individual, after saving substantially, gets into the habit of frequently lending coins to other villagers, charging interest and keeping careful records of all money exchanges. Villagers entrust him with safekeeping their money, because (1) he keeps the money in a safe place; (2) he keeps detailed records and is trustworthy; and (3) he offers to pay depositors interest. He becomes the village's banker.

When a creditworthy villager requests a loan, the banker adds a double mark in his books: a deposit in the new creditor's account, which becomes that person's liability towards the banker, and an asset in the banker's balance sheet. When a villager deposits money, the banker adds a double mark in his books, the addition of money in the depositor's account, and a liability in the bank's balance sheet. If a borrower requests to pay someone with coins, the banker gives out coins, confident that the money usually comes back to the safe, when the payee deposits it into his own account, such that liquidity remains the same. Frequently, the banker either issues notes of credit that can be exchanged, or makes two marks in the books to exchange money directly, without using any coins at all, while the size of the bank's balance sheet increases. In fact, what matters is that coins in the safe are in the legal ownership of the bank, and loans and deposits are recorded as assets and liabilities

14 For that very reason, all computable general equilibrium models do not represent inflation, while dynamic stochastic general equilibrium models ascribe inflation to frictions, sticky prices and delays in reaching equilibrium.

on the bank's balance sheet (Werner, 2014). It is to be noted that under the law, the banker owns the deposited money entrusted to him, even though he owes an equal amount of money to his depositors.

A key question then is whether the sum of deposits plus money in circulation always matches the quantity of coins created by the mint, or if there is any relationship between the two. In fact, it probably never does, practically or legally: the numbers in the books far exceed the quantity of coins in the economy, but not necessarily by any conserved or exogenously decided ratio. Authorities do not have control over the quantity of money, because lending activity is done by the bank, where the money is lent and re-lent arbitrary numbers of times, as it only involves the creation of legal documents stating liability between agents and the bank (loans) or the reverse (deposits).

To account fully for all the money written in the books and equate it back to the quantity of coins in the safe (the bank's liabilities), one has to account for all the money that is expected to be paid to the bank in the foreseeable future (the bank's assets). However, some of it never will, since returns on investment are fundamentally uncertain (Fontana, 2008), as all sorts of unpredictable events can lead agents to default, with probabilities not fully known. Even if the quantity of physical coins is well defined, the quantity of money in the economy can only at best be estimated subjectively, but not accurately. Users of the bank can only estimate for themselves, using public statements from the bank, whether they believe the bank is sustainable or not. The amount of money in the economy is not a well-defined quantity, for two reasons: (1) anyone can lend money using promissory notes denominated in gold coins as unit of account, and this is not necessarily recorded by the state or the bank (e.g., bar tabs); (2) money flows between a certain present and an uncertain future.[15] In that sense, money appears to have the properties of information, or 'memory' (Kocherlakota, 1998), rather than of a tangible commodity or fiat currency in fixed supply.

The banker can in principle 'create' as much credit as fellow villagers are willing to take, by expanding his bank's balance sheet (adding assets and liabilities in equal value). The banker has incentive to maximise the amount of money lent. However, if he lends too much, too many projects may not deliver, as he could be financing projects with dubious business cases.[16] Standard fractional banking theory

[15] As will be seen in Section 9.3, probabilities of default have heavy tails and therefore expected values are heavy-tailed uncertain and do not always exist. While the sum of loans made is not contingent on future events and thus not heavy-tailed uncertain, expected returns are heavy-tailed uncertain and insolvencies happen at every moment, at which point arbitrary amounts of money can vanish instantaneously as assets are auctioned off to repay creditors.

[16] A key assumption here is that there is a limited supply of projects in each risk-return category that an economy of a certain size can supply. When this is depleted, projects in each return

(Abel et al., 2014) would suggest that he is losing other people's money. But in reality, there is no actual record of whose money goes into whose hands through the bank, since all contracts are signed between the bank and users of the bank, deposits are loans made to the bank and depositors are in fact the bank's creditors (Werner, 2014).[17] The state may or may not impose limits (reserve requirements) to how much can be lent;[18] however, that does not ensure that the bank always operates at or below the limit, since the ratio of lending to any reserves is a probabilistic quantity that can drift up and down following uncontrollable economic activity, while the banker always has the option to borrow reserves from the state. Lastly, it may not be realistically possible to regulate small-scale lenders (e.g., bar tabs).

When projects fail, the 'primitive' bank may be forced to restrict its ability to either lend, or to give back deposits, or both, in order not to run out of coins. That is because the bank is in continuous expectation of cash flow from future loan repayments, which it uses for lending and giving deposits back when requested, and if this dries up, as it can since it is heavy-tailed uncertain, its activities can become compromised.

The 'primitive' bank remains in business according to two rules: (1) it must be able to give money deposited back to villagers when demanded, and (2) it must be able to lend money to villagers when demanded. In that sense, it is primarily cash flow-constrained. This means maintaining the trust of villagers who use its services. Anthropological evidence (in what follows) supports this model of borrowing and lending for over most of recorded history (in fact preceding the use of coins), while econophysics suggests that the whole monetary system is an unstable pyramid made out of relationships of trust.

9.2.3 *Empirical Evidence*

Evidence for financial systems dating back 5,000 years can be found in economic anthropology literature, which resemble remarkably how modern monetary systems work (Graeber, 2014). Reliance is made on Graeber for a comprehensive review of the economic anthropology literature, since no other recent empirically based work exists to our knowledge that comprehensively covers the nature of debt over such a long span of human history.

category will have higher risk. This is assumed sensible but without definite empirical evidence, challenging to establish since risk is a subjective quantity subject to fundamental uncertainty.

17 As opposed to investment funds, where money is invested on behalf of individuals (transactions are made off-balance sheet) but the money remains in the individuals' ownership, for banks, deposits are owned by the banks and owed by them to depositors (the deposits are on the bank's balance sheet). Institutions create money when they leverage their own balance sheets, but they do not if they invest on behalf of others.

18 Reserve or capital requirements, which some countries have (e.g., the USA), and others don't (e.g., the UK).

(i) Complex Financial Systems Pre-date Metal Currency

Graeber (2014) shows that anthropological evidence over the existence of barter, before the invention of currency, is thin, and that in fact, systems of credit existed instead. The textbook myth of double coincidence of wants never actually existed, because it is too easily resolved by using credit: delaying in time the moment at which one pays back for something received, such that debts could be cancelled off by the provision of various goods at various times. That is, as long as trust exists along with a measurement accounting system to compare the value of goods. Indeed, barter, in which agents exchange goods at the same moment in time, only ever existed between tribes that did not know or trust each other, since they had no expectation of seeing debts paid off.

Graeber also shows that complex financial systems existed since long before coins appeared in Greece, India and China during antiquity. In Mesopotamia, systems of clay tablets existed in which contracts of debt between legal entities were inscribed and kept, to be broken once such contracts were fulfilled. These contracts thus had value, could change hands, were traded and were used as payment. Although 'money' did not exist in the form of government-minted currency, lending could be done, and thus 'horizontal' money was created and destroyed (see Wray, 2016). Mesopotamia is where some of the oldest records of interest bearing loans originate from. However, substantial evidence also shows that societies dating back to the Upper Paleolithic made use of tally sticks to record debts and liabilities, which were inscribed and split lengthwise when contracts were made.

In fact, there never really has been any important difference between primitive promises to pay and modern digital currency: 'money is not a commodity but an accounting tool' (Graeber, 2014, p. 46), just like the kilogram or the centimetre, where 'one of X equals six of Y'. According to Graeber, money apparently has always been as ephemeral then as it is today: it is a gauge of trust, or contract, between two legal entities, and a metric to measure and record debt.

(ii) Metal Currency Was Invented as a Tool for War

Graeber traces the invention of metal currencies in various parts of antiquity, in ancient Greece, India and in China. Currency in the form of lumps of precious metal stamped with official markings from local authorities have been invented to raise armies and wage war, and emerged through taxation. Local authorities needed to incentivise inhabitants under their territories to either enlist as soldiers, and to provide soldiers with supplies. They would distribute to soldiers coins stamped with an official mark, while creating a tax for everyone else to be paid using coins figuring that very mark. Civilians, needing coins to pay the tax, would have to find soldiers and supply them with something that they wanted in exchange for coins. The soldiers could then spend these coins buying supplies from villagers, who would agree to such exchange through the fact that the payment of taxes was enforced by the army itself. By increasing the money supply, the government would be able to increase the number of soldiers active in its army. Governments typically ended up searching for increasing sources of precious metal in order to expand their armies, without which their armies would stop growing, villagers would stop cooperating and warfare would have to stop.

Coins had value because they would be accepted as means of paying taxes (vertical money, see Wray, 2016). Graeber cites evidence indicating that for equivalent weight in precious metal, stamped coins carried more value than equivalent but unstamped lumps of metal. However, coins could also be melted and made into other currencies, and most importantly, coins could be stolen with that very purpose in mind. Thus coins were useful in times of war and political instability.

(iii) Institutions Have Taken the Function of Banks since the Earliest Organised Societies

In early societies such as in Mesopotamia, temples or other institutions that were not local authorities have held functions common to banks. Villagers and citizens would provide tribute to temples, in the form of goods, which would be re-distributed or re-invested into development projects, for instance, for building and for maintaining trade routes.

> Temple administrators invented the idea [of interest-bearing loans] as a way of financing the caravan trade. [...] Temple administrators developed the habit of advancing goods to local merchants – some of them private, others themselves Temple functionaries – who would then go off and trade overseas. Interest was just a way for the Temples to take their share of the resulting profits. (Graeber, 2014, p. 64)

In Medieval India,

> The key innovation was the creation of what were called the 'perpetual endowments' or 'inexhaustible treasuries'. Say a lay supporter wished to make a contribution to her local monastery. Rather than offering to provide candles for a specific ritual, or servants to attend to the upkeep of the monastic grounds, she would provide a certain sum of money – or something worth a great deal of money – that would then be loaned out in the name of the monastery, at the accepted 15 per cent annual rate. The interest on the loan would then be earmarked for that specific purpose [...]. We have to assume that in most cases the money is an accounting unit: what were really being transacted were animals, wheat, silk, butter, fruit and all the other goods whose appropriate rates of interest were so carefully stipulated in the law-codes of the time. (Graeber, 2014, p. 253)

In fact, Graeber finds that whether metal currency existed or not, and whether the trade of lumps of precious metals was widespread or not, temples often had the ability to lend and finance activities. Temples accumulated substantial amounts of wealth over time, which enabled them to play that role, whether with metal money or with goods and services, including in periods in which metal currency disappeared following the decline of empires.

(iv) Alternation between Virtual and Metal-Based Money

Some scholars talk of a 'return to barter' in medieval times. Graeber explains that there is no credible evidence for this, and instead, there is substantial evidence suggesting a return to credit economies. In fact, in Medieval Europe, even though Roman coins went out of circulation following the collapse of the Roman Empire and the mints that it operated, people continued to use virtual Roman coins as units of account, without using real metal coins at all, as if they still existed. This was possible because the Middle Ages mark a period of relative peace, without expansionary empires, in which large armies were not needed and the trust in institutions could be sufficiently high to develop the use of credit systems again, as metal money disappeared. Anyone could create credit denominated in imaginary Roman coins, but he/she needed to be trusted and to trust borrowers.

History has seen an alternation between ages of relative peace in which economies predominantly used credit systems without metal currencies, and ages of war in which economies operated based on metal currencies used to provide and supply large armies and cities. The old agrarian empires in Mesopotamia and Egypt used credit, before the invention of metal currency. Following this, the use of metal currency appeared in ancient Greece, India and China, where they became widespread, during the development of large expanding empires. Following the decline of large empires, metal currencies went out of circulation and credit systems developed again in a world in which political systems became fragmented and regionalised. Metal currencies were revived again during the age of the 'great capitalist empires' after 1450, with the expansion of European empires into the new world searching for precious metals. Finally, this ended for good in the seventies with money largely becoming 'fiat currency' again, setting the stage for a new period of pure credit money, which is now digital.

Graeber argues that the primary difference between credit systems and metal currency, at least in early history, is that metal currency can be stolen, while elaborate credit systems cannot. A key aspect of war is the capture of loot in the form of portable objects of value, which in general meant precious metals. The main difference between periods dominated by credit and periods dominated by currency may be the importance of the state (which mints metal currencies and raises taxes) relative to that of financial institutions (which create money in metal or virtual form). Whether or not money was redeemable in gold and silver, the total quantity of gold did not necessarily (or in general) match the total money supply. Notably, during the British gold standard starting in 1844, in which 100% of bank notes were fully redeemable in gold, the standard did not cover bank deposits, and thus, only a small fraction of the real money supply could be converted to gold.

9.2.4 *An Imaginary Simple Economy with Currency*

A second thought experiment is made to explore whether the quantity theory of money can be a self-consistent description of either monetary systems, using Figure 9.1.

(a) A Metal Currency-Based Wartime Economy

Based on the anthropological evidence assembled by Graeber, one can draw the micro-foundations of a synthetic, or imaginary, 'primitive' economy with a government and taxes, that uses metal or paper money as currency, whether redeemable into gold or not, and whether the money is made of metal or not. At one end of the spectrum (Figure 9.1a), a Kingdom, with expansionary ambitions, mints, with the effigy of the King, metal coins that it gives to its army, and taxes the local population with these very coins, so that this army can supply itself in local markets. This creates a market and a flow of coins, that, without the enforcement of the tax, would be valueless. Peasants and merchants also deposit or donate their savings to the local Temple, and the Temple lends money to entrepreneurs for the development of infrastructure business and overseas trade projects, to the King for public works and various extravagant expenses, and to peasants if they fail to raise sufficient funds to pay the taxes, for instance when crops fail. The Temple accumulates and commands over time substantial amounts of wealth, in the form of coins or other commodities, thus assembling sufficient collateral to function as a bank. The Temple creates loans when needed, and keeps safe everyone's money, including the Treasury's, through the use of careful bookkeeping and the hiring of powerful guards.

The government intervenes in the economy by financing a large public force (the army) and demanding taxes from peasants and merchants. As the army expands with conquests and plunder, the total money supply expands as more and more precious metal enters the economy; the metal is melted and minted into ever larger quantities of coins to fund an ever larger army. However, the real money supply is not entirely determined by this, since the Temple can also create money through its issuance of loans, written in its books, so long as it is confident that loans will be paid back with interest. This means that the money supply also expands with the inclusion of money or value to be obtained in the future.

However, whether the money circulating is made of actual coins of precious metal, of promissory notes or marks in a book, may not make an important difference. In the case of promissory notes, the Temple may allow the citizen to redeem notes into a certain quantity of precious metal by weight (or coins), so long as it has a sufficient reserve of metal to cover the occasional demands from citizens. But given that it is able to create loans and transfer money between accounts, the total money supply is not determined solely by the quantity of gold mined and plundered by the King. If ever larger quantities of precious metal appear needed to sustain the Kingdom's expansion, it is primarily to make the coins, and coins are more convenient for maintaining soldiers on a campaign, away from the temple. But the value of the

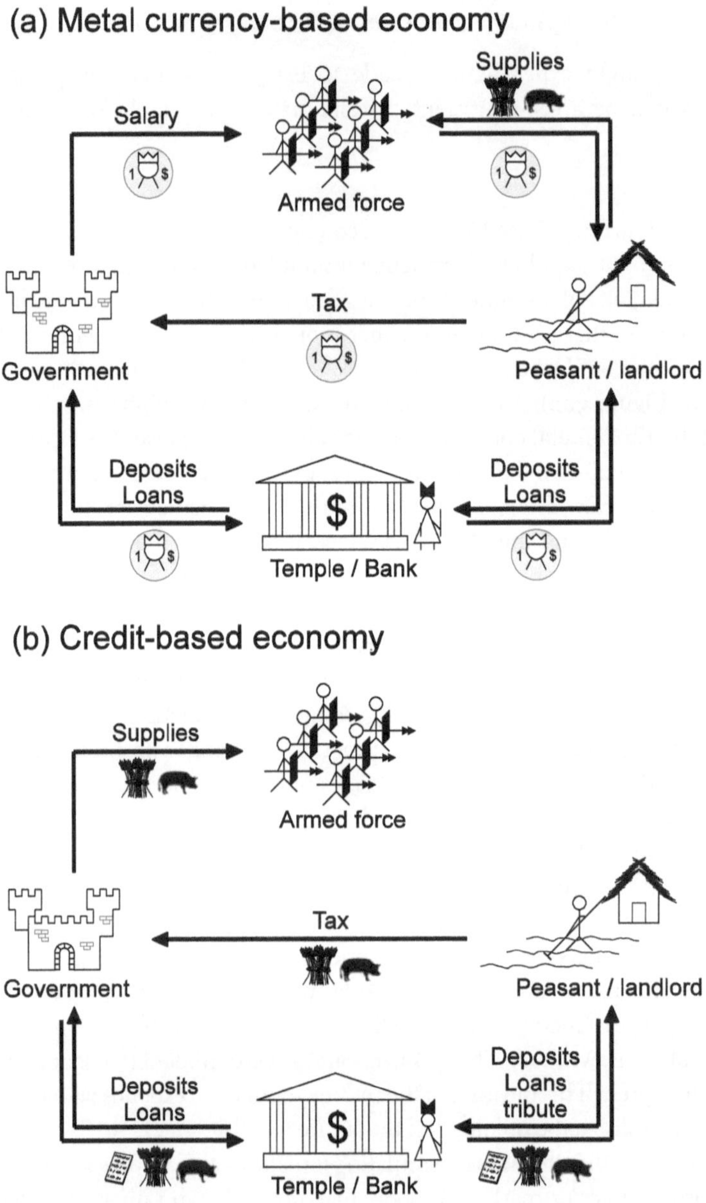

FIGURE 9.1 Two imaginary 'primitive' economies, (a) with a metal currency, a government, an army, taxes, banks and peasants, and (b) a credit-based economy in which exchanges and debts are recorded in books, tabs and clay tablets.

coins is driven by the value of the tax, since it is the tax that incentivises peasants and merchants to engage in commerce with the soldiers.

(b) A Peacetime Credit-Based Economy

The other end of the spectrum describes a credit-based economy (Figure 9.1b). The Kingdom does not have expansionary ambitions, and supplies itself its armed force, while all goods are traded on the basis that their value is recorded in books, clay tablets, promissory notes, bar tabs and/or tally sticks. One finds that apart from the fact that the army is not growing and not in a position to capture loot to expand the supply of money, the resulting economy is not fundamentally different from the metal currency-based economy. The Temple plays the role of money-lender in a similar way to the metal currency case. The only difference is that there are no metal coins to be exchanged, money is instead virtual. Debts are recorded, and paid back with goods at different moments in time, using a currency by name as metric. It is likely that promissory notes or clay tablets make their appearance, especially if these become accepted by the Government for the payment of taxes, but this makes no fundamental difference.

9.2.5 *Money Is Trust*

The empirical evidence from anthropology thus suggests that the quantity of money may never have been determined by the quantity of money printed, but instead, by endogenous activities in the credit system, whether in wartime currency or peacetime credit monetary systems. The allocation of credit and finance by financial institutions may not in fact be limited by savings, or to the size of the money supply. That is, not in any other way than through the risk that these activities add to the balance sheet of financial institutions concerned. Whether or not someone can obtain credit from a financial institution is not exactly related to whether the bank has run out of deposits to lend. It may be more related to whether the bank already has excessive amounts of risk on its balance sheet, or whether it considers itself in a position to take on further risk, and whether the lender is creditworthy. There thus appears to be no formal limit to the amount of money that can in principle be created.

In this perspective, money is trust, and anyone can create it. Imagine that Lori lends a cow to Andrew. Andrew hands Lori a note that indicates that the bearer is owed the value of a cow, denominated in units of cowrie shells, which need not exist. Lori wants to buy broccoli from Hillary, handing Hillary Andrew's note. As long as Hillary trusts that Andrew is going to pay, she may be fine with this. It does not matter whether Hillary wants a cow or not, or whether the actual cow still exists or not, it is the value denoted in cowrie shells that matters to her, which enables Hillary to trade Andrew's note onwards in exchange for other goods. Ultimately, if everyone trusts that Andrew will one day pay back, then the note can be traded indefinitely. Andrew has added to the cowrie shell money supply, without handling any sea shells at all. He did not create actual cowrie shells either, he only created a contract under his name.

The existence of a financial system thus appears, according to the empirical evidence gathered by Graeber, reliant on the trust that all agents have towards each other and towards financial institutions. First, agents must trust that other agents and institutions are long-lived and going to be around for the foreseeable future. That may be why complex financial systems did not survive in times of war, but appear to have been replaced by precious metal currency systems as store of value, since people would not trust institutions to remain long-lived. Second, agents must also have trust in the solvency and willingness to pay back of most other agents, in particular banks, since if they did not, depositors would not entrust banks with their savings, nor be willing to trade with other agents, given that barter is difficult and trade requires loans. It is understandable that in times of war, peasants would not trust soldiers to honour debts. Furthermore, legal assurances are critical for maintaining trust in systems, such as the rule of law for enforcing property rights, as well as laws on liability, such as the limited liability for enterprises, and bankruptcy laws, in order to ensure agents that contracts are enforceable.

9.3. MONEY AS AN UNSTABLE SCALE-FREE NETWORK

9.3.1 *The Scale-Free Network of Money Creation*

Econophysics offers a complementary view on the nature of money. According to the preceding section, all agents in a financial network exist as legal entities that have to meet solvency requirements in order to engage in business. Following Graeber, all agents can in principle create their own 'money', 'the only problem is to get it accepted' (Minsky, 1986, p. 228). Money is created when people take out loans, and destroyed when loans are repaid. Assuming this from now on, a complex double-layered network (equity and debt) endogenously develops, linking financial institutions through liability and ownership contracts. As this network develops, the size of the money system endogenously grows.

This network is known to be scale free (Figure 9.2), similarly to citation, innovation, social and many other types of networks.[19] Scale-free networks are pervasive in nature, and arise when processes of network creation involve 'preferential attachment', in which new nodes preferentially attach to existing nodes the larger they are.[20] In the case of financial agents, the larger their expected income is, the more they can lend. The scale-free nature of the financial network means that nodes with

[19] Barabási and Bonabeau (2003); Katz (2016); Thurner et al. (2018).

[20] See Chapter 5 and Barabási and Albert (1999).

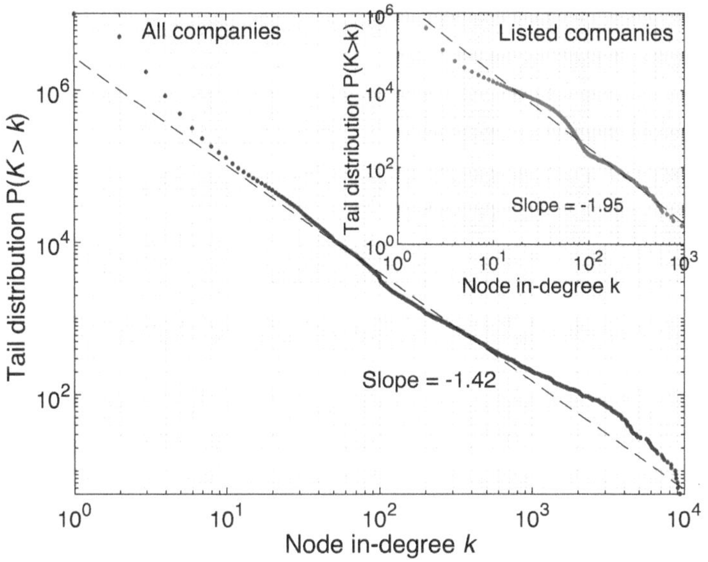

FIGURE 9.2 Scale-free nature of financial networks, derived from the ORBIS dataset (see Semieniuk et al., 2022). Cumulative histograms of the number of links going to each node weighted by its financial capitalisation for various financial networks (main panel, with power-law fit) while restricted networks involving listed companies only are given in the inset.

more connections to other nodes exist in lower numbers than nodes with fewer connections, following a power law, and the measured exponent lies between one and two (Garlaschelli et al., 2005).

The financial network can be considered as a pyramid in which each financial institution or agent interacts with a subset of the network, and has its own 'lender of last resort' (see Figure 9.3, left panel). The lenders of last resort for private individuals are normally commercial banks or investment funds, while the lenders of last resort for small banks and funds are generally larger banks. The lender of last resort of the largest banks is the central bank, the ultimate lender of last resort. Private individuals cannot normally interact with the central bank, nor can small investment funds. Thus, this network is to some degree hierarchical. It is not a tree network, however, since banks lend to each other, and companies can lend to each other as well, allowing for closed paths. Investment takes place under many forms of money, including bonds, equity, insurance contracts, futures, or simply promissory notes. This network is generally treated as multi-layered for that reason (Thurner et al., 2018).

When money is created, both a liability and an asset are created (Wray, 2016), expanding the balance sheets of a pair of agents. Since both assets and liabilities

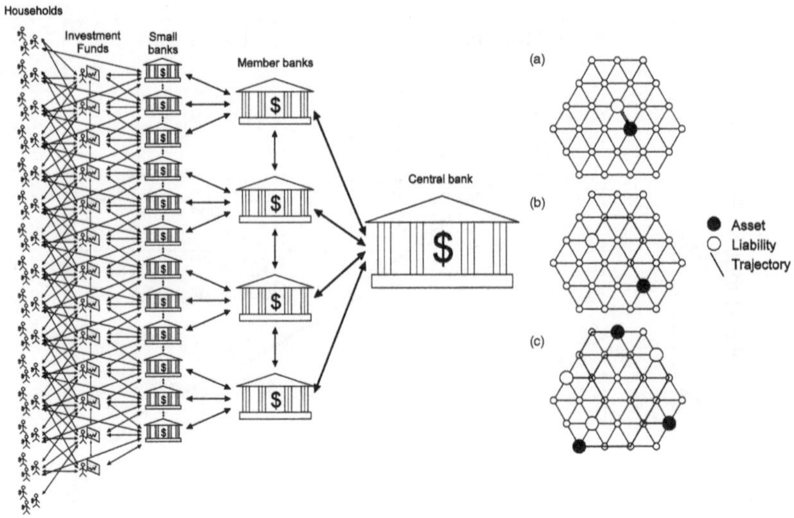

FIGURE 9.3 (Left) Hierarchical network of financial institutions and financial agents. (Right) Illustration of the creation of an asset-liability pair on a financial network between two institutions. (a) The pair is created when one institution lends to another with promise of later payment. The asset is the promise to pay (as a black circle), the asset is the money owed (as a white circle). (b) Once the asset and the liability are created, they can travel on the network, with agents buying and selling assets and liabilities from each other. Ultimately, whoever owns the liability owes money to whoever owns the asset. (c) A real network features a complex entanglement of asset-liability pairs travelling on the network.

are tradable, they may travel on the network from one agent to another (Figure 9.3 right panel). The asset and liability remain linked to one another, however, since they are 'destroyed' when debts are paid back. Lending can thus be understood as endogenously creating the network links between nodes themselves which may otherwise not be linked.

This setup would suggest that the financial sector endogenously builds itself via a process of preferential attachment[21] where creditworthy institutions borrow to finance real assets, using their existing assets as collateral (as in Kiyotaki and Moore, 1997). The more they are creditworthy, the more they can borrow. Higher leverage, however, generates network nodes that are more susceptible to become insolvent under external shocks generating shockwaves travelling across the ownership network. The more money is created, the more real assets are built, but also, the more fragile the financial network may become, since, as is generally observed (see below), the value of all financial assets is affected by heavy-tailed noise. Thus, the more

[21] This is ensured by the facts that the network is scale-free, see Barabási and Bonabeau (2003), and that financial institutions lend proportionally more the larger they are.

'financialised' an institution is (its ratio of financial vs physical assets), the more vulnerable it is to fluctuations travelling across the network (Thurner, 2011).

As loans are gradually repaid, assets and liabilities disappear, and thus without continuous lending for investment, the money supply would endogenously shrink over time. However, as observed in normal times, investment occurs such that the size and complexity of the financial network increases with time. Since the ability of nodes to invest depends on the size of their balance sheet, financial value appreciation implies increasing ability to raise finance and liquidity, while value contraction implies a declining ability to do so (Kiyotaki and Moore, 1997), both of which lead to respective self-reinforcing feedback in times of boom and recession.

9.3.2 *Recurrent Instability as Self-Organised Criticality*

There exists evidence to suggest that the financial network may be a 'self-organised critical' (SOC) system, similar to earthquakes, sand piles and evolutionary ecosystems.[22] The SOC model explains the key features of the dynamics of these systems.

Earthquakes make a good analogy with financial instability. In earthquakes, points in the earth's crust accumulate pressure gradually with slow tectonic plate movement until breaking point occurs, which allows movement and emits travelling shock waves. These waves trigger other pressure points to break in their wake, that in turn emit more shock waves, and so on, creating cascades and aftershocks (Bak et al., 2002). The SOC model explains why the frequency and magnitude of individual earthquakes follows a power law (the Gutenberg-Richter law), and the magnitude of fluctuations following a fluctuation follows a power law decay over time.[23]

Both of these stylised facts are widely observed in finance (Yamasaki et al., 2005), and not many other processes can generate such behaviour in time series. In the financial sector, highly leveraged agents are susceptible to insolvency induced by natural fluctuations, and emit shock waves through the financial network that can induce other leveraged agents to become insolvent. The frequency–magnitude distribution of financial fluctuations, and their decay, follows a power law as well. It is not necessary for neighbours in the network to become insolvent for a node to 'feel' the shock, as changes of value are transmitted through the valuation of assets (Battiston et al., 2016a).

This is represented in Figure 9.4, which analyses the type of noise observed in financial markets, using recent data and following the data of Gopikrishnan et al. (1999). The noise observed in asset prices is not normally distributed; in fact, it has heavy tails well described by power laws over several orders of magnitude. Power-law distributed noise, self-similar (fractal) noise over all scales, represents smoking-gun evidence of strongly interacting elements in a complex network. It is not necessarily

[22] Bak et al. (1987, 1988); Bak (1996), see also Thurner et al. (2018).

[23] Omori's law (Omori, 1895); see Utsu et al. (1995).

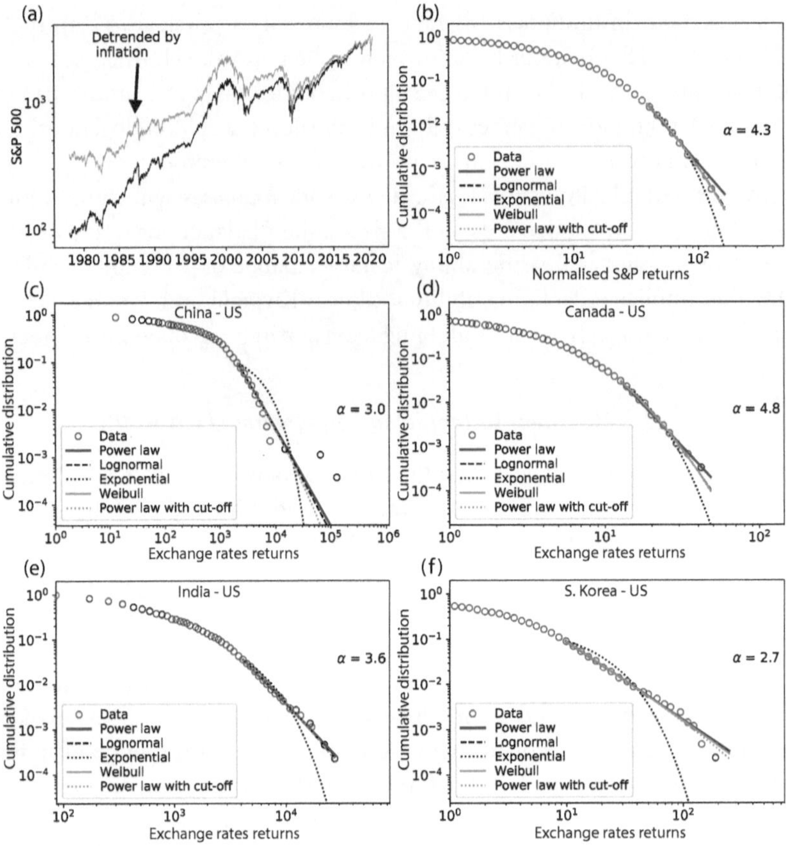

FIGURE 9.4 (a) Price index for the S&P 500 index. (b) Cumulative distribution of normalised returns from the S&P 500 price index, showing a scale-free linear tail for large events. Fits to various distributions are made, where a power law with cutoff, accounting for finite system size and maximum event magnitude, generally giving the best fit. Weibull distributions are very similar. (c)–(f) Same for exchange rates between the US dollar and various major currencies (for the method, see Gopikrishnan et al., 1999).

smoking-gun evidence of SOC specifically (Watkins et al., 2016); however, not many processes other than SOC can transform normally distributed (ergodic) noise into power-law (non-ergodic) distributed noise. For this to happen, a mechanism by which the system acquires memory, and become non-ergodic, must exist, and SOC is one such possibility.

The problem of heavy-tailed financial fluctuations meets the required criteria for a system to display the punctuated equilibrium and recurrent instability that is described by so-called 'sandpile' models of SOC:[24]

24 Bak et al. (1987, 1988); see Watkins et al. (2016) for a review.

1. contingency between financial agents;[25]
2. intermittent avalanches (price declines) of all magnitudes between lulls at all timescales;
3. avalanche thresholds (solvency limits);
4. a slow driving force, the leverage build-up over time;
5. power-law distributions of price declines.

The microeconomic foundation for SOC and the above criteria would stem from the fact that when financial agents lend to each other and buy stakes in each other, their ability to do so is based on their creditworthiness which is itself derived from the value of their own equity. In this picture, as agents borrow to invest using their assets as collateral, they collectively build, in an uncoordinated way, a taller and taller, and they ever more precarious, complex cathedral-like financial structure. While all agents individually may be solvent, fluctuations naturally arise due fundamental uncertainty over asset values, and they become amplified by the ownership network itself (see Battiston et al., 2016a). If for any reason, returns or prices decline, leveraged units can be accidentally forced into speculative or 'Ponzi'-like financing (Minsky, 1982), since these states are contextual and contingent on the financial environment. Large and small parts of the precarious cathedral collapse, triggering more insolvencies and creating self-perpetuating local or global instabilities.

9.3.3 *Characterising the Creep towards Self-Organised Criticality*

Under the SOC model, the mechanism by which the financial network may creep towards the metastable SOC state is borrowing regulated by the rate at which past debt is validated by present-day returns. But the rate at which debt is acquired to add to and/or improve the capital stock of the economy is also controlled by financial regulation through capital requirements. It is hypothesised here that the more liberal financial regulation is, the quicker the system can drive itself towards criticality, while if financial regulation is very strict, returns on investment tend to be limited, but the creep towards SOC is also slower. Financial innovation may also contribute to accelerating the creep towards SOC, as it searches for ways around existing regulations to increase investment in high-risk high-returns ventures.[26] Financial regulation tends to be relaxed in eras of boom, times at which old lessons tend to be forgotten, and tightened after crises, when memory is fresh (Perez, 2001).

Although when aggregate debt is high, chances are higher that the system is close to instability (Keen, 1995, 2017), aggregate debt may not be a good metric for the

[25] By this we mean that agents' net worth and ultimately solvency is constrained by the net worth and solvency of their neighbours in the financial network. An agent's ability to operate financially is contingent on the ability of some peers to lend him money, and others to meet their financial commitments towards him.

[26] Minsky (1982); Guttmann (2015, 2016).

distance of the financial network to instability. It is too coarse a metric: a network can be close to instability due to the presence of a restricted number of highly leveraged nodes, while it may not be if all nodes are leveraged but none are in a highly leveraged state. Furthermore, if leveraged nodes are not well connected, their insolvency may not cause much propagation. Measuring the distance to instability can be done using a stress-test method on an artificial representation of the financial network in which nodes are shocked externally and propagation is observed (Battiston et al., 2016a, 2017). Stress-testing is, of course, something that is regularly done by central banks.

Three parameters control this putative gradual creep towards instability:

1. the amount that can be borrowed at any time by any financial institution given the liabilities and assets it already possesses;
2. the amplitude of background financial noise relative to the equity of firms;
3. the proportion of nodes affected by financial noise.

These three parameters have a respective financial regulation control lever associated to them:

1. the amount that banks, companies and individuals can borrow, as a ratio of their existing wealth and expected cumulated future income, can be limited;
2. higher requirements for collateral can be demanded from companies and institutions, limiting leverage ratios, itself limiting their susceptibility to respond to and propagate noise, while the base interest rate can be raised to cool off a growing financial bubble;
3. the amount of failures can be limited by more carefully choosing who can borrow.

This offers some rationale for the structure that financial regulation can take to control the creep towards instability. It is stressed that this model is entirely based on classic complex networks signatures recurrently observed in financial times series.

9.4. A COMPLEXITY MODEL FOR INFLATION AND THE FINANCIAL INSTABILITY

A third 'primitive' economy thought experiment is developed to illustrate macroeconomic dynamics that result from understanding money as a scale-free network of trust relationships. Based on the evidence cited above, a simple theory for money, trade, foreign exchange and inflation, is constructed in order to suggest possible mechanisms for the endogenous emergence of financial instability, hyperinflation, debt deflation and depression, none of which are adequately explained by standard theory.

9.4.1 The 'Primitive' Economy: Banking and the State

To maintain trust in financial institutions, creditors are required by law to pay off their debts or spend time in prison. As the economy grows, more banks are set up, and lending is widespread. Since 'everyone can create money; the problem is getting it accepted' (Minsky, 1986, p. 228), agents create money when they write promissory notes, but being accepted depends on their financial credentials. As it becomes common for agents to own both financial assets and liabilities, the money supply grows with lending, creating a scale-free network of debt relationships.[27]

The state itself occasionally needs to borrow money to pay for the salary of the security forces when tax receipts are insufficient, or of builders for large infrastructure projects, and thus requests bankers to create money, or sells treasury bonds to villagers, and repays loans using future tax income. The state also maintains its balance sheet within certain bounds of solvency, as otherwise, banks could decide to refuse to loan money to the state: although it makes law, the state is bound by the same requirements to repay loans as any other legal entity in the village, citizen or enterprise, for the same reasons of trust and justice. However, banks may also consider that it is not in their interest to stop lending money to the state even when it is in deep deficit, since the state going bankrupt would likely create too much chaos for the good of business, while rolling over loans generates interest, and state deficit spending increases private sector income.[28]

If there is more than one banker in the village, bankers must lend to each other, since when a citizen borrows money from one banker and spends the money buying goods from a villager whose bank account is with another banker, this leads to imbalances in both bankers' balance sheets, which is solved by inter-bank loans. If one bank is less successful than others, inter-bank loans may not cancel out, liquidity may decline to the extent that it may fail to provide money on demand for deposits or loans, in which case a bank run could occur.

A 'primitive' credit economy is now assumed in which banks trade not in actual gold coins, but using promissory notes issued using the bankers' personal signatures, redeemable in gold coins, and bank accounts denominated in gold coins. The macroeconomy functions based on the trade of a number of types of financial assets as money, which have a trading value.[29] The economy effectively has more than one type of money. Some of these monies can be used to settle accounts, pay taxes, while all can be traded for one another, the balance being settled between bankers using inter-bank loans. It is possible that, in the event of one bank running out of liquidity or losing the trust of villagers, the value of its promissory notes declines over time or suddenly, villagers developing a preference for holding the notes of the other

[27] Whether the economy is coin and credit-based or credit only-based.
[28] Minsky (1982); Wray (2016).
[29] Inside money, see Cavalcanti and Wallace (1999a).

banks.[30] This could develop into an instability in which the value of these notes crashes to near zero. In this case, the banker must file for bankruptcy.

If, for any reason, one bank becomes preferred to all others, and its business grows to such an extent that it controls most of the trade in notes with villagers, the state and the other banks, and that even other banks begin to use its notes rather than their own as currency,[31] then this bank has effectively become the lender of last resort. This is so since if all banks run out of liquidity, and this bank also finds itself unable to lend, then no-one else can. The largest bank effectively underwrites the activities of all other banks and of all economic activity in the village: it is de facto the central bank. Central banks under that denomination have not always existed but are a natural outcome of a financial system based on credit and trust (Galbraith, 2017, Ch. 4). The Bank of England was created as a private institution in 1694 when public subscribers collectively loaned £1,200,000 in gold to the King's Government, in exchange for a monopoly on the creation of bank notes, effectively promissory notes that can be traded indefinitely. Whether the central bank is considered to be an integral part of the state or not is not in principle important (the Bank of England has been a private institution for a long period of history), although it is difficult to imagine there not being close collaboration between the state and the central bank, since the state is also the spender of last resort.[32]

9.4.2 *Inflation*

The central bank underwrites the activities of all other banks and of large corporations, but does not lend to individual villagers. A certain amount of economic activity in the village is then dependent on the central bank financing the state to employ a substantial number of villagers, and this money ends up in the accounts of villagers held with the commercial banks, coming back to the central bank through the state collected as taxes. The state, however, also borrows directly from villagers, companies and other banks by selling them treasury bonds, its own form of money.

The state thus appears in a position to spend indefinite amounts of money by borrowing from the central bank or other banks, who do not want to see the state fail. Since all of that spending employs villagers, this increases economic activity. The question is where that leads to, since one intuitively assumes that the state cannot keep borrowing indefinitely. Assuming indefinite support from the central bank, one possibility is that excessive public spending leads to the state bidding up prices of

30 Households preferring to hold the instruments they see as a better store of value is referred to as Gresham's Law and has appeared numerous times throughout history (see Galbraith, 2017).

31 Banks can in fact create promissory notes that are to be repaid in the form of promissory notes of the other bank, thus effectively trading in units of the other banks.

32 Notably, the state spends on building basic infrastructure, which no other entity may be willing to do, since it is the largest institution in the village and is able to do so, adopting a long-term view of society.

local goods and services in the economy as it competes to obtain these with villagers and enterprises, when the employment of villagers reaches maximum capacity (as happens, notably, in times of war). As prices and wages increase substantially without production increasing proportionally, this effectively devalues the central bank's promissory notes, with respect to, for example, other financial assets or goods and services in the economy. However, this means that bank deposits and loans of all villagers denoted in that currency devalue as well. If most villagers are creditors rather than debtors (notably, creditors towards the state), they lose more wealth through their assets (their deposits) than they gain wealth by devaluing their liabilities (their loans). In this case, they effectively pay for the state's expenditures through inflation, as a form of indirect tax on their total wealth. Those who are debtors (including the state) increase their relative wealth by devaluing their liabilities. This can explain, it is argued here, how inflation can happen in times near to full employment.

If, instead, it is villagers who are in debt and the state makes a surplus, then it is commercial banks who may have created excessive amounts of money for private companies. If many companies find themselves becoming insolvent,[33] potentially creating domino chains of insolvencies in their wake, commercial banks may find themselves running into liquidity problems as villagers fail to repay their loans. If they do become insolvent, the central bank faces the choice between letting commercial banks fail, in which case some villagers lose their deposits, or bailing out the commercial banks by lending to them or buying a stake in them, in the latter case acquiring the failing assets. If villagers lose trust in the central bank's ability to repay their deposits, then they may decide to purchase other types of assets or simply goods, and this flight from money leads to a devaluation of the currency with respect to goods in the economy. However, most importantly, banks may decide to begin charging higher interest rates to cover for some of the losses from bad debts and recover some liquidity. Since the failing enterprises have been bailed out, debts remain and the economy remains highly leveraged (debt to income ratios remain high) and since these assets have not been allowed to fail, the costs of financing and refinancing are charged by borrower companies by increasing mark-ups on prices of goods and services. The ensuing inflation is a mechanism through which the cost of failing assets is redistributed ('socialised') to villagers, mostly to creditors, to the benefit of lenders. This can explain, as argued here, periods of high inflation that follow financial turbulence, but not near full employment ('stagflation' as described by Minsky, 1986).

[33] Notably, if banks have lent excessively to villagers who did not have well thought through business plans, if decreasing returns were appearing at the tail end of a frenzy of innovative activity, or if agents were using much of the available finance to speculate on the price of capital assets and a change of expectations of return led to a capital asset price decline.

9.4.3 *Foreign Exchange and Hyperinflation*

The existence of a neighbouring village is now introduced, with its own state, central bank and production of various speciality goods. Two situations can arise:

1. the villages are at war and/or do not trust each other and/or see no need for goods produced in the opposite village;
2. the two villages are at peace and trust each other and have a desire for the goods produced in the opposite village.

Notably, goods in opposite villages may be desired by villagers due to their lower prices, themselves associated to specialised methods of production. The question is how import prices are formed.

In the case of war, since a constant threat exists of invasion of one village by the other, villagers of one village may not trust the use of the other village's promissory notes, since in the event of an invasion, the rule of law is likely to collapse and property rights not enforced. Trade between villages must then take place using one of several mutually trusted commodities such as precious metals, since these maintain their value even if institutions fail as they can be melted and re-minted or made into all sorts of items. Effectively, in times of war, trade can only take place on the basis of barter or metal currency (Graeber, 2014).

In the case of peace, a foreign exchange value arises, that depends on each village's current account in the books of the central bank in the opposite village, and what the currency can be exchanged for. If one village acquires more desires for goods from the exporter village than the reverse, a trade deficit develops. The central bank of the exporter village accumulates promissory notes from the importer's central bank.[34] Foreign importer notes, since they cannot be spent in the exporter village, unless its villagers need them to travel to the importer village, nor can they be deposited in any bank, so they can only be used to buy directly from the importer village. However, since there is relatively little desire to import from the importer village, a lack of trust as to what can be obtained with importer notes develops in the exporter village, and thus since many exporter villagers see no value in these notes, anyone in the trade of foreign exchange will only offer a low price for importer notes. This in turns means increasing import prices for importers and decreasing import prices for exporters, despite that price levels remain the same in each village when measured with their own currencies.

Since the state will not accept payment of taxes in foreign currency, then it remains impractical for villagers to trade between each other in foreign notes, even

34 The exporter central bank obtains these notes since when exporter villagers sell items to importer villagers, they accumulate importer notes, which they mostly exchange for exporter notes with their local bank, keeping a small quantity to allow for reverse transactions. The latter then exchanges these for exporter notes with the central bank, and the central bank ends up owning most of the foreign currency.

if they have full trust in their likelihood of repayment. They convert this money to local currency at their local bank, who then deposits this foreign money at the central bank.

Decreasing demand for the foreign currency, leading to its devaluation, can induce an increase in demand for foreign goods and services and increase the demand again for the foreign currency, generating a negative stabilising feedback on the currency value. However, if other banks accept deposits in foreign currency, villagers can use that for investment opportunities in the foreign village, notably to buy government bonds. In that case, decreasing demand for foreign goods leading to devaluation of the foreign currency leads to decreased returns on, and decreasing appetite for, investment in the foreign village, further decreasing demand for foreign currency, a positive re-inforcing feedback. A stable foreign exchange necessarily requires that the negative feedback is stronger than the positive feedback.

It is possible that an instability in the currency value develops. This can happen if state expenditures are substantially denominated in foreign currency while its income is in local currency. As the central bank and other banks run out of foreign currency reserves, they have to buy them at discount. Any fluctuation in the exchange rate can trigger an overall self-reinforcing feedback where the dropping value of the local currency increases the state deficit and debt in foreign currency, and the increasing debt affects the confidence of foreigners and citizens holding assets in the local currency in the ability of the central bank to prevent inflation, causing an accelerated flight from the local currency towards the foreign currency, leading to hyperinflation.

9.4.4 *Financial Instability and Debt Deflation*

Another set of phenomena can take place in the 'primitive' economy: bubbles, financial crises and debt deflation. Fisher (1932) was the first to offer a detailed description of such dynamics in their 1929 episode, while a detailed analysis was given by Minsky (1982).

It is imagined that institutions and enterprises sell two types of financial assets: fixed term money deposits (bonds) and parts of the ownership of an enterprise (equity). Their prices can substantially vary according to changing perceptions of expected returns, since money can be made by either waiting for returns, or through trading and price differentials. Villagers will typically own both real and financial assets, and borrow in order to lend by leveraging existing assets. This means that everyone is some sort of a banker, since everyone can create liabilities.

This implies that (1) agents endogenously create a complex network of finance, and (2) changes of value somewhere in the network immediately trigger changes in the value of the enterprises who own them, and the enterprises who own those, and so on, and thus in the value of the financial assets they issue as well: shocks are transmitted as travelling waves on the network. This is not a feature solely of modern economies; Graeber (2014) shows that such complex financial systems with their inherent instability have existed since as far as economic history can be traced.

Minsky (1982) defines four possible states of finance activity: hedge financing, where liquidity is sufficient to cover shortfalls in returns from investments in all foreseeable scenarios; speculative financing, in which some periods of activity require borrowing to meet commitments, but overall activity over the foreseeable future yields positive returns, while borrowing declines over time; Ponzi financing, where speculative financing in which borrowing needed to meet commitments increases over time; insolvency, where the present value of expenditure on debt servicing of liabilities exceeds the present value of returns from assets in most foreseeable scenarios, and refinancing is not available.

Key to this is that hedge finance can become speculative, and speculative finance can become ponzi finance under changes of the economic context, notably increases in interest rates or declines in aggregate demand (Minsky, 1982). When most agents are involved in hedge finance, leeway exists to absorb losses without affecting their ability to borrow or their equity, and fluctuations remain localised. When the proportion of Speculative finance increases, the network becomes brittle.

Following the evidence shown in the preceding section, it would be reasonable to suppose that a substantial amount of network nodes are involved in speculative and ponzi finance, the financial network approaches the edge of instability, in which small financial fluctuations can propagate very far across the network, in the same way that a disease epidemic can propagate across a human population. Exactly at the instability, fluctuations diverge in magnitude. This is because insolvencies cause insolvencies with a self-reinforcing feedback. At the edge of instability, the economy functions normally, except that any arbitrarily small but widespread disturbance can develop into a major financial crisis of any kind of magnitude, self-similar fluctuations with power-law probabilities. This is a self-organised critical state of 'punctuated equilibrium', in which the economy amplifies small fluctuations.

According to Minsky (1982), when the economy is prosperous, returns on existing assets validate past decisions of borrowers by reinforcing their expectations of returns. With trust in the economy, banks allow borrowers (including households, see Lavoie, 2020) to gradually increase their leverage ratios, under expectations that the apparent peaceful stability of the economy makes losses improbable. This gradual creep brings the economy towards the edge of financial stability, a point at which the leverage of too many nodes are collectively subject to go in negative equity territory even if they are not individually, due to their equity value being contingent on other nodes' equity value. The economy begins to observe price instabilities, each generated by other internal or external events of arbitrary large or small magnitude (e.g., elections, financial failures, news, discoveries). While driving factors may appear exogenous, it is the unstable state of the financial network that can transform these external events into major financial instabilities.

Firms with negative equity face the choice between borrowing more or selling existing assets to cover shortfalls, which leads to further asset price declines, and three self-reinforcing types of feedback:

1. the value of existing assets to be used as collateral declines, restricting what can be borrowed (Heinsohn and Steiger, 2005);
2. as asset prices (and prices in general) fall, the value of the currency effectively increases as well as the face value of all debt contracts, enlarging debt payments of all companies triggering even more asset sales (Battiston et al., 2016a);
3. with the currency value increasing, hoarding can occur, restricting further spending and income.

The overall effect is that as companies and individuals sell off assets to repay debt, their debt situation effectively worsens rather than improves. This has been observed in the years following the 1929 and 2007 financial crises (Fisher, 1932; Wray, 2016). A recession usually follows debt deflation, with the recession lasting significantly longer if it was prompted by a financial crisis (Reinhart and Rogoff, 2009).

9.5. CONCLUSION: IMPLICATIONS FOR A NEW UNDERSTANDING OF MACROECONOMICS AS A COMPLEX NETWORK

This chapter developed a complexity theory basis for better understanding the monetary system, credit creation and finance and their observed unstable dynamics. Empirical evidence from anthropology and econophysics was used to describe money as having the nature of trust (and legal) relationships of debt between agents, denominated using currency as metric, without supply limits as standard theory would normally suggest. The evidence shows that agents collectively build precarious pyramids of trust relationships, in the form of scale-free networks, which occasionally collapse with frequency–magnitude probabilities described by scale-free heavy-tailed distributions. The build-up of systemic risk is controlled by financial regulation.

This contrasts with the view expressed by the New Monetarist literature, which, for its part, claims the benefit of basing theory upon strict micro-foundations using game theoretical arguments. There is, however, no fundamental constraint in New Monetarism to allow credit instruments to be used to settle payments, nor any fundamental requirement for there to be exogenous limits to credit creation (Cavalcanti and Wallace, 1999a). Thus, it may be argued, the complexity theory of money presented here is not in principle at odds, but may in fact be seen as broadly consistent with the game theoretical arguments of New Monetarism.[35]

[35] E.g., as in Kiyotaki and Wright (1989); Kiyotaki and Moore (1997).

Key implications of using a complexity theory of money as opposed to a quantity theory of money are that (1) money (debt) is created endogenously by financial agents; and (2) the impact of increasing debt, whether public, private, or both, gradually brings the system towards a brittle state close to recurrent instability, or punctuated equilibrium. According to what can be inferred from the empirical evidence reviewed, debt does not lead to just simple growth limitation effects, as has been suggested in now widely discredited analysis.[36] This has led to a potentially crucial misunderstanding in current mainstream economic thought and in current rules of monetary policy: increasing public and private debt may not decrease but increase economic activity (Keen, 2017), while it makes the system more prone to amplify fluctuations and recurrent instability.

The empirical evidence suggests that a more adequate metaphor to consider is that of tectonics and earthquakes.[37] In earth systems, the slow movement of tectonic plates increases pressure at specific points of the earth's crust, lifting entire mountain ranges over time. The way mountains lift is through sudden slips of tectonic plates against one another, which causes shockwaves that travel along the crust, relieving accumulated pressure. Travelling shockwaves, however, also trigger other slips in the crust that are already near to breaking point, adding energy to the shockwave as it comes by. Depending how many such slips are triggered in the wake of the shockwave, the overall event can be very large or very small. The magnitude of earthquakes is self-similar (or fractal) and described very precisely by power-law statistical distributions (the Richter scale) and aftershocks by exponential decay.

Equivalents of the Richter scale and Omori's law for aftershocks are as accurately observed in financial systems, modern or antique. Credit and purchasing power appear to be created without limit by agents, in many forms, with expectations of return, as allowed by the balance sheets of commercial banks, individuals and companies who create liabilities bought by other companies, banks and individuals. In this model, as financial agents acquire assets by issuing liabilities, they expand their balance sheets, which generally includes equity in or liabilities of other institutions, gradually increasing their leverage. However, the larger and the more connected their balance sheets are, the more exposed their solvency is to travelling shockwaves of value loss, which can be triggered by other firms declaring insolvency or sending profit warnings. Travelling shockwaves can become amplified when they trigger further insolvencies in their wake. If too many firms are highly leveraged, chains of insolvencies can appear, and with it recurrent instabilities.

Most of the time, most companies can absorb most types of shocks. It may not therefore be the average degree of leverage that is the enabling condition for recurrent instability to set in, as financial agent positions may be highly heterogeneous. It may be the existence of a sufficient number of highly leveraged firms connected

36 Originally proposed by Reinhart and Rogoff (2010); later discredited by Herndon et al. (2014).

37 Sornette and Sornette (1989); Bak (1996); Bak et al. (2002).

directly or indirectly in chains, in the context of changes of financial context, that can tip the system into instability, even when average leverage is low. Systemic risk may thus not be a simple unique function of total debt (public or private), which requires substantial further research using complex networks methods.

Effective policies to take control of the price stability of the financial system and currency might therefore have little to do with limiting the amount of money created by the central bank, nor reducing public spending, nor even private debt. In fact, what could, in this model, manage price stability is simply what limits the build-up of systemic risk in the form of chains of directly or indirectly connected highly leveraged nodes too close to insolvency. The financial system may gradually build itself into precarious states over time, but regulation could prevent it from reaching the edge of instability. This includes reducing how much can be borrowed according to the value of existing assets, increasing collateral requirements and more carefully choosing who can borrow using more sophisticated financial assessment methods and better data. Coordinating this can be done by assessing systemic risk in addition to assessing individual institution risk.

The next chapter will develop this theory into a SOC model of the stability of the financial sector, that can be used computationally. The goal of that model is to reproduce qualitatively the features of scale-free noise observed in financial asset price time series. But for a broader use in this book regarding environmental governance, one has to go back to Chapter 3. It was established there that how one understands the allocation of finance for energy-related innovation determines what one predicts the macroeconomic impacts of the low-carbon transition will be. The transition influences the trends of macroeconomic variables, but also the risk of asset price instability. Financing low-carbon innovation implies expanding the balance sheet of a substantial number of financial institutions, while at the same time, the possible stranding of fossil-fuel assets could cause shocks that could become amplified and destabilise those same balance sheets. But before this can be really explored, the overall macroeconomic theory must be developed, and this is done in Chapter 11.

10

Micro-foundations for Credit Creation and the Business Cycle

In this chapter, a self-organised criticality model of financial networks is developed mathematically and is applied computationally. It first establishes a complex network model of the equity identity of balance sheets. This is used to simulate various possible modes of operation of the financial system under different levels of stress and states of criticality, according to the distributions of the distance to insolvency of financial agents. This model can explain how the economy amplifies some small fluctuations into large scale financial crashes. It explains when and how the economy may be vulnerable to instability according to the topology of its financial network, and its distance to criticality according to the quantity of leverage that its financial agents have undertaken. Lastly, it identifies policy instruments effective at controlling the rate of growth of borrowing, systemic risk accumulation and collective risk-taking.

10.1. INTRODUCTION: FRAMING THE PROBLEM

The 2007–2008 financial crisis featured a number of interesting stylised facts, notably an emergent long-range correlation of asset prices for assets that seemed previously uncorrelated, heavy tails, volatility clustering, and a correlation between volatility and volumes traded (Cont, 2005). Fund managers in the network typically diversify their portfolios to minimise their own risk. They typically do this by measuring correlations between asset prices using time series, implicitly assuming that price variations follow normal distributions. When portfolios are fully diversified, risk is assumed minimised. Option and asset prices are often set using the Black and Scholes (1973) option pricing and the capital asset pricing models, which also assumes that price returns follow normal distributions. As seen in Chapter 9, it is quite notable that asset returns *do not* follow normal distributions, but instead have heavy tails which are often power-law distributions. The likelihood of extreme events is orders of magnitude larger than what is assumed when using normal distributions. And during these extreme events, asset prices move together downwards.

It is notable that fund managers make their clients substantial returns using standard models, assuming normally distributed returns. The Black-Scholes options pricing and the capital asset pricing models have been celebrated as highly effective. In that sense, no-one could dispute the validity of these methods when assessing strategies to generate profits, as people have been making real money. What is also notable is that these are clearly incorrect scientific representations how the financial sector works, and thus, while these models are apparently very effective for making money, they do not describe actual reality.[1] More specifically, they cannot predict or describe the onset of financial crises, and therefore, fund managers will make profits until the financial crisis hits so long as they were able to get out in time. In reality, the use of these wrong models may even have contributed to *increasing* the very vulnerability of the financial system, not least by ignoring where the instability lies. By diversifying portfolios using the standard method for risk assessment, the mixing up of different types of risk profiles may have effectively minimised 'perceived' risk for individual funds in the opinion of fund managers and according to their models, but it apparently contributed to increasing systemic risk for the whole system.[2] What this is symptomatic of, naturally, is the practical need for methods when none are empirically established, and where not having a solution is not an option.

There is an interesting tension between *normative and descriptive models of finance*, and it must be emphasised the degree to which *they are not equivalent*. They have a different purpose, and the divide between the two matches the difference in objective between the fund manager, who seeks to maximise profit, and the financial regulator, who seeks to minimise instability. Econophysics[3] has in recent years provided useful methods to analyse long-range correlations in financial networks and their topology. This type of analysis could not be achieved with standard methods used in economics, which are primarily based on multiple linear regressions or vector autoregressions. But here again, one needs to distinguish the strands of econophysics that seek to maximise profit for funds and traders, and those that seek to understand systemic risk, which are at odds with each other.[4]

Specifically, one strand of econophysics focuses on analysing the stability of financial networks and its methods are beginning to be used by central banks and financial regulators. It has first been a question of what topology financial

[1] Adams and Thornton (2013); Cont et al. (2010).

[2] Helleiner (2011); Haldane and May (2011).

[3] See, for instance, Cont et al. (2010); Raddant and Wagner (2016); Battiston et al. (2016a); Gopikrishnan et al. (1999).

[4] They cannot logically be the same, because there is no reason to expect that minimising risk/maximising profit for one node of the financial network minimises the risk/maximises return for the whole network. And indeed, a trade-off exists between performance and systemic brittleness.

networks have, and whether that matters. As discussed in Chapter 9, it has been demonstrated that financial networks are scale-free (Garlaschelli et al., 2005), but also that changing their topology by design would not make them necessarily more or less robust with respect to instability (Roukny et al., 2013). In that context, it is therefore the *distance to criticality* (the distance to the SOC state) over which agency and control matters.

The distance to criticality in any financial network changes continuously, as debt levels change. According to Minsky, there tends to be a gradual creep towards the critical state until instability occurs, as confidence grows and debt levels rise. The state of the financial network can be observed using present-day data. However, it is to be noted that given that financial networks are scale-free, the data requirement to have a full picture is extremely large. Notably, the number of 'leaves' (nodes with one link only) and small hubs in the hierarchical network, which features 'small worlds',[5] is substantial and data is largely unavailable, since these represent primarily individuals and small enterprises. Thus not all scales can be observed. But furthermore, exploring the time evolution of these networks is even more challenging, as it would require one to have representations of whole networks as a time series, and re-building the present-day picture already requires a large amount of work. Thus it is mostly realistic to primarily observe the present-day network topology, and use asset price trends for time series.

Network models of finance exist[6] and are used to study the stability of financial systems. What is of interest in this field of enquiry is the so-called 'stress test': to model the propagation of hypothetical shock waves of all kinds through the network in order to observe which nodes may be vulnerable, which parts of the network may not be resilient, and how large collapses of value could be. The resilience of banks to financial shocks are of particular interest, and the 'unobserved' correlation between asset values, asset prices that do not seem correlated at all in the price time series, but that do follow each other during extreme events. These asset prices follow each other for the following reason: financial distress induces financial distress and the fire-sale of assets, whatever they are. This part is not included in normative models of finance, since clearly, financial instability is not of great interest as it is not a moment when money can be made, and nothing can be done about it.

But a bigger picture is also at play. Every agent in a financial network participates with the purpose of accumulating wealth, and to do so faces financial commitments towards others, as yet others face financial commitments towards them, and they are thus continuously exposed to systemic risk. Take, for example, someone taking out a mortgage to buy and let out a flat. That person must, every month, pay his creditor

5 Small networks nested in a larger structure of similar topology (Barabási and Bonabeau, 2003).
6 Leading in the field is work by Battiston et al. (2012, 2016b, 2017).

(the bank), using a combination of funds from rent and possibly his salary or other income. If, due to unemployment, his tenants become unable to pay rent, he could become forced to default.

House prices rise as a result of banks creating money for individuals to buy property. Homeowners enjoy house prices going up as this generates return on everyone's investments, above the investment for which they borrowed from banks. Thus their wealth increases, but it only does so if new market entrants with financial credentials create the demand for houses, and new market entrants can only enter the market if banks create more loans for them to buy houses. To close the circle, banks will lend if new entrants can be expected to pay back, and new entrants will only show interest if house prices can be expected to rise. During a financial crisis, this whole construction unravels as banks fail to create more money, new entrants and demand for houses disappear, houses sell at discount and prices dip, which leads some homeowners' property value to decline below the value of their loans, which in some cases the homeowners may even never be able to pay off and where they become technically insolvent. As they become insolvent, they sell or hand over their properties to banks who put them on the market at further discount, which contributes to make prices dip further. It is clear that to operate normally, housing markets require the self-fulfilling promise of house price rises.

In the housing market, every agent is constrained by his/her financial commitments and position in the property pyramid they hope to climb, where their wealth only increases if younger and less wealthy agents can be persuaded to take out loans and enter the pyramid at its base. Wealth growth is a collective emergent phenomenon, as is its collapse. This is why public policy facilitating access to finance for young workers to buy property can easily lead to bubbles and price instability rather than form a sustainable solution to housing crises (Schelkle, 2012).

The 2007–2008 financial crisis concerned mainly housing markets but contaminated and consumed the entire financial system. Financial crises do not necessarily have to originate from housing markets, and notably, they often originated from technology innovation (Perez, 2001). An open question is whether financial instability can find its source in a rapid low-carbon transition. The value of assets that could be prematurely depreciated in principle far exceeds what triggered the 2007–2008 financial crisis[7] Whether the decline in 'sunset' industries can trigger financial stability through stranded assets is a point of current debate (Semieniuk et al., 2021), but there is no fundamental reason why they should not. In other words, if industries in high-carbon activities suddenly see their future profitability curtailed by changes in policy, markets or consumer behaviour, they could face large losses

[7] See Mercure et al. (2018c); Caldecott (2018); Fisch-Romito et al. (2021); Battiston et al. (2017) in comparison with Blanchard (2009).

and even default on their loans,[8] which in some cases could be substantial (e.g., shale oil producers). Those losses could further destabilise banking lending networks and lead to a similar situation as in 2007–2008 (Battiston et al., 2017).

In this chapter, a complex network model is developed based on the simplest possible identity equation that represents the interconnected balance sheets of agents. The model is allowed to endogenously grow itself, as links are added every time an agent borrows funds from another agent or acquires financial assets. Exogenous noise exists on the network, reflecting non-financial world events. The most important, fundamental finding is that if one applies normally distributed noise to the value of assets in this network, the equity value on the balance sheet of agents does not remain normally distributed, but rather, becomes heavy-tailed, scale-free *power law*-distributed (and *non-ergodic*, i.e. with memory). Different modes of evolution are identified, an ordered phase, in which the network grows uninterrupted, a disordered phase on the edge of chaos, in which a punctuated equilibrium arises interrupted recurrently by clustered instability, and a chaotic phase, in which nothing grows much. The evolution of the system between these three phases is controlled by three parameters: ease of access to finance, the magnitude of the exogenous noise with respect to the value of assets, and the degree of carefulness to which financial institutions choose to allocate loans to agents. These three parameters are readily associated respectively to three types of financial regulation: the size of loans in relation to existing assets and expected income, collateral requirements and better use of data and more detailed balance sheet disclosure by all financial agents to improve investment choice. The model suggests that it is the way in which the financial pyramid evolves that generates the type of recurrent instability behaviour that financial markets display, a quantitative demonstration of Minsky's financial instability hypothesis.

10.2. A NETWORK MODEL OF DISTRESS PROPAGATION

10.2.1 *The Equity Identity*

The goal in this chapter is to develop a positive model of financial dynamics and instability. Stefano Battiston[9] and colleagues have devised a method to carry out stress-tests of the financial network that is relatively effective at representing how financial shock waves travel across a financial network, especially given the scarcity of data available to work with. Earlier stress-test models primarily looked at chains of defaults in the network following a disturbance, and assumed that only defaults induced defaults. This clearly limits how shock waves can travel across networks, as

8 See reports by the Bank of England and Banque de France: BoE (2015, 2018); Bolton et al. (2020).

9 Battiston et al. (2012, 2016b, 2017).

in general, even in deep depressions, not all institutions become insolvent, while they still lose substantial value, and those losses can induce more losses and default. Furthermore, value losses can travel across the network without necessarily leaving a trail of insolvencies: nodes can communicate value losses across the network without declaring bankruptcy.

Battiston and colleagues focused on how changes of the value of equity of one node induces changes in the equity of network neighbours. The solvency of nodes is assumed to be determined by the value of assets relative to that of liabilities, not considering issues of cash flow. The valuation of firms is considered to follow changes in their balance sheet instantaneously, the so-called 'mark to market' assumption.

However, losses are not necessarily transmitted linearly only, as they may become amplified. Amplification suggests non-linearity, and ownership through equity cannot on its own generate such non-linearity. However, the suddenness of insolvencies past the zero equity threshold can play that role. Thus, intuitively, one can suggest that sudden insolvencies in the wake of loss shockwaves travelling along the network can amplify the magnitude of those shocks, as in the earthquake example given in Chapter 9.

Here, a model loosely following Battiston et al. (2016b) is described. A balance sheet is defined using the fundamental equity identity, where the equity of institution or company i (E_i) is defined as the difference between its assets (A_i) and its liabilities (D_i), which evolve over time,

$$E_i(t) = A_i(t) - D_i(t). \tag{10.1}$$

Insolvency occurs when E_i becomes negative. Since through equity ownership (shares in other companies), for each company, A_i may depend on the value E_i of other companies, changes in equity somewhere induces changes of equity elsewhere. Naturally, the effect that institution A has on institution B is not the same as the effect that institution C has on A, as it depends on the amount of equity that each company owns from other companies. Typically, companies own relatively small fractions of the equity of other companies, and thus the exposure of one company to the distress of another is relatively limited, and shocks disperse rapidly in the network. Distress can happen typically when equity shocks from several network neighbours arrive at the same time. This would not arise if the source of shock is isolated, as it would disperse quickly; however, it can happen if some nodes amplify the shock as it travels.

Companies can also lend money to other companies, either through loans or by issuing bonds, and thus A_i can depend on the value of the liabilities of other companies, and is affected by those companies defaulting. Loans are different from equity since their value collapses to zero when creditors come to realise that their debtors are going to default payment on their loans, while equity is a reflection of what investors think a company is worth. Under fluctuations in the value of its assets (hard assets, money lent and equity and bonds owned), the equity of a company can fluctuate substantially. The 'distance' to insolvency can be measured using the 'leverage' ratio, equal to debts divided by equity, $L_i = D_i/E_i$. When debts exceed equity several times over, a company is at risk of insolvency as a result of any relatively small fluctuation in the value of its assets.

This then suggests that the equity of company i, E_i, can in principle depend on the equity and the debt of any other company, and on the value of its own physical assets. The full set of equity ownership for any financial agent in an economy in relation to all other financial agents in that economy can be thought of as a matrix in which all owning financial agents are rows and all owned financial agents are columns, and the entries are the percentage share ownership.[10] Similarly, a matrix of debt ownership can be determined in which the rows are creditors and columns are debtors. Zero entries in the matrices indicate no equity or debt connection between two companies. This then means that the relationship between equity, debt and assets in the economy is recursive, and this is shown in the mathematical appendix at the end of this chapter. Lastly, as shown in Chapter 9, financial agents are connected to one another through scale-free networks of ownership.

10.2.2 *The Basic Theoretical Model*

Figure 10.1 shows the basic building block of the model developed here. The proposition is that this one single simple building block can in fact represent every possible relevant financial agent in the economy, and when connected to other such blocks, every possible relevant financial relationship. It can thus be used to construct the whole financial network with a good amount of its relevant intricacies, while remaining parsimonious and easy to understsand. Here, financial agents are assumed to borrow from each other and/or to raise equity funds (selling shares) from each other in order to invest in financial or real assets. Real assets are ultimately what generates value in the economy, underpinning all other activities, but the lending and share

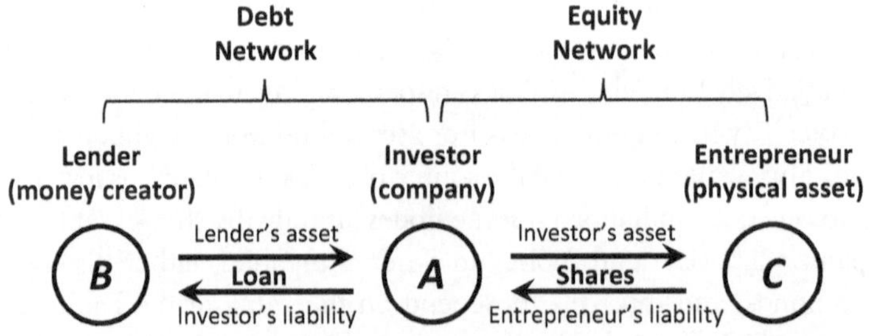

FIGURE 10.1 Diagram showing the model's representation of financial relationships between financial agents in the model.

[10] Here, owned financial agents are companies since of course persons cannot be owned but can own.

ownership is what happens to achieve this. The assumptions of the model in relation to lending and ownership are as follows:

1. every financial agent is considered to be either, some or all of the following: a lender who creates loans, an investor who borrows to invest, and/or an entrepreneur who builds physical assets;
2. each time an investment is made, a loan is created and a physical asset is built;
3. this involves a lender *B* creating a liability-asset relationship between him/herself and an investor A who takes out the loan;
4. the investor A uses the funds to buy ownership in a company C that builds a physical asset with expected return.

If the lender *B* buys ownership in the entrepreneur C directly, then A and *B* are the same financial entity, and this is therefore implicitly covered by the model. If the lender *B* lends directly to the entrepreneur C, then A and C are the same entity and this is also covered by the model.[11]

Thus, by applying this basic *A–B–C* construct over and over like Lego, one can build a whole artificial financial network, using random agents gradually lending to each other and buying stakes in each other. Further rules are necessary in order for the networks to be scale-free as required by the empirical evidence, and meanwhile, rules of insolvency have to be added:

1. both the equity and debt networks develop through a 'preferential attachment' process (see Chapter 5), where the larger a lender is, the more it lends, while the larger an investor's balance sheet is, the more it can borrow and own stakes in other companies, and the larger an entrepreneur's company is, the more it receives investment to build more assets;
2. the amount that can be borrowed by one agent is proportional to that agent's existing stock of assets;
3. the value of physical assets, as they mature, is affected by stochastic variations, where the assets may turn out to be worth more or less than they initially cost;
4. changes in asset values accrue to their immediate and ultimate owners through a constant revaluation process involving inter-agent ownership of equity and debt;

[11] Here, inspiration is taken from Minsky in imposing that 'everyone can create money, the challenge is to get it accepted' and assume that many firms issue debt in the form of bonds, such that those buying the bonds are lenders, while banks also lend. Therefore, no distinction is made between types of firms and assume that all firms can borrow and lend, as long as their balance sheet allows it. However, the distribution of sizes of firms follows a scale-free network, or in other words, a power-law (Pareto) distribution.

5. when the equity of an agent crosses into negative territory due to changing asset values, this agent is considered insolvent, and its assets are auctioned off and liquidated, while its debts are written off. This agent disappears from the network, while its owners incur a loss. This could lead to further insolvencies.

These rules imply that starting from one set of *A*–*B*–*C* agents, applying the concept over and over, creating relationships either between existing agents or with new agents who are thereafter included in the model, both equity and debt networks will be scale-free and will connect all agents in the system, where all agents have at least one financial relationship with someone else, but potentially many. Naturally, due to preferential attachment, a few agents will become highly connected nodes who are either lending to many others or owning stakes in many others, while many will have only one financial relationship.

The value of physical assets (only) is affected by exogenous stochastic variations (or financial noise) due to fundamental uncertainty, markets and uncertain entrepreneurial success. Since agents owning physical assets are connected by equity ownership, these variations are felt by owners, who suffer endogenous financial noise. Furthermore, since agents can default, and since insolvencies means writing off loans from lender balance sheets whose equity is owned by others, the value of these lost loans can be felt by various agents in the network. Thus, everyone's equity value is connected to everyone else's one way or another.

Crucially, if some physical assets generate important losses to some entrepreneurs, they could become insolvent if their leverage ratio is very high (as they may also have borrowed money in addition to selling equity). Some of the investors owning large equity stakes in those entrepreneurs may happen to also be in highly leveraged positions, and these losses could in principle push them into insolvency. Alternatively, entrepreneurs who are not insolvent but who suffer large losses in expected revenue could push some of their highly leveraged equity owners into negative equity territory. At this stage, when either or both these agents become insolvent, all of the loans taken out either by entrepreneurs or investors are written off, not just those that have a relationship to the physical assets generating the losses. This is where the loss becomes amplified and passed on. The lenders inevitably suffer a sudden loss in equity value that can in principle be much larger than the original loss in physical assets. The lender may pass this loss on to its equity owners; however, if the lender becomes insolvent, it will add to this shockwave the value of all of its own losses too and pass that on to the owners of its debt in addition to the loss of equity it passes on to its equity owners.

It is easy to see that in such a model, financial shockwaves generate further financial shockwaves. If most financial agents are not highly leveraged, it is likely that insolvencies are rare and that shockwaves are quickly absorbed and do not travel far. However, if many financial agents are highly leveraged, they perpetuate and add energy to the shockwaves, which then affect more and more financial agents.

10.2.3 *Three Rounds of Losses*

Battiston et al. (2016b) classifies the above more formally between three rounds of losses that can happen during a financial crash:

1. *First-round* losses are direct losses, as initially recorded when shocks take place. Since institutions have in the short run fixed commitments on liabilities, they reduce their equity value accordingly. This is transmitted through the equity owner network.
2. *Second-round* losses arise due to the possible distress of some institutions which are suddenly expected to become unable to meet their debt commitments, and thus losses arise through the devaluation of debt assets. This is initially transmitted through the debt network, followed by the equity owner network.
3. *Third-round* losses arise due to the process in which institutions begin to sell assets to generate cash to meet debt commitments or redress balance sheets. The resulting downwards pressure on asset prices (with respect to money), due to the collective movement, induces further sales of assets to generate cash, which results in further reductions in asset prices.

The first round of losses takes place directly through equity owned. This is a linear process, where the value of a company changes proportionally to the value of its stake in other companies, and the total value lost is divided between all owners without amplification. Second-round losses take place through expectations that debtors may default on their loans, decreasing the value of the debt owned, a non-linear process. This can amplify the original losses as it adds the bankrupt debt and distributes that across owners. Third-round losses take place when distressed firms sell assets in order to generate cash to repay their loans, in an effort to redress their balance sheet and avoid bankruptcy, the collective effect of which leads to general asset price declines, which appear, in the perspective of firms, as the value of their debt increasing, where the value of the currency in which it is written appreciates against assets, worsening their financial position generally.

Typically, second-round losses are at least as large compared to first-round losses, while round-three losses may be of a similar order to round one and two combined, although in principle, it can also trigger a vicious cycle, a contagion of what Fisher (1932) called the 'money disease'.

As is becoming clear, the change in equity for firm i is a function of the changes in equity of all other firms j to which firm i is connected, whether through debt or equity ownership. A loss of \$Xbn by firm k in principle implies losses for all other firms, assuming that the whole network is connected. But the total value of losses may not equate \$Xbn once distributed across the network. It is generally counted multiple times by the network, for the following reason.

As a first highly exaggerated example, imagine that Phil discovers oil, and issues shares for the total value of £1bn to raise the capital necessary to extract and sell that oil. Gregor decides to buy all of that equity, setting up a fund that specialises in that type of asset. Pablo decides to invest £1bn in this fund, which looks promising. And finally, Neil, who manages a pension fund, invests £1bn of its member's accumulated wealth in Pablo's firm, which owns £1bn of fossil fuel assets. When Phil realises that, after acquiring £1bn worth of physical capital for oil extraction, following a drastic oil price crash, he will be making a loss for each barrel of oil that he produces, he declares bankruptcy, which implies that his equity collapses to zero. Everyone loses some money, and therefore, the total loss is of somewhere lower than £4bn but higher than £1bn. The trading of assets and their use for leveraging finance across the network has led to counting multiple times the same value. This arises only just through accounting convention, and thus, perhaps one should not consider this 'real' loss amplification, but rather, a leverage effect.

As a second example, imagine that Phil discovers oil, and issues once again shares for the total value of £1bn. Gregor, who is already indebted, borrows £1bn from Pablo, who runs a bank, to buy those shares, leveraging existing assets, and assume that Neil owns £1bn of equity in that bank. Now imagine that Phil loses 10% of his equity value as he issues a profit warning following technical problems. Assume that Gregor's balance sheet is so leveraged that a 50% loss on equity invested in Phil's company makes his equity negative. Pablo writes off the bad loan of £1bn to Gregor as the latter declares bankruptcy. Despite that the starting shock is only of £0.1bn, the loss felt by Pablo is of £1bn and Neil somewhere under £1bn (depending on the total value of Pablo's Bank), and thus it has been amplified by a factor of more than 10 through the debt network. In reality, the magnitude entirely depends on the value of assets owned by Gregor as they are auctioned off to repay creditors. Nevertheless, the loss is generally amplified when bankruptcies happen, making the system non-linear.

The difference between first- and second-round losses is that in a world without lending, equity losses would be losses of real physical value as accounted in books, and could not exceed that. However, with lending, losses on debt assets are losses of value that has been expected to materialise in the future. The first round has to do with loss allocation, while the second has to do with expectations. The third round could be understood as related to general confidence in financial markets relative to the currency metric of value on the basis of which rules of solvency operate, where inflation erases debts while deflation increases debts.

10.2.4 *An Applied Network Model of Financial Instability*

Computational experiments can be made remarkably easily based on very general principles of financial accounting, the equity identity and the insolvency criterion, and generate a particular type of behaviour very similar to that of financial markets, reproducing many stylised features. There is no need to invoke any behavioural rules, complex or simple, for traders of financial assets.[12] The result is that simple normally distributed stochastic variations affecting the value of physical capital assets (equipment, real estate, etc.) become transformed into *non-ergodic, heavy-tailed* and *scale free* variations. A transition to the SOC state can readily be observed. This finding suggests that financial markets are almost certainly governed by SOC dynamics.

A scale-free network is grown endogenously by using a process of preferential attachment with the *A–B–C* process above: pick a random existing or new node (a random number in the index of nodes) and connect it to an existing node in both networks. The topology (the slope of the exponent) can be controlled. Observations[13] suggest (see Figure 9.2) that the equity network is characterised by an exponent of -1.4, while the debt network is reported to have an exponent of -2.1 (Cont et al., 2010). However, the two networks should ideally be consistent, in that larger institutions in the domain of equity are likely also large in the domain of debt. In order to achieve a double linked network with the specified exponents, it is constructed as follows.

A simulation is created in which at each 'time step' one asset-liability pair is created, the ownership of which passes through intermediaries, using preferential attachment. The value of the asset created is a random number the upper limit of which depends on the total value of hard assets already owned by that node. The value of some or all assets is shocked using either 'white noise' or normally distributed stochastic variations.[14] Following this, the equity value of all companies is updated by applying the equity identity over and over onto itself until all the values converge, at which point all variables become self-consistent and losses are reflected in equity values. Finally, a check is made every time step for equity values that dip below zero, in which case they are deleted, and for simplicity, their liabilities and the value of their ownership by others written off entirely. This write-off can push owners in turn into negative equity territory, in which case the calculation process continues, and this can lead to long chains of insolvencies. In fact, it leads to clustered volatility.

12 It is known that behavioural rules, and especially adaptive ones, can lead to highly complex dynamics including heavy tails, see, e.g., Palmer et al. (1994); Cont (2005). However, ownership links are not speculative and therefore matter to first order, while trading behaviour is speculative and thus matters only to second order.

13 Inferred from equity data from the ORBIS dataset.

14 White noise is defined here as noise of which the probability distribution is constant between -1 and 1. For such a symmetric range, the standard deviation of white noise is of around 0.58. The assumption of white or normal noise is not realistic, as financial noise is effectively never short-tailed, but this is used here to show that *even if* external noise were short-tailed, heavy-tailed noise would nevertheless emerge spontaneously.

The value variations applied to some or all hard assets reflect exogenous real (non-financial) world events, such as changes in consumer tastes and demand, political events, changes in trade relationships or the appearance of disruptive innovations. Meanwhile the endogenous noise reflects what happens inside the financial network as a result. Lastly, the network is grown from one node to tens or hundreds of thousands, or to the limit of the available computing power.[15]

The model is controlled by three parameters: (1) the amplitude of the variations applied to the value of assets (denoted *sig*), (2) the number of nodes variations are applied to (denoted *NR*), and (3) the amount that can be borrowed according to a node's balance sheet size (denoted *LR*). What is observed is that in certain circumstances (certain combination of parameters), avalanches of insolvencies arise endogenously as the network grows. This is shown in Figures 10.2 and 10.3, where the total value of assets $\sum A_i$ across the economy, and the sum of debt and asset written off during bankruptcy avalanches are shown, respectively. The former grows exponentially and sees noise, while the latter sees clustered peaks. The total asset value changes as noise is applied, and assets are either created with borrowing or destroyed with bankruptcies. The magnitude-frequency distributions of clustered volatility are heavy-tailed, in some cases nearly scale-free.

This model shows very clear signs of behaviour very similar to self-organised criticality discussed in Chapter 5. These are:

1. heavy-tailed distributions of value variations;
2. clustering of avalanches in time;
3. heavy-tailed distributions of waiting times between avalanches;
4. an endogenous creep towards the edge of instability.

Avalanches are typically clustered, something similar to the Bak and Sneppen (1993) model of evolution discussed in Chapter 5. Here, however, the system connecting elements to one another is made of two scale-free networks, and nodes accumulate risk over time, and thus it also has similarities with the Bak–Tang–Wiesenfeld model of sandpiles (Bak et al., 1987).

The above three parameters generate different outcomes, and are kept constant in each simulation here for simplicity. In this three-dimensional parameter space, a phase transition boundary exists, but the phase transition can also happen with increasing likelihood with increasing size of the network. Under certain conditions in terms of the three parameters above, one of three possible phases can be observed: (1) the ordered phase, where growth occurs without any bankruptcies (panels a, b, c, d); (2) the SOC phase in which avalanches of clustered bankruptcies arise at all

[15] The network can be grown to arbitrarily large values, and to reflect the real world, it should be of order 10^7–10^9 nodes; however it becomes computationally slow past 10^5–10^6 on an ordinary desktop computer using Matlab. The experiments shown are preliminary and require deeper and systematic analysis.

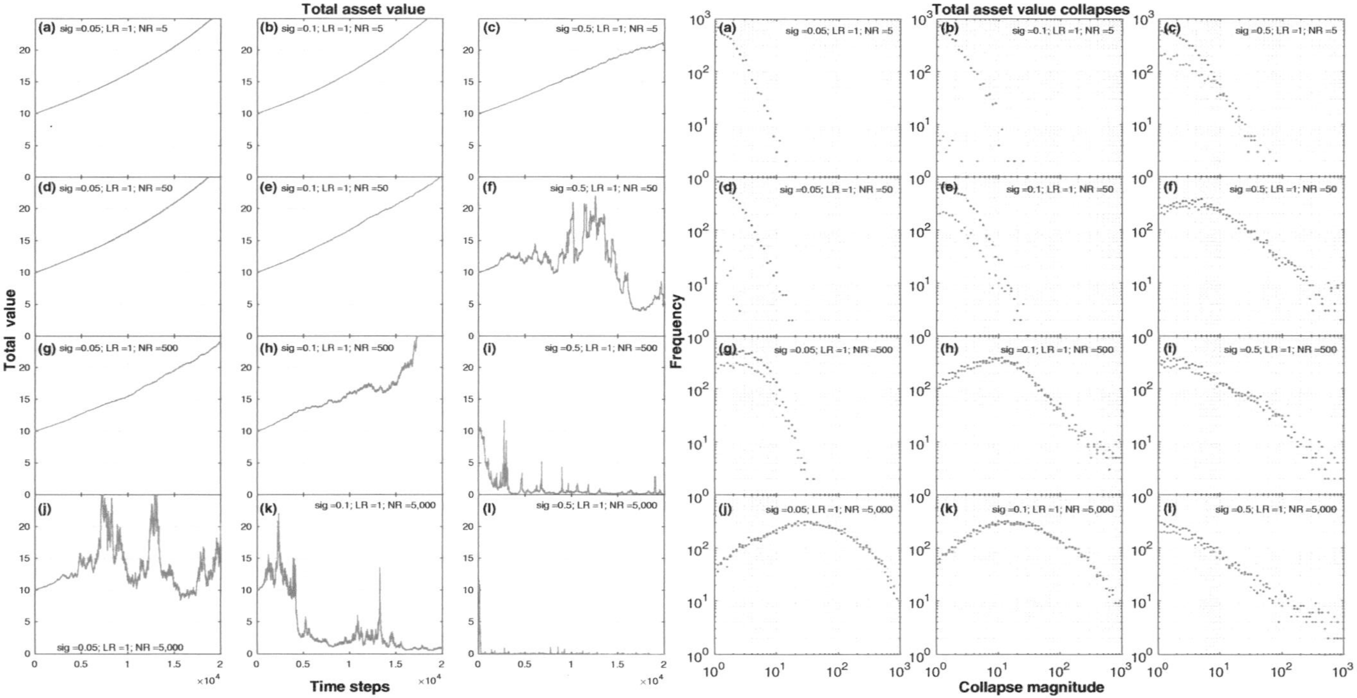

FIGURE 10.2 Evolution of the total value of assets in a network model for various amplitudes (sig) of white noise applied to various numbers (NR) of nodes. Investors are allowed by banks to borrow up to a value equal to their current wealth (LR = 1).

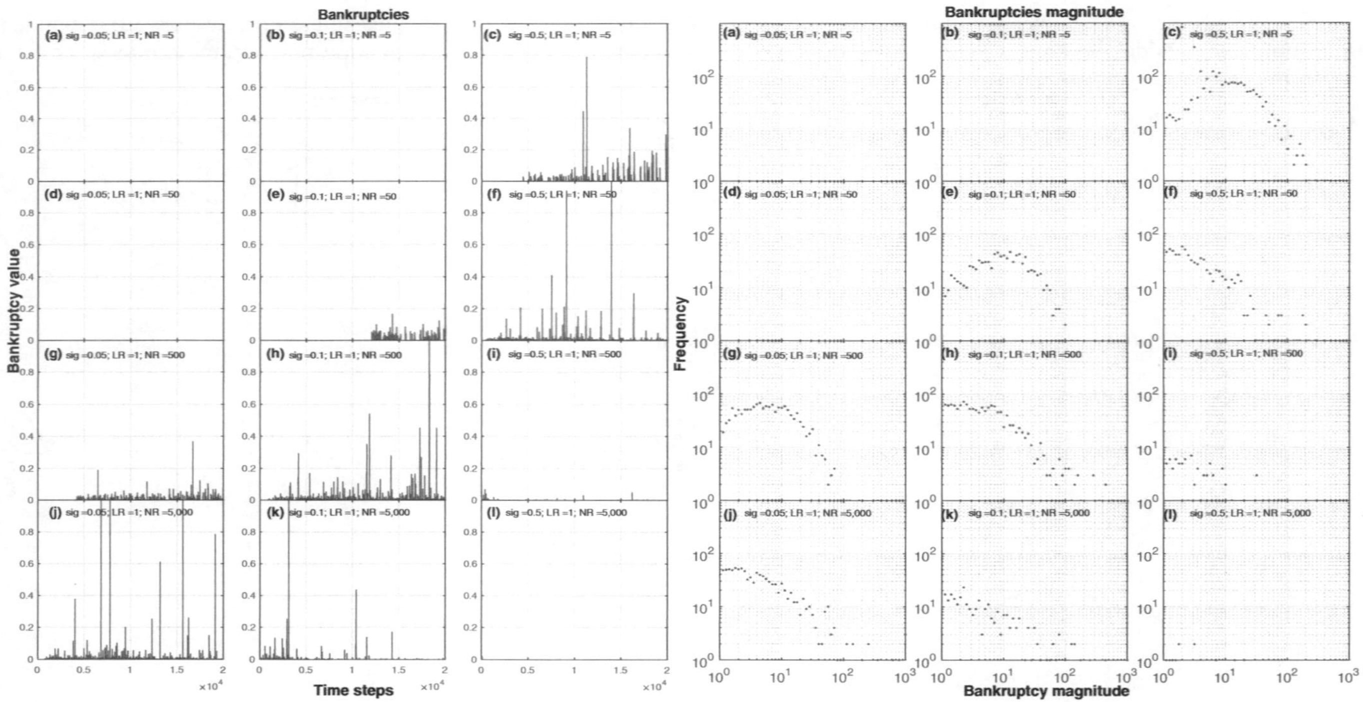

FIGURE 10.3 Bankruptcies in a network model for various amplitudes (sig) of white noise applied to various numbers (NR) of nodes. Investors are allowed by banks to borrow up to a value equal to their current wealth (LR = 1).

scales (panels e, f, g, h, j); and (3) a chaotic phase in which the network self-destructs too quickly to be able to build to any size, when noise driving bankruptcies is too high (panels i, k, l).

The transition thus goes from an ordered state in which the network gradually grows in value exponentially, with noise commensurate with the noise patterns introduced on asset values. Past the transition, avalanches of bankruptcies begin to appear, clustered in time, of all possible magnitudes.[16] These clustered insolvencies generate in the model large fluctuations in equity values, total debt and total asset value in the economy. The resonating noise induced is of amplitude orders of magnitude larger than what is applied to asset values. However, the structure of the noise is also different: it tends towards a scale-free power-law power spectrum. This is a peculiar type of noise: that typical of earthquakes. In fact, both the clustering and the noise type is the same as with earthquakes. Fluctuations in debt are also heavy-tailed, as well as those in the equity value of individual network nodes. The numbers of nodes collapsing also follows a heavy-tailed distribution, and in fact form a 'devil's staircase'. Lastly, as the chaotic phase develops, the amplitude of the noise declines again.

It can be shown with further simulations (not shown here) that the system can go in and out of the SOC phase from and back to the ordered state, albeit with some degree of hysteresis. This can be observed by gradually increasing and decreasing the amplitude of the white noise applied to asset values. This suggests that the phase transition line, although blurry in parameter space, is relatively well defined and stationary.

10.2.5 *Interpretation of the Computational Experiment*

This model has enormous explanatory power regarding the evolution of financial networks with all the features of the real-world financial system. It does not take many assumptions to discover that the network must become SOC due to the interconnectedness and threshold effects. It is to be noted that each trajectory of this simulation is unique and extremely path-dependent. Thus the transition to the SOC state features hysteresis and is not always reproducible with the exact same characteristics, even for identical model parameters. This nature of non-ergodic recursive stochastic systems has only recently started to be discussed in the context of

[16] The distributions of avalanches do not form exactly straight lines on the log-log graphs and are therefore not exactly power laws; this is likely due to a lack of statistics, where large numbers of bankruptcies are needed, requiring to run the model for very long times. However, the fact that the heavy tails appear and disappear is clear.

economics and finance.[17] This model experiment would suggest that the economy enters the SOC state under the following conditions:

1. the magnitude of financial noise on hard assets is high, implying that '*too many projects*' do not deliver expected returns;
2. the amount that is being borrowed according to balance sheet sizes '*is too high*';
3. the number of assets and interconnections between institutions '*is large*'.

To determine 'how large is too large', one would need to apply this simulation to real-world data, a complex but achievable challenge,[18] although outside of the scope of this book. What is remarkable is the parsimony of this model, which has no need to invoke any behavioural rules for financial agents, other than declaring insolvency when their equity becomes negative.

The interpretation of this computational experiment is as follows. As the financial sector grows, by gradually creating money in order to build physical assets, a financial bubble grows in which the value of physical assets is counted multiple numbers of times throughout the chains of ownership across the financial network. The increasing number of such chains increase the amount of money and value available in the economy, or in other words, the size of the money supply. However, they also gradually make the system more and more fragile, depending how leveraged the system as a whole is, and how many nodes are at or near Minsky's speculative and perhaps Ponzi states. When many nodes find themselves in such states, relatively small fluctuations lead them to insolvencies and they fall over, they pull their neighbours down with them in avalanches, and each avalanche sets the stage for more insolvency chains to develop. The system self-organises towards the critical state.

However, the self-organised critical state has a phase transition, and this is an important observation. It means that there is an ordered state in which the financial network is stable as it grows. All agents remain in Minsky's hedge finance state, with plenty of buffer to absorb shocks. It is the comparison between leverage and the magnitude of financial noise that determines when the economy enters the critical state, at which point all assets suddenly become substantially more risky than before. However, financial risk is not straightforward to calculate, as it involves knowing the detailed topology of the network, and no agent in the system has that capacity.

[17] See, for instance, Peters (2019).

[18] Comprehensive data exists that can readily be used to recreate international equity networks for the present day, for instance, the ORBIS database (see Battiston et al., 2017; Semiemiuk et al., 2022). However, comprehensive data is more difficult to find that covers debt networks. Furthermore, the evolution of these two networks in time is not clear, and thus the temporal nature of change cannot be compared against data (and the data requirement to do so would be enormous). Time dependences can instead be analysed against time series of asset prices, in other words financial noise (e.g., see Figure 9.4). Lastly, 'time' in the model does not correspond to real time, but rather, corresponds to the number of financial exchanges.

The amplitude of the noise that makes the system critical can indicate how near to insolvent many companies are. When private debt is generally high, or frequently high across the network, the system becomes fragile to any arbitrarily small financial losses incurred by any particularly highly leveraged company. Meanwhile, when entrepreneurs begin to become collectively unsuccessful in too many ventures (such as may happen towards the end of waves of innovation), the financial system becomes unstable. Lastly, the chaotic state is not a state that is likely to be frequently observed, but could be understood to represent something such as an economy that is repeatedly hit by natural disasters, to the extent that assets are destroyed as quickly as they are built.

It is to be noted that instability arises endogenously in the model, but it could also be induced directly using exogenous factors such as external losses, causing the start of avalanches, but amplified by the degree of leverage. It then seems clear that while the cause may be exogenous (e.g., some particular bank failing, or a pandemic causing loss of demand, or stranded fossil fuel assets), it is the leveraged state of the network that enables exogenous events to cause a more explosive financial crisis, the magnitude of which follows a heavy-tailed distribution. This is consistent with observation.

The last question therefore revolves around how to control the creep towards the critical state, or avoid it altogether. Again, all three parameters discussed can be used to maintain the system within the ordered state of finance. This was already stated in Chapter 9: (1) Limits to the amount that companies and individuals can borrow, as a ratio of their existing wealth and expected cumulated future income; (2) the amount of failures can be limited by more carefully choosing who can borrow; and (3) higher collateral requirements can be demanded from companies. All three parameters essentially correspond to some form of financial regulation.

10.3. CONCLUSION AND OUTWARDS LOOK

The goal of this chapter was to study how and why the financial system is inherently unstable, and drives itself naturally towards financial instability. In the broader picture of this book, this has implications in relation to environmental governance. In particular, it provides insights over what can be expected for the financial system during a disorderly low-carbon transition in which capital write downs are sudden and unexpected.

The literature over the macroeconomic impacts of the low-carbon transition, with its standard equilibrium economics normative basis and framing, estimates the percentage of GDP that could be expected to be lost due to green investments crowding out other productive investments. The reality of complex financial networks is not at all like that. What this chapter shows is that it is financial stability that is at stake, not GDP losses.

Capital-intensive technological and innovation transitions are inherently intertwined with the creeping of the financial system towards self-organised criticality, by simply increasing the stock of private debt to potentially high levels in order to finance innovation in the new technological paradigm, while at the same time devaluing specific classes of assets in the old technological paradigm.[19] This combination, as can be gathered from concepts presented in this chapter, could be a recipe for disaster in generating financial instability. Indeed, as the financial system creeps towards self-organised criticality, fluctuations that arise due to losses in stranded assets could become amplified by the financial network, notably through losses in the interbank lending market and through various insolvencies, into fluctuations of all magnitudes. In other words, if the transition is very rapid, large amounts of high-carbon capital could become written off suddenly by a change of sentiment of investors regarding what they believe is the profitability of their investments. Such sudden losses could push the system into (or further into) an unstable regime of clustered insolvencies and high financial volatility. The greater the micro-fluctuations from stranded devalued assets are, the larger the system-wide macro-fluctuations become. An analysis of financial contagion due to stranded fossil fuel assets and other transition risks is therefore warranted.

More broadly, it may be the case that the economy recurrently enters and exits the disordered SOC state following fluctuations in the success of innovation. First, the model is clearly consistent with the narrative of Minsky (1986). But even more importantly, this appears consistent with observations in economic history.[20] Thus, it may not be entirely under the control of policy-makers to avoid economic instability if it is the innovation system that is partly driving the system towards the critical state. Carlota Perez notably suggests that new waves of innovation and the growth of 'sunrise' industries always cause bubbles that crash every time (Perez, 2001). However, less evidence exists to suggest that the accumulation of risk in 'sunset' industries causes financial instability (Semieniuk et al., 2021). Looking back at the low-carbon transition, it is clear that it is bound to generate substantial amounts of stranded assets, and the question that remains unsolved is whether this could be sufficient to drive the economy into further financial instability than it is now, following the 2007 financial crash and the crash caused by the COVID-19 pandemic (Semieniuk et al., 2021). It may well be the case that the economy is now in the SOC state and will remain unstable until highly leveraged financial institutions are cleared out or re-structured, rapid inflation erases debt levels and/or new sources of revenues from new technological sectors allow the economy to outgrow debt levels.

[19] Perez (2001); Semieniuk et al. (2021).

[20] Schumpeter (1939); Freeman and Louçã (2001); Perez (2001); Semieniuk et al. (2021).

10.4. MATHEMATICAL APPENDIX

Eq. 10.1 can be unpacked in terms of the equity and debt of all financial agents in the network (companies henceforth for simplicity). The matrix expressing equity ownership is denoted α_{ij} and the one for debt ownership is β_{ij}, forming two distinct networks, both assumed scale-free. The assets A_i of company i can be of three possible natures, shares α_{ij} in the equity of all other firms j, the fraction β_{ik} of loans taken by any other firms k, and physical capital assets A_i^{ext} (e.g., real estate, factories):

$$A_i = \sum_j \alpha_{ij} E_j + \sum_k \beta_{ik} D_k + A_i^{ext}. \qquad (10.2)$$

Denoting D_i as debts of firm i owned by financial agents in the network, and D_i^{ext} debt owned by financial agents outside of the network (e.g., abroad), Eq. 10.1 becomes

$$E_i = \sum_j \alpha_{ij} E_j + \sum_j \beta_{ik} D_k + A_i^{ext} - D_i - D_i^{ext}. \qquad (10.3)$$

(i) First-Round Losses

In the first round of losses, changes in the equity of firms ΔE_j are transmitted directly to the equity of their owners ΔE_j, by the amount specified by their shares α_{ij},

$$\Delta E_i^{(1)} = \sum_j \alpha_{ij} \Delta E_j \qquad (10.4)$$

If losses took place only through this process (if D_i is constant), there would always exist a vector E_i that solves the recursive equation

$$E_i = \sum_i \alpha_{ij} E_j - D_i \qquad (10.5)$$

in a steady state following a shock to one or more elements of E_j. Once E_i changes, Eq. 10.4 is applied to E_i over and over until it stops changing, at which point a new steady state is reached, and losses have dissipated (although the sum of E_i has changed). Experiments with data readily show that this is true in scale-free networks as long as there are no 'rings' of ownership in the network.[21] This system is linear, and without threshold effects, it cannot on its own generate SOC behaviour, nor amplify shocks. As such, it can only disperse shocks among the nodes.

(ii) Second-Round Losses

In the second round, the value of debt assets (bonds, loans) declines due to expectations of default by owners. Expectations are subjective and therefore it is not

[21] Ownership constructions of the form firm A owns B that owns C that owns A and some small share of another firm D. Any arbitrarily small loss in the equity of D leads to a slow unravelling of the value of firms A, B, C. This construction is, however, clearly illegal, since these firms have an equity value underpinned only by each other only and thus by nothing at all.

possible to express these exactly in equations. It is assumed that a non-linear value function f exists that expresses the change in the value of debt $\Delta D'_i$ given change in equity E_i through a perceived likelihood of default $P_i = f(E_i, D_i)$, where bank managers are assumed to value debt on the basis of this.

The expectation of default by firm i of firm k depends on how close to insolvency firm k is (i.e. how close to zero E_k is). The value of the debt D'_k in terms of its original face value D_k can be expressed as

$$D'_k = (1 - P_k)\, D_k. \tag{10.6}$$

This implies changes in the value of debt, due to changes in the financial position, as

$$\Delta D'_k = -P_k D_k. \tag{10.7}$$

The change in equity due to a change in the valuation of debt owned is

$$\Delta E_i^{(2)} = \sum_k \beta_{ik} \Delta D'_k = \sum_k \beta_{ik} P_k D_k. \tag{10.8}$$

In a simplified model, debts could be assumed to be immediately written off as companies' equity reaches zero,

$$P_k = \delta_k(E_k) = \begin{cases} 1 & E_k \leq 0 \\ 0 & E_k > 0 \end{cases},$$

in which case

$$\Delta E_i^{(2)} = -\sum_k \beta_{ik} \delta(E_k) D_k. \tag{10.9}$$

Whether a non-linear function is used or this step function, a non-linear threshold effect arises, which can give rise to amplification of shocks and the SOC state, as shocks trigger sudden debt losses that amplify existing equity shockwaves. This means that equity shockwaves do not necessarily dissipate and die down. The reason the behaviour of the debt network is different from the equity network is that debts are written down in terms of specific dollar values on contracts, and therefore do not change value in balance sheets until unambiguous evidence indicates default, at which point they are worthless.[22]

(iii) Third-Round Losses

In the third round, losses are related to a collective fire-sale of existing assets in order to avoid defaulting on financial commitments. By selling assets, firms reduce A_i in

22 Banks may in principle calculate their balance sheet using an expected value of debts on the basis of some perceived likelihood function, rather such a step function, but that function is necessarily non-linear as it is not likely to be simply proportional to the equity of borrowers. The higher the non-linearity, the more of a threshold effect it generates.

order to repay part of their debts D_i, thereby decreasing their leverage (increasing their equity to assets ratio), and thus decreasing their likelihood of default (the change in E_i relative to A_i that would lead to insolvency). By doing so, firms attempt to improve their financial position; however, as a collective movement, this may make the price of financial assets decline so fast that firms do not succeed in reducing their leverage, as assets flood the market and fewer and fewer buyers can be found. The effect of asset prices rapidly declining, as agents seek the relative safety of owning cash, is that the value of the debts of firms, written in nominal monetary terms, increases with respect to the value of non-monetary assets. In real terms, this implies debt that increases in value relative to the value of the firms themselves, decreasing their equity and increasing their leverage despite their best efforts to decrease it.

This is equivalent to the value of the currency increasing, hence the term 'deflation'. The change in the perceived value of debt D_i' is inversely related to the change in the average asset price π, itself proportional to the aggregate change in value of assets across the financial sector $\pi \propto \sum_i E_i$:

$$\frac{\Delta D_i'}{D_i'} = -\gamma \frac{\Delta \pi}{\pi} = -\gamma \frac{\sum \Delta E_j}{\sum E_j}. \tag{10.10}$$

The equity loss associated with effectively increasing debt as asset prices collapse is directly proportional to the change in perceived debt value, which creates an amplification effect:

$$\Delta E_i^{(3)} = \Delta D_i' = \gamma \left(1 - \delta(E_i)\right) D_i \frac{\sum \Delta E_j}{\sum E_j}. \tag{10.11}$$

(iv) All Losses Combined

Using a first-order approximation, the sum of losses can thus be summarised as

$$\Delta E_i \simeq \sum_j \alpha_{ij} \Delta E_j + \sum_k \beta_{ik} \delta\left(E_k\right) D_k + \gamma \left(1 - \delta(E_i)\right) D_i \frac{\sum \Delta E_\ell}{\sum E_\ell}, \tag{10.12}$$

an equation that is recursive in the vector E_i. This equation can be applied over and over onto itself and all three loss rounds will be represented following an initial seed shock, until a steady state is reached. When using this equation recursively, it can propagate losses, sometimes for many iterations, if losses cause insolvencies that cause further insolvencies and so on. But the model *always* reaches a steady state again eventually, whether it involves many chains of loss propagation or very few. That is, unless a chain of events were to push all companies into insolvency, but this has a vanishingly small likelihood when the network is large, as the results indicate, with a power-law probability distribution.

11

A Macroeconomic Model for Growth and Creative Destruction

This chapter is the final component of this book's complexity theory of economic evolution, but not the least: it brings together all the elements developed in previous chapters to build a general macro theory of innovation and economic growth. As debated in Chapter 3, in economic theory, there is no real consensus across schools on the nature of growth. There is, however, consensus on the idea that growth originates from the cumulative effect of innovation. In Chapter 8, a theory of creative destruction was developed that explains, at the very least, productivity growth from cumulative process innovation. To a lesser degree, it explains product innovation and diversity growth. In this chapter, it is shown that process and product innovation have a co-evolutionary role in generating economic growth in a demand-led model of economic evolution. From there, a closed set of relationships is derived to represent the macroeconomic connection and causation between innovation, productivity, employment, production, investment and demand, offering a complete model of endogenous economic growth based on innovation.

11.1. SCHUMPETER'S PLEA FOR REASONED HISTORY

Joseph Schumpeter is known for his account of the role of the entrepreneur for economic development, productivity change and economic growth. However, one of his main points of contention was a methodological one: he insisted that not all of economic theory should be constructed on the basis of regressions applied to measured data, as it tends to downplay the role of historical events, and of the broader economic and socio-political context. Notably, sectoral technical and productivity change is clearly related to broader contextual and systemic change in a variety of sectors simultaneously, something that may not be easily captured in simple regressions.

Schumpeter thus pleaded for what Freeman and Louçã (2001) termed a 'reasoned history' approach, in which one uses history as well as sophisticated data analysis to construct economic theory.[1] He had early on made a claim, in his *Theory of Economic Development* (Schumpeter, 1934), that innovation '*clusters*' in time, giving rise to a half-century long business cycle. He adopted and extended work initially developed by Kondratieff (1928), which provided powerful historical narratives regarding how innovation has developed over the years and given rise to waves of prosperity separated by periods of depression, dividing history into various '*industrial revolutions*'. Schumpeter's theory of business cycles remains insightful to this day, and since it was published, more of that has been observed with the development of the IT revolution, something that Schumpeter himself could not have foreseen, but that still broadly follows his general narrative.

More recently in the 80s–90s, Freeman and Perez (1988) and Freeman and Louçã (2001) adopted Schumpeter's reasoned history approach and applied it to produce a comprehensive account of the development of each great wave of innovation, their transformational impact from the technological, social, economic and financial perspectives. They clarify the process in which great waves have formed and transformed society using very detailed accounts of history. From these insights can be gathered a broader understanding of the dynamics of economic systems that could not otherwise be inferred easily from data alone, in part due to the extreme complexity of the changes observed in data when not using a historical narrative, and in part due to lacking a sufficiently long time series to cover several centuries. In other words, the general rule uncovered is that while ideally one would infer rules of economic evolution from data, in practice the exercise is too complex while one can infer much more by incorporating historical accounts. It is clear that Schumpeter's reasoned history approach did not exclude the use of quantitative models, if they are used in conjunction with a historical narrative. But this obviously requires a reliable theory of macroeconomics that is broadly consistent with key features of the historical account, and notably, that can reproduce business cycles endogenously, whereas the latter do not arise in systems of agents with rational expectations.[2]

In this narrative, innovation, and its clustering in space and time, has given rise to almost all economic transformation that has been observed for the last three hundred years at least. Schumpeter also provided a powerful if incomplete, narrated, model of macroeconomic evolution and of business cycles, that has inspired generations of economists. However, there still has to be a generally accepted quantitative theoretical translation that can be used on computers to make

[1] Notably, see his argument in Business Cycles (Schumpeter, 1939). See also the interpretation of Schumpeter by Freeman and Louçã (2001) in chapter 2.

[2] That agents have rational expectations is almost certainly ruled out by the existence of heavy-tailed noise in financial price series, since, according to Chapter 10, heavy-tailed noise is symptomatic of complexity, and agents would require foresight that even very fast computers cannot have due to the sheer complexity of financial networks.

quantitative predictions.[3] Notably, such a model would ideally be consistent with Keynes and post-Keynesian followers such as Minsky and more recent authors, since many believe that both theories are essentially the same but with different emphases. As reviewed by Keen (2013), standard equilibrium models did not foresee the 2007 financial crisis, but some post-Keynesian models do produce the type of instabilities observed. Lastly, a Schumpterian model of growth necessarily has to be demand-led, given the structure of his theory of the entrepreneur and, most importantly, of credit creation, and this is necessarily consistent with post-Keynesian models.

In this chapter, a general model of macroeconomic evolution is constructed based on the historical narrative of Kondratiev, Schumpeter, Keynes, Freeman, Louça, Perez and Minsky. In this model, a narrated and quantitative dynamical demand-led model is designed for economic growth describing productivity change from entrepreneurial activity that conceptually matches Schumpeter's *Theory*, in which a virtuous cycle emerges between investment in technology and R&D, competitiveness and prices, income and demand, and expectations of return by entrepreneurs. A key element is to make a distinction between process innovation, which increases productivity, and product innovation, which induces consumers to spend, both of which motivate the creation of purchasing power.

In a converse perspective, this model also explains the important reverse situation in which previously productive sectors of industry go into decline, due to changes in the direction that innovation takes, sending the economy into periods of financial instability. Schumpeter's '*creative destruction*' leads to sectors of industry, cities, and groups of people all together suffering dwindling affluence. Such periods of history can be readily observed through the fascinating vestiges of the industrial revolution in northern cities of Great Britain, and in the Great Lakes region of North America where the internal combustion engine and personal mobility revolution took place. This post-industrial decline is an endogenous phenomenon that has always been part of the industrial process, and that has periodically created economic and political upheaval of important scale. The Thatcher government of the UK in the eighties, with its free market ideology, led to trapping large groups of manual workers into perpetual unemployment, leaving them behind while the rest of British society moved on. However, there exist strategies that can mitigate the negative impacts that the later stages of industrial revolutions can have on social systems, discussed in Chapter 12. Thus, some attention is given here to the phenomenon of creative destruction in its various dimensions.

3 This is not to say that there have not been valiant attempts, but no quantitative theory is, as of now, generally accepted by all followers of Schumpeter, if one compares, for instance, evolutionary economics to general equilibrium theory, for which consensus exists. Notable examples of work that translates Schumpeter's macroeconomic theory quantitatively includes agent-based modelling by Dosi et al. (2010, 2013, 2015), and work by the author and colleagues (Mercure et al., 2018a,c). More becomes available if one considers post-Keynesian theory as consistent with Schumpeter, see Chapter 3.

11.2. ECONOMIC EVOLUTION, GROWTH AND INSTABILITY

As discussed in Chapter 8, Schumpeter (1934) describes economic evolution as a circular flow, in equilibrium, that is continuously pushed out of equilibrium by the profit-making innovations that entrepreneurs create. It is an evolutionary economy in constant change, but change that is not evenly distributed in time. Schumpeter does not give a very clear reason why innovation should cluster in time, other than perhaps claiming that there is a depletion of ideas taking place after each 'gale of creative destruction'. Furthermore, Schumpeter places the financial institution at the heart of the process, where, as described in Chapters 3 and 8, entrepreneurs borrow funds in order to invest in research and innovation. While the entrepreneur's profit is his (and perhaps his shareholders'), when he fails, he typically loses someone else's money, thus affecting the financial sector (Chapters 9 and 10).

As observed recurrently, great waves of innovation evolve following a profile that goes through four overlapping phases:[4]

1. innovation into radically new directions is developed by 'visionary' entrepreneurs, in the background, during the mature phase of an existing socio-technical regime, building onto its developments and those of earlier waves of innovation;[5]
2. a 'constellation' of related innovations begins a massive and pervasive diffusion process across industry, each reinforcing the others. These innovations benefit from radical cost reductions as their diffusion progresses, which become reinforced, as related innovations and investment upstream make their whole value chain increasingly competitive; they displace or disrupt over time one or more existing socio-technical regimes; creative destruction and possible investment bubbles based on exaggerated expectations of return can lead to financial instability;[6]
3. the new technological revolution consolidates itself and pervades many aspects of a society that is from then on radically transformed; as the new technology sees a golden age, expectations of return become stable and moderate;
4. as the new constellation of socio-technical regimes ages, its productivity and profit generation limits become visible, leading to stagnating investment, limited returns on investment and a declining contribution to broader prosperity; this may be accompanied by social, political and financial instability, sectoral decline or even recession or depression.

4 This framework is best described by Perez (2001), but appears in other works including Freeman and Perez (1988); Freeman and Louçã (2001); Semieniuk et al. (2021).

5 Geels' notion of the socio-technical regime is used (Geels, 2002). The use of 'visionary' in the present context does not intend anything normative; instead entrepreneurs are qualified as having sufficiently good foresight based on which innovations can be reasonably expected to generate profits.

6 See Semieniuk et al. (2021) for theory on the macroeconomics of rising and declining industries.

Schumpeter's clustering of innovation is thus explained by the fact that in specific domains of application, sets of innovations typically enable each other. For example, during the third industrial revolution, the development of the Bessemer steel process enabled the production of very low-cost steel, which enabled the development of numerous innovations in the electrical domain at competitive costs. This demand for steel in the electrical domain reinforced activity in the steel sector that enabled further cost reductions. Innovation takes place as a cluster that is more pervasive than any of its components, and none of the innovations can be seen as independent. It is as a whole cluster that innovation can make its way through the technical landscape to transform the way things are done across the economy.

It is to be noted that the process described above is relatively regular and takes place over a long period of time (approximately fifty years). While one cannot predict the future of innovation, if one believes that there exists such a cycle and that, due to a recurrent endogenous mechanism, it will repeat itself in the same shape in the future, if one can tell where in the current cycle society finds itself, then one can expect to some degree to be able to predict the evolution of the macroeconomy. That is, one could do this with the appropriate quantitative theory and model that understands this endogenous mechanism of innovation. However, as shown in discussions of the Adjacent Possible (Chapters 5 and 6), the economy cannot be conceived of as in equilibrium, because it never has time to explore all of its possible states and trajectories, which grow much faster than the number of possibilities it eliminates. Therefore, this theory must be one of evolutionary and adaptive navigation into the nearest unknown.

History, however, is riddled with events that one does not know, a priori whether to classify as endogenous or exogenous (e.g., wars, some types of financial crashes). It would be tenuous to argue that one could predict endogenously all this detail. However, despite this, it may be possible to aspire to, for example, develop the ability to predict the onset of instability or of stable growth, based on observation. And furthermore, such narratives, if credible, could find strategic use in policy-making. For example, how long is financial instability, induced by the COVID-19 pandemic and its aftermath, going to last? Will large-scale automation and artificial intelligence generate its own contribution to instability, or lead to stable growth? Will the low-carbon transition extend such financial instability even longer, or even generate its own financial instability impediments? Or alternatively, could the low-carbon transition generate stable long-term growth?

11.2.1 *Aggregate Productivity Change, Spillovers and the Design Space*

If one follows the narrative of Freeman and Louçã (2001) and Perez (2001), productivity growth in the economy takes place through a complex, uncoordinated but interlinked innovative effort across various domains and even sectors. As argued by Perez (1983) and Freeman and Perez (1988), one important recurrent finding is that important declines in the cost of key inputs characterised each technological revolution. It notably took the form of materials (e.g., steel), fuels (e.g., coal, oil, electricity), infrastructure (e.g., canals), modes of mobility (railways, cars) and media of exchange or communication (e.g., the internet). While such things typically already existed for some time when they entered the mainstream, these game-changing innovations led to cost reductions that radically changed the industrial possibilities that they offered. And such activity upstream of supply chains took place under the incentive that returns could be made out of expanding activity that was observed to take place downstream.

For example, the invention of the spinning jenny during the first industrial revolution required the use of iron, and its mass diffusion demanded substantial expansion in the production of iron. Innovations, investment and expansion upstream in iron and coal production generated cost reductions that opened up endless possibilities for the production of textiles-related *and* unrelated iron-made final and intermediate goods. Production possibilities based on existing materials and methods has been termed the '*design space*' (Stankiewicz, 2000), the source of the Adjacent Possible. Thus, cost reductions in key inputs leading to new possibilities expanded and transformed the design space in which entrepreneurs found themselves operating. New materials at lower costs, in conjunction with changing levels of income for households, companies and the government opened the space of possibilities for profit-motivated entrepreneurs typically full of innovative ideas.

There is thus a process that goes back and forth up and down supply chains for the production of goods and services. Expectations of downstream expansion (e.g., in iron-made goods) motivates investment for expansion upstream (e.g., coal mining), which leads to cost reductions in key inputs from upstream for production downstream. These cost reductions downstream lead to further investment upstream in a virtuous cycle, leading to an emergent cooperative expansion across several sectors of the economy, increasing competitiveness across large sections of the economy. Take, for example, Henry Bessemer, the inventor of the Bessemer process for steel production, and the investor it attracted, Andrew Carnegie, who oversaw the manifold expansion of steel production in the USA. Carnegie became one of the richest men the world has ever seen, as the successive innovations in steelmaking led to continuous reductions in production costs over several decades, continuously expanding the design space of entrepreneurs, leading to ever growing demand for his company's steel products, thereby making a fortune, but also enabling a substantial amount of related economic activity.

Steelmaking is not nearly as profitable in the present day, as much of the novelty of steel products has passed, expansion has turned into decline, and new, lower cost materials have gradually replaced steel in many (though by no means all) applications. The iron and steel sector suffers nowadays from chronic overcapacity worldwide, which implies that current capacity growth exceeds demand growth. In other words, the steel sector still expands, as emerging economies use increasing amounts of steel for an expanding urbanisation and growing vehicle fleets; however, productivity growth in the use of steel and steel products exceeds demand growth, and profits are not nearly as substantial as they were in Carnegie's time.

The simultaneous growth of production and final demand for new goods and services is explained by a simultaneous growth in the money supply, real household income, production capacity and pervasively declining real prices for many products. This virtuous cycle is typically explained in standard equilibrium theory as a growing total factor productivity due to technical change.[7] However, this does not explain in any way the emergence of any kind of business cycles nor of unemployment, as it generally remains exogenously defined, as if economists assumed that the future was pre-written in God's Grand Book of Things. But in an evolutionary theory, as seen earlier, if one was to replay the tape of history, one should obtain a different story every time.

Instead, here, productivity change is explained as an emergent process of cooperative innovative activity between uncoordinated entrepreneurs collectively participating in giving rise to whole new 'constellations' of innovations and their pervasive diffusion that transforms productivity across the economy. Many of these innovations generate cost reductions in myriads of existing applications (e.g., everything that used steel in the late nineteenth century), and these cost reductions lead to either reductions in the prices of final products, or in the commercial availability and affordability of new products that overall allow improvements in living standards, and increases in aggregate demand.

Take again, for example, the emergence of the availability of low-cost iron during the late eighteenth century, and steel in the late nineteenth century. In both cases, it led to the possibility of developing new types of machinery for agriculture, which increased ever more the productivity of workers in agriculture, decreasing production costs for food products. Mechanisation of agriculture put out of work large numbers of workers on farms across Britain, who then converged to cities, contributing to social, economic and political instability. However, urban concentration later allowed the expansion of a new workforce that became available to factories, good or bad, which employed new management structures, increasing the productivity of these workers. This process of structural change was not coordinated by anyone's vision in particular, and occurred over more than a century.

7 The production function used in equilibrium theory, in which output growth is split between its contributions from labour, capital and productivity change, was shown many years ago, to be a numerical artefact of the accounting identity for valuing capital used in national accounts (see Shaikh, 1974). The residual ascribed to productivity, normally understood as improving technology, essentially depends on how capital is valued. It is known since the 'Cambridge capital controversies' that there is no unambiguous definition for the quantity (or valuation) of capital. Notably, it is defined as both cumulated past investment, or expected revenue, depending on the application and context, but these are not equal, which signals an issue of fundamental nature.

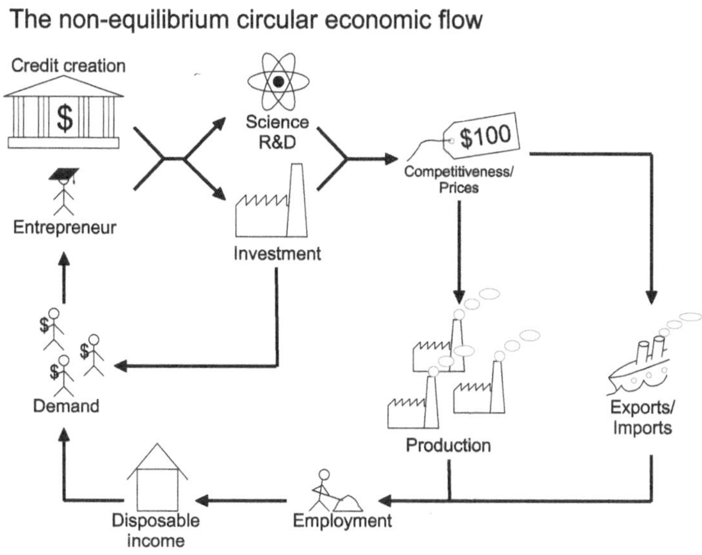

FIGURE 11.1 Illustration of the circular flow in a Schumpeterian economy out of equilibrium.

A key element in these developments is, as Schumpeter insisted, the availability of the creation of purchasing power by financial institutions (Schumpeter, 1934). Indeed, entrepreneurs typically did not have at hand large amounts of idle financial capital, and did not necessarily need or want to accumulate such capital from existing enterprises for carrying out experiments for increasing productivity or developing new products. Instead, a climate of optimism would develop in the economy, as all sorts of new successful ventures would emerge across the economy, and financial institutions developed an increasing sense of confidence in the success of such ventures. As argued in Chapters 3 and 10, since according to Minsky (1982, 1986), 'everyone can create money, the problem is to get it accepted', banks could create most of the finance that entrepreneurs required, within the extent to which bank managers believed loans would be paid back with interest. That finance, in a context of growing productivity, income and output, led to a money supply growing faster than the population, and a growing purchasing power per capita without necessarily going through a compensating price inflation. It is this increasing purchasing power, validated by successful return from investment in productivity increasing ventures, that leads to increasing aggregate demand across the economy, reinforcing growth during the Kondratiev upswings.

Figure 11.1 shows this in more stylised and formalised form. The entrepreneur, sensing an unmet need in the economy, outlines an idea and business plan for creating a new product, carrying out some process innovation and/or increasing his scale of production, and submits this plan to a financial institution. Based on a combination of his personal creditworthiness and history of past success, the bank's balance sheet and the general degree of optimism in the economy, the financial institution decides whether or not to create finance for the entrepreneur. If it does, the entrepreneur carries out his plan, and if he is successful, he generates productivity improvements or the availability of new products, repaying his creditor. If he is not successful and fails to repay the bank, he may end up defaulting and declaring bankruptcy. With cumulative productivity improvements, prices decline in real terms across the economy, leaving households with unspent income according to their usual spending patterns. This allows them to expand their spending towards either new products or increased quantities of existing products. Rising aggregate demand sectorally motivates entrepreneurs to further carry out R&D and industrial expansion.

This process can go wrong if something breaks this virtuous cycle of productivity growth. Symptoms would emerge such as increasing overcapacity in various sectors, a sign that either entrepreneurs have expanded production beyond the reach of aggregate demand, or aggregate demand growth is falling relative to entrepreneur expectations. Overcapacity rapidly sends a warning signal to financial institutions that the outlook of markets is deteriorating and, crucially, that in worsening economic conditions, some of the entrepreneurs they have provided finance with will fail in their plans.[8] This leads financial institutions to suddenly start to restrict lending to projects that they might have lent to before. It can also lead to increases in lender interest rates, turning some entrepreneurial activities from profitable to unprofitable, or in the language of Minsky, from hedge to speculative and from speculative to Ponzi. A financial crisis typically follows along the dynamics described in Chapter 10 (see Semieniuk et al., 2021).

11.2.2 *Two Types of Innovation Co-evolving*

Entrepreneurs can apply for finance for two different types of innovation, which are thus classified more for their structural impact on the macroeconomy rather than their return for entrepreneurs. Entrepreneurs can seek to either carry out *process* or *product innovation*.

[8] Carlota Perez (2001) insists that it is a reality check on widespread exaggerated expectations in the possibilities of new innovations that lead to this change of sentiment in financial institutions. Notably, during the railway mania, many projects were started with differing rail gauges, or expanded to reach cities where demand did not meet expectations. Thus she argues that a technological bubble arose during each great surge of innovation. While this may be at least partially correct, this is not the entire account given by Freeman and Louçã (2001), in which it is clear that overcapacity with technology from older regimes may have also contributed to bursting financial bubbles and waves of optimism and prosperity. Here, the viewpoint is taken that both effects happen more or less simultaneously, and may in fact reinforce each other, where losses made in industrial activities of older regimes may have sufficient impact on aggregate demand through household income to impose a limit on production in new regimes, a case in which creative destruction becomes self-limiting.

Process innovation is well described in Chapter 8, where a micro-scale effect of creative destruction takes place as new ideas, within existing technological constellations, or as components of existing technologies, replace older ways of doing things, yield production cost reductions as technologies achieve the same at lower cost or achieve more at constant cost. The cumulative effect of innovation and small-scale creative destruction leads to a gradual and recurrent learning-by-doing effect characterised by a learning rate that may be related to the topology of the network of ideas. Process innovation results in a gradual replacement of indefinite operational expenditures (wages, inputs to production) by one-off capital expenditures, generating either a profit, or enabling to sell at lower price. In the former, capitalists are left with excess money, while in the latter, it is consumers, after they have purchased 'the usual basket of goods'. Since returns on typically incremental process innovation are moderate, investment in process innovation can also only be moderate and incremental, otherwise they are not justified by the near-term profits that can be expected.[9]

The macroeconomic effect of process innovation is that by definition, it reduces either or both employment and inputs to production, the latter reducing employment elsewhere, notably upstream, and in a potentially pervasive way. As employment declines, the direct macroeconomic impact is that less income becomes available for consumers to maintain demand, which leads to economic slowdown. However, it critically depends on what happens to the profit, whether it is spent in the economy or not. Since process innovation increases productivity, income and profit together allow purchasing more than what the same amount of money would have bought before the innovation happened. Thus, if capitalists save their profit by paying back their debts, or by increasing their stock of wealth (e.g., feeding real estate price bubbles), the economy slows down, while if they spend it on goods in the real economy (e.g., cars, restaurant meals), the economy grows. However, with cumulative process innovation, consumers could eventually run out of ways to spend their money, as they may not be satisfied with purchasing ever larger quantities of the same basket of goods.

Product innovation, less well described in Chapter 8, is where radically new ideas and products are developed and sold. These products do not increase the productivity of the economy, instead they create new ways for consumers to spend their money. However, consumers must have excess income to spend on new products, otherwise new products may not sell if consumer budgets can only afford 'the usual basket of goods'. If consumers spend on new products, new jobs are created and the economy grows accordingly.

[9] Following the example of Carnegie, it is clear that in the long term, if competitive advantage is maintained by continuous process innovation compounded with industrial growth, substantial returns can be generated. This may now be happening with solar photovoltaics and electric vehicles.

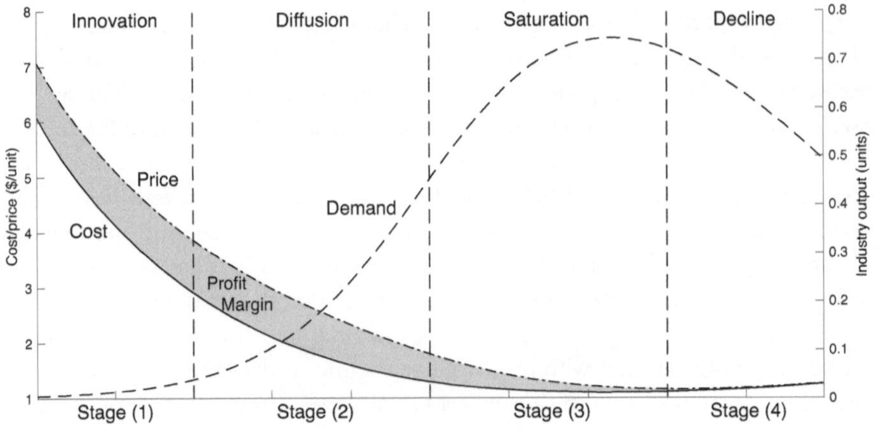

FIGURE 11.2 Illustration in four stages of the lifecycle of products and their industries, through continuous process innovation following initial product innovation.

The key issue is that the money needed to spend on new products can only originate from profits generated by process innovation. Meanwhile, what avoids capitalists using profits solely for increasing their wealth (e.g., investing in financial assets, accumulating in a bank account) is the emergence of new attractive products to spend their profits on, or alternatively, for consumers to spend their increased wages on. Without product innovation, spending would slow down, while without process innovation, income growth would slow down. With excessive process innovation, demand growth would decline, due to wealth accumulation, while with excessive product innovation, many products would go unsold, to the loss of their manufacturers. The two types of innovation must inevitably work together, but a key question is whether this is a stable coevolutionary process.

11.2.3 A *Model of the Economic Life-Cycle of Products*

The interplay of process-product innovation is complex as its impacts travel upstream and downstream value chains continuously. But it can be simplified through a simple four stage model of the innovation life-cycle of products based on the above concept of the design space (Figure 11.2).

stage(1) Product innovation leads to creating a new product (e.g., steel). Market demand is created.

stage(2) Costs go down drastically with increasing scale, and declining prices generate substantial increases in demand that fuel further expansion. Product innovation at the end-use level increases the demand (e.g., new products made of steel). Process innovation focuses on making the product ever cheaper to maintain or increase comparative advantage (e.g., Carnegie in the USA). Large corporations form, raking in huge profits. Lenders drown entrepreneurs with finance. Profit margins are large and volumes increase exponentially, and industry relies on large margins despite relatively low volumes. Fortunes are made.

stage(3) Innovation depletes at the product level, while other process innovation takes place at the end-use level, where users of the product seek to become more efficient in order to reduce their costs (e.g., car manufacturers using less steel as an input). Competition (e.g., from abroad) pushes prices down close to costs. The industry relies on large volumes despite low profit margins. Any further end-use innovation becomes a danger.

stage(4) Overcapacity becomes chronic and destroys part of the industry. Factories move to countries where wages are lower. Unemployment develops and some companies go bankrupt, volumes stagnate while profit margins remain low, sometimes negative, and interest from investors or lenders for any expansion or innovation remains low.

This is not to say that sectors disappear at Stage 4, as most products remain in use indefinitely, for example, steel. But past Stage 3, such products cease to attract the attention of investors and lenders, and growth, if there is any, follows aggregate demand minus what is taken out by process innovation at the product level. The interest of investors turns towards other new products.

Table 11.1 provides a summary of all six great waves of innovations that the world has seen since the start of the eighteenth century. It provides examples of applications, key inputs and dates of upswings and downswings. This was reproduced from Freeman and Louçã (2001) with additions to complete the table beyond the nineties. The more speculative current wave of innovation was included involving machine learning and artificial intelligence based on so-called 'big' data. What can be observed is that each of these waves involved really new areas of application and that as opposed to some interpretations of Schumpeter's 'creative destruction' concept, each wave *did not* replace an earlier wave or earlier innovations.

11.2.4 *Creative Destruction: The Dying Industries*

Each great wave made the economy become substantially more productive such that productivity grew faster than wages at certain times. Guttmann (2015) explains that it is when productivity growth exceeds real wage growth that a lack of aggregate demand materialises, since real income follows real wages which may not be able to buy the whole of the economy's product if the income share of capital versus wages becomes too high and remains invested in more capital assets.

TABLE 11.1 *The great waves of innovation*[a]

Constellation of technical and organisational innovations	Examples of visible, successful, profitable innovations	'Carrier' branch or sector	Core and key inputs	Transport and communication infrastructure	Managerial and organisational changes	Timings of upswings/ downswings
1. Water-powered mechanisation of industry	Arkright's Cromford mill (1771) Henry Cort's 'puddling' process (1784)	Cotton spinning, iron products, water wheels, bleach	Iron Raw cotton Coal	Canals Turnpike roads Sailing ships	Factory systems Entrepreneurs Partnerships	1780–1815 1815–1848
2. Steam-powered mechanisation of industry and transport	Liverpool–Manchester railway (1831) Brunel's 'Great Western' steamship (1838)	Railways and railway equipment, steam engines, machine tools, alkali industry	Iron Coal	Railways Telegraphs Steam ships	Joint stock companies Subcontracting to responsible craft workers	1848–1873 1873–1895
3. Electrification of industry, transport and the home	Carnegie Bessemer steel plant (1875) Edison's New York Electric Power station (1882)	Electrical equipment, heavy engineering, heavy chemicals, steel products	Steel Copper Metal alloys	Steel railways Steel ships Telephone	Specialised professional management systems 'Taylorism' Giant firms	1895–1918 1918–1940
4. Motorisation of transport, civil economy and war	Fort's Highland Park assembly line (1913) Burton process for cracking heavy oil (1913)	Automobiles, trucks, tractors, tanks, diesel/petrol engines, aircraft, refineries	Oil Gas Synthetic materials	Radio Motorways Airports Airlines	Mass production and consumption 'Fordism' Hierarchies	1941–1973 1973–1980
5. Computerisation of entire economy	IBM 1401 and 360 series computers (1960s) Intel microprocessor (1972)	Computers, software, telecommunication equipment, biotechnology	Integrated circuits Recording magnetic media	Internet Email Wireless telecom	Networks Email systems Digitisation of archives	1980s–2007 2007–2019
6. Machine learning, artificial intelligence and genetics	IBM/Google artificial go/chess players (1990s–2010s) Google self-driving car (2010s)	Intelligent machines, social media, personalised cancer treatment	Integrated circuits Personal and other 'big' data	Social media 'Smart' phones/computers	Big data management Targeted advertising Firm automation	2019–??

[a]Reproduced from Freeman and Louçã (2001) with the author's additions.

When overcapacity sets in, as aggregate demand really fails productive capacity by a substantial amount, some uncompetitive firms may fold and productive capital may be written off. In standard equilibrium theory, capital not used in a sector becomes available to other sectors. But this assumption is not appropriate in a situation of overcapacity and structural change or recession in the economy. As stated earlier, 'That the theorist's teaching, according to which capital "migrates" from declining to rising industries, is unrealistic is obvious: the capital "invested" in railroads does not migrate into trucking and air transportation but will perish in and with the railroads' (Schumpeter, 1947, see Chapter 8).

Indeed, the capital that is written off is value that will never be recovered. In the stylised model of the entrepreneur above, this incurs a loss, not only to the entrepreneur, who loses his enterprise, but also to the financial institution, which financed innovation and expansion. Capital is written off when the present and expected future value becomes less than its cost of operation and, crucially, the costs of servicing debt incurred for the initial investment. Stranded railways, tankers, pipelines, oil rigs, cannot be re-used for anything else than they were designed for, and in a situation of overcapacity and contracting market, can most likely not be sold to anyone.

Downwards expectations of return are self-fulfilling, as the negative sentiment generates reductions in investment, which reduces employment, which reduces aggregate demand, which reduces profits, which reduces expected returns, and so on. There is no known formal limit to this downwards cycle. In the 1930s, at its worse, unemployment in the USA affected one quarter of the population, and it took years to re-start the economic engine. A similar situation has been encountered with the 2007–2008 crisis and ensuing Great Recession.

The Great Depression saw various strategies adopted to help restart the economic engine. With Keynes, at the time, it was understood that government expenditure could contribute. For instance, it was felt intuitively that work should be found for the workers of the deeply depressed steel industry, as well as other newer sectors such as the automotive industry. The quiet arms buildup in Germany and the New Deal in the USA did just that: provided work to the depressed heavy industries, which generated income to workers to spend to increase aggregate demand again. While the war effort did provide the steel industry with something new to do, it also motivated new innovative activity based on the new technologies of the new age of oil, automobiles and aircraft.

The Great Depression also led to, first, political instability, and later, entirely new political dynamics, with notably the rise of Nazism in Germany, and other movements towards protectionism and nationalism in many other nations. The situation of economic stagnation provided a fertile ground for populist movements. In Germany, the plan was specifically to revive the steel industry by building weapons in preparation for war, and the plan did support these workers economically, and raised substantial support for the party (see Freeman and Louçã, 2001, p. 267).

A similar situation may have been happening in recent times, with US President Trump, in truly populist manner, scrapping policies to reduce greenhouse gas emissions and pulling out of the Paris Agreement, in order to support workers in the coal, oil, gas and steel industries, where workers feel that globalisation, environmental policy and bankers have robbed them of their livelihood. In reality, these industries have become victims of increasing productivity across the economy through the usual process of technological change domestically and internationally, where workers are increasingly replaced by robots, while demand growth demand growth for products of the heavy and mining industries, and fossil fuel products, products of the last few Kondratiev cycles, is declining. It is notable that no amount of domestic support for the consumption of fossil fuels in the USA will revive the heavy and mining industries if most of the rest of the world attempts to achieve emissions reductions and climate change objectives, as the price of fossil fuels would unavoidably plummet (later discussed in Chapters 14 and 15).

11.3. THE MACROECONOMIC IMPLICATIONS OF CREATIVE DESTRUCTION

11.3.1 A *Quantitative Model of Economic Growth*

The mathematical appendix of this chapter describes the equations for a complete and closed quantitative model of economic evolution, growth and instability. The model simulates demand, investment, output, employment and trade on a sectoral level following national accounts. It is demand-led and meant to be established on a traditional post-Keynesian macroeconometric basis. It is a variant of the well established E3ME model,[10] adding innovative components for Minskian financial instability and elements for product and process innovation. E3ME is used again in Chapter 15.

Modelling aggregate global growth is not what should be the focus in the use of this macroeconomic model. It would appear that global growth has been hovering around a remarkably stable attractor near 3% per year (Jarvis, 2018), despite the occasional and recurrent crises, something akin to a punctuated equilibrium. However, more surprisingly, growth in different regions does not appear to hover around any kind of attractor, where some regions, such as China, have been growing at more than twice the growth rates observed in economies such as the EU and USA. Many economists have been trying to predict the behaviour of a putative catching-up process between developing and developed economies,[11] but that remains yet to be observed. Catching up is imposed to models as it perhaps appears otherwise 'unethical not to', especially in a normative neoclassical frame. Therefore, it is the

[10] See Mercure et al. (2018a) and `www.e3me.com`.

[11] Using notably the Solow–Swan model or the Romer model.

stability of the global growth attractor that is the remarkable feature, since the global economy shows no sign of stagnation nor convergence despite the distributional differences arising internally.

What is special about the global scale? Its only special feature is that it is a closed economy. Is it trade that somehow causes deviations from 3% therefore? This is a good question. What defines regions are political divisions, areas of application of law, regulations and tariffs. Otherwise, the global economy can be seen as a single evolutionary system in which agents continuously develop 'new ways of making a living', increasing their productivity. And since the economy has not had time to explore all of its possible states, there are always 'new ways of making a living' that can be discovered within the Adjacent Possible.

In a demand-led model, what is ultimately accumulated, if anything? In the sandpile model of financial networks given in Chapter 10, it is effectively the degree of confidence in the solvency of the agents involved, individually, as the model has no representation of the aggregate degree of confidence in the whole economy. Of course, in reality, agents also have a degree of confidence in the whole economy, the loss of which re-inforces instabilities. Nevertheless, it is not the quantity of physical capital *per se* that is accumulated, since the value of capital is not a function of its mass of material and there is no unambiguous way to quantify this.[12] But the value of capital is a pyramid of belief, which is why it can collapse so easily. What appears accumulated therefore is knowledge, in the economy, of its own capacity at growing and achieving certain things, notably surviving. It is some sort of inventory of all the 'past, present and new ways of making a living' that exist.

11.3.2 *The Structural Crisis of Adjustment*

Where macroeconomics plays a useful role for policy analysis is primarily in identifying sectoral and regional trends and distributional issues. It primarily concerns assessing whether policy proposals are likely to exacerbate existing distributional issues or to create new ones. With standard equilibrium models, inevitably modellers assume that they (or their models) have knowledge of all the possible states in which the economy can find itself, to the extent that models are based on utility optimisation. Optimising implies that someone, somewhere, must have a good understanding of all of the states that exist within the Adjacent Possible. However, it is not just a case of whether the representative agent knows all of that, but more importantly, whether the modeller, designing the model, does. In equilibrium models, disturbances are always followed by return to a 'normal' state in the economy.

[12] Take, for example, the value of capital following the COVID-19 pandemic. Since the behaviour of firms, workers and consumers changed discontinuously with the advent of movement restrictions, the production capital became instantaneously inadequate for the newly structured demand, where shortages and overcapacity arose simultaneously. The quantity and value of capital is context-dependent and contingent on subjective views of future usefulness.

Just as in medical science: one identifies symptoms of a disease, deviations from the 'normal' mode of operation, for which various remedies are known to exist that eliminate these symptoms. In the real world, there is no 'normal' mode of operation since no one can enumerate the Adjacent Possible; there are too many possible path-dependent possibilities.

The difference between demand-led evolutionary macroeconomic models, and standard equilibrium models, can in general be summarised by the existence of path-dependence that exacerbates existing differences and distributional issues. For example, in stagnating economies, evolutionary models will assume that growth stagnation induces investment stagnation, which exacerbates the overall situation, whereas booms will be reinforced by attracting more investment. This is possible since the creation of money and purchasing power is not limited by savings in evolutionary and post-Keynesian models. Money is created precisely in ways that exacerbate existing differences, since this is where returns are deemed to be.

Meanwhile, investment in equilibrium models is imposed as equal to savings, generally assumed to equal a fixed share of total output determined by the propensity to save. The result of this is that a pool of liquid capital is assumed to exist, growing gradually according to the savings rate, and this pool of capital is shared between all sectoral users of capital.[13] When one sector requires more capital, notably when the public sector invests in some particular projects, capital is crowded-out from other uses, and this leads to lower total output, simply due to the basic premise that the economy operates optimally as a starting point (see Chapter 3). Conversely, if a sector goes into decline, due to regulation or to consumer preferences, capital is 'liberated' from that sector and can be used in other sectors. This results in a pronounced damping of distributional effects that would otherwise appear in a non-equilibrium model, and all the structural change disappears. A large part of the reason for structural change to disappear in equilibrium models that if this positive feedback was included in optimisation calculations, the models could not be solved, and therefore, this crucial feedback is ignored.

The structural crises of adjustment that follows the great waves of innovation is an important effect to understand, and its source is internal structural change. Structural change arises during economic transformations due to the tendency of the economy, in its evolutionary behaviour, to explore the Adjacent Possible through many 'ways of making a living' that turn out not to be sustainable, and frequently this ends up into bursting and crashing bubbles. It is a process of exploration of an Adjacent Possible that is not known a priori. Sectors grow, and later decline, not because better 'ways of making a living' have been discovered that crowd-out the old ones in terms

[13] Some models impose vintage capital constraints. This comes in as constraints in the utility optimisation calculation, in that it prevents some of the otherwise possible configurations. This is generally understood as generating sub-optimal allocations, in the sense that capital 'lumpiness' behaves similarly to frictions or distorsions in the market.

of resource allocation, but rather, that these 'new ways of making a living' are so successful that they outnumber and outgrow the old ones, but also, make many of them obsolete and unfit.

Furthermore, sectoral decline is not generally gradual or predictable, due to inter-sectoral teleconnections, where decline generates instabilities in the 'ways of making a living' that depend on others and become unsustainable in whole chains. In fact, it is clear that supply chains in the economy also possess the conditions to behave following self-organised criticality (Bak et al., 1993). It is also clear from the great waves literature[14] that periods of relative tranquility, during booms, expansions and Kondratiev upswings, are interrupted by periods characterised by financial, economic and political instability, even armed conflict and substantial transformations.

The pending low-carbon transition, in which policy aims at accelerating technological change, industrial decline and transformation, may be likely to precipitate this process of structural change at a large scale. Semieniuk et al. (2021) (Figure 11.3)

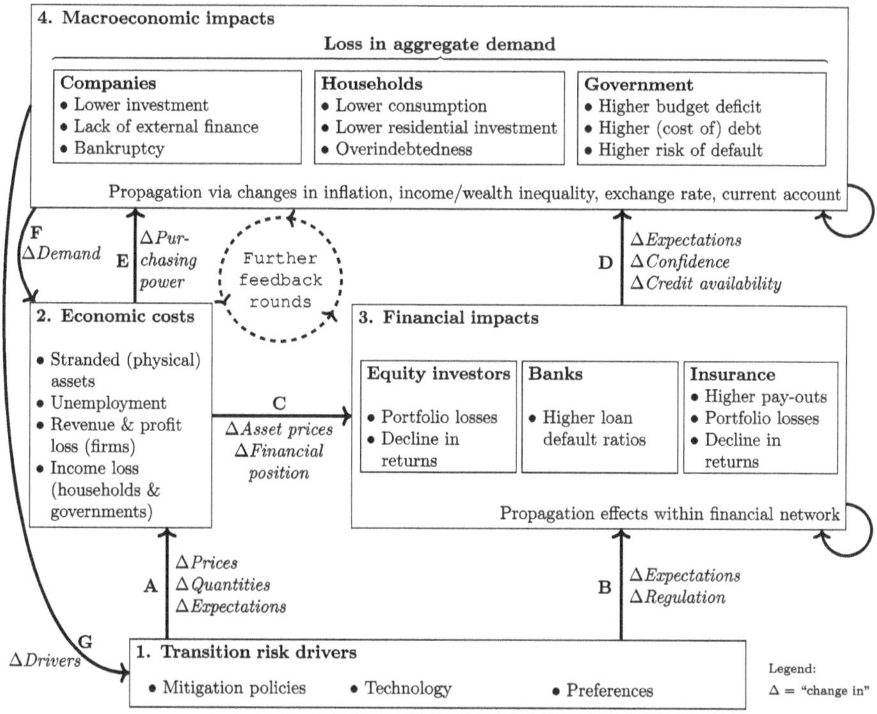

FIGURE 11.3 Illustration of the channels of transmission of financial risk during a rapid low-carbon technological transition (Semieniuk et al., 2021).

[14] Schumpeter (1934, 1939); Freeman and Louçã (2001); Perez (2001); Minsky (1986); Semieniuk et al. (2021).

provide a model for tracing the connections in the macroeconomics of a rapid low-carbon transition threatening the high-carbon sunset industries, accumulating systemic risk through gradual or perhaps sudden decline. In that model, climate policy influences preferences for high-carbon technology as well as the competitiveness in their use. Agent preferences also play a role in driving technological change. The changes in the type of fuel used and technology demanded results in changes in the economic viability of many industries, accumulating individual and systemic risk across the economy. As suggested earlier, it remains to be seen whether the low-carbon transition will take place in an orderly fashion, or whether it will trigger instability across the economy.

11.4. CONCLUSION: CULTURES AND SOCIO-TECHNICAL REGIMES

The substantial social implications of structural crises of adjustment, structural change and economic change in general may be argued the whole reason for economists to develop economic models at all. These social implications generally have to do with the fact that once agents have developed successful 'new ways of making a living', they are likely to seek to settle in and maintain that way of life for their lifetime, perhaps that of their children and potentially indefinitely (Zenghelis et al., 2018). Agents form cultures around ways of making a living. This notably defines social classes and groups.[15] The destruction of ways of making a living is frequently unavoidable and occupations become obsolete, given that once developed, innovations cannot be readily prevented from being used or diffusing, creatively destroying their way through the economy. And hence lies the tragedy of structural change in the economy. Some occupations may become highly resilient to change, finding evolutionarily stable states, such as restaurant staffing, catering, singing, painting and other arts and services. Other occupations may become at great risk of being replaced, such as car manufacturing, coal mining, oil and gas drilling, petrochemicals.

A key feature of structural change is that it does not care for geography. New employment in new, sunrise industries often has no geographical relationship with employment in older, sunset industries. This implies that unless the workforce is willing to abandon its home and migrate,[16] some workers are trapped into unemployment as older occupations disappear, while other workers elsewhere benefit from high wages generated by new local labour shortages in the new

[15] Wilk and Cliggett (2007); Douglas and Isherwood (1979).
[16] See the account of US migration during the Great Depression in John Steinbeck's novel '*The grapes of wrath*'.

occupations. This is strongly reinforced by house price declines against unaffordable house prices where the jobs are.

The scars and marks of structural change can be readily observed, for instance, in the rich British landscape. Britain is a good example since so much of the early industrial revolution has taken place on that small island which once ruled the largest empire in history. For example, remains of tin mines litter the Cornwall landscape, dating from as far back as the bronze age, when tin was used to mix with copper to form bronze, to make tools and weapons harder. Tin mining saw its golden age during the nineteenth century, but declined and disappeared completely in the 1890s, leaving a population of miners behind, some of whom moved to the New World in search of other mining jobs. Manchester, Bristol, Birmingham, Leeds, Sheffield and other northern cities display a red-brick industrial landscape of factories, canals and warehouses from the nineteenth century, now gradually converted into housing due to its popular historical character. Very little of the old industrial activities, initially revolving around textiles, now remain in those cities, which have suffered long decades of post-industrial decline until they became revived by activity in the new knowledge economy. The knowledge economy did not, however, employ the old coal miners who went on strike against the closure of the mines in the 1980s. New, fresh young workers with modern skills took up those new opportunities, coming straight out of university, leaving the coal miners ever farther behind.

11.5. APPENDIX: A QUANTITATIVE MODEL OF ECONOMIC GROWTH AND BUSINESS CYCLES

11.5.1 A *Demand-Led Macroeconomic Model*

Schumpeterian and post-Keynesian, and therefore by necessity, complexity economic models, take as a starting point the demand for goods and services, estimated empirically. Following standard national accounts conventions, this demand is classified between the purposes of final consumption C_i, investment I_i, government G_i or exports X_i, while part of the demand may be imported M_i. Inter-sectoral relationships must be considered since sectors purchase from each other in the process of supplying final demand (e.g., vehicles or machinery purchased and used for production purposes). It is standard to represent this using the Leontief inverse $(I - A_{ij})^{-1}$, itself derived from Input-Ouput tables A_{ij}, which is a matrix that converts vectors of demand for product types (subscript i) to matrices of production by industry sector (subscript j). The macroeconomic identity for an open economy can therefore be written as (omitting a country subscript)

$$Y_j = \sum_i (I - A_{ij})^{-1} (C_i + I_i + G_i + X_i - M_i) . \tag{11.1}$$

In this convention for macroeconomics, information flows from generating demand vectors first, and deriving production vectors from those through the Leontief inverse, and there is therefore no production function in a demand-led model.[17]

The final demand for products is estimated differently depending on whether the products are for final consumption or investment, while the demand from the government is taken as exogenous, and the demand for exports originates from the demand for imports in similar models for other regions. By connecting sufficient numbers of national models, one can obtain a global model in which all imports and exports are endogenously determined and sum up consistently. It is to be noted, however, that the demand for investment products I_i is not identical to investment I_j, in that sectors investing are not necessarily the same as sectors producing the investment goods. Thus a second matrix B_{ij}, different from the Leontief inverse, connects I_i with I_j.

$$I_i = \sum_i B_{ij} I_j. \tag{11.2}$$

Consumption is defined as a function of product prices P_i^C, import prices P_i^M, personal income PI and population N:[18]

$$C_i = F_C\left(-P_i^C, -P_i^M, +PI, +N\right). \tag{11.3}$$

Investment demand for products is derived from investment by sector I_j, function of prices of investment goods P_j^I, output in that sector Y_j, and a 'capacity factor' CF_j,

$$I_j = F_I\left(-P_j^I, +Y_j, +CF_j, -D_j, +AS_j\right). \tag{11.4}$$

The terms for debt D_j and 'animal spirits' or enthusiasm AS_j will be discussed below, in relation to finance. The capacity factor CF_j corresponds to the degree of utilisation of current production capacity. Expressed as a percentage of utilisation, when this variable approaches 100%, investment happens for expanding production capacity under the expectation that demand and production needed to supply the demand, could otherwise exceed production capacity, at which point the economy could become unstable with inflation. Due to fundamental uncertainty (Chapter 6), industrialists seek to maintain a degree of flexibility in meeting the demand, which

17 Keynesian demand-led macroeconomics reject Say's law that states that production generates its own demand. Production equals demand by definition, but production is generally lower than what could potentially be produced were the demand to be higher, since fundamental uncertainty-facing investors are assumed to expand capacity when it comes close to full employment.

18 '+' before variables indicates positive relationships or correlations, and '–' indicates negative relationships or anti-correlations. The functions F themselves can be flexible, but may typically be of the form of linear regressions over relative changes, e.g., $\frac{\Delta Z}{Z} = \beta_X \frac{\Delta X}{X} + \beta_Y \frac{\Delta Y}{Y}$, the βs being elasticities (e.g., price/income elasticities, substitution elasticities) with the above sign restrictions.

could fluctuate.[19] The capacity factor is thus the ratio between current output and potential output Y_j^N,

$$CF_j = \frac{Y_j}{Y_j^N}. \quad (11.5)$$

Y_j^N is defined according to accumulated past investments made τ years ago minus depreciation with exogenous sectoral depreciation rate δ_j, a representation of accumulated 'capital' or capabilities for production, according to its value depreciated since investment,

$$Y_j^N = \int_0^\infty (1 - \delta_j)^\tau I_j(t - \tau) d\tau. \quad (11.6)$$

Imports concern a demand for products either not available from domestic production, or less expensive when imported, and thus resemble in form consumption in Eq. 11.3,

$$M_i = F_M \left(+P_i^C, -P_i^M, +PI, +N \right). \quad (11.7)$$

Exports originate from the demand for imports M_{ki} from other regions k, through a bilateral export matrix BT_{ki},

$$X_i = \sum_k BT_{ki} M_{ki}. \quad (11.8)$$

Up to this point, it is the personal income PI variable that drives demand, according to prevailing prices. The population and government demand are assumed exogenous. However, before defining PI, how prices change due to both innovation and inflation must be defined.

11.5.2 *Cumulative Causation and Accumulation of Knowledge*

In the above 'circular flow' model, innovation plays no role, where Input–Output coefficients and prices are exogenous or constant and not explained. There is no growth. As discussed above, growth is assumed to happen through a combination of process innovation, reducing inputs to production and therefore either reducing prices or increasing profits, leaving income to be spent on more goods and services after the 'usual basket of goods' has been consumed, and product innovation, creating new products on which the leftover income can be spent. In macroeconomic reality, the impact of innovation involves reducing inputs to production; this implies reducing production of primary or intermediate products, which reduces output,

[19] As has been observed with goods shortages of all sorts during the COVID-19 crisis, an economy operating near to full employment is incapable of adapting to altered demand profiles if they happen suddenly, and this leads to losses.

employment and income upstream of supply chains, while it concurrently reduces real prices for goods and increases demand downstream.

First, sectoral technological progress indicators TPI_j are defined, which resemble cumulative production used in learning curves (Chapter 8). However, with a possible depreciation of past represented through a survival function $\ell_j(\tau)$ for investments in capacity and R&D made τ years ago,

$$TPI_j = \int_{-\infty}^{t} \left(I_j^{R\&D}(\tau) + I_j(\tau) \right) \ell_j(t-\tau) d\tau. \tag{11.9}$$

When introduced into regressions, notably prices, the TPIs make the equations become just like learning curves, with the regression parameter, in a log difference regression, corresponding to the learning exponent at the sector level. The TPIs influence not only prices, in which input costs are reflected, but also employment, where capital and innovation replace workers, as well as, in principle, the Input-Output relationships between sectors, reflecting reductions in inputs to production, although this is more difficult to establish.

Prices depend on two effects. They increase non-linearly with capacity factors when the demand requires production that makes capacity factors come close to 100%. Industry prices decrease with cumulated knowledge and investment, but increase with unit costs UC_j determined by Input-Output relationships, and input/commodity/energy prices on which technological progress operates,

$$P_j = F_P\left(+UC_j, +CF_j, -TPI_j, +\alpha_j S_j\right), \tag{11.10}$$

where $\alpha_j S_j$ is a debt servicing term, defined below in Eq. 11.16. Industry prices P_j are converted to final goods prices P_i through a correspondence matrix, and value-added tax (VAT) rate can also be included,

$$P_i = \sum_i PP_{ij} P_j * \left(1 + T^{VAT}\right). \tag{11.11}$$

Technological progress has international impacts, since import prices stem from the domestic prices of other regions, and thus technological progress in other regions can have an impact on domestic imports and be detrimental to domestic production, and conversely, technological progress can lead to an expansion of exports, an important contributor to domestic growth.

Lastly, the Input–Output coefficients A_{ij} should generally decline in input sectors with increasing TPIs, reflecting where the savings originate from, although this is generally difficult to infer due to a scarcity of time series on IO tables,

$$A_{ij} = A_{ij}^{o} \left(\frac{TPI_j(t)}{TPI_j(t_o)} \right)^{-b_j}. \tag{11.12}$$

It is assumed that industry sector j improves uniformly the use of its inputs i according to a power law function of the TPIs.

11.5.3 *Employment, Wages and Income*

Industrial production leads to industrial employment E_j, which depends on output, sectoral wages W_j and technological progress,

$$E_j = F_E\left(+Y_j, -W_j, -TPI_j\right). \tag{11.13}$$

Wages depend on local employment conditions, wages in other sectors W_j^{oth}, and sales. Unemployment is $1 - \frac{E_j}{N}$, while industrial income per worker employed is $\frac{P_j Y_j}{E_j}$,

$$W_j = F_W\left(+W_j^{oth}, -\left[1 - \frac{E_j}{N}\right], +\frac{P_j Y_j}{E_j}\right). \tag{11.14}$$

Personal income, derived from wages, depends on income taxes T^I

$$PI = \sum_j \frac{E_j W_j}{N}\left(1 - T^I\right). \tag{11.15}$$

With personal income defined, the set of equations is nearly closed, in that demand leads to production, which leads to employment, which leads to income that drives demand again. Several more variables nevertheless remain to be defined.

11.5.4 *The Financial Sector*

Investment takes place motivated by expectations of return, but plagued by limited foresight. As discussed earlier, in non-equilibrium complex evolutionary systems, agents cannot foresee in which direction the economy will collectively evolve, of all the possible directions it could take within the vast Adjacent Possible. However, since the costs of new technology go down with investment, once a new technology is proven to have a market, it attracts investment, and therefore, it is clear that agents in the Adjacent Possible revolve and cluster around specific locations (or technology constellations), rather than disperse in different directions. This is evoked by the saying *'the path is made by walking it'*, which literally suggests that once a path is created by visionary entrepreneurs in the Adjacent Possible, that path becomes feasible in the imagination of others, and as costs come down, many agents begin to walk it, while other directions remain unexplored and prohibitively costly.

Despite their lack of foresight, rather than sitting there pondering about the vastness of the Adjacent Possible and the limits of the knowable, entrepreneurs take their bets and invest to make a profit, even though they cannot estimate probabilities of return. One of their guides for forming their expectations is, good or bad, past success, and therefore, in a Minskian framework, present-day returns validate past investment decisions and present-day investment decisions are guided by validated success. This introduces a time teleconnection in the model, a new dynamical relationship. It creates a positive reinforcement when returns grow, and a negative reinforcement when returns decline. It intensifies financial contexts as it makes things both better and worse. When returns have been high for some time, investors invest more, which generates its own demand that re-inforces output and profits, while when returns have been bad for some time, investors hold investment up, which slows the economy down even more. This is what Keynes termed 'animal spirits'.[20]

As defined above, investment depends on accumulated debts D_i and animal spirits AS_j,

$$I_j = F_I\left(-P_j^I, +Y_j, +CF_j, -D_j, +AS_j\right).$$

Debts are serviced through the debt servicing term in the prices equation. D_j is defined in terms of the difference between past investments and past shares of output used to repay debt incurred $\pi_i(\tau)$, τ years back, with exogenous base interest rate r,[21]

$$D_j = \int_0^\infty \left(I_j(t-\tau) - \pi_j(t-\tau)Y_i(t-\tau)\right)(1+r)^\tau d\tau. \qquad (11.16)$$

Animal spirits (or investor confidence) are defined in terms of a memory function $h(t-\tau)$, similar to a survival function, that determines the length in time investors look back to validate present investment decisions,

$$AS_j = \left[\int_0^\infty I_j(t-\tau)CF_j(t-\tau)h(\tau)d\tau\right]AS_j^{ext}. \qquad (11.17)$$

Here, the capacity factor is used as a proxy for return on investment, since when overcapacity occurs, assets become unproductive, which signals investors to stop investing. Meanwhile, AS_j^{ext} represents external shocks on investor confidence that override the rest, due to, for example, a financial crisis. Alternatively, Eq. 11.17 could be replaced by the network model of finance of Chapter 10.

11.5.5 *Virtuous/Vicious Economic Cycles*

The Minskian equations added in relation to finance, although speculative, introduce important dynamical connections, in addition to those related to technological progress. These three equations (Eqs. 11.9, 11.16 and 11.17) are the only ones that connect the past with the present. All three are cumulation functions, that combine past and present-day information. They are the sources of path-dependence and of

20 This section of the model is more speculative and requires tests to be established, where the rest of the model already works without this Minskian addition.

21 Interest rates are not assumed to clear money markets, since as shown in Chapter 9, money is created on demand by financial institutions if they deem investors creditworthy based on the projects they propose, in the investment equation. Increased demand for money does not, in post-Keynesian or evolutionary theory, lead to increased interest rates, as opposed to standard neoclassical models. Creating an endogenous interest rate that varies according to perceived risk is challenging and not attempted here, where instead it is whether projects go ahead or not that is modelled.

irreversibility, defining the model as non-equilibrium. The dynamics they imply are as follows.

1. *TPI.* Technological progress in sectors stems from cumulative causation from past investment, which itself is motivated by output in those sectors. This forms a self-reinforcing cycle in which technological progress causes lower prices that attract more demand in progressing sectors, causing higher output, which induces further investment and technological progress. This implies to some degree a race between sectors as it intensifies competitiveness differences. It also leads, however, to declines in employment and intermediate demand, which dampen positive effects to some degree through their impact on income and ultimately aggregate demand, but this is generally overcome by the price effects attracting demand, maintaining a positive economic growth. TPIs are the source of endogenous growth in this model, but also, the source of structural change, since loss of output due to innovation does not occur in the same sectors or locations as the gains of output related to innovation.
2. *Debt.* Excessive debt accumulated in previous periods restricts borrowing for investment since investors become concerned about possible insolvency. Restricted credit impacts sectors such as construction and the manufacturing of investment and intermediate goods, which leads to economic slowdown. The debt term can slow down investment following booms if returns do not justify further expansion.
3. *Animal Spirits.* Animal spirits lead to increased investment when sectors have rising output, and to restricted investment when sectors have stagnating output. This reinforces trends both ways, up and down. This adds inertia to the economic engine, and is in part the reason for the economy to remain trapped in recessions or rise into bubbles. Here, financial crashes can only be generated by a shock in investor confidence AS_j^{ext}. In reality, these shocks should come as a result of shockwaves through an ownership network model (Chapter 10).

Ultimately, the dynamics lead towards a virtuous cycle of growth despite occasional slowdowns caused by external shocks, or shocks on investor confidence due to a self-organised critical financial sector. Growth that is approximately exponential arises essentially due to the fact that investment is proportional to output, or in other words, the capabilities of the economy.

However, more importantly than global aggregate growth, this model generates perpetual internal structural change due to technological progress, as some sectors attract increasing demand caused by their own success, while others stagnate. Additional issues could arise, however, that can be modelled through more specific technological progress, such as, for instance, reduced reliance on fossil fuels, due to policy and increasing fuel efficiency, causing structural change in fossil fuel sectors, or due to a capital-intensive transition in automating production to replace part of the labour force. Therefore, this model represents a non-equilibrium economy in perpetual change.

However, it does not model an endogenous exploration of the Adjacent Possible in the form of new technologies, since this model can only explore what its equations allow it to explore, which is a range of states pre-specified by its internal calibration against past observation. Its internal equations can be regressed in various ways against empirical data, but that does not generate any information on the Adjacent Possible and the ability of agents to discover 'new ways to make a living'. Therefore it is a partially evolutionary model, but one that is fully post-Keynesian.

PART III

Applied Complexity Economics for Environmental Governance

MAP FOR PART III

Part III is where the new economic theory of Part II is applied, solving the issues raised in Part I. Part III proposes a new normative approach for informing environmental and climate change policy-making on the basis of a complexity economics approach. This is called 'Risk-Opportunity Analysis'. This approach was co-created with policy-makers in the UK government through many months of collaboration and communication. It is meant to offer improved thinking and ways to develop evidence bases for problems of deep transformational change such as climate policy, in which the goal is to radically transform the energy system and the economy to make it environmentally sustainable. Transformational change cannot be informed using the traditional methods of equilibrium economics designed to analyse marginal change. Following this, case studies are given exploring the full complexity of a dynamically changing coupled global environmental and economic system.

Part III is divided along a methodological chapter, and three case studies:

(1) a formulation for risk-opportunity analysis to complement cost-benefit analysis (Chapter 12);
(2) an exploration of the complexity of the coupled economy-environment-food system in Brazil (Chapter 13);

(3) policies for a low-carbon energy transition (Chapter 14);
(4) the macroeconomic and structural change and financial impacts of the low-carbon transtion (Chapter 15).

Part III is also partly written for non-technical decision-makers, who may seek to understand issues of decision-making involving deep transformational change. In large parts, it responds to demands made in public policy-making for improved methods of policy appraisal looking towards the low-carbon transition, and mitigating its impacts for the common citizen.

Lastly, a conclusion is offered with reflections and ways forward.

12

Risk-Opportunity Analysis for Transformative Policy Design and Appraisal

The current global climate policy agenda requires technological change, innovation, labour markets and the financial system to be led towards an orderly and rapid low-carbon transition. Yet progress has been slow and incremental. Inadequacies of policy appraisal frameworks used worldwide may be significant contributors to the problem, as they frequently fail to adequately account for the dynamics of societal and technological change. Risks are underestimated, and the economic opportunities from innovation are generally not assessed in practice. In this chapter, the root causes of those inadequacies are identified and linked to structural features of standard analysis frameworks. A generalisation of existing frameworks for policy analysis and the appraisal of outcomes of proposed policy strategies is formulated, to help better identify and frame situations of transformational change. The term 'risk-opportunity analysis' is used to capture the generalised approach, in which conventional economic cost-benefit analysis is a special case. New guiding principles for policy-making during dynamic and transformational change are offered. This work was originally published in Mercure et al. (2021b) and as part of Grubb et al. (2021a).

12.1. THE LOW-CARBON INNOVATION POLICY PROBLEM

The urgency of climate change and the inadequacy of the global response has led some to ask, 'why are we waiting?' (Stern, 2015). Part of the answer may lie in the inadequacy of the tools most commonly used to guide decision-making processes.[1] The problem of reducing global emissions of greenhouse gases pose three challenges that standard and prevailing welfare economics policy assessment

[1] Mercure et al. (2016a); Farmer et al. (2015).

methods, cost-benefit analysis (CBA),[2] and general economic equilibrium analysis, are generally not in an adequate analytical position to address: the pervasive and transformative nature of the necessary changes[3] including non-marginal elements; the highly heterogeneous interests of different actors, stakeholders and decision-makers; and the high uncertainty regarding costs, benefits and path-dependence in the outcomes of policy strategies.[4] Conventional textbook welfare economic methods, as applied in current policy appraisal, are designed to analyse changes of marginal nature with relatively uniform stakeholders. Change that is structurally transformative change may not, however, be successfully triggered by informing policy using a paradigm designed for managing marginal change. Furthermore, as could be observed during both the 2008 financial crisis and the COVID-19 crisis, marginal analysis, ignoring systemic risk may also be leading policy-makers to design fragile systems with insufficient resilience to handle increasingly frequent extreme events (Schwarcz, 2019).

As discussed in Chapters 1 and 2, Climate change policy epitomises a need for change in approach felt in several domains of policy-making where substantial change is desired, as expressed in current policy objectives in various constituencies, but not materialising. Other areas include innovation policy, industrial strategy, finance, infrastructure, regional development, productivity growth and the response to structurally disruptive events such as pandemics. Marginal analysis is useful to inform policy over a vast domain. But in these areas of transformative policy-making, marginal analysis is not suitable to handle the complex dynamics involved. These problems of transformational change require a more general approach with corresponding definitions and methods.

A more general set of social scientific methods, both quantitative and qualitative could serve as part of a general paradigm for policy appraisal (Kattel et al., 2018). An appropriate approach would admit the limits to available knowledge to adaptively guide the approximate direction of change of a complex transition, rather than attempt to identify a highly uncertain distant end point with false precision. As discussed in Chapter 6, a practical scientific handling of deep uncertainty emerges more naturally from complexity science than it does from traditional welfare economics (Arthur, 1999).

In this chapter, the scientific basis is identified to manage information flow in a policy appraisal framework theoretically compliant with structurally transformative situations, which we call 'risk-opportunity analysis' (ROA). It is not a policy or political proposition; rather, building upon all preceding chapters of this book, it identifies suitable scientific methods, drawn from the sciences of complexity

[2] See for instance the UK's guidelines for policy analysis (the 'Green Book' HM Treasury, 2020a) and those of the EPA in the United States (EPA, 2014).

[3] See Fouquet (2016), and more generally see the IPCC (2018).

[4] For these three elements, see respectively Dietz and Hepburn (2013); Geels et al. (2016); Hughes et al. (2013).

and dynamical systems, that are coherent with observed features and properties of problems of structurally transformative change. A number of methodologies in fact exists (e.g., robust-decision-making, Marchau et al., 2019) for analysing decision-making options under deep uncertainty, to which ROA is to some degree related. What these lack, however (see Chapter 4), is the broad philosophical pedigree that welfare economics possesses going back to eighteenth century, through which much of our present day understanding of legitimacy-building in the eyes of the public and public institutions during policy appraisal has been developed, as well as the mechanisms of the science–policy interface itself. ROA is a generalisation of widely used CBA, and therefore benefits from the same intuitive philosophical background, while avoiding the most important flaws of CBA when applied to problems of structural change.

The root causes of the inadequacy of marginal analysis are first considered here in relation to the appraisal of policy design for structurally transformative change, using climate change policy as the main testing ground. Next, the scientific basis of ROA is set out. The methodological framework of analysis itself is then given. Lastly, examples of application are explored before a conclusion.

12.2. CHALLENGES IN POLICY APPRAISAL

12.2.1 *Preamble*

Basic welfare economic principles, as applied in finance ministries, are most useful when

1. An intervention does not substantially change the background economic situation (e.g., prices of goods and services and GDP growth) nor the relationships between variables;
2. The heterogeneity of affected stakeholders, and of the dimensions of policy outcomes, is not highly relevant for the objectives to be considered achieved;
3. All parameters and outcomes involved in policy analysis are sufficiently confidently known, with quantified uncertainty, such that expected values are considered robust.

For many situations, including notably policy that concerns innovation, these requirements do not hold, invalidating any conclusions based on the application of basic welfare economics, either as descriptions of reality, or as normative principles. Going back to Chapter 6, three useful definitions relate to the reliability of the knowledge that decision-makers use: *heavy-tailed* and *fundamental uncertainty*, as well as *systemic risk*.

Heavy-tailed uncertainty is characterised by a probability distribution where very impactful events are sufficiently likely that the variance fails to exist. This means that if one tries to compute it, the estimated value of the variance becomes larger and larger and diverges to infinity as the sample size becomes large. In extreme cases the mean also fails to exist, but even if it does exist, averages converge very slowly with the addition of data, which makes it unreliable.

Fundamental uncertainty about the future involves unknown unknowns, arising when one cannot enumerate and rank all possible futures. It is proposed here that fundamental uncertainty is generally related to heavy-tailed uncertainty.

Systemic risk is associated with complex interdependencies within a system and can precipitate systemic collapse based on the cumulative contribution of certain actions by the individual entities that collectively compose that system. It can arise when the actions of any individuals do not necessarily pose a risk to themselves directly, but contribute to forming risks at the community level. Systemic risk is not the aggregation of individual risk but rather an emergent property of the system that arises as an amplification of any such aggregate risk (see Cont and Schaanning, 2017).

There exists of a discrepancy between the definition of 'risk' used in economics, as the impact of uncertainty on objectives quantifiable with probabilities (following Knight), and the definition used in most other spheres of society (such as public health, engineering, or national security, e.g., the ISO risk management standard), which does not require probability to be quantifiable in order for something to be considered as a risk. For the sake of communicating with policy-makers, the latter definition is adopted here, recognising that probabilities are rarely quantifiable in practice. Meanwhile, the term 'uncertainty' is used to refer to the range of possible variations in the accuracy of existing knowledge and predictions (see Chapter 6), and not in the sense used by economists meaning unquantifiable risk.

12.2.2 *Understanding Rapid Pervasive Change*

According to the UK's Green Book for policy appraisal (HM Treasury, 2020a), marginal analysis is 'generally most appropriate where the broader environment (e.g., the price of goods and services in the economy) can be assumed to be unchanged by the intervention'. By contrast, it works 'less well where there are potential non-marginal effects or changes in underlying relationships'. Meanwhile, general equilibrium economic models are designed to handle marginal demand, supply and price changes, but do not handle deep structural changes in the economy, as they take the structure of the economy to be fixed.

To understand the mismatch that occurs when a marginal analysis technique is applied to a problem of non-marginal change, it is necessary to identify the relevant system dynamics and their potential path-dependence.

Dynamics of Economic Systems

The economy is characterised by inertia, which implies understanding it as a dynamical system.[5] Inertia in the economy stems from two broad processes: the

[5] Mokyr (1992); Grübler et al. (1999).

long-lived nature of productive capital assets required for generating return, and the interconnectedness of agents, firms, industrial systems and supply chains/trade networks.[6] Production requires building physical and human capital assets, and this takes time, and such investment occurs with the expectation they will be used for an even longer period of time. Rapidly changing economic circumstances can lead to a devaluation of capital before it has paid for itself. Thus, for problems that potentially involve transformative change, understanding dynamics is of primary concern, where the dynamic effectiveness of policies can be analysed instead of their static efficiency. The static efficiency of complex systems is only ever knowable *ex ante* for as long as change is marginal, beyond which it loses clear meaning.

Path Dependence

Policy action in certain domains almost always has the outcome of changing to some degree the problem at hand, creating the need for further analysis and further policy action (Rittel and Webber, 1973). Playing the game may change the game. For example, research suggests that it has been the German introduction of feed-in tariffs that created a market for solar photovoltaics, which allowed Chinese manufacturers to justify expanding production at a large scale, which subsequently resulted in substantial cost reductions and the availability of low-cost solar energy to the rest of the world (Yu et al., 2016). A relatively benign climate policy decision transformed the whole low-carbon industry and climate change problem, affecting the policy strategy of all nations, by opening new opportunities and closing older ones.

Path-dependence is intrinsically difficult to represent in equilibrium-based economic analysis, because as discussed in Chapters 5 and 6, the notion of equilibrium erases the impact of history, the memory that is embedded in economic structure. Seen as an evolutionary metabolic system, as time passes, economic evolution identifies the range of what were past possibilities of what the economy will not become, while it expands the range of what it could become – but neither can be exhaustively enumerated with certainty.[7] In the language of marginal analysis, the constraints of the allocation problem that must be solved in path-dependent systems keep changing according to the solution that was reached in previous time positions. This is a difficult to solve, infinitely recursive problem when framed using standard economic optimisation.

12.2.3 *Addressing Normatively Highly Differentiated and Heterogeneous Interests*

A common criticism levelled against methods embedded in current policy appraisal is that it requires normative valuation elements to be included in an otherwise

[6] See earlier theoretical work on the topic in Mercure (2015, 2018).

[7] See Chapters 5 and 6 where the concept of the 'Adjacent Possible' is discussed. See also Kauffman (2000); Arthur et al. (1997a); Day (1992).

descriptive quantitative analysis,[8] valuation that is often ultimately interpreted as objective science. As detailed in Chapter 4, the mainstream theory is ambiguous over whether it aims to describe reality or moral values. Indeed in CBA, moral values, in other words beliefs, are effectively quantified in monetary terms using methods that have frequently been argued as an arbitrary choice of the analyst, since beliefs are, strictly speaking, not reliably measurable quantities.[9] Aggregating the value of moral choices with real flows of economic quantities is scientifically inconsistent and it often leads to internal philosophical contradictions and challenges. For example, the Stern Review involved measuring the statistical value of life of people affected by climate change impacts, and this method generated different values according to ethnicity and social background (Aldred, 2009). Not least, this is inconsistent with other widely accepted human rights-related principles, both derived from normative principles and not objectively observable, but also, inconsistent with each other. But this is ultimately just a case of conflicting moral theories, which has nothing to do with scientific analysis.

More importantly, welfare economic valuation methods ascribe value to multiple dimensions of policy impacts using only one monetary metric combining all real and moral costs and benefits, with stated interpretation that the resulting quantity represents their normative value to society as a whole. Where that quantity remains constant, society is interpreted as indifferent, but this can involve substantial underlying structural changes, with winners and losers. The normative weighting of different actors' interests is inevitably a political choice, and, where one takes a positivist view of science, this cannot be the outcome of any scientific assessment.[10] In other words, by including normative elements into objective analysis, current appraisal methods take the value judgment, and thus agency, away from the policy-maker, and gives it to the analyst. The former may meanwhile be in need of guidance for policy design on how to pursue a range of goals, while the latter may end up under undue political pressure to shape the subjective component of the assessment in particular ways.

12.2.4 *Working Scientifically with Uncertainty*

The concept of Pareto-optimal policy-making, in a strict sense, may in some instances be scientifically tenuous, since the possible outcomes of policy action cannot usually be exhaustively enumerated and ranked.[11] It was sugested in Chapter 1 that the aim to deliver optimality may be too restrictive as it involves unrealistically high demands

8 E.g., the monetary value of risk to life or the willingness to pay for beauty or pollination services, see Bateman et al. (2002); Hanley and Barbier (2009), and the official guidelines in HM Treasury (2020a); HSS (2016).

9 This criticism is long established; see Baram (1979); Ackerman and Heinzerling (2001).

10 See Ackerman and Heinzerling (2001); Pindyck (2017).

11 Baram (1979); Ackerman and Heinzerling (2001); Weitzman (2009).

on information availability and reliability, while in practice, it frequently leads to the use of some untestable proxies for inferring missing information. At the same time, the role, value and information content of uncertainty as the generator of both risk and opportunity is generally missed. By alleviating requirements for optimality, uncertainty could in fact be seen as an ally rather than as an enemy.

Uncertainty Is Fundamental

As discussed in Chapter 6, fundamental uncertainty is an essential characteristic of the economy[12] and is present in most policy decisions. Its sources include the development of new technologies; the intentions and investment decisions of economic agents; the outcomes of entrepreneurial ventures; the future costs and prices of all traded goods and services; and the behaviour of the economy as a whole. Possibilities are in general not exhaustively known, and therefore probability distributions around these possibilities are not knowable. Arbitrarily assigning probabilities to unknowable quantities can lead to scientific inconsistency.

That fundamental uncertainty cannot be represented using probability distributions is closely related to the degree of path-dependence inherent in the economy. For example, a range of possible values for auctioned connectivity broadcasting licences did not exist until the mobile phone was created. But moreover, many futures may either be distinctly advantageous or clearly disastrous. That probability distributions could be heavy-tailed implies that expected values – and therefore discounted costs and benefits – are generally unreliable quantities, as they involve adding up large uncertain values with small relatively well-known values.

One crucial consequence of fundamental uncertainty is that knowledge about a system after a non-marginal transformation has taken place is inherently less robust than knowledge of the status quo. As a natural consequence, the valuation of the predominantly long-term direct and indirect benefits of policy action is more prone to uncertainty than the valuation of the predominantly short-term direct costs of the same policy action. Thus, mis-handling uncertainty may generate, in marginal analysis, a status quo bias if the tendency of analysts is to avoid including uncertain quantities, or a confidence bias if uncertainty is underestimated. This affects particularly innovation and regional development policy.

Experience tells us[13] that the standard response of welfare economics analysts to fundamental uncertainty is to make proxies for missing knowledge, and impose short-tailed distributions to missing data, since marginal analysis requires users to quantify probabilistically all real and moral costs and benefits (e.g., measuring the statistics of rare events involves long waiting times and is not commonly done). Some of these

[12] Going back to Keynes (1921); see also Fontana (2008).

[13] The experience of the policy-making process in government by colleagues is referred to in this statement.

quantities inevitably have heavy-tailed or unknown probabilities, such as the social cost of carbon, or the benefits of hypothetical technologies that do not yet exist. The political pressure on analysts that results from the requirement to make proxies when data is unavailable potentially politicises the policy analysis process, and could ultimately undermine it.

Uncertainty Has Value

The economy naturally evolves through its attraction towards productivity increasing novelty.[14] Entrepreneurs and venture capitalists in fact make practical use of fundamental uncertainty, since business opportunity frequently arises through unpredictable events that allow capturing competitive advantage, for instance successful innovation. This notion contrasts with normative probability-based standard portfolio optimisation (Markowitz, 1952), which requires fully quantified risks. Venture capital would likely not exist if probabilities of entrepreneurial success were equally known by everyone, as there would be less opportunity for creating comparative advantage out of innovative industrial ventures.

Entrepreneurs do not typically focus on single sources of cash flow (excluding monopolies), as they strive to future-proof one's enterprise by creating new products and capture new markets (Porter et al., 1996). Figure 12.1a illustrates a typical business perception of returns on investment in research and development (R&D) at the firm level, drawing from empirical findings.[15] Investing insufficient resources into innovation leads an enterprise towards obsolescence and eventual failure. Meanwhile, too high an investment of available resources into too many risky ventures is a gamble that leads to a relatively high chance of successive strategic mistakes, unproductive investments, and failure. A middle-ground thus exists.

This behaviour is observed empirically in innovation portfolio analysis, where it is observed that a combination of breadth, selectiveness and innovative intent increases return on R&D investment, due to its generation of options.[16] This can coincide with some types of normative portfolio analysis in the context of innovation (Way et al., 2019). It may be understood as the entrepreneur's adaptive response to strong path-dependence, where strategic re-adjustment takes place as information is gathered and expectations are recurrently re-formed (Figure 12.1b). A similar logic is known empirically to apply to public innovation policy-making:[17] although pressure arises for policy-makers to identify 'optimal policies', in practice not all policies succeed, while objective value exists in trial and error, investing in both high and low risk ventures.

[14] Freeman and Louçã (2001); Schumpeter (1939).
[15] Klingebiel and Rammer (2014); Meifort (2016).
[16] Klingebiel and Rammer (2014); Meifort (2016).
[17] Mazzucato (2013); Mazzucato and Penna (2016).

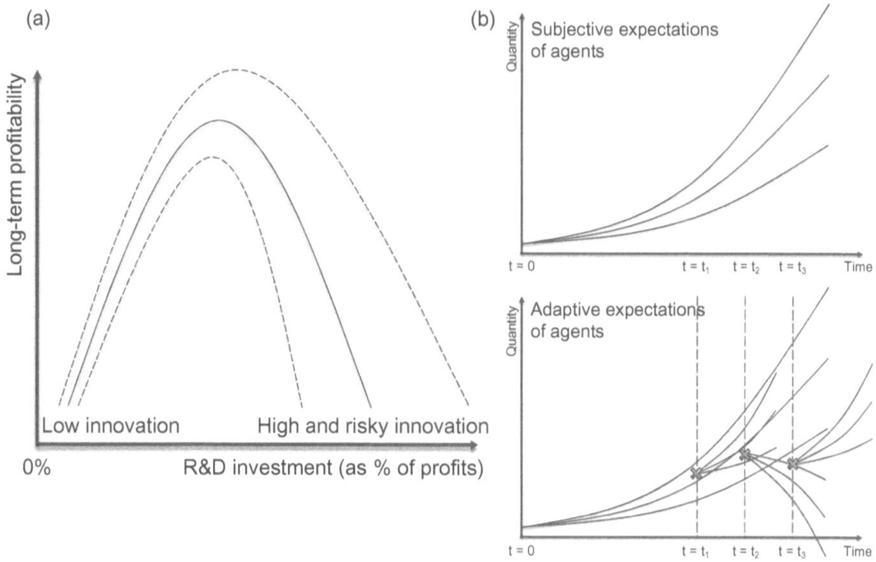

FIGURE 12.1 (a) Illustration of the profitability of companies in relation to their degree of commitment of resources to R&D investment for the development of new products. Dashed lines illustrate degrees of uncertainty. (b) Illustration of the process of expectations creation and readjustment by agents to capture opportunities as time passes. (Top panel) Agents in practice form subjective expectations of the future, with central scenario and limit cases. (Bottom panel) As time passes, agents re-form their expectations adaptively according to new information. Crosses are actual realisations, while curves delimit ranges of possibilities expected by agents.

12.3. RISK-OPPORTUNITY ANALYSIS FOR INFORMING POLICY-MAKING

In this section, a risk-opportunity analysis (ROA) framework is defined, designed to inform policy-making for problems involving non-marginal change, that can be used within existing science–policy interfaces. ROA is a generalisation, in fact possibly the only self-consistent generalisation one can make, of CBA when in the presence of dynamics and strong path-dependence in the economy, of fundamental uncertainty and heterogeneity of stakeholders. ROA requires abandoning the standard use of expected values on the basis that detailed probabilities are unknowable in general, and demands appropriate treatment of uncertainty in each domain of analysis.

12.3.1 *Methodological Steps in ROA*

Building upon the standard guidelines of common policy appraisal frameworks including the Green Book and the European Commission guidelines for policy appraisal,[18] as well as on the above descriptive principles of dynamical systems, ROA involves the following steps:

(1) Identify the boundaries of the system considered and map out all relevant feedback between components, considering their magnitudes and directions. Choose or develop suitable dynamical quantitative and/or qualitative analysis models and datasets accordingly.
(2) Estimate median (not mean) outcomes and impacts on the process and direction of evolution and on the structure of the system itself, in a chosen relevant set of qualitatively or quantitatively measurable metrics, associated with each comprehensive policy portfolio proposed, under various plausible scenarios of economic evolution through time. Establish ranges of uncertainty or degrees confidence for each outcome metric.
(3) Carry out, using a stress test or other method, a risk assessment for each policy portfolio under study, to identify all possible extreme unintended detrimental consequences and worst-case scenarios, estimating their severity and likelihood, under each dimension considered. This should identify notably the possibility of reaching tipping points and rapid non-linear changes, and their dependence on known variables.
(4) Carry out, using scenario variation analysis or other methods, an opportunity assessment, identifying all possible option creation potentials for each policy portfolio under study, under each dimension considered. Option creation potentials are elements of scenarios and systems that expand the ranges of possible desirable futures.
(5) Report to decision-makers median impacts, direction of system change feedback, risks and opportunities, in all dimensions considered, along with uncertainty ranges and/or confidence levels. Report both qualitative and quantitative evidence, against current regulatory norms and risk tolerances. The normative weighting or valuation of outcomes is not considered part of ROA.

12.3.2 *Taking a Systems Perspective*

The intended and unintended impacts of policy-making are typically felt across several dimensions, such as income, inequality, access to stable services, environmental quality, financial stability, health and so on. To minimise the chance of missing important impact transmission mechanisms, establishing a holistic systems view and system boundaries is required, identifying feedback between system components using multiple outcome indicators that cover the main possible intended and

[18] HM Treasury (2020b); EC (2015).

unintended outcomes. Furthermore, system changes can include structural changes in which the system gradually changes its mode of operation. Given the structure of uncertainty, what can reliably be analysed is the direction of whole system change in multiple domains, with the understanding that the end point is uncertain. Lastly, important background changes may exist superimposed onto the outcomes of policy action, where the latter may exacerbate or synergise with existing background evolution trends.

For example, from this perspective, imposing a particular policy measure to achieve a certain objective (e.g., carbon price to reduce carbon emissions) should not be understood to lead to a new static equilibrium state of society, technology and the economy, but rather, to a new state of change of behaviour, technology and the economy. That direction of change may suit some stakeholders and groups thereof, while others not, depending on their individual circumstances, motives, and aspirations. Particularly, some social groups may have vulnerabilities or states of resilience in various domains, which may be created, exacerbated, or mitigated by the policy initiative.

By taking a holistic systems view, the methodology encompasses the broader direction of change induced by possible policy strategies, including unintended impacts on different groups of stakeholders, as well as the wider range of possible extreme events and vulnerabilities associated with newly created systems. Thus, the use of models of complex systems by definition generates ranges of path-dependent outcomes, feedback and structural changes useful to populate a risk-opportunity analysis by generating both median outcome projections and tail risk analyses.

In practice this means that policy options are to be assessed in combination, rather than individually, and assessed for a whole system, rather than limiting the analysis to a subset. Relationships between system components are to be mapped and reinforcing and balancing feedback identified. As opposed to assessing the expected outcome of a policy at a moment in time, these approaches can be used to assess whether a policy decision changes things in the direction sought by decision-makers (the direction of change), how much it changes things (the effectiveness), how quickly change happens, how confident one can be that this new direction would be taken, and what the risks and opportunities are, as defined below.

12.3.3 *Costs and Benefits Become Risks and Opportunities*

Governments as well as other organisations generally find to be part of their remit to consider tail risks, in various domains, generated by their actions, although the focus varies depending on the purpose of the policy or decision appraisal exercise. Strategic, regulatory, and budget policy- and decision-making are interested in different aspects of uncertainty (Figure 12.2). On the strategy side, the focus is on the most likely outcome and direction of change induced by a strategic decision. However, regulatory decision-making (for example with safety, regulatory norms,

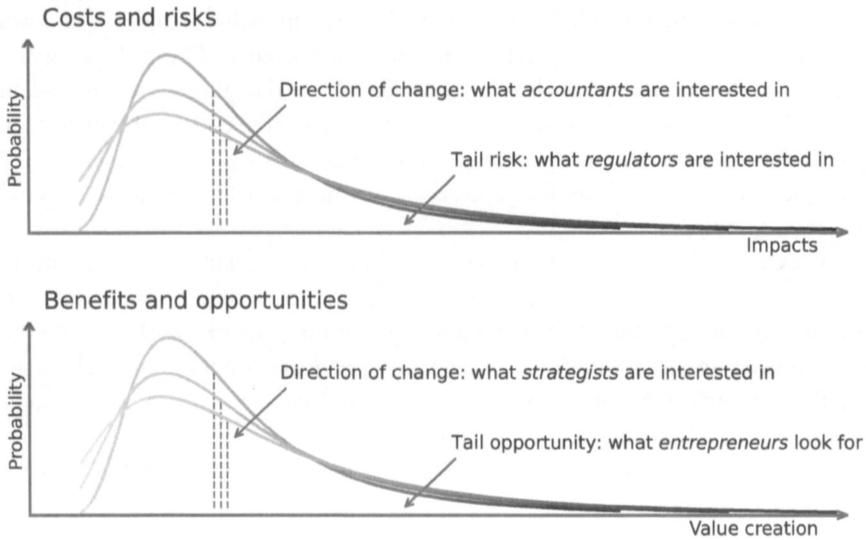

FIGURE 12.2 Illustration of heavy-tailed probability distributions for risks and opportunities. In complex systems, one can rarely accurately determine probability distributions, and thus these are shown with truncated unknown heavy tails. Expected values either do not converge or cannot be reliably calculated, but risks and opportunities can nevertheless be critically appraised.

compliance, quality assurance and insurance), will typically focus on ensuring that the system evolves within certain bounds away from extremes, maintaining sufficient capacity to absorb the impacts of unexpected events (e.g., based on estimates of tail events such as the likelihood of electricity black-outs, financial crashes, flooding, pandemics). Yet another category of policy action will assess whether a strategy fits within existing budgets and priorities. For the purpose of the present text, the three classes of policy-making functions will be denoted, respectively, 'strategy', 'regulation' and 'accounting'. All three functions and purposes of decision-making can make use of risk-opportunity analysis for different but related reasons.

Generalising welfare economics to complex dynamical systems, an accurate and comprehensive interpretation of non-linear dynamics and fundamental uncertainty suggests that comparing costs and benefits in fact implies a comparison of risks and opportunities. In that generalisation, the standard concept of 'externality' encompasses systemic risk, and the risk of reaching a tipping point due to collective action (and conversely for systemic opportunity). Probability distributions cannot be assumed to be fully known since due to emergence in complex systems, one cannot confidently enumerate and rank all possibilities and have comprehensive knowledge, even if one can be confident about what is likely and what is less likely. Since they cannot be assumed known, due to the possible emergence of extreme events, probability distributions for costs and benefits must therefore allow for the possibility of heavy tails for any systems with moderately high degrees of complexity. Therefore, expected values do not always exist and are not reliably calculated, and thus risk is not reliably quantifiable (Figure 12.2). This is particularly important in the context of the common and standard imposition, in present methodologies, of arbitrary probability distributions onto existing data, especially short-tailed distributions, since they potentially lead to wrong inferences and underestimation of real risks. Where multiple plausible scenarios are generated but expected values are not reliable, three useful elements can be informed:

(1) The confidence that the strategist can have over whether a policy adoption will reach a certain outcome and send the system in movement in a desired direction that fits current objectives;
(2) The confidence that the regulator can experience as to whether a system will avoid becoming prone to collapse in ways that exceed existing regulatory norms;
(3) The accountant can also assess whether costs, negative outcomes, and tail risks of unintended negative consequences overshadow benefits and opportunities, and whether outcomes fit within or contribute to current fiscal priorities.

System stress tests can be used to assess risk. Indeed, as is clear in the practice of stress-testing, tail risk can be estimated without probability distributions necessarily being fully known, notably using network models (Battiston et al., 2017). This complements the estimate of costs with an assessment of risks. However, in addition to these standard practices, the strategist, taking the role of an entrepreneur, can also assess, using this methodology, whether policy action is likely to open options for further economic and innovation opportunities. That is, without this being the main focus, some innovation strategies may offer further potential for opportunity generation and economic spillovers than others. This complements the estimate of benefits with an assessment of opportunity.

For example, a particular low-carbon transition policy strategy could have, compared to an alternate approach, different simultaneous types of outcomes: (1) it increases/decreases the likelihood of meeting stated emissions target; (2) it is more profitable/costly; (3) it makes the financial system more/less resilient (systemic risk decreases/increases); (4) it decreases/increases energy poverty; (5) as side effects, it creates/destroys, industrial capabilities with more/less potential to generate new products, markets and jobs.

In practice this means that policy options are proposed to be assessed upon knowledge of their broader risks and opportunities, not just their costs and benefits, and avoid aggregating outcomes over arbitrary probability distributions. Specifically, the assessment encompasses 'tail' risks and opportunities (e.g., tipping points), which may include very high impact outcomes, positive and negative. Reducing systemic risks generally implies increasing systemic resilience. The assessment also considers outcomes that can only be qualitatively assessed. The assessment is likely to rely on relevant expert knowledge and judgment; where this is the best available form of evidence it can be retained in its pure form, and not be converted to monetary values.

12.3.4 *Defining Risk and Opportunity*

Systemic risk is well defined and managed in risk assessment methodologies (HM Treasury, 2020b). Managing systemic risk is done in policy-making in order to design and shape systems in resilient ways, which allows them to withstand unexpected situations without leading to a likelihood of systemic failure. Systems typically need spare capacity to absorb such situations (e.g., during pandemics, or speculative bubbles). In many if not most systems, seeking to maximise performance is known to affect stability and increase systemic risks.[19] Underplaying heavy-tailed uncertainty, and optimising systems based on incomplete knowledge, can lead strategists to design brittle systems prone to failure. Regulators, if not involved in the design, can inherit a built-in fragility challenging to manage, at potentially high costs for accountants and society. Uniting risk and cost assessments in the same policy analysis framework, including unintended consequences of design, logically leads to focusing on improving the resilience of systems. It may help plan the direction of development of the economy in resilient ways. The risk-opportunity methodology therefore incentivises strategists, regulators and accountants to work coherently together.

Opportunity, however, is a more diffuse concept. Whereas 'risk', as normatively understood, concerns the likelihood of 'harm' to existing components of a well-understood system (i.e. the one prevailing at decision-making time), 'opportunity' concerns the likelihood of decisions resulting in a system which is considered 'better' (under certain normative criteria) by stakeholders, and/or features more option generation potential, than the prevailing one. Since a putative 'better' system (as normatively understood in the relevant context), after transformation, is by definition less well known than the prevailing system, a 'better' outcome is naturally surrounded by more fundamental uncertainty than the status quo. However, the economy and markets are systems in continuous change, and entrepreneurs generally embrace that dynamism in their search for opportunities.[20] Uncertainty is ultimately inseparable from innovation and productivity growth.

[19] E.g., reducing capital requirements in finance accelerates investment and systemic risk. For more on the resilience-optimisation tradeoff see Carlson and Doyle, (2002) Doyle and Carlson, (2000).

[20] Klingebiel and Rammer (2014); Meifort (2016).

In practice this means that, for example, policy choices with higher near-term costs and high near-term uncertainty (such as investing in innovation) are identified in ROA for their potential to generate options to capture future opportunities with economic returns, while in comparison, other policies that have low near-term costs with low uncertainty but characterised only by moderate long-term return can characterised as such in ROA. ROA can also caution against policies that generate high short-term return with high confidence (such as focusing on natural resource exports, or deregulating finance) but that are damaging to the economy in the long run as they concurrently lead to a systemic risk build-up. Such strategic insights resulting from ROA are not commonly obtained using marginal analysis. This information can allow relevant stakeholders to more effectively achieve stated normative objectives.

12.3.5 *Complex Dynamics*

Fundamental uncertainty implies that distant outcomes are uncertain, success is not guaranteed, and decision-makers can at best reliably control the direction of change, rather than the endpoint, and adaptively adjust policy over time to achieve stated outcomes. Figure 12.3 illustrates as an example the understanding of the effectiveness of a pricing policy for supporting the diffusion of low-carbon products (green) and the phase out of high carbon products (black), from the perspectives of both static equilibrium (top row) and a dynamic complexity policy (bottom row) assessment frameworks. In the static framework, the driver is typically a tax that intends to 'internalise' a stated externality and is understood, in the parent theory, to change the relationship between supply and demand accordingly. The expected outcome, such as the level of adoption of low-carbon technologies, is understood to be a unique static outcome of the driver, as it settles in a new equilibrium.

In a scientific context of complex dynamics, a policy change shapes driver variables that are themselves dynamic (e.g., vehicle prices declining with learning-by-doing cost reductions, which reinforce dynamic diffusion processes, which reinforce learning-by-doing processes). Scenarios are generated in which uncertainty encompasses a range of directions of change rather than a range of static end points. Heavy-tailed uncertainty over outcomes exists due to the compounding effect of interactions between system components. Thus, a risk-opportunity assessment identifies central-, worst- and best-case scenarios, without generating a false sense of knowledge and certainty.

In practice this means that as opposed to identifying new theoretical equilibria reached by pricing policy signals, ROA identifies feedback that controls the dynamics of evolution of a system, in order to identify a range of new trajectories that a system could take following the introduction of a policy portfolio. This makes use of scenario analysis: whether some or all of the scenarios achieve a stated objective; and whether opportunities can arise; and whether worst case scenarios fall within established

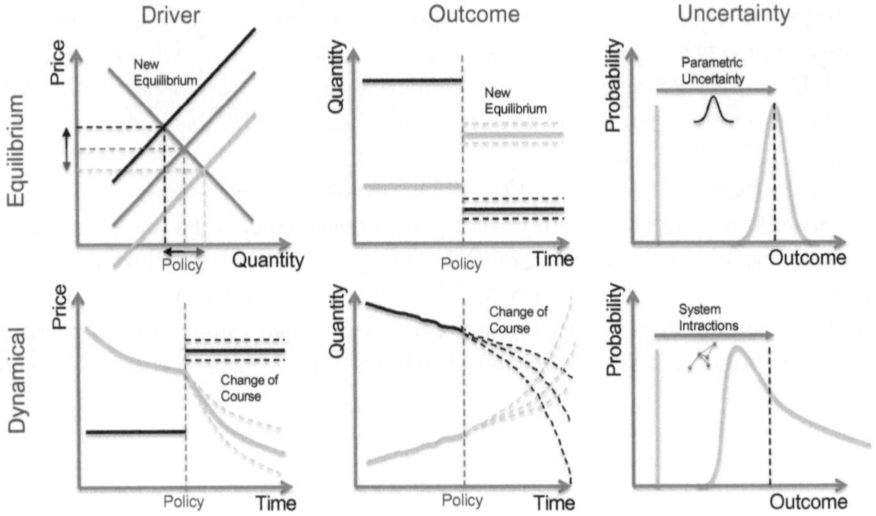

FIGURE 12.3 Comparison of the process of assessing change in policy impact assessment, between the marginal analysis framing (top row), and the complexity science framing (bottom row), in terms of its drivers (left), outcomes (middle) and uncertainty (right). This illustrates a situation of impact assessment of hypothetical policies for the diffusion of low-carbon innovations. In marginal analysis, pricing policies are typically used, which change the position of the equilibrium between supply and demand of green and brown products. The outcome is a well-defined function of the driver, with assumed short-tailed probability distribution, giving a potentially false sense of knowledge and certainty. In complex systems analysis, the driver itself is dynamic, the outcome process can take a range of directions, and the true uncertainty, compounding system interactions, is frequently heavy-tailed.

accepted bounds of failure. Based on establishing system feedback and sensitive intervention points, policy space can be searched by policy-makers until all stated objectives and standards are met under all dimensions of analysis.

12.3.6 *From One-Dimensional to Multi-dimensional Assessment*

Different stakeholders value different outcomes of policy decisions, measured using different metrics, differently (e.g., GDP, health, jobs, environment), leading to political debates. In complex systems, each dimension has different degrees of uncertainty and tail lengths. Combining all metrics into one would also lead to combining their uncertainties, which could obscure uncertainty analysis unnecessarily from the perspective of users. For example, the health impacts of reducing vehicle pollution in cities and its uncertainty is increasingly well characterised, however the economic impacts of reducing petrol and diesel use in certain countries, due to job losses, may be substantially less well characterised. Aggregating highly uncertain outcomes with relatively well-known outcomes leads to a valuation that is overall highly uncertain, substantially undermining the analysis and not making best use of the information.

The assessment of impacts of a policy can be made individually on each metric chosen for the analysis, considering (1) intended and unintended outcomes, (2) alignment with the direction expected/desired, (3) its magnitude, (4) the degree of uncertainty or confidence in the outcome, (5) the likelihood of extreme events taking place, and (6) the option generation potential. In order to separate assessment from politics, a multidimensional analysis, estimated independently for each relevant dimension, is used. A relative normative valuation of policy outcomes can subsequently be carried out separately, with or without sophisticated quantitative methods, by independent actors who possess the political legitimacy to do so, which lies outside of the ROA methodology.[21]

In practice this means that analysts report risks and opportunities in multiple dimensions relevant to the problem and leave the valuation of each of these dimensions to be done by policy-makers. The latter can evaluate the information and choices to be made in the context of stated multidimensional objectives and their knowledge of stakeholder needs and their diversity.

12.3.7 *Normative Principles for Policy-Making in a Context of Risk and Opportunity*

While this chapter is methodological and does not make a policy recommendation, some normative principles can be derived from complexity science analysis that can usefully frame policy problems in the context of structurally transformative change and become part of official guidelines.

Whether to Act at All

The foundational normative principle for policy-making under the Coase Theorem and market failure framework is to develop one policy response per identified market failure.[22] In a complex system with continuous endogenous change, or where the exogenous context changes faster than equilibrium can be reached, finding the optimal policy requires a search through an infinitely large set of possible futures branching out from one another: it cannot be identified in practice.

A foundational normative principle suitable for dynamical systems, inferred from the use of ROA, is to act to prepare for change that is likely, to bring about options for change that is desirable, and to avoid change that is undesirable. This is conceptually connected to the central normative principle of the 'market shaping' framework (Mazzucato and Penna, 2016) that has been used to support the development of

[21] Such as Multi-Criteria Analysis (MCA). E.g., see the European Commission's impact assessment guidelines (EC, 2015), where this is the practice.

[22] Coase (1960); Lehmann et al. (2019); Hanley et al. (2016).

so-called 'mission-oriented policies'.[23] It is applicable as a rationale for any policy that is intended to achieve structurally transformative change, or that takes place in a context of structurally transformative change.

How Much Effort to Make

A basic normative principle of welfare economics is that effort to correct a market failure should be applied up to the level at which the marginal benefits of action are equal to the marginal costs of that action, thereby suggesting that this should be reliably identified. This is generally defended on the basis of an idealised normative utilitarian moral philosophy framework of social justice. However, given that real world agents are not necessarily utilitarians,[24] it is not an empirically validated description of human behaviour.

For non-marginal change, 'optimality' cannot reliably be identified because outcomes are heavy-tailed uncertain. A second normative principle inferred from ROA methodology is that sufficient policy effort may be applied to kick-start self-generating change over time. This considers the observed effectiveness of policy in relation to the dynamic processes that it aims to influence in its stated objective. For example, if a government invests in the development of a new low carbon technology but abandons support for it before it is successfully commercialised, self-generating increasing returns may never materialise, and the investment could be wasted. For example, UK offshore subsidies (initially £140/MWh $\simeq$ £300/tCO2e at the prevailing carbon intensity, see Chapter 14) successfully brought the technology to market parity, while the official value of emissions reductions in the UK at the time was £14/tCO2e for the power sector and £59/tCO2e in other sectors. Had the official value been used to design the policy following a market failure rationale, it would likely have failed.

Where to Direct the Effort

When a single marginal market failure is identified, standard economic theory contends that externality pricing or compensation mechanisms can be applied after which the market is expected to allocate resources optimally. In cases where structurally transformational change is possible, optimal states are not reliably identifiable, while some policies may be more effective in incentivising change towards stated objectives than others. A suitable normative principle is therefore not allocative efficiency, but dynamic effectiveness (Kattel et al., 2018). It is simply more effective to act on known points of greatest leverage.

Applied to the pricing value of externalities, this principle suggests that the most effective approach may not necessarily be a uniform price across the whole economy,

23 Including for example the 'Grand Challenges' in the UK government's Industrial Strategy (Government, 2017).

24 Graeber (2014); Douglas and Isherwood (1979); Sahlins (1972).

as would be inferred from welfare economics, but could instead be prices targeted in specific sectors, set at specific levels that are estimated likely to catalyse change, or combinations with regulations and other policies.[25] Indeed, this principle also suggests that there is no reason to expect, a priori, pricing itself to be an effective policy, and that other forms of targeted policy may be equally or more effective (notably, regulation). That policy should be 'technology neutral' does not appear to be supported by the evidence; what appears to matter is to be effective at picking winners not losers.[26]

Economic Change, Systems Design and Future-Proofing

There exists a trade-off between optimising the performance of a system under constant observed conditions, and maintaining its resilience to unforeseen circumstances.[27] Take for example the Coronavirus pandemic: what may be have been deemed, before the event, an 'optimal' level of bed capacity in national health systems, according to available resources and an assumed recurrence frequency of pandemics, could potentially have less than expected resilience to actual pandemics, since these are rare events for which the probabilities are not well characterised. A second example is technology choice in climate policy. Recent debate focused the need for substantial negative emissions occurring late century compensating for near-term emissions, scenarios developed on the basis of systems optimisation (IPCC, 2018). This may be a risky and false narrative underplaying real systemic risk, where emissions today contribute to the accumulation of risk of possible future climate tipping points being triggered, a risk not mitigated by future negative emissions.

12.4. POLICY DOMAINS WHERE ROA COULD MAKE A DIFFERENCE

In this section, we provide three examples of domains of policy that could benefit from the ROA approach in generating and incorporating more relevant information its appraisal than the incumbent methods. We explain the rationale for using ROA and the difference ROA makes in comparison to standard approaches.

12.4.1 *Climate Change Mitigation and Low-Carbon Innovation*

Achieving stringent climate targets involves a deep transformation of most of its industries and systems, and a large-scale re-organisation of economic and industrial activity. This does not necessarily imply negative consequences for the economy; it

25 See Chapter 14, as well as Kay et al. (2012); King (2015). For example, in UK electricity, dramatic emissions reductions have been achieved with a carbon price of £35/tCO2e. Meanwhile, the existing petrol fuel duty is equivalent to a staggering £238/tCO2e, and has not induced comparable change.

26 Klingebiel and Rammer (2014); Mazzucato and Penna (2016); Carreras (2020).

27 Carlson and Doyle (2002); Doyle and Carlson (2000).

may however involve distributional impacts, with winners and losers.[28] Winners will arise in new industries where high wage occupations are created; workers in existing high-carbon industries being phased out will be at the losing end.

This Policy Objective Does Not Meet the Criteria for Marginal Analysis:

(1) Stakeholders and their aspirations and needs are heterogeneous, over several dimensions and variables: different industries, sectors, interests, perspectives.
(2) Low-carbon innovation is a non-linear process, featuring strong positive feedback and possible tipping points.[29] Notably, the diffusion of innovations concurrent with learning-by-doing cost reductions have strong potential for rapid disruption.
(3) The impacts of climate change, as well as the outcomes of low-carbon innovation policy, are both characterised by heavy-tailed uncertainty (Weitzman, 2009) and generate important social, financial and economic systemic risks.

Risk-Opportunity Analysis Can Address Targeted Low-Carbon Innovation Policy

Technological costs for addressing climate change are path-dependent, where the state of the technology is conditioned by the story of its development, and will be so in the future (Farmer and Lafond, 2016). This process is taking place with all key components of low-carbon technology, including batteries for electric vehicles. Since the costs and diffusion profiles of those technologies is highly dynamic, to understand their trajectories, feedback must be mapped and understood, and dynamical models must be used to project the ranges of possibilities as results of deliberate policy in the UK and abroad. Notably, substantial first mover advantages can be captured when investing in innovation and technological change.[30]

Opportunities, in the perspective of policy-makers, for economic co-benefits from innovation policy exist (Peñasco et al., 2021), in which the deployment of new technologies involves and enables the development of new capabilities nationally, which allows for the development of new industries and occupations that can become part of the makeup of the future economy and prosperity. The potential for new technologies to promote growth in key sectors can be estimated using detailed dynamical models of industrial transformation and capability on a scenario basis. This option generation potential can be assessed in ROA.

Risks emerging from a rapid low-carbon transition arise, where substantial financial value, labour and capital, invested in high-carbon industry and fossil fuel

[28] Discussed in depth in Chapter 15; see also Mercure et al. (2018a,c, 2021a).
[29] E.g., see Grübler et al. (1999); Grübler (1998).
[30] Rennings (2014); Quitzow et al. (2014).

extraction, transformation, transportation and use across the economy, can become stranded, with substantial financial and socioeconomic implications.[31] Furthermore, further investment now in high-carbon capital through lack of coordination can make the system more fragile. Estimating the accumulation of systemic risk in financial, economic and social networks is increasingly seen by policy-makers as an important part of low-carbon policy appraisal.[32]

Risk-Opportunity Analysis Reaches Different Conclusions to Marginal Analysis

Marginal analysis of climate policy first and foremost recommends pricing the carbon externality. ROA may recommend any combination of sectoral carbon pricing, targeted investment, regulation, or other measures, depending on those measures' likely effectiveness at reducing emissions in their respective contexts and their ability to generate options for economic diversification in sectors and regions affected by post-industrial decline.

12.4.2 *Multi-sector Policy in Response to a Pandemic*

Challenges encountered during the COVID-19 pandemic, and through the government response, have highlighted key salient issues in the need for and use of scientific information for guiding policy decisions (Cheng et al., 2020). Challenges have included determining the level of preparedness that society should continuously maintain, the structure of the health system response, the structure of the economic response and the structure of the stimulus package post-crisis.

Preparedness and Response to Pandemics Do Not Meet Marginal Analysis Criteria:

(1) The likelihood and frequency of pandemics is not a well-known distribution, has a probability tail (a heavy tail) that is not well characterised.[33]
(2) The propagation of diseases is highly non-linear, such that delays in acting result in higher than proportional impacts, damages and loss of life.
(3) Under social distancing policy, the economy falls so far under full-employment equilibrium that the impact of the economic response and stimulus is not well described by equilibrium economic theory.

[31] Battiston et al. (2017); Mercure et al. (2018c).
[32] Bolton et al. (2020); BoE (2018).
[33] For the three points here, see respectively Fan et al. (2016); Dai and Locasale (2020); Coibion et al. (2020).

Risk-Opportunity Analysis Can Address Preparedness, Response and Economic Stimulus

Preparedness. The frequency and magnitude of pandemic events is not known, which makes choosing a suitable level of preparations complex. ROA can help determine the normative balance between what is excessive and likely never to be used, and what is likely necessary to avoid a serious breakdown of the health system, including the adaptive capacity of the existing system. A system that is highly economical is also highly brittle, breaking down at every shock.

Lockdown response. The propagation of diseases is highly non-linear, reflecting the fact that the more people are ill and contagious, the more people are at risk of contracting the disease, and different response timings lead to radically different outcomes. ROA, which is arguably what has in effect been used in the public policy response of many countries, is a suitable framework to integrate outcome data from non-linear epidemiological models, such as those that were used by scientists informing policy-makers, to predict the outcomes and assess the direction of change of contagion in various scenarios of lockdown and social distancing policy.

Economic response. Offering no economic support would have led to systemic loss of aggregate demand and further job losses, which can lead to widespread insolvencies. Excessive support leads to accumulation of public debt that can have an impact on foreign investor confidence and the economy's ability to service debt in the future. ROA could integrate a dynamic economic and financial analysis, under different dynamic scenarios of contagion and response, to evaluate suitable levels of support.

Post-crisis stimulus. How to prioritise the allocation of resources post-crisis should be addressed using dynamical modelling. Some sectors may face higher systemic economic and financial risk than others, notably the energy and heavy industries as well as transport (e.g., aviation). ROA can help determine whether reviving these sectors helps contribute to aggregate demand and restart the economy or leads to stranded investments due to rapid obsolescence or lack of sustained demand.

Risk-Opportunity Analysis Reaches Different Conclusions to Marginal Analysis

An extensive review of cost-benefit methods to determine pandemic preparedness revealed that none of 34 studies included non-marginal system transformations (Kellerborg et al., 2020). Studies of the CBA of lockdown response typically compare the value of lost life against lost GDP, but indicate that the methodology critically depend on the value assigned to quality-adjusted life years, without consensus on the strategy to follow.[34] ROA however offers a deeper sense of the system dynamics at play. For example, due to the non-linearity of disease propagation, early and brief lockdown intervention may have widely different impacts on GDP and contagion

34 Miles et al. (2020); Schonberger et al. (2020); Broughel and Kotrous (2021).

than delayed action of the same or longer duration, analysis that can be done using detailed dynamical modelling over a wide range of possible strategies.

12.4.3 *Regional Development Policy*

Regional development is highly path-dependent, since local industrial, innovation and development capabilities build, to first order, on existing local capabilities. Just as success breeds success, regional development allows the creation of ever higher wage occupations and living standards, which attract further highly skilled labour, which helps fuel development further. Wages typically follow steep spatial gradients between highly and less developed regions across and within countries. Assessing regional development policies based on comparing local productivity, wages and prices can inadvertently exacerbate the typical winner-take-all positive feedback that already exists in the process of development.

Levelling-Up Policy Does Not Meet the Criteria for Marginal Analysis:

(1) Positive feedback exists between the level of development of a region, and its ability to attract resources necessary for further development.
(2) Reverse negative feedback exists where slowdown in regional development drives highly skilled labour away, reinforcing economic decline.
(3) Regional development policy and infrastructure investment affects wages, which attracts new workers and change the fundamental economy in a path-dependent way.
(4) Stakeholders are heterogeneous and many dimensions are involved, notably inequality.

Risk-Opportunity Analysis Can Address Regional Development policy
Targeted investment can catalyse and crowd-in private investment. ROA can analyse whether public authorities can signal a direction of travel to the private sector through local infrastructure investment that may or may not crowd-in further private sector investment. Leadership signals can help companies decide where to locate and access the skills they require. ROA with systems dynamics models can simulate local capability accumulation investment through cumulative causation.

Path-dependence and heavy-tailed uncertainty. The winner-take-all nature of regional development implies that the outcome of intervention is uncertain, depends on history and the way in which it is carried out, and is therefore heavy-tailed uncertain. In ROA, scenarios of development are developed focusing on best and worst case scenarios to determine clearly the bounds of the problem and where the risks lie.

Maximising option generation instead of near-term income. Investing where expected return is highest does not necessarily mean investing where opportunities are highest, since some strategies with lower near-term direct returns can increase the potential for business creation generating higher longer-term indirect returns, compared to strategies with high direct near-term returns but low option generation potential. This is particularly true for the spontaneous emergence of new industry clusters following infrastructure developments or investment in innovation and higher education.

Risk-Opportunity Analysis Reaches Different Conclusions to Marginal Analysis

Infrastructure investment policy appraisal based on static CBA frameworks can identify near-term direct costs and benefits, but indirect, longer-term dynamical outcomes are not identified. Urban simulation models, for example, can help identify indirect, path-dependent impacts and offer a sense of urban planning strategy, while non-equilibrium regional economic models can track the development of capabilities and supply chains in wide ranges of policy strategies.

12.5. CONCLUSION

The next steps in proposing a risk-opportunity analysis framework to replace welfare economics-based policy assessment lie in laying out a framework development roadmap. This roadmap should be co-created in close collaboration with stakeholders and users of the framework. Ideally, this should include actors involved in purposes such as regulating, accounting and strategising. Indeed, such a framework must respond to existing needs in existing science–policy interfaces which must be identified using an expansive engagement program between scientists and decision-makers.

A first part of the roadmap must involve an intensive dissemination program for concepts of complexity science applied to decision-making (dynamics, heterogeneity, uncertainty). A second part should involve developing clear context-dependent guidelines on how to use this framework under diverse situations and problems. The risk-opportunity assessment framework proposed here is as defensible on grounds of social justice and legitimacy as are cost-benefit analyses, multi-criteria assessments and other welfare-economics based policy assessments. However, it makes better and more honest use of available information and uncertainty.

It may be argued that welfare economics and equilibrium-based analysis and decision-making methods have not helped governments see clearly the best opportunities to drive the rapid, structural economic change that is needed to meet climate change goals. As Stern writes, 'The economic response [to climate change] has to be very large, involve dynamic increasing returns, changed economic and urban organisation and design, and the avoidance of potential lock-ins' but 'we have seen models predominate where these elements, the guts of the story, are essentially assumed away' (Stern, 2018). When society faces great challenges, economic analysis that assumes away the most important considerations can lead to unease and distrust of economics and economists on the part of policy-makers (Mercure, 2019) and the public (Haldane and Turrell, 2018). A stronger science-based decision framework may be an important part of the solution.

The next three chapters of this book explore further the relationship between the use of complexity science and ROA in different domains of policy, which will illustrate how to do this in practice.

13

A Science–Policy Interface for the Energy–Water–Food Nexus

This chapter uses as a case study the energy–water–food Nexus, one of the most complex sustainability challenges faced by the world, to propose an effective mode of operation of the science–policy interface for addressing 'wicked' policy problems. This case involves Brazil, where insufficiently well-understood interactions within the Nexus are contributing to large-scale deforestation and land-use change, water and energy scarcity, and increased vulnerability to climate change. The reason is a combination of global and local environmental and economic change, putting unprecedented pressures on the Brazilian environment and ecosystems. The complex interdependence of developments at the global and local levels are analysed, highlighting the impact of global environmental and economic change on Brazil and, conversely, that of developments in Brazil for other countries and the world. A need is thus identified to adjust the scientific approach to these challenges as an enabling condition for stronger science–policy bridges for sustainability policy-making. This chapter is adapted from Mercure et al. (2019b), which was developed as part of research carried out in Brazil.

13.1. INTRODUCTION

Income growth, industrialisation, economic change and globalisation are bringing global demand for energy, water and food to a point increasingly beyond the Earth's carrying capacity.[1] This, in turn, is causing environmental degradation in many tropical natural resource-exporting countries such as Brazil. Such degradation could be seen as a simple management problem but, on closer examination, it results from far more complex interconnections between energy, water and food,[2] referred to as

[1] Beddington (2012); Rockström et al. (2009); Steffen et al. (2015).
[2] Beddington (2012); Hertel (2015); Hoff (2011); Liu et al. (2015).

the Energy–Water–Food Nexus.[3] The term 'complex' is used for Nexus governance to highlight that the problem displays, in particular, four key characteristics typical of so-called 'wicked' problems:[4] first, the pervasive nature of uncertainty in every aspect of the problem, notably both climate and socio-economic change; second, the existence of many different stakeholders with distinct and potentially conflicting values and views; third, the interdependence of all aspects; and finally the limited success of existing governance structures in implementing proposed solutions. Nexus governance is a true 'wicked problem', a practical expression on the ground of the issues discussed in Chapter 1.

This chapter explores the Brazilian Nexus case study to develop and propose the form and structure of an effective science–policy interface that can address the full complexity of complex sustainability policy problems, as a complementary framework to risk-opportunity analysis described in the previous chapter. This structure could be used to address many other domains of unstable complex interacting socio-economic, technology and environmental problems, especially those related to climate change.

Here, Brazil provides a textbook example of the challenges arising from the Nexus. On one hand, it is one of the regions of the planet that will be most affected by climate change. On the other, it is an economy highly driven by and tied to global economic change, through exports of agricultural and energy commodities. Both climate and economic change drive environmental degradation and social challenges, at all scales of analysis, which are allowed or amplified by the shortcomings of the governance system. Moreover, the situation of Brazil is also a relevant comparator for other countries that face Nexus-related challenges (e.g., large-scale land-use change, water scarcity, energy crises) or may face them in the future. Furthermore, it is very likely that tipping points in Brazil could have far-reaching consequences across the world: for the global climate system, food supplies and land-use change emissions.[5] Therefore, policy-makers in all nations could pay attention.

Nexus governance can be supported by robust science, but robust science does not automatically lead to effective policy implementation. Engineering-oriented views focus on searching for optimal policy solutions in order to internalise system-wide externalities, maximise system efficiency and minimise waste.[6] The application of such an approach requires the existence of sufficiently good models to optimise Nexus governance choices. But complexity science warns of the dangers in such assumptions. Indeed, as seen in earlier chapters, complex interactions may lead to new and unpredictable phenomena. As discussed in Chapter 12, human knowledge and predictive power over a complex system is always limited, while decisions must

3 Nexus henceforth, see Bazilian et al. (2011); Keairns et al. (2016); Kurian (2017); Leck et al. (2015); Weitz et al. (2017).
4 Rittel and Webber (1973); Head and Alford (2015).
5 Brando et al. (2014); Lenton et al. (2008); Piesse and Thirtle (2009); Baccini et al. (2012).
6 For instance Hoff (2011); Bazilian et al. (2011); Bajželj et al. (2014); Garcia and You (2016).

be taken using available resources. It is unrealistic to assume the existence, even theoretically, of an ultimate Nexus planner that could optimise such a complex system. Reliance on optimisation has the effect of downplaying path-dependent phenomena, such as behavioural feedback. Path-dependence, representing the influence of developmental, technological and socio-political histories, is not limited to what has happened in Brazil. The range of realistic options is highly dependent upon paths taken elsewhere. The global–local interaction is therefore a necessary component of the analysis, which tends to be overlooked by a focus on a hypothetical Nexus planner optimising conditions in one country.

A new approach for Nexus analysis is proposed for formulating integrated Nexus policy strategies in the presence of partial knowledge and understanding, and substantial uncertainty. This includes integrating science deeply in the process of policy-making, developing a science–policy–law interface to identify Nexus-resilient public policy solutions, which could be determined on the basis of, for instance, risk-opportunity analysis (Chapter 12). The chapter first summarises the general context of global environmental and economic change as drivers of the Nexus challenges faced by Brazil. This is followed by four case studies that combine economic, scientific, legal and policy data to illustrate the intricate environmental and social interconnections between each node of the Nexus in Brazil: energy–water, food–energy, water–food and energy–water–food. Significantly, the four case studies highlight the role of complexity in Nexus challenges. A proposal is made on how a change in the scientific approach to the Nexus could contribute to a more functional science–policy bridge, and how this bridge could enable the design and implementation of Nexus-resilient public policies.

13.2. REVIEW OF THE GENERAL CONTEXT

13.2.1 *Global and Local Environmental Change*

Brazil is likely to experience amongst the most pronounced of the effects of climate change. Figure 13.1 shows maps of changes in mean temperatures and rainfall for low and high emissions scenarios. In a scenario of continued high global emissions, temperature changes of up to 3–6°C could occur over the Amazonian region, potentially severely degrading vegetation and ecosystems. Meanwhile, in such a scenario, rainfall could be significantly disturbed, increasing by 60% in the southern regions while it could decrease by 40% in arid regions of the north. These changes would have serious impacts on agriculture and food production in Brazil. However, these projections also rank amongst the least certain globally, partly because the Amazon rainforest is intimately connected with the local and global climate, and land use, making it complex to predict.[7] Brazil has recently faced several droughts, with

7 Christensen et al. (2013); Malhi et al. (2008); Phillips et al. (2009).

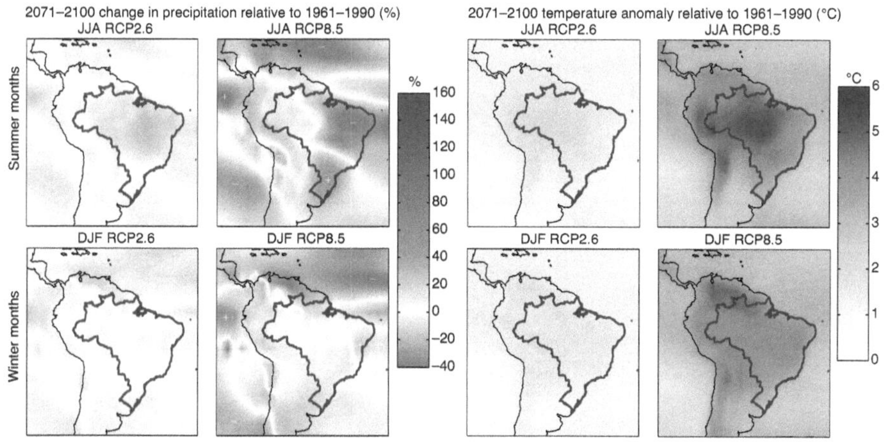

FIGURE 13.1 Changes in annual average rainfall (as a % change to annual averages) and mean temperature, in the summer (top panels) and the winter (bottom panels), for low cumulative global GHG emissions (left panels) and high cumulative emissions (right panels). In scenarios of high emissions, temperature changes of up to 6°C are expected over the Amazonian region, and rainfall changes of +60% and −40% are expected in North-Eastern and Southern Brazil, respectively (Mercure et al., 2019b).

evidence suggesting that changing rainfall patterns will lead to reduced river flows in several catchment areas.[8] The Brazilian rainforest is particularly sensitive to drought events. A self-reinforcing interaction exists between temperature change, drying, forest fires, deforestation and a collapse of the Amazonian rainforest.[9] In particular, drought-fire interactions generate one of the possible tipping points.[10] However, here tipping points come about through a combination of direct and indirect anthropogenic factors.

In recent years, Brazil's Cerrado biome and the Amazon have both been exposed to increased rainfall intensity during the wet season followed by longer-than-usual dry seasons. In 2014–2015, the state of São Paulo experienced a severe water crisis driven by below-average rainfall. Water in this region is supplied by moisture from the Amazon and the South Atlantic through low-level easterly jets.[11] During the drought period, the regional atmospheric circulation was blocked by a high-pressure system in the mid-troposphere.[12] This barrier changed moisture transport from the Amazon to South-Eastern Brazil. These changes were unpredictable, but most likely have anthropogenic roots, and could become recurrent.

8 Marengo and Bernasconi (2015); Lewis et al. (2011); Escobar (2015); Davidson et al. (2012).
9 Phillips et al. (2009); Nobre et al. (2016); Nepstad et al. (2008).
10 Brando et al. (2014); Lenton et al. (2008).
11 Fearnside (2005); Zemp et al. (2017).
12 Marengo et al. (2016); Nobre et al. (2016).

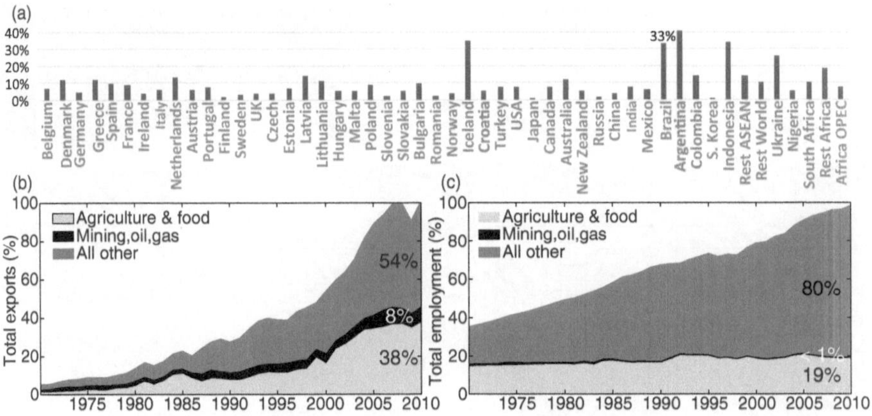

FIGURE 13.2 (a) Current share of total exports consisting of agricultural products and food by country (33% for Brazil). (b) Total exports, normalised to 2010. (c) Corresponding shares of employment, normalised to 2010. Data from Eurostat, OECD, national statistics, Asian Dev. Bank, UN prodcom (Mercure et al., 2019b).

A changing climate leads plant and animal species to migrate and/or evolve. In Brazil, this phenomenon affects agricultural activities, as land productivity changes with the climate, primarily as a result of rainfall changes and water availability.[13] Under severe climate change, this could involve large-scale land-use change, which would mean significant biodiversity loss. As agricultural activities re-organise themselves, Brazilian society itself is affected. Thus, climate change would result in pronounced pressures on Brazilian food production, itself accounting for a large component of economic activities in Brazil, and of the world's food-supply sources.

13.2.2 *Global Economic Change Driving Environmental Degradation*

The Brazilian economy benefits from lucrative exports of agricultural and food products (Figure 13.2). These account for around one third of total Brazilian exports making Brazil one of the countries with the highest export shares in that sector. These goods have traditionally accounted for a major component of Brazilian exports and their production employs a significant portion of the entire Brazilian labour force. These figures place Brazil in a context of growing wealth associated to exports of natural resources, driven by growing purchasing power worldwide. However, these data also signal the significant vulnerability of the Brazilian economy. Voluminous exports of natural resources are made lucrative by international prices, supported

[13] Burrows et al. (2011); Jump and Penuelas (2005); Wheeler and Von Braun (2013).

by high demand in many other nations around the world (particularly Chinese imports of soybeans), and export growth is thus strongly driven by economic growth in other large emerging economies. This economic pressure is well known to strain the Brazilian environment through man-made deforestation and land-use change that creates space to expand agriculture,[14] a phenomenon often involving indirect land-use change (ILUC).

ILUC refers to the phenomenon in which an event of land-use change in one place induces another event of land-use change elsewhere, mediated by commodity and land prices.[15] In Brazil, this typically involves a hierarchy of production associated to land productivity, where the most productive land is converted to produce new lucrative crops for exports (e.g., soybeans, sugar cane), displacing cattle farming, which itself moves to occupy other areas that are deforested before use. Deforestation in the Amazon has declined from 2004 to 2014 as authorities have managed to regulate farmers' behaviour partly by law enforcement and partly by economic measures. Intensification and commoditisation of agriculture also contributed to reduced rates of deforestation. However, the deforestation in the Amazon has increased again from August 2015 to July 2016, and then dramatically under the Bolsonaro government after 2018. Over the thirty years prior to 2018, the Cerrado has lost 50% of its native vegetation cover. Deforestation is likely to continue mostly because it is linked to global markets growth for agricultural commodities, mediated by prices, and made possible by globalisation, giving rise to powerful incentives for agribusiness to acquire new land in Brazil.[16]

Agricultural products, grown either as feedstock for biofuel production or to feed animals, contribute to this phenomenon.[17] Under climate change mitigation policy following the Paris Agreement, global markets for biofuels could virtually be unbounded. Meanwhile, under growing affluence and increasingly meat-intense diets in middle-income countries, global markets for soy as animal feed can become very large. Concerns over the sustainability of biofuel mandates have raised sufficient concern in Europe to revise this policy trajectory,[18] but this may not necessarily deter policy-makers in other large economies. Indeed, despite sustainability concerns,[19] biofuels remain a key component of the national strategy of many countries to mitigate climate change.[20] Thus a large global market for liquid biofuels for transport could be expected to emerge by 2050, notably for land and air transportation.

14 E.g., see Nepstad et al. (2008).
15 Barona et al. (2010); Arima et al. (2011); Lapola et al. (2010); Morton et al. (2006).
16 Lapola et al. (2014); Lambin and Meyfroidt (2011).
17 Nepstad et al. (2008); Lapola et al. (2010); Nepstad et al. (2006); Searchinger et al. (2008).
18 See, e.g., Bowyer and Kretschmer (2010).
19 Lapola et al. (2010); Searchinger et al. (2008); Fargione et al. (2008).
20 Bowyer and Kretschmer (2010); Harvey and Pilgrim (2011); IEA (2021).

Estimates of the world's carrying capacity for biofuel production consider only land leftover after global food demand has been supplied.[21] However, no evidence exists to suggest that food demand will be supplied before energy demand, since biofuel consumers in some regions can easily, and inadvertently, outbid food consumers in others. Brazil could very likely face this intricate problem.

13.2.3 *The Policy Landscape Addressing the Nexus*

The government has recently acknowledged the need to adapt existing regulation and to create new policies to manage these challenges. Although Brazil has comprehensive water, energy and food governance frameworks, each sector has evolved separately and is organised independently from the other two. The law and policy pertaining to each sector only occasionally and marginally refer to issues arising in other sectors. Such fragmentation is what makes Nexus challenges pressing.

The climate change framework in Brazil includes some integrative guidance and instruments to deal with the Nexus. Since the 2000s, Brazil has adopted climate change legislation and policies that establish the country's voluntary emissions reduction target and incorporate laws and policies relating to climate change.[22] The development of new and existing legal and policy instruments will require capacity building, intergovernmental coordination, monitoring systems, and the improvement of the climate change projections to be better reflected in public policies.

Measures from international law also have influence in Brazil at the supply-chain governance level, to improve sustainability in agricultural commodity production. These measures include regulating or incentivising global market access by certain products. This includes certification requirements for producers to respect sustainability standards or the use of specific labels reflecting abidance by such standards. They result from a coordinated effort between local governments, producers, consumer groups, others directly involved in commodity supply-chains and civil society groups. Brazil has also received international finance as a result of its verified emissions reductions.

13.3. NEXUS ANALYSIS: FOUR CASE STUDIES

13.3.1 *Selection of Case Studies of Cross-Sectoral Interactions*

Four case studies are selected to chart the most important Nexus interactions relevant for Brazil as well as the shortcomings of the existing governance framework:

[21] Hoogwijk et al. (2009); Smeets et al. (2007); Mercure (2012); GEA (2012).

[22] A full overview of the policies as they were in 2018 is given in Mercure et al. (2019b) and Paim et al. (2020). This landscape has been changing rapidly, however, following the populist approach of the government that followed.

1. the **Water–Energy** (W–E) link, focusing on water use for hydroelectricity under increasing climate change constraints;
2. the **Energy–Food** (E–F) link, focusing on the competition for land between energy and food production sparked by biofuels policy;
3. the **Food–Water** (F–W) link, focusing on the impact of climate change on food production in Brazil;
4. simultaneous **Water–Energy–Food** (W–E–F) links, focusing both on ILUC generated by global demand for agricultural and bio-energy commodities produced in Brazil, and on the scarcity of suitable land resulting from climate change.

13.3.2 W–E – *Hydroelectricity and Climate Change*

Climate change is modifying rainfall patterns in Brazil.[23] A water crisis has emerged in recent years, which has resulted in record low levels in hydroelectric dam reservoirs, where persistent drought has also affected agriculture in the North-East region.[24] In the São Paulo region, where 10% of the Brazilian population live and one third of GDP is produced, water scarcity from 2014 to 2016 generated both electricity blackouts and a drinking water crisis leading to the rationing of both. The water crisis is a problem of water management and efficiency of use, but it is related to local and global environmental change, while it affects and is governed by policy in both the water and energy sectors simultaneously. In particular, electricity policy encouraging the use of water for generation of energy directly affects drinking water availability. According to the water policy, the water management must promote multiple uses of water including for the generation of energy and direct human use, except in case of water scarcity, when priority is given to the latter. In practice, the lack of definition of water allocation priorities causes increasing water competition conflicts between the energy and water supply sectors, especially during water shortage periods and before scarcity is reached.[25]

The Brazilian electricity system is largely based on hydroelectricity,[26] making it low-carbon, but also vulnerable to changes in climate and rainfall.[27] The Brazilian electricity system features 219 hydroelectric dams, one of the largest systems in the world. The vast majority of the large-scale generators (99.5%) are connected by the National Interconnected System. Modelling suggests that in most hydrological basins, river flows will decline in all climate change scenarios. These projections

[23] IPCC (2013); Davidson et al. (2012).
[24] Escobar (2015); Nobre et al. (2016); Marengo and Bernasconi (2015).
[25] Benjamin et al. (2004).
[26] Greater than 62.6% according to IEA data.
[27] De Lucena et al. (2009); Prado Jr et al. (2016); da Silva Soito and Freitas (2011); da Silva et al. (2016); Paim et al. (2019).

place constraints on the future composition of the Brazilian electricity sector, and technological diversification appears inevitable. This is challenging if the objective is to simultaneously maintain low CO_2 emissions, although non-hydro renewables could contribute to alleviate pressure on water resources.

The country's overreliance on hydro became conspicuous in 2001, when a combination of below-average rainfall and insufficient investments in new generation capacity culminated in a major electricity supply crisis. In order to avoid blackouts, a 20% demand reduction was required at short notice, and twenty-two of the twenty-seven Brazilian states were instructed to implement rationing policies.[28] These measures were in place for less than a year, but had a lasting effect on people's energy-use: 90% of households changed their consumption habits, with a 14% reduction in electricity use that remained ten years later. This suggests a large potential for efficiency improvements in the Nexus that can be realised by targeted policies. But also, the 'energy efficiency gap' unveiled an underlying 'water efficiency gap'.[29]

Hydropower projects have continued to obtain the go-ahead from authorities since the Ten Year Plan 2024 was released in 2015. The majority of new dam projects are in the Amazon basin, where most of Brazil's remaining hydroelectric potential lies, demanding comparatively large investments to connect these to the transmission grid, with environmental impacts associated with flooding areas of rich biodiversity and often under indigenous occupation. The implementation of the Belo Monte hydropower power plant offers a good illustration of the emerging complexity.[30] The Ten-Year Energy Plan 2026, released in 2017, features less dependency on hydropower, and aims at increasing non-hydro renewables (wind, solar, biomass).

It is clear that diversification of the power grid could improve water security, by giving hydro dams better flexibility to regulate water supplies. The national adaptation plan envisions that the electricity sector planning follows climate change projections. However, it does not indicate how this goal is to become operative in the context of long-term power plans oriented towards the expansion of hydroelectricity. Aligned with the climate policy pledge, reserving a proportionate role for large hydropower systems and taking into account Brazil's vast potential for low-cost solar and wind resources, could be an approach for tackling risks to water availability. This strategy responds to the environmental concerns surrounding backup thermal power plants used during periods of water shortage to secure energy supply in the national grid interconnection. Meanwhile, establishment of water policy priorities or criteria for allocating water amongst different users could ultimately mitigate competition for the water supply, especially coming from the energy sector.

28 Using quotas, financial incentives and information campaigns, see Maurer et al. (2005).
29 Costa (2013); Lynham and Tarui (2014).
30 Berchin et al. (2015).

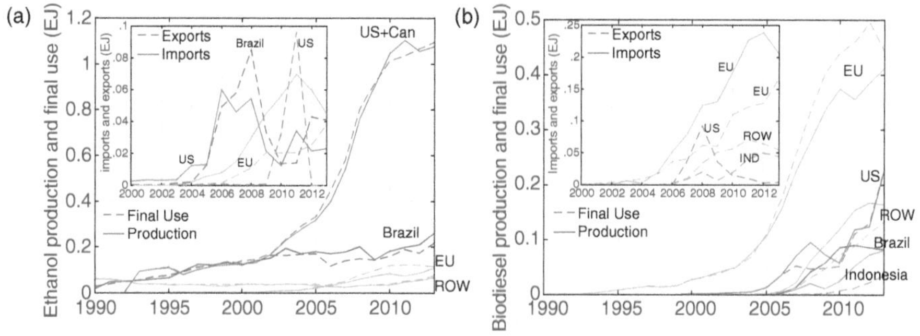

FIGURE 13.3 Biofuel production, final use, imports and exports worldwide. (a) Ethanol. (b) Biodiesel. The main charts show production and final use, while the insets show imports and exports. Data from IEA World Energy Balances (2017) (Mercure et al., 2019b).

13.3.3 *E–F – Biofuels and Competition for Land*

The global demand for first generation liquid biofuel feedstocks such as sugar cane, maize and soy has grown rapidly in the past decade due to the increasing adoption of policies to decarbonise transport fuels and to support local biofuel industries (e.g., in the USA; see Figure 13.3). This new demand requires a dedicated supply of agricultural products, which has the potential to partially displace existing food production. Brazil produces a substantial share of the global supply for agricultural commodities for biofuels, notably sugar cane and soybeans (see below). Prices for internationally traded agricultural commodities can fluctuate widely, in connection to oil and biofuels, leading to complex interdependencies.

Since 2008, a significant body of research has developed issuing a stark warning regarding (i) the carbon sustainability of biofuels and (ii) the competition for land that the development of large biofuel markets could generate, with the potential to price out local agriculture for food and lead to food price volatility as well as restrict access to food.[31] These studies primarily emphasise the effects of ILUC as a driver of linkages across activities, environmental impacts and markets, mediated by commodity and land prices.

The complexity of these linkages is appreciated and debated in both science and policy circles. However, it has not yet been translated into consensus over appropriate policy solutions, which creates uncertainty for the development of the sector. Yet, large-scale biofuel use is considered as a necessary component of climate change mitigation scenarios consistent with the Paris Agreement.[32]

[31] E.g., see Liu et al. (2015); Nepstad et al. (2008); Lapola et al. (2014); Searchinger et al. (2008); Fargione et al. (2008).

[32] E.g., see IPCC (2018); Rose et al. (2014); Mercure et al. (2018b).

In order to implement the Paris Agreement, biofuel mandates are thus likely to be substantially increased worldwide. Global liquid biofuel use in transport could easily exceed 5–10 EJ,[33] which would entail that, given land availability, comparatively low production costs and the current advanced development of the sector, Brazilian agriculture could be incentivised to supply a substantial fraction of these bioenergy feedstocks. This would require large areas of additional land for sugar cane for ethanol and/or soybeans for biodiesel. Land areas currently available for biofuels production in Brazil amount to 85.6 Mha excluding cropland and pastures, 41.8 Mha when safeguarding protected areas, and 37.8 Mha when excluding the Amazon altogether. Land requirements for biofuel feedstocks are between 20.2 and 2.3 ha/1,000 GJ for soybeans and sugar cane. Thus, between less than 37 EJ (sugar cane ethanol) and less than 2 EJ (soybean biodiesel) of liquid biofuels can be produced in Brazil depending on the crop used. Several EJ of biofuel demand in Brazil could incentivise farmers to produce beyond current limits, especially if other demands for land are simultaneously growing, causing ILUC cascades.[34]

Brazil's biofuel policies date back to the oil shock of 1973, and have been historically geared towards energy security and rural development, with limited concerns for their ecological impact and potential competition with food production.[35] It was only with the commodity and biofuels boom of the mid-2000s that increased production and exports raised questions of competition with food production and of deforestation in the Cerrado and the Amazon.

In this context, Brazilian authorities took some measures to promote the sustainable development of biofuels. At the federal level, the main framework regulating sugar cane expansion is the Agro-Environmental Zoning. Based on agricultural potential, land vulnerability, climate risks and environmental regulations, it defines suitable areas for the expansion of sugar cane, and excludes cultivation in areas with original vegetation cover or highly bio-diverse regions, including the Amazon and Pantanal biomes and others (e.g., indigenous land, conservation areas). It prioritises expansion in under-used areas, areas occupied by livestock and degraded pastures. However, one major limitation is that it does not consider potential competition between sugar cane and food production within those areas. It does not address issues relating to water availability, energy planning or socio-economic aspects.

The development of biofuels policy was interrupted in the EU due to sustainability concerns. However, the attraction to low-carbon fuels may not necessarily be limited by sustainability concerns in other emerging economies such as China and India, and thus this may change again. Although the current policy framework goes some way towards addressing environmental issues, it has serious limitations and does

33 $5\text{–}10 \times 10^{18}$ J of thermal energy; global primary energy use $\simeq$ 500 EJ.

34 See Mercure et al. (2018b); Adami et al. (2012); Lossau et al. (2015); Miller (2010) for the values used.

35 Garcez and de Souza Vianna (2009); La Rovere et al. (2011); Wilkinson and Herrera (2010).

not adequately address the potential displacement of food production by energy crops. ILUC cascades are likely to intensify from further biofuel expansion and affect deforestation.

13.3.4 *F–W – Climate Change Impacts*

In future climate change scenarios, large areas of land may be at risk of degradation as a result of more frequent drought in the North and North-East of Brazil, while lands in the South are likely to suffer from more frequent flooding and erosion.[36] A tipping point involving the collapse of the Amazon through droughts and fires could also be on the horizon.[37] Inhabitants of the North-East of Brazil (the Caatinga) traditionally cope with frequent droughts, but this area could undergo desertification as a result of climate change. Under scenarios of productivity collapse, people migrate, and thus agricultural activities also effectively migrate, as some farmers abandon their land to find work in cities while other farmers plant crops that used to be grown elsewhere. Climate change will lead to substantial regional economic losses for the North-East and other areas.[38]

The effects of climate change will likely push maize, soybeans and sugar cane grown over much of the territory to migrate, as land productivity evolves. Scenarios of land productivity changes and yield of crop types in Brazil are shown in Figure 13.4, generated using a global dynamic vegetation model, which simulates the transient changes in carbon and water cycles due to land use, specific phenology and seasonal CO_2 fluxes in carbon and water cycles of agricultural-dominated areas, as well as the production of crops and grazing lands. Effectively, the model allows for assessing a broad range of feedback within the terrestrial biosphere as increasingly shaped by human activities such as climate change and land use.

Simulations of crop yields show that under a high emissions scenario (RCP 8.5), land productivity for all four commodities decreases substantially, except for sugar cane, which may find more suitable conditions in the South. Productivity loss under a low emissions scenario (RCP 2.6) is less pronounced but still likely to occur. Maize declines steeply in the North and North-East, which could induce substantial socio-economic changes. Soybeans, grown in the South and in the Cerrado, could be constrained to the South, with substantial impacts on exports. The cane industry, traditionally rain-fed and situated in the São Paulo area, is currently expanding to drier areas in the North where irrigation is required.[39] Finally, pastures could also be displaced from their traditional southern heartland.

36 Marengo and Bernasconi (2015); Marengo et al. (2013); Barros et al. (2013).
37 Malhi et al. (2008); Davidson et al. (2012); Cook et al. (2012).
38 Barbieri et al. (2010); Confalonieri et al. (2014); de Souza Ferreira Filho and De Moraes (2015).
39 Fachinelli and Pereira Jr (2015); Rudorff et al. (2010).

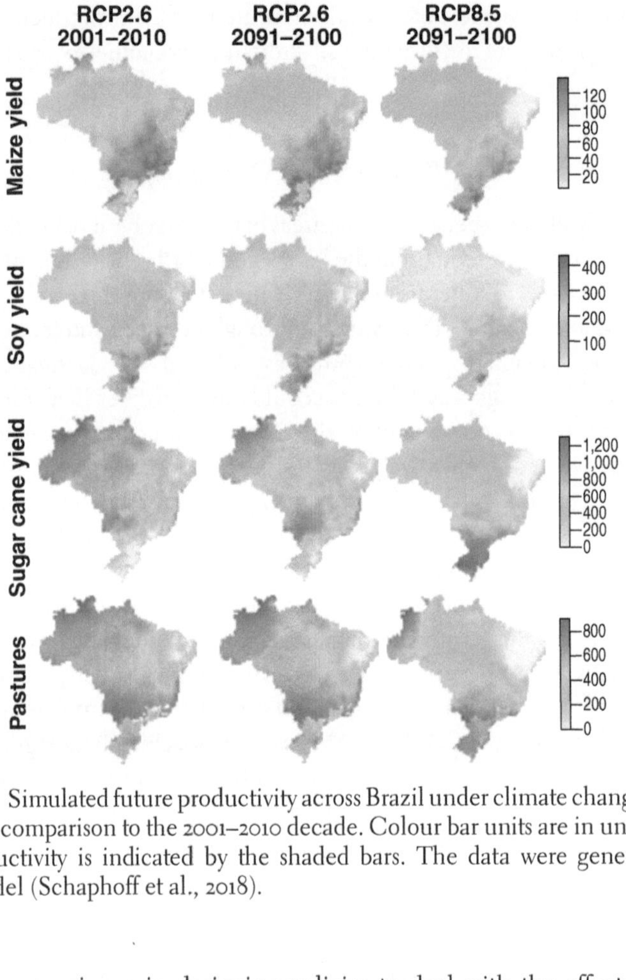

FIGURE 13.4 Simulated future productivity across Brazil under climate change for various land-uses in comparison to the 2001–2010 decade. Colour bar units are in units of gC/m^2, where productivity is indicated by the shaded bars. The data were generated by the LPJml4 model (Schaphoff et al., 2018).

Brazil has experience in designing policies to deal with the effects of climate variability on the farming sector. In 1996, the Agricultural Climate-Risk Zoning was implemented to minimise risks from adverse climate events on crops. At that time, it was designed to reduce the large number of payment claims faced by the rural public insurance as a result of crop losses caused by either floods or droughts. It comprises a crop year calendar with the zoning of the most suitable crops for each region and the best period for planting, considering the soil conditions and the crop cycling capacities.

The Low-Carbon Plan was created in 2011 to reduce agricultural GHG emissions, and it includes the provision of low-interest loans for farmers who implement low-carbon agricultural practices. It provides for climate change adaptation measures to ensure food security, including the development of projects, research, and the transfer of technologies to increase efficiency and resilience of agro-ecosystems, to maintain productivity under biotic and abiotic climate change pressures, to foster sustainable and integrated uses of water and soil, and to consider the climate modelling of different agricultural systems. Although several years have elapsed since its creation, the Plan is not yet fully implemented, mostly due to lack of awareness by farmers, lack of skilled technical assistance amongst farmers to implement new technologies, insufficient technical support from public or private agencies, regional disparities in the allocation of credits, and lack of monitoring to ensure compliance.[40] Projected climate variations call for further agricultural risk-management policies. Some steps have been taken to integrate climate change scenarios when amending existing public policies that address climate risks in agriculture. However, implementation challenges remain, mainly as regards the ability of the public sector to put in practice the required policy adjustments and to address social and regional economic disparities. Meanwhile, more sound water and electricity policy could contribute in alleviating risks of food availability crises, while land-use policy itself affects the land's water recycling ability and thus influences the availability of water and energy.[41]

13.3.5 *W–E–F – ILUC and Deforestation*

The deforestation of the Amazon was initially attributed, besides infrastructure extension and selective logging, to expanding cattle and soy industries. Deforestation was shown to be statistically related to changes in the international soy price. However, it was later established that the expansion of soybean crops takes place at the expense of pastures, which are less profitable, and that it is the increasing search for new pastureland that predominantly accounts for forest clearing.[42] In other words, soybean producers are not directly responsible for setting fire to the forest for clearing purposes. Yet, soybean producers are not merely displacing cattle ranchers; they are also acquiring newly deforested land from them. Indeed, cattle ranchers often speculate on the future sale price of the land they want to deforest and the land is used for grazing until it is sold to soybean farmers. How illegally deforested land is initially acquired is not fully clear, although it seems to be a combination of deficient land registration, poor law enforcement, legal loopholes, bribes and risk-taking.

A close relationship exists between the Brazilian soybean industry and the Chinese meat industry.[43] China imports over half of Brazil's production of soybeans to supply fast growing pork and poultry industries (Figures 13.5 and 13.6), for direct human consumption of derivatives (oil, flour, etc.), and to produce biodiesel. China's demand for meat follows its fast domestic income growth, allowing consumers to eat meat more frequently. Due to their high protein content, soybeans are predominantly

40 Marengo et al. (2011); Newton et al. (2016).
41 Zemp et al. (2017); Spera et al. (2016).
42 Garcia (2011); Morton et al. (2006); Barona et al. (2010); Arima et al. (2011).
43 See, e.g., Brown-Lima et al. (2010b).

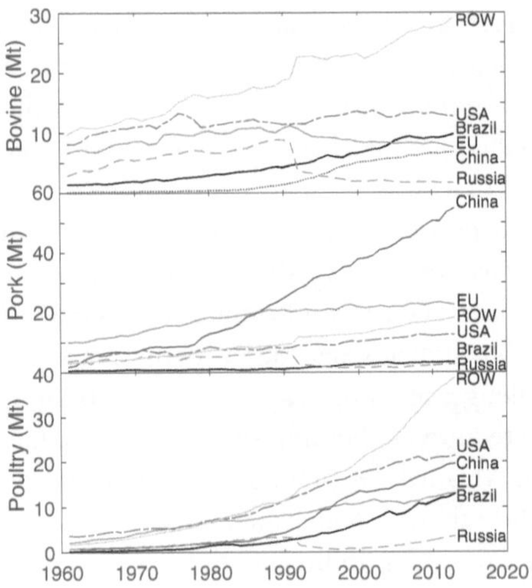

FIGURE 13.5 Meat production around the world, for bovine, pork and poultry (Mercure et al., 2019b).

used to feed animals. China's consumption of soybeans has far outpaced its domestic production, partly as a result of its water shortages. Increasing desertification in areas previously used to grow this crop has indirectly transferred production to Brazil. Under climate change scenarios, larger amounts of land-use may be transferred from China to Brazil in this way.

The USA is the largest producer of soybeans in the world. However, its soybean cropland area is not expanding, and thus production growth allocates itself to Brazil and Argentina, which have historically been able to accommodate it. Meanwhile, the sugar cane-based ethanol industry is also growing in Brazil, expanding far outside of its traditional growing region in the State of São Paulo. It could potentially occupy land currently used for soybean crops or cattle, depending on prices, and trigger ever more complex cascades of ILUC and deforestation.

Deforestation of the Amazon and of the Cerrado could in fact also explain changes in the water cycle that have led to water scarcity in cities and in the hydroelectric system. It is well established that cutting trees down reduces evapotranspiration. Roots pump below-ground water vertically upward, it then transpires through the leaves and the resulting humidity rises to the atmosphere to form clouds. Over the Amazon this biotic pump is so powerful that the resulting pressure difference attracts additional humidity from the Atlantic, which in return falls down as rain in the Eastern and North-eastern Amazon. Deforestation has recently been shown to alter the feedback between land and atmosphere in the water cycle.[44] While this is not

44 Fearnside (2005); Zemp et al. (2017).

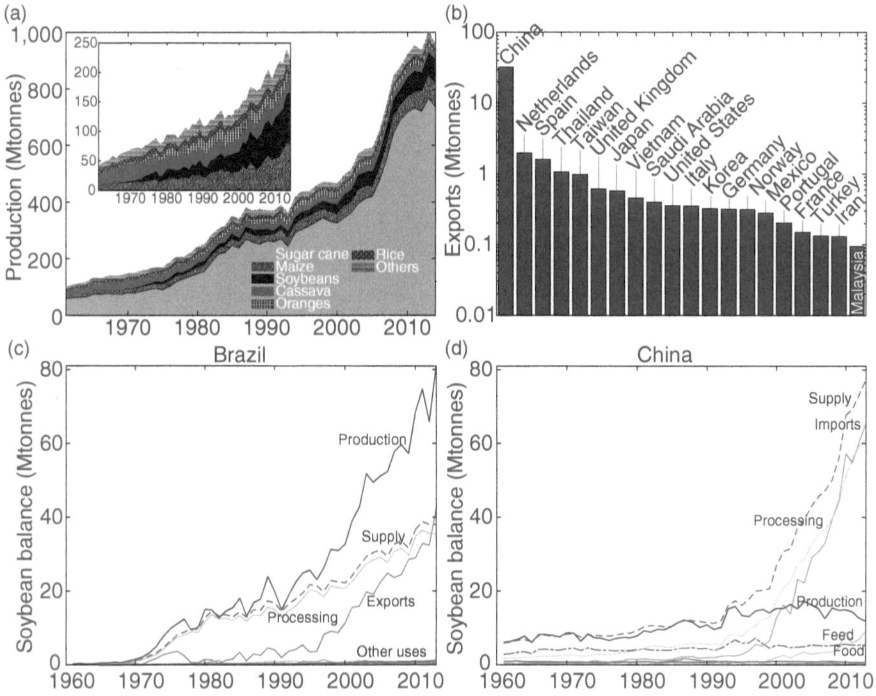

FIGURE 13.6 (a) Main crops produced in Brazil. The inset shows the same data for clarity. (b) Main export destinations for soybeans. (c) and (d) Balance of soybeans in Brazil and China. The 'domestic supply' equals 'production' plus 'imports' minus 'exports', while 'food' denotes domestic consumption as food. 'Feed' denotes direct (unprocessed) use to feed animals, although soybeans mostly go through 'processing' before they are used as feed. Over 50% of soybeans produced in Brazil are destined for the Chinese market, processed there for feeding pigs. Data from FAOSTAT 2017 (Mercure et al., 2019b).

fully established, water scarcity events could potentially ultimately be associated with ILUC and with the expansion of food commodity production for exports.

From 2004 to 2014, deforestation in the Amazon Forest slowed down in Brazil due to a complex combination of factors. Amongst the public policies adopted by Brazilian authorities, the 2004 Action Plan for Prevention and Control of Deforestation in the Legal Amazon has achieved effective results in monitoring, controlling and taking enforcement actions in areas affected by deforestation. It includes the regularisation of occupied federal public lands, the expansion of protected areas, the granting of legal status to indigenous land, and some restrictions in access to credit from public financial institutions imposed on those who have infringed environmental legislation.

Whereas such policies partly explain the slowing down in deforestation in the Amazon during that period, other important factors include a temporary slowdown in the demand for soy and beef, intensification of beef production, and measures targeting the supply-chain governance of these commodities. Amongst the latter, of note are the moratoria on soy and beef produced on recently deforested land and steps to meet technical standards in foreign markets,[45] including a certificate system for sustainable soy. These developments are encouraging but, realistically, their effectiveness has been truly tested when international demand for soy and beef rose again. Deforestation has become widespread again as the Bolsonaro government relaxed laws regulating the agribusiness.

The combination of climate change, climate policy and growing food consumption internationally may have been unleashing a new complex deforestation storm in Brazil post-2018, due to how it has been governed since. Deforestation rates in the Amazon have been increasing again, and in the Cerrado it has never been under control. Climate change will reduce land productivity, which could force rent-seeking farmers to source additional cropland, which would likely be supplied through ILUC. Climate policy, inside and outside Brazil, could develop a substantial global demand for biofuels, which could induce larger expansion of sugar cane plantations leading to additional ILUC. Globally growing demand for meat and biofuels can give rise to unprecedented pressures on remaining natural resources and forests in Brazil.

Brazil has been taking measures to fight deforestation. However, while crucial, the approach does not tackle international demand for commodities as an underlying driver, further affected by climate change pressures. The combination of intersectoral agriculture, forest policies and trade measures, at the global level, could be part of a broader and more effective solution. The moratoria on soy is an example of the supply-chain governance of commodities that has helped reduce deforestation for soy in the Amazon, although it does not in fact prevent ILUC. The supply-chain governance can include other policies, such as certification and labelling requirements, although the certificate system for sustainable soy in Brazil has not been as effective as the moratorium on soy, mainly due to higher risks for producers not selling their produce.[46]

In conclusion, what emerges from studying ILUC and Amazon and Cerrado deforestation in Brazil is that many processes contribute to this effect, all of which are Nexus-related and involve all scales from local to global:

1. global demand for agricultural commodities (notably soybeans going to China for meat production) requires increasing amounts of land;
2. existing policies prevent direct land-use change but not ILUC, incentivising the use of loop-holes in which complex ILUC cascades emerge;

45 Lapola et al. (2010); Nepstad et al. (2014); Tollefson (2015).
46 Gibbs et al. (2015); Meijer (2015).

3. climate change, deforestation and associated changes in the water cycle lead to changes in the productivity of the land, and crop yields that may exacerbate land scarcity and accelerate the process of ILUC and deforestation;
4. insufficiently resilient governance structures are made weaker by strong economic incentives for land grabbing to produce ever larger amounts of food commodities for export.

Deforestation could lead to the ultimate downfall of the whole Brazilian agribusiness as the Amazon and Cerrado biomes are irreversibly altered. Thus, the issue of ILUC and deforestation affects all nodes and aspects of the Nexus in Brazil: water security (deforestation destabilises the water cycle), food security (competition for land between the agribusiness and other uses) and energy security (water instability affecting rainfall and hydropower, land availability for biofuel feedstocks).

13.4. POLICY IMPLICATIONS

It is challenging to devise clear policy implications when faced with a 'wicked' problem such as the Nexus, precisely for the reasons that define a 'wicked' problem: knowledge is incomplete, and optimal solutions can by definition not be identified. Possible optimal solutions identified with current knowledge are only ever illusory, as new information and scientific advances change the constraints of optimisation problems, leading to different solutions, while ad hoc assumptions that could be used to cover for missing knowledge can lead to misleading conclusions. A profound recognition of the complexity of the Nexus and of our limited understanding is paramount to making any progress addressing the Nexus with public policies. Table 13.1 summarises the Nexus challenges surveyed here. Figure 13.7 illustrates the Brazilian Nexus with its external influences related to global economic and environmental change, and relevant institutions at various scales, with a proposed science–policy interface.

For this degree of complexity, where the feedback at play is not even all known, even the framework of risk-opportunity analysis (previous chapter) becomes challenging to carry out, and further institutional developments are needed. Nexus-resilient policy-making requires integration and consistency of action across sectors according to current scientific knowledge. It is important to note, however, that Nexus integration does not actually recommend the creation of integrated ministries, or of a 'Nexus' government department. By contrast, it recommends an enhancement of the science–policy interface for all governance institutions in order to make it Nexus-savvy. This can be achieved in two main forms. First, making use of a scientific board of Nexus experts to check for Nexus feedback in proposed policies, using a standardised procedure that makes use of Nexus modelling tools, that promotes finding empirical evidence and makes use of qualitative studies on the coherence of

TABLE 13.1 *Summary of Nexus challenges in Brazil.*

	Challenges		
Case study	Environmental	Socio-economic	Policy
W–E: Hydro-electricity	• Water scarcity • Competition among users • Reserve thermoelectric plants increase GHG emissions • Dam projects in the Amazon affect biodiversity and indigenous land	• Energy security • Over-reliance on hydroelectricity • Diversification of the energy matrix • Investment in new capacity due to increasing energy demand	• Improving policy coherence • Incorporating climate change impacts in long-term energy planning • Reducing reliance on water resources in long-term energy planning • Elaborating plan for high potential renewables
E–F: Biofuels	• Crop expansion beyond traditional areas • ILUC • Water use • Unsustainable agricultural practices including sugar cane burning for manual harvesting	• Biofuel crops displace food crops • ILUC leading to deforestation • Competition for land can threaten food security (non-cash crops)	• Defining protected areas and areas suitable for expansion for energy crop production • Reducing burning practices and developing mechanisation • Linking national policy with the international framework of global commodities governance, including certification schemes
W–F: Food production	• Rise in frequency of extreme weather events, floods, droughts • Changes in temperature and rain patterns affect crop yield	• Changes in land productivity produces crop and people migration and changes in agricultural output	• Adapting existing policies (e.g., ZARC) and creating new policies that incorporate climate change uncertainty and risk management
W–E–F: Deforestation	• Deforestation • Land degradation • Potential Amazon collapse	• Expansion of soy plantations • Displacement of pastures • ILUC leading to deforestation • Unclear or absent property rights • Land grabbing	• Strengthening national policies against deforestation, including law enforcement, monitoring, regulation of property ownership and land tenure rights • Linking national policy with the international framework of global commodities governance

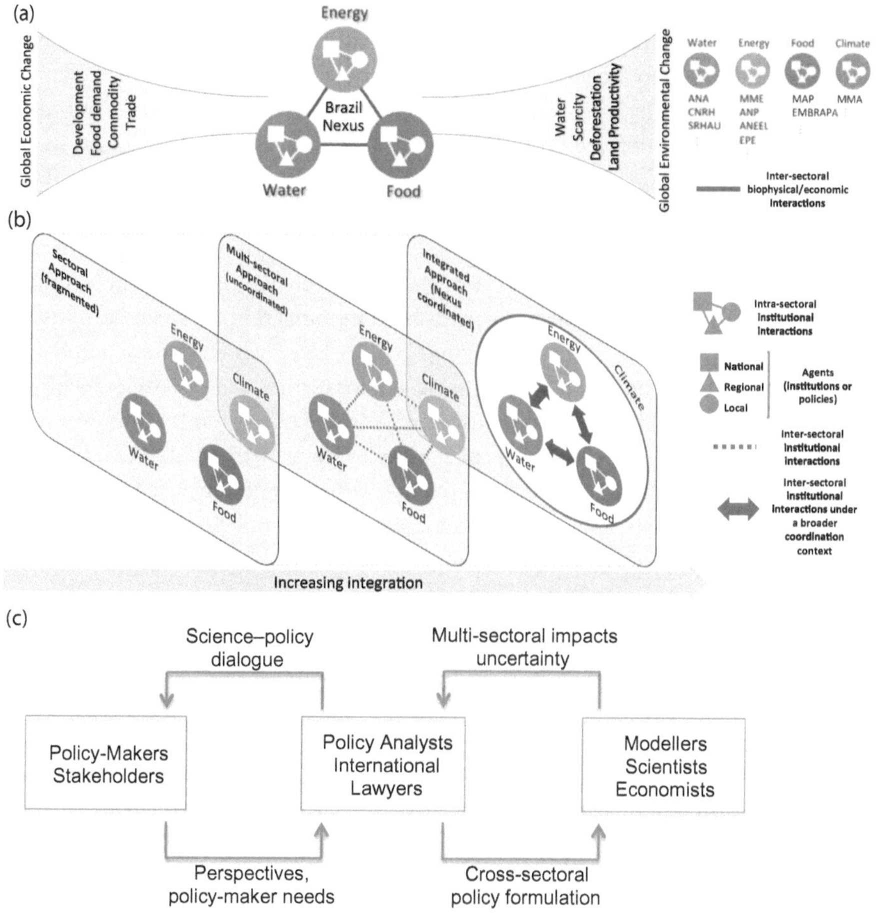

FIGURE 13.7 Schematic representation of the Nexus and relevant Brazilian institutions, and of the science–policy interface. (a) The Nexus involves global to local interactions, and strong interactions between the actions of each institution in each of its nodes. Each institution is attached to one of the sectors. (b) In the fully fragmented current policy situation, interactions exist between institutions and frameworks for each node of the Nexus and climate change, without interactions across nodes. In a situation of improved degrees of communication, interactions could exist between institutions. However, in an ideal Nexus integrated framework, coordinated interaction could take place between nodes of the Nexus in a framework defined by climate policy. (c) The science–policy–law interface involves an iterative dialogue between policy-makers and scientists, mediated/translated by policy analysts and legal experts (Mercure et al., 2019b).

new and existing regulations and law. Second, a similar interface, and possibly the same board, could be used to design policies based on knowledge of Nexus feedback. A possible example, in the Brazilian case, would be the adoption of an export duty on soybeans, the rate of which could be progressive so as to counteract exports that are 'excessive' in terms of the pressure on land use they are likely to cause.

The Nexus-savvy input provided by the proposed boards or other similar networks of Nexus experts could be organised in different ways according to the structure of the science and policy interface in a given country. One key consideration in making such interfaces functional and useful to policy-makers and other stakeholders is the interface's iterative nature or 'bidirectional' character. It should involve policy-makers and stakeholders expressing their needs and normative views to policy-analysts, department experts and legal experts, who would interpret this information to either develop or test detailed policy proposals within existing windows of opportunity and build an evidence-base that will ultimately support these proposals under a parliament vote. By obtaining results, Nexus experts can convey their findings to policy-makers and stakeholders, who can then adjust their requirements and strategies or, alternatively, ask for further analysis under additional political parameters. Through an iterative process, the policy frameworks eventually identified would be supported by a substantial evidence-base, which can be politically tested in parliament. The science–policy interface should be used continuously as policy is implemented, its effectiveness evaluated over time, more data and better models become available, and as the nature of policy problems evolve.

13.5. CONCLUSION

The structure of the science–policy interface proposed for Brazil in this chapter requires close integration of scientific knowledge with governance structure. Recent experience with populist governments that typically refuse to rely on, or make selective choice of scientific knowledge, notably in Brazil, the USA and the UK, has revealed during the COVID-19 pandemic how problematic and dramatic a dysfunctional science–policy interface can be. Indeed, the virus spread most easily, and led to most deaths, in those countries with governments who refused to follow scientific advice, allowed disinformation to thrive or relied excessively on public opinion which may itself have been misinformed. Addressing COVID-19 effectively required policy-makers to 'understand' the virus and its complex dynamics of contagion. It required a responsive and adaptive approach to policy, recurrently adjusted following new scientific discoveries. Dramatically different effectivenesses at tackling contagion have been observed around the world between countries, with notably a stark difference between Eastern and Western countries. Populism in Brazil has similarly allowed a disastrous 'contagion' of deforestation by again refusing to engage in dialogue with scientists. Nobody will be made better if the Amazon collapses as a result of misunderstanding the Nexus, even the large land-owners and the currently profitable agribusiness in Brazil.

The science–policy interface proposed here is possibly the only broad type of approach that can address the complexity of the Nexus or other complex 'wicked' problems in modern society. The approach strives to understand the full breadth of the problem at various scales, from global to local, and in various domains that are integrated, from socio-economic to physical and environmental complex dynamics, where obviously no equilibrium or steady state can be assumed. Within that scope, finding solutions to problems involves the same process as making science progress, and policy instruments and laws are tested with a very high degree of granularity before implementation. It should be complemented with the risk-opportunity approach discussed in Chapter 12. The analysis must encompass all relevant interacting systems in order to make sure solving a problem somewhere does not just translate into creating another problem elsewhere. And ultimately, this involves a robust system in which science becomes part of the policy-making and political deliberative process, just as most countries have had to face during the COVID-19 crisis.

14

Technology Dynamics in a Rapid Low-Carbon Transition

This chapter explores technology dynamics, and policies to influence the direction of technological change, for addressing climate change. 'Optimal' policy to address climate change has been the topic of substantial debate. In the standard environmental economics framework, one pricing policy should be used per market failure, and that policy is expected to exactly fix the externality and solve the problem. For climate change, this is a carbon price. Socio-technical systems are, however, never in equilibrium, but rather are in constant change. Here, insights from Chapters 6–8 are brought together to formulate a dynamic model of co-evolutionary technology diffusion and learning. The model is used to analyse policy design in key sectors that matter for climate change. Synergies and interference effects exist between different types of policy approaches, and this indicates that for technological change policy, welfare economics is a poor framework to design technology policy, as optimality is ambiguous. Instead, simulations can help identify smart and effective policy strategies that accelerate technological change in desired directions.

14.1. TECHNOLOGICAL CHANGE IS PATH-DEPENDENT

Socio-technological change in the energy sector is what is mostly needed to reduce greenhouse gas emissions and reduce the likelihood of damaging climate change, while pure behavioural change is not likely to contribute sufficient emission reductions on its own to achieve climate targets. This means that, for instance, most people would likely be acquiring electric vehicles rather than stop driving altogether. But furthermore, in many situations, new technologies are needed to enable behavioural change. For instance, an increasing availability and range of low-carbon technologies allow consumers and manufacturers to co-shape low-carbon lifestyles.

Technological change is path-dependent, and different agents, notably the government and the wider public sector, can contribute to shaping it. Socio-technological change does not happen by magic, nor does it originate entirely from heroic entrepreneurs in their garages. It originates from basic research in research institutions, goes through iterative development, and crosses the technology valley of death before taking over mass markets.[1]

The case for technological change in the energy sector comes from the urgent need to end all fuel combustion in order to reduce carbon dioxide emissions. Classical economists have called this the 'greatest market failure ever faced by humanity' (Stern, 2007). In around 2018, climate scientists suggested that reaching net-zero emissions by 2050 would likely lead to peak warming not exceeding 1.5°C ,[2] and this has decisively shaped the net-zero policy objective of many regions. Eliminating fuel combustion in all technological applications supplying the goods and services that people use is a tremendously ambitious task.

Thus it seems clear that the Age of Oil, the Kondratiev wave that started in the 1920s with the internal combustion engine and petrochemicals, must effectively come to an end now. However, the sector has already been struggling. Visible signs of instability have arisen in oil and gas markets, with wide price fluctuations not seen since the oil crises of the 70s, while coal markets have been already in full decline since the 2010s. Indeed, following a historic decision by OPEC in 2015, in relation to quotas, to let the oil flow (van de Graaf and Bradshaw, 2018), prices fell from above $100/bbl to below $30/bbl and remained comparatively low, and more volatile, until new geopolitical conflict involving Russia, Ukraine and other countries brought oil prices back up to new highs above $100/bbl. Oil demand does not grow as much as it used to, or as producers would have expected it to, perhaps due to increasing efficiency of the use of oil all through its value chain, and overcapacity has been developing. More recently, during the first wave of COVID-19 lockdowns, as oil production continued but mobility came to a standstill worldwide, oil prices that were already low overnight turned negative, something never seen before.[3]

Electric vehicles (EVs) and vehicles of higher efficiency are currently eating away at the dominant market share of petrol and diesel vehicles in car markets. Solar photovoltaics panels (PVs) and wind power are quietly chipping away their way into power generation with some hard economics. Many low-carbon technologies that seemed far-fetched and unnecessarily costly are now more than just demonstration projects. What has been happening? It seems that some of these technologies, such as EVs and PVs, have gained sufficient market share to become self-sustaining, or

[1] See Chapter 8, as well as Grübler and Wilson (2013); Gallagher et al. (2012); Grubb et al. (2014).

[2] See IPCC (2018), and notably, Millar et al. (2017) and Holden et al. (2018).

[3] 'US oil prices turn negative as demand dries up', BBC story 20 April 2020, see `www.bbc.co.uk/news/business-52350082`.

are becoming close to. This is due to the cumulative effect of past climate policies having had irreversible impact: technology is decisively changing.

Under a classical environmental economics analysis, those technologies would be static entities that can be used or abandoned according to the economic context and agent preferences. Therefore, if a climate policy had to be terminated, or if the carbon price was lowered, these technologies would disappear again from markets as quickly as they came. Thus, in the classical frame of mind, adopting support policies such as subsidies is a choice to be taken seriously, as the policy support must become a permanent fixture, and the latter can be expensive. But is this really how it works? Or would these technologies not eventually become the new normal, potentially even *less* costly than their old fossil fuel counterparts? After all, PVs have no fuel costs, and EVs substantially less moving parts that can break or wear out or require maintenance. What could be so special about the *status quo* fossil fuel technologies, that new technologies could not achieve?

By looking at the data (next section), it would seem that a low-carbon new normal may be near a tipping point. This suggests that while policies such as subsidies and carbon prices brought these technologies to the mainstream, they may not need to be maintained in place forever, and these technologies are here to stay. They will not need to be subsidised indefinitely, due to their performance, because they will likely outperform fossil technologies. This would suggest that the externality need not even be priced forever.

The reason for this is innovation dynamics and path-dependence. In Chapter 7, the structure of the diffusion of innovations was discussed, which results from inter-agent interactions, leading to typical S-shaped diffusion patterns with early and late adopters. In Chapter 8, a theory of innovation was derived from creative destruction in the connected network of ideas that expands within the Adjacent Possible, which ultimately result in learning curves. These two phenomena interact, in that as consumers buy into a new technology driving demand up typically exponentially, producing firms receive income that they partly re-invest in expanding production capacity to meet expected rising sales, as well as in improving methods of production, in order to increase profit. The result is that as scale expands, costs decline, which enables firms to attract more consumers and expand scale further, which leads to more demand, in a virtuous cycle, until market saturation is reached. The larger the scale that is achievable in markets, the lower the costs can become. The global markets is the ultimate scale that energy technologies can reach, and it is large. Since the expansion of the innovation system into the world of ideas is irreversible,[4] technological change is strongly path-dependent.

For policy-making, the result is that supporting market entry to a technology, using subsidy or other demand pull or supply push mechanisms, can provide sufficient

4 Once knowledge is developed, it is not usually forgotten, thus technology improvements only ever go forwards as agents avoid repeating past errors.

scale and learning for a technology to eventually fare on its own and potentially beat the competition with its own merits, not least its price, which it could not have achieved without the temporary support and without the expanded scale. However, it could also simply fail to achieve market parity, if, for instance, its potential is just not good enough, or it is inconsistent with the broader direction of change. This policy narrative, drawn from innovation systems, starkly contrasts with the market failure and externality pricing narratives that are currently most frequently used in environmental policy-making (Chapter 4). The latter theory has no mechanism that could suggest that the externality would stop needing to be priced.

This is particularly true for climate change, where since CO_2 takes thousands of years to clear from the atmosphere, the social cost of carbon can only increase and never decrease, which suggests that the carbon price, if determined on the basis of pricing the climate change externality, can only ever increase. Meanwhile, the cost of solar electricity has declined by orders of magnitude in recent years,[5] which suggests that were the cost of solar to break through parity with fossil technologies, carbon pricing and once costly feed-in tariffs would cease to matter, as solar PV would become unstoppable even if the social cost of carbon remains high and increasing. In truth, the value of the subsidy that can bring a technology to the market has no relationship with the social cost of carbon, and may in fact initially be much higher. The economic returns, meanwhile, could be very large and in reality incalculable, as people gradually realise all the neat things that can be done with solar energy, not least in communities and developing countries devoid of electricity infrastructure, who could thus rapidly leapfrog. And lastly, since existing carbon prices are low while the road to bring solar PV to mass markets has been long and costly, one cannot attribute the success of PV deployment to a pricing of the climate externality. Success must be attributed to national R&D programs that themselves mostly began around the time of the 1970s oil crisis, a time when climate change was not much of a topic.

In this chapter, a new strategy of analysis for technological change policy is proposed, based on innovation systems as opposed to market failure, which understands the degree of path-dependence involved. First, the technology narrative is developed looking at past tipping points in technology market breakthroughs. Second, the analysis method is demonstrated using examples based on the 'Future Technology Transformations' (FTT) model of technology diffusion dynamics that combines the principles of innovation and diffusion developed in Chapters 7 and 8. Lastly, the narrative for technology policy-making is reframed in terms of path-dependence and these analysis methods, with focus on climate change policy.

5 Farmer and Lafond (2016); Yu et al. (2016).

14.2. TECHNOLOGY SUPPORT TOWARDS TIPPING POINTS

A great success story of government support for innovation leading to market parity can be told about offshore wind power in the UK.[6] A renewables obligation scheme was initially established by the UK government targeting primarily onshore wind. Through this mechanism, which offered an effective subsidy per MWh of electricity produced to renewables operators, offshore wind benefited from £140 to £150 per MWh, which corresponds to a subsidy of around £280–£310/tCO_2e,[7] in comparison to the carbon price at the time, and the value of carbon emissions in UK policy appraisal of £14/tCO_2e in the power sector and £59/tCO_2e in other sectors, used in UK government cost-benefit exercises. This seemed disproportionately large and terrible value for money to the adherents of the market failure framework and cost-benefit analysis (CBA), notably for civil servants at HM Treasury, especially under the prospect where the subsidy would be needed indefinitely. And indeed, CBA indicated that other emissions reductions options existed at much lower prices.

However, the decision was nevertheless taken, due to the need to meet overarching legal EU commitments, and with strategic considerations regarding which sectors and technologies would be most appropriate to achieve these commitments, by decision-makers in UK government who did not expect to subsidise offshore wind forever. And indeed, costs have gone down dramatically as a result of the policy, from over £200/MWh back in 2008 to around £120/MWh in 2015, going down steeply to £60/MWh in 2020 and a forecast between £30 and £50/MWh for 2030. This is below the cost of gas electricity that lies between £60 and £100/MWh. The policy will indeed not be needed forever, as a tipping point may have been reached, and the UK is now even in a position where it could export offshore wind technology and related services.

Another similar story happened with solar and wind energy policy in Germany, which has been labelled 'spectacularly inefficient' by economists of the German Council of Economic Experts.[8] As stated in Chapter 12, the German introduction of the 'expensive' and 'inefficient' feed-in tariffs effectively created a market for solar PV, which allowed Chinese manufacturers to justify expanding production at a massive scale, which subsequently resulted in substantial cost reductions, creating the availability of low-cost solar energy to the rest of the world, including Germany itself. Notably, CBA is not commonly used in Germany for *ex-ante* appraisal of policies, which allowed policymakers to implement the feed-in tariffs on a strategic basis without formal comparison of cost and benefits. It was retrospectively evaluated to be a policy failure by economists because Germany was not on track to deliver

[6] Documented in Jennings et al. (2020).

[7] This conversion uses the UK's 2008 carbon intensity of electricity generation.

[8] The criticism is documented in Ch. 11 of their 2016 annual report (GCEE, 2016), while the story of solar PV cost reductions is documented in Yu et al. (2016).

necessary emission reductions, and thus they recommended a return to technology neutral carbon pricing (the EU-ETS) as a leading instrument. However, it can now be seen with hindsight that the policy has in fact changed the game for renewables globally, and made the transition much more achievable, by giving the technology the needed deployment scale to reach necessary cost reductions. The failure, if any, is not having successfully kept the PV industry in Germany, which has become large and highly profitable.

These two cases can be seen as public investment in R&D to lower costs. However, policy-makers in the UK and Germany have been surprised by the success of these two bold and highly risky ventures. Uncertainty was in both cases very large and there were many ways in which this could have gone wrong. Thus, the narrative can neither be framed as one of successfully pricing carbon emissions or knowledge spillover externalities, as neither of these caused the success. Furthermore, while supply push policies targeting R&D were used directly, most of the supporting cash flow took the form of demand pull policy clearing space in the market by making offshore wind and PV compete with other system types. The sheer scale of deployment brought the costs down. One advantage that offshore wind has over onshore wind is that while its engineering complexity is higher, obtaining planning permission is in some sense easier offshore than onshore.

The general policy narrative therefore is to support promising technologies by offering opportunity for upscaling up to a point where they could break through in markets and survive without further support. However, since this is never guaranteed, it is not wise to back just one horse, and as demonstrated in innovation scholarship,[9] a combination of breadth of innovation, commitment and weeding out unproductive ventures is likely the most productive. In other words, back several horses, if and only if they make progress, until one or more breakthroughs are made and returns are generated in comparison to the alternatives. Once the tipping point is reached, it is irreversible, and the technology may well transform markets completely. This is not new of course, it is the narrative used by venture capitalists.

For the sake of this chapter, it might seem that modelling this quantitatively for use in policy appraisal, for example, in risk-opportunity analysis (Chapter 12), could be challenging as it requires to forecast the future on systems inherently non-linear, complex and path-dependent. However, it turns out that the two recurrent organising principles of technology evolution, the S-shaped diffusion curve (or Lotka-Volterra), and the learning curve (Wright's law), are highly robust, and relatively straightforward to model in time step simulations, and do not actually involve debilitating amounts of uncertainty, as shown next.

9 Meifort (2016); Klingebiel and Rammer (2014).

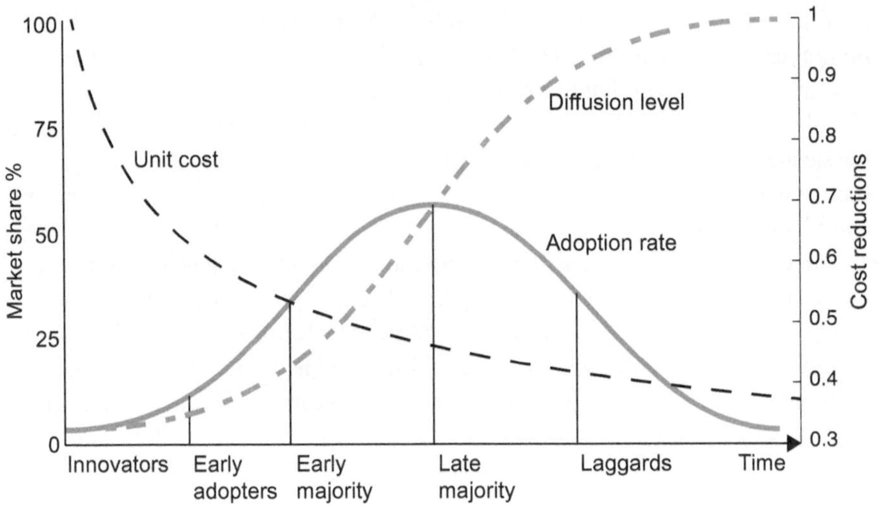

FIGURE 14.1 Illustration of the co-evolving diffusion of innovations and cost reductions.

14.3. FORECASTING TECHNOLOGICAL CHANGE

14.3.1 *Combining Diffusion and Learning-by-Doing*

Technology diffusion follows a self-reinforcing feedback: upscaling leads to cost reductions, which attract more upscaling; this generates more cost reductions, in a self-fulfilling avalanche (Figure 14.1). In a model, combining diffusion with learning-by-doing dynamics is straightforward in time step simulations. The diffusion progresses following an S-shaped curve, and for each exponential capacity increments in the early phases, costs go down rapidly following the learning curve and its exponent. In early phases costs go down rapidly, while in the later phase of market saturation, costs stop declining as the technology matures.

However, the closing feedback of declining costs generating further diffusion as it attracts consumers is more complex to model, since it involves agent behaviour and choices. Choices depend on the 'fitness' of the technology in its market in relation to competitors, its ability to attract sales and beat competitors. Analytical solutions for this dynamical system do not exist, since there are as many possible outcomes as one is willing to simulate, and no equilibrium exists under the simulation timescale, because it is comparable to the evolution timescale.[10]

[10] The evolution timescale can also be called the time span of autocorrelation: it is a representation of inertia, a period of time characterising how much change is physically possible. When the observation timescale is much shorter than this, no significant change can be expected, while when the observation timescale is much longer, one can in some cases expect to reach a steady state. Here, physical structures such as cars and buildings survive for a time span of ten to eighty

An almost exact analogy exists in biology, in models of competing species in ecosystems. This is called the 'Lotka-Volterra' system of equations,[11] which is the same as the replicator dynamics equation of evolutionary theory discussed in Chapter 7. When several species compete in ecosystems, their survival depends on their reproduction and death rates, as well as how they interact and compete with other species, whether they interfere with themselves and others. For example, an invasive bird species may expand its population rapidly and as a result, begin to occupy habitats normally used by other bird species that might grow less quickly and have therefore a lower capacity to capture those habitats, and with limited habitat opportunities, end up declining in numbers.[12]

Here, it is assumed that technology grows according to three rates:

1. rate at which the overall market is growing;
2. rate at which production capacity for the technology is scaled up;
3. rate at which technology comes to the end of its life.

The rationale is as follows.[13] The demand for a certain consumer end-use energy service is assumed to be growing (e.g., mobility, heating, connectivity/data), and accordingly, sales of equipment providing that service naturally grow at that rate (e.g., vehicles, heating systems, mobile phones). Sales, which would be births in biology, are divided between different types of competing technologies (e.g., electric vs petrol vehicles), according to their ability to capture the attention of consumers, in other words their fitness. However, technology fleet sizes depend not only on sales, but also on items coming to their end of life, which would be deaths in biology. Those are likely indiscriminate, but depend on the size of technology fleets (e.g., cars scrapped in the fleet due to end of life breakdowns and accidents). Thus there is a continuous in-flow and an out-flow of units in technology fleets, due to births and deaths. Deaths are determined by a survival function, representing the likelihood of survival of units past a certain age, from which the life expectancy can be determined. How do births come about?

In biology, the number of births of one species depends on the number of potential parents and their likelihood of conceiving and delivering. In economics, it depends on the dynamics for industry to expand output given sales and returns on prior investment. The production capacity is itself built out of income from the sale of units, and therefore scales with it: the larger the sales, the larger the expansion, and the larger sales can become afterwards. The maximum rate of growth of industry thus depends on the whole lifecycle of the technology. Seen alternatively from

years, similar to the simulation time span of around fifty years, and thus no equilibrium or steady state can be reached.

11 Derived in Lotka (1925); Volterra (1939); see Morris and Pratt (2003); Bhargava (1989); Karmeshu et al. (1985) for applications.

12 See, e.g., mathematical biology in Kot (2001).

13 The detailed mathematical argument is given in Mercure (2015).

the consumer end, as discussed in Chapter 7, it may be social influence, visibility and other network effects that determine the growth rate. In reality, both industry expansion and market popularity co-evolve together.

However, some competing technologies or brands may be winning market share while others may be losing ground, thus not all industries are expanding. Usually, outdated technologies are in outright decline. This is easiest understood in terms of market shares, where, normalising sales by the total number of units, some 'species' absorb market share at the expense of other who are losing it, and the flow of shares they absorb depends simultaneously on the growth rate of industry, the survival rate of technology and consumer preferences. However, what ultimately determines whether 'species' are advancing or retreating in the competition is preferences. These can be determined by examining markets, agent purchasing behaviour and by making some assumptions over the process of decision-making that heterogeneous agents use. The mathematics to use were derived in Chapter 7 and are summarised more simply in the Appendix.

Different concepts can be used for determining preferences and choices, all of which are challenging to fully substantiate against data, especially given that preferences under social influence or other industry bandwagon effects, as discussed in Chapter 7, suffer from an identification problem, and linear regressions cannot reliably be used.[14] However, one way to decompose the problem is to carry out pairwise comparisons of options in markets, and to weigh the importance of those comparisons by the frequencies at which they actually take place.

For example, imagine a case in which agents facing a repeated choice, recurring every technology lifetime, between three options, and have, on average, transitively ordered preferences where option C has enormous tangible advantages over options A and B, while agents also prefer option A to option B, but B starts off as dominant. However, in that particular market, many of the agents do not have access to or are not aware of option C, which has only recently made its appearance, but A is relatively common. In that case, C will not be the preferred option in practice, as agents in effect have to wait to gain access to or learn of the existence of C, and thus choose A more often. Knowing the starting market shares, it is possible to determine fairly clearly what flow of shares from A would go to B and C, while some limited amounts of market shares also flow from B to C. This can be done using the 'Lotka-Volterra' equations. Adding agent heterogeneity to this primarily requires assuming that all perceptions are distributed, rather than single-valued.[15] This is

14 See Manski (1993) and discussions in Chapter 7.

15 See the Appendix; this is discussed at length in the original description of the FTT modelling principle (Mercure, 2012).

different from standard multinomial logit modelling, as the latter assumes equal access to technology for all options, which thus skips diffusion dynamics.

In this model, declining costs in relative terms due to the learning curve can attract increasing preferences towards the less established technologies if their cost reductions justify it. Typically, new technologies have rapidly declining costs, while older technologies have stagnating costs. This contributes to determining the rates of exchange of shares between technologies in their ecosystem, where learning attracts preferences, preferences push up diffusion, and diffusion leads to lower costs, and the preferred technologies take over the market in a self-reinforcing avalanche. The FTT model, based on this principle, has been used to study the diffusion of innovations in various carbon-intense sectors of the global economy.[16] In practice, the model involves iterating over and over between

1. Estimating the market progress and retreat of each technology given prior preferences;
2. Estimating the cost reductions due to the learning curve, progress and retreat for all options;
3. Re-evaluating the preferences, including updated costs and including other external changes from elsewhere in the economy.

14.3.2 *Policy Analysis: Creating Multiple Storylines*

Policy plays a key role in the FTT diffusion process, naturally, by influencing costs and the degrees of diffusion freedom. Early intervention in the technology lifecycle can trigger a technological avalanche, if it brings its cost below parity with competitors. However, policy can also alter the way technologies win and lose market share in non-financial ways, for instance with regulations, industry mandates and public procurement, or other programs that aim at shaping industry and markets. All of these will leave path-dependent marks on markets. Notably, it is clear that for a policy to have impact, for example a tax or a subsidy, choice must exist for consumers, as otherwise, they have no way of responding to the policy signal. For example, if the acquisition of petrol and diesel vehicles is taxed, in a situation where electric vehicles remain difficult for consumers to get their hands on, then most of the impact of the policy is to make vehicles more expensive. Now, if a second policy can increase the availability of electric vehicles, then while that policy on its own might not have that much impact until it becomes prohibitively expensive, it can potentially multiply the impact of the tax, where the two policies work most effectively when applied together.

[16] See Mercure (2012); Mercure et al. (2014) for use of the FTT model in power generation, Mercure et al. (2018b) for vehicles, and Knobloch et al. (2018) for household heating. The model has been used in various policy appraisal processes.

Such a proposition is very different from the market failure narrative in which one expects to use just one policy instrument per market failure. The reason is that the diffusion process is highly non-linear, and consumers must have options and degrees of freedom available in order for a tax to effectively change their choice behaviour.[17]

A detailed analysis of the impacts of policies on vehicle markets was done using the FTT model for road transport (FTT:Transport) by Aileen Lam, in which she systematically analysed the effectiveness of multiple combinations of policies on the diffusion of low-carbon vehicles in five major economies characterised by radically different vehicle markets. To do this, she gathered very large datasets on vehicle models and market composition.[18]

Figure 14.2 shows vehicle markets in different countries, displaying substantial agent heterogeneity through heavy-tailed purchasing behaviour distributions with standard deviations as large as their medians. Figure 14.3 shows the impacts of different types of policies over time on these five markets starting from their present day configuration.

What can be seen is that, first, the diffusion of vehicles is path-dependent and never in an equilibrium, with or without policies, as different technologies with different fitnesses compete in markets with evolving contexts. Second, taxes and subsidies, on their own, have some impact at re-orienting the direction of diffusion, by re-scaling relative preferences. However, the addition of fuel economy or phase out regulations can help shape that direction further. But interestingly, it is the so-called 'kick-start' policy that really magnifies the effect of the taxes: it is interpreted as an exogenous addition of low-carbon vehicles in the mix, as a result of either a procurement policy, or a regulation that forces manufacturers to sell a certain percentage of low-carbon models (e.g. EV mandates). Without that, the taxes and subsidies have substantially less grip on markets. This appears to be a robust finding irrespective of the geography; however the shapes of the policies themselves, for example the rate of taxes, are highly geography-dependent, since even the technologies themselves are market specific as they have been influenced by different regulatory histories.[19]

17 Here the reader could argue that a system of multiple market failures should be used, such as in Lipsey and Lancaster (1956). Here, one could invoke a coordination or inertia market failure as impeding the diffusion from reaching the 'normative' rate, in addition to the climate change market failure, allowing for two policy instruments. With two market failures, there is no limit to the number of combinations of solutions that can address the market failures, which is loosely consistent with work in this chapter. It is not clear, however, that effective combinations of policy instruments necessarily match the number of market failures even in the framework of the second best, and how informative this in fact is.

18 See Lam and Mercure (2021) for details, and earlier work in Mercure et al. (2018b) and Mercure and Lam (2015).

19 Notably, US vehicle markets are typically different than European markets, with larger vehicles with substantially lower fuel efficiency, while Japanese vehicles have the highest fuel efficiency in the world (Knobloch et al., 2020) due to an explicit policy objectives to reduce dependence on imported oil.

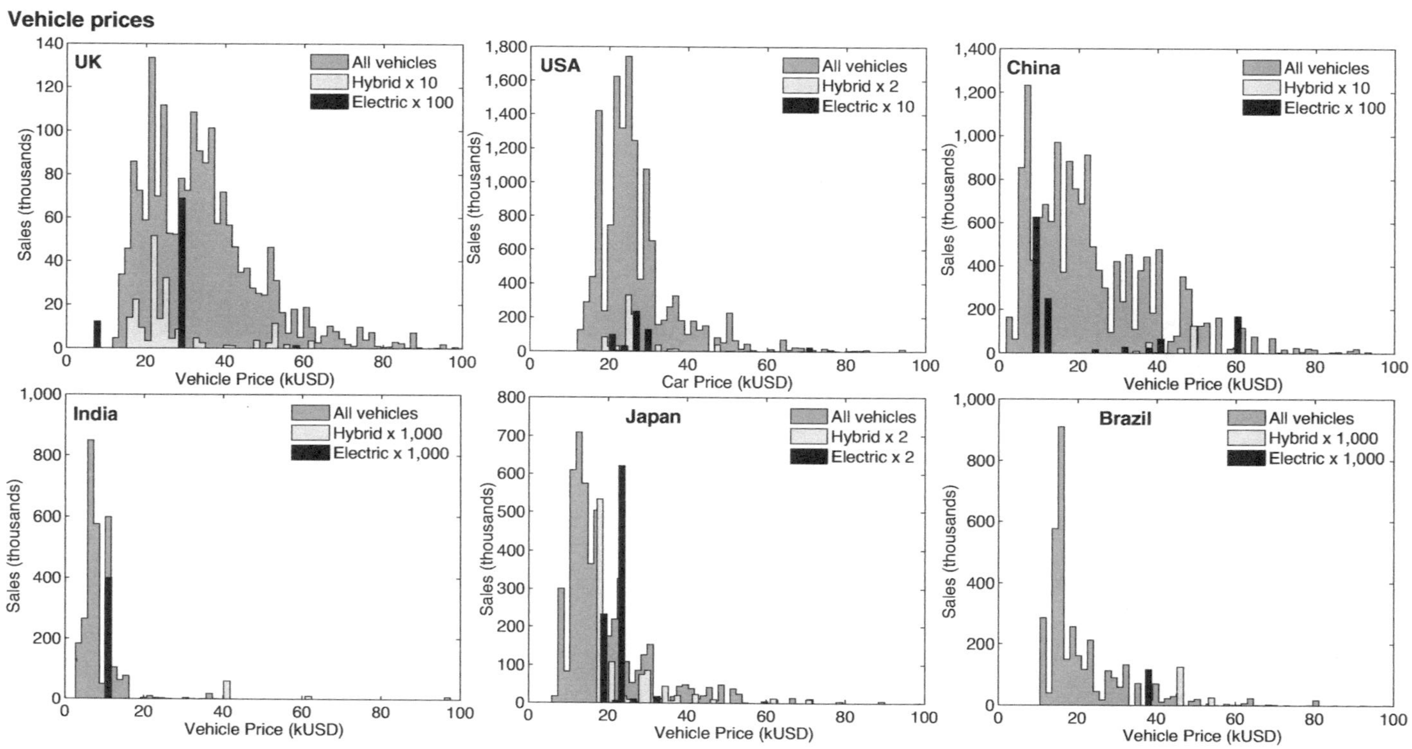

FIGURE 14.2 Heterogeneity of vehicle markets in six major economies in 2015 (Mercure and Lam, 2015).

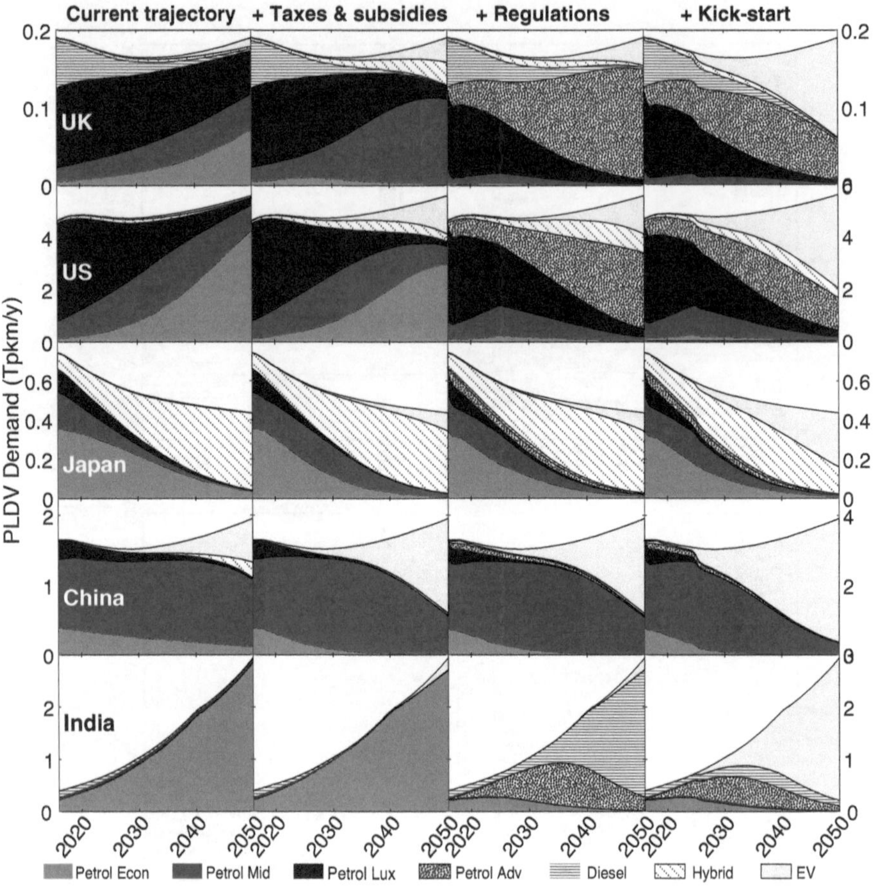

FIGURE 14.3 Evolution of vehicle fleets in the current trajectory (first column), and with the successive addition of various layers of policies (other columns). Kick-start policies multiply the impact of the taxes for EV uptake (Lam and Mercure, 2021).

Figure 14.4 shows a similar analysis carried out in power generation. Here, it is clear that power technology is highly dependent on geography, but in this case primarily due to the availability of natural resources that has shaped regional engineering capabilities. Coal prevails in China and India, hydroelectricity in Brazil, and natural gas in the USA and Europe. Meanwhile, solar and wind energy have had their longest history in Europe and the USA, where they were developed as a result of fears of energy shortages following the 1970s oil shocks following the formation of OPEC.

First, it is found that optimisation as a driver of technology choice does not reproduce diffusion trajectories consistent with recent history (first column[20]), where

[20] The optimisation data were generated by exogenously scaling FTT to values published by in IEA (2019), which themselves were generated by the IEA's cost-optimisation energy model. That the IEA systematically understimates the diffusion rates of solar and wind in its projections is well

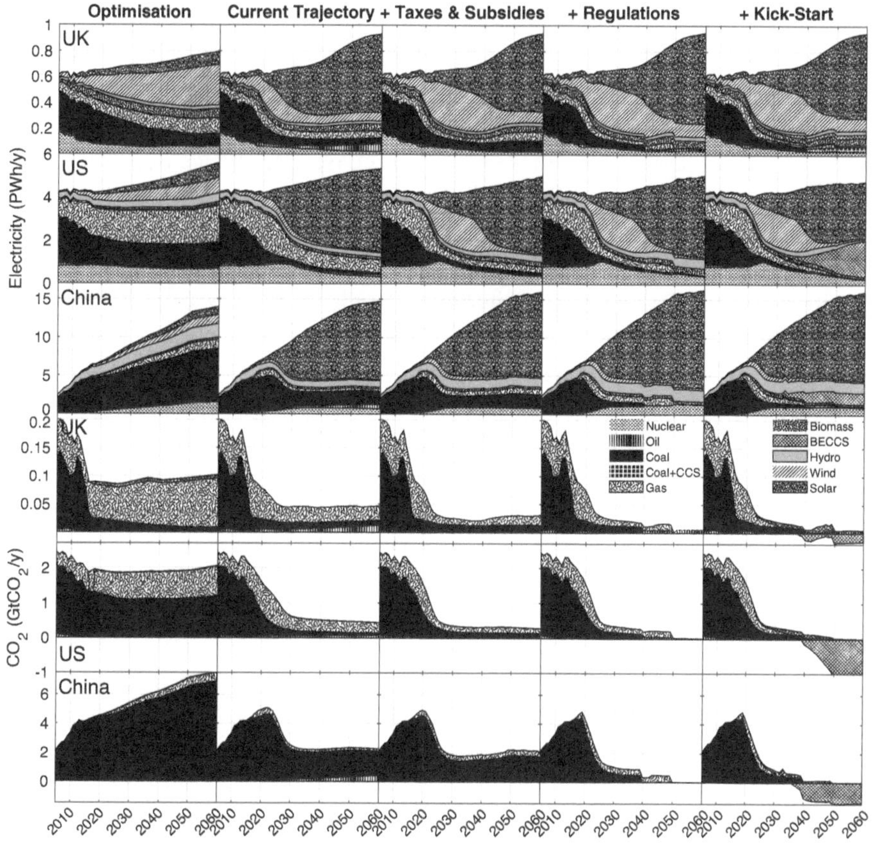

FIGURE 14.4 Evolution of electricity systems globally with different added layers of policies. The optimisation column is the result one obtains with cost-optimisation models that do not take account of diffusion dynamics, while the current trajectory FTT simulation does. Taxes and subsidies include a steep carbon price going up very steeply to \$500/tCO_2 in 2033 and remaining there afterwards. Regulations corresponds to shutting down remaining coal and gas plants in 2040 and 2050 respectively. The kick-start program can be seen as exogenous interventions to scale up CCS such as public procurement. BECCS contributes negative emissions.

diffusion rates of new technologies are much lower in the simulation than in actual recent history. Tuning FTT to follow closely the trajectories of existing new and old technologies (see the Appendix), the picture is radically different, as it would seem that a tipping point for solar PV might have been reached, where its cost reductions have become unstoppable barrelling down towards parity with coal.[21]

documented online by Prof Auke Hoekstra, see for example `https://maartensteinbuch.com/2017/06/12/photovoltaic-growth-reality-versus-projections-of-the-international-energy-agency/`.

[21] This is also a finding in Farmer and Lafond (2016); Lafond et al. (2018).

Second, in power generation, it is clear that carbon taxation (second column[22]) is an important driver of change, as it pushes coal generators out of the market, making space for natural gas and renewables. However this on its own is not sufficient in FTT to achieve net-zero emissions, despite the standard notion from environmental economics that it should be sufficient to price the climate change externality. The carbon price must become unrealistically high to really get rid of fossil fuel electricity, and here they are instead banned using a regulatory instrument. For similar reasons as in vehicle markets, market kick-start can play an important role in improving the effectiveness of the carbon price by offering options to investors away from fossil fuels, as otherwise they may just pass carbon costs on to electricity consumers. Here, it is the carbon capture and storage (CCS) technology that is first deployed through national programs, and then scaled up by the market under the carbon price. Emissions become negative through the combination of bioenergy and CCS.

As a last example, Figure 14.5 shows a similar picture for household heating. Here, a choice also exists between taxing high-carbon fuels, subsidising low-carbon technology, banning certain practices and systems, and procuring new systems to expand the market. It is not at all clear that carbon taxation maximises welfare as suggested by standard welfare economics, since ultimately it reduces the income of poorer families, and the way the tax is recycled does not necessarily alleviate this burden imposed on them. Poor families may not have the capacity to assemble the capital necessary to invest in heat pumps, and thus may end up just paying the more expensive fuels without reducing their emissions. Or alternatively, they may decide to burn all sorts of things in old wood stoves and coal fireplaces instead of highly taxed fuel. Other approaches can incentivise technological change without necessitating moving so much money around.

In FTT, a baseline was constructed for the trajectory of heating technology in 53 regions or countries of the world, according to their costs and their existing market shares. Those baselines are already dynamic, to the extent that some EU member states, although not all, achieve their sectoral target in the baseline.[23] To those baselines are added various policy packages in various forms, and once again, it is a combination of taxes, technology-specific subsidies and a market kick-start policy that achieves the target most effectively.

14.3.3 *Policy Interactions and Portfolio Design*

The earlier experimentations with the FTT model combining diffusion and learning-by-doing dynamics suggest that in non-linear technology diffusion processes, one should expect that policies interact with one another. They may either enable each

22 A carbon tax has been applied with feed-in tariff for wind power and other technology subsidies for nuclear, geothermal, ocean and other renewables.

23 For an analysis of EU member states, see Knobloch et al. (2017, 2021).

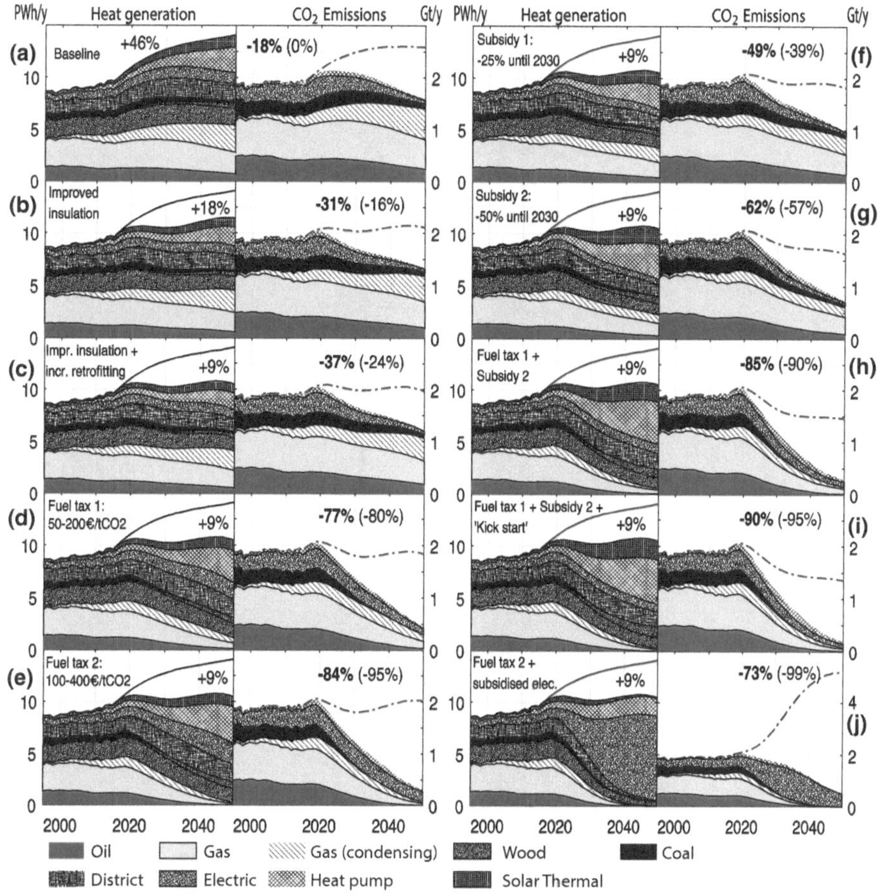

FIGURE 14.5 Evolution of home heating systems globally with different types of policies (Knobloch et al., 2018).

other, or they may interfere with one another. Notably, it is quite clear that for the successful diffusion of electric vehicles in fleets, government procurement or EV mandates can multiply the effect of taxes and subsidies, where taxes on engine sizes or carbon-intense fuels would otherwise just make driving more expensive without leading to substantial changes in the carbon intensity of the fleet. Reducing transport demand may be one way of reducing emissions, but not necessarily needed if other policy approaches can accelerate the diffusion of electric vehicles.

In her work, Aileen Lam explored systematically every possible combination of policies in a set of seven, and she found, by analysing the impact of individual and pairs of policies, that generally, the effectiveness of combined policies is not the linear sum of the effectivenesses of individual policies (Lam and Mercure, 2021). She determined that this is the case for both the cost-effectiveness and the

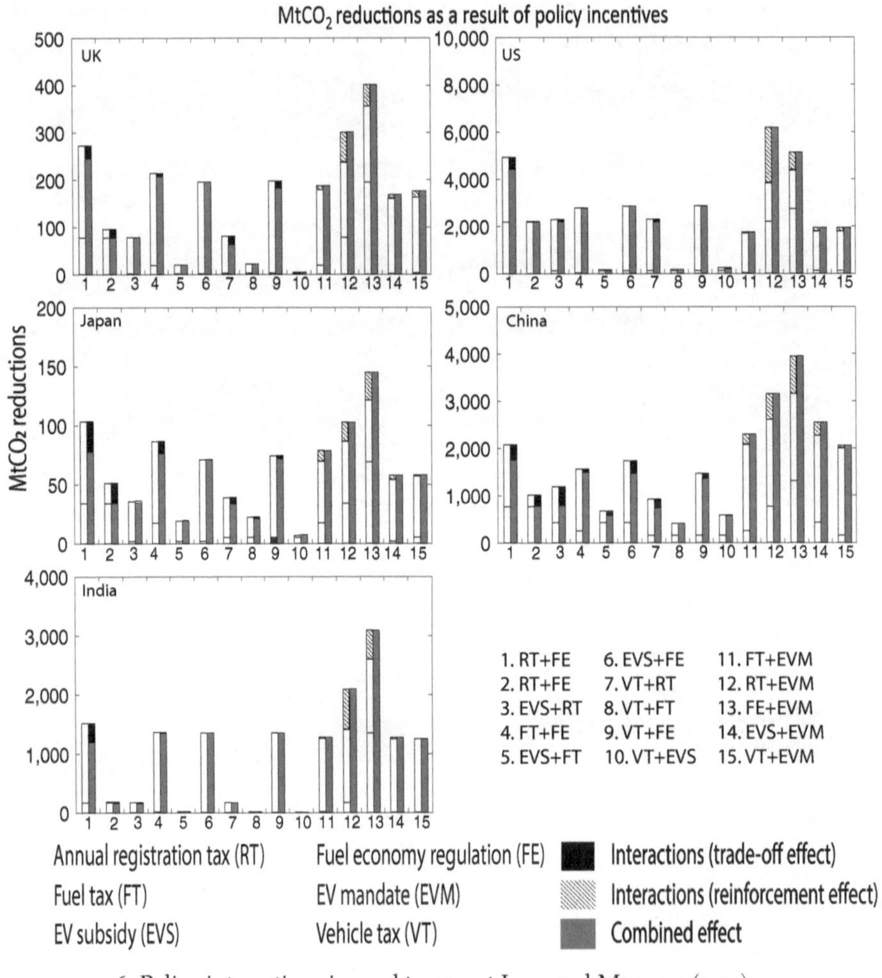

FIGURE 14.6 Policy interactions in road transport Lam and Mercure (2021).

absolute effectiveness on emissions. Her main findings are twofold (Figure 14.6). First, combining taxes and subsidies leads to interference effects, where the overall effectiveness is less than the sum of its parts. Second, combining financial (taxes, subsidies) with non-financial policies (regulations, EV mandates) leads to important synergies, where the non-financial policies typically increase choice for consumers which offer them ways to avoid the taxes imposed and benefit from the subsidies. This is a combination that enables to break the technology lock-in.

That there exists synergies and interference effects between policies suggests that clever combinations can be searched for and identified that very effectively change the course of evolution of a technology system. It is not possible *a priori* to determine how many such strategies there can be, but intuition can be used to guide the identification process. Aileen's findings make intuitive sense. The system's enormous dimensionality and non-linearity make it impossible to identify the optimal policy package with an optimisation calculation. Indeed, it is quite unlikely that anyone could prove that any particular combination of policies is optimal, largely because one would have to show that nothing better exists within that huge complex policy landscape. But one could determine that a strategy is *good enough* as it achieves the objectives set.

What is clear is that notions of efficiency on the basis of pricing externalities do not apply in technology policy for situations where slow diffusion interacts with learning. As discussed in Chapter 12, using standard marginal analysis to design policy would likely only lead to very marginal change on the basis of existing degrees of freedom. For example, only those agents with access to options would be incentivised by a pricing policy, while all other agents, not having this level of choice, can do nothing else but pay the tax. And indeed, as discussed in Chapter 12, welfare economics is indeed a theory of marginal evolution, and the theory cannot see beyond change that is marginal.

14.4. REFRAMING TECHNOLOGY POLICY NARRATIVES

To summarise, the findings shown here have important implications for standard welfare economics framing of policy design, which imposes as a dogma that a single pricing policy instrument should be used to address the externality in each observed market failure. Here, it would suggest that using only just a carbon tax should be sufficient and most efficient to reduce emissions by addressing the climate change market failure. Welfare economists might at the limit argue that an additional policy instrument, such as the EV mandate, address a second externality regarding inertia and diffusion dynamics restricting access of agents to low-carbon technologies, in the theory of second best (Lipsey and Lancaster, 1956). But there really is a limit to which the market failure framework remains a useful narrative to guide policy design in systems far from equilibrium, and questions arise on whether it is not instead misleading, while ultimately, it is not justified by any empirical evidence. And since all socio-technical systems are in perpetual movement far from equilibrium, and that public policy more often than not deals with socio-technical systems, this framing issue is problematic, and potentially in the way of achieving the changes necessary.

Here, as seen in Figure 14.3, it is clear that the policy-maker could instead take the driving seat and play a responsive role as the system evolves. This happened in the UK with offshore wind policy, which was updated regularly according to the results achieved. Since uncertainty is very high, a policy-maker could begin his policy design journey with a strategy based on a diffusion analysis of the type shown here. By observing how far the system's direction of evolution diverges from model projections, the policy-maker could either or both adjust the stringency, shape and structure of the policy framework, and at the same time ask the analyst to improve the model. Ultimately, the policy-maker will be learning as much as the analyst through the experience accumulated in this one-off policy experiment. As suggested is the case in 'wicked problems' by Rittel and Webber (1973), the process of solving the policy issue is the same as the process of understanding the problem, where both the scientist and the policy-maker learn and adapt.

As discussed in Chapter 12, fundamental uncertainty implies that policy-makers should be much better at steering the direction of travel of evolving complex socio-technical systems than at pre-determining their destination, which can only be identified with false certainty in standard environmental economics framework. The lack of equilibrium means that the range of possible outcomes is very large, although it is limited by the rate of change itself. Here, the range of possible outcomes in 2050 of a policy adopted in the present day depends strongly on the rate of turnover of capital in technology fleets, reflected by their lifetimes and the ability of industry to scale up the production of new systems. Meanwhile, technology systems can also get trapped into situations of lock-in where the dominance of one type of system makes it lengthy and difficult for innovations to replace them, both due to cost considerations as well as industrial scale up dynamics. Breaking lock-ins will not happen on the basis of marginal change.

14.5. MATHEMATICAL APPENDIX

This appendix complements Chapter 7 by applying its theory to practical technological analyses. The diffusion process follows the Lotka-Volterra competition equation, which for a population of N technology units divided bewteen competing species, with numbers N_i, is

$$\frac{dN_i}{dt} = r_i \left[N_i + \sum_j \alpha_{ij} \frac{N_i N_j}{N} \right]. \tag{14.1}$$

The first term describes exponential population growth in each species, with growth rate r_i, and the second describes the interaction between species, where some species grow at the expense of others, mediated by the interaction parameter α_{ij} that expresses each possible pair of species' relative fitness and determines which species is winning over which within each pair. This is a competition system if α_{ij} is antisymmetric, but can become 'predator-prey' in other cases. If one normalises N_i by the total population N to obtain population shares $S_i = N_i/N$, one obtains approximately (Mercure, 2015)

$$\frac{dS_i}{dt} = \sum_j \alpha_{ij} S_i S_j. \tag{14.2}$$

This suggests that the growth of shares in i depends on shares of i (larger grows faster) and the shares of j (larger has more to lose).

Take for example the case of two species competing, $S_1 + S_2 = 1$. This leaves

$$\frac{dS_1}{dt} = \alpha_{12} S_1 (1 - S_1), \tag{14.3}$$

where by definition $\alpha_{11} = \alpha_{22} = 0$. The solution is a logistic diffusion curve,

$$S_1(t) = \frac{1}{1 + \exp\left[\alpha_{12}(t - t_0)\right]}. \tag{14.4}$$

This is an S-shaped curve that starts off exponentially, then crosses 50% linearly, and then saturates exponentially as it goes towards 100% That technology diffuses this way has been verified empirically in countless studies since as far back as the 50s.[24]

In cases of more than two interacting species, there are no analytical solutions, but one can observe, depending on the starting shares and parameters, successions of diffusion patterns. However, where the diffusion process becomes more interesting is when the parameters α_{ij} become dynamic, and for technologies they must, since costs and fitnesses change all the time with diffusion scale. Thus it is useful to decompose α_{ij} into its different components.

Two main components of α_{ij} can be defined, one that concerns agent preferences and choices F_{ij}, and one that concerns possible rates of change A_{ij}. Furthermore, α_{ij} should be split into its share in-flow and out-flow contributions, which can be analysed separately. One can considers the share in-flow for technology i originating from technology j, during a unit time Δt,

$$\Delta S_{j \to i} = \frac{S_i}{t_i} \frac{S_j}{\tau_j} F_{ij} \Delta t. \tag{14.5}$$

The interpretation of F_{ij} is the relative preference for i relative to j, as a fraction of 1, where $F_{ij} + F_{ji} = 1$. For example, if agents were surveyed, one might find that 70% prefer i and 30% prefer j. F_{ij} is thus a matrix comparing every pair of options. For shares to flow from j to i, at least some agents must prefer i, and the rate of flow happens according to the frequency at which agents get the opportunity to replace units of j, τ_j, and the rate at which they can expand their population, t_i. A reverse flow exists following opposite preferences,

$$\Delta S_{i \to j} = \frac{S_j}{t_j} \frac{S_i}{\tau_i} F_{ji} \Delta t. \tag{14.6}$$

The net flow $\Delta S_{j \to i} - \Delta S_{i \to j}$, between technology i and all other options in the market is thus

$$\Delta S_i = \sum_j S_i S_j \left(F_{ij} A_{ij} - F_{ji} A_{ji}\right) \Delta t. \tag{14.7}$$

[24] To save using substantial space here, see the references in Grübler (2003); Mercure (2012); Mercure et al. (2014).

Thus the matrix A_{ij} contains the time constants, the rates of exchange between each possible pairs of technologies. Notably, when some technologies have very long lifetimes, they are only very slowly replaced, even when they have low fitnesses. These values can be obtained using survival analysis and survival functions.[25]

The most interesting component comes through the preference parameter F_{ij}. Figure 2.1 shows the principle schematically. It is assumed that agents are heterogeneous, as shown in Figure 14.2. As discussed in Chapter 2, the heterogeneity of agents explains the fact that under most situations, preferences are not clear cut between options, as even if a majority of agents prefer option i, there generally remains a minority who prefers option j. If preferences are Gumbel-distributed in a binary choice, then choices are represented by a logistic (logit) function of the relative 'utility' between options. The concept of 'utility' then requires to be defined.

In standard multinomial logit regressions, utility is a non-measured internal variable that serves to express all of the components that matter to agents making decisions. The same is used here, but outside of a logit framework, since regressing the evolutionary equation above is not possible given that it is never in equilibrium.[26] The trick is to define some reasonable representation of disutility 'costs' to agents, gather sufficient data to cover all components, and insert that in to the F_{ij} framework, assuming that some cost components will be missing. The missing components γ_i can be estimated by 'tuning' the output of the simulation, using Eq. 14.1, to the trajectory observed in historical data (Mercure et al., 2018b). A unique set of values γ_i exists that achieves this, and these values are interpreted as missing 'non-pecuniary' costs. Using this ensures that the model respects observed technological trajectories, but values of γ_i identified should be small in comparison to measured costs, otherwise the responsiveness of the simulation to policy inputs becomes low and highly uncertain.

Take for example power generation (Mercure, 2012). One defines a 'levelised cost of generating electricity' (LCOE) for each technology, and assume that this is the approximate basis upon which heterogeneous power sector investors make decisions. They are heterogeneous for various reasons, for example, projects considered involve varying natural landscapes, technical requirements, and investors have varying risk tolerance and discount rates. The levelised cost involves capital costs at the start of the project I_i, which is normalised by the capacity factor $CF(t)_i$ to obtain the cost per

[25] Mercure (2015, 2018); Mercure et al. (2018b).

[26] As discussed in Chapter 7, actual technology adoption choice trajectories of the collectivity of agents is not a unique function of the utility driving it, as it can have hysteresis and is path-dependent, depending on what happened before. This is why a linear regression of the Lotka-Volterra system, in the form of a multinomial logit with agent interactions, will not converge to unique parameter values (i.e. due to the identification problem of Manski, 1993). The regression could be done using Eq. 14.1 and a non-linear algorithm, but this has no guarantee that unique parameters for α_{ij} can be identified, and indeed, experiments show that the optimisation landscape is not simple nor smooth.

electricity produced. It also incurs possible fuel costs during the generator's lifetime $F(t)_i$ (which are zero for renewables), operation and maintenance $OM(t)_i$, and a possible carbon tax $CO2(t)_i$, and generates income $E(t)$:

$$LCOE_i = \frac{\sum_t \frac{I_i/CF_i + F(t)_i + OM(t)_i + CO2(t)_i}{(1+r)^t}}{\sum_t \frac{E(t)}{(1+r)^t}} + \gamma_i, \tag{14.8}$$

where r is a discount rate that investors are assumed to use. All of these values are naturally dynamic, and thus are calculated at every time step. Notably, the capital cost I_0 can change rapidly due to the learning curve of technology-specific exponent b_i,

$$I_i(t) = I_i(t=0)\left(\frac{W_i(t)}{W_i(t=0)}\right)^{-b_i}, \quad W_i(t) = W_i(t=0) + \sum_t Q_i(t), \tag{14.9}$$

where W_i is the cumulated capacity Q_i ever installed as defined in the learning curve framework. As more and more units are installed, W_i increases and investment costs I_i decline, notably for solar PV and wind turbines. Learning does not necessarily make other cost components decline.

The existence of agent perception heterogeneity implies that the LCOE is distributed, and the best way to represent that is to assume a distribution function, such as the Gumbel distribution, and to calculate a variance for the LCOE:

$$\Delta LCOE_i^2 = \frac{\sum_t \frac{\Delta I_i^2/CF_i^2 + \Delta F(t)_i^2 + \Delta OM(t)_i^2 + \Delta CO2(t)_i^2}{(1+r)^t}}{\sum_t \frac{E(t)^2}{(1+r)^t}}. \tag{14.10}$$

This variance controls what relative cost difference is necessary for net change to become visible.

There remains the parameter γ_i to define, which captures everything missed by the chosen cost framework which could lead the simulations to fail to reproduce observed diffusion trajectories. All one needs to do is iteratively adjust by hand the vector of values γ_i until the projections have equal slope at the start of the simulation as the historical time series have for each technology. If, for example, the model projects PV to remain constant or decline while reality sees PV grow exponentially, then the cost representation is not very good and a large component can be interpreted to be missing, and γ_i will be large relative to the LCOE. This cost could be identified and inserted into the LCOE to reduce the uncertainty; however it is likely related to the fact that people investing in PV are not always the same as those investing in other power technologies, as they may be homeowners or farmers, for example.

In the case of transport, the γ_i can be high and diverse across the types of technologies, but especially, between engine size classes (Mercure et al., 2018b). In road transport, cost differences between vehicles purchased by consumers can span orders of magnitude between luxury and economy vehicles, and these differences stem from income and social group differences. They are adequately captured using the γ_i framework.

Lastly, the sequence of tasks in the simulation is as follows:

(1) Calculate initial LCOEs for all technologies and preferences F_{ij} between all pairs;
(2) Evaluate shares using the Lotka-Volterra Eq. 14.1, from shares at $t - 1$ and LCOEs;
(3) Estimate capacities, service (e.g., power) generation and other quantities (e.g., GHG emissions) for time t;
(4) Calculate learning cost reductions to re-estimate investment costs;
(5) Re-calculate LCOEs for all technologies and preferences F_{ij} between all pairs;
(6) Go back to 2 and iterate this list at each time increment Δt.

This can easily be written in any programming language or integrated within other simulation frameworks, such as E3ME-FTT-GENIE in this case. This forms the core of the FTT technology diffusion modelling framework.

15

Macroeconomics and Structural Change in a Rapid Low-Carbon Transition

The world is on the verge of undergoing a large-scale energy system transformation. Past and present climate policies have had sufficient impact on technology that energy systems will unavoidably be transformed. Governments nevertheless face a choice between whether to support climate policy in their countries to accelerate the transition, or attempt to slow down progress in the climate agenda. No government can fully control the World's energy system, while innovation is global. An important political economy issue emerges with the impending peaking in fossil fuel use and the likely start of the decline of the fossil fuel socio-technical regimes. Financial, economic and political instability lies in the balance. Different countries are affected very differently by this technological transition, where fossil fuel exporters stand to lose substantial economic activity while energy importers have no regrets and only see opportunities. In this chapter, an in-depth analysis is made of the economic and financial impacts of the end of the Age of Oil and other fossil fuels. Risks and opportunities are identified, revealing striking narratives of disruptive structural change and an evolution of economic and geopolitical power across the world. Reflections made regarding policy to mitigate the socio-economic and financial impacts of the transformation. This chapter is partly adapted from Mercure et al. (2021a) and Semieniuk et al. (2022).

15.1. DEFINING STRUCTURAL CHANGE IN THE ENERGY TRANSITION

Policy for a low-carbon transition is making progress, following pledges made as part of the Paris Agreement, through which over 189 countries have agreed targets for greenhouse gas (GHG) emission reductions. GHG reductions equate directly with reductions of demand for fossil fuels. Energy systems are currently over 80% based on the combustion of fossil fuels, for activities from mobility to industrial production to heating homes and communicating. Everything humans do relies on energy, and thus energy generation plays a critical role in enabling society to function. Most decarbonisation policy plans start with decommissioning coal electricity plants, high-carbon industrial plants, and then vehicles, as well as heating systems. However, as of late 2021, detailed policy plans were still not yet in place in all countries. Transforming the energy sector is a substantial challenge that is likely to have enormous ramifications that are not fully understood.

These ramifications arise because the end of fossil fuels implies the end of a whole constellation of technologies and innovations that date from around 100 years. It is the end of the Age of Oil and the internal combustion engine, as well as the end of the Age of Coal and the heavy industry. As discussed in Chapter 11, the technologies related to the internal combustion engine, petrochemicals and aviation date from the 1920s innovation system and Great Wave, which reached their growth peak and began their innovative decline in the 1970s with the oil shocks. Meanwhile, the technologies related to coal combustion for electricity generation and steelmaking date from the 1880s Great Wave. To avoid climate change, these technologies must come to the end of their lives so that GHG emissions cease. This has provided substantial motivation in some parts of the world to promote low-carbon innovation. But furthermore, it is very possible that low-carbon innovation becomes a desirable product in itself, beyond climate change considerations, from an economic standpoint. After all, thermal conversion of fossil energy is wasteful at best, in comparison to new non-combustion ways of capturing energy, and the extraction of fossil fuels is itself labour and energy-intensive, while process innovation for lowering fossil fuel conversion losses has come to its limits. With or without climate policy, these technologies from earlier eras are now entering a full decline.

Quite the opposite, low-carbon energy production and end-use is capital-intensive and characterised by low operational costs. Solar panels and wind turbines require labour to install them, but operate largely unsupervised and rarely require maintenance as they simply feature less components and are automated. This is particularly true for solar photovoltaics, which do not even have moving parts, and can just sit under the sun producing electricity at no effort. Electric vehicles have substantially less moving parts too, and are expensive solely due to the cost of manufacturing their battery, complex technological components with costs that are declining very rapidly.[1] Domestic and industrial heat pumps generate well over 100% efficiency of use of electricity, sometimes even in excess of 300%, which offers broad possibilities. A low-carbon economy will necessarily involve a much higher energy efficiency than an economy based on thermal combustion. The decline of the ages of oil and coal are irreversible, as it may not be economically desirable for anyone to go back to thermal conversion once high-carbon capital has depreciated.

[1] Knobloch et al. (2020); Ziegler and Trancik (2021).

As with all technological transitions from one Kondratiev to another, new value chains arise, and old value chains decline and die with creative destruction. With value chains come complex networks of occupations, trades, business models and 'ways of making a living', which come to an end in whole clusters. As discussed in Chapter 11, such declines are never very peaceful, as they lead to 'sailing ship effects' in which agents trapped in the old regimes attempt to hinder or slow down the transition in order to avoid what eventually becomes inevitable. Such agents may perceive the situation as involving unnecessary change and a failure of governance, as happened at the onset of every Kondratiev (Freeman and Louçã, 2001). It is also because agents operating in the 'sunset' industries begin to compete for a dwindling demand for their products and suffer from over capacity (Semieniuk et al., 2021). Here, it is the oil, gas and coal extraction, transformation, transportation, distribution, as well as petrochemicals, steelmaking, car manufacturing, aviation and many other applications that must disappear or undergo substantial change, where potentially many companies may not survive but instead become replaced. Meanwhile, the economy takes the opportunity to leave behind old inefficient 'ways of making a living', in which little additional innovation could be made, for new powerful methods of economic production. In this case, it is inexpensive, capital-intensive, efficient and perhaps intelligent or automated electricity generation, mobility and industrial production.

In this chapter, the risks and opportunities that emerge in the low-carbon transition are explored in detail using a highly disaggregated global macroeconomic, technology diffusion, financial and climate model, called E3ME-FTT-GENIE, introduced in Chapter 2, and largely based on the equation systems given in Chapters 7, 11 and 14 for technological evolution and macroeconomics, respectively.[2] The decline of the Age of Oil is first explored through a quantitative closed analysis of global energy markets, demand and supply. Second, the macroeconomic, geopolitical and political economy implications of the low-carbon transition are explored through macroeconomic modelling. Third, the economic and financial risks and opportunities are explored that result from this transition. Lastly, as Minsky (1986) famously suggested, capitalism is inherently unstable, and thus a conclusion is given regarding the policy approaches that can mitigate the volatility and instability to be expected in what could otherwise become a turbulent low-carbon transition.

15.2. THE DECLINE OF THE AGE OF OIL

15.2.1 *Geopolitical Context*

It is useful to first provide some context of geopolitics. Global climate negotiations have traditionally been framed as a 'Prisoner's Dilemma' (PD) game, where the

[2] See Mercure et al. (2018a) for a detailed description of the integrated model.

objective of curbing emissions of CO_2 is plagued by 'free-riding' by those not doing so, but who nevertheless benefit from global mitigation, without the economic burden of environmental regulation.[3] However, this motive is not actually supported by the evidence.[4] More fundamentally, the nature of the incentives is misrepresented by the PD: the game may now be more about industrial strategy, job creation and success of trade.[5] The costs of generating solar and wind energy, depending on location, have in fact, or will soon reach parity with the lowest-cost traditional fossil alternatives, while investment in low-carbon technologies is generating substantial new employment.[6]

The notion that a country should benefit from free-riding on other countries' climate policies can also be challenged. Incremental decarbonisation, increasing energy efficiency, and the economic impacts of COVID-19 have led oil and gas demand and prices to decline substantially, affecting the viability of extraction in less competitive regions. Fossil fuel exporters can be economically impacted by climate policy decisions of other countries through lower global demand and lower prices, and abandoning climate policies to boost domestic demand or maintain high prices is not sufficient to compensate for declining exports.

The transition to a low-carbon economy has raised major questions of geopolitics in the international relations literature.[7] Here Vakulchuk's definition of 'geopolitics' is used, as the connection between geography, resources, space and the power of states. It has become increasingly clear, with the pace at which renewables are growing, that traditionally fossil fuel dominated energy geopolitics must be revisited. With the prospects of renewable energies capturing markets previously dominated by fossil fuels, energy commodity exporters, in some cases affected by the resource curse (Ross, 1999), lose export markets. Concurrently, importers improve their trade balances.[8] Revenues losses could lead to political instability in fossil fuel exporting economies and, although robust evidence indicates that climate change could increase conflict at all scales, it is unclear whether the transition will increase or reduce conflict overall.[9]

Bazilian and Goldthau et al.[10] describe four scenarios of geopolitical evolution, based on whether successful climate action is taken and on how geopolitical rivalries in fossil fuels and renewables are addressed. They call for short to mid-term quantitative scenario creation that could describe the geopolitical dynamics and narrow

3 IPCC (2014); Hurlstone et al. (2017); Barrett (1994); Nordhaus (2015).
4 Aklin and Mildenberger (2020); McEvoy and Cherry (2016).
5 E.g., see HM Treasury (2021); European Commission (2019); White House (2021).
6 Farmer and Lafond (2016); Lafond et al. (2018); Wei et al. (2010); Fragkos and Paroussos (2018); Garrett-Peltier (2017).
7 IRENA (2019); Hafner and Tagliapietra (2020); Scholten (2018); Goldthau et al. (2019); O'Sullivan et al. (2017); Vakulchuk et al. (2020).
8 IRENA (2019); Hafner and Tagliapietra (2020).
9 IRENA (2019); O'Sullivan et al. (2017); Vakulchuk et al. (2020); Hsiang et al. (2013).
10 Goldthau et al. (2019); Bazilian et al. (2020).

down the possibilities. A key question is whether low-carbon technology development is globally cooperative or fragmented, and whether the emerging renewable energy geopolitics comes to replace fossil energy geopolitics.[11]

Most nations possess sizeable technical potentials for one or more types of renewable energy sources, reducing the likelihood of any state gaining significant control over future energy supplies. However, the production of renewables technology is increasingly concentrated in a few regions, including China, Europe and the United States, generating new types of geopolitical rivalry. Concerns over access to critical materials for making renewables technology have been raised, and although debated, remain a concern for policy-makers. Lastly, the possibility of new resource curse situations linked to renewables has also been also raised.[12]

Scholarship in geopolitics thus paints a much more complex picture than the PD suggests. Despite this, the PD remains the prevailing framing of global climate policy,[13] underpinning debates such as those on 'carbon leakage' (the relocation of carbon-intensive industries to countries with no or limited climate policy), and the historical 'free-riding' of developed nations and the right to emit of developing nations. These hypotheses can be verified using quantitative modelling evidence to help narrow down possibilities, something that is explored next.

15.2.2 *Technological Change*

Four are created representing very different possible ways one could conceptualise future economic evolution. According to simulations using the GENIE earth system model, these scenarios achieve very different climate outcomes. The scenarios were created as follows:[14]

1. **Technological Diffusion Trajectory (TDT)**: The current trajectory of technology and the economy is simulated based on recently observed trends in technology, energy markets and macroeconomics, exploring the direction of technology evolution not contingent on the adoption of new climate policies. This generates a median global warming of 2.6°C .
2. **Global Net-Zero (Net-Zero)**: Detailed climate policies are added to the model by either increasing the stringency of what already exists or by implementing policies that may be reasonably expected in each regional context. The UK, EU, China, Japan and South Korea reach net-zero emissions independently in 2050. Moderate amounts of negative

[11] Scholten (2018); Scholten and Bosman (2016).
[12] Overland (2019); Hafner and Tagliapietra (2020); Scholten (2018).
[13] Nordhaus (2015); Aklin and Mildenberger (2020); Weitzman (2017).
[14] The Appendix provides a summary of the policies assumed. In short, a carbon price is imposed, along with additional sector-specific technologies that achieve a rapid rate of transition.

emissions are used to offset residual emissions in industry. This achieves a median warming of 1.5°C.

3. **EU and East Asia Net-Zero (EU-EA Net-Zero)**: The same policies to achieve net-zero emissions for Europe and East Asia (China in 2060, Japan, the EU and South Korea in 2050) but assume TDT policies elsewhere. This reaches a median warming of 2.0°C.
4. **Investor Expectations (InvE)**: The energy–economy system is assumed to follow high-carbon trajectories similar to outputs of current standard equilibrium models,[15] which predict a technological status quo and an undisturbed continued growth in fossil fuel demand. The transition fails to go ahead, to reflect expectations of delayed or abandoned decarbonisation by a major subset of investors in energy systems. This scenario leads to global average temperature warming of 3.5°C.

Figure 15.1 shows projected technology evolution in four sectors, as well as global CO_2 combustion and industrial emissions, in four scenarios of future energy and economic evolution. The low-carbon transition is already underway in several sectors, as can be seen in technology data. The modelling results suggest that a transition is in the making in the TDT scenario, in comparison to InvE, with both solar PVs and EVs diffusing very rapidly without additional policy support. This diffusion is generated by the interaction between diffusion and learning-by-doing cost reductions, which lead costs to achieve parity with other technologies during the 2020s. Naturally, in the partial and global net-zero scenarios, the decarbonisation is more rapid, as it is imposed by scenario construction. East Asia and the EU together accounting for a sizeable fraction of global energy demand, their decarbonisation has large impacts on energy markets, not least due to the scale of markets for PVs, EVs and other low-carbon technologies that are created.

15.2.3 *Energy Markets*

The TDT technology transition underway, if one believes the modelling, leads to a rapid and drastic re-organisation of energy markets (Figure 15.2). Fossil fuels are highly traded, since they originate from a restricted set of locations, where they can be found due to geological history, in places such as the USA, Canada, Australia, the Middle East and Russia. Thus most countries of the world are importers, and a few are exporters. Meanwhile, quality renewable resources, especially the sun and wind, are available literally everywhere, and increasingly so as technological costs decline. Although some areas are clearly more productive for renewables than others, for sufficiently inexpensive solar panels and wind turbines, it becomes possible for

[15] For instance, RCP 8.5, see Riahi et al. (2011).

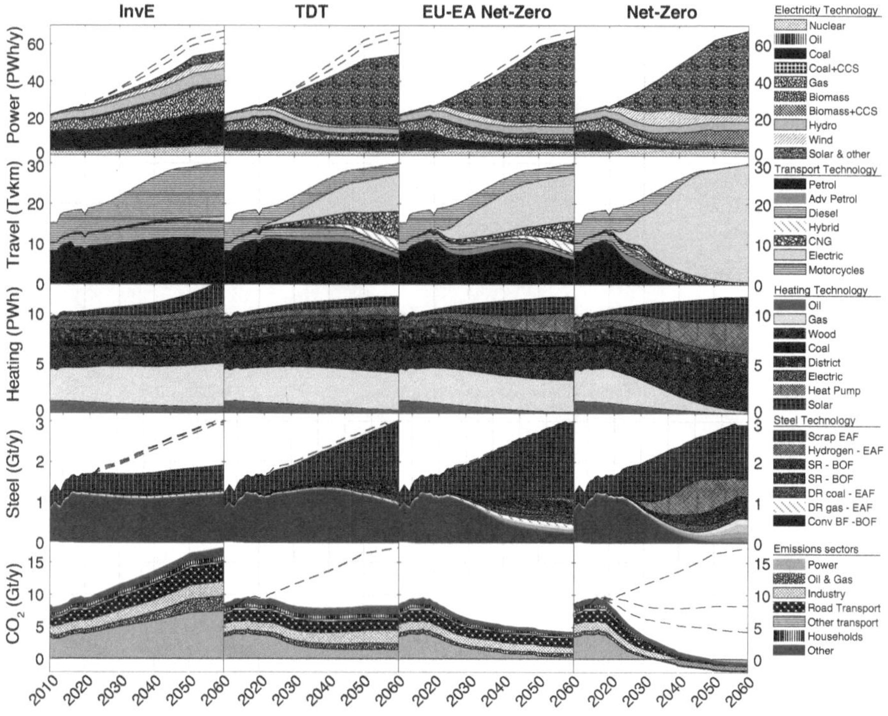

FIGURE 15.1 Technological change in the four high-carbon sectors of power generation, road transport, household heating and steelmaking (Mercure et al., 2021a). Key: CCS: Carbon Capture and Storage; CNG: Compressed Natural Gas; EAF: Electric Arc Furnace; BF: Blast Furnace; BOF: Basic Oxygen Furnace; DR: Direct Reduction; SR: Smelt Reduction

anyone with enough land to produce energy. In that sense, renewable energy is much more democratically distributed around the world than fossil fuels. There is no real reason for renewable electricity to be as substantially traded as fossil fuels are, as this saves substantial infrastructure transport costs which would not be justified by relatively small inter-region renewables cost differences. The old model of centralised energy production and sparse network distribution may well disappear, replaced by decentralised production and consumption.

Thus it is clear that decarbonisation leads to a drastic change in trade balances of nearly all countries of the world, depending on whether they are importers or exporters, in something that amounts nearly to a zero-sum game. Importer countries gain from reducing imports, as their inhabitants can spend the money domestically on other domestically made goods instead, while exporter countries lose equal amounts of exports, money not spent domestically anymore. This re-organisation of energy trade, if it happens, is of such a large scale that global geopolitical power could be on the edge of becoming fundamentally destabilised.

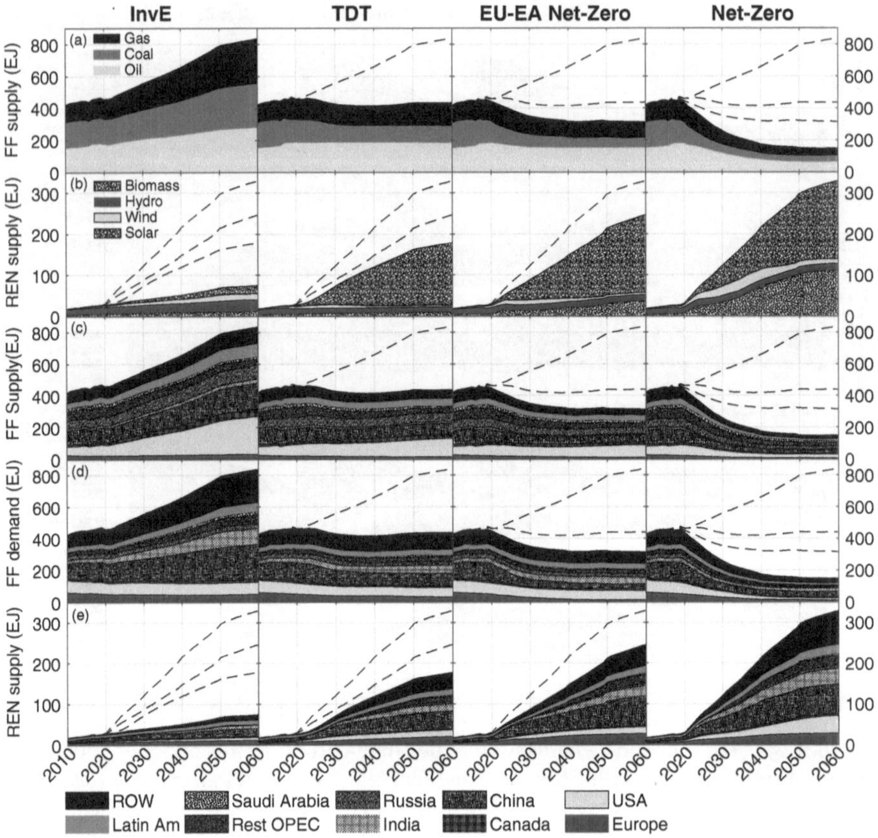

FIGURE 15.2 Evolution of global energy demand and supply, for (a) fossil fuels by fuel type and (b) renewables by resource type, (c) fossil fuels by producing country and (d) using country, and (e) renewables by country of supply, which is approximately equal to demand by country (Mercure et al., 2021a).

Figure 15.2 shows the supply of fossil fuels and renewables by sources, the supply and demand for fossil fuels by region, and the supply of renewables by region only, since it is nearly identical to its demand as net international trade of electricity is currently comparatively small. The supply of fossil fuels is, if one is led to believe the technological forecasts simulated from data by the FTT model, likely to peak in the 2020s. It is uncertain at which rate a subsequent decline could arise after this, as policy-makers will be making further energy policy decisions. As demonstrated below, a likely scenario may be the EU-EA Net-Zero, where EU and Chinese energy policy decisions lead to drastic declines in demand for all three fossil fuels, as these regions comprise of over 1.7bn people and industries with high energy demand. The result is a substantial shrinking in global fossil fuel markets. Here, peaking of fossil fuels is not related to their availability,[16] as it is clear that fossil fuel reserves far exceed the carbon budget for a 2°C scenario, let alone net-zero emissions in 2050.[17]

All scenarios except InvE drastically affect the quantities of fossil fuels produced and exchanged, relative to expectations formed on the basis of energy and economic scenarios produced using standard equilibrium models. Standard models, as currrently used by international institutions, do not produce technology diffusion scenarios that are consistent with observed reality.[18] But furthermore, this transition will unavoidably lead some companies to bankruptcy as their core business becomes affected. As discussed in Chapter 10, insolvencies can trigger further insolvencies when nodes of the financial network are leveraged, which is likely to be the case. Thus, further questions arise as to whether not only economic stability could be affected by this re-organisation of production and trade, but financial stability as well. Financial instability could arise in the financial network if enough companies are leveraged and high-carbon companies are suddenly re-valued by pricing in future fossil sector losses, for example, on the basis of changing expectations towards TDT or EU-EA Net-Zero relative to InvE.

It should also be noted from Figure 15.2 that total energy demand in a low-carbon economy is much lower than in a high-carbon, combustion-based economy, by a factor of just above two. This partly reflects accounting ambiguity, and partly the vast inefficiency of thermal conversion in comparison to energy produced without any combustion. Notably, the electricity demand of electric vehicles, in energy units, is a very small fraction of the thermal content of petrol and diesel used for the same distance driven, the excess energy lost as heat from the engine. The same is true of LED lights and heat pumps in comparison to incandescent bulbs and fuel combustion heating systems, while electricity plants simply waste around 50% of the thermal content of fossil fuels.

15.3. MACROECONOMICS OF THE ENERGY TRANSITION

15.3.1 *Political Economy of Oil*

Oil markets are controlled and managed since the 1970s on the basis of political economy considerations rather than simple economics. In the 1970s, the OPEC cartel formed with the explicit intention of restricting Middle Eastern supply, reducing competition, driving up prices and acquiring monopolistic rents as it forced the rest of the world to look for more expensive oil elsewhere than in the Middle East.

16 As in peak oil theory, see Hubbert (1962); Rehrl and Friedrich (2006); Reynolds and Baek (2012).
17 See Meinshausen et al. (2009).
18 Farmer and Lafond (2016); Lafond et al. (2018); Ives et al. (2021).

OPEC has operated in this way since then until recently, when it suddenly switched to a different strategy (van de Graaf and Bradshaw, 2018). In 2015, OPEC let the oil flow more freely, which led to an oil price crash that never recovered to the pre-2015 prices above $100/bbl, but reached prices below $30/bbl in 2016, and even negative for one day in 2020. It will never be possible to fully know what change of spirit took place with OPEC leaders, but one possibility is that under the expectation of reduced future expected demand, due to increasing efficiency and environmental policy, OPEC has decided that their oil would take priority in energy markets, even if this meant that prices were going to be lower from then on. Following this, in 2022, new conflicts involving Russia, Ukraine and other countries began that were almost certainly partly motivated by energy-related geopolitics, leading to oil prices well above $100/bbl again.

Before 2015, OPEC had been maximising rent by restricting supply and maintaining spare capacity while the market was growing, which led other producers to explore for ever more technically challenging resources, such as deep offshore, arctic oil and oil sands. This drove prices up as the marginal cost of the last barrel needed to supply the demand became increasingly costly to extract, and the price ultimately had to justify its extraction, so long as output at lower-cost production sites was deliberately restricted. However, under expected limited future demand, OPEC could lose out in the long run if part of its resource base, which remains very large, ends up never used, while more return can be obtained by following a strategy based on lower prices but substantially higher volumes. Effectively, the expectation of climate policy and peak demand implies that the old Hotelling (1931) rule, if it was ever followed, breaks down for good.

The political economy of oil and gas can be summarised by examining resource data as shown in Figure 15.3, where the world's production, proved reserves and known resources are shown distributed along an estimated break-even production cost axis, for all major producer countries and the rest of the world. Total reserves and resources are indicated in the legends. In the TDT scenario, the E3ME-FTT model projects cumulative global oil and gas use up to 2050 of 890 and 630 Gbbl respectively (and 480 and 370 Gbbl in the Net-zero scenario). OPEC countries together possess over 650 and 202 Gbbl of resources of oil and gas, at substantially lower break-even costs of production below $20 per barrel. In comparison, resources left in the USA, Canada and Russia occur at substantially higher production costs between $20 and $80 per barrel. Even without additional climate policies, peak oil demand is on the horizon and the latter countries cannot compete with OPEC, who can on their own cover most of global demand until the time when oil and gas markets come to an end. Chances are that by restricting supply as they have done in the past, their rents would turn out lower than what they can obtain at lower prices but substantially higher volumes while demand lasts.

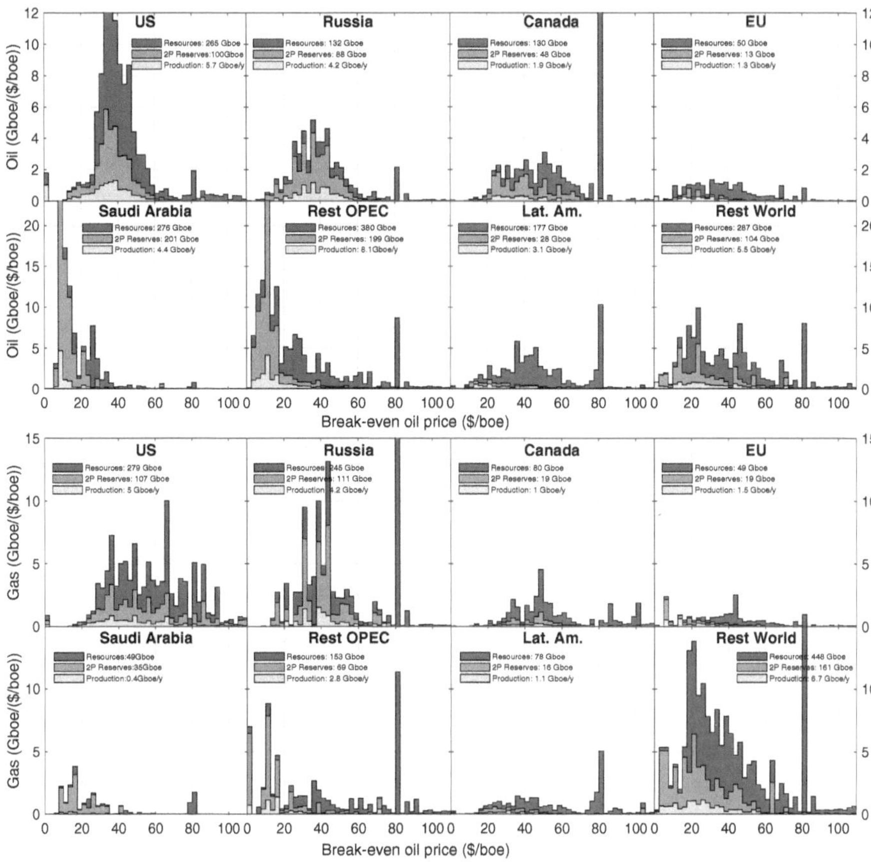

FIGURE 15.3 Resources, 2P reserves and production of oil and gas across the world in 2020, according to the Rystad dataset (Mercure et al., 2021a). Note that production histograms are scaled up by a factor 5 for visibility. Totals are given in the legends.

That this is indeed most likely correct has been determined using the E3ME-FTT model, by creating the two extreme sub-scenarios of OPEC decision-making.

1. **Quotas (QU)**: OPEC restricts output such that it maintains a constant share of peaking and declining global oil and gas output. This implies declining production to reserve ratios as output follows global demand.
2. **Sell-off (SO)**: OPEC increases output such that it maintains a constant production despite that demand is peaking and declining. This implies that OPEC gradually acquires the market until its production reaches global demand.

Figure 15.4, left-hand panels, shows the impact of those decisions on oil and gas markets. The top two panels show price trajectories across all scenario variants. Prices rise in InvE, but stagnate in the TDT and decline in the net-zero scenario. The method with which prices are determined, explained in the Appendix, is to find the marginal cost value, among the data shown in Figure 15.3, that clears the global demand generated by E3ME, while those resources are gradually depleted. The model does not, however, simulate the discovery of new reserves, but exploration is very likely to stop entirely anyway. It also does not take account of the impact of armed conflict and thus will simulate changes smoother than what is observed. The lower panels show the loss in oil and gas output suffered by various countries, in the likely EU-EA Net-Zero scenario relative to InvE, according to the QU and SO scenario variants. Fossil export losses are by definition more evenly distributed in the QU scenario than in the SO scenario. This implies that economic impacts of decarbonisation on non-OPEC producers is likely higher in the SO scenario. In the full Net-Zero scenario, the same trends are observed but intensified.

15.3.2 *Macroeconomics and Employment*

Figure 15.4, right-hand side panels, shows the macroeconomic impacts of the transition, in the EU-EA Net-Zero scenario relative to InvE. Critically, the model assumes credit creation by banks for projects (see Chapters 3 and 9). Quantities shown are declines in government royalties from fossil fuel extraction, and changes in GDP and aggregate employment. Here it becomes quite clear: importers have positive GDP changes while exporters have negative GDP changes, for all exporters except OPEC. OPEC can essentially recover all of their GDP and employment losses through the adoption of the SO strategy. Therefore it is clear that it makes sense for them to do so, assuming that they are endowed by that level of foresight. Meanwhile, there is little that the USA, Canada and Russia can do to protect their very large fossil fuel industries from decline caused by decarbonisation in the EU and East Asia.

The importers, notably the EU, China, India and Japan, in fact gain in macroeconomic terms as they get rid of costly imports of fossil fuels and are assumed not to replace those imports by other imports, and instead spend the money domestically, which strengthens domestic employment and production. Decarbonisation boosts investment for two reasons: first, firms in importer countries invest in the low-carbon capital that allows them to eliminate energy imports, and this trickles down through the local industry, and second the surge in domestic income not spent on energy but spent on domestically produced goods and services,[19] drives investment across sectors of consumption goods. This double dividend effect pushes economic activity

[19] Including low-carbon energy, although primary energy demand is drastically reduced, despite that useful energy demand is not reduced, due to the elimination of fuel combustion.

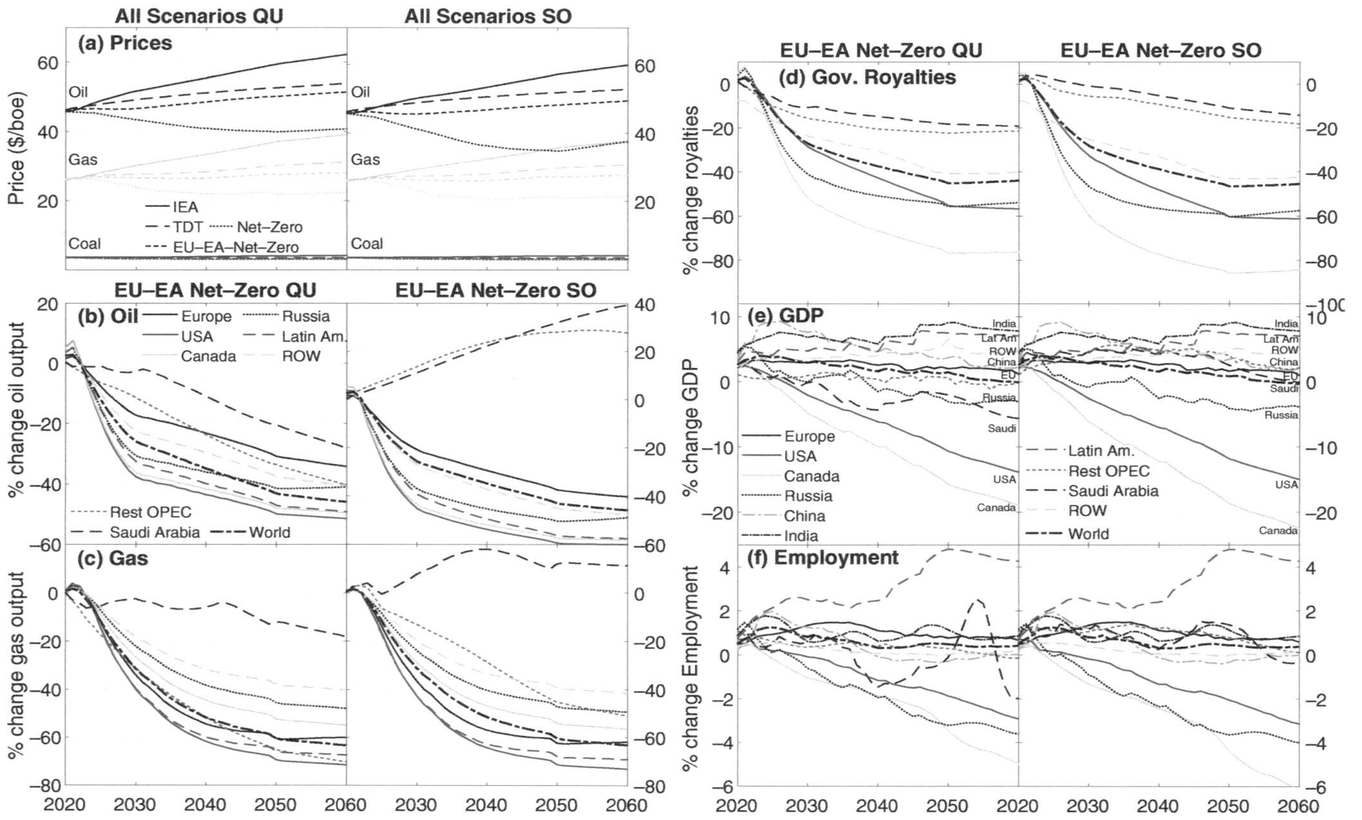

FIGURE 15.4 (Left panels) Absolute price changes, production losses in oil and gas markets in the 'Quotas' (QU) and 'Sell-off' (SO) scenarios, expressed as a % change from the InvE scenario. (Right panels) Changes in government revenues from oil and gas activities through royalties, changes in GDP and employment, all expressed as % changes from the InvE scenario. Saudi Arabia is separated from the rest of OPEC for clarity, 'ROW' stands for Rest of the World for regions and countries not otherwise included, while 'World' refers to changes at the global level. Government revenues are assumed deficit-neutral for clarity of analysis (Mercure et al., 2021a).

up, as construction and manufacturing increases activity, and the income spent by workers in those sectors increase activity in all other sectors.[20]

The exporters excluding OPEC, notably the USA, Russia, Canada, lose in macroeconomic terms in roughly a mirror image compared to the importers. Under limited expectations of economic return in the visibly declining high-carbon sectors, firms restrict investment, which reduces activity in construction, manufacturing, materials and others, and loss of income in those sectors leads to reduced spending in all other sectors of the economy. However, the loss of government royalties plays an important role too as it further reduces spending and income in social services, education, defence and other public services and the areas in which these sectors traditionally procure their services. Crucially, no realistic increase in domestic demand for fossil fuels can replace losses of exports, even if climate policies are abandoned and fossil fuel use promoted. In fact, low-carbon technology may even become adopted in those countries despite the lack of policy to support those, as costs are brought down by investment by the importers. However, with climate policies, exporters can still benefit from a low-carbon investment stimulus while if they abandon all climate policies, they forgo this last opportunity for economic activity.

Hence, two very distinct patterns emerge according to this importer-exporter classification of countries, which can be observed in Figure 15.5. Here, while aggregate investment increases in all countries with the low-carbon transition in the EU-EA Net-Zero, with or without climate policies, exporters have a loss of GDP related to their losses of fossil fuel output and dependent industries.

15.3.3 *Reframing the Climate Policy Game*

An analysis of agency in this system can be made on the basis of the macroeconomic outcomes shown above, using a simple classical game theory framework. One cannot assume that decision-makers in all those countries have all of the knowledge included in the projections of the E3ME-FTT model, nor that they decide solely on the basis of discounted future GDP; however, one can imagine that decision-makers are aware of the sectors and regions in which unemployment is currently emerging, and may be able to have a sense of where this is heading. Assuming that artificial decision-makers were to decide according to the GDP outcomes of E3ME-FTT model scenarios as payoffs, the game that emerges is as follows.

It is a two level game (Figure 15.6), in which at the top level, importers decide whether or not to decarbonise, linked to a decision by OPEC whether or not to flood markets. At the bottom level, depending whether OPEC floods markets or not, high-cost producers decide whether or not to follow importers in decarbonising. It is important to see that decisions about low-carbon technologies are not directly related

[20] This assumes that crowding-out, as traditionally assumed in equilibrium models, does not occur, i.e. that finance in low-carbon capital does not crowd out finance elsewhere in the economy. See Chapters 9 and 3.

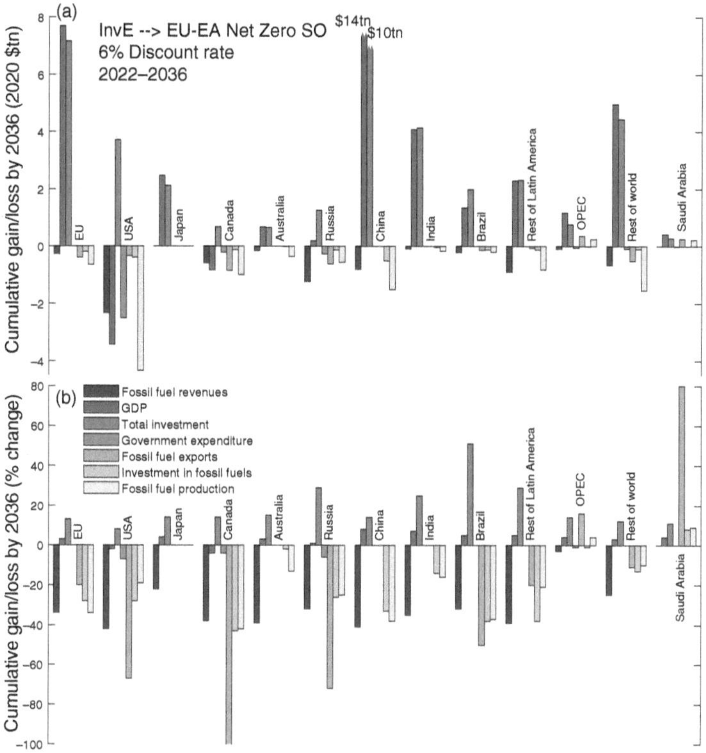

FIGURE 15.5 Cumulated gains and losses in the EU-EA Net-Zero SO scenario relative to InvE, in various economic quantities cumulated between 2022 and 2036 and discounted by 6%, in (a) absolute value and (b) relative changes (Mercure et al., 2021a). Bars for each country going left to right are in the order of the legend going top to bottom.

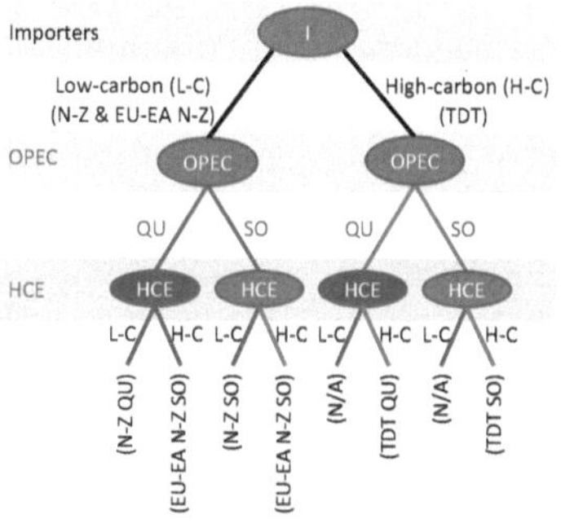

Payoff matrix
Importers vs OPEC

		OPEC			
		QU		SO	
		Importers	OPEC	Importers	OPEC
Importers	EU-EA N-Z	26889	243	26521	1182
	TDT	8367	−40	8171	410

Payoff matrix
OPEC vs HCE

		High-Cost exporters (HCE)			
		EU-EA Net-Zero		Net-Zero	
		HCE	OPEC	HCE	OPEC
OPEC	QU	−2590	243	−4595	1551
	SO	−4042	1182	−6350	2748

FIGURE 15.6 Reframed climate policy game. Values are cumulated GDP between 2022 and 2036 discounted by 6% (Mercure et al., 2021a).

to decisions about energy production, since countries (e.g., Norway) could decide to reduce domestic emissions while exporting fossil fuels. The result is that the decision by importers to decarbonise is dominant as it does not depend on what exporters do, and thus they can do this unilaterally. Following that, the decision by OPEC whether or not to flood markets is also dominant, since a decision by non-OPEC countries to flood markets has no impact and OPEC has no regrets whatever other countries decide. Finally, the decision by high-cost exporters to postpone climate policies indefinitely is also dominant. Therefore, the EU-EA Net-Zero SO scenario would dominate, due to all the combined incentives, if decisions were really taken on that GDP payoff basis.[21] In the long run, however, as fossil fuel markets collapse, it would not seem sensible for any country to continue postponing joining the low-carbon economy. It will make sense for as long as there are people to believe that fossil fuel industries will rebound.

Whether or not this game is a realistic depiction of existing incentives, the storyline is insightful. It says that importers such as China and the EU cause damage to exporters such as the USA and Russia. The only way the non-OPEC exporters can avoid the damages caused by decarbonisation is if they put political pressure on other countries to abandon climate action. But this is not likely to work in Europe, nor in China, given that there are no economic advantages anymore in doing so, while there is a new low-carbon innovation race to be won.

15.4. MACROECONOMIC RISKS AND OPPORTUNITIES

15.4.1 *Structural Change*

Arguably the most important impact of the low-carbon transition is one of structural change caused by creative destruction. In effect, some workers and investors become trapped in sections of the economy that are going in decline, without an escape route. Coal mining towns, as there used to be in England but still exist in Poland, Germany, China, India and Australia, enter post-industrial decline. Large petrochemical processing hubs, such as those in Rotterdam, Houston and Taiwan, that employ large numbers of people with relatively high wages, could become largely unemployed. Take Rotterdam, for example: oil tankers arrive from overseas and unload oil directly into an enormous petrochemical complex, which becomes immediately transformed into myriads of fuels and derivatives, to be loaded again onto barges on the Rhine River headed to Germany, France, Switzerland and Austria.

As EVs become widely adopted by Western and Central Europeans, as may be on the verge of happening, for lack of demand for transport fuels, the volume processed in Rotterdam should unavoidably decline drastically. One could imagine that in a low-carbon economy, non-transport petrochemicals would become replaced by a bio-economy, in which plastics and fuels originating from plant matter are

[21] Clearly this is not the case as since Joe Biden took over the US Presidency, his first decision was to rejoin the Paris Agreement, which may have been taken on grounds other than GDP and employment. Russia appears unlikely to adopt climate policies, while Canada is likely to follow as usual whatever the USA decides.

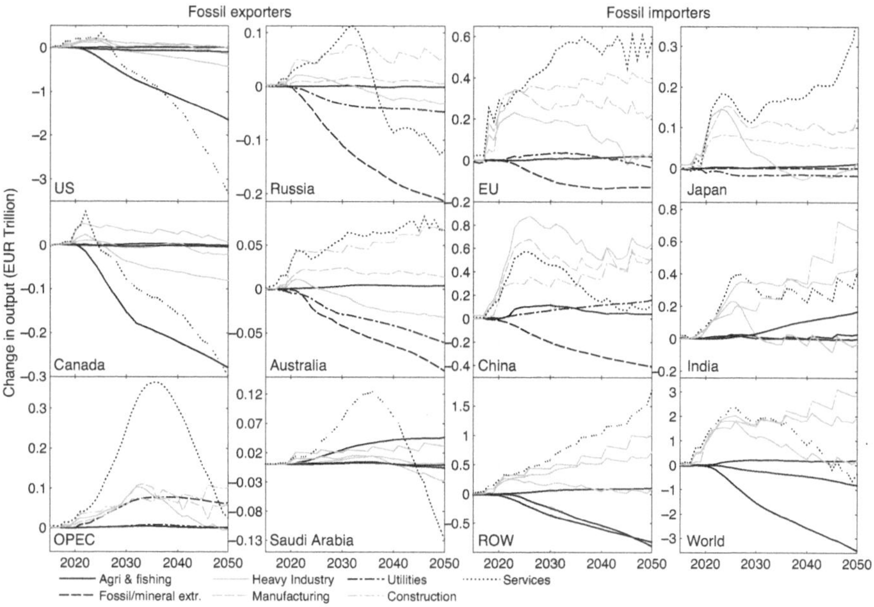

FIGURE 15.7 Structural change in different economies classified between importers and exporters of fossil fuels. Differences in sectoral output are taken between a Net-Zero emissions scenario globally with oil and gas fire sale from OPEC.

processed in similar chemical hubs. Unfortunately, there is no practical reason to expect that those new chemical industries would necessarily locate themselves where petrochemicals have traditionally been, or have anywhere near the same volumes. Meanwhile, further impacts could also arise in the car industry in Germany, simply because even if a successful EV industry emerges, all companies involved in making parts for internal combustion engines would still gradually disappear, as EVs require substantially less components than traditional vehicles. Thus it is clear that the transition will generate socio-economic impacts that are geographically concentrated.

Figure 15.7 shows more generally the structural change that can be expected around the world as a result of the transition. Three recurrent patterns emerge again, between the high-cost exporters, OPEC, and the importers. Importers will be affected by the transition, in areas such as Rotterdam, but importer countries nevertheless have substantially less such value chains at risk. Meanwhile, investment in new technology more than compensates economic activity, thus increasing aggregate demand and raising economic activity overall despite localised situations of post-industrial decline. In contrast, exporters have larger and more dominant value chains becoming at risk, affecting and being affected by stagnating aggregate demand and fiscal regimes; this leads to general slowdown across those economies and areas of disastrous regional decline.

What is clear is that as opposed to common belief and debates based on equilibrium economics[22] the impacts of the declining industries will be much more disruptive to economies than the effect of investment in new technologies (Semieniuk et al., 2021). It appears to be the decline of what already exists that becomes more destructive than the re-allocation of existing and new resources into new directions.

15.4.2 *Transition Financial Risks*

The impacts of the ongoing transition on the economy goes much further than just creating structural change. In fact, although a formal accepted model does not yet really exist, the decline of industries has rarely been orderly in history.[23] This may be because humans, when cornered, perhaps tend to believe in their luck until the time of redemption comes when they must admit that they are ruined. In finance, as discussed in Chapters 9 and 10, one profit warning leads to the next due to complex chains of ownership, while in declining industries, it is possible that firms attempt to increase their leverage as much as lenders will allow them to in a last bid for survival, which would just increase the systemic impact of their losses. In a rapid low-carbon transition, bankruptcies must unavoidably take place, but the degree to which financial losses would be sudden could strongly depend on policy and behaviour.

The discussion over 'Transition Risks' originated with the Bank of England and its then Governor Mark Carney, kicked off by a very influential speech at the Lloyds of London alongside a landmark report (BoE, 2015). This was followed by a flurry of activity and debate focused on defining and quantifying climate change-related risks, so-called physical and transition risks.[24] Meanwhile, large institutions have announced publicly plans to divest from fossil fuels, including the Church of England, the Norwegian Sovereign Wealth Fund. Banks have begun to take serious notice, and it has become in 2021 a very fluid and fast-changing situation. Through new requirements over disclosure of climate change-related risks, the information about real risks of post-industrial decline in fossil fuel-related activities that many companies face directly or indirectly could become easier to access. Divestment from these companies could happen on the basis of more than just environmental or ethical reasons, such as evidence of financial risk.

22 See, for instance, van Vuuren et al. (2020), and more generally Clarke et al. (2014); Stern (2007).

23 See the great waves literature, especially Freeman and Louçã (2001); Perez (2001). A model of decline of 'sunset' industries is given in Semieniuk et al. (2021).

24 See, for example, TCFD (2017); BoE (2018); Bolton et al. (2020); UNEP (2018); NGFS (2019); Mercure (2019); Campiglio et al. (2018).

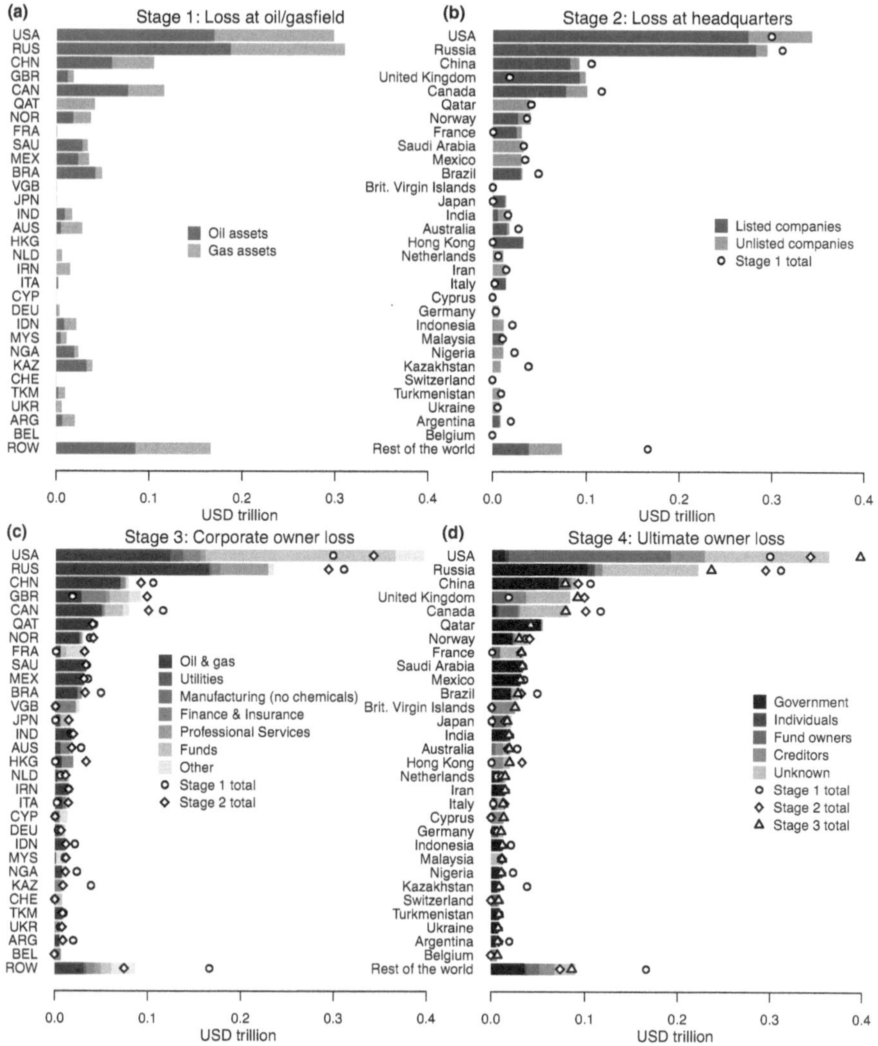

FIGURE 15.8 Propagation of financial risks from wells to owners, starting from losses of expected revenue at (Stage 1) oil and gas assets, (Stage 2) company headquarters, (Stage 3) ultimate corporate owners, (Stage 4) ultimate owners. Reproduced from Semiemiuk et al. (2022).

Figure 15.8 shows the flow of transition risks in the global financial sector that stems from oil and gas activities during the transition.[25] The risk is calculated by assuming that investors believe in the InvE scenario but suddenly realise that the

[25] This work was carried out by a consortium of researchers that includes contributors to this chapter (Semiemiuk et al., 2022).

global energy system is instead on an EU-EA Net-Zero SO trajectory, and re-value all their assets accordingly. To estimate company risk, a large scale-free network of equity ownership was created using the Bureau van Dijk ORBIS database, which documents the 100 largest shareholders for several millions of companies worldwide. This is similar in concept to the artificial equity network used in Chapter 10; however, equivalent data on the topology of the global debt network was not available to the team, and thus a SOC model could not be built on empirical data, and a linear model of loss propagation used instead. Losses of fossil fuel companies are traced through the global equity ownership network, and bankrupt companies are identified globally. Losses to ultimate owners at corporate level are quantified, as well as for governments, funds (e.g., pension funds) and individuals.

Panel (a) shows the geographical distribution of revenue lost at the fossil fuel asset level (oil and gas wells). Total losses (not shown), calculated using E3ME-FTT data, range from $3tn (TDT) and $7tn (EU-EA Net-Zero) to $11tn (global Net-Zero). However, it is only expected profits that in fact travel on the network, in this case $1.4tn, the rest going into wages and other inputs to production. The largest risk is unsurprisingly situated in the USA, Canada, Russia and to a lesser degree Saudi Arabia and the rest of OPEC. While in Saudi Arabia, the SO strategy prevents very substantial losses, losses nevertheless arise due to a lower oil price relative to InvE. Panel (b) shows the corresponding equity value losses at the level of fossil fuel company headquarters. This involves a different geography as the operations of companies are not all situated in the same countries as their headquarters. A similar geographical ranking is observed nevertheless. Panel (c) shows the losses at the level of the ultimate corporate owner, organised by sector. Lastly, panel (d) shows the distribution of losses between governments, funds and individuals.

The number of bankrupt companies is large, and follows this ranking order. What is not calculated is what happens to all of the debt that has been incurred by all of these companies, that must be written off by banks and other creditors, and what the impact of doing so is on those companies, whether those companies could in turn go bankrupt, and whether those bankruptcies would generate further runaway bankruptcy chains as was simulated in Chapter 10. It would appear that a change of sentiment could, in principle, trigger enough chains of bankruptcies to threaten global financial stability, a situation similar to what happened in 2007–2008, which was then followed by the Great Recession of the 2010s. Clearly, whether this can happen must be determined in time, and policies to promote an orderly transition must be adopted and enforced to avoid this type of disaster scenario.

15.5. CREATING RESILIENCE THROUGH ECONOMIC DIVERSIFICATION

A discussion was reported between a colleague of the author and the Canadian Minister of Environment and Climate Change towards the end of 2020. A national political debate had emerged over what to do with the oil industry in Mid-West

Canada where tar sands were being extracted. The persistent low oil prices had put the whole industry in jeopardy, and since the provincial government of Alberta used to rely on substantial royalties from oil and gas extraction for its public budget, the decline had led to very drastic cut in public expenditure, notably in higher education and public services. The decline also had impacts at the federal level, and future financial stability was being questioned. The country seemed to have painted itself in a corner in recent years by trying to save the ailing oil industry, on the expectation that oil prices were soon going to recover. The cancellation by newly elected Joe Biden of the Keystone XL pipeline project to bring oil down through the USA may have been the last straw for Prime Minister Justin Trudeau. The Environment and Climate Change minister was in fact saying that what was needed was not more fear-mongering regarding the oil industry in Canada, as the dire situation was now well known and acknowledged. The question he wanted answered was what to do now.

Indeed, what to do? The reliance of public finances on an increasingly volatile oil and gas sector as the global economy approaches the end of the Age of Oil was not wise. It could have been understood that just like the car industry in the Great Lakes region has been struggling for decades to the extent that people have accepted it, despite that cars still have a privileged place in people's daily lives, a similar decline may now be arising in the oil sector, despite that mobility and energy demand still grow. History is littered with similar examples of areas suffering from post-industrial decline following a wave of activity that turned out temporary. The financial sector in Canada trapped itself by the ramifications of the oil sector's grip and the latter's very survival becoming conditional to support from the government, such as nationalising pipelines that no one else can afford to fix. Heated debates were raging on the radio in 2018 regarding whether or not it was wise to nationalise the Westwards Trans Mountain pipeline given the trade wars waged by the Trump administration.[26]

Just like in any other situation of post-industrial decline, offering work to unemployed workers is what is needed in the very short term to avoid dire socio-economic problems. But intervention can be better planned than that. It is economic diversification for long-term resilience that must also take place. The best approach, as this book suggests, is to carry out a risk-opportunity analysis to identify the current trajectory of the system, largest risks and opportunities, and the interventions that could steer the economy, within the very thick fog of uncertainty that it faces, towards economic diversification and investment towards a new paradigm of technology and innovation. The onset and nature of the new great wave of innovation is obvious to everyone: information, automation, electrification, artificial intelligence. This has made great strides in leading centres such as Toronto and Montreal, and many parts of the world. But what can the trapped oil workers from the Mid-West expect? It is unlikely that tar sand mining hub Fort McMurray becomes a hub of

[26] All of the above insights were gathered by the author through personal communications with relevant persons and taking part in radio interviews, and thus may well just be circumstantial, but they came from real actors.

innovation in artificial intelligence or biotech, if the predominant skill set revolves around operating oil extraction machinery. And thus the tragedy, there are not many opportunities for a former oil town. To find the next cluster of innovation, one must just search for the nearest university. Fort McMurray perhaps cannot be saved, but Edmonton and Calgary definitely have a bright future, although that will not be achieved by defunding its universities to reduce the deficit created by the declining tax intake. More broadly, economic resilience in Canada would require diversification of its innovation portfolio regionally. Concentration of skills and work around oil and gas in Alberta was perhaps, with hindsight, never a great idea.

The same issue faces various other economies worldwide, notably the USA, where the California Bay and the Boston areas will be stealing the thunder from every other region, notably Texas and the Great Lakes. The former are the forward looking areas of innovation and growth while the latter are the areas of technological decline looking towards the past. The wise trick would be to use financial capital and accumulated return from the old regime and invest it to plan equitably the new regime. The key issue lies with skills and whether workers are happy to transition from an industry in which they have accumulated experience and receive high wages, for becoming junior employees in new industries they know very little of. Workers from the old regimes may well prefer to go for early retirement instead. But it is not clear that the pension schemes will remain in sufficiently good form to support early retirement for such a large number of people. Meanwhile, in California, employers can never find enough skilled workers in the new ventures.[27]

In OPEC countries, diversification appears very slow, despite claims and announcements that have been made. Despite that OPEC will likely succeed in remaining the 'last man standing' in the oil and gas sector, the same economic diversification logic holds. Wanting to remain the 'last man standing' may well be what ultimately leads to ruin, if it deters financial executives to seek diversification from within. The problem remains the same, new skills fit for the new regime of technology must be developed, and the opportunity exists to do so as long as oil money still flows, while these options will evaporate once the innovation train has been missed and oil money runs out.

Economic resilience in a rapid low-carbon transition can be created by a combination of three elements:

1. divestment from fossil fuels;
2. industrial and innovation policy with a clear direction and narrative;
3. regional economic development policy for areas of post-industrial decline.

Divestment from fossil-related assets must happen with a logic that seeks to avoid a disorderly transition, as has been discussed by the central banks and members

[27] Markkanen and Anger-Kraavi (2019); Green and Gambhir (2020).

of the NGFS.[28] If diversification and divestment happen too rapidly or too slowly, a chance remains that a contagion of financial instability develops. Divestment means to gradually reduce the components of financial portfolios that are afflicted by substantial transition risks, and to replace those by other types of assets, to promote financial resilience. Neither the risks nor the assets will disappear in the near term as a result of divestment, but they will be re-branded as junk bonds which could be dealt with by those able to absorb such risks.

Industrial policy, in the form of coordinated innovation policy using technology push and pull strategies, can help create new activities to replace the old ones, at the national or broader regional level.[29] This enables to create economic and financial value towards which workers and financial capital can be oriented. This should ideally target whole ranges of sectors, with a focus on public sector driven innovation such as what emerges from universities. The proper functioning of innovation systems should be ensured.[30]

Regional economic development policy should be used to level up economic development in areas afflicted by post-industrial decline to avoid self-reinforcing cycles of economic decline and avoid forcing residents to re-locate in more productive areas. Typically, workers become trapped in those areas because they simply cannot afford high house prices in affluent areas where innovation systems thrive and new industries are located. Without thought-through policy, those regions are likely to suffer from chronic unemployment and socio-economic exclusion. Regional economic policy can take the form of creating opportunities through the education sector (e.g., training programs), decentralising government activities towards those regions to provide public sector jobs, and economic incentives for industries to relocate in declining areas.

15.6. APPENDIX: MODEL ASSUMPTIONS

The E3ME-FTT-GENIE integrated framework is described below. The full set of equations underpinning the framework is given and explained in Mercure et al. (2018a). Assumptions for all scenarios are also given.

E3ME

The Energy–Economy–Environment Macro Econometric model (E3ME) is a highly disaggregated multi-sectoral and multi-regional, demand-led macroeconometric and dynamic input-output model of the global economy. It simulates the

28 Network for Greening the Financial System, see NGFS (2019); BoE (2018); Bolton et al. (2020).

29 See Kattel et al. (2018); Mazzucato and Penna (2016); Mazzucato (2013, 2018).

30 For instance, see Hekkert et al. (2007); Bergek et al. (2008) and the functions that enable innovation systems to thrive.

demand, supply and trade of final goods, intermediate goods and services globally. It is disaggregated along harmonised data classifications worldwide for forty-three consumption categories, seventy (forty-three) sectors of industry within (outside of) the EU member states and the UK, sixty-one countries and regions including all EU member states and G20 nations covering the globe, twenty-three types of users of fuels and twelve types of fuels. The model features fifteen econometric regressions calibrated on data between 1970 and 2010, and simulates on yearly time steps onwards up to 2070. The model is demand-led, which means that the demand for final goods and services is first estimated, and the supply of intermediate goods leading to that supply is determined using input-output tables and bilateral trade relationships between all regions. The model features a positive difference between potential supply capacity and actual supply (the output gap), as well as involuntary unemployment of the labour force. This implies that when economic activity fluctuates, short-term non-equilibrium changes in the employment of labour and capital can arise, and notably, unemployed resources can become employed. The model follows the theoretical basis of demand-led post-Keynesian and Schumpeterian (evolutionary) economics[31] in which investment determines output, rather than output determining investment and capital accumulation as done in general equilibrium models. This implies that purchasing power to finance investment is created by banks on the basis of the creditworthiness of investors and investment opportunities, and repaid over the long term. The model therefore possesses an implicit representation of banking and financial markets, in which the allocation of financial resources is not restricted by crowding-out from other competing activities, as the creation of money in the form of loans can accelerate during periods of optimism, and decline in periods of depression. For that reason, E3ME is the ideal model to study the business cycle dynamically, as it does not assume money neutrality and is path-dependent.

The closed set of regressions includes estimating, as dependent variables, demand (by construction equal to supply), investment, labour participation, employment, hours worked, wages, prices (domestic and imports), imports and the expansion of industrial productive capacity. Endogenous growth is generated by the inclusion of technology progress factors in several equations, which represent sectoral productivity growth as the economy accumulates scale, knowledge and knowhow with cumulative investment. Final energy demand and the energy sector as a whole is treated in detail similarly but separately in physical energy quantities (Mercure et al., 2018a).

FTT

E3ME estimates energy demand and related investment in all sectors and fuel users of the global economy with the exception of the four most carbon-intensive

[31] Mercure et al. (2019a); Pollitt and Mercure (2017).

sectors (power, transport, heat, steel), for which technological change is modelled with substantially higher definition using the Future Technology Transformations (FTT) family of models. FTT is a bottom-up representation of technological change that reproduces and projects the diffusion of individual technologies calibrated on recent trends. FTT:Power[32] represents the market competition of 24 power technologies including nuclear, coal/oil/gas-based fuel combustion (with carbon capture and storage (CCS) options), photovoltaic and concentrated solar (PV/CSP), onshore/offshore wind, hydro, tidal, geothermal and wave technologies. FTT:Transport represents the diffusion of petrol, diesel, hybrid, compressed natural gas and electric vehicles and motorcycles in three engine size classes, with twenty-five technology options. FTT:Heat looks at the diffusion of oil, coal, wood and gas combustion in households as well as resistive electric heating, electric heat pumps and solar heaters in thirteen technology options. Lastly, FTT:Steel represents all existing steel-making routes based on coal, gas, hydrogen and electricity in twenty-five types of chains of production. Technologies not represented in FTT currently have very low market shares, which necessarily implies, in a diffusion framework, that their diffusion to such levels that would invalidate the present scenarios is highly unlikely within the policy horizon of 2050 (e.g., nuclear fusion, hydrogen mobility).

FTT is a general framework for modelling technology ecosystems that is in many ways similar to modelling natural ecosystems, based on the replicator dynamics equation. The replicator equation (or Lotka-Volterra system) is a ubiquitous relationship that emerges in many systems featuring non-linear population dynamics such as in chemical reactions or ecosystem populations. It is related to discrete choice models and multinomial logits through adding a term in the standard utility model representing agent interactions (e.g., technology availability limited by existing industry sizes, social influence) that gives it the distinctive S-shaped diffusion profile.[33]

The direction of diffusion in FTT is influenced by the economic and policy context on the basis of suitable sector-specific representations of decision-making, by comparing the break-even (levelised) cost of using the various technology options, in a discrete choice model weighted by the ubiquity of those technology options. The various levelised costs include a parameter representing the comparative non-pecuniary costs and advantages of using each technology. This parameter is used to calibrate the direction of diffusion to match what is observed in recent trends of diffusion, notably important for PV, wind, EVs and heat pumps.[34]

A key recent innovation in FTT:Power is a detailed representation of the intermittency of renewables through the introduction of a classification of generators along

[32] The FTT models below are described in Mercure et al. (2014, 2018b); Mercure and Lam (2015); Knobloch et al. (2018).

[33] See, for instance, Safarzynska and van den Bergh (2010); Mercure (2018) and Chapter 7.

[34] See the Appendix of Chapter 14 and the references there.

six load bands, following the method of Ueckerdt et al. (2017) with the addition of an allocation of production time slots to available generators according to intermittency and flexibility constraints. This ensures that the level of grid flexibility to allow the introduction of large amounts of renewables are respected, maintaining model results within a range deemed to represent a stable electricity grid. Intermittency, optimal intermittent renewable curtailment and energy storage parameters are estimated by Ueckerdt based on solar and wind data and optimisation modelling results. The result in FTT is that the main obstacle for solar and wind penetrating grids is the rate at which the required flexibility can be accommodated. The addition of this electricity market model has implied, in comparison to earlier work based on cruder and more restrictive stability assumptions, that renewables can penetrate the grid more rapidly and effectively.

GENIE

GENIE, an intermediate complexity earth system model, simulates the global climate carbon cycle to give the future climate state driven by CO_2 emissions, land-use change and non-CO_2 climate forcing agents. It comprises the GOLDSTEIN (global ocean linear drag salt and temperature equation integrator) 3-D frictional geostrophic ocean model coupled to a 2-D energy moisture balance atmosphere, a thermodynamic-dynamic sea-ice model, the BIOGEM ocean biogeochemistry model, SEDGEM sediment module, and the ENTSML (efficient numerical terrestrial scheme with managed land), dynamic model of terrestrial carbon storage and land-use change. GENIE has the resolution of $10^\circ \times 5^\circ$ on average with sixteen depth levels in the ocean and has here been applied in the configuration set by Holden et al.[35] (see references therein).

The probabilistic projections are achieved through an ensemble of simulations for each emissions scenario using an 86-member set that varies twenty-eight model parameters in order to produce an estimate of the full parameter uncertainties. Each ensemble member simulation is continued from an AD 850 to 2005 historical transient spin-up. Post-2005 CO_2 emissions are provided by E3ME, scaled by 9.9/X to match actual emissions in 2019 (where X = 9.3 GtC is E3ME 2019 emissions), to correct for missing processes in E3ME. The emissions trajectories are then extrapolated to 2100 (InvE and TDT scenarios) or until they reach net-zero (EU-EA N-Z scenario). The net-zero scenario reaches zero emissions during the E3ME simulation in 2050. Trace gas radiative forcing and land-use-change maps and land-use emissions are taken from Representative Concentration Pathway (RCP) 2.6 (net-zero and EU-EA N-Z scenarios) and RCP 6.0 (InvE and TDT scenarios).

[35] Holden et al. (2013a,b).

The GENIE ensemble has been validated through comparing the results of 86-member ensemble simulations for the RCP scenarios with CIMIP5 (coupled model intercomparison project phase 5) and EMIC (earth system model of intermediate complexity) ensembles.

The Energy Market Model Using Rystad Data

The geographical allocation of oil and gas production is estimated by integrating to the model data from the substantial Rystad Ucube dataset in the form of breakeven cost distributions (as in Figure 15.3, aggregated into 61 regions). The Rystad dataset documents over 120,000 oil and gas production sites worldwide, which covers the large majority of current global production and existing reserves and resources. It provides each site's breakeven oil and gas prices, reserves, resources and production rates.

The energy market model assumes that each site has a likelihood of being in producing mode that is functionally dependent on the difference between the prevailing marginal cost of production and its own breakeven cost. The marginal cost is determined by searching, iteratively with the whole of E3ME, for the value at which the supplies match the E3ME demand, which is itself dependent on energy carrier prices. Dynamic changes in marginal costs are interpreted as driving dynamic changes in energy commodity prices.

The regional production to reserve ratios are exogenous parameters representing producer decisions. Initial values are obtained from the data to reproduce current regional production according to the reserve and resources database. Future changes in production to reserve ratios for each region are determined according to chosen rules for the QU and SO scenarios. Changes are only imposed to production to reserve ratios of OPEC countries, in order to either achieve a production quota that is proportional to global output (QU scenario, thereby reducing production to reserve ratios accordingly), or attempting to maintain constant absolute production while global demand is peaking and declining (SO scenario, thereby increasing production to reserve ratios). Only oil and gas output in OPEC are thus affected by these parameter changes, which affects the allocation of the overall markets.

Renewables are limited through resource costs by technical potentials determined in earlier work.[36]

The Formation of Scenarios and Choices of Regional Decarbonisation Policy Portfolios

TDT – All policies are implicit through the economic, energy and technology diffusion data, with the exception of an assumed explicit carbon price for the EU-ETS region and other carbon markets covering the projection period, covering

[36] See Mercure and Salas (2012, 2013) for all information on energy resources in E3ME-FTT.

all industrial but not consumer, mobility, household nor agriculture emission sources, following current policy. Regulations are applied in some regions such as on coal generation in Europe, which cannot increase due to the Large Combustion plant directive. Hydro, comparatively resource-limited, is regulated in many regions to avoid large expansions that could otherwise be politically sensitive.

Net-Zero – To the implicit policies of the TDT are added explicit policies as follows, with the exception of the carbon price, which is replaced by more stringent values. Emissions reach net-zero independently in the UK, the EU, South Korea and Japan by 2050, and China by 2060, following current legally binding targets, as well as in the rest of the World as a whole.

Power Generation:

- Feed-in tariffs for onshore and offshore wind generation, but not solar PV.
- Subsidies on capital costs for all other renewables (geothermal, solar CSP, biomass, wave and tidal) with the exception of hydro and solar PV.
- Hydro is regulated directly in most regions to limit expansion, given that in most parts of the world the number of floodable sites is limited and flooding new sites faces substantial resistance from local residents.
- Coal generation is regulated such that no new plants not fitted with CCS can be built but existing plants can run to the end of their lifetimes. However, all remaining coal plants are shut down in 2050.
- Public procurement is assumed to take place to install CCS on coal, gas and biomass plants in many developed and middle income countries where this does not already exist, notably in the USA, Canada, China and India.
- The use of BECCS is supported by existing policies and the introduction of further public procurement policies to publicly fund the building of BECCS plants in all countries endowed by solid biomass resources.

Road Transport:

Policy portfolios were designed tailored to five major economies characterised by different vehicle markets (UK, USA, China, India and Japan), according to what policies are already in place and the composition of local vehicle markets. Policies in other countries were designed by using proxies to the most similar of the five markets above. Portfolios include combinations of the following:

- Regulations on the use of inefficient petrol and diesel vehicles, with increasing efficiency targets over time.
- Capital cost subsidies on EVs.
- Taxes on petrol and diesel and/or on the purchase price of high-carbon vehicles.

- Public procurement programs for supporting the diffusion of EVs.
- Yearly vehicle taxes linked to emissions.

Household Heating:

- Taxes on household use of fuels for heating (coal, oil, gas).
- Capital cost subsidies for heat pumps and solar water heaters.
- Public procurement policies to increase the market share of the heat pump industry.
- Regulations on the sale of new coal, oil and inefficient gas boilers.

Steelmaking:

- Regulations on the construction of new inefficient coal-based steel plants.
- Capital cost subsidies on new lower carbon plants such as biomass and hydrogen-based iron ore reduction and smelting, and to fit CCS to existing high-carbon plants.
- Public procurement to build new low-carbon steel plants in order to develop markets where they do not exist.

Cross-Sectoral Policies:

- Energy efficiency: the energy efficiency of non-FTT sectors are assumed to change in line with the IEA, with corresponding investments in the respective sectors.
- Carbon price: applied to all industrial fuel users with the exception of road transport, household heating, agriculture and fishing, which are covered by other sector-specific fuel taxes, and are not expected to participate in emissions trading schemes. The carbon price is exogenous and increases in the EU from its 2020 value, in nominal EUR, until EUR1955/tC in 2033 and remains there thereafter. Deflating these values using E3ME's endogenous price levels into 2020USD (since E3ME operates in nominal EUR) and converting to CO_2, these carbon prices are equivalent to between $300–500/tCO2 in 2033, going down thereafter following different country inflation rates to $250–350/tCO2 in 2050 and $150–200/tCO2 in 2070.

EU-EA Net-Zero – The net-zero scenario was designed by creating a cross between the TDT and the Net-Zero scenario in which the EU, UK, Japan, South Korea and China adopt the Net-Zero policies as defined above and achieve their respective targets, while every other country follows the TDT. Note that technology spillovers (e.g., learning) in the model imply that this scenario is not a simple linear combination of the parent scenarios, since low-carbon technology adoption in countries without net-zero policies is higher than in the TDT.

SO and QU Scenario Variants – These scenarios were generated by varying the exogenous production ratio to reserve ratio of OPEC countries including Saudi Arabia (given that OPEC is disaggregated between Saudi Arabia, OPEC countries in Africa and the rest of OPEC), assuming that only OPEC has the freedom and incentive to do so. Production in the model is proportional to existing reserves in each producing region, the proportionality factor being determined by the data such that production data is consistent with reserve data. The production to reserve ratios in the three OPEC regions are modified by applying the values that achieve either production quotas that remain proportional to global oil and gas outputs (QU scenario) or constant in absolute value (SO scenario). In the central scenarios, production to reserve ratios are maintained constant.

SO scenarios could be defined for other regions, notably the USA and Russia; however, we consider those unlikely to materialise without SO response from OPEC, which, due to its higher competitiveness according to Rystad data, in the model, always wins price wars. Thus such SO scenarios for regions other than OPEC add little information to what is already shown here. In reality, SO strategies could be plagued by refining capacity bottlenecks or strategic stockpiling behaviour. We assume that refining and fuel transport capacity remains undisrupted (e.g., by regional conflict), and that current capacity outlives peak demand. This is reasonable given existing capacity, and the fact that demand growth declines. We furthermore assume that incentives for stockpiling drastically decline in situations of peak demand, as overproduction is likely, reducing opportunities for arbitrage. Trade tariffs on oil and gas could be imposed to protect domestic industries, notably in the USA, decoupling them from global markets, but are not modelled here.

InvE scenario – This scenario involves no other assumptions than policies present in the TDT and replacing all FTT outputs (energy end-use and energy sector investment) with exogenous data consistent with the IEA's WEO 2019 current policies scenario. This scenario, qualitatively similar to RCP8.5, sees growth in all fossil fuel markets, and was chosen over the newer IEA's WEO 2020 scenarios which are qualitatively different. The InvE scenario cannot be reached under any realistic set of assumptions in E3ME-FTT projections, as it would violate the model premise of near-term continuity in observed technology diffusion trajectories. This scenario was chosen as a proxy for recent past expectations for the future of fossil energy markets, of investors who may still entertain beliefs of indefinite growth in future fossil fuel markets. Since it is not possible to determine which investors entertain which expectations, the realism of the InvE scenario as a proxy for expectations cannot be assessed; therefore, it is used only to develop a what-if comparative narrative.

16

Conclusions and Outlook

This chapter concludes the book by offering a vision over the next problems of environmental governance to solve as the world undertakes a low-carbon transition. The first key point is that the sustainability transition is already underway. The second is that it will not lead to lower economic growth, but rather, faster economic growth with a weakening of economic, financial and political stability globally. These important findings should underpin a radically different policy conversation than has happened up to now, looking to understand risks and opportunities rather than estimating costs and benefits. It is quite clear that the low-carbon transition will leave some people behind through structural change in the economy, creating new inequalities or reinforcing existing ones. Economic agents are classified here into two overarching supergroups, the 'optimists', forward-looking agents who operate in the new economic paradigm with rising expectations, and the 'sceptics', who look towards the past and are becoming trapped in the old technological paradigm, with depressed expectations. Institutions of governance and policy advocates will have to move on from persuading the world to adopt climate policy, and go towards developing effective and equitable governance modes for the sustainability transition that has been put in motion.

16.1. WHAT THIS BOOK SET OUT TO ACHIEVE

This book has set out to develop a robust and reliable scientific basis on which to ground an improved science–policy interface to inform resilient environmental governance. It has avoided the common trap of basing governance solely on normative axioms, as it instead advocates the creation of a reliable scientific theory of complexity economics, grounded into observation, empirics and knowledge of complex dynamically changing systems. The goal has been to formulate a theory of economics that can actually tackle the 'wickedness' of contemporary environmental issues through public policy. The key question is whether it achieves this goal. And what does this all mean in practice?

In a nutshell, what this book finds is that addressing environmental issues, in particular climate change, will not lead to simple generalised costs and benefits, and society does not face a binary choice between going for it or not according to whether benefits exceed costs. In fact, first, the low-carbon transformation of the global economy is already happening, and is irreversible, while the fossil fuel technological paradigm is under full creative destruction, and will not last much longer. Second, this transition can lead to a large range of possible futures, some of them unexpected. It will interact notably with other large changes taking place, such as automation and artificial intelligence, to produce an economy that takes advantage of the ongoing innovation and technological opportunities. Third, if this ongoing transition carries on in a way that remains disorderly, it will lead, for a period, to political, economic and financial instability, with new geopolitical dynamics, and generate deep distributional issues between those who catch the low-carbon train before it leaves the platform, looking towards the future, and those who are left behind, with an eye to the past.

This book it delivers robust methods to study and understand those implications, and it delivers insights on how to mitigate negative impacts or avoid them altogether. As Schumpeter made it clear as far back as the early 20th century, the economy always changes, in great movements with great upheaval, and this always leaves people behind. This is due to the work of entrepreneurs, who push the economy forward, but at the same time destroy some people's 'ways of making a living'. Kauffman, meanwhile, offers the deep insights needed to understand the evolutionary mechanisms through which this process operates. Thus this book and its proposal of a risk-opportunity analysis framework for policy assessment, provides methods to govern the transition as it unfolds, recognising with humble honesty the huge uncertainties involved, and that humans are better at steering change adaptively than at predicting the future.

16.2. CHANGING THE MODE OF CONVERSATION

A first critical step in 'evidence-based policy-making' is to move on from basing governance solely on normative principles, going towards co-creation while learning. When using normative principles only, one makes an implicit critical assumption that one knows all the outcomes of all possible courses of action without uncertainty, and therefore, that the thinking that is needed concerns ethics and values regarding what outcomes society as a whole desires. In both the deontological or consequential schools of moral philosophy, the assumption is made that one can fully know the causal link between an action or policy choice and its full implications. This is simply not the case in an economy with any degree of complexity.

Decision-making made with cost-benefit analysis or any other equilibrium economics thinking and analytical framework makes the same assumption that one can know with certainty, or known probabilities, the outcomes of policy action, and remains therefore grounded primarily into normative principles, rather than in assessing actual causation and processes of transformation.

It is typically causation more than morals that requires scientific investigation. The uncertainty that is faced by decision-makers, over outcomes of their possible choices, is fundamental, heavy-tailed and not fully characterised with numbers. Policy action is only but one element amongst a large number of interacting components in a complex system. Policy can address one problem here and create another one there. While most of standard economics interrogates itself on what norms to aspire to, it is primarily causation that must be investigated, more so than values. And furthermore, it seems desirable to separate robust scientific work from normative economic valuation, in order to keep both processes clean from undue political pressure, and avoid at all costs the policy process becoming 'policy-based evidence-making', which makes the analyst a slave of the political process.

16.3. FOUNDATIONS FOR THE LOW-CARBON ECONOMY

Schumpeter popularised the term 'creative destruction' in the 1920s and studied it onwards into the forties. But economists seem to have abandoned the concept in the seventies up until now. It is a good question why, as it seems never a good idea to forget lessons learned. By the time the 2007–2008 financial crash happened, many economists had forgotten what financial instability and debt deflation look like, assuming that the 1929 episode could never happen again due to lessons learned. After that major failure of macroeconomics, all of a sudden, people started to read Minsky again, who had been relegated to the shelves in dark corners of quiet university libraries.

According to Minsky, humans live in the future. Humans take decisions in the present according to the future they see, in their minds, and they form those futures according to the past they have experienced. Minsky is quite clear that this is how investment decisions are taken. A company is valuable if it has a bright future, more so than if it has a bright present. And humans, possibly, function in the same way, where they can endure quite significant suffering in the present if they can keep the faith that this will provide them with a bright future. This explains why young persons can spend so many years at school under the promise of the broader pleasures of adult life.

The economy evolves through great waves of innovation and upheaval, and many economists and policy-makers seem to have recently woken up and suddenly remembered this. Times are changing, and it is becoming very visible, for both economic agents who happen to be working on the modern new technology, and those trapped in the declining industries. The Great Waves literature, following in the footsteps of Schumpeter, documents how every fifty or so years, a change in socio-technical regime takes place, at which time a period of socio-economic and political instability arises.

Normatively, many want to see the onset of a low-carbon great wave of innovation, and the old concept of the 'S-shaped' diffusion curve has become popular again. This stems from the cumulative effects of past low-carbon policy becoming increasingly visible. Electric vehicles are seen on the streets. Solar panels are everywhere in fields in the countryside. Wind turbines are being built across the seas. The oil price is volatile and has for the first time in history even turned negative. This is not anymore just a fancy dream of some green activists. This is real, the world is changing, business is taking shape and people are making money with the changing times.

Schumpeter was always clear that each great wave leaves some people behind, and even creates some kind of 'social convection', a movement of people across the social classes. This evokes the concept of the 'nouveau riche', or the 'parvenu', accumulating enormous wealth out of the new regimes of technology, beyond the dreams of those holding the 'old money', who, attached to the old regimes, follow their decline. Minsky's proposition that humans live in the future would suggest that the former, happy-go-lucky, have everything to hope for, while the latter, experiencing very bleak expectations, will be incessantly insecure. Creative destruction has generated over history endless grievances as power and wealth moved from one social group to another. Naturally, if this was not the case, entrepreneurs would not have quite the same motivation. Thus, without expressing normative views over whether this is good or bad, 'social convection' in fact allows some degree of social mobility which is in part what motivates financiers to invest, entrepreneurs to create and makes the economy tick.

It is challenging to see the low-carbon transition through any other lens than that of the great waves of innovation, even if this frame is radically different from that of equilibrium economics. The transition involves such a typical constellation of powerful, related innovations, like pieces of a puzzle of which the world is gradually coming to see the picture. Low-carbon electricity technology generates without wasteful fuel combustion, and nearly without wage costs. Batteries enable the transport and highly efficient use of this pure form of energy at next to no conversion loss. Automation and artificial intelligence enable further radical reductions of wage bills across sectors. Bio-tech innovations enable an ever longer life to people, including a lengthening working life, and therefore a longer preservation of knowledge and skills by economic agents. Scientists, engineers and research funding agencies appear to increasingly accept this as an inevitable future, due to all the operational cost reductions that these innovations will together deliver, which raises the question why economists persist in suggesting that this transition will be costly and reduce economic productivity.

The new economy is forming under our eyes through the work of unstoppable entrepreneurs. They are almost certainly set to become the next 'nouveau riche', through some yet unknown combination of business models, battling each other in the high-tech and low-carbon innovation jungle. Enormous 'cleantech' innovation systems are seen hovering around the great universities, and the money is there, plenty of it. Going back to Carolta Perez, if history is to be a guide to the future, banks will not hesitate to open the lending floodgates to finance all of that new low-carbon tech, all the way until a green bubble forms and bursts. Meanwhile, the 'old (brown) money' will, as ever, pour its remaining resources into every possible attempt to stop the new low-carbon regime, because, ultimately, power and prestige trump money.

For this book, the key question remains, is it possible to equitably co-create the foundations of the new low-carbon economy?

16.4. A NEW WORLD ORDER OF ECONOMIC POWER

The new low-carbon economy will generate upheaval with far-reaching consequences for geopolitical power relations worldwide. The decline of export markets for hydrocarbons and high-carbon-related goods, knowledge, equipment and infrastructure will painfully affect those regions of the world that currently focus their economic activities and 'ways of making a living' in the high-carbon sectors. In those regions, the historical legacy of wealth generation from fossil fuel extraction has in many cases led to a neglect of innovative activity in unrelated sectors, the so-called resource curse, simply because everyone wanted a piece of the pie, and got used to feeding on it.

It is slowly becoming obvious that what used to be considered national wealth in the form of fossil fuel natural resource endowments could become an enormous liability. Those countries and powerful individuals holding the wealth and power (notably military power) will become kings ruling houses of cards when nobody wants fossil fuels anymore. What is worse is that the decline will become ever more clear day by day, and by that point it will have become too late to diversify those economies. If Minsky is correct that financial agents live in the future, it should logically become impossible to finance diversification once a contagion of pessimism begins to eat through those financial systems. This implies that power will slip between those leaders' fingers like sand if they procrastinate any further.

The less cost-competitive fossil fuel producers will be out of the game of musical chairs first, as peak oil demand sets in, having no choice but to mitigate post-industrial decline and diversify immediately. This includes the USA, Canada and Russia. A sharp and early blow might, however, be better in the long run than a long and drawn-out painful decline. The 'last man standing' in the Middle East may well see nothing better to do than to hang on to those markets, pushing everyone else out, carrying on with the diseased industry until there is nothing left of demand for it, prisoners of the resource curse.

In the meantime, power may accrue to those unlikely figures, those who used to be the underdogs not endowed with resources. Where reserves of fossil fuels used to signify wealth and power, it will be technical knowledge that fuels those. Through a drastic change in trade balances as importers stop importing expensive fossil fuels from the old price-controlling foreign cartel of producers, the money unspent on imports will reinforce the domestic industries that will increasingly underpin their growing economic power. Like tectonic plate movements suddenly changing direction, trade balances will rapidly and radically change their levels and direction of change. A key remaining question is the direction that international capital flows will take once the oil stops flowing globally, and how this could affect currencies. But it is intuitively clear who might benefit and who might lose in the currency game.

16.5. LOOKING FORWARDS WITHOUT FORGETTING THE PAST

Two current observations might in time matter for the test of this book through time. First, the transition is clearly already underway. Second, resistance to climate change policy is but one aspect of deep divisions and polarisation currently observed in societies across the world. The latter divisions seem to group people between two very distinct clans, associating on both sides two very distinct packages of beliefs and attitudes on topics as varied as political affiliation, immigration, social inclusion and racism, attitude towards science, including medical science and vaccines. The reflections in this section are opinionated, uninformed, not supported by any evidence and based on intuition. But they could potentially have explanatory power, even if qualitative in nature, and they stem from the overall findings of this book.

An important divide is emerging in many countries worldwide. This division does not match anymore the traditional *left* and *right*, or socialist and conservative spectrum. The political arena has in recent years rotated 90°. On one side of the divide, call them the '*sceptics*', people are at the same time sceptical of climate policy, of international multilateralism, of science and medicine, of government institutions, of mainstream media and, afraid of regressing in social status, tend towards promoting policies that reinforce existing privileges and inequalities. *Sceptics* see living as a zero sum game in which gains by one person necessarily comes at the expense of losses for another. *Sceptics* will vote for populist strongmen that thrive on nostalgia and explicitly or implicitly promise to bring back past glories. They do not match the traditional conservative right as they include a combination of formerly ageing working class socialists in deprived regions, older individuals with accumulated wealth and more to lose than to gain, wealthy conservatives and holders of 'old money'.

On the other side of the divide are people, call them the '*optimists*', who see the exact opposite, seeking to address existing inequalities, believing more enthusiastically in science and medicine, knowledge and government institutions, and weary of climate change. *Optimists* vote for consensus-seeking leaders who promise to create a bright future out of the ashes of a past not to be revived. They are not exactly the old socialist left, as they include an odd combination of younger leftist socialists, environmentalists, businessmen, entrepreneurs, bankers and city dwellers, and self-made holders of 'new money'.

A hypothesis, admittedly ambiguous, unsupported by evidence and difficult to prove, is proposed here, as follows. The *sceptics*' way of looking at the world is shaped by realities that look towards the past, because in those realities, the future looks less bright than the past. Meanwhile, the *optimists*' view is shaped by realities that look towards the future, because in those realities, the future looks brighter than the past. What the *optimists* consider 'progress' makes the *sceptics*' lives worse off, since their prospects become ever more limited. But that 'progress' clearly improves the lives of the *optimists*. Neither the *optimists* nor the *sceptics* are really aware of what is going on as they may both be oblivious to the true underlying economic process; all they see is a changing world through the lens of their respective experiences, which are radically different. They live in different worlds, even though they run into each other all the time. These divisions worsen, with lack of opportunity increasing for the *sceptics*, while the opportunities flood towards the *optimists*.

In this analogy, the 'optimists' are those who happen to be driving the new technological regime, while those trapped in the decline are the 'sceptics'. These two overarching supergroups transcend the traditional social classes, nationalities and old political affiliations, since in all of these, there are winners and losers. One day, however, those racing ahead with the high-tech innovation train will inevitably have to slow down and let those who missed the train back in. Otherwise, there will eventually be too few happy affluent citizens to fuel the rise of the new technological regime. With insufficient aggregate demand, the economic outlook will turn bleak, when the rentiers (investors in the Facebooks, Googles and Teslas of this world) run out of ways to spend their savings in the real economy of goods and services, while the common citizen runs out of income to even buy a car. Inequality is ultimately not good for business.

16.6. A LOT LEFT TO LEARN

Governing the low-carbon transition will be very different from making the case for it. A generation of climatologists and climate change economists have spent their working lives making the case for the adoption of climate policy. The focus has been so much on convincing stakeholders to agree that many (although not all) forgot to think deeply about how the transition should be governed once it is going. Economic history tells us that when change starts, it is rapid and disruptive, and generates instability and inequality, not least due to a concentration of ownership of the new capital. Political history also tells us that when inequality is too high, political instability arises, and sometimes conflict. Each wave of innovation has had its dose of instability and conflict.

Thus as the low-carbon transition sets in, the new knowledge that is needed by institutions of governance will concern how to manage the impacts of the transition, more so than the reasons why this transition was needed in the first place. It is clear that the environment and the climate will become increasingly monitored, and the transition may need to be substantially accelerated according to how well the natural environment is managed, and how it responds to resulting changes in human environmental footprint. But equally if not more challenging will be managing the socio-economic transformation that inevitably follows socio-technical change.

References

Abel, Andrew B., Bernanke, Ben S., and Croushore, Dean. 2014. *Macroeconomics (8th ed.)*. Pearson.

Abrahamse, Wokje, and Steg, Linda. 2013. Social influence approaches to encourage resource conservation: A meta-analysis. *Global Environmental Change*, **23**(6), 1773–1785.

Acemoglu, Daron. 2002. Directed technical change. *The Review of Economic Studies*, **69**(4), 781–809.

Acemoglu, Daron, Aghion, Philippe, Bursztyn, Leonardo, and Hemous, David. 2012. The environment and directed technical change. *American Economic Review*, **102**(1), 131–166.

Ackerman, Frank, and Heinzerling, Lisa. 2001. Pricing the priceless: Cost-benefit analysis of environmental protection. *University of Pennsylvania Law Review*, **150**, 1553.

Adami, Marcos, Rudorff, Bernardo Friedrich Theodor, Freitas, Ramon Morais, Aguiar, Daniel Alves, Sugawara, Luciana Miura, and Mello, Marcio Pupin. 2012. Remote sensing time series to evaluate direct land use change of recent expanded sugarcane crop in Brazil. *Sustainability*, **4**(4), 574–585.

Adams, Michael, and Thornton, Barry. 2013. Black swans and VaR. *Journal of Finance and Accountancy*, **14**, 1.

Aghion, Philippe, Howitt, Peter, Brant-Collett, Maxine, and García-Peñalosa, Cecilia. 1998. *Endogenous Growth Theory*. MIT Press.

Akerlof, G. A. 1970. The market for 'lemons': Quality uncertainty and the market mechanism. *The Quarterly Journal of Economics*, **84**(3), 488–500.

Aklin, Michaël, and Mildenberger, Matto. 2020. Prisoners of the wrong dilemma: Why distributive conflict, not collective action, characterizes the politics of climate change. *Global Environmental Politics*, **20**(4), 4–27.

Aldred, Jonathan. 2009. Ethics and climate change cost-benefit analysis: Stern and after. *New Political Economy*, **14**(4), 469–488.

Alesina, Alberto, and Passarelli, Francesco. 2019. Loss aversion in politics. *American Journal of Political Science*, **63**(4), 936–947.

Amunts, Katrin, Ebell, Christoph, Muller, Jeff, Telefont, Martin, Knoll, Alois, and Lippert, Thomas. 2016. The human brain project: Creating a European research infrastructure to decode the human brain. *Neuron*, **92**(3), 574–581.

An, Sungbae, and Schorfheide, Frank. 2007. Bayesian analysis of DSGE models. *Econometric Reviews*, **26**(2–4), 113–172.

Anas, A. 1983. Discrete choice theory, information theory and the multinomial logit and gravity models. *Transportation Research Part B: Methodological*, **17**(1), 13–23.

Anderson, P. W. 1972. More is different. *Science*, **177**(4047), 393–396.

Anderson, P. W., Pines, D., and Arrow, K. J. 1989. *The Economy as an Evolving Complex System*. Santa Fe Institute Studies in the Sciences of Complexity. Westview Press.

Anderson, S. P., de Palma, A., and Thisse, J.-F. 1988. A representative consumer theory of the logit model. *International Economic Review*, **29**(3), 461–466.

1992. *Discrete Choice Theory of Product Differentiation*. MIT Press.

Anderson, Soren T., and Newell, Richard G. 2004. Information programs for technology adoption: The case of energy-efficiency audits. *Resource and Energy Economics*, **26**(1), 27–50.

Anthoff, D., and Tol, R. 2014. *Climate Framework for Uncertainty, Negotiation and Distribution*. www.fund-model.org.

Aoki, Masanao, and Yoshikawa, Hiroshi. 2007. *Reconstructing Macroeconomics: A Perspective from Statistical Physics and Combinatorial Stochastic Processes*. Cambridge University Press.

Arima, Eugenio Y., Richards, Peter, Walker, Robert, and Caldas, Marcellus M. 2011. Statistical confirmation of indirect land use change in the Brazilian Amazon. *Environmental Research Letters*, **6**(2), 024010.

Arrow, Kenneth J. 1962a. The economic implications of learning by doing. *The Review of Economic Studies*, **29**(3), 155–173.

1962b. Economic welfare and the allocation of resources for invention. Pages 609–626 of: *The Rate and Direction of Inventive Activity: Economic and Social Factors*. Princeton University Press.

Arthur, W. B. 1989. Competing technologies, increasing returns, and lock-in by historical events. *The Economic Journal*, **99**(394), 116–131.

1999. Complexity and the economy. *Science*, **284**(5411), 107–109.

2014. *Complexity and the Economy*. Oxford University Press.

Arthur, W. B., Durlauf, S. N., and Lane, D. A. 1997a. *The Economy as an Evolving Complex System II*. Santa Fe Institute Studies in the Sciences of Complexity. Westview Press.

Arthur, W. B., Ermoliev, Yu M., and Kaniovski, Yu M. 1987. Path-dependent processes and the emergence of macro-structure. *European Journal of Operational Research*, **30**(3), 294–303.

Arthur, W. B., Holland, John H., LeBaron, Blake Dean, Palmer, Richard, and Tayler, Paul. 1997b. Asset pricing under endogenous expectations in an artificial stock market. Pages 15–44 of: Arthur, W. B., Durlauf, S. N., and Lane, D. A. (eds.), *The Economy as an Evolving Complex System II*. Addison-Wesley.

Arthur, W. B., and Lane, D. A. 1993. Information contagion. *Structural Change and Economic Dynamics*, **4**(1), 81–104.

Arthur, W. B., and Polak, W. 2006. The evolution of technology within a simple computer model. *Complexity*, **11**(5), 23–31.

Awaya, Yu, and Fukai, Hiroki. 2017. A note on 'money is memory': A counterexample. *Macroeconomic Dynamics*, **21**(2), 545–553.

Axsen, Jonn, Mountain, Dean C., and Jaccard, Mark. 2009. Combining stated and revealed choice research to simulate the neighbor effect: The case of hybrid-electric vehicles. *Resource and Energy Economics*, **31**(3), 221–238.

Baccianti, Claudio, and Löschel, Andreas. 2014. *The Role of Product and Process Innovation in CGE Models of Environmental Policy*. Tech. rept. WWWforEurope Working Paper.

Baccini, A. G. S. J., Goetz, S. J., Walker, W. S., Laporte, N. T., Sun, M., Sulla-Menashe, D., Hackler, J., Beck, P. S. A., Dubayah, R., Friedl, M. A., et al. 2012. Estimated carbon dioxide emissions from tropical deforestation improved by carbon-density maps. *Nature Climate Change*, **2**(3), 182–185.

Bajželj, Bojana, Richards, Keith S., Allwood, Julian M., Smith, Pete, Dennis, John S., Curmi, Elizabeth, and Gilligan, Christopher A. 2014. Importance of food-demand management for climate mitigation. *Nature Climate Change*, **4**(10), 924–929.

Bak, P., Tang, C., and Wiesenfeld, K. 1987. Self-organized criticality: An explanation of 1/f noise. *Physical Review Letters*, **59**, 381–384.

Bak, Per. 1996. *How Nature Works*. Springer Verlag.

Bak, Per, and Sneppen, Kim. 1993. Punctuated equilibrium and criticality in a simple model of evolution. *Physical Review Letters*, **71**(24), 4083.

Bak, Per, Tang, Chao, and Wiesenfeld, Kurt. 1988. Self-organized criticality. *Physical Review* A, **38**(1), 364.

Bak, Per, Chen, Kan, Scheinkman, José, and Woodford, Michael. 1993. Aggregate fluctuations from independent sectoral shocks: Self-organized criticality in a model of production and inventory dynamics. *Ricerche Economiche*, **47**(1), 3–30.

Bak, Per, Christensen, Kim, Danon, Leon, and Scanlon, Tim. 2002. Unified scaling law for earthquakes. *Physical Review Letters*, 88(17), 178501.

Bala, Venkatesh, and Goyal, Sanjeev. 1998. Learning from neighbours. *The Review of Economic Studies*, **65**(3), 595–621.

Banerjee, A. V. 1992. A simple model of herd behavior. *The Quarterly Journal of Economics*, 797–817.

Barabási, Albert-László, and Albert, Réka. 1999. Emergence of scaling in random networks. *Science*, **286**(5439), 509–512.

Barabási, Albert-László, and Bonabeau, Eric. 2003. Scale-free networks. *Scientific American*, **288**(5), 60–69.

Baram, Michael S. 1979. Cost-benefit analysis: An inadequate basis for health, safety, and environmental regulatory decision-making. *Ecology Law Quarterly*, 8, 473.

Barbieri, Alisson F., Domingues, Edson, Queiroz, Bernardo L., Ruiz, Ricardo M., Rigotti, José I., Carvalho, José A. M., and Resende, Marco F. 2010. Climate change and population migration in Brazil's Northeast: Scenarios for 2025–2050. *Population and Environment*, **31**(5), 344–370.

Barona, Elizabeth, Ramankutty, Navin, Hyman, Glenn, and Coomes, Oliver T. 2010. The role of pasture and soybean in deforestation of the Brazilian Amazon. *Environmental Research Letters*, **5**(2), 024002.

Barrett, Scott. 1994. Self-enforcing international environmental agreements. *Oxford Economic Papers*, **46**, 878–894.

Barros, Vicente R., Garavaglia, Christian R., and Doyle, Moira E. 2013. Twenty-first century projections of extreme precipitations in the Plata Basin. *International Journal of River Basin Management*, **11**(4), 373–387.

Bass, F. M. 1969. New product growth for model consumer durables. *Management Science Series A-Theory*, **15**(5), 215–227.

Bateman, I. J., Carson, R. T., Day, B., Hanemann, M., Hanley, N., Hett, T., Jones-Lee, M., Loomes, G., Mourato, S., Özdemiroglu, E., Pearce, D. W., Sugden, R., and Swanson, J. 2002. *Economic Valuation with Stated Preference Techniques: A Manual*. Edward Elgar.

Battiston, Stefano, Puliga, Michelangelo, Kaushik, Rahul, Tasca, Paolo, and Caldarelli, Guido. 2012. Debtrank: Too central to fail? Financial networks, the FED and systemic risk. *Scientific Reports*, **2**, 541.

Battiston, Stefano, Farmer, J. Doyne, Flache, Andreas, Garlaschelli, Diego, Haldane, Andrew G., Heesterbeek, Hans, Hommes, Cars, Jaeger, Carlo, May, Robert, and Scheffer, Marten. 2016a. Complexity theory and financial regulation. *Science*, **351**(6275), 818–819.

Battiston, Stefano, Caldarelli, Guido, D'Errico, Marco, and Gurciullo, Stefano. 2016b. Leveraging the network: A stress-test framework based on DebtRank. *Statistics & Risk Modeling*, **33**(3–4), 117–138.

Battiston, Stefano, Mandel, Antoine, Monasterolo, Irene, Schütze, Franziska, and Visentin, Gabriele. 2017. A climate stress-test of the financial system. *Nature Climate Change*, **7**(4), 283.

Baumol, William J. 1996. Entrepreneurship: Productive, unproductive, and destructive. *Journal of Business Venturing*, **11**(1), 3–22.

Bazilian, Morgan, Rogner, Holger, Howells, Mark, Hermann, Sebastian, Arent, Douglas, Gielen, Dolf, Steduto, Pasquale, Mueller, Alexander, Komor, Paul, Tol, Richard S. J., et al. 2011. Considering the energy, water and food nexus: Towards an integrated modelling approach. *Energy Policy*, **39**(12), 7896–7906.

Bazilian, Morgan, Bradshaw, Michael, Gabriel, Johannes, Goldthau, Andreas, and Westphal, Kirsten. 2020. Four scenarios of the energy transition: Drivers, consequences, and implications for geopolitics. *Wiley Interdisciplinary Reviews: Climate Change*, **11**(2), e625.

Beddington, John. 2012. *Food, Energy, Water and the Climate: A Perfect Storm of Global Events?* Tech. rept. Chief Scientific Adviser to HM Government, `webarchive.nationalarchives.gov.uk/20121206120858/www.bis.gov.uk/assets/goscience/docs/p/perfect-storm-paper.pdf`.

Bell, Stephanie. 2001. The role of the state and the hierarchy of money. *Cambridge Journal of Economics*, **25**(2), 149–163.

Bellais, Renaud. 2004. Post Keynesian theory, technology policy, and long-term growth. *Journal of Post Keynesian Economics*, **26**(3), 419–440.

Ben-Akiva, Moshe E., and Lerman, Steven R. 1985. *Discrete Choice Analysis: Theory and Application to Travel Demand*. MIT Press.

Benhabib, J., Bisin, A., and Jackson, M. O. 2010. *Handbook of Social Economics*. Vol. 1. Elsevier.

Benjamin, Antonio Herman, Marques, Claudia Lima, and Tinker, Catherine. 2004. The water giant awakes: An overview of water law in Brazil. *Texas Law Review*, **83**, 2185.

Berchin, Issa Ibrahim, Garcia, Jéssica, Heerdt, Mauri Luiz, Moreira, Angélica de Quevedo, da Silveira, Ana Clara Medeiros, and de Andrade Guerra, José Baltazar Salgueirinho Osório. 2015. Energy production and sustainability: A study of Belo Monte hydroelectric power plant. Pages 224–237 of: *Natural Resources Forum*. Vol. 39. Wiley Online Library.

Berentsen, Aleksander, Camera, Gabriele, and Waller, Christopher. 2005. The distribution of money balances and the nonneutrality of money. *International Economic Review*, **46**(2), 465–487.

Bergek, Anna, Jacobsson, Staffan, Carlsson, Bo, Lindmark, Sven, and Rickne, Annika. 2008. Analyzing the functional dynamics of technological innovation systems: A scheme of analysis. *Research Policy*, **37**(3), 407–429.

Bertram, Christoph, Luderer, Gunnar, Pietzcker, Robert C., Schmid, Eva, Kriegler, Elmar, and Edenhofer, Ottmar. 2015. Complementing carbon prices with technology policies to keep climate targets within reach. *Nature Climate Change*, **5**(3), 235–239.

Besley, T., and Hennessy, P. 2009. *Letter from the British Academy to Her Majesty the Queen, 'The Global Financial Crisis ? Why Didn?t Anybody Notice?'*.

Bezemer, Dirk J. 2009. 'No one saw this coming': Understanding financial crisis through accounting models. *MPRA Paper* 15892.

Bhargava, S. C. 1989. Generalized Lotka-Volterra equations and the mechanism of technological substitution. *Technological Forecasting and Social Change*, **35**(4), 319–326.

Bigoni, Maria, Camera, Gabriele, and Casari, Marco. 2020. Money is more than memory. *Journal of Monetary Economics*, **110**, 99–115.

Bikhchandani, S., Hirshleifer, D., and Welch, I. 1992. A theory of fads, fashion, custom, and cultural change as informational cascades. *Journal of Political Economy*, **100**(5) 992–1026.

1998. Learning from the behavior of others: Conformity, fads, and informational cascades. *Journal of Economic Perspectives*, **12**(3), 151–170.

Black, Fischer, and Scholes, Myron. 1973. The pricing of options and corporate liabilities. *Journal of Political Economy*, **81**(3), 637–654.

Blanchard, Olivier J. 2009. The crisis: Basic mechanisms and appropriate policies. *IMF Working Papers*.

BoE. 2015. *The Impact of Climate Change on the UK Insurance Sector*. Tech. rept. Bank of England, `www.bankofengland.co.uk/prudential-regulation/publication/2015/the-impact-of-climate-change-on-the-uk-insurance-sector`.

2018. *Transition In Thinking: The Impact of Climate Change on the UK Banking Sector*. Tech. rept. Bank of England, `www.bankofengland.co.uk/prudential-regulation/publication/2018/transition-in-thinking-the-impact-of-climate-change-on-the-uk-banking-sector`.

Bolton, Patrick, Despres, Morgan, Pereira Da Silva, Luiz Awazu, Samama, Frédéric, and Svartman, Romain. 2020. *The Green Swan: Central Banking and Financial Stability in the Age of Climate Change*. Tech. rept. Banque de France.

Bouwman, A. F., Kram, T., and Klein, K. 2006. *Integrated Modelling of Global Environmental Change: An Overview of IMAGE 2.4*. Tech. rept. Netherlands Environmental Assessment Agency, `www.rivm.nl/bibliotheek/rapporten/500110002.pdf`.

Bovari, Emmanuel, Giraud, Gaël, and Mc Isaac, Florent. 2018. Coping with collapse: A stock-flow consistent monetary macrodynamics of global warming. *Ecological Economics*, **147**, 383–398.

Bowyer, Catherine, and Kretschmer, Bettina. 2010. Anticipated indirect land use change associated with expanded use of biofuels and bioliquids in the EU: An analysis of the national renewable energy action plans. *Institute for European Environmental Policy*, http://tov.skavt.net/baza_znanja/biogoriva/ILUC_porocilo_IEEP_november2010.pdf.

Brando, Paulo Monteiro, Balch, Jennifer K., Nepstad, Daniel C., Morton, Douglas C., Putz, Francis E., Coe, Michael T., Silvério, Divino, Macedo, Marcia N., Davidson, Eric A., Nóbrega, Caroline C., et al. 2014. Abrupt increases in Amazonian tree mortality due to drought–fire interactions. *Proceedings of the National Academy of Sciences*, **111**(17), 6347–6352.

Brantle, T. F., and Fallah, M. H. 2007. Complex innovation networks, patent citations and power laws. *PICMET 2007 Proceedings*, 540–549.

Brock, W. A., and Durlauf, S. N. 2001. Discrete choice with social interactions. *The Review of Economic Studies*, **68**(2), 235–260.

Broughel, James, and Kotrous, Michael. 2021. The benefits of coronavirus suppression: A cost-benefit analysis of the response to the first wave of COVID-19 in the United States. *PLoS One*, **16**(6), e0252729.

Brown-Lima, Carrie, Cooney, Melissa, and Cleary, David. 2010a. An overview of the Brazil-China soybean trade and its strategic implications for conservation. *The Nature Con-*

servancy Latin America Region.(Citing figures from the Secretariat of Foreign Trade (SECEX)) The Nature Conservancy, Brazil, 40.

2010b. An overview of the Brazil-China soybean trade and its strategic implications for conservation. *Brazil: The Nature Conservancy Latin America Region.(Citing figures from the Secretariat of Foreign Trade (SECEX)) The Nature Conservancy,* 40.

Bull, Ivan, and Willard, Gary E. 1993. Towards a theory of entrepreneurship. *Journal of Business Venturing*, 8(3), 183–195.

Burke, Mary A., and Young, H. Peyton. 2011. Social norms. Pages 311–338 of: Benhabib, Jess, Bisin, Alberto, and Jackson, Matthew O. (eds.), *Handbook of Social Economics*. Vol. 1. Elsevier.

Burrows, Michael T., Schoeman, David S., Buckley, Lauren B., Moore, Pippa, Poloczanska, Elvira S., Brander, Keith M., Brown, Chris, Bruno, John F., Duarte, Carlos M., Halpern, Benjamin S., et al. 2011. The pace of shifting climate in marine and terrestrial ecosystems. *Science*, **334**(6056), 652–655.

Caldecott, Ben. 2018. *Stranded Assets and the Environment: Risk, Resilience and Opportunity*. Routledge.

Cambridge Econometrics. 2013. *Employment Effects of Selected Scenarios from the Energy Roadmap 2050*. Tech. rept. European Commission (DG ENER), `http://ec.europa.eu/energy/sites/ener/files/documents/2013_report_employment_effects_roadmap_2050_2.pdf`.

2014. *E3ME: Energy-Economy-Environment Macroeconometric Model*. `www.e3me.com`.

2015. *Assessing the Employment and Social Impact of Energy Efficiency*. Tech. rept. European Commission (DG ENER), `http://ec.europa.eu/energy/sites/ener/files/documents/CE_EE_Jobs_main18Nov2015.pdf`.

Campiglio, Emanuele, Dafermos, Yannis, Monnin, Pierre, Ryan-Collins, Josh, Schotten, Guido, and Tanaka, Misa. 2018. Climate change challenges for central banks and financial regulators. *Nature Climate Change*, 8, 462.

Capros, Pantelis, Karadeloglou, Pavlos, and Mentzas, Gregory. 1990. An empirical assessment of macroeconometric and CGE approaches in policy modeling. *Journal of Policy Modeling*, **12**(3), 557–585.

Capros, Pantelis, Paroussos, Leonidas, Fragkos, Panagiotis, Tsani, Stella, Boitier, Baptiste, Wagner, Fabian, Busch, Sebastian, Resch, Gustav, Blesl, Markus, and Bollen, Johannes. 2014. Description of models and scenarios used to assess European decarbonisation pathways. *Energy Strategy Reviews*, **2**, 220–230.

Carbon Trust. 2005. *The UK Climate Change Programme: Potential Evolution for Business and the Public Sector*. Tech. rept. Carbon Trust.

Carlson, J. M., and Doyle, John. 2002. Complexity and robustness. *Proceedings of the National Academy of Sciences of the United States of America*, **99**(suppl. 1), 2538–2545.

Carney, Mark. 2015. *Breaking the Tragedy of the Horizon: Climate Change and Financial Stability*. Tech. rept. `www.bankofengland.co.uk/publications/Pages/speeches/2015/844.aspx`.

Carreras, Marco. 2020. Investigating the Role of BNDES as a Tool to Transmit Countercyclical Policy Decisions: Evidence from 2002–2016. *SSRN*.

Castelvecchi, Davide. 2020. First room-temperature superconductor excites-and baffles-scientists. *Nature*, **586**(7829), 349.

Cavalcanti, Ricardo de O., and Wallace, Neil. 1999a. Inside and outside money as alternative media of exchange. *Journal of Money, Credit and Banking*, **31**(3), 443–457.

1999b. A model of private bank-note issue. *Review of Economic Dynamics*, **2**(1), 104–136.

Chapin III, F. Stuart, Zavaleta, Erika S., Eviner, Valerie T., Naylor, Rosamond L., Vitousek, Peter M., Reynolds, Heather L., Hooper, David U., Lavorel, Sandra, Sala, Osvaldo E., Hobbie, Sarah E., et al. 2000. Consequences of changing biodiversity. *Nature*, **405**(6783), 234.

Cheng, Cindy, Barceló, Joan, Hartnett, Allison Spencer, Kubinec, Robert, and Messerschmidt, Luca. 2020. COVID-19 government response event dataset (CoronaNet v. 1.0). *Nature Human Behaviour*, **4**(7), 756–768.

Christensen, Jens Hesselbjerg, Kanikicharla, Krishna Kumar, Aldrian, Edvin, An, Soon Il, Cavalcanti, Iracema Fonseca Albuquerque, de Castro, Manuel, Dong, Wenjie, Goswami, Prashant, Hall, Alex, Kanyanga, Joseph Katongo, et al. 2013. Climate phenomena and their relevance for future regional climate change. Pages 1217–1308 of: *Climate Change 2013 the Physical Science Basis: Working Group I Contribution to the Fifth Assessment Report of the Intergovernmental Panel on Climate Change*. Cambridge University Press.

Christiano, Lawrence J., Eichenbaum, Martin S., and Trabandt, Mathias. 2018. On DSGE models. *Journal of Economic Perspectives*, **32**, 113–140.

CIRED. 2018. *The IMACLIM model*. `www.centre-cired.fr/en/imaclim-r-monde/`.

Clarke, Leon, Weyant, John, and Edmonds, Jae. 2008. On the sources of technological change: What do the models assume? *Energy Economics*, **30**, 409–424.

Clarke, Leon, Jiang, Kejun, Akimoto, Keigo, Babiker, Mustafa, Blanford, Geoffrey, Fisher-Vanden, Karen, Hourcade, J.-C., Krey, Volker, Kriegler, Elmar, and Löschel, Andreas L. B. 2014. Chapter 6: Assessing transformation pathways, in Climate Change 2017, Working Group III, Fifth Assessment Report of the Intergovernmental Panel on Climate Change. Tech. rept. IPCC.

Coase, Ronald Harry. 1960. The problem of social cost. *The Journal of Law and Economics*, **56**(4), 837–877.

Coibion, Olivier, Gorodnichenko, Yuriy, and Weber, Michael. 2020. The cost of the covid-19 crisis: Lockdowns, macroeconomic expectations, and consumer spending. *National Bureau of Economic Research*.

Commission, European. 2019. *The European Green Deal*. Tech. rept. European Commission.

Confalonieri, Ulisses E. C., Lima, Anna Carolina L., Brito, Isabela, and Quintão, Ana Flávia. 2017. Social, environmental and health vulnerability to climate change in the Brazilian Northeastern Region. *Climatic Change*, **127**(1), 123–137.

Cont, Rama. 2005. Long range dependence in financial markets. Pages 159–179 of: Lévy-Véhel, Jacques, and Lutton, Evelyne (eds.), *Fractals in Engineering*. Springer London.

Cont, Rama, and Schaanning, Eric. 2017. Fire sales, indirect contagion and systemic stress testing. *Indirect Contagion and Systemic Stress Testing (June 13, 2017)*.

Cont, Rama, Moussa, Amal, and Santos, Edson B. 2010. Network structure and systemic risk in banking systems. *SSRN*.

Cook, Brian, Zeng, Ning, and Yoon, Jin-Ho. 2012. Will Amazonia dry out? Magnitude and causes of change from IPCC climate model projections. *Earth Interactions*, **16**(3), 1–27.

Coronese, Matteo, Lamperti, Francesco, Keller, Klaus, Chiaromonte, Francesca, and Roventini, Andrea. 2019. Evidence for sharp increase in the economic damages of extreme natural disasters. *Proceedings of the National Academy of Sciences*, **116**(43), 21450–21455.

Costa, Francisco. 2013. Can rationing affect long run behavior? Evidence from Brazil. *SSRN* DOI:10.2139/ssrn.2028684.

Crabbé, Ann, and Leroy, Pieter. 2008. *The Handbook of Environmental Policy Evaluation*. Earthscan.

da Silva, Rodrigo Corrêa, de Marchi Neto, Ismael, and Seifert, Stephan Silva. 2016. Electricity supply security and the future role of renewable energy sources in Brazil. *Renewable and Sustainable Energy Reviews*, **59**, 328–341.

da Silva Soito, João Leonardo, and Freitas, Marcos Aurélio Vasconcelos. 2011. Amazon and the expansion of hydropower in Brazil: Vulnerability, impacts and possibilities for adaptation to global climate change. *Renewable and Sustainable Energy Reviews*, **15**(6), 3165–3177.

Dafermos, Yannis, Nikolaidi, Maria, and Galanis, Giorgos. 2017. A stock-flow-fund ecological macroeconomic model. *Ecological Economics*, **131**, 191–207.

Dai, Ziwei, and Locasale, Jason W. 2020. Cooperative virus propagation in COVID-19 transmission. *medRxiv DOI:10.1101/2020.05.05.20092361*.

David, Paul A. 1985. Clio and the Economics of QWERTY. *The American Economic Review*, **75**(2), 332–337.

Davidson, Eric A., de Araújo, Alessandro C., Artaxo, Paulo, Balch, Jennifer K., Brown, I. Foster, Bustamante, Mercedes M. C., Coe, Michael T., DeFries, Ruth S., Keller, Michael, Longo, Marcos, et al. 2012. The Amazon basin in transition. *Nature*, **481**(7381), 321–328.

Day, Richard H. 1992. Complex economic dynamics: Obvious in history, generic in theory, elusive in data. *Journal of Applied Econometrics*, 7(S1), S9–S23.

De Lucena, André Frossard Pereira, Szklo, Alexandre Salem, Schaeffer, Roberto, de Souza, Raquel Rodrigues, Borba, Bruno Soares Moreira Cesar, da Costa, Isabella Vaz Leal, Júnior, Amaro Olimpio Pereira, and da Cunha, Sergio Henrique Ferreira. 2009. The vulnerability of renewable energy to climate change in Brazil. *Energy Policy*, **37**(3), 879–889.

de Palma, A., and Kilani, K. 2009. Transition choice probabilities and welfare analysis in additive random utility models. *Economic Theory*, **46**(3), 427–454.

de Souza Ferreira Filho, Joaquim Bento, and De Moraes, Gustavo Inacio. 2015. Climate change, agriculture and economic effects on different regions of Brazil. *Environment and Development Economics*, **20**(1), 37–56.

DG ECFIN. 2015. *The QUEST III Model*. `http://ec.europa.eu/economy_finance/research/macroeconomic_models_en.htm`.

Dietz, Simon, and Hepburn, Cameron. 2013. Benefit–cost analysis of non-marginal climate and energy projects. *Energy Economics*, **40**, 61–71.

Dixon, Peter B, and Jorgenson, Dale. 2013. *Handbook of Computable General Equilibrium Modeling SET, Vols. 1A and 1B*. Newnes.

Domencich, T. A., and McFadden, D. 1975. *Urban Travel Demand: A Behavioural Analysis*. North-Holland Publishing.

Dosi, G., Freeman, C., Nelson, R., Silverberg, G., and Soete, L. 1988. *Technical Change and Economic Theory*. Pinter Publishers.

Dosi, Giovanni. 1982. Technological paradigms and technological trajectories. *Research Policy*, **2**(3), 147–62.

Dosi, Giovanni, Fagiolo, Giorgio, and Roventini, Andrea. 2010. Schumpeter meeting Keynes: A policy-friendly model of endogenous growth and business cycles. *Journal of Economic Dynamics and Control*, **34**(9), 1748–1767.

Dosi, Giovanni, Fagiolo, Giorgio, Napoletano, Mauro, and Roventini, Andrea. 2013. Income distribution, credit and fiscal policies in an agent-based Keynesian model. *Journal of Economic Dynamics and Control*, **37**(8), 1598–1625.

Dosi, Giovanni, Fagiolo, Giorgio, Napoletano, Mauro, Roventini, Andrea, and Treibich, Tania. 2015. Fiscal and monetary policies in complex evolving economies. *Journal of Economic Dynamics and Control*, **52**, 166–189.

Douglas, M., and Isherwood, B. 1979. *The World of Goods: Towards an Anthropology of Consumption*. Routledge.

Doyle, John, and Carlson, Jean M. 2000. Power laws, highly optimized tolerance, and generalized source coding. *Physical Review Letters*, 84(24), 5656.

Durlauf, S. N., and Ioannides, Y. M. 2010. Social interactions. *Annual Review of Economics*, **2**(1), 451–478.

E3M. 2018. *The GEM-E3 Model*. www.e3mlab.eu/e3mlab/index.php?option=com_content&view=category&id=36%3Agem-e3&Itemid=71&layout=default&lang=en.

E3MLab. 2018. *The PRIMES Model*. www.e3mlab.eu/e3mlab/index.php?option=com_content&view=category&id=35&Itemid=80&lang=en.

EC. 2009. *Impact Assessment Guidelines*. Tech. rept. European Commission, http://ec.europa.eu/smart-regulation/impact/commission_guidelines/docs/iag_2009_en.pdf.

2015. *Better Regulation Guidelines*. Tech. rept. European Commission, http://ec.europa.eu/smart-regulation/guidelines/docs/swd_br_guidelines_en.pdf.

2017. *The Economic Rationale for Public R&I Funding and Its Impact*. Tech. rept. https://ri-links2ua.eu/object/document/326/attach/KI0117050ENN_002.pdf.

Edenhofer, O., Lessmann, K., Kemfert, C., Grubb, M., and Köhler, J. 2006. Induced technological change: Exploring its implications for the economics of atmospheric stabilization: Synthesis report from the Innovation Modeling Comparison Project. *Energy Journal*, 57–107.

Edenhofer, O., Knopf, B., Barker, T., Baumstark, L., Bellevrat, E., Chateau, B., Criqui, P., Isaac, M., Kitous, A., Kypreos, C., et al. 2010. The Economics of Low Stabilization: Model Comparison of Mitigation Strategies and Costs. *Energy Journal*, **31**(1), 11–48.

Ekins, P., Pollitt, H., Barton, J., and Blobel, D. 2011. The implications for households of environmental tax reform (ETR) in Europe. *Ecological Economics*, **70**(12), 2472 – 2485.

EPA. 2014. *Guidelines for Preparing Economic Analyses*. Tech. rept. National Center for Environmental Economics Office of Policy U.S. Environmental Protection Agency.

Escobar, Herton. 2015. Drought triggers alarms in Brazil's biggest metropolis. *Science*, **347**(6224), 812–812.

Fachinelli, Natália Pezzi, and Pereira Jr, Amaro Olimpio. 2015. Impacts of sugarcane ethanol production in the Paranaiba basin water resources. *Biomass and Bioenergy*, **83**, 8–16.

Falkner, Robert. 2016. The Paris Agreement and the new logic of international climate politics. *International Affairs*, **92**(5), 1107–1125.

Fan, V.Y., Jamison, D.T. and Summers, L.H., 2016. *The inclusive cost of pandemic influenza risk*, Working Paper No. w22137, National Bureau of Economic Research.

Fargione, Joseph, Hill, Jason, Tilman, David, Polasky, Stephen, and Hawthorne, Peter. 2008. Land clearing and the biofuel carbon debt. *Science*, **319**(5867), 1235–1238.

Farmer, J. Doyne, and Foley, Duncan. 2009. The economy needs agent-based modelling. *Nature*, **460**(7256), 685–686.

Farmer, J. Doyne, and Lafond, François. 2016. How predictable is technological progress? *Research Policy*, **45**(3), 647–665.

Farmer, J. Doyne, Hepburn, Cameron, Mealy, Penny, and Teytelboym, Alexander. 2015. A third wave in the economics of climate change. *Environmental and Resource Economics*, **62**(2), 329–357.

Farrell, C. J. 1993. A theory of technological progress. *Technological Forecasting and Social Change*, **44**(2), 161–178.

Fearnside, Philip M. 2005. Deforestation in Brazilian Amazonia: History, rates, and consequences. *Conservation Biology*, **19**(3), 680–688.

Fisch-Romito, Vivien, Guivarch, Céline, Creutzig, Felix, Minx, Jan C., and Callaghan, Max W. 2021. Systematic map of the literature on carbon lock-in induced by long-lived capital. *Environmental Research Letters*, **16**(5), 053004.

Fisher, Irving. 1932. *Booms and Depressions*. Adelphi.

Fisher, J. C., and Pry, R. H. 1971. A simple substitution model of technological change. *Technological Forecasting and Social Change*, **3**(1), 75–88.

Foley, A. M., Holden, P. B., Edwards, N. R., Mercure, J.-F., Salas, P., Pollitt, H., and Chewpreecha, U. 2016. Climate model emulation in an integrated assessment framework: A case study for mitigation policies in the electricity sector. *Earth System Dynamics*, **7**, 119–132.

Fontana, Giuseppe. 2008. *Money, Uncertainty and Time*. Routledge.

Fouquet, Roger. 2016. Historical energy transitions: Speed, prices and system transformation. *Energy Research & Social Science*, **22**, 7–12.

Fragkos, Panagiotis, and Paroussos, Leonidas. 2018. Employment creation in EU related to renewables expansion. *Applied Energy*, **230**, 935–945.

Freeman, C. 1994. The economics of technical change. *Cambridge Journal of Economics*, **18**(5), 463–514.

Freeman, C., and Perez, C. 1988. Structural crises of adjustment: Business cycles and investment behaviour. Pages 38–66 of: Dosi, G., Freeman, C., Nelson, R., Silverberg, G., and Soete, L. (eds.), *Technical Change and Economic Theory*. Pinter Publishers.

Freeman, C., and Louçã, F. 2001. *As Time Goes By*. Oxford University Press.

Friedlingstein, Pierre, O'Sullivan, Michael, Jones, Matthew W., Andrew, Robbie M., Hauck, Judith, Olsen, Are, Peters, Glen P., Peters, Wouter, Pongratz, Julia, Sitch, Stephen, et al. 2020. Global carbon budget 2020. *Earth System Science Data*, **12**(4), 3269–3340.

Friedman, Milton. 1953. The methodology of positive economics. *Essays in Positive Economics*, **3**(3), 145–178.

Friedman, Milton, and Schwartz, Anna J. 1965. Money and business cycles. Pages 32–78 of: NBER (ed.), *The State of Monetary Economics*, Publisher: NBER, pp 32–78.

Gaechter, Simon, Johnson, Ej, and Herrmann, Andreas. 2007. Individual-level loss aversion in riskless and risky choices. *IZA Discussion Paper*, **2961**.

Galbraith, John Kenneth. 2017. *Money: Whence It Came, Where It Went*. Princeton University Press.

Galí, Jordi. 2015. *Monetary Policy, Inflation, and the Business Cycle: An Introduction to the New Keynesian Framework and Its Applications*. Princeton University Press.

Gallagher, Kelly Sims, Grübler, Arnulf, Kuhl, Laura, Nemet, Gregory, and Wilson, Charlie. 2012. The energy technology innovation system. *Annual Review of Environment and Resources*, **37**, 137–162.

Gallos, Lazaros K., Cohen, Reuven, Argyrakis, Panos, Bunde, Armin, and Havlin, Shlomo. 2005. Stability and topology of scale-free networks under attack and defense strategies. *Physical Review Letters*, **94**(18), 188701.

Garcez, Catherine Aliana Gucciardi, and de Souza Vianna, João Nildo. 2009. Brazilian biodiesel policy: Social and environmental considerations of sustainability. *Energy*, **34**(5), 645–654.

Garcia, Beatriz. 2011. *The Amazon from an International Law Perspective*. Cambridge University Press.

Garcia, Daniel J., and You, Fengqi. 2016. The water-energy-food nexus and process systems engineering: A new focus. *Computers & Chemical Engineering*, **91**, 49–67.

Garlaschelli, Diego, Battiston, Stefano, Castri, Maurizio, Servedio, Vito D. P., and Caldarelli, Guido. 2005. The scale-free topology of market investments. *Physica A: Statistical Mechanics and Its Applications*, **350**(2–4), 491–499.

Garrett-Peltier, Heidi. 2017. Green versus brown: Comparing the employment impacts of energy efficiency, renewable energy, and fossil fuels using an input-output model. *Economic Modelling*, **61**, 439–447.

GCEE. 2016. *Chapter 11: 'Energiewende: Umsteuern zu einer globalen Klimapolitik' ('The Energy Transition: Shifting towards a Global Climate Policy')*. Tech. rept. German Council of Economic Experts.

GEA (ed.). 2012. *Global Energy Assessment*. Cambridge University Press, Cambridge, UK and New York, NY, USA and the International Institute for Applied Systems Analysis, Laxenburg, Austria.

Geels, F. W. 2002. Technological transitions as evolutionary reconfiguration processes: A multi-level perspective and a case-study. *Research Policy*, **31**(8–9), 1257–1274.

2005. The dynamics of transitions in socio-technical systems: A multi-level analysis of the transition pathway from horse-drawn carriages to automobiles (1860–1930). *Technology Analysis & Strategic Management*, **17**(4), 445–476.

2006. Co-evolutionary and multi-level dynamics in transitions: The transformation of aviation systems and the shift from propeller to turbojet (1930–1970). *Technovation*, **26**(9), 999–1016.

2011. The multi-level perspective on sustainability transitions: Responses to seven criticisms. *Environmental Innovation and Societal Transitions*, **1**(1), 24–40.

Geels, F. W., Berkhout, F., and van Vuuren, D. P. 2016. Bridging analytical approaches for low-carbon transitions. *Nature Climate Change*, 576–583 (2016).

Genus, Audley, and Coles, Anne-Marie. 2008. Rethinking the multi-level perspective of technological transitions. *Research Policy*, **37**(9), 1436–1445.

Gibbs, Holly K., Rausch, Lisa, Munger, Jacob, Schelly, Ian, Morton, Douglas C., Noojipady, Praveen, Soares-Filho, Bitraldo, Barreto, Paulo, Micol, Laurent, and Walker, Nathalie F. 2015. Brazil's soy moratorium. *Science*, **347**(6220), 377–378.

Gillingham, Kenneth, and Palmer, Karen. 2014. Bridging the energy efficiency gap: Policy insights from economic theory and empirical evidence. *Review of Environmental Economics and Policy*, 8(1), 18–38.

Gillingham, Kenneth, Newell, Richard G., and Pizer, William A. 2008. Modeling endogenous technological change for climate policy analysis. *Energy Economics*, **30**(6), 2734–2753.

Giraudet, L.-G., Guivarch, C., and Quirion, P. 2012. Exploring the potential for energy conservation in French households through hybrid modeling. *Energy Economics*, **34**(2), 426–445.

Godley, Wynne, and Lavoie, Marc. 2006. *Monetary Economics: An Integrated Approach to Credit, Money, Income, Production and Wealth*. Springer.

Goldthau, Andreas, Westphal, Kirsten, Bazilian, Morgan, and Bradshaw, Michael. 2019. How the energy transition will reshape geopolitics. *Nature*, **569**(7754), 29–31.

Goodwin, Richard. 1982. A growth cycle. Pages 165–170 of: *Essays in Economic Dynamics*. Springer.

Gopikrishnan, Parameswaran, Plerou, Vasiliki, Amaral, Luis A. Nunes, Meyer, Martin, and Stanley, H. Eugene. 1999. Scaling of the distribution of fluctuations of financial market indices. *Physical Review E*, **60**(5), 5305.

Gould, Stephen Jay, and Eldredge, Niles. 1977. Punctuated equilibria: The tempo and mode of evolution reconsidered. *Paleobiology*, **3**(2), 115–151.

Goulder, Lawrence H., and Schneider, Stephen H. 1999. Induced technological change and the attractiveness of CO2 abatement policies. *Resource and Energy Economics*, **21**, 211–253.

Goulder, Lawrence H., Hafstead, Marc A. C., and Williams III, Roberton C. 2016. General equilibrium impacts of a federal clean energy standard. *American Economic Journal: Economic Policy*, 8, 186–218.

Government, HM. 2017. *Grand Challenges: Building a Britain Fit for the Future*. Tech. rept. HM Government.

Graeber, David. 2014. *Debt-Updated and Expanded: The First 5,000 Years*. Melville House.

Grübler, Arnulf. 1998. *Technology and Global Change*. Cambridge University Press.

Green, Fergus, and Gambhir, Ajay. 2020. Transitional assistance policies for just, equitable and smooth low-carbon transitions: Who, what and how? *Climate Policy*, **20**(8), 902–921.

Gritsevskyi, Andrii, and Nakićenovic, Nebojša. 2000. Modeling uncertainty of induced technological change. *Energy Policy*, **28**, 907–921.

Grubb, M., Carraro, C., and Schellnhuber, J. 2006. Technological change for atmospheric stabilization: Introductory overview to the Innovation Modeling Comparison Project. *Energy Journal*, **1**, 1–16.

Grubb, M., Hourcade, J.-C., and Neuhoff, K. 2014. *Planetary Economics*. Taylor & Francis / Routledge.

Grubb, M., Drummond, P., Mercure, J.-F., and Hepburn, C. 2021a. *The New Economics of Innovation and Transition: Evaluating Opportunities and Risks*. Tech. rept. Economics of Innovation and System Transition (EEIST), www.eeist.co.uk.

Grubb, Michael, Edmonds, Jae, Ten Brink, Patrick, and Morrison, Michael. 1993. The costs of limiting fossil-fuel CO2 emissions: A survey and analysis. *Annual Review of Energy and the Environment*, **18**, 397–478.

Grubb, Michael, Köhler, Jonathan, and Anderson, Dennis. 2002. Induced technical change in energy and environmental modeling: Analytic approaches and policy implications. *Annual Review of Energy and the Environment*, **27**, 271–308.

Grubb, Michael, Bashmakov, Igor, Drummond, Paul, Myshak, Anna, Hughes, Nick, Biancardi, Andrea, Agnolucci, Paolo, and Lowe, Robert. 2018. *An Exploration of Energy Cost, Ranges, Limits and Adjustment Process*. Tech. rept. `https://discovery.ucl.ac.uk/id/eprint/10047775/1/An%20exploration%20of%20energy%20cost,%20ranges,%20limits%20and%20adjustment%20process.pdf`.

Grubb, Michael, Drummond, Paul, Poncia, Alexandra, McDowall, Will, Popp, David, Samadi, Sascha, Penasco, Cristina, Gillingham, Kenneth T., Smulders, Sjak, Glachant, Matthieu, et al. 2021b. Induced innovation in energy technologies and systems: A review of evidence and potential implications for CO2 mitigation. *Environmental Research Letters*, **16**(4), 043007.

Grübler, A., Nakicenovic, N., and Victor, D. G. 1999. Dynamics of energy technologies and global change. *Energy Policy*, **27**(5), 247–280.

Grübler, Arnulf. 2003. *Technology and Global Change*. Cambridge University Press.

2012. Energy transitions research: Insights and cautionary tales. *Energy Policy*, **50**, 8–16.

Grübler, Arnulf, and Wilson, Charlie. 2013. *Energy Technology Innovation*. Cambridge University Press.

Guttmann, Robert. 2015. The heterodox notion of structural crisis. *Review of Keynesian Economics*, **3**(2), 194–212.

2016. *Finance-Led Capitalism: Shadow Banking, Re-regulation, and the Future of Global Markets*. Springer.

Hafner, Manfred, and Tagliapietra, Simone. 2020. *The Geopolitics of the Global Energy Transition*. Springer Nature.

Haldane, Andrew G., and May, Robert M. 2011. Systemic risk in banking ecosystems. *Nature*, **469**(7330), 351–355.

Haldane, Andrew G., and Turrell, Arthur E. 2018. An interdisciplinary model for macroeconomics. *Oxford Review of Economic Policy*, **34**(1–2), 219–251.

Hall, Lisa M. H., and Buckley, Alastair R. 2016. A review of energy systems models in the UK: Prevalent usage and categorisation. *Applied Energy*, **169**, 607–628.

Hanley, Nick, and Barbier, Edward B. 2009. *Pricing Nature: Cost-Benefit Analysis and Environmental Policy*. Edward Elgar Publishing.

Hanley, Nick, Shogren, Jason F., and White, Ben. 2016. *Environmental Economics: In Theory and Practice*. Macmillan International Higher Education.

2019. *Introduction to Environmental Economics*. Oxford University Press.

Harvey, Mark, and Pilgrim, Sarah. 2011. The new competition for land: Food, energy, and climate change. *Food Policy*, **36**, S40–S51.

He, Ping, Huang, Lixin, and Wright, Randall. 2005. Money and banking in search equilibrium. *International Economic Review*, **46**(2), 637–670.

Head, Brian W., and Alford, John. 2015. Wicked problems: Implications for public policy and management. *Administration & Society*, **47**(6), 711–739.

Heilbroner, Robert L. 1973. Economics as a 'value-free' science. *Social Research*, **40**(1), 129–143.

Heinsohn, Gunnar, and Steiger, Otto. 2005. Alternative theories of the rate of interest: A reconsideration. Pages 67–81 of: *The Monetary Theory of Production*. Springer.

Heisenberg, Werner. 1958. *Physics and Philosophy: The Revolution in Modern Science*. Harper & Row Publishers.

Hekkert, M. P., Suurs, R. A. A., Negro, S. O., Kuhlmann, S., and Smits, R. E. H. M. 2007. Functions of innovation systems: A new approach for analysing technological change. *Technological Forecasting and Social Change*, **74**(4), 413 – 432.

Helleiner, Eric. 2011. Understanding the 2007–2008 global financial crisis: Lessons for scholars of international political economy. *Annual Review of Political Science*, **14**, 67–87.

Herndon, Thomas, Ash, Michael, and Pollin, Robert. 2014. Does high public debt consistently stifle economic growth? A critique of Reinhart and Rogoff. *Cambridge Journal of Economics*, **38**(2), 257–279.

Hertel, Thomas W. 2015. The challenges of sustainably feeding a growing planet. *Food Security*, **7**(2), 185–198.

Hicks, John. 1932. *The Theory of Wages*. Springer.

HM Treasury. 2020a. *The Green Book: Central Government Guidance on Appraisal and Evaluation*. Tech. rept. UK HM Treasury, `www.gov.uk/government/publications/the-green-book-appraisal-and-evaluation-in-central-governent`.

2020b. *The Orange Book: Management of Risk – Principles and Concepts*. Tech. rept. UK HM Treasury, `www.gov.uk/government/publications/orange-book`.

2021. *Net Zero Review*. Tech. rept. UK HM Treasury.

Hofbauer, Josef, and Sigmund, Karl. 1998. *Evolutionary Games and Population Dynamics*. Cambridge University Press.

Hoff, H. 2011. *Understanding the Nexus. Background Paper for the Bonn 2011 Conference: The Water Energy and Food Security Nexus*. Tech. rept. Stockholm Environment Institute, `www.sei.org/publications/understanding-the-nexus/`.

Hofstede, Geert. 2001. *Culture's Consequences: Comparing Values, Behaviors, Institutions and Organizations across Nations*. Sage Publications.

Holden, P. B., Edwards, N. R., Gerten, D., and Schaphoff, S. 2013a. A model-based constraint on CO2 fertilisation. *Biogeosciences*, **10**(1), 339–355.

Holden, P. B., Edwards, N. R., Müller, S. A., Oliver, K. I. C., Death, R. M., and Ridgwell, A. 2013b. Controls on the spatial distribution of oceanic δ 13 C DIC. *Biogeosciences*, **10**(3), 1815–1833.

Holden, Philip B., Edwards, Neil R., Ridgwell, A., Wilkinson, R. D., Fraedrich, K., Lunkeit, Frank, Pollitt, Hector, Mercure, J.-F., Salas, P., Lam, A., et al. 2018. Climate–carbon cycle uncertainties and the Paris Agreement. *Nature Climate Change*, 8(7), 609.

Hoogwijk, Monique, Faaij, André, de Vries, Bert, and Turkenburg, Wim. 2009. Exploration of regional and global cost–supply curves of biomass energy from short-rotation crops at abandoned cropland and rest land under four IPCC SRES land-use scenarios. *Biomass and Bioenergy*, **33**(1), 26–43.

Hotelling, H. 1931. The economics of exhaustible resources. *Journal of Political Economy*, **39**, 137–175.

Hottenrott, Hanna, and Rexhäuser, Sascha. 2015. Policy-induced environmental technology and inventive efforts: Is there a crowding out? *Industry and Innovation*, **22**(5), 375–401.

Houghton, J. 2015. *Global Warming*. Cambridge University Press.

Hsiang, Solomon M., Burke, Marshall, and Miguel, Edward. 2013. Quantifying the influence of climate on human conflict. *Science*, **341**, 6151.

HSS. 2016. *Guidelines for Regulatory Impact Analysis*. Tech. rept. U.S. Department of Health & Human Services.

Hubbert, M. K. 1962. *Energy Resources. A Report to the Committee on Natural Resources*. Tech. rept. Publication No. 1000-D. National Academy of Science, Government Printing Office.

Hughes, Nick, Strachan, Neil, and Gross, Robert. 2013. The structure of uncertainty in future low carbon pathways. *Energy Policy*, **52**, 45–54.

Hung, Shiu-Wan, and Wang, An-Pang. 2008. A small world in the patent citation network. Pages 1–5 of: *2008 IEEE International Conference on Industrial Engineering and Engineering Management*. IEEE.

Hurlstone, Mark J., Wang, Susie, Price, Annabel, Leviston, Zoe, and Walker, Iain. 2017. Cooperation studies of catastrophe avoidance: Implications for climate negotiations. *Climatic Change*, **140**(2), 119–133.

IEA. 2019. *World Energy Outlook 2019*. IEA/OECD.

2020. *World Energy Balances 2020*. IEA/OECD.

2021. *IEA Policies Database*. `www.iea.org/policies`.

IEA-ETSAP. 2016. *IEA-ETSAP Optimization Modeling Documentation*. `http://iea-etsap.org/index.php/documentation`.

IIASA. 2013. *The MESSAGE Model*. `www.iiasa.ac.at/web/home/research/modelsData/MESSAGE/MESSAGE.en.html`.

Innes, A. M. 1913. What is money? *Banking Law Journal*, **May**, 377–408.

IPCC. 2007. *Climate Change 2007: Mitigation of Climate Change*. Cambridge University Press.

2013. *Climate Change 2013: The Physical Science Basis*. Cambridge University Press.

2014. *Climate Change 2014: Mitigation of Climate Change*. Cambridge University Press.

2018. *Special Report: Global Warming of 1.5°C*. Cambridge University Press.

IRENA. 2019. *A New World: The Geopolitics of the Energy Transformation*. Tech. rept. IRENA.

Ives, M. C., Righetti, L., Schiele, J., De Meyer, K., Hubble-Rose, L., Teng, F., Kruitwagen, L., Tillmann-Morris, L., Wang, T., Way, R., and Hepburn, C. 2021. The prospects for Paris: Behavioral insights into unconditional cooperation on climate change. *Oxford INET Working Paper Series No. 21-04*.

Jaffe, Adam B., and Stavins, Robert N. 1994. The energy-efficiency gap: What does it mean? *Energy Policy*, **22**(10), 804–810.

Jarvis, A. J., Jarvis, S. J., and Hewitt, C. N. 2015. Resource acquisition, distribution and end-use efficiencies and the growth of industrial society. *Earth System Dynamics*, **6**(2), 689.

Jarvis, Andrew. 2018. Energy returns and the long-run growth of global industrial society. *Ecological Economics*, **146**, 722–729.

Jaxa-Rozen, Marc, and Trutnevyte, Evelina. 2021. Sources of uncertainty in long-term global scenarios of solar photovoltaic technology. *Nature Climate Change*, **11**(3), 266–273.

Jennings, T., Tipper, H. A., Daglish, J., Grubb, M., and Drummond, P. 2020. *Policy, Innovation and Cost Reduction in UK Offshore Wind*. Tech. rept. Carbon Trust.

Jevons, William Stanley. 1876. *Money and the Mechanism of Exchange*. Vol. 17. D. Appleton.

Jochem, Eberhard, and Gruber, Edelgard. 2007. Local learning-networks on energy efficiency in industry: Successful initiative in Germany. *Applied Energy*, **84**(7–8), 806–816.

Johnson, Eric J., and Goldstein, Daniel. 2003. Do defaults save lives? *Science*, **302**(5649), 1338–1339.

Jorgenson, Dale W., and Wilcoxen, Peter J. 1993. Energy prices, productivity, and economic growth. *Annual Review of Energy and the Environment*, **18**, 343–395.

Jump, Alistair S., and Penuelas, Josep. 2005. Running to stand still: Adaptation and the response of plants to rapid climate change. *Ecology Letters*, 8(9), 1010–1020.

Kadanoff, Leo P. 2000. *Statistical Physics: Statics, Dynamics and Renormalization*. World Scientific Publishing Company.

Kahneman, D. 2003. Maps of bounded rationality: Psychology for behavioral economics. *American Economic Review*, **93**(5), 1449–1475.

Kahneman, D., and Tversky, A. 1979. Prospect theory: An analysis of decision under risk. *Econometrica*, **47**(2), 263–291.

Kaldor, N. 1957. A model of economic-growth. *Economic Journal*, **67**(268), 586–624.

Kapur, Sandeep. 1995. Technological diffusion with social learning. *The Journal of Industrial Economics*, **43**(2), 173–195.

Karmeshu, Bhargava, S. C., and Jain, V. P. 1985. A rationale for law of technological substitution. *Regional Science and Urban Economics*, **15**(1), 137–141.

Kattel, Rainer, Mazzucato, Mariana, Ryan-Collins, Josh, and Sharpe, Simon. 2018. The economics of change: Policy and appraisal for missions, market shaping and public purpose Policy Report. *Institute for Innovation and Public Purpose WP 2018-06*.

Katz, J. Sylvan. 2016. What is a complex innovation system? *PLoS One*, **11**(6), e0156150.

Kauffman, Stuart A. 2000. *Investigations*. Oxford University Press.

Kay, John, Nash, David, Silim, Amna, Ormerod, Paul, Hallsworth, Michael, Fisher, Greg, Hodgson, Geoffrey M., Dolphin, Tony, Westlake, Stian, Watson, Jim, et al. 2012. Complex new world: Translating new economic thinking into public policy. *Institute for Public Policy Research, London*.

Keairns, D. L., Darton, R. C., and Irabien, A. 2016. The energy-water-food nexus. *Annual Review of Chemical and Biomolecular Engineering*, **7**, 239–262.

Keen, Steve. 1995. Finance and economic breakdown: Modeling Minsky's 'financial instability hypothesis'. *Journal of Post Keynesian Economics*, **17**(4), 607–635.

2011. *Debunking Economics – Revised and Expanded Edition*. Zed Books.

2013. Predicting the 'Global financial crisis': Post-Keynesian macroeconomics. *Economic Record*, **89**(285), 228–254.
2017. *Can We Avoid Another Financial Crisis?* John Wiley & Sons.
Kellerborg, Klas, Brouwer, Werner, and van Baal, Pieter. 2020. Costs and benefits of interventions aimed at major infectious disease threats: Lessons from the literature. *The European Journal of Health Economics*, **21**, 1329–1350.
Keynes, John Maynard. 1921. *A Treatise on Probability*. Macmillan & Co.
1930. *Treatise on Money: Pure Theory of Money*. Vol. I. Macmillan.
1936. *The General Theory of Employment, Interest and Money*. Palgrave-Macmillan.
King, D., Shrag, D., Dadi, Z., Ye, Q., and Ghosh, A. 2015. *Climate Change: A Risk Assessment*. Tech. rept. Cambridge University Centre for Science and Policy.
King, J. E. 2015. *Advanced Introduction to Post Keynesian Economics*. Edward Elgar.
Kirman, Alan P. 1992. Whom or what does the representative individual represent? *The Journal of Economic Perspectives*, **6**(2), 117–136.
Kishore, Vimal, Santhanam, M. S., and Amritkar, R. E. 2011. Extreme events on complex networks. *Physical Review Letters*, **106**(18), 188701.
Kiyotaki, Nobuhiro, and Moore, John. 1997. Credit cycles. *Journal of Political Economy*, **105**(2), 211–248.
Kiyotaki, Nobuhiro, and Wright, Randall. 1989. On money as a medium of exchange. *Journal of Political Economy*, **97**(4), 927–954.
Klingebiel, Ronald, and Rammer, Christian. 2014. Resource allocation strategy for innovation portfolio management. *Strategic Management Journal*, **35**(2), 246–268.
Knetsch, Jack L. 1989. The endowment effect and evidence of nonreversible indifference curves. *The American Economic Review*, **79**(5), 1277–1284.
Knight, Frank H. 1921. *Risk, Uncertainty and Profit*. Houghton Mifflin Company.
Knobloch, F., and Mercure, J.-F. 2016. The behavioural aspect of green technology investments: A general positive model in the context of heterogeneous agents. *Environmental Innovation and Societal Transitions*, **21**, 39–55.
Knobloch, F., Mercure, J.-F., Pollitt, H., Chewpreecha, U., and Lewney, R. L. B. 2017. *A Technical Analysis of FTT:Heat – A Simulation Model for Technological Change in the Residential Heating Sector*. Tech. rept. European Commission, DG Energy, `https://ec.europa.eu/energy/sites/ener/files/documents/technical_analysis_residential_heat.pdf`.
Knobloch, Florian, Pollitt, Hector, Chewpreecha, Unnada, Daioglou, Vassilis, and Mercure, Jean-Francois. 2018. Simulating the deep decarbonisation of residential heating for limiting global warming to 1.5 C. *Energy Efficiency*, **12**(2), 521–550.
Knobloch, Florian, Huijbregts, Mark A. J., and Mercure, Jean-Francois. 2019. Modelling the effectiveness of climate policies: How important is loss aversion by consumers? *Renewable and Sustainable Energy Reviews*, **116**, 109419.
Knobloch, Florian, Hanssen, Steef V., Lam, Aileen, Pollitt, Hector, Salas, Pablo, Chewpreecha, Unnada, Huijbregts, Mark A. J., and Mercure, Jean-Francois. 2020. Net emission reductions from electric cars and heat pumps in 59 world regions over time. *Nature Sustainability*, **3**, 437–447.
Knobloch, Florian, Pollitt, Hector, Chewpreecha, Unnada, Lewney, Richard, Huijbregts, Mark A. J., and Mercure, Jean-Francois. 2021. FTT: Heat – A simulation model for technological change in the European residential heating sector. *Energy Policy*, **153**, 112249.
Kocherlakota, Narayana R. 1998. Money is memory. *Journal of Economic Theory*, **81**(2), 232–251.

Köhler, J., Grubb, M., Popp, D., and Edenhofer, O. 2006. The transition to endogenous technical change in climate-economy models: A technical overview to the Innovation Modeling Comparison Project. *Energy Journal*, **1**, 17–55.

Köhler, J., Whitmarsh, L., Nykvist, B., Schilperoord, M., Bergman, N., and Haxeltine, A. 2009. A transitions model for sustainable mobility. *Ecological Economics*, 68(12), 2985–2995.

Kondratieff, Nikolai. 1928. *The Long Wave Cycle*. Russian Association of Social Research Institutes.

Kot, Mark. 2001. *Elements of Mathematical Ecology*. Cambridge University Press.

Kreindler, Gabriel E., and Young, H. Peyton. 2013. Fast convergence in evolutionary equilibrium selection. *Games and Economic Behavior*, 80, 39–67.

2014. Rapid innovation diffusion in social networks. *Proceedings of the National Academy of Sciences*, **111**(Supplement 3), 10881–10888.

Kriegler, Elmar, Weyant, John P., Blanford, Geoffrey J., Krey, Volker, Clarke, Leon, Edmonds, Jae, Fawcett, Allen, Luderer, Gunnar, Riahi, Keywan, Richels, Richard, et al. 2014. The role of technology for achieving climate policy objectives: Overview of the EMF 27 study on global technology and climate policy strategies. *Climatic Change*, **123**(3–4), 353–367.

Kriegler, Elmar, Petermann, Nils, Krey, Volker, Schwanitz, Valeria Jana, Luderer, Gunnar, Ashina, Shuichi, Bosetti, Valentina, Eom, Jiyong, Kitous, Alban, Méjean, Aurélie, et al. 2015a. Diagnostic indicators for integrated assessment models of climate policy. *Technological Forecasting and Social Change*, 90, 45–61.

Kriegler, Elmar, Riahi, Keywan, Bauer, Nico, Schwanitz, Valeria Jana, Petermann, Nils, Bosetti, Valentina, Marcucci, Adriana, Otto, Sander, Paroussos, Leonidas, and Rao, Shilpa L. B. 2015b. Making or breaking climate targets: The AMPERE study on staged accession scenarios for climate policy. *Technological Forecasting and Social Change*, 90, 24–44.

Kurian, Mathew. 2017. The water-energy-food nexus: Trade-offs, thresholds and transdisciplinary approaches to sustainable development. *Environmental Science & Policy*, 68, 97–106.

Kwasnicki, W., and Kwasnicka, H. 1996. Long-term diffusion factors of technological development: An evolutionary model and case study. *Technological Forecasting and Social Change*, **52**(1), 31–57.

Kymlicka, Will. 2002. *Contemporary Political Philosophy: An Introduction*. Oxford University Press.

La Rovere, Emilio Lèbre, Pereira, André Santos, and Simões, André Felipe. 2011. Biofuels and sustainable energy development in Brazil. *World Development*, **39**(6), 1026–1036.

Lacopetta, Maurizio. 2019. The emergence of money: A dynamic analysis. *Macroeconomic Dynamics*, **23**(7), 2573–2596.

Lafond, François, Bailey, Aimee Gotway, Bakker, Jan David, Rebois, Dylan, Zadourian, Rubina, McSharry, Patrick, and Farmer, J. Doyne. 2018. How well do experience curves predict technological progress? A method for making distributional forecasts. *Technological Forecasting and Social Change*, **128**, 104–117.

Lakka, Spyridoula, Michalakelis, Christos, Varoutas, Dimitris, and Martakos, Draculis. 2013. Competitive dynamics in the operating systems market: Modeling and policy implications. *Technological Forecasting and Social Change*, 80(1), 88–105.

Lam, Aileen, and Mercure, Jean-Francois. 2021. Which policy mixes are best for decarbonising passenger cars? Simulating interactions among taxes, subsidies and regulations for the United Kingdom, the United States, Japan, China, and India. *Energy Research & Social Science*, **75**, 101951.

Lambin, Eric F., and Meyfroidt, Patrick. 2011. Global land use change, economic globalization, and the looming land scarcity. *Proceedings of the National Academy of Sciences*, **108**(9), 3465–3472.

Lamperti, Francesco, Dosi, Giovanni, Napoletano, Mauro, Roventini, Andrea, and Sapio, Alessandro. 2018. Faraway, so close: Coupled climate and economic dynamics in an agent-based integrated assessment model. *Ecological Economics*, **150**, 315–339.

Lane, David. 1997. Is what is good for each best for all? Learning from others in the information contagion model. Pages 105–128 of: *The Economy as an Evolving Complex System II*. Santa Fe Institute studies in the sciences of complexity. Vol. 27. Westview Press.

Lapola, David M., Martinelli, Luiz A., Peres, Carlos A., Ometto, Jean P. H. B., Ferreira, Manuel E., Nobre, Carlos A., Aguiar, Ana Paula D., Bustamante, Mercedes M. C., Cardoso, Manoel F., Costa, Marcos H., et al. 2014. Pervasive transition of the Brazilian land-use system. *Nature Climate Change*, **4**(1), 27–35.

Lapola, David M., Schaldach, Ruediger, Alcamo, Joseph, Bondeau, Alberte, Koch, Jennifer, Koelking, Christina, and Priess, Joerg A. 2010. Indirect land-use changes can overcome carbon savings from biofuels in Brazil. *Proceedings of the National Academy of Sciences*, **107**(8), 3388–3393.

Laughlin, R. B., and Pines, David. 2000. The Theory of Everything. *Proceedings of the National Academy of Sciences*, **97**(1), 28–31.

Lavoie, Marc. 2014. *Post-Keynesian Economics: New Foundations*. Edward Elgar Publishing.

2020. Was Hyman Minsky a post-Keynesian economist? *Review of Evolutionary Political Economy*, **1**(1), 85–101.

Leck, Hayley, Conway, Declan, Bradshaw, Michael, and Rees, Judith. 2015. Tracing the water–energy–food nexus: Description, theory and practice. *Geography Compass*, **9**(8), 445–460.

Lee, S., Pollitt, H., and Park, P.-S. 2015. *Low-Carbon Sustainable Future in East Asia*. Routledge.

Lehmann, Paul, Sijm, Jos, Gawel, Erik, Strunz, Sebastian, Chewpreecha, Unnada, Mercure, Jean-Francois, and Pollitt, Hector. 2019. Addressing multiple externalities from electricity generation: A case for EU renewable energy policy beyond 2020? *Environmental Economics and Policy Studies*, **21**(2), 255–283.

Lenton, Tim, and Watson, Andrew. 2011. *Revolutions That Made the Earth*. Oxford University Press.

Lenton, Timothy M. 2020. Tipping positive change. *Philosophical Transactions of the Royal Society B*, **375**(1794), 20190123.

Lenton, Timothy M., Held, Hermann, Kriegler, Elmar, Hall, Jim W., Lucht, Wolfgang, Rahmstorf, Stefan, and Schellnhuber, Hans Joachim. 2008. Tipping elements in the Earth's climate system. *Proceedings of the National Academy of Sciences*, **105**(6), 1786–1793.

Lewis, Simon L., Brando, Paulo M., Phillips, Oliver L., van der Heijden, Geertje M. F., and Nepstad, Daniel C. 2011. The 2010 amazon drought. *Science*, **331**(6017), 554–554.

Li, Xin, Chen, Hsinchun, Huang, Zan, and Roco, Mihail C. 2007. Patent citation network in nanotechnology (1976–2004). *Journal of Nanoparticle Research*, **9**(3), 337–352.

Libet, Benjamin, Wright Jr, Elwood W., and Gleason, Curtis A. 1983. Preparation-or intention-to-act, in relation to pre-event potentials recorded at the vertex. *Electroencephalography and Clinical Neurophysiology*, **56**(4), 367–372.

Lipsey, Richard G., and Lancaster, Kelvin. 1956. The general theory of second best. *The Review of Economic Studies*, **24**(1), 11–32.

Liu, Cixin. 2014. *The Three-Body Problem*. Head of Zeus.

Liu, J., Mooney, H., Hull, V., Davis, S.J., Gaskell, J., Hertel, T., Lubchenco, J., Seto, K.C., Gleick, P., Kremen, C. and Li, S., 2015. Systems integration for global sustainability. *Science*, **347**(6225), p.1258832.

Löschel, Andreas. 2002. Technological change in economic models of environmental policy: A survey. *Ecological Economics*, **43**(2–3), 105–126.

Lossau, Selma, Fischer, Günther, Tramberend, Sylvia, van Velthuizen, Harrij, Kleinschmit, Birgit, and Schomäcker, Reinhard. 2015. Brazil's current and future land balances: Is there residual land for bioenergy production? *Biomass and Bioenergy*, **81**, 452–461.

Lotka, Alfred J. 1925. *Elements of Physical Biology*. Williams and Wilkins Company.

Lucas Jr, Robert E., et al. 1976. Econometric policy evaluation: A critique. Pages 19–46 of: *Carnegie-Rochester Conference Series on Public Policy*. Vol. 1.

1996. Nobel lecture: Monetary neutrality. *Journal of Political Economy*, **104**(4), 661–682.

Lutz, Christian, Meyer, Bernd, and Wolter, Marc Ingo. 2009. The global multisector/multicountry 3-E model GINFORS: A description of the model and a baseline forecast for global energy demand and CO2 emissions. *International Journal of Global Environmental Issues*, **10**(1–2), 25–45.

Lynham, John, and Tarui, Nori. 2014. What can water demand programs learn from electricity demand programs. Pages 217–233 of: *Routledge Handbook of Water Economics and Institutions*. Routledge.

Malhi, Yadvinder, Roberts, J. Timmons, Betts, Richard A., Killeen, Timothy J., Li, Wenhong, and Nobre, Carlos A. 2008. Climate change, deforestation, and the fate of the Amazon. *Science*, **319**(5860), 169–172.

Mansfield, E. 1961. Technical change and the rate of imitation. *Econometrica*, **29**(4), 741–766.

Manski, Charles F. 1993. Identification of endogenous social effects: The reflection problem. *The Review of Economic Studies*, **60**(3), 531–542.

Marchau, Vincent A. W. J., Walker, Warren E., Bloemen, Pieter J. T. M., and Popper, Steven W. 2019. *Decision-Making under Deep Uncertainty: From Theory to Practice*. Springer Nature.

Marchetti, C., and Nakicenovic, N. 1978. *The Dynamics of Energy Systems and the Logistic Substitution Model*. Tech. rept. IIASA, `http://pure.iiasa.ac.at/id/eprint/1024/`.

Marengo, Jose A., and Bernasconi, Mauro. 2015. Regional differences in aridity/drought conditions over Northeast Brazil: Present state and future projections. *Climatic Change*, **129**(1), 103–115.

Marengo, J. A., Tomasella, J., Alves, L. M., Soares, W. R., and Rodriguez, D. A. 2011, The drought of 2010 in the context of historical droughts in the Amazon region, *Geophys. Res. Lett.*, 38, L12703.

Marengo, Jose A., Alves, Lincoln M., Soares, Wagner R., Rodriguez, Daniel A., Camargo, Helio, Riveros, Marco Paredes, and Pabló, Amelia Diaz. 2013. Two contrasting severe seasonal extremes in tropical South America in 2012: Flood in Amazonia and drought in northeast Brazil. *Journal of Climate*, **26**(22), 9137–9154.

Marengo, José A., Williams, Earle R., Alves, Lincloln M., Soares, Wagner R., and Rodriguez, Daniel A. 2016. Extreme seasonal climate variations in the Amazon basin: Droughts and floods. Pages 55–76 of: *Interactions between Biosphere, Atmosphere and Human Land-Use in the Amazon Basin*. Springer.

Markkanen, Sanna, and Anger-Kraavi, Annela. 2019. Social impacts of climate change mitigation policies and their implications for inequality. *Climate Policy*, **19**(7), 827–844.

Markowitz, Harry. 1952. Portfolio selection. *The Journal of Finance*, **7**(1), 77–91.

Mas-Colell, A., Whinston, M. D., and Green, J. R. 1995. *Microeconomic Theory*. Oxford University Press.

Mass, William, and Robertson, Andrew. 1996. From textiles to automobiles: Mechanical and organizational innovation in the Toyoda enterprises. *Business and Economic History*, **25**(2), 1–13.

Matêjka, F., and McKay, A. 2015. Rational inattention to discrete choices: A new foundation for the multinomial logit model. *American Economic Review*, **105**(1), 272–98.

Maurer, Luiz, Pereira, Mario, and Rosenblatt, José. 2005. *Implementing Power Rationing in a Sensible Way: Lessons Learned and International Best Practices*. World Bank.

Mazzucato, Mariana. 2013. The Entrepreneurial State: Debunking the Public vs. Private Myth in Risk and Innovation. *Anthem*.

2018. *The Value of Everything: Who Makes and Who Takes from the Real Economy*. PublicAffairs.

Mazzucato, Mariana, and Penna, Caetano C. R. 2016. Beyond market failures: The market creating and shaping roles of state investment banks. *Journal of Economic Policy Reform*, **19**(4), 305–326.

Mazzucato, Mariana, and Semieniuk, Gregor. 2017. Public financing of innovation: New questions. *Oxford Review of Economic Policy*, **33**, 24–48.

2018. Financing renewable energy: Who is financing what and why it matters. *Technological Forecasting and Social Change*, **127**, 8–22.

McCollum, D. L., Wilson, C., Pettifor, H., Ramea, K., Krey, V., Riahi, K., Bertram, C., Lin, Z., Edelenbosch, O. Y., and Fujisawa, S. 2016. Improving the behavioral realism of global integrated assessment models: An application to consumers' vehicle choices. *Transportation Research Part D: Transport and Environment*, **55**, 322–342.

McCollum, D. L., Zhou, Wenji, Bertram, Christoph, De Boer, Harmen-Sytze, Bosetti, Valentina, Busch, Sebastian, Després, Jacques, Drouet, Laurent, Emmerling, Johannes, Fay, Marianne, et al. 2018. Energy investment needs for fulfilling the Paris Agreement and achieving the Sustainable Development Goals. *Nature Energy*, **3**(7), 589.

McDonald, Alan, and Schrattenholzer, Leo. 2001. Learning rates for energy technologies. *Energy Policy*, **29**(4), 255–261.

McEvoy, David M., and Cherry, Todd L. 2016. The prospects for Paris: Behavioral insights into unconditional cooperation on climate change. *Palgrave Communications*, **2**, 16056.

McFadden, D. 1973. Conditional logit analysis of qualitative choice behavior. Pages 105–142 of: Zarembka, Paul (ed.), *Frontiers in Econometrics*. Academic Press.

2001. Economic Choices. *The American Economic Review*, **91**(3), 351–378.

McGlade, Christophe, and Ekins, Paul. 2015. The geographical distribution of fossil fuels unused when limiting global warming to 2°C. *Nature*, **517**, 187–190.

McLeay, M., Radia, A., and Thomas, R. 2014. *Money Creation in the Modern Economy*. Tech. rept. Bank of England, `www.bankofengland.co.uk/quarterly-bulletin/2014/q1/money-creation-in-the-modern-economy`.

McNerney, James, Farmer, J. Doyne, Redner, Sidney, and Trancik, Jessika E. 2011. Role of design complexity in technology improvement. *Proceedings of the National Academy of Sciences*, **108**(22), 9008–9013.

McShane, Blakeley B., Bradlow, Eric T., and Berger, Jonah. 2012. Visual influence and social groups. *Journal of Marketing Research*, **49**(6), 854–871.

Meifort, Anna. 2016. Innovation portfolio management: A synthesis and research agenda. *Creativity and Innovation Management*, **25**(2), 251–269.

Meijer, Karen S. 2015. A comparative analysis of the effectiveness of four supply chain initiatives to reduce deforestation. *Tropical Conservation Science*, 8(2), 583–597.

Meinshausen, M., Meinshausen, N., Hare, W., Raper, S. C. B., Frieler, K., Knutti, R., Frame, D. J., and Allen, M. R. 2009. Greenhouse-gas emission targets for limiting global warming to 2°C. *Nature*, 458(7242), 1158–1162.

Mercure, Jean-Francois. 2012. FTT: Power : A global model of the power sector with induced technological change and natural resource depletion. *Energy Policy*, 48(0), 799–811.

2015. An age structured demographic theory of technological change. *Journal of Evolutionary Economics*, **25**, 787–820.

2018. Fashion, fads and the popularity of choices: Micro-foundations for diffusion consumer theory. *Structural Change and Economic Dynamics*, **46**, 194–207.

2019. Toward risk-opportunity assessment in climate-friendly finance. *One Earth*, **1**(4), 395–398.

Mercure, Jean-Francois, and Lam, Aileen. 2015. The effectiveness of policy on consumer choices for private road passenger transport emissions reductions in six major economies. *Environmental Research Letters*, **10**(6), 064008.

Mercure, Jean-Francois, and Salas, P. 2012. An assessment of global energy resource economic potentials. *Energy*, **46**(1), 322–336.

2013. On the global economic potentials and marginal costs of non-renewable resources and the price of energy commodities. *Energy Policy*, **63**, 469–483.

Mercure, Jean-Francois, Karmouch, R., Anahory, Y., Roorda, S., and Schiettekatte, F. 2005. Dependence of the structural relaxation of amorphous silicon on implantation temperature. *Physical Review B*, **71**(13), 134205.

Mercure, Jean-Francois, Goh, S. K., O'Farrell, E. C. T., Perry, R. S., Sutherland, M. L., Rost, A. W., Grigera, S. A., Borzi, R. A., Gegenwart, P., and Mackenzie, A. P. 2009. Quantum oscillations in the anomalous phase in $Sr_3Ru_2O_7$. *Physical Review Letters*, **103**(17), 176401.

Mercure, Jean-Francois, Rost, A. W., O'Farrell, E. C. T., Goh, S. K., Perry, R. S., Sutherland, M. L., Grigera, S. A., Borzi, R. A., Gegenwart, P., Gibbs, A. S., et al. 2010. Quantum oscillations near the metamagnetic transition in $Sr_3Ru_2O_7$. *Physical Review B*, **81**(23), 235103.

Mercure, Jean-Francois, Bangura, A.F., Xu, Xiaofeng, Wakeham, N., Carrington, A., Walmsley, P., Greenblatt, M., and Hussey, N. E. 2012. Upper critical magnetic field far above the paramagnetic pair-breaking limit of superconducting one-dimensional $Li_{0.9}Mo_6O_{17}$ single crystals. *Physical Review Letters*, **108**(18), 187003.

Mercure, Jean-Francois, Pollitt, H., Chewpreecha, U., Salas, P., Foley, A. M., Holden, P. B., and Edwards, N. R. 2014. The dynamics of technology diffusion and the impacts of climate policy instruments in the decarbonisation of the global electricity sector. *Energy Policy*, **73**(0), 686–700.

Mercure, Jean-Francois, Pollitt, H., Bassi, A. M., Vinuales, J. E., and Edwards, N. R. 2016a. Modelling complex systems of heterogeneous agents to better design sustainability transitions policy. *Global Environmental Change*, **37**, 102–115.

Mercure, Jean-Francois, Knobloch, F., Pollitt, H., Lewney, R., Rademakers, K., Eichler, L., van der Laan, J., and Paroussos, L. 2016b. *Policy-Induced Energy Technological Innovation and Finance for Low-Carbon Economic Growth. Study on the Macroeconomics of Energy and Climate Policies*. Tech. rept. European Commission, `https://ec.europa.eu/energy/sites/ener/files/documents/ENER%20Macro-Energy_Innovation_D2%20Final%20%28Ares%20registered%29.pdf`.

Mercure, Jean-Francois, Pollitt, Hector, Edwards, Neil R., Holden, Philip B., Chewpreecha, Unnada, Salas, Pablo, Lam, Aileen, Knobloch, Florian, and Vinuales, Jorge E. 2018a. Environmental impact assessment for climate change policy with the simulation-based integrated assessment model E3ME-FTT-GENIE. *Energy Strategy Reviews*, **20**, 195–208.

Mercure, Jean-Francois, Lam, A., Billington, S., and. Pollitt, H. 2018b. Integrated assessment modelling as a positive science: Private passenger road transport policies to meet a climate target well below 2°C. *Climatic Change*, **151**(2), 109–129.

Mercure, Jean-Francois, Pollitt, Hector, Viñuales, Jorge E., Edwards, Neil R., Holden, Philip B., Chewpreecha, Unnada, Salas, Pablo, Sognnaes, Ida, Lam, Aileen, and Knobloch, Florian. 2018c. Macroeconomic impact of stranded fossil fuel assets. *Nature Climate Change*, 8(7), 588.

Mercure, Jean-Francois, Knobloch, Florian, Pollitt, Hector, Paroussos, Leonidas, Scrieciu, S. Serban, and Lewney, Richard. 2019a. Modelling innovation and the macroeconomics of low-carbon Transitions: Theory, perspectives and practical use. *Climate Policy*, **19**(8), 1019–1037.

Mercure, Jean-Francois, Paim, Maria-Augusta, Bocquillon, Pierre, Lindner, Soeren, Salas, Pablo, Martinelli, Paula, Berchin, II, de Andrade Guerra, J. B. S. O., Derani, Cristiane, de Albuquerque Junior, C. L., et al. 2019b. System complexity and policy integration challenges: The Brazilian Energy-Water-Food Nexus. *Renewable and Sustainable Energy Reviews*, **105**, 230–243.

Mercure, Jean-Francois, Salas, P., Vercoulen, P., Semieniuk, G., Lam, A., Pollitt, H., Holden, P. B., Vakilifard, N., Chewpreecha, U., Edwards, N. R., et al. 2021a. Reframing incentives for climate policy action. *Nature Energy*, **6**, 1133–1143.

Mercure, Jean-Francois, Sharpe, Simon, Vinuales, Jorge E, Ives, Matthew, Grubb, Michael, Lam, Aileen, Drummond, Paul, Pollitt, Hector, Knobloch, Florian, and Nijsse, Femke J. M. M. 2021b. Risk-opportunity analysis for transformative policy design and appraisal. *Global Environmental Change*, **70**, 102359.

Miles, David K., Stedman, Michael, and Heald, Adrian H. 2020. 'Stay at Home, Protect the National Health Service, Save Lives': A cost benefit analysis of the lockdown in the United Kingdom. *International Journal of Clinical Practice*, e13674.

Millar, Richard J., Fuglestvedt, Jan S., Friedlingstein, Pierre, Rogelj, Joeri, Grubb, Michael J., Matthews, H. Damon, Skeie, Ragnhild B., Forster, Piers M., Frame, David J., and Allen, Myles R. 2017. Emission budgets and pathways consistent with limiting warming to 1.5°C. *Nature Geoscience*, **10**(10), 741–747.

Miller, Shelie A. 2010. Minimizing land use and nitrogen intensity of bioenergy. *Environmental Science & Technology*, **44**(10), 3932–3939.

Minsky, Hyman. 1982. *Can 'It' Happen Again?* Routledge.

1986. *Stabilizing an Unstable Economy*. Yale University Press.

Miyoshi, H., and Kii, M. 2011. *Technological Innovation and Public Policy*. Palgrave Macmillan Asian Business Series.

Mokyr, Joel. 1992. Technological inertia in economic history. *Journal of Economic History*, 325–338.

Monasterolo, Irene, and Raberto, Marco. 2018. The EIRIN flow-of-funds behavioural model of green fiscal policies and green sovereign bonds. *Ecological Economics*, **144**, 228–243.

Montoya, Jose M., and Solé, Ricard V. 2002. Small world patterns in food webs. *Journal of Theoretical Biology*, **214**(3), 405–412.

Moran, T. A., Brede, M. A. I., and Noble, J. 2013. The origin of money: An agent-based model. *The Twelfth European Conference on Artificial Life*, 472–279.

Morgenstern, Oskar, and Von Neumann, John. 1953. *Theory of Games and Economic Behavior*. Princeton University Press.

Morris, S. A., and Pratt, D. 2003. Analysis of the Lotka-Volterra competition equations as a technological substitution model. *Technological Forecasting and Social Change*, 70(2), 103–133.

Morton, Douglas C., DeFries, Ruth S., Shimabukuro, Yosio E., Anderson, Liana O., Arai, Egidio, del Bon Espirito-Santo, Fernando, Freitas, Ramon, and Morisette, Jeff. 2006. Cropland expansion changes deforestation dynamics in the southern Brazilian Amazon. *Proceedings of the National Academy of Sciences*, **103**(39), 14637–14641.

Muth, John F. 1961. Rational expectations and the theory of price movements. *Econometrica: Journal of the Econometric Society*, **29**(3), 315–335.

Nagel, Thomas. 1974. What is it like to be a bat? *The Philosophical Review*, 83(4), 435–450.

Nakicenovic, N. 1986. The automobile road to technological change: Diffusion of the automobile as a process of technological substitution. *Technological Forecasting and Social Change*, **29**(4), 309–340.

NCE. 2018. *Unlocking the Inclusive Growth Story of the 21st Century: Accelerating Climate Action in Urgent Times*. Tech. rept. New Climate Economy.

Nelson, R. R., and Winter, S. G. 1982. *An Evolutionary Theory of Economic Change*. Harvard University Press.

Nepstad, Daniel C., Stickler, Claudia M., and Almeida, Oriana T. 2006. Globalization of the Amazon soy and beef industries: Opportunities for conservation. *Conservation Biology*, **20**(6), 1595–1603.

Nepstad, Daniel C., Stickler, Claudia M., Soares-Filho, Britaldo, and Merry, Frank. 2008. Interactions among Amazon land use, forests and climate: Prospects for a near-term forest tipping point. *Philosophical Transactions of the Royal Society B: Biological Sciences*, **363**(1498), 1737–1746.

Nepstad, Daniel C., McGrath, David, Stickler, Claudia, Alencar, Ane, Azevedo, Andrea, Swette, Briana, Bezerra, Tathiana, DiGiano, Maria, Shimada, João, da Motta, Ronaldo Seroa, et al. 2014. Slowing Amazon deforestation through public policy and interventions in beef and soy supply chains. *Science*, **344**(6188), 1118–1123.

Newton, Peter, Gomez, Angelo Eduardo Angel, Jung, Suhyun, Kelly, Timothy, de Araújo Mendes, Thiago, Rasmussen, Laura Vang, dos Reis, Júlio César, Rodrigues, Renato de Aragão Ribeiro, Tipper, Richard, van der Horst, Dan, et al. 2016. Overcoming barriers to low carbon agriculture and forest restoration in Brazil: The Rural Sustentável project. *World Development Perspectives*, **4**, 5–7.

NGFS. 2019. *A Call for Action: Climate Change as a Source of Financial Risk*. Tech. rept. Central Banks and Supervisors Network for Greening the Financial System, `www.ngfs.net/sites/default/files/medias/documents/synthese_ngfs-2019_-_17042019_0.pdf`.

NIES. 2012. *Asia-Pacific Integrated Model*. `www-iam.nies.go.jp/aim/`.

Nobre, Carlos A., Sampaio, Gilvan, Borma, Laura S., Castilla-Rubio, Juan Carlos, Silva, José S., and Cardoso, Manoel. 2016. Land-use and climate change risks in the Amazon and the need of a novel sustainable development paradigm. *Proceedings of the National Academy of Sciences*, **113**(39), 10759–10768.

Nordhaus, William D. 1973. Some skeptical thoughts on the theory of induced innovation. *The Quarterly Journal of Economics*, 87(2), 208–219.

2007a. Critical assumptions in the Stern review on climate change. *Science*, **317**(5835), 201–202.

2007b. A review of the Stern review on the economics of climate change. *Journal of Economic Literature*, **45**(3), 686–702.

2010. Economic aspects of global warming in a post-Copenhagen environment. *Proceedings of the National Academy of Sciences*, **107**(26), 11721–11726.

2014. The perils of the learning model for modeling endogenous technological change. *The Energy Journal*, **35**, 1–13.

2015. Climate clubs: Overcoming free-riding in international climate policy. *American Economic Review*, **105**(4), 1339–70.

2017. Revisiting the social cost of carbon. *Proceedings of the National Academy of Sciences*, 201609244, **114**(7), 1518–1523.

2020. *DICE/RICE Models*. https://williamnordhaus.com/dicerice-models.

Nordhaus, William D., and Samuelson, P. 2009. *Economics. 19th ed.* McGraw-Hill/Irwin.

OECD. 2015. *System Innovation: Synthesis Report*. Tech. rept. OECD, www.pte.pl/pliki/2/1/OECD%20System.pdf.

Omori, F. 1895. On the aftershocks of earthquakes. *Journal of the College of Science, Imperial University of Tokyo*.

O'Neale, Dion R. J., and Hendy, Shaun C. 2012. Power law distributions of patents as indicators of innovation. *PLoS One*, 7(12), e49501.

O'Sullivan, Meghan, Overland, Indra, and Sandalow, David. 2017. The geopolitics of renewable energy. *SSRN HKS Working Paper No. RWP17-027*.

Overland, Indra. 2019. The geopolitics of renewable energy: Debunking four emerging myths. *Energy Research & Social Science*, **49**, 36–40.

OXFAM. 2012. *A Safe and Just Space for Humanity*. Tech. rept. OXFAM, www.oxfam.org/sites/www.oxfam.org/files/dp-a-safe-and-just-space-for-humanity-130212-en.pdf.

Paim, Maria-Augusta, Dalmarco, Arthur R., Yang, Chung-Han, Salas, Pablo, Lindner, Sören, Mercure, Jean-Francois, de Andrade Guerra, José Baltazar S. O., Derani, Cristiane, da Silva, Tatiana Bruce, Viñuales, Jorge E., et al. 2019. Evaluating regulatory strategies for mitigating hydrological risk in Brazil through diversification of its electricity mix. *Energy Policy*, **128**, 393–401.

Paim, Maria-Augusta, Salas, Pablo, Lindner, Sören, Pollitt, Hector, Mercure, Jean-Francois, Edwards, Neil R., and Viñuales, Jorge E. 2020. Mainstreaming the Water-Energy-Food nexus through nationally determined contributions (NDCs): The case of Brazil. *Climate Policy*, **20**(2), 163–178.

Palmer, R. G., Arthur, W. B., Holland, J. H., LeBaron, B., and Tayler, P. 1994. Artificial economic life: A simple model of a stockmarket. *Physica D*, **75**(1–3), 264 – 274.

Pavlov, Ivan Petrovitch, and Gantt, William. 1928. *Lectures on Conditioned Reflexes: Twenty-Five Years of Objective Study of the Higher Nervous Activity (Behaviour) of Animals*. Liveright Publishing Corporation.

Peñasco, Cristina, Anadón, Laura Díaz, and Verdolini, Elena. 2021. Systematic review of the outcomes and trade-offs of ten types of decarbonization policy instruments. *Nature Climate Change*, **11**(3), 257–265.

Perez, Carlota. 1983. Structural change and assimilation of new technologies in the economic and social systems. *Futures*, **15**(5), 357–375.

2001. *Technological Revolutions and Financial Capital*. Edward Elgar.

Perman, Roger, Ma, Yue, McGilvray, James, and Common, Michael. 2003. *Natural Resource and Environmental Economics, 3rd ed.* Pearson Education Limited.

Peters, Ole. 2019. The ergodicity problem in economics. *Nature Physics*, **15**(12), 1216–1221.

Pettifor, Hazel, Wilson, Charlie, McCollum, David, and Edelenbosch, O. Y. 2017a. Modelling social influence and cultural variation in global low-carbon vehicle transitions. *Global Environmental Change*, **47**, 76–87.

Pettifor, Hazel, Wilson, C., Axsen, J., Abrahamse, W., and Anable, J. 2017b. Social influence in the global diffusion of alternative fuel vehicles: A meta-analysis. *Journal of Transport Geography*, **62**, 247–261.

Phillips, Oliver L., Aragão, Luiz E. O. C., Lewis, Simon L., Fisher, Joshua B., Lloyd, Jon, López-González, Gabriela, Malhi, Yadvinder, Monteagudo, Abel, Peacock, Julie, Quesada, Carlos A., et al. 2009. Drought sensitivity of the Amazon rainforest. *Science*, **323**(5919), 1344–1347.

Piesse, J., and Thirtle, C. 2009. Three bubbles and a panic: An explanatory review of recent food commodity price events. *Food Policy*, **34**(2), 119–129.

Piketty, Thomas. 2013. *Le capital au XXIe siècle*. Le Seuil.

Pindyck, Robert S. 2017. The use and misuse of models for climate policy. *Review of Environmental Economics and Policy*, **11**(1), 100–114.

Pollitt, H., and Mercure, J.-F. 2017. The role of money and the financial sector in energy-economy models used for assessing climate and energy policy. *Climate Policy*, 1–14.

Popp, David. 2002. Induced innovation and energy prices. *American Economic Review*, **92**, 160–180.

2006. Innovation in climate policy models: Implementing lessons from the economics of R&D. *Energy Economics*, **28**(5–6), 596–609.

Popp, David, and Newell, Richard. 2012. Where does energy R&D come from? Examining crowding out from energy R&D. *Energy Economics*, **34**(4), 980–991.

Porter, Michael E. 1991. America's green strategy. *Scientific American*, **264**(4), 168.

Porter, Michael E., and van der Linde, C. 1995. Toward a new conception of the environment-competitiveness relationship. *Journal of Economic Perspectives*, **9**(4), 97–118.

Porter, Michael E., et al. 1996. What is strategy? *Harvard Business Review*, **74**(6), 61–78.

Prado Jr, Fernando Almeida, Athayde, Simone, Mossa, Joann, Bohlman, Stephanie, Leite, Flavia, and Oliver-Smith, Anthony. 2016. How much is enough? An integrated examination of energy security, economic growth and climate change related to hydropower expansion in Brazil. *Renewable and Sustainable Energy Reviews*, **53**, 1132–1136.

Quitzow, Rainer, Walz, Rainer, Köhler, Jonathan, and Rennings, Klaus. 2014. The concept of 'lead markets' revisited: Contribution to environmental innovation theory. *Environmental Innovation and Societal Transitions*, **10**, 4–19.

Raddant, Matthias, and Wagner, Friedrich. 2016. Phase transition in the S&P stock market. *Journal of Economic Interaction and Coordination*, **11**(2), 229–246.

Rai, Varun, and Henry, Adam Douglas. 2016. Agent-based modelling of consumer energy choices. *Nature Climate Change*, **6**(6), 556–562.

Rehrl, T., and Friedrich, R. 2006. Modelling long-term oil price and extraction with a Hubbert approach: The LOPEX model. *Energy Policy*, **34**(15), 2413–2428.

Reinhart, Carmen M., and Rogoff, Kenneth S. 2009. *This Time Is Different: Eight Centuries of Financial Folly*. Princeton University Press.

2010. Growth in a time of debt. *American Economic Review*, **100**(2), 573–578.

Rennings, K. L. B. 2014. Global diffusion of environmental innovations. *Environmental Innovation and Societal Transitions, special issue*, **10**, 1–94.

Reynolds, D. B., and Baek, J. 2012. Much ado about Hotelling: Beware the ides of Hubbert. *Energy Economics*, **34**(1), 162 – 170.

Riahi, Keywan, Rao, Shilpa, Krey, Volker, Cho, Cheolhung, Chirkov, Vadim, Fischer, Guenther, Kindermann, Georg, Nakicenovic, Nebojsa, and Rafaj, Peter. 2011. RCP 8.5: A scenario of comparatively high greenhouse gas emissions. *Climatic Change*, **109**(1), 33–57.

Rittel, Horst W. J., and Webber, Melvin M. 1973. Dilemmas in a general theory of planning. *Policy Sciences*, **4**(2), 155–169.

Rivers, Nic, and Jaccard, Mark. 2006. Useful models for simulating policies to induce technological change. *Energy Policy*, **34**(15), 2038–2047.

Rockström, Johan, Steffen, Will, Noone, Kevin, Persson, Åsa, Chapin, F. Stuart, Lambin, Eric F., Lenton, Timothy M., Scheffer, Marten, Folke, Carl, Schellnhuber, Hans Joachim, et al. 2009. A safe operating space for humanity. *Nature*, **461**(7263), 472–475.

Rogelj, Joeri, McCollum, David L., Reisinger, Andy, Meinshausen, Malte, and Riahi, Keywan. 2013. Probabilistic cost estimates for climate change mitigation. *Nature*, **493**(7430), 79–83.

Rogelj, Joeri, Luderer, Gunnar, Pietzcker, Robert C., Kriegler, Elmar, Schaeffer, Michiel, Krey, Volker, and Riahi, Keywan. 2015. Energy system transformations for limiting end-of-century warming to below 1.5°C. *Nature Climate Change*, **5**(6), 519.

Rogelj, Joeri, Popp, Alexander, Calvin, Katherine V., Luderer, Gunnar, Emmerling, Johannes, Gernaat, David, Fujimori, Shinichiro, Strefler, Jessica, Hasegawa, Tomoko, Marangoni, Giacomo, et al. 2018. Scenarios towards limiting global mean temperature increase below 1.5°C. *Nature Climate Change*, 8(4), 325.

Rogers, Everett M. 2010. *Diffusion of Innovations*. Simon and Schuster.

Romer, Paul M. 1986. Increasing returns and long-run growth. *Journal of Political Economy*, **94**(5), 1002–1037.

Rose, Steven K., Kriegler, Elmar, Bibas, Ruben, Calvin, Katherine, Popp, Alexander, van Vuuren, Detlef P., and Weyant, John. 2014. Bioenergy in energy transformation and climate management. *Climatic Change*, **123**(3), 477–493.

Ross, Michael L. 1999. The political economy of the resource curse. *World Politics*, **51**(2), 297–322.

Rotmans, J., Kemp, R., and Van Asselt, M. 2001. More evolution than revolution: Transition management in public policy. *Foresight*, **3**(1), 15–31.

Roukny, Tarik, Bersini, Hugues, Pirotte, Hugues, Caldarelli, Guido, and Battiston, Stefano. 2013. Default cascades in complex networks: Topology and systemic risk. *Scientific Reports*, **3**, 2759.

Rudorff, Bernardo Friedrich Theodor, Aguiar, Daniel Alves, Silva, Wagner Fernando, Sugawara, Luciana Miura, Adami, Marcos, and Moreira, Mauricio Alves. 2010. Studies on the rapid expansion of sugarcane for ethanol production in São Paulo State (Brazil) using Landsat data. *Remote Sensing*, **2**(4), 1057–1076.

Ryan, Bryce, and Gross, Neal C. 1943. The diffusion of hybrid seed corn in two Iowa communities. *Rural Sociology*, 8(1), 15.

Safarzynska, K., and van den Bergh, J. C. J. M. 2010. Evolutionary models in economics: A survey of methods and building blocks. *Journal of Evolutionary Economics*, **20**(3), 329–373.

Sahlins, Marshall. 1972. *Stone Age Economics*. Taylor & Francis.

Schaphoff, Sibyll, Bloh, Werner von, Rammig, Anja, Thonicke, Kirsten, Biemans, Hester, Forkel, Matthias, Gerten, Dieter, Heinke, Jens, Jägermeyr, Jonas, Knauer, Jürgen, et al. 2018. LPJmL4 – a dynamic global vegetation model with managed land – Part 1: Model description. *Geoscientific Model Development*, **11**(4), 1343–1375.

Schelkle, Waltraud. 2012. A crisis of what? Mortgage credit markets and the social policy of promoting homeownership in the United States and in Europe. *Politics & Society*, **40**(1), 59–80.

Scholten, Daniel. 2018. *The Geopolitics of Renewables*. Springer.

Scholten, Daniel, and Bosman, Rick. 2016. The geopolitics of renewables: Exploring the political implications of renewable energy systems. *Technological Forecasting and Social Change*, **103**, 273–283.

Schonberger, Robert B., Listokin, Yair J., Ayres, Ian, Yaesoubi, Reza, and Shelley, Zachary R. 2020. Cost benefit analysis of limited reopening relative to a herd immunity strategy or shelter in place for SARS-CoV-2 in the United States. *medRxiv*.

Schumpeter, Joseph A. 1934. *The Theory of Economic Development: An Inquiry into Profits, Capital, Credit, Interest and the Business Cycle*. Harvard University Press.

1939. *Business Cycles*. McGraw-Hill.

1942. *Capitalism, Socialism and Democracy*. Martino Publishing.

1947. The creative response in economic history. *The Journal of Economic History*, **7**(2), 149–159.

1991. Money and currency. *Social Research*, 499–543.

2014. *Treatise on Money*. Worldbridge.

Schwarcz, Steven L. 2019. Systematic Regulation of Systemic Risk. *Wisconsin Law Review*, **1**, 1–54.

Searchinger, Timothy, Heimlich, Ralph, Houghton, Richard A., Dong, Fengxia, Elobeid, Amani, Fabiosa, Jacinto, Tokgoz, Simla, Hayes, Dermot, and Yu, Tun-Hsiang. 2008. Use of US croplands for biofuels increases greenhouse gases through emissions from land-use change. *Science*, **319**(5867), 1238–1240.

Semieniuk, G., Campiglio, E., Mercure, J.F., Volz, U. and Edwards, N.R., 2021. Low-carbon transition risks for finance. *Wiley Interdisciplinary Reviews: Climate Change*, 12(1), p.e678.

Semieniuk, G., Holden, P.B., Mercure, J.F., Salas, P., Pollitt, H., Jobson, K., Vercoulen, P., Chewpreecha, U., Edwards, N.R. and Viñuales, J.E., 2022. Stranded fossil-fuel assets translate to major losses for investors in advanced economies. Nature Climate Change, 12, 532—538.

Shackle, George Lennox Sharman. 2010. *Uncertainty in Economics and Other Reflections*. Cambridge University Press.

Shaikh, Anwar. 1974. Laws of production and laws of algebra: The Humbug production function. *The Review of Economics and Statistics*, **56**(1), 115–120.

Sharif, M. N., and Kabir, C. 1976. Generalized model for forecasting technological substitution. *Technological Forecasting and Social Change*, 8(4), 353–364.

Sharpe, Simon. 2019. Telling the boiling frog what he needs to know: Why climate change risks should be plotted as probability over time. *Geoscience Communication*, **2**(1), 95–100.

Silverberg, Gerald, Verspagen, Bart, et al. 1999. *Long Memory in Time Series of Economic Growth and Convergence*. MERIT, Maastricht Economic Research Institute on Innovation and Technology.

Simon, H. A. 1955. A behavioral model of rational choice. *The Quarterly Journal of Economics*, **69**(1), 99–118.

Small, K. A., and Rosen, H. S. 1981. Applied welfare economics with discrete choice models. *Econometrica*, **49**(1), 105–130.

Smeets, Edward M. W., Faaij, André P. C., Lewandowski, Iris M., and Turkenburg, Wim C. 2007. A bottom-up assessment and review of global bio-energy potentials to 2050. *Progress in Energy and Combustion Science*, **33**(1), 56–106.

Smil, Vaclav. 2019. *Energy in World History*. Routledge.
Smith, Wendell R. 1956. Product differentiation and market segmentation as alternative marketing strategies. *The Journal of Marketing*, **21**(1), 3–8.
Snider, Elliot, Dasenbrock-Gammon, Nathan, McBride, Raymond, Debessai, Mathew, Vindana, Hiranya, Vencatasamy, Kevin, Lawler, Keith V., Salamat, Ashkan, and Dias, Ranga P. 2020. Room-temperature superconductivity in a carbonaceous sulfur hydride. *Nature*, 586(7829), 373–377.
Solow, R. M. 1957. Technical change and the aggregate production function. *The Review of Economics and Statistics*, **39**(3), 312–320.
Sornette, A., and Sornette, D. 1989. Self-organized criticality and earthquakes. *EPL (Europhysics Letters)*, **9**(3), 197.
Sornette, Didier. 2017. *Why Stock Markets Crash: Critical Events in Complex Financial Systems*. Vol. 49. Princeton University Press.
Sorrell, S., Mallett, A., and Nye, S. 2011. *Barriers to Industrial Energy Efficiency: A Literature Review*. Working Paper 10/2011. United Nations Industrial Development Organization, `http://sro.sussex.ac.uk/id/eprint/53957/1/WP102011_Barriers_to_Industrial_Energy_Efficiency_-_A_Literature_Review.pdf`.
Spera, Stephanie A., Galford, Gillian L., Coe, Michael T., Macedo, Marcia N., and Mustard, John F. 2016. Land-use change affects water recycling in Brazil's last agricultural frontier. *Global Change Biology*, **22**(10), 3405–3413.
Stankiewicz, Rikard. 2000. The concept of 'design space'. Pages 234–247 of: *Technological Innovation as an Evolutionary Process*. Cambridge University Press.
Stassinopoulos, Dimitris, and Bak, Per. 1995. Democratic reinforcement: A principle for brain function. *Physical Review E*, **51**(5), 5033.
Steffen, W., Richardson, K., Rockström, J., Cornell, S. E., Fetzer, I., Bennett, E. M., Biggs, R., Carpenter, S. R., de Vries, W., de Wit, C. A., Folke, C. et al. 2015. Planetary boundaries: Guiding human development on a changing planet. *Science*, **347**(6223).
Steg, Linda, Perlaviciute, Goda, and van der Werff, Ellen. 2015. Understanding the human dimensions of a sustainable energy transition. *Frontiers in Psychology*, **6**, 805.
Stern, Nicholas. 2007. *The Economics of Climate Change*. Cambridge University Press.
2015. *Why Are We Waiting?: The Logic, Urgency, and Promise of Tackling Climate Change*. MIT Press.
2018. Public economics as if time matters: Climate change and the dynamics of policy. *Journal of Public Economics*, **162**, 4–17.
Stern, Nicholas, and Taylor, Chris. 2007. Climate change: Risk, ethics, and the Stern review. *Science*, **317**(5835), 203–204.
Steyaert, Chris, and Hjorth, Daniel. 2008. *Entrepreneurship As Social Change: Third Movements in Entrepreneurship Book*. Vol. 3. Edward Elgar Publishing.
Sunstein, Cass R. 2015. The ethics of nudging. *Yale Journal on Regulation*, **32**, 413.
TCFD. 2017. *Recommendations of the Task Force on Climate-Related Financial Disclosures*. Tech. rept. Task Force on Climate-Related Financial Disclosures, `https://assets.bbhub.io/company/sites/60/2021/10/FINAL-2017-TCFD-Report.pdf`.
Thaler, Richard H. 2016. Behavioral economics: Past, present, and future. *American Economic Review*, **106**(7), 1577–1600.
Thaler, Richard H., and Sunstein, Cass R. 2009. *Nudge: Improving Decisions about Health, Wealth, and Happiness*. Penguin.
Thurner, Stefan. 2011. *Systemic Financial Risk : Agent-Based Models to Understand the Leverage Cycle on National Scales and its Consequences*. Tech. rept. OECD.

Thurner, Stefan, Windischberger, Christian, Moser, Ewald, Walla, Peter, and Barth, Markus. 2003. Scaling laws and persistence in human brain activity. *Physica A: Statistical Mechanics and Its Applications*, **326**(3–4), 511–521.

Thurner, Stefan, Hanel, R., and Klimek, P. 2018. *Introduction to the Theory of Complex Systems*. Oxford.

Tollefson, Jeff. 2015. Stopping deforestation: Battle for the Amazon. *Nature News*, **520**(7545), 20.

Trutnevyte, Evelina. 2016. Does cost optimization approximate the real-world energy transition? *Energy*, **106**, 182–193.

Trutnevyte, Evelina, Hirt, Léon F., Bauer, Nico, Cherp, Aleh, Hawkes, Adam, Edelenbosch, Oreane Y., Pedde, Simona, and van Vuuren, Detlef P. 2019. Societal transformations in models for energy and climate policy: The ambitious next step. *One Earth*, **1**(4), 423–433.

Turnheim, B., Berkhout, F., Geels, F., Hof, A., McMeekin, A., Nykvist, B., and van Vuuren, D. 2015. Evaluating sustainability transitions pathways: Bridging analytical approaches to address governance challenges. *Global Environmental Change*, **35**, 239–253.

Tversky, Amos, and Kahneman, Daniel. 1974. Judgment under uncertainty: Heuristics and biases. *Science*, **185**(4157), 1124–1131.

Tversky, Amos, and Kahneman, Daniel. 1991. Loss aversion in riskless choice: A reference-dependent model. *The Quarterly Journal of Economics*, **106**(4), 1039–1061.

Ueckerdt, Falko, Pietzcker, Robert, Scholz, Yvonne, Stetter, Daniel, Giannousakis, Anastasis, and Luderer, Gunnar. 2017. Decarbonizing global power supply under region-specific consideration of challenges and options of integrating variable renewables in the REMIND model. *Energy Economics*, **64**, 665–684.

UNEP. 2018. *Extending Our Horizons: Assessing Credit Risk and Opportunity in a Changing Climate: Outputs of a Working Group of 16 Banks Piloting the TCFD Recommendations; PART 1: Transition-Related Risks & Opportunities*. Tech. rept. UNEP, `www.unepfi.org/wordpress/wp-content/uploads/2018/04/EXTENDING-OUR-HORIZONS.pdf`.

UNFCCC. 2015. *Paris Agreeement. 22 April 2016, art 2(1)(a)*. Tech. rept. UNFCCC, `http://unfccc.int/files/essential_background/convention/application/pdf/english_paris_agreement.pdf`.

Utsu, Tokuji, Ogata, Yosihiko, et al. 1995. The centenary of the Omori formula for a decay law of aftershock activity. *Journal of Physics of the Earth*, **43**(1), 1–33.

Utterback, James M., and Abernathy, William J. 1975. A dynamic model of process and product innovation. *Omega*, **3**(6), 639–656.

Vakulchuk, Roman, Overland, Indra, and Scholten, Daniel. 2020. Renewable energy and geopolitics: A review. *Renewable and Sustainable Energy Reviews*, **122**, 109547.

Valverde, Sergi, Solé, Ricard V., Bedau, Mark A., and Packard, Norman. 2007. Topology and evolution of technology innovation networks. *Physical Review E*, **76**(5), 056118.

van Asselt, Marjolein B. A., and Rotmans, Jan. 2002. Uncertainty in integrated assessment modelling. *Climatic change*, **54**(1–2), 75–105.

van Buskirk, R. D., Kantner, C. L. S., Gerke, B. F., and Chu, S. 2014. A retrospective investigation of energy efficiency standards: Policies may have accelerated long term declines in appliance costs. *Environmental Research Letters*, **9**(11), 114010.

van de Graaf, Thijs, and Bradshaw, Michael. 2018. Stranded wealth: Rethinking the politics of oil in an age of abundance. *International Affairs*, **94**(6), 1309–1328.

van de Waal, Erica, Borgeaud, Christèle, and Whiten, Andrew. 2013. Potent social learning and conformity shape a wild primate's foraging decisions. *Science*, **340**(6131), 483–485.

van Vuuren, D. P., Edmonds, J. A., Kainuma, M., Riahi, K., and Weyant, J. 2011. A special issue on the RCPs. *Climatic Change*, **109**(1–2), 1–4.

van Vuuren, D. P., van der Wijst, Kaj-Ivar, Marsman, Stijn, van den Berg, Maarten, Hof, Andries F., and Jones, Chris D. 2020. The costs of achieving climate targets and the sources of uncertainty. *Nature Climate Change*, **10**(4), 329–334.

Vespignani, Alessandro. 2012. Modelling dynamical processes in complex socio-technical systems. *Nature Physics*, **8**(1), 32–39.

Viñuales, Jorge E. 2012. *Foreign Investment and the Environment in International Law*. Cambridge University Press.

2015. The Paris climate agreement: An initial examination. *C-EENRG Working Papers*.

Volterra, Vito. 1939. The general equations of biological strife in the case of historical actions. *Proceedings of the Edinburgh Mathematical Society*, **6**(1), 4.

Walker, Warren E., Harremoës, Poul, Rotmans, Jan, Van Der Sluijs, Jeroen P., Van Asselt, Marjolein B. A., Janssen, Peter, and Krayer von Krauss, Martin P. 2003. Defining uncertainty: A conceptual basis for uncertainty management in model-based decision support. *Integrated Assessment*, **4**(1), 5–17.

Walras, Léon. 1956. *Elements of Pure Economics*. Routledge. Translated by W. Jaffé from original 19th century French version.

Warren, R., Watkiss, P., Wilby, R. L., Humphrey, K., Ranger, N., Betts, R., Lowe, J., and Watts, G. 2017. *UK Climate Change Risk Assessment Evidence Report: Chapter 2, Approach and Context*. Tech. rept. Report prepared for the Adaptation Sub-Committee of the Committee on Climate Change.

Watkins, Nicholas W., Pruessner, Gunnar, Chapman, Sandra C., Crosby, Norma B., and Jensen, Henrik J. 2016. 25 years of self-organized criticality: Concepts and controversies. *Space Science Reviews*, **198**(1–4), 3–44.

Way, Rupert, Lafond, François, Lillo, Fabrizio, Panchenko, Valentyn, and Farmer, J. Doyne. 2019. Wright meets Markowitz: How standard portfolio theory changes when assets are technologies following experience curves. *Journal of Economic Dynamics and Control*.

Webb, Colin, Dernis, Hélène, Harhoff, Dietmar, and Hoisl, Karin. 2005. *Analysing European and International Patent Citations*. Tech. rept. OECD.

Wei, Max, Patadia, Shana, and Kammen, Daniel M. 2010. Putting renewables and energy efficiency to work: How many jobs can the clean energy industry generate in the US? *Energy Policy*, **38**(2), 919–931.

Weiss, Martin, Junginger, Martin, Patel, Martin K., and Blok, Kornelis. 2010. A review of experience curve analyses for energy demand technologies. *Technological Forecasting and Social Change*, **77**(3), 411–428.

Weitz, Nina, Strambo, Claudia, Kemp-Benedict, Eric, and Nilsson, Måns. 2017. Closing the governance gaps in the water-energy-food nexus: Insights from integrative governance. *Global Environmental Change*, **45**, 165–173.

Weitzman, Martin L. 2009. On modeling and interpreting the economics of catastrophic climate change. *The Review of Economics and Statistics*, **91**(1), 1–19.

2017. On a world climate assembly and the social cost of carbon. *Economica*, **84**(336), 559–586.

Werner, Richard A. 2014. Can banks individually create money out of nothing? The theories and the empirical evidence. *International Review of Financial Analysis*, **36**, 1–19.

2016. A lost century in economics: Three theories of banking and the conclusive evidence. *International Review of Financial Analysis*, **46**, 361–379.

Wheeler, Tim, and Von Braun, Joachim. 2013. Climate change impacts on global food security. *Science*, **341**(6145), 508–513.

White House. 2021. *FACT SHEET: President Biden Sets 2030 Greenhouse Gas Pollution Reduction Target Aimed at Creating Good-Paying Union Jobs and Securing U.S. Leadership on Clean Energy Technologies.* www.whitehouse.gov/briefing-room/statements-re0000000000000leases/2021/04/22/fact-sheet-president-biden-sets-2030-greenhouse-gas-pollution-reduction-target-aimed-at-creating-good-paying-union-jobs-and-securing-u-s-leadership-on-clean-energy-technologies/.

Wilk, Richard R., and Cliggett, Lisa C. 2007. *Economies and Cultures: Foundations of Economic Anthropology*. Westview press.

Wilkinson, John, and Herrera, Selena. 2010. Biofuels in Brazil: Debates and impacts. *The Journal of Peasant Studies*, **37**(4), 749–768.

Wilson, C., Grubler, A., Bauer, N., Krey, V., and Riahi, K. 2013. Future capacity growth of energy technologies: Are scenarios consistent with historical evidence? *Climatic Change*, **118**(2), 381–395.

Wilson, Charlie, Grubler, Arnulf, Bento, Nuno, Healey, Stephen, De Stercke, Simon, and Zimm, Caroline. 2020. Granular technologies to accelerate decarbonization. *Science*, **368**(6486), 36–39.

Wray, L. Randall. 2016. *Modern Money Theory: A Primer on Macroeconomics for Sovereign Monetary Systems*. Palgrave-Macmillan.

Wright, Theodore P. 1936. Factors affecting the cost of airplanes. *Journal of the Aeronautical Sciences*, **3**(4), 122–128.

Yamasaki, Kazuko, Muchnik, Lev, Havlin, Shlomo, Bunde, Armin, and Stanley, H. Eugene. 2005. Scaling and memory in volatility return intervals in financial markets. *Proceedings of the National Academy of Sciences of the United States of America*, **102**(26), 9424–9428.

Young, H. P. 2001. *Individual Strategy and Social Structure: An Evolutionary Theory of Institutions*. Princeton University Press.

2009. Innovation diffusion in heterogeneous populations: Contagion, social influence, and social learning. *The American Economic Review*, **99**(5), 1899–1924.

Yu, Hyun Jin Julie, Popiolek, Nathalie, and Geoffron, Patrice. 2016. Solar photovoltaic energy policy and globalization: A multiperspective approach with case studies of Germany, Japan, and China. *Progress in Photovoltaics: Research and Applications*.

Zemp, Delphine Clara, Schleussner, Carl-Friedrich, Barbosa, Henrique M. J., Hirota, Marina, Montade, Vincent, Sampaio, Gilvan, Staal, Arie, Wang-Erlandsson, Lan, and Rammig, Anja. 2017. Self-amplified Amazon forest loss due to vegetation-atmosphere feedbacks. *Nature Communications*, 8(1), 1–10.

Zenghelis, Dimitri, Fouquet, Roger, and Hippe, Ralph. 2018. Stranded assets: Then and now. In: *Stranded Assets and the Environment: Risk, Resilience and Opportunity*. Routledge.

Ziegler, Micah S., and Trancik, Jessika E. 2021. Re-examining rates of lithium-ion battery technology improvement and cost decline. *Energy & Environmental Science*, **14**(4), 1635–1651.

Index